Pastoral Lessons

A Study in
Pastoral Theology, Theory and Practice

Fr. Richard O Connor, D.D.

En Route Books and Media, LLC

Saint Louis, MO

En Route Books and Media, LLC
5705 Rhodes Avenue
St. Louis, MO 63109

Cover credit: Sebastian Mahfood

Copyright © 2025 Richard O Connor

ISBN-13: 979-8-88870-421-9
Library of Congress Control Number: 2025946275

No part of this book may be reproduced, stored in a retrieval system, or transmitted in any form, or by any means, electronic, mechanical, photocopying, or otherwise, without the prior written permission of the author.

Dedication

This work is dedicated to the students
of my *Pastoral Theology* class at the Angelicum
in Rome from 2008 to 2023.

Their dedication to their work
and their good humour
was an inspiration for me.

Acknowledgements

Thanks to Fr Sean Sheehy, Listowel, Co Kerry Ireland; to Fr Dominic Nguyen, Sydney; Fr Thomas Rzempoluch, Naples; and Mr. Chris Hogan, Kerry who proofread this study and offered valuable points of correction.

Abbreviations

AA	*Apostolicam Actuositatem*
Acts	*Acts of the Apostles*
Cor	*Corinthians 1 or 2*
CCC	*Catechism of the Catholic Church*
CC	*Casti Conubii*
C.I.C	*Code of Canon Law*
CL	*Christifideles Laici*
CT	*Catechesi Tradendi*
EN	*Evangelii Nuntiandi*
FC	*Familiaris Consortio*
GE	*Gravissimus Educationis*
GS	*Gaudium et Spes*
IM	*Inter Mirifica*
Jn	*Gospel of John*
LG	*Lumen Gentium*
Lk	*Gospel of Luke*
Mt	*Gospel of Matthew*
Mk	*Gospel of Mark*
PDV	*Pastores Dabo Vobis*
Re. Dim.	*Religious Dimension of Education in a Catholic School*
Rm	*Letter to the Romans*
RP (or R et P)	*Reconciliatio et Paenitentia*
OT	*Optatam Totius*
PO	*Presbyterorum Ordinis*
Rev	*Revelations*
SC	*Sacrosanctum Consilium*
S.Th	*Summa Theologiae*
Thess	*Letter to the Thessalonians*
TMHS	*Truth and Meaning of Human Sexuality*
VC	*Vita Consacrata*

Where a portion of a quotation is <u>underlined</u>, it means that emphasis is being added by the author of this study, not by the author of the particular quotation. Scripture quotations are given in italics, so also words and phrases in the main text which the author wishes to emphasize.

Table of Contents

Abbreviations v

General Introduction 1

Part A: The Mysteries and the Church 9

Chapter I: The Mysteries of the Faith and Models of the Church—Trinity, Incarnation, Redemption, Second Coming and the Church 11

Chapter II: The Church, Universal and Local—The Universal Church, the Diocese and the Parish 29

Part B: King 41

Chapter III: The Kingly Office—The Shepherd, his Authority and Role 43

Chapter IV: The Kingship of the Laity and of the Ordained—History, Difference, Harmony 65

Chapter V: Shepherding the Flock—Priestly Duties; Visitation, Ecumenism 73

Chapter VI: Parish Pastoral Council—Purpose, Membership, Consultative Vote 83

Chapter VII: Parish Finance Councils and Buildings—Purpose, Building Projects, Spirit of Poverty 97

Chapter VIII: The Role of the Laity in the World—Dialogue on Involvement, Living the Mysteries, Catholic Action 107

Chapter IX: The Priest in the Vineyard of the World: Areas of Priestly Involvement, Witness to the Incarnation 121

Part C: Prophet 143

Chapter X: Evangelization and Preaching—Importance of Evangelization; Aim of Preaching and its Agent 145

Chapter XI: The Sources of Preaching—Scripture and Tradition; Subject Matter of Preaching 159

Chapter XII: Preparation for Preaching—remote, proximate and immediate Preparation. 175

Chapter XIII: Evangelization in The Home and the School—The Catholic School, Pluralism in the Classroom, the Catholic Teacher 189

Chapter XIV: The School and Catechetics—Content and Method in Catechetics, Inculturation 205

Chapter XV: Education for Chastity—Changed Context; Content and Method, Chastity explained, the Priest and the School. 221

Chapter XVI: The School and the State—Good Catholics make good Citizens; Catholic Schools undermined; Lessons from History' 241

Chapter XVII: The Church, the Priest and the Media—Media and Morals; going on air; Media Vigilance. 251

Chapter XVIII: A Love for Truth—Truth and Realism; Truth undermined and reinstated; bearing Witness 269

Part D: Priest 279

Chapter XIX: The Sacraments in a secularist World— Decline of the Sacred, Sacraments and Liturgy, the overall Unity of the Sacraments. 281

Chapter XX: The Sacrament of Baptism—Matter, Form, Effects, Minister, Recipients, Catholic Upbringing 293

Chapter XXI: The Sacrament of Confirmation—History, Doctrine, a big Day, the Fall Off, Solutions 303

Chapter XXII: The Sacrament of Eucharist—Real Presence, Mass, Sacrament and Sacrifice 317

Chapter XXIII: Eucharist – Pastoral Considerations, Decline in Mass Attendance and Solutions 331

Chapter XXIV: The Loss of the Sense of Sin—Causes, Solutions, the Demonic 349

Chapter XXV: The Sacrament of Penance—Nature, Parts, Effects, Seal, Children's Confessions 365

Chapter XXVI: The Pastoral Care of the Sick—The Psychosomatic, Christ as the Meaning of Suffering and Death.. 385

Chapter XXVII: The Sacrament of the Sick—The Sacrament Itself, Moral and Medical Problems, the Patient's Family 401

Chapter XXVIII: The Sacrament of Holy Orders—Origin, Nature, Decline in Vocations 417

Chapter XXIX: The Spirituality of the Secular Priest—Configuration to Christ, a distinctive Spirituality, Stages in spiritual Growth, The Evangelical Counsels, An underlying Metaphysics.. 431

Chapter XXX: The Sacrament of Marriage—Definitions, Properties, Ends, Goods, Effects, pastoral Care 449

Chapter XXXI: Marriage Undermined—Causes, the Church's Position, the great Let Down 461

Chapter XXXII: Marriage Supported—Preparation, ongoing Care of the Family, different Situations 477

Chapter XXXIII: Marriage in the Wider View—Bring God back, Housing, Media, Legislation, The Way Forward, Spirituality... 497

Part E: Towards the Kingdom.. 515

Chapter XXXIV: The Celtic Cross—Whither goes the Parish? – a Dialogue 517

Chapter XXXV: The Kingdom of God—The Church and the Kingdom, the Kingdom and the Parish, the Vision of *Gaudium et Spes,* Preparing the World for the Kingdom, the Kingdom Existence of our Achievements... 533

Chapter XXXVI: The Dawn of a new Christendom—*Fuga Mundi*, New monastic Witness, Islands of Faith.. 551

End Notes 563

Reading: Church Documents 571

The Author.. 575

General Introduction

Simon Son of John, do you love me ?………….Feed my sheep. Jn. 21:17.

……we must bear in mind that Christ is not alone. The whole meaning of His earthly life lay in His building for Himself a 'fullness'. Since Christ's body truly belongs to Him, encounter with Christ takes place in encounter with those who are Christ's, because they are His body. J. Ratzinger. *Eschatology: death and eternal life, p207.*

The Blessed Trinity, one God in three persons, is the starting point of this study. God is eternal but He freely chose to create the world and the entire universe at the first moment of time. He created the world though the Son by the power of the Holy Spirit. At a certain moment in time, about two thousand years ago, He sent His Son, Jesus Christ, truly God and truly man, into the world to redeem it from sin, and He sent His Holy Spirit to sanctify those redeemed. While on earth Christ gathered a people to Himself, the Church, His mystical body of which He Himself is the head. He is still extending Himself in time and space, calling people to Himself in this body and will continue to do so until the end of time when He will come again to judge the living and the dead on their response to His call. As head, Christ is complete in Himself but He is still growing in His mystical body, this body being further completed every day until it reaches its fulness at a future time unknown to us.

Subject Matter

Our subject matter in this presentation of pastoral lessons is the body of Christ as it attains this "fullness" when being built up daily by the power of the Holy Spirit working through her pastors and their helpers all for the glory of the Father. One can also say that it is the life and work of the ordained pastor, along with his lay helpers, as he is instrumental in fostering the growth of the mystical body, leading the people of God to their goal of union with Him.

St Thomas Aquinas put it simply by saying that the task of the pastor is the care of the body of Christ. This refers both to the Eucharistic Body of Christ, the Blessed Sacrament, (and the other sacraments by extension) and to the mystical body of Christ as the Church because the Church lives from the Eucharist, and the Eucharist comes to be in the context of the Church when Mass is offered by the priest with his people gathered round him.

Christ, a divine person, truly God and truly man, has three offices (*munera*) or roles, those of king, prophet and priest, and the pastor, because he is conformed to Christ in holy orders, shares in these three offices and his work can be studied in light of them. Accordingly, we will study him in his work of shepherding the flock entrusted to him (king), of preaching to them, instructing them in the faith, (prophet) and of sanctifying them by the administration of the sacraments (priest). He does this principally at parish level but also at diocesan level in the sense that he does not act independently of his bishop and fellow priests and may have duties assigned to him which take him outside the boundaries of his own parish at times. Indeed, if he is using radio or television and other media to proclaim the faith he will be reaching people in places very far away. Within the parish he meets people in schools, hospitals and prisons. He meets them in their homes when he visits families and as individuals in the confessional, in counselling and in various other situations.

But because the pastor is not alone in this work but is helped by lay people in various ways, we must also look at the part they play in this building up of the Church. Pope John Paul II says:

> The Church's mission of salvation in the world is realized not only by the ministers in virtue of the Sacrament of Orders but also by all the lay faithful; indeed, because of their Baptismal state and their specific vocation, in the measure proper to each person, the lay faithful participate in the priestly, prophetic and kingly mission of Christ. *Christifideles Laici, (CL), On the Vocation and Mission of the Laity*, #23.

Though the Church is not a democracy, all of the laity share in the building up of the mystical body in various ways according to their different positions in the Church and their different callings in life: those who are members of the parish pastoral council, the catechists, the teachers in the schools, the spiritual councillors in the hospital, those on home visitation teams or the bereavement teams are different examples. They too are furthering this work of building up the Church. But so also are other good Christians in their care of their families at home and in their places of work. We will be looking at these different roles of the laity in due course.

The goal of this great effort to build up the Church has often been described as the salvation of souls so that people reach heaven individually. But people are more than souls and they do not live as isolated individuals, nor do they float above the earth like angels. So, a more comprehensive statement of the goal of all this pastoral effort is to prepare individuals for heaven by having them live good lives in a state of grace here on earth, but also to prepare the entire people of God and the world itself for the coming of the kingdom of God which will be realized fully after the resurrection of the dead, at the eschaton, when Christ will come again. The ultimate purpose of all pastoral effort is the glory of God when the Son will have handed over the world to the Father at His second coming and *God will be all in all. (1 Cor.15:28)*.

Pastoral theology studies this building up of the body of Christ as the Church strives for this fulness which it will have in the kingdom.

Pastoral Theology as a Science

We must first see if pastoral theology is a science in the widest sense of the word meaning a growth in knowledge by logical deduction from true premises to certain conclusions. If it is, one might then expect that it would have always been taught in a formally academic way in Church institutions. But a brief look at the history of priestly formation shows that this was not always what happened though in more recent times it *is* happening.

In the gospels we see Christ forming His twelve apostles by instruction and example when He walked with them along the roads of Israel. Chapter 10 of St John's gospel, where Christ is speaking about the good shepherd and how he should be willing to lay down his life for his sheep, might be seen as a little lecture in pastoral theology. They were privileged to hear such instruction from the mouth of Wisdom incarnate. Then we see St Paul doing something similar when he instructs Timothy and Titus in his pastoral letters, and we have St Peter giving instructions of a pastoral kind in his first letter.

After the apostles, as the Church began to be structured as diocese, first in the cities around the Mediterranean and later in the country places, the elders or bishops, who were the earliest successors of the apostles, ordained others as helpers - the presbyters and deacons. But we do not have much now by way of evidence of what kind of formation they received or if it can be called "science" apart from occasional bits of instruction in letters. We can presume that the form of formation was what we might call the "apprenticeship model", with the younger man learning both doctrine and practical skills from an older man who was his mentor.

When we come to the Fathers we have St Gregory the Great with his *Pastoral Rule*. Its framework is that of a study of virtues and vices and it shows the pastor how he might promote the former and curb the latter. Then there is St Augustine with his sermons on the shepherds wherein he compares the good shepherd who is concerned for the flock with the hireling shepherd who exploits them for his own gain. Fittingly, the Church puts those sermons before us in the breviary to be read every year. There is also the great example and instruction of St John Chrysostom.

For much of the Church's history in the first millennium the monasteries were the major centres of Church life and indeed of social life also in many places. So, people in the surrounding areas went to the monks for the sacraments, for instruction in their preaching and for many other kinds of help like education which they received in the monastery schools, healing in the monastery hospitals and the hospitality those on journeys received in the monastery hostels. The monks took care of most things, spiritual and even temporal at a time when civil life had largely collapsed after the fall of the Roman empire. Because the monks had time for study we can take it that those who heard them preach and attended their schools did indeed receive good formation in the faith, and that some of those students would have gone on to become priests ministering in the surrounding parishes. But we still cannot say that they received formal training in pastoral theology taught as a science.

Whatever about those young men who were able to gain from the preaching and teaching of the monks, many more did not have that advantage and were formed solely by apprenticeship. The young apprentice priest was assigned to a parish priest from whom he learned the minimal rudiments of Latin needed for the valid administration of the sacraments, some practical advice on how to handle family and social problems and the more earthly skills such as how to keep house, plant a garden, care for the horses, maintain church buildings and so on. He learned good things from a good pastor but he might also learn bad things from a bad pastor: there was a certain amount of concubinage in those times, often tolerated by the laity as being inevitable, the bottle of alcohol was never too far away and that was not all. I can leave the rest to the imagination of my reader.

The Protestant revolt gave a jolt to this apprenticeship system. The reformers were well versed in the scriptures but their interpretations of them varied so that they often contradicted each other. Despite this, however, they were persuasive and succeeded in carrying off whole hoards of Catholics to their side. This posed a challenge for the Church.

The Council of Trent sought to remedy this situation by the founding of seminaries, houses of training for students for the priesthood with a military style of discipline, a monastic style of detachment from the outside world and a definite course of studies which was uniform throughout the Catholic world. It certainly improved the standard of theological formation which the new priests received in scripture, dogma and morals, and it gave them time to pray and study. However, its monastic-style detachment from the outside world, by means of the high walls that surrounded those seminaries, led to the paradox of priests being prepared for the "big, bad world" outside the walls by having them cut off from that world entirely. But it was assumed that the pastoral experience which the young priest would gain soon after ordination would make up for any such shortcomings.

Though formal instruction had now begun, still, it was only in the 18th century that some attempts were made to write manuals of pastoral theology in Southern Germany and Austria and, even then, many of those books were mostly concerned with the administration of the sacraments, especially the celebration of Mass and penance, and with teaching the rudiments of canon law as it was to be had then. It was taken for granted that, if one were well versed in such subjects, that that was sufficient so that a specific science of pastoral theology was not needed. And when it did begin to be introduced as a separate study it was often regarded as a minor subject which didn't fetch many credits in exams, and many of those teaching it had little or no experience of parish life apart from doing some summer supply here and there. In the seminary I went through it was referred to as a "pup" subject! Pastoral theology, where it was taught at all, was not seen as a science but mostly as technique, as the "tricks of the trade of parish work", so to speak, the "know-how" of doing different things such as the administration of the sacraments, the keeping of accounts, the chairing of meetings, fundraising for schools *etc.*, things which were given some airing in some seminaries, perhaps, but best picked up, it was believed, when the student was ordained and put to work with an experienced parish priest. As for instruction that could be called "science", that was seen as being taken care of in the study of dogmatic and moral theology.

So then, how do we answer the question of whether or not pastoral theology is a science or if it is anything more than technique picked up more by practice than by any kind of theoretical study? Pope St John Paul II answers our question affirmatively: he says that pastoral theology *is* a science and more than mere technique or art even though this is important also because, though a science, it is one that must have practical application also. He says:

> Pastoral or practical theology is a scientific reflection on the church as she is built up daily, by the power of the Spirit, in history…it is not just an art. Nor is it a set of exhortations, experiences and methods. It is theological in its own right, because it receives from the faith the principles and criteria for the pastoral action of the church in history… *Pastores Dabo Vobis, (PDV),* #57; *Cf. The Code of Canon Law, (C.I.C), Canon 258.*

It is a science because the pastoral has to be grounded in the doctrinal and cannot be dissociated from it. So, again, St John Paul says:

> ...what is pastoral is not opposed to what is doctrinal. Nor can pastoral action rescind from doctrinal content, from which in fact it draws its substance and real validity. *Reconciliatio et Paenitentia, (RP), #26.*

If pastoral practice were to be dissociated from solid dogmatic principles, on the grounds that practice is guided entirely by a compassion that is determined by circumstances, then one is giving into a morality of mere situation ethics in which just about everything is permitted and in which feeling, and no longer reason or the true faith, comes to be the guiding light.

Pastoral theology, says the pope, finds application in pastoral activity, which activity, conversely is an expression of the Church in action in her everyday life in her work of salvation:

> Pastoral activity is always the dynamic expression of the reality of the church, committed to her ministry of salvation. *Familiaris Consortio, (FC), #69.*

If this is so, if it is an expression of the reality of the Church in her work of salvation, then it presupposes a knowledge of the Church, of ecclesiology, which in turn presupposes a knowledge of all the other branches of theology and the mysteries from which they derive. It shows how they are to be given practical application in daily life for the building up of the Church. Far from being a marginal subject, then, it is really the meeting point of all the other branches of theology as they are given effect in the life of the parish. It is what can be called "applied" or "practical" theology. This study, therefore, will not attempt anything like providing a comprehensive account of the various branches of theology - an impossible task in any case – rather it will presuppose such knowledge in the reader and draw on its main principles and show their application.

The Aim of this Study

The aim of this study, accordingly, is to provide students for the priesthood and other pastoral workers with a theoretical basis for their work of caring for and building up the Church, showing the practical application of what they have been learning in other areas in theology. It will draw also from the experience of pastors past and present and I wish to offer a little from my own limited experience in parish work also.

Though more than an art, as just explained, I hope also, nonetheless, to be able to pass on some tips of practical advice to those willing to learn. In other words, while I aim to be scientific in the sense of drawing conclusions from certain principles of

Catholic teaching, my presentation will also have somewhat of the style of an older priest passing on observations and practical things learned from experience to seminarians and younger priests and their lay helpers. That will make it somewhat informal or casual in places, something the strictly academic theologian might not appreciate.

As to method, I hope to be deductive but also to use such devices as dialogue and story and anecdote. This might be called "the apprenticeship method" to some degree and I make no apologies for that because, for all its faults, it did have its benefits also. In any case, my hope is that what might be called my "mix of methods" would be of some help in forming new shepherds modelled on Christ the good shepherd. What I am aiming at is best summed up by St John Paul's again when he says:

> The whole training of the students should have as its object to make them true shepherds of souls after the example of Our Lord Jesus Christ, teacher, priest and shepherd. *Pastores Dabo Vobis*, (quoting *Optatam Totius*, #4; cf. also *Code of Canon Law, Canon 255*).

Ecclesiology, the study of the Church, makes no sense apart from the study of Christ who founded the Church, who in turn cannot be understood except as the Son of God, incarnate in human nature. This takes us back to the Trinity, the first doctrine in the hierarchy of truths. Hence, as to the outline of this study, in the next chapter we will first see how the mystery of the Trinity and the other mysteries of the faith are foundational for a study of pastoral theology and for the spirituality of all Christians and in a special and distinctive way for the priest in his care of his people. Then we will look at the Church, using some models that are useful for a pastoral understanding of it; and after that, in subsequent sections, we will look at the work of the priest and the laity in light of Christ's three offices of king, prophet and priest. We will conclude with a study of the kingdom of God of the end time and its relevance for pastoral life in the present.

As for sources, I will be drawing mostly on the scriptures, some of the Fathers, St Thomas Aquinas, the documents of Vatican II, the *Catechism of the Catholic Church (CCC)*, the *Code of Canon Law, (CIC)* and the writings of St John Paul II to a considerable extent. But the documents of some other councils, popes and theologians will be cited also.

Conclusions:

1. Pastoral theology is a science and not just a set of pastoral techniques because it proceeds from the truths of the faith and examines how these are given

practical application in the daily life of the Church as she is being built up and nourished by her pastors and their lay helpers.

2. Because it is such a science it requires a knowledge of theology and the mysteries of the faith. It is like a bowl into which all the branches of theology will flow. It also requires a love of Christ, truly God and truly man, which calls for a true spirituality on the part of the priest and his helpers. They need to unite themselves to Christ in faith, hope and love by prayer, penance and good living.

Part A

The Mysteries and the Church

Chapter I

The Mysteries of the Faith and Models of the Church

Trinity, Incarnation, Redemption, Second Coming and the Church

I am the good shepherd; I know my own and my own know me as the Father knows me and I know the Father; and I lay down my life for the sheep". Jn. 10:14,15.

The mystery of the Most Holy Trinity is the central mystery of Christian faith and life. It is the mystery of God in Himself. It is therefore the source of all the other mysteries of the faith, the light that enlightens them. *Catechism of the Catholic Church, (CCC), #234.*

The church is a sheepfold whose one and necessary door is Christ. *Lumen Gentium, (LG), The Church, Vatican II, #6*

Moral living is underpinned by dogmatic belief. So also is liturgy in as much as it is the mysteries re-enacted and celebrated. Pope Leo the Great says that what Christ did visibly on earth in the mysteries has passed over into the sacraments. (*Sermon 2 on the Ascension*). Spirituality, then, can be described as the living out of the mysteries in the events of ordinary, daily life. To try to have doctrine lived out in morals, liturgy and spirituality makes up a great part of what can be called " the pastoral endeavour". In this chapter we will first give a simple presentation of the central mysteries of the faith and see how pastoral practice follows from them. After speaking of the mysteries we will go on to talk about the Church, the extension of Christ's incarnation in His mystical body wherein His paschal mystery is celebrated every day, and seek for models to understand it.

The Mysteries

We admire people with simple faith: *Blessed are those who have not seen but still believe. Jn 20:29.* However, to accept the mysteries with simple faith does not mean taking them for granted and then forgetting about them in daily life. But this often happens, and when it does it reduces religion to being a thing of mere convention, a merely cultural thing which soon loses itself in whatever happens to be the ideology of the day, instead of it being a thing of conviction because based on solid doctrine, firmly accepted, and thus being counter cultural at times.

<u>The Trinity</u>

In the hierarchy of truths in theology the doctrine of the Blessed Trinity is the highest: one God in three persons, the Father, the Son and the Holy Spirit. The Son proceeds from the Father by generation, and the Holy Spirit proceeds from the Father and the Son by spiration in the eternal processions of knowing and loving respectively. We say also in the *Creed* that the Son is "begotten" of the Father before time began. These words "generated" and "begotten" mean a coming forth eternally, due to the Father's knowledge of Himself, and they rule out any suggestion of carnal generation as with us humans or that the Son was created at some early point in time which was the heresy of Arius in the fourth century. We use a different word, "spiration", for the coming forth of the Holy Spirit because He is the fruit of the love of the Father and the Son for each other and also because the Father and the Son together are one principle of His coming forth.

The doctrine of one God in three persons, with one of those persons coming on earth to suffer and die and rise and come again at the end of time, gives Christianity a distinctiveness with sets it apart from all other religions and which should accordingly have its followers live in a way that sets them apart from any ideologies which the world might offer at a given time.

This doctrine was the subject of some heated controversies in the early centuries of the Church but is not of such interest today. I don't expect to see mention of any dispute about the Trinity in any newspaper heading in the near future! This lack of interest could be due to the fact that those controversies have long been settled and that people today are quite solid and happy in their belief in the Trinity now. But more likely it is due to the fact that in an age of materialism and secularism many, even those who are Christians, give no thought at all to this great and foundational mystery. They will say that it is "too far up in the clouds for them" and that they have "more important concerns down here on the ground"!

But if people give no thought to the Blessed Trinity, how can we then conclude that their faith in this mystery is quite solid? And how can we blame them then for becoming purely secularist in their thinking if the mystery of the Trinity is not put before them because secularism is, very simply, a world view which discards God and settles for the material and the visible as being the sum total of reality? One cannot relate the world to God if there is no thought of God in His inner being in people's minds to begin with nor can one make an excuse for this failure by saying that the Trinity is too abstract a topic for most people. But then, one must ask: who allows it to happen that the Trinity and the other mysteries of the faith are "left up in the clouds" if that is where some people deem them to be? Some priests feel they might be over taxing their hearers if they talk about such supposedly difficult things. As a result, these priest confine themselves to preaching pious, moral platitudes which have no basis in dogma. Furthermore, dogma is left aside as having a bad name in an age of relativism and scepticism.

The mystery of the Holy Trinity is of the greatest relevance not just because it is a foundational doctrine in the hierarchy of truths but also because in daily Christian living it gives us the first model of Christian love. God is infinite being and also infinite goodness because being and goodness are convertible terms in metaphysics – what exists is good to the degree that it exists. Goodness tends to diffuse itself, to give of itself, to "spread itself out" as it were. In the Trinity the Father gives of Himself to the Son by knowing Himself, and the Father and the Son give themselves to each other by love, which love is not a mere emotion or sentiment but a third person, the Holy Spirit, the bond between the Father and the Son. This self-giving love of the persons of the Trinity, one to another, is the first model for our way of loving as Christians: to love for the Christian is to give of oneself generously to others. The inner life of the Trinity is one of *communio* love, self-giving love (*koinonia* in Greek). Accordingly, as said above, Christians live the life of the Trinity in their daily lives if there is this kind of love in their families and in all their other communities. Such love is then an image here on earth of the love that exists eternally between the persons of the Trinity "up above", a self-giving love of one for the other. To the extent that people look upwards towards this model of love their lives will be truly Christian and to the extent that they fail to do so they will be self-centred or they may even look to a model below them, the model of the animals, and become debauched.

The priest should be an example of this love when he exercises pastoral charity towards his people. He grows himself spiritually when he pours himself out unreservedly for his people in this way.

The Incarnation

This self-giving which is the inner life of the Trinity does not stop there. It also goes "outside" of the Trinity, as it were, when God created the universe - infinite Being giving rise to contingent, finite being - by a free act of will. The Father creates through the Son in the love of the Holy Spirit. The apex of that creation is man; but God did not stop at merely creating man; He willed to join Himself to man, so He sent His Son to become one of us in the incarnation. The incarnation, then, is the second most fundamental mystery of our faith when God the Son became man in the womb of the Virgin Mary by the power of the Holy Spirit.

Christ Himself posed the question of His own identity when He asked: *Who do men say that I am?* And He answered it when He confirmed Peter's answer which came not from below but from above: *You are the Christ, the Son of the living God. Mt. 16:13-20.*

It is important to be clear and accurate on the doctrine of the incarnation, otherwise we will be like men building a house on shifting foundations. If the priest is configured to Christ by holy orders but does not know who or what Christ is he will not be able to represent Him correctly to people. The *Catechism of the Catholic Church* says:

> The unique and altogether singular event of the Incarnation of the Son of God does not mean that Jesus Christ is part God and part man, nor does it imply that He is the result of a confused mixture of the divine and the human. He became truly man while remaining truly God. Jesus Christ is true God and true man. During the first centuries, the church had to defend this truth of faith against the heresies that falsified it. *Catechism of the Catholic Church, (CCC), #464*

In brief, we are talking about one person, a divine person, the second person of the Trinity who is "God from God, light from light, true God from true God, consubstantial with the Father" as we say in the *Creed*, becoming "a man like us in all things but sin". So, we have one person in two natures, which means that Christ was a man, human, very human if we consider His compassion for those who suffer or weep, but not a human *person* because then He would be two persons in two natures which would land us in the old heresy of Nestorianism.

There were major controversies about the incarnation also in the early centuries of the Church which went on for hundreds of years and even had Christians taking to the streets in riots in places. These controversies were closely related to those pertaining to the Trinity because one of the central issues of debate was whether or not Christ was truly God. Different councils of the Church in those early centuries confronted and settled those controversies. Looking back now from today's lack of interest in those controversies some people will laugh at how people in those times got so hot about them. Gibbon, for example, the well-known English historian, of the eighteenth century, laughed at how Christians in the fourth century at the time of the Arian heresy could get so upset about that one *iota* which differentiated the terms *homoousios* and *homoiousios,* the former saying that Christ was truly God of the *same* substance with the Father, which is Catholic truth, and the latter saying that He was only of a *like* substance with the Father, which is heresy. But in his old age Gibbon admitted that on that one *iota* hung the whole fabric of Catholic doctrine and with it the Church's very future.

Today, as I said above, one does not find people arguing over such matters; but those heresies keep on surfacing in various forms. In the days before Vatican II great stress was put on the divinity of Christ but sometimes at the expense of His humanity. To illustrate this I can remember an argument in my childhood days between an elderly couple in which the old man was using some strong language, to which his wife replied "now Dan, Our Lord would not use language like that"; to which Dan replied "fine for Him, He was God and didn't have to put up with what I have to put up with"! So, according to Dan, Christ was God and therefore not really human and so was able to glide blissfully above the problems of life which he, poor Dan, had to put up with! This is a mini example of Docetism – the heresy that Christ was truly God indeed but not truly man. By way of a reaction against that, then, after Vatican II – but not on account of the council - the pendulum swung the other way towards a new Arianism without the name of Arius even being mentioned. This happened mostly in the field of catechetics where Christ was presented as a "jolly chap palling around with His twelve buddies" smiling at everyone. He is depicted in cartoon fashion in the children's schoolbooks even though experienced teachers will tell you that children will take very well to biblical figures being presented to them in the traditional style of sacred art. It happens also at second level when students of comparative religion are presented with Christ as just one other religious leader on a par, more or less, with Mohommed or Buddha or some other such religious leader.

If Christ was not truly God but merely a man - perhaps a very holy man - then He would not have been able to redeem us. If He was not truly man then He would not have shared our lot here in this troubled world. In an effort to reconcile His having two natures in one person there is a temptation to "play up" one of those natures by "playing down" the other. So, to ensure His divinity one mistakenly "plays down" His humanity and *vice versa*. The model being used here is that of a glass in which there is oil and water. The more oil there is in the glass the less water there can be, and *vice versa*. But that is a false model. Nor do we mix the two natures like milk and water in the one glass. Instead, we can play up both natures without any fear of contradiction: Christ was truly God, and in that respect infinite; but He was also truly man, more delicately and beautifully human than any other man, and that, not *in spite* of being divine but precisely *because* His human nature was so closely united to His divine nature. We see that clearly at the grave of Lazarus, a scene of delicate beauty, where He cries truly human tears at the sorrow He saw in the eyes of Martha and Mary over the loss of their brother but where also, a few minutes later, He raises Lazarus by His power as God. *(Jn.11)*.

Students for the priesthood need to study these ancient heresies and be clear on what Catholic truth teaches about Christ. But sadly, I have often found that young priests studying even at post graduate level are often unclear on these things which, I argue, must affect their ministry negatively. For example, could there be any such thing as adoration of the Blessed Sacrament in the life of a priest if he thought that Christ was not truly God; and if there is no adoration in his life, what then?

We live the incarnation in our parish communities when we allow Christ the fullness He desires in the extension of His mystical body in ourselves and in those around us in our families and our parishes and do so in practice by frequenting the sacraments, by living in the state of grace, by doing our duty faithfully and with charity and by evangelizing others by good example and in various other ways. The grace of the incarnation affects the world around us, the cultural, the social, the economic and even matter itself because of man's close relationship to the world which is his dwelling.

The priest gives a lead in this when he administers the sacraments and preaches and catechises. He also lives the incarnation in his own life when he gets "stuck in" to the lives of his people, becomes *incarnate* in them, as it were, when he takes time to get to know them, visits their homes, shares their concerns and makes them his own in prayer.

The Redemption

Christ came on earth to save us from sin. His incarnation had a redemptive purpose. *Christ died for our sins in accordance with the scriptures. I Cor. 15:3.*

As man He was both priest and also victim offering Himself on the cross so that by dying and rising we too could die and rise with Him and share His glory in both soul and body. Let's hear what the *Catechism of the Catholic Church* says:

> The cross is the unique sacrifice of Christ, the "one mediator between God and men". But because in his incarnate divine person he has in some way united himself to every man, "the possibility of being made partners, in a way known to God, in the paschal mystery" is offered to all men. He calls his disciples to "take up [their] cross and follow (him)", for "Christ also suffered for (us), leaving (us) an example so that (we) should follow in his steps." In fact,

> Jesus desires to associate with his redeeming sacrifice those who were to be its first beneficiaries. *#618.*

The cross is central to Christianity, yet as individuals and as whole societies we try to evade it in various ways. Archbishop Fulton Sheen once said that in the East in the 20th century under communism, people had the cross without Christ because the Soviet Union was atheistic and because of the suffering communism imposed on those whose unhappy lot it was to be subject to it, whereas in the West we try to have a Christianity which is without the cross because of the way we sugar-coat religion to make it more palatable to the secular world, seldom speaking about sin or the penance it requires in atonement.

A consideration of the cross should bring us to a realization of the evil that is sin if such a cruel death, suffered by the Son of God, was the price He paid to redeem us. Sadly, today there is much sentimental talk about God's forgiveness and mercy but very little about the evil of sin, which has some people, who are living habitually in sin, ask why they need forgiveness at all! The sense of sin is being lost. We must see later why this is so.

Christ carried His cross, and because we are His members in His mystical body, He gives us a share in that cross when we willingly take up our own daily sufferings and unite them with His in reparation for our own sins and those of others (a central part of the Fatima message).

In practice Christians live the redemption when they carry the crosses that are sent to them in God's providence and offer up their sufferings with the sacrifice of Christ on the cross for the saving of the world. Thereby their sufferings too come to have a redemptive power because of and along with His.

The priest lives this mystery in a very special way when he re-enacts this sacrifice on the altar at Mass and then lives it out during the day when he helps his parishioners to carry their crosses and he may have to suffer a lot himself in doing so such that this suffering will be *his* cross and *his* path to holiness.

<u>The Second Coming of Christ</u>

Finally, Christians should be looking forward to the second coming of Christ when He will call all men from their graves to judge them and establish His kingdom. *You will see the Son of Man seated at the right hand of the Almighty and coming on the clouds of heaven. Mk. 14:62.* And the Creed says: *He will come again to judge the living and the dead.*

Christians should live in such a way as to be always ready to face judgment at the end of their individual lives, but also, as a people, Christians should be influencing the world around them so that Christ will be king in every area of life. An awareness of the second coming and the kingdom of God is not something that is strong in the minds of many Christians at present even though it is an event that awaits us as at the end of history but could happen at any time: *You do not know the day when your master is coming. Mt.24:42.*

In practice this means that all Christians and the entire church strain forward in expectation of the kingdom of God by praying for it and by striving to make our world a more human place for all.

The priest is one who is out in front, in this forward movement of the Church, the bride, as she runs towards the Christ the bridegroom at His second coming, and meanwhile he is leading his people in preparing the world for that kingdom.

The Church - Models

Given that Christ is extended in His mystical body, the Church, and that He continues to live His mysteries in the Church, mention of His mysteries as above leads on to a study of the Church herself.

The priest, configured to Christ and imitating Him, has the task of caring for the Church, the mystical body of Christ. He is a representative of Christ standing before the Church and a representative of the Church standing before Christ to plead for her and offer sacrifice. He works at building up the Church. This requires of the priest an understanding of ecclesiology which is a vast study in itself but which we cannot engage in fully here. I will limit myself to drawing on a work by Cardinal Avery Dulles, his book *Models of the Church*, in which, as the title says, he presents different models of the Church which I find are helpful for a pastoral study.

First let us go to Vatican II which gives us a wide variety of images of the Church in *Lumen Gentium*.

> The church is a sheepfold whose one and necessary door is Christ. She is the flock of which God himself foretold he would be the shepherd …a tract of land to be cultivated, the field of God. On that land grows the ancient olive tree whose holy roots were the patriarchs…the vine… the edifice of God…the house of God in which dwells his family…. the temple…the holy city, the new Jerusalem… the bride…the mother…the body of Christ…the sacrament of salvation… a priestly people, a holy and royal people…People of God, of the new covenant, messianic people, pilgrim people". #6.

Why so many images for one thing? Because we are dealing with mystery. The Church is indeed a human organization but it is much more. It is also a divine entity. It is the extension of Christ, who is God and man, in His members in this world and it exists also in heaven and in purgatory. It is a body whose very soul is none other than the Holy Spirit who is God. Consequently, even a hundred images will not be enough to capture this mystery fully, but we must use some images nonetheless. Rather than labour through each of the images above let us try to make use of a few basic models provided by Cardinal Dulles that will serve as various windows on the Church and see how the priest might relate to each of them.

The Institutional model

Christ, as founder and head of the Church, structured it as an institution. He did so in order to enable it to endure. It is a structure of a very simple kind: the twelve and the disciples with Peter as head. The Holy Spirit would guide its development from the beginning. So let us look first at what Dulles calls "the institutional model". If the Church is a living body the institution, we might say, is the skeleton or visible structure of the organism. *Lumen Gentium* again:

> They are fully incorporated in the society of the church who, possessing the Spirit of Christ, accept her entire system and all the means of salvation given to her, and through union with her visible structure are joined to Christ, who rules her through the supreme pontiff and the bishops. This joining is effected by bonds of professed faith, of the sacraments, of ecclesial government, and of communion". *Ibid. #14. (cf.* also *CIC, canons 204-210).*

Here the Church is presented as an institution, for so it is. It is organized, structured, visible, external. St. Charles Borromeo even went so far as to compare it to the Republic of Venice of his day. This emphasis on the external and visible was strong after the reformation precisely because the Protestants were denying this and instead were speaking of the Church as an inward, invisible reality only.

Today it is quite fashionable, even for Catholics, to bash the institutional Church and to demand that it must change, by which these critics usually mean that it must throw off its hierarchical structure and become a simple democracy like some of the reformation sects. But the same people will also argue for women's ordination, which would then give us a hierarchy of a feminine kind which, seemingly, presents them with no problem! They ignore the fact that Christ Himself gave His Church a male, hierarchical structure with Peter at the head and the apostles with and under him; that shortly after, but still within apostolic times, the orders of priest and deacon came to be and that this structure is normative for all time even if there will always be ongoing development on how we understand these orders and how they function in relation to each other and in relation to the laity whom they serve. So, this structure is of divine ordinance and cannot be revamped at will as could happen in civil society if, for example, a country with a constitutional monarchy like England were to be changed into a republic like France due to some new party of republican minded people coming to power there.

Even reasoning in a purely sociological way one can say that if the Church were not an institution it would merely be a movement and, like all movements which, if they don't soon provide themselves with a structure, will rise on a wave of enthusiasm for a while due to the influence of a charismatic founder, and fall away again when this leader gets old, or will fragment if the leader is opposed by a rival in a power struggle.

The institutional Church is made visible at diocesan level by the bishop and at local or parish level by the presence of the parish priest and his flock. So, those who join in the fashionable chorus of bashing the institutional Church are, in effect, mostly hitting at their own parish priest because he is their nearest point of contact with the institutional Church. But then, if due to a shortage of priests, he is withdrawn from them they will be up in arms protesting at the bishop for robbing them of their priest! Or they will try to run an exclusively lay parish with no need of a priest at all. In which case one is no longer talking about a *Catholic* community! These are some of the contradictory results of institutional bashing. [1]

Our particular interest here is the priest as servant of the institutional Church. It requires of him that he be an efficient administrator in the sense of providing good leadership with properly organized liturgy in the first place; that he then be able to manage parish finances and see after the maintenance of church buildings and parish schools; that he have an up-to-date filing system with the names of the families in his parish documented and that he be a capable leader able to organize various parish events.

But if that is the *full* extent of his vision or his capabilities then he won't be much different to the manager of any other merely human institution or business. Indeed, he could become materially minded, seeing his parish as nothing more than another business venture to be run efficiently and for profit. The care of souls, the channelling of grace and the exercise of true, sincere charity are not likely to be priorities of his. He could become arrogant in his style and authoritarian, thinking that the Church is there solely for the wellbeing of the priest, which is what is called "clericalism". Yet, the efficient administration of a parish is important. Indeed, the failure of a parish priest to maintain church buildings can be grounds for his removal in canon law (*cf can. 1741 #5*). But granting this much, the institutional model, though important in its own right, has to be supplemented by other models, and not just for sociological reasons but for theological reasons also. If the institution is like the skeleton of the body of the Church that body will also need inner life, heat and the circulation of blood if it is to have life, which, in the case of the Church, means having the life of grace due to the indwelling of the Holy Spirit.

This brings us to our next model, the mystical communion model.

Mystical Communion Model

Christ has the grace of union whereby His human nature is taken up into union with the divine nature. He also has an abundance of habitual sanctifying grace in His human nature as head of the Church, His mystical body. This grace overflows into the members of His body so that they can become by participation what He is by nature: divine. This grace, we might say, is the inner life or blood-flow of the living organism. The mystical communion model has us look at the Church in this way. Let us go to *Lumen Gentium* again:

> This was to be the new People of God. For, those who believe in Christ, who are reborn not from a perishable but an imperishable seed through the Word of the living God (*1 Pet.1:23*), not from flesh but from water and the Holy Spirit (*Jn.3:5-6*), are established firmly as 'a chosen race, a royal priesthood, a holy nation, a purchased people…You who in times past were not a people, but are now the people of God' (*1 Pet.2:9-10*). That messianic people has for its head Christ 'who was delivered up for our sins…..' The heritage of this people are the dignity and freedom of the sons of God, in whose hearts the Holy Spirit dwells as in His temple. Its law is the new commandment to love as Christ loved us. Its goal is the kingdom of God… #9.

The Church's inner life of sanctifying grace begets faith, hope and especially charity in its members, thus making the Church a place of welcome for newcomers and of warmth for everyone. This grace, present in souls in this life, is meant to blossom into glory in the next. Dulles maintains that this was also the vision of the church which St Thomas Aquinas had primarily:

> For Aquinas the church essentially consists in a divinizing communion with God, whether incompletely in this life or completely in the life of glory. The grace that is the seed of glory is the grace of Christ and hence the church is

made up of all who are brought into union with God by supernatural grace flowing from Christ as head. Aquinas' view of the church is 'theological' rather than institutional. *Models of the Church, p. 47.*

But, of course, St Thomas did not reject the institutional and hierarchical aspect of the Church.

This mystical communion aspect of the Church was expressed by St John Paul II when commenting on Vatican II in this regard. Here again we have the term *communio* in Latin (or *koinonia* in Greek):

> Much was done by the Second Vatican council to bring out a clearer understanding of the church as *communion* and its concrete application to life. What then does this complex word *'communion'* mean? Its fundamental meaning speaks of the union with God brought about by Jesus Christ, in the Holy Spirit. *Christifideles Laici, (CL), #19.*

This *communio* is no superficial friendship; rather it is the very love that is the inner life of the Trinity now become the inner life of the Church because one of the Trinity, the Son, became man and became head of the Church, His body.

The priest who has this vision of the Church will have a keen sense of the supernatural and of the workings of grace. He will celebrate the sacraments with a sense of the sacred and promote charity in his people. So, he is likely to be a warm-hearted fellow able to draw people together and make them feel at home and be charitable himself in his dealings with them. He will say that finances and material things – necessary indeed - should be at the service of the building up of a charitable community.

But if understood in an unbalanced way, if he forgets the institutional side of things, this kind of priest will be weak on authority and tempted to seek popularity from being friendly; nor will he be discerning as to who may or may not receive the sacraments so long as he "keeps them all happy" as if that were the goal of all pastoral work, in which case, paradoxically and ironically, he also becomes somewhat like the priest who is merely a business administrator in the sense that he is always seeking to keep his customers happy but in this case at the expense of faith.

Let us look now at another model that can be said to combine both of the above models.

The Sacrament Model

Christ, the head of the Church is also its high priest who offered Himself as a sacrifice on Calvary and continues to make that same sacrifice present every day in the

Chapter 1: The Mysteries of the Faith and the Models of the Church

Church through the ministry of His priests. Hence, we have the Church's liturgy. The sacramental model, one could say, combines the above two, the institutional and the mystical communion models, because the sacraments are visible signs, administered in a structured way, of the invisible grace which is the inner life of the Church.

> ...the church is a kind of sacrament of intimate union with God and of the unity of all mankind; that is she is a sign and instrument of such union and unity. *LG,* #9, #48.

A sacrament is a visible sign of an invisible grace. It effects what it signifies and signifies what it effects. Before the council we thought mostly of the seven specified sacraments beginning with baptism, confirmation etc., but the council gave us a wider view as Henri de Lubac explains:

> If Christ is the sacrament of God, the church is for us the sacrament of Christ; she represents him, in the full and ancient meaning of the term, she really makes him present. She not only carries on his work, but she is his very continuation, in a sense far more real than that in which it can be said that any human institution is its founder's continuation. *Catholicism,* p. 29.

The visible aspect of the Church as a sacrament requires the Church to be institutional indeed, but the invisible aspect, the working of grace in souls, also belongs to the Church as a mystical communion.

The priest who would see this model as primary will be very devoted to good liturgy. He will see to the correct and valid administration of the sacraments and respect the rubrics laid down by Church authorities. He will celebrate Mass with great dignity, but with humility also, and have a keen sense of the sacred. We can expect that things on the altar and in the sanctuary will always be clean and decorous where he is in charge. This is important because the most important contact that most parishioners have with their parish is when they attend Sunday Mass which is only for the duration of one hour in the week; so, it is important that things be right at that time. A sloppy, ill prepared liturgy is a sure turn off and it raises questions in peoples' mind about the faith of the priest himself.

But, if limited in his vision, it may happen that this priest will not be able to see further than the sanctuary in terms of space or farther than Sunday in terms of time; that he will have little regard for the problems of the poor and needy at the outer edges of his parish. At worst, he may see himself as some kind of entertainer or showman in the sanctuary, seen now as a stage, in which case he is putting himself in the way as an obstacle between the Lord and His people. He must indeed relate to his people but not as an entertainer, rather, instead, as a pastor leading his sheep home to the Lord. He must preach so as to form them in faith which will make him unpopular at times.

This takes us to another model, closely related to the sacrament model, what can be called the "herald model" because preaching is an important part of it.

The Herald Model

Christ our head is the Word made flesh. He referred to Himself as the "Truth". His Church does not exist for herself but to proclaim Him to the world. There is perfect unity between Christ and His teaching. Hence, we can see the Church as a herald of what God has first said to us in Christ and revelation.

> The holy People of God shares also in Christ's prophetic office. It spreads abroad a living witness to him…For, by this sense of faith which is aroused and sustained by the Spirit of truth, God's people accept not the word of men but the very Word of God (*cf. 1 Th.2:13*). It clings without fail to the faith once delivered to the saints (*cf. Jude 3*), penetrates it more deeply by accurate insights, and applies it more thoroughly to life. All this it does under the lead of a sacred teaching authority to which it loyally defers". *LG, #12.*

If Christ is a prophet, as well as being priest and king, then the Church must be prophetic also in the widest sense of the word of bearing witness to Him in word and deed, not only in Church on Sunday but in the secular world of work also during the week and in family life. This prophetic role belongs especially to the priest when he is preaching. In fact, it is through the word of God that the people are united and held together because "faith comes from hearing". So the council says:

> The People of God finds its unity first of all through the word of the living God… *Presbyterorum Ordinis, (PO), #4.*

Pope Saint Paul VI put great emphasis on this especially in his letter *Evangelii Nuntiandi*. Prior to Pope Paul the entire protestant tradition had put great emphasis on preaching the word of God. Karl Barth in the last century is an example.

The priest who likes this model will undoubtedly be a good preacher and will prepare his sermons with thought and with care. He will inspire his people with a love for the word of God as found in scripture and the doctrines of tradition, but he will also instil in them a desire for fundamental human rights in defence of the weak. He will be like the prophets of old calling people to repentance, or, one could say, he will be the conscience of society in his time.

But if concerned with this exclusively this priest will tend to neglect the daily nuts and bolts of parish administration and fail to see the importance of the sacraments. Or, he will fail to see how the liturgy of the word is meant to announce the Christ who then becomes present in the Eucharist, in which case he becomes like a Christian preacher who does not have a valid Eucharist. Worse still, he might take a wrongful pride in his own eloquence or descend to being a funny man entertaining the audience with his jokes or to preaching himself instead of the Lord, or, worst of all, he might use his powers of preaching to divide his people on political matters or other such matters which might best be left to others. We will be looking at this model more closely in the prophet section of this study coming later.

The Servant Model

Christ spoke of Himself as one who came to serve, and He taught this in His parable of the good Samaritan and more vividly by His washing of the disciples' feet. Hence, another model, related to the prophet model, is what can be called the "servant model", a necessary supplement, because it wants to see what is preached being given practical effect in charitable deeds and in the kind of social reform that will promote the common good of society and foster the union of all men in Christ. Hence the council says:

> …this sacred synod proclaims the highest destiny of man and champions the godlike seed which has been sown in him. It offers to mankind the honest assistance of the church in fostering that brotherhood of all men which corresponds to this destiny of theirs. *Gaudium et Spes, (GS), #3.*

The document from which this quote is taken, *Gaudium et Spes,* begins by saying that the Church makes her own the joys and hopes of mankind today. She states that she wants to be involved in the struggle for justice, in feeding the hungry and in every other worthy, lawful endeavour that seeks to make the life of mankind more genuinely human and open to grace.

The priest who likes this model will want to go outside of the sanctuary to the outermost parts of his parish to visit the poor in their homes and in the back alleys if that is where they are to be found. Within his parish he will organize various programmes of social aid for various worthy causes, even if doing so may take him beyond the bounds of his parish at times. He will be interested in what his people are doing, not just on Sunday but on Monday and the other days in their various occupations, and will want to champion the rights of those who are oppressed in any way. He will give great credibility to the Church as a body truly concerned about people and their needs and not just as a spiritual club for pious people concerned only with the heavenly. In other words, he will rob Marxists and such people of their excuse for saying that religion is just the opium of the people and that the Church does not care about their lot.

But, taken to extreme, this priest simply becomes a social worker or a politician or trade union activist. He forgets that the root evil is sin, not just social sin but personal sin, and that the root liberation is not by means of social agitation but is that which was won for us by Christ's sacrifice on the cross, a sacrifice made present every day in the Mass. So, this priest may indeed see the connection between his prophetic role and his servant role but may fail to see any link between either of these and his sacramental role. In the course of time such a priest will neglect the Mass and the sacraments entirely. In presenting himself as a social activist he forgets that, however worthy may be the causes for which he struggles, the people he is serving want their priest to be more than a social activist. They want him to be a man of God first and foremost.

Other Models or Images

In addition to these five models of the church listed by Avery Dulles there are other models or images which can prove useful such as those we saw already in *Lumen Gentium*. A simple image is that of the Church as the family of God with the bishop as His principal representative in the diocese. This image goes back to Ignatius of Antioch. He used it to call for unity of the clergy round their bishop. (*cf.*, his letters to the *Philadelphians* and to the *Magnesians*). In a given parish an elderly, saintly parish priest might be seen in this light with his parishioners coming to him for his prayers in their time of need and for advice in their difficulties. But a young priest is also a father to his people, even to those older than himself. They may come to him expecting him to have a wisdom that comes from above – which he will have if he is faithful to prayer, especially prayer to the Holy Spirit, and study – but he should also be respectful of age and the wisdom of age that one often finds in senior lay people.

There is then the classic image or model of St Paul of the Church as the body or the temple of Christ with the priest nourishing this body or building up this temple; and then there is his image of the Church as the bride of Christ whom He loves so that the priest will love her in the place of Christ to the point of giving himself totally for her in a life of self-sacrifice. This was an image often used by St John Paul II:

> According to the Letter to the *Ephesians* (*Ch. 5*), the bride is the church, just as for the prophets the bride was Israel. She is therefore a collective subject and not an individual person. This collective subject is the People of God, a community made up of many persons, both women and men. *Mulieris Dignitatem*, #25-27. (*cf.* St Thomas, *Summa Theologiae*, III, Supplement, q95, a3).

St John Paul himself loved the Church in this way, and then, in his later years he came across to people as a great, fatherly figure caring for the family of God worldwide and was loved by the young in particular. This model of the Church as the bride of Christ should enrich the priest's understanding of celibacy. He forgoes having an earthly bride, not for a life of lonely individualism but in order to give himself fully to his people, thereby representing Christ in His union with His bride the Church.

An important pastoral point in relation to the above models is that, since all have value, the individual priest should be open to all and be competent in some measure in exemplifying all of them. This, in turn, will depend to some extent on his talents, his style of leadership and on his personality. A priest who is a great preacher but who totally neglects parish finances is unbalanced in his work, so also a great liturgy priest who has no care for the poor in his parish. It is likely that in a given rectory there could be two or three priests one of whom better exemplifies one model and another some other model by very temperament. That happens. But it need not be a ground for disagreement between them. Rather, it should be grounds for co-operation and complementarity from which everyone in the parish will benefit.

Can we find any one, over all model that will catch and subsume all these other models? Dulles wisely says "no" to that because he is mindful of the fact that the Church, at the end of all analysis, is still a mystery of the divine in the human which will never be fully captured by any one model or image. Pope Paul VI said the same at the council:

The church is a mystery. It is a reality imbued with the hidden presence of God. It lies, therefore, within the very nature of the church to be always open to new and ever greater explorations". *Council Speeches of Vatican II* (Opening of Second Session).

But then, one should also remember that the same pope gave Mary the title of "Model and Mother of the Church" which means that if one cares to examine the matter one will find in her life aspects of all the models presented above and lived out in a perfect way.

Conclusions:

1. Pastoral theology has to be founded on the mysteries of the faith, beginning with the Trinity. It is the study of the practical application of the mysteries in the life of the parish. The priest is a man of God, representing God to his people and bringing the mysteries to them especially by his preaching and administration of the sacraments. Christians grow in holiness by living the mysteries in their daily lives and in the liturgy.

2. The priest is also a man of the Church, representing his people before God. There are many possible, inclusive models of the Church, no one of which will exhaust her meaning entirely, because she is divine as well as human because of Christ her head who is truly God and truly man, and the Holy Spirit who lives in her. So, this should have us see the different models as complementary and also the work of those who give effect to them in the parish. A priest should try to embody all of the models as best his talents or temperament will allow.

3. Being a good pastor requires a love of the Church despite the failings of its members. There have always been problems in the Church and sin in its members, with the great exception of Mary, but an attitude of negative criticism only makes matters worse. The attitude of what is sometimes called "loyal dissent" does not help either. It is, in fact, a contradictory notion if one is dissenting from sound teaching in either faith or morals. The pastor will love the Church if he has a love for Christ the head of the Church which love is nourished by time spent in prayer before the Blessed Sacrament.

4. We should remember that Mary has been given the title of "Model and Mother of the Church" and implore her help in all our pastoral endeavours.

The study of the different models of the Church gives us different ways of looking at the Church in itself. Next, we will try to say something about its origin, not so much historically - because we all know it was founded by Christ - but ontologically, that is to see whether it originates with the universal and leads down to the particular or *vice versa*, and then look at its structure as found in the diocese and the parish.

Chapter II

The Church, Universal and Local

The Universal Church, the Diocese and the Parish

We want you to know, brothers, what God's grace has done in the churches in Macedonia. 2 Cor.8:1.

The Roman Pontiff, as the successor of Peter, is the perpetual and visible source and foundation of the unity of bishops and of the multitude of the faithful. (*cf. CIC #227*). The individual bishop, however, is the visible principle and foundation of unity in his particular church, <u>fashioned after</u> the model of the universal church. <u>In and from</u> such individual churches there comes into being the one and only Catholic Church. *Lumen Gentium, #23. (cf. also St. Cyprian).*

Having looked at the different models of the Church let us return to the first one, the Church as an institution, as a body having an organized, visible structure spread throughout the world which is universal with a unity made visible in the papacy and in the college of bishops and made visible locally also whenever a parish community gathers for Mass with their priest, especially on a Sunday. But where do we begin – at the top with the universal Church or at the bottom with the local Church? Which comes first? It is a bit like the old riddle of which comes first - the hen or the egg!

The universal Church and the local Church

The quote above from *Lumen Gentium* seemingly tries to have it both ways! If, as it says, the particular Church is fashioned "after the model of the universal Church" then it would seem to follow that the universal Church is prior. But then when it says that "in and from such individual Churches there comes into being the one and only Catholic Church" one gets the impression that the particular Church comes first and that the many such Churches are building blocks of the universal Church which then comes into being afterwards when these are put together. *Lumen Gentium* also speaks of the particular Church under the bishop as "a portion of the universal Church". (cf. *#23*). Pope John Paul II throws some light on this problem when he says:

> The particular church does not come about from a kind of fragmentation of the universal church, nor does the universal church come about by a simple

> amalgamation of particular churches. But there is a real, essential and constant bond uniting each of them and this is <u>why the universal church exists and is manifested in the particular churches</u>. For this reason the council says that the particular churches 'are constituted after the model of the universal church; it is <u>in and from these particular churches</u> that there comes into being the one and only Catholic church'. *Christifideles Laici,* #25, (*cf.* also *General Directory of Catechesis, 1997,* #217).

This gives priority to the universal Church but he also quotes *Lumen Gentium* again which seems to give priority to the particular church. However, what we gain from this quote is that in talking about the Church and how it comes to be we are not talking about a simple breaking down or building up of material entities. We are dealing with a sacramental reality which requires a different kind of language. The word "manifested" is the key because a sacrament is something that makes manifest by sign a supernatural reality. The next quote from John Paul II makes this clearer again:

> ...sacred ministers must always be aware that <u>the universal Church "is a reality which is ontologically and temporally prior to every particular Church"</u>. Indeed, the universal Church is not the sum total of all particular Churches. The particular Churches, in and with the universal Church, must be open to the reality of a true communion of persons, charisms, and spiritual traditions which transcends geographical, psychological or intellectual boundaries. It should be perfectly clear to priests that the Church is one. Universality or catholicity should always pervade the particular. A profound, genuine and vital bond of communion with the See of Peter is the guarantee and necessary condition for this. Acceptance, diffusion, and conscientious application of papal documents, and of other documents published by the Dicasteries of the Roman Curia, are its concrete expression. *Priest, Pastor and Leader,* # 17.

The universal Church is ontologically and temporally prior to every particular Church. It was not the case that the Church sprang up here and there in different places under different pastors who then came together and made Peter their head. No, it began with Christ's calling of Peter and the twelve at a particular time so that today the pope and the college of bishops have an ontological priority. But one can indeed speak of a coming together or a building up in a *material* sense if one is doing some kind of census of the Church and tots up the number of parishes in each diocese and then the number of dioceses in the world, or if at some great liturgical event like a papal installation, one sees people coming to Rome from the different diocese of the world. So once again the following quote should clear up the matter:

> The particular Church is constituted by the community of Christ's disciples who live incarnated in a definite socio-cultural space. Every particular Church 'makes present the universal Church together with all of its essential elements'. In reality the universal Church, made fruitful by the Holy Spirit on the first Pentecost, 'brings forth the particular Churches as children and is expressed in them'. The universal Church, as the Body of Christ, is thus made manifest as 'a Body of Churches'. *General Directory on Catechesis, #217.*

By the term "particular Churches" in the above quotes is meant the diocese under the bishop who is a member of the college of bishops with and under Peter. But can we take this manifesting of the universal Church a step further analogically and say that the universal Church is also made manifest in the local parish church building when the faithful are gathered with their priest around the altar on a Sunday for Mass? We can. The office of bishop, and hence his particular Church, follows from its divine institution by Christ but logistical necessity requires that the bishop then divide up his diocese into parishes with a priest in charge of each parish:

> Because it is impossible for the bishop always and everywhere to preside over the whole flock in his church, he cannot do other than establish lesser groupings of the faithful. Among these, parishes set up locally under a pastor who takes the place of the bishop are the most important: for in a certain way they represent the visible Church as it is established throughout the world" *Sacrosanctum Consilium, (SC), #42.*

So, the analogy continues downwards – the local parish Church also manifests the universal Church, and *Lumen Gentium* finds a basis for this not just in historical development but in the New Testament itself:

> This church of Christ is truly present in all legitimate local congregations of the faithful which, united with their pastors, are themselves called churches in the New Testament. *LG, #26. (cf. Acts 8:1; 14:22-3; 20:17).*

And again, further *on Lumen Gentium* says:

> As they [priests] sanctify and govern under the bishop's authority that part of the Lord's flock entrusted to them, they make the universal church visible in their own locality and lend powerful assistance to the up building of the whole body of Christ. *#28.*

The implications of this are very ennobling for the small, remote parish and its community. If we use sacramental language and accept that the universal Church is "manifested" in the local Churches then it follows that whenever there is a lawful gathering of the faithful around the altar with their priest for Mass that there we have the Church made present and visible. Even if it is in a little church building on the side of a hill in a faraway country with little resources materially - with only a small congregation because of its minority status or because of persecution - that what we have there is not merely a *portion* of the universal Church but the universal Church itself made visibly present in one place.

This reminds me of Cardinal Newman when he became a Catholic and was able to say that it was not in any of the great Protestant cathedrals, with their elaborate liturgies, that the Church of the apostles was to be found in his day but in the Catholic Church even if that Church was to be found in a small congregation gathered with their priest in some small, humble chapel off the beaten track.

An analogy for this can be found in the sacred Hosts at Holy Communion at Mass; the entire Christ is present in every consecrated Host in the ciborium and even in every "portion" of the Host (if considered materially). Another analogy might be that of the sun in the sky, a thing of immense magnitude in itself, but something which can, nonetheless, be made present in whole in small mirrors held in the hands of a hundred different people. This means that Catholics everywhere, no matter how small in numbers in their local Church, are not just a part, out on the edges, of the universal Church, poor relations of the universal Church compared, let us say, to the Catholics of Rome or of some other big city, but are in themselves the locus of the universal Church in their own communities. It is another way of saying that the Church is very directly a mother to all. It also says that the Church, though a divine and therefore a spiritual thing, is also an earthly thing; it is not "up in the clouds" but very much rooted in the earth, localized, and that is because it is incarnated like its Head. The Church, being a sacrament, elicits the divine and makes it present in a way that is as visible and as tangible as a crowd of people whom one can count and physically touch, though all the while the divinity present in it is invisible in itself. That is why also all of the sacraments require the physical presence of both the minister and the recipient and why an electronic Mass – Mass by TV for example – can never take the place of a localized Mass even though for those who are housebound it is the best they can do. Yet, even when localized, we cannot touch or measure what takes place in the souls of those gathered at Mass, their *communio*, the workings of grace in them because that is due to the indwelling of the Holy Spirit who is the third person of the transcendent God.

The Parish – its Development

If then the parish has this great dignity, if it is the universal Church made manifest locally, if it is the place "where it all happens" in the daily life of the Church we should give some time to studying it. St. Pope Paul VI had a great regard for the parish. He saw it as indispensable and listed the many things that happen in it:

> We believe simply that this old and venerable structure of the parish has an indispensable mission of great contemporary importance: to create the basic community of the Christian people; to initiate and gather the people in the accustomed expression of liturgical life; to conserve and renew the faith in the people of today; to serve as the school for teaching the salvific message of Christ; to put solidarity into practice and work the humble charity of good and brotherly works". *Discourse to the Roman Clergy, 1963.*

The parish is an "old and venerable structure" according to the pope. It goes back to the early days of the faith. At first Christianity was a religion of the cities – Antioch, Rome, Corinth and other big centres around the Mediterranean and usually the religion of the lower classes in such places. The people in the countryside were referred to as "pagans". Today it is be mostly the other way around: people in country places generally hold on to the faith and practice it better than those in the cities for the simple reason that traditions hold more firmly in such places. The particular Church in a city was headed by an apostle such as St Peter when he was in Antioch and later in Rome, and after his generation it was headed by those on whom the apostles had laid hands and put in their place as overseers, *episcopoi*. These *episcopoi* were the successors of the apostles and later came to be known as bishops. These *episcopoi*, in turn, were surrounded by a group of *presbuterio*, presbyters, whom today we call "priests" or "pastors". Then there were also the deacons, assistants of the bishops in liturgy and in administration and works of charity.

One could say that in these cities – using our terms today – that the diocese and the parish were synonymous at first. But as numbers of the faithful grew, the city territories had to be broken down into smaller units with a priest placed in charge of each under the overall jurisdiction of the bishop. In today's language we call those units "parishes". To show the unity that was there between all of these parishes under the bishop it was customary to take a piece of the consecrated Host, that which is broken off just before Communion at Mass, and send it from one parish Mass to another to be put in the chalice in the other parish.

Later, when persecutions ceased and the Church expanded out from the cities into the countryside more parishes, each with its own priest, had to be established. And when the territory expanded further new diocese had to be set up to make for groupings of these new parishes and so on as the expansion went further which, in turn, led to the establishing of metropolitan areas under patriarchs or archbishops as we still have today.

This development was mostly in the countries round the Mediterranean and upwards into Gaul (France today). But in places like Ireland and England the structure of the monasteries developed – a monastery being the central unit of Church structure for a whole clan or tribe.

The Parish – Definition

How can we define what a parish is? Normally we think of it as a unit of the Church in a designated territory and, in fact, it is nearly always such. But that is not its principal defining mark. Instead, it is its character as a Eucharistic community as St John Paul makes clear. The parish is not principally a structure, a territory, or a building, he says, but rather:

> …the family of God, a fellowship afire with a unifying spirit, a familial and welcoming home, the community of the faithful. Plainly and simply, the parish is founded on a theological reality, because it is a Eucharistic community.
> *Christifideles Laici*, #26

The Eucharist is central in the life of the parish. But it does not follow that every group of people gathered for Mass thereby form a parish. Other elements are also needed. Let us turn to the *Code of Canon Law* for further help:

> A parish is a certain community of Christ's faithful stably established within a particular Church, whose pastoral care, under the authority of the diocesan Bishop, is entrusted to a parish priest as its proper pastor. The diocesan Bishop alone can establish, suppress or alter parishes. He is not to establish, suppress or notably alter them unless he has consulted the council of priests. *Canon 515.*

If a parish is to be "stably establish" it needs some material resources such as finance and some buildings, a church building and perhaps some schools and equipment and it must be foreseen that these resources will be able to endure for a foreseeable time ahead.

The parish is also a legal entity. It is a juridical person. "A lawfully established parish has juridical personality by virtue of the law itself". *Ibid., #3*. So, if Mrs Jones slips on a banana skin on her way into Mass, and claims it was left carelessly on the steps of the church building, she can sue the parish, not in the sense of taking a law-case against each and every parishioner nor against the parish priest as a private individual but against the parish itself as a juridical personality who will be represented in court by the current parish priest.

> In all juridical matters, the parish priest acts in the person of the parish, in accordance with the law. *Canon 532.*

The parish can also be described as the place where an individual or family has domicile, a stable residence, even if their work during the day calls them to places outside the parish. *(cf. CIC #205/6)*. It is the place where one feels at home and beds down at night. Domicile has a legal aspect to it also in regard to baptisms, confirmations, weddings, funerals *etc*. Normally one receives these sacraments in one's own parish, or, if for some reason, people wish to receive them in another parish the consent of the priest of one's place of domicile is sought. And if one is to feel at home in a given parish, we should be able to say that it is a place where one is first made to feel welcome and is then invited to be part of what is going on there. This requires that the parish priest and his assistant(s) be welcoming people and that perhaps they have some pastoral team who will make an outreach to new comers.

Flowing from the parish as a religious entity there is the parish as a social and cultural entity. I say "flowing from the religious" because the religious dimension is the deepest in man even if some people are unwilling to admit that. The parish, accordingly, is that place which people of faith are proud of as their home; the place they sing about in their songs and long for when they are in exile. That faith and sense of parish is the locus of all true patriotism. The man who is all enthusiasm for his country or for the international community but has no regard for the place of his birth or upbringing does not impress me. The parish has also often been the locus or geographical unit of sporting teams which also fosters local patriotism when people cheer for the team that represents their home place. This is good for building community spirit provided it does not go to the extreme of begetting hostility towards teams from other places. The home parish is the place which at the beginning of our lives sets us on the road to our final home in the kingdom of God. [1]

I am stressing the importance of the home parish here for the added reason that such emphasis will serve as a corrective to the over emphasis we have nowadays on globalism understood as a one-world regime in which all national and local boundaries are due to be abolished. That is nothing other than neo-Marxism, a denial of the basic truth that man is a "localized" being, that life for most people is lived locally in their home place for the simple reason that earthly living anchors us in place and time. That will continue to be true even if telecommunication and trade are now fast uniting all parts of the world in one large network and when foreign travel is becoming ever more easy. Globalism can be enriching when it opens us to what is good in other cultures but if that is at the expense of one's own home culture, a culture flowing from the faith that is lived in one's parish, then it is bad. [2]

It is the parish priest who has full and proper care of a parish under his bishop. He may have assistant priests with him but his authority is not then divided or "parcelled out" even if an assistant priest is assigned a portion of the parish for his special care, or even if he has special duties in that parish or in a number of nearby parishes. (cf. *Canon 545*).

It is for the bishop to appoint the parish priest – and his assistant priests - and remove them. It is not for any council of laity in the parish to do so. The bishop can also establish, suppress or alter parishes but he should consult the council of priests when doing so. Priests who have served in such parishes in times past can give him good advice on such rearrangements. (cf. *Cans. 515, 523*).

Other Kinds of Parish Structures and Personal Parishes

The parish we are most familiar with is the territorial parish but there are other kinds of parishes such as the personal parish when a priest with the office of pastor has care of some minority group which transcends the borders of a number of territorial parishes, perhaps an ethic or language group who are Catholics, or Catholics of a different rite or a group who are always on the move because of their profession, e.g., those in the air force or navy. The same happens with personal prelatures as when a bishop has care of such people.

Then there is the *quasi* parish which is "a certain community of Christ's faithful within a particular church, entrusted to a priest as its proper pastor, but because of special circumstances not yet established as a parish." It is usually legally the equivalent of a parish. (cf. *Can 518*). A quasi parish might be established in expanding missionary territory when a priest or deacon or catechist goes out to a district outside his own parish and helps in setting up a new parish there. People from that district might be coming in to the established parish for some time beforehand already. The hope is that the quasi parish will soon be able to stand on its own two feet as a stable entity. There is the opposite situation, then, where one parish or more has lost a priest due to retirement or some other cause and vocations are low in that country. If the population is not too high the neighbouring pastor may be able to take over the care of both parishes, or the bishop may put in a deacon or religious or even a lay person into the vacant parish to manage such things as the organizing of time-tables for services, the taking of Mass offerings or the looking after church maintenance. But such a person, even if very competent, can not have the full care of that parish because he/she is not the pastor. He works under the direction of the pastor of a nearby parish. Widening out on this arrangement, one can have what is called a "cluster" or union of three or four or more parishes put together under a team of priests each of whom is a pastor in his own parish but all of whom help out in the whole area and take care of the parish (or of two or more parishes) where there is no resident pastor. Even though all those priests are of equal standing as parish priests, good order requires that one of them takes overall charge to co-ordinate teamwork. He is called the "moderator". (*cf. Canon 517*).

As to the duties of the moderator *vis a vis* the others canon law says the following:

Each of the priests to whom the care of a parish or of a number of parishes together is jointly entrusted, is bound to fulfil the duties and functions of a parish priest mentioned in canons *528, 529* and *530*. They are to do this according to a plan determined among themselves. The faculty to assist at marriages, and all the faculties to dispense which are given to a parish priest by virtue of the law itself, belong to all, but are to be exercised under the direction of the moderator. *Canon. 543 #1.*

The duties of the moderator are similar to those of the vicar forane as outlined in *Canon 555.*

Canon 553 goes on to say that parish priests are obliged to live in the area assigned to them. That is important in many respects. It cuts across the old abuse of absenteeism of former times which often led people to believe that their priest was away having a good time with their dues (and, sadly, sometimes that was the case). In any case, because, again, the Church is an incarnate reality and because people are attached to the place they call "home" the faithful in any given parish want their priest to be in their midst. There is also the aspect of the spousal nature of the priest-people relationship. When parishes are being clustered for reasons of necessity people will still be heard to say "Yes, we know there is a shortage of priests but nonetheless we'd like to have our own priest". This is particularly true of old people who want the consolation of having their priest nearby when they are drawing near to life's end.

A parish priest in his own parish, or the moderator for the cluster of parishes, is bound to offer Mass weekly for the faithful in his care – *the missa pro populo*. The principal Sunday Mass is the most suitable occasion (if a funeral does not make this impossible) and the faithful should be told that this Mass is for them. It is a source of comfort for them to know that their parish priest is offering Mass for them and praying for them at other times also. More than that, to intercede for his people is one of the defining notions of priesthood, something we see in the Old Testament as when Moses intercedes for his people.

This clustering of parishes is happening a lot now in the Western world where vocations have declined. It works to some degree, so long as the situation does not arise where there are too few priests for too many parishes in a given cluster. When this happens, lay people have to conduct Eucharistic services themselves and sometimes preach also, even though this is an exceptional measure.

Should we then conclude that this is going to be the shape of the future Church – lay leaders and ministers because of the shortage of priests? I knew of a situation in the middle of France where there were many parishes with no resident priest and where the lay leaders came together for a meeting. The bishop sent them a message expressing his regret that he did not have a priest to send to them for the foreseeable future. But they sent him a reply telling him that he need not worry, that they were doing fine without any priest! Again, I knew of a situation in Switzerland where a deacon was insisting on conducting his own service on the first Sunday of every month even when a priest *was* available! He was insisting on having "his own show" at all costs! Should we *resign* ourselves to this kind of thing? The answer is definitely No. Here is what St John Paul II says on the matter:

> It would be a fatal error to despair in the face of present difficulties and adopt an attitude which, *de facto*, would prepare a Church of the future which would be almost bereft of priests. Measures adopted in this light to counter present shortages of priests, notwithstanding the good intentions motivating them, would, in fact, be seriously prejudicial for the ecclesial community. *Priest, Pastor and Leader, #24; cf.* also his *Address to Congregation for Clergy, 2001.*

Priests should be willing to seek the help of good lay people in a time of shortage and they should be appreciative of the help they can give, most especially in countries of persecution. And, indeed, priests who are under strain do appreciate this. But to resign ourselves to such a situation would, in fact, amount to adopting a kind of congregationalism, a protestantizing of the Church, because it would mean a departure from the original divinely-given structure of the Church, given to her by Christ Himself when He established her as a hierarchy of priest and people. So also, calling for the ordination of women or married priests or the re-installing of priests who left the priesthood is not the answer because it is to avoid looking for the root of this problem of the shortage of priests which is a lack of faith consonant with the rise of secularism and hedonism and of a general atheism whether that be official atheism as in communist countries or practical atheism as in the West.

Conclusions:

1. The parish can be seen as a part of the diocese and of the universal Church, but the last is ontologically prior. The parish is a manifestation, a presence, of the universal Church at local level especially when the people of God are gathered round the altar to celebrate the Eucharist with their pastor.
2. Theologically the parish is a family-type community under God the Father, centred on Christ in the Eucharist. Materially the parish is a geographic unit centred round the church building, stable financially. Legally it is a juridical person under the care of a pastor who is a priest. Socially it is the place where people have a sense of belonging and are helped to grow in faith, hope and love.
3. The parish structure has had a varied history in the past. Today, due to rapidly changing circumstances and various needs such as the shortage of priests, canon law allows for flexibility in structure and in the provision of personnel, clerical and lay, for the care of souls. However, because by divine will the Church lives from the Eucharist, celebrated by ordained priests, one must not make the shortage of priests an excuse for developing parish structures which will function entirely without priests.

We have been looking at the Church as it is structured institutionally. In the coming sections we will look at the work of the pastor in his parish as king, prophet and priest, along with his lay helpers. The next chapter will look at his work as shepherd, his kingly role.

Part B

King

Introduction

We have said that the pastor is conformed to Christ by his ordination, Christ who is truly God and truly man in one person and who has three offices *(munera)* those of king/shepherd, prophet/teacher and priest/sanctifier. As to which of these three is primary theologians differ. Pope Benedict XVI would give priority to that of prophet because faith comes from hearing and outside of a context of faith administering the sacraments so as to sanctify – a priestly function – makes no sense. But others, like Jean Galot, former professor at the Gregorianum in Rome, would give priority to the shepherding role because the shepherd feeds his flock with both the word of God and the sacraments and holds them together. And then many pastors on the ground would give priority to the priestly role because they would hold that the most important functions of the pastor, -why we usually call him a "priest" - is to say Mass and then to hear confessions. St John Paul II in his various writings gives priority to one office here and to another there at different times without coming down definitively on any one of them. The *Code of Canon Law* takes the order of king, prophet and priest, (the order I am taking in this study). I do so for the very basic reason that a priest, when appointed to an existing parish, takes over an organized structure of things which he has to maintain, that he administers the sacraments there and prepares his people there for the sacraments by preaching the word of God to them.

Chapter III

The Kingly Office

The Shepherd, his Authority and Role

"I will give you shepherds after my own heart" Jer.3:1.

"And He appointed twelve to be with Him and to be sent out to preach and have authority to cast out demons." Mk. 3:13-15.

Also, the function of guiding the community as shepherd, the proper function of the parish priest, stems from his unique relation to Christ the Head and Shepherd. It is a function having a sacramental character. *Address by Pope John Paul II in Priest, Pastor and Leader of the Parish Community, #5*

If we begin by looking at the pastor's kingly office we must first see why such an office is needed at all, why the Lord has instituted such; then we will look at the source and nature of the pastor's authority and the kind of style of leadership it should give rise to in his daily work of shepherding the flock.

Why Shepherds?

<u>St Thomas</u>

St. Augustine famously said: "For you I am a bishop, with you I am a Christian," *Sermon 340*.

The word "bishop" used here by St Augustine is, of course, inclusive of the three offices of king, prophet and priest. When we come to St Thomas Aquinas we find him asking "whether there should be order in the Church?" The method of St Thomas when examining some question is, first, to present us with some *objections* to the position he will be advocating. Then he states his position briefly in his *sed contra*. Then he expounds on that position in a full article, and finally he gives replies to the objections which he had posed at the beginning.

We will look at his article on this question of whether there should be a structured order of personnel in the Church in full, looking at both the objections he poses and the replies he gives to them because it is very relevant today. By an "order" is meant a class or group of people in a given society or community who are set apart and have authority or functions in relation to the rests of the community. The order understood in this article below is that of the hierarchy of ordained men in the church.

Objection 1. "It would seem that there should not be Order in the church. For Order requires subjection and pre-eminence. But subjection seemingly is incompatible with the liberty whereunto we are called by Christ. Therefore, there should not be Order in the Church".

This objection relies on a pagan understanding of authority whereby those in command lord it over those under them, tyrannically, for their (the rulers') own selfish gain. The gospel, by comparison, talks of the *freedom* of the children of God. But this freedom is not a reckless liberty that refuses all authority.

Objection 2. "Further, he who has received an Order becomes another's superior. But in the church everyone should deem himself lower than another (*Philippians 2:3*): "Let each esteem others better than themselves." Therefore Order should not be in the church".

This objection relies on a false equation made between the subjective moral worth of a person and the objective position of authority he has in the church.

Objection 3. "Further, we find order among the angels on account of their differing in natural and gratuitous gifts. But all men are one in nature, and it is not known who has the higher gifts of grace. Therefore Order should not be in the church".

This objection relies on a denial of any authority on the grounds that we are all equal in nature as compared to the angels who are unequal in nature.

Bearing in mind that St Thomas was writing in the mid 13th century one can see that the first two objections here are strangely prophetic of the reformation still to come three hundred years later, because one could say that Protestantism was a call for democracy in religion, a call that soon after would be taken up in civil life with the enlightenment and the French revolution.

On the contrary, "Those things that are of God, are in order [Vulg: 'Those (powers) that are, are ordained of God.']." Now the church is of God, for He Himself built it with His blood. Therefore there ought to be Order in the church".

Chapter 3: The Kingly Office

"Further, the state of the church is between the state of nature and the state of glory. Now we find order in nature, in that some things are above others, and likewise in glory, as in the angels. Therefore there should be Order in the church".

I answer that, "God wished to produce His works in likeness to Himself, as far as possible, in order that they might be perfect, and that He might be known through them. Hence, that He might be portrayed in His works, not only according to what He is in Himself, but also according as He acts on others, He laid this natural law on all things, that last things should be reduced and perfected by middle things, and middle things by the first, as Dionysius says (Eccl. Hier. v). Wherefore that this beauty might not be lacking to the church, He established Order in her so that some should deliver the sacraments to others, being thus made like to God in their own way, as co-operating with God; even as in the natural body, some members act on others".

In simple terms: if there is hierarchical order above us in heaven and below us in nature it is to be expected that God would arrange for the same in His Church.

Reply to Objection 1. "The subjection of slavery is incompatible with liberty; for slavery consists in lording over others and employing them for one's own profit. Such subjection is not required in Order, whereby those who preside have to seek the salvation of their subjects and not their own profit".

Reply to Objection 2. "Each one should esteem himself lower in merit, not in office; and orders are a kind of office".

Reply to Objection 3. "Order among the angels does not arise from difference of nature, unless accidentally, in so far as difference of grace results in them from difference of nature. But in them it results directly from their difference in grace; because their orders regard their participation of divine things, and their communicating them in the state of glory, which is according to the measure of grace, as being the end and effect, so to speak, of grace. On the other hand, the Orders of the church militant regard the participation in the sacraments and the communication thereof, which are the cause of grace and, in a way, precede grace; and consequently our Orders do not require sanctifying grace, but only the power to dispense the *sacraments*; for which reason order does not correspond to the difference of sanctifying grace, but to the difference of power". *Summa Theologiae III, q34. a1.*

Nature, grace and glory are three levels of being according to St Thomas, the Church being a community of those living by grace. Now if there is order, hierarchy, below at the level of nature and above at the level of glory there should also be order or hierarchy at the level in between, that of those living by grace in the Church. It is fitting then that some should be appointed to administer this grace with authority to others.

As to the objections, the first one would hold up if we assumed that authority in the Church was entirely for domination, for the benefit of those on top so that they could exploit or oppress those under them. This indeed happens at times when a pastor is a hireling shepherd intent only on his own well-being. This is clericalism. Authority in the Church is for service so that those exercising it will take good care of those in their charge for their good and in faithfulness to Christ who appointed them to do this. Authority might still need to be firm and strict at times, but if so, it is still for the good of the flock and should be exercised with moderation and pastoral charity.

The reply to the second objection becomes clear when we distinguish between merit and office. Those in high office might well be much lower than those in low office in their inner souls in the sight of God - who knows except God alone – but gradation of office is still necessary for right order in the Church and indeed in any organized community.

The reply to the third objection sees the hierarchy of the angels as being based primarily on their different levels of grace and secondarily on their different levels of nature, but office in the Church is for the administration of grace which is a different thing to the possession of grace because even a priest in a sinful state of soul can still administer the sacraments validly.

I think this article by St Thomas with both the objections and replies is important because we live in a democratic age now in civil life and we are undoubtedly influenced by this in our ecclesial life also. Hence the many calls today for the involvement of the laity, co-responsibility, shared decision making and so forth. All of these ideas are good and have their rightful place in due measure. Indeed, they are encouraged in the documents of Vatican II. But if by this is meant the restructuring of the Church in a non-hierarchical way, they will then be examples of good things taken to extremes which will turn out to be bad. It would mean a democratizing or protestantizing of the Church. Christ in His wisdom gave His Church a definite hierarchical structure with Peter and the twelve having authority and then the disciples who will be served by being governed by the former, and that must stand by divine ordinance even if it will have a history of development as to how it is applied in practice in the course of time. As to what a rightful involvement of the laity means we will see as we go on.

Chapter 3: The Kingly Office

Protestant Objection

Protestants, especially of an evangelical kind, see Catholic hierarchy, more particularly a hierarchy of men calling themselves priests, as an attempt at setting up another layer of mediatorship between God and His people, thereby bypassing the one mediator who is Christ Himself. But this is not what is happening as the council makes clear in relation, first, to the role of Mary and then that of the priest:

> But just as the priesthood of Christ is shared in various ways both by sacred ministers and by the faithful, and as the one goodness of God is in reality communicated diversely to his creatures, so also the unique mediation of the Redeemer does not exclude but rather gives rise among creatures to a manifold co-operation which is but a sharing in this unique source. *Lumen Gentium, # 62.*

The surgeon doing an operation is assisted by others around him, junior doctors and nurses, even if perhaps he could perform the operation all by himself. We do not see these others as rivalling him or as pushing him aside or as presenting themselves as another layer of medics between the doctor and the patient. This is only a rough analogy because the doctor does not have the omnipotence of God, but I hope it makes the point.

Protestants of some denominations also see this hierarchy as an attempt by men at controlling or monopolizing the gift of grace as if priests were the owners of grace or its absolute dispensers. Thus they will argue that:

> Church and ministers are at the service of God and his work and cannot be presented as if they were proprietors and dispensers of the grace of God. *Waldensian and Methodist Churches in Italy in Churches Respond to BEM, Vol II, p. 247.*

Not so. Grace indeed "belongs" to God alone and He is not tied to His own sacraments and can bestow His grace on anyone anywhere, even on those who never heard of the sacraments. But He did set up this structure and willed it as the normal means of bestowing His grace and therefore appointed His apostles and their validly ordained successors as its administrators which requires that they have authority in this matter. We do indeed live in a democratic age now but the Church does not follow sooth unquestioningly. Nonetheless, these Protestant objections serve as a warning to priests who might try to demand financial reward for the dispensing of the sacraments or who might unjustly withhold the sacraments from people who are rightly disposed and entitled to them by reason of their baptism and who seek them at times that are reasonable or in emergencies.

The philosophical basis of St Thomas' position is that God not only communicates a likeness to Himself in the very being of the things He created but that He goes further and gives those things an additional likeness to Himself in being the cause of other things:

> But actually to do follows on actually to be: thus God is at once pure actuality and the first cause. If then God has communicated to other beings His likeness in respect of being it follows that he has communicated to them his likeness in respect of action. St Thomas, *Summa Contra Gentiles Bk. III, Ch. 69.*

And again:

> The last perfection to supervene upon a thing is its becoming the cause of other things. While then a creature tends by many ways to likeness of God, the last way left open to it is to seek the divine likeness by being the cause of other things, according to what the Apostle says: 'we are God's co-adjutors'. *1Cor.3:9; S .Cont. Gent., Ch. 21.*

God, in Christ, gives to ordinary men, frail and often sinful though they be, a part to play in His own great work of saving people when He appoints them as shepherds of the flock. In doing this they have a certain likeness to God Himself, the first cause of everything and the shepherd of all.

<u>Order in Vatican II</u>

The council clearly affirmed the governing role of the pope and bishops:

> Continuing in the same task of clarification begun by Vatican I, this council has decided to declare and proclaim before all men its teaching concerning bishops, the successors of the apostles, who together with the successor of Peter, the Vicar of Christ and the visible Head of the whole Church, govern the house of the living God. *Lumen Gentium, #18.*

As well as pope and bishops there are the other orders such as those of priests and deacons and there are other ministries of a non-sacramental kind:

> For the nurturing and constant growth of the people of God, Christ the Lord instituted in his church a variety of ministries, which work for the good of the whole body. *Ibid., #18.*

The Church has a variety of ministries each in need of the others:

> Consequently, the ordained priesthood ought not to be thought of as existing prior to the church, because it is totally at the service of the church. Nor should it be considered as posterior to the ecclesial community, as if the church could be imagined as already established without this priesthood. *St John Paul II, Pastores Dabo Vobis, #16.*

This last quote is important as a kind of consequence of what precedes: the priesthood or hierarchy is not to be seen as prior to the Church as if the Church were essentially the hierarchy with the laity tacked on below at the bottom of the pyramid and put there for the benefit of the former - clericalism again. But neither then should we go to the other extreme by way of reaction and conclude that the Church is entirely a self-sufficient laity with priests as scarcely needed except perhaps to say the words of consecration at Mass occasionally, if even that much. This kind of thing has been happening in some places where priests are scarce and where a priest who does arrive is told he is not needed at all! In both cases the divinely given hierarchical structure of the Church is being set aside in favour of passing ideologies borrowed uncritically from civil society.

The Shepherd's Authority

<u>From Above</u>

Given the divinely willed hierarchical structure of the Church, a structure which must persist in every age, be it monarchic or democratic or other, we must see next where or what is the source of authority in this structure. Is it from above or below? If we turn to scripture and begin with the papacy we see that it is from above: Christ, who is God, gives Peter the keys:

You are Peter and on this rock I will build my church……I will give you the keys of the kingdom of heaven and whatever you bind upon earth will be bound in heaven and whatever you lose upon earth loosed in heaven. Mt. 16:18-19.

But Peter was first amongst the twelve, all of whom were called by Christ, not appointed by any group of disciples; and the authority given to Peter was to be shared by the twelve with and under him for the good of the entire Church.

Even if we move from the Church to the civil sphere we still see that authority is from above. Recall Christ's words to Pilate at His trial: *You would have no authority over me were it not given you from above. Jn.19.11.* Hence Christians who submit to the authority of the Church should submit to that of the state also provided civil legislation does not conflict with the moral law. *Let every soul be subject to higher powers, for there is no power but from God, and those that are, are ordained from God. Romans 13:1-2.* We will see more on this later when we are talking about models of Church authority. But let us return to our present concern which is that of authority in the Church. We said above that it is from above. Let us hear St John Paul on this:

> ...the priest, by virtue of the consecration which he receives in the sacrament of orders, is sent forth by the Father through the mediatorship of Jesus Christ, to whom he is configured in a special way as head and shepherd of his people, in order to live and work by the power of the Holy Spirit in the service of the church and for the salvation of the world. *Pastores Dabo Vobis #12; cf.* also *Directory on the Ministry and Life of Priests, Ch.1*

The Trinity, as we saw, is the first and most fundamental of the mysteries. Literally everything has its beginning there and so also the authority and sacramental power of the priest. It comes to him from Christ, through the apostles down along in apostolic succession to the bishop who actually ordains him. This needs to be said in a democratic age when all authority and political power is thought to come from the people as its ultimate source. So, St John Paul II says:

> <u>It [the priest's authority] is not entrusted to the priest by the community, but, through the bishop, it comes to him from the Lord</u>. To reaffirm this clearly and exercise this function with humble authority is an indispensable service to truth and to ecclesial communion. The collaboration of others, who have not received this sacramental configuration to Christ, is hoped for and often necessary. *Address by Pope John Paul II in Priest, Pastor and Leader of the Parish Community, #5*

And again:

> …the ministerial priesthood is rooted in the apostolic succession, and vested with *potestas sacra* consisting of the faculty and responsibility of acting in the person of Christ, the head and the shepherd. *Instruction on certain Questions, #1.*

The Christian community may ask for a priest to be sent to them or for a priest to be removed or they may propose some young man as suitable for ordination as often happened in the early centuries and, sometimes, they are consulted on a candidate's suitability, but they do not confer authority or sacramental power on him. Only the bishop may do that and he may go against their wishes or recommendations if he thinks that is the right thing to do in a given case. There is a false logic in thinking that because a priest is ordained for the service of the community that therefore it is the community that gives him the authority to do this:

> Our sacramental priesthood, therefore, is both 'hierarchical' and 'ministerial'. It is a particular 'ministerium', that is a 'service', with regard to the community of the faithful. <u>It does not, however, derive from that community</u> nor from its 'call' or 'delegation'. Rather, the ministry is a gift for the community which comes from Christ himself and from the fullness of his priesthood … Conscious of this reality, we understand how our priesthood is 'hierarchical', that is, how it is connected with the power to form and govern a priestly people, and how, precisely because of this, it is also 'ministerial'. We exercise an office through which Christ himself incessantly 'serves' the Father in the work of our salvation. Our entire priestly life is, and ought to be, deeply imbued by this service if we wish adequately to offer the Eucharistic Sacrifice 'in persona Christi'. *Adress by Pope John Paul II in Priest, Pastor and Leader, #7*

Hierarchy and *ministerium* (or service) are not contradictory concepts. In a pagan society those in high positions in a hierarchy would not see themselves as serving anyone but rather would see those in their charge as being there to serve *them*, the rulers. In a democratic society those in service would see their authority as coming "up" from those whom they serve. But in Catholicism the two ideas of hierarchy and service are complimentary: hierarchy, with its authority coming from God, is there for service of His people. Priests who are authoritarian in the wrong sense of the word, i.e., who are dictatorial, cloud this truth and do great harm.

Authority, Obedience and Humility

I would present it as a maxim that one should not exert authority in any kind of government, ecclesial or civil, who has not first learned to obey which, in turn, requires the virtue of humility. Obedience in the Church is not merely a matter of social logistics, as, for example, one finds in a secular organization like the army – a thing required by good order and efficiency. It has a deep theological root in ecclesiology that takes us back to the mystery of the redemption again. Very simply, Christ redeemed the world by His obedience to the Father's will which had Him die a terrible death on the cross, an obedience which was motivated by love. So also in the Church, the priest should obey his bishop and the curate his pastor not merely because "he is the boss" and there might be consequences for going against him but because doing so is one aspect of the living out of the mystery of the redemption in one's own life. One is obliged to obey except when the order given is sinful. The Nazis did horribly immoral things on orders from the Furher and tried to justify themselves later at Nuremberg by claiming they were good soldiers obeying their commander but it did not save them from the gallows. Because the order given might be unpleasant or different to what one might have wished, it would be a dishonest rationalizing of conscience to call that "sinful". "What a *sin* that the bishop should assign a young man like me to the care of a retirement home when he knows how talented I am at playing music and basketball with the teenagers of the parish"!!! One should also realize that there are times when a bishop gives what seems to be a strange command with no explanation because of a background situation that he cannot explain without doing great harm. That still does not entitle the recipient to deem that command to be sinful. The bishop may also be acting on a genuine impulse of the Holy Spirit which the young man does not understand. The individual's understanding of a given situation is not always the full measure of what is at issue. That requires the humility of knowing and accepting one's place in the order of things in the Church.

That said, it is easy to see how a superior might yield to the temptation to take advantage of the commitment to obedience and humility of those under him merely to assert his authority, which amounts to sheer bullying. "I will show him who is boss around here, and that will teach him humility also". That kind of bullying happened all too often in the days before the council. I don't need to give examples. It sometimes led to breakdowns in timid souls or caused them to leave the priesthood entirely. Paradoxically, it caused some others, who stayed the course, to bide their time until they themselves came into positions of authority and would then inflict the same tyranny on those coming after them, thereby perpetuating the evil further still. "Now it is my turn to put down the boot and I sure will do so" was their thinking.

Because of the cast-iron face of right order which this presented externally to the world the impression was given that all was well within in the Church when, in fact, a lot of resentment was boiling under the surface waiting to explode. This is just what happened with the shake-up of the council, but was not the fault of the council. The lid was blown off the pot and a lot of angry steam came out. This steam did not cool down without giving rise to a similar abuse but this time aimed in the opposite direction. The shoe went onto the other foot as it were: curates and junior religious began openly defying their superiors and thereby begot a knock-on spirit of rebellion in all areas of Church life which persisted for a long time. This happens at times even when the superior is a truly humble, caring person because the junior is a self-willed person taking advantage of the former's gentleness.

Order is necessary, but right order can exist only when superiors learn that authority in the Church is for service, for the spiritual good of those in one's care as we saw above, never for domination but, nonetheless, that it be exercised with patience and firmness. They should realize that to humiliate anyone is not the way to inculcate the virtue of humility; that it merely begets resentment and rebellion. Then, on the other side, it requires that juniors learn the true meaning of obedience and humility so that they will be willing to obey without grumbling, even when the command is unpleasant, for the simple reason that Christ did so to begin with, even unto death; that they will accept that He makes His will known to them mostly through their superiors and that to rebel is merely a mark of pride.

Given the right understanding of authority and obedience in the pastors let us see how they exercise it for the good of those in their care and what models of authority they will need in order to do so.

Models of Church Authority

In an earlier chapter we sought some models for the being itself of the Church. Let us see here if we can find some models for the *exercise* of authority in the Church.

We are all influenced by the ideologies and trends of the age we live in, and so also is the Church when it comes to models of authority. But to be influenced is one thing, to slavishly borrow is another. She borrows at times, not slavishly but as transforming.

> She (the church) fosters and takes to herself, insofar as they are good, the ability, resources and customs of each people. Taking them to herself she purifies, strengthens and ennobles them.... *Lumen Gentium, #13.*

This will be true also of "the customs of each people" as regards the exercise of authority. She fosters and takes them to herself but not in a purely passive or slavish way but in ways consistent with her own nature making that to be her starting point:

> In order to serve the church, which is an organically structured community of the faithful invested with the same baptismal dignity and diversity of charisms and functions, it is necessary to know and love her as she is willed by Jesus Christ, her founder <u>and not as passing philosophies or different ideologies would fashion her</u>. *Priest, Pastor and Leader of the Parish Community, #16.*

With the exercise of authority, as with many other things, people tend to be influenced by those who went before them or by those around them or by whatever happens to be the fashion of their times. Thus, in past ages, when monarchy was the "fashion" in government it happened at times that the pope saw himself as the "emperor" of the Church and that the parish priest saw himself as the "king" of the parish. Taken to extremes this led to sheer arrogance and gave poor witness to the Shepherd of the gospel who was *gentle and lowly of heart. (Mt. 11: 29)*. But we must not tar all former popes or parish priests with that same brush. There were saints in those times also in those positions who did indeed wield great power spiritually and even temporally but who were also lowly, humbly serving their people.

Then, in a democratic age, the parish priest may see himself as there to serve, service now wrongly understood as complying with the wishes of the more vocal people in his parish. When taken to extreme this means he will go along with anything that some people propose, good or bad, so that he himself comes to be nothing more than a spineless wimp or he may become a cunning manipulator when he foresees the people proposing something he does not like but has not the courage to oppose them. It is hard to say which kind of leader is the more off-putting: the dictator or the wimp. The mistake is the same in the two extremes: the pope or bishop or priest is slavishly borrowing his model of leadership from the model he sees in civil society around him when instead he should be taking it from the Church as willed by her founder, Christ Himself.

> For a community of the faithful to be called a church, and indeed to truly be a church, it **cannot be guided according to political criteria of those of human organizations**. Every particular church owes its guidance to Christ since it was He who fundamentally linked apostolic mission to the church and hence no community has the power to grant that mission to itself or to delegate it. *Instruction on certain Questions, #3. (emphasis original).*

Chapter 3: The Kingly Office

Yes indeed, the Church will be influenced by the world of her times and she will borrow from that world. That is because she too is incarnate in the world and not floating above it in abstraction. But hopefully she will not borrow in any slavish way. Instead, she will take up and use profitably whatever the world offers her but will do so by purifying and transforming it in accordance with her own inner nature as given to her by Christ.

Despite some aberrations she has been doing this from the beginning. Her law makers took up and transformed old Roman law and made of it a basis for her own canon law. She took over the Roman basilicas, places of business, and re-designed them to be places of worship. She even took over some of the old pagan temples and made churches of them. With St Augustine she took over Platonist philosophy and put it at the service of the faith and so also with St Thomas Aquinas she took over, purified and developed Aristotelianism and put it so wonderfully at the service of truth, guided by the light of faith. St Thomas was criticized and even condemned for doing so in his time and accused of paganising the faith, of diluting the wine of the gospel with the water of Aristotle. He replied by an appeal to what Christ did at the wedding feast of Cana:

> ...a mixture is not thought to have occurred when one of two items comes into the possession of the other, but when both of them are changed in their nature. So those who use the works of the philosopher in sacred doctrine, by bringing them into the service of the faith, do not mix water with wine, but rather change water into wine. *Commentary on Boethius on The Trinity, q2, a3, ad 5.*

In brief the Church is in the world but not of the world because then she could not be the light of the world or the salt of the earth.

The Shepherd's Style of Leadership

What are the implications of the above for the style of leadership of the priest in the parish? Here we have some good advice from St John Paul II again:

> The parish priest, 'in close communion with his Bishop and with his faithful... should avoid introducing into his pastoral ministry all forms of authoritarianism and forms of democratic administration which are alien to the profound reality of the ministry. *Priest, Pastor and Leader of the Parish Community, #18.*

I once knew a priest who had been an army chaplain and the trainer of a hurling team. So, his style as a parish priest was that of issuing very direct commands: "you do this and not that" *etc*. He thought his people were soldiers in the army or players on the field. He was gruff to the point of being what some saw as tyrannical. But there were some people who liked that style, claiming that it was clear-cut and that it got things done speedily. Then, by contrast, I also knew of a parish priest who was so weak and democratic that he could hardly pick a new colour for the wall of his sitting room without calling a meeting of parishioners and having a vote on it. On one occasion, at the time of the transition from Latin to the vernacular in the Mass, he held a meeting to consult with the people as to how he should introduce the new responses. Five minutes into the meeting an army officer who happened to be in the audience piped up and said: "Father, are you in charge or are you not? If you are in charge then will you just get on with it. Say what you intend to do and stop wasting our time with these useless meetings"! Obviously, *he'd* fit in better in the parish of the ex-army chaplain and some of those others in the army priest's parish would feel more at home in the parish of this latter priest. One cannot please everyone!

All of this means that, to some extent, leadership depends on the style and personality of the one exercising it which must leave room for variety. I once worked with a priest whose style of leadership was one that I would describe as being utterly chaotic. But he was a humble soul and was suffering in various ways and had a great understanding of those who were suffering in the parish and they loved him in return. So, when it came to organizing something they willingly rallied round him and took ninety percent of the work on themselves, and things would somehow fall into place on the night even if it was at the last minute. His style was not mine but I would be the last to criticize him. The style of leadership will be different with different priests, but whatever the style it will require virtues, such as strength combined with gentleness, and firmness combined with patience. It also requires foresight, planning, an overall view of the big picture as well as attention to small detail, and charity over all for the good of those he is serving, all for the Lord.

A young priest, whatever his style, still needs the example of other models before him. I would direct him to some of the great pastors of the past, men like St John Chrysostom, St Augustine, to name but two from the times of the Fathers and then to later men like St Vincent de Paul or St Francis de Sales or St John Vianney in later times and, more recently still, to St John Paul II himself, a great pastor first in the small theatre as a curate in a Polish parish and then, later, in the great world theatre as pope of the universal Church. But in every diocese, hopefully, a young priest should be able to find good models in some of the older priests even if such men never got the spotlight in any theatre. Pope Benedict XVI was once asked about this matter and he said

Chapter 3: The Kingly Office

that the right kind of leadership should be that of a "Christocracy" which, of course, takes us back to Him who is the good shepherd *par excellence* and who washed the disciples' feet, but also one who could also be very definite with His authority and fearless with His opponents.

Two-way Influence of Models of Authority in Church and State

Let us now look at styles of leadership in the Church *viz a vis* those in the state in what might be called a "reverse line of influence". The Church in her style of leadership will, as I said, be influenced by the kind of society in which she finds herself and by the form of civil government which prevails there. Some such forms will come nearer to and others be further off from the form that is in line with her own essential nature, just as Aristotelianism as a philosophy proved to be a better instrument for explaining the faith than Platonism had been, though the latter served the faith fairly well also.

Monarchy and aristocracy in the state as a form of government "agrees" with hierarchy in the Church. Democracy in the state agrees with lay involvement in the Church. I have a special liking myself for the tribal model of leadership as one still finds it in many African countries and such as existed in my own country in times past. The chief had great authority but he was close to his people, much more so than was the king in European countries in former times. The chief was not a dictator because he had his council of elders around him who were very representative of the people, each elder being the head of a family as he was himself. This too was the model of government of the people of Israel for a long time, until they demanded a king, something God did not favour but which He conceded to them and which turned out to be tough medicine when they were given Saul as king. But tribal times are gone in Europe and going fast in Africa because of the rise of the big cities there. So also, monarchy has been on the wane since the French revolution, as regards having effective power, and democracy is now, the "in-thing" in the West. But democracy has not always produced good fruit. People with their free vote have often put some very evil and incompetent rulers in power, and have themselves often directly voted for some terrible evils in referenda as, for instance, when they legalized abortion and sodomy, the former undermining the most fundamental of human rights, the right to life, and the latter being completely contrary to nature. Democracy descends to being merely the rule of emotion and expediency, in fact to being mob rule, when moral principles are lost sight of so that no one is safe after a while. (*cf.* John Paul II, *Centesimus Annus*)

A lesson from all of this for any shepherd who will sheepishly want to borrow from whatever happens to be the accepted form of government around him is that he should first examine that form and see both its strengths and its weaknesses. He should also bear in mind the words of Mahatma Ghandi in India who said that people are always looking for a system of government that is so perfect that those running it do not even need to be good. How wise! Bad rulers will tear holes in the best constitutions and manipulate every organ of government for their own selfish ends, no matter how well devised those organs are with checks and balances. By comparison, good, upright rulers will try to promote the common good even if there is no parliament or constitution, and their people will love them because they know that they are caring rulers and that they are being heard when they make known their needs. History gives examples of both.

From stones, taken from old secular buildings which are used for new church buildings, to philosophical systems, to different forms of civil government or whatever else may be to hand, the Church takes up and uses what she finds useful in such things provided that it is in accord with her own God-given nature and then that she can purify and elevates it with her grace. The Church has her own essential structure given to her by Christ, *a structure which will have to remain normative even if it can be flexible within limits.* So, if her rulers are to borrow somewhat from civil forms of government around them they must keep this in mind and be critical and selective.

It is worth noting that St Thomas Aquinas had the theory that the best form of civil government would be a combination of monarchy, aristocracy and democracy, a combination that should be tailored to the genius of a given people in the amount of power it would give to each of these three. But the best kind of government for the Church has to be that which Christ willed for her, a hierarchy with authority directly from God at the service of the people so as to lead them to God in the truth and sanctify them in grace but which allows them their rightful say and participation also (*cf. canon 212*).

But let us now look at this matter the other way round: if we had the confidence that our faith should give us in the wisdom of the Church's divinely instituted structure we would hold that up as the norm against which civil structures could be evaluated and not *vice versa*. The flow of influence would then be in the other direction: the Church giving a lead to civil society in matters of government structures and morals. I am not suggesting that democracy be abolished and that we return to absolute monarchy – putting back the clock. The Church's form of government, which has the principal aim of the salvation of souls, can not be expected to fit the state like a glove as *its* form of government whose principal (but not exclusive) aim is the common good of the earthly city. I am saying that whatever the form of government of the state, possibly something like what St Thomas proposed above with due adaptations, it would have a regard for God as the source of its authority and for the moral law as the basis of civil law, see every citizen as being in God's image and likeness and try to promote justice with equity and charity for the common good. Rulers would have regard for the Church also as speaking for God and as interpreting the moral law but not in such a way as to discriminate against other religions if they also have regard for God and the moral law. (*cf.* The Vatican II document on *Religious Freedom* for more on this).

One could say that this did happen at times, at least, in the Middle Ages when some who were saints of the Church were rulers of kingdoms also, e.g., St Louis IX of France, St Elizabeth of Hungary, and ruled with justice and charity though they did not have our understanding of religious freedom today (because they lived prior to the reformation). They drew inspiration from the Church and they saw themselves as answerable to God for the way they served the people He entrusted to them, just as good shepherds in the Church will do with regard to *their* flock. The use of the word "minister" to designate the person who *serves* though he/she be the *head* of a government department today is a relic of this influence of Church government on state government from the past. All I am advocating is that something similar be promoted today but in ways that take account of the developments that have happened in forms of government since the time of these saintly rulers.

For this to happen the Church's leaders, from their side, would have to be credible witnesses in the eyes of the civil leaders: men of clear, sound, moral teaching backed up by integrity of life and action. Failures from this side does immense harm to the Church, of course, but also to society and accounts for some, at least, of the revolt of the state against the Church which is often seen today.

This flow of influence would need to happen "on the ground" also by priests and catechists teaching good morals and Catholic social teaching to those in their charge, to pupils and adults, be they Catholics or non-Catholics, to all who are or will be citizens of the state, so that they will live lives that are chaste, honest, truthful, hardworking and charitable as citizens, all the more necessary for those of them who come to hold office in government. The state and the common good will benefit from such influence and the Church will be given the freedom it needs to continue its good influence.[1]

<u>Authority is from God</u>

I said above that the authority of the rulers comes from God. This is a forgotten truth today and needs emphasis. Regardless of the form of government, democracy or not, authority in the state, as well as in the Church, comes from God in the first place because God is the ultimate source of all authority, that of the king on his throne, that of the prime minister in parliament, that of the parents in the home, that of the teacher in school, that of the policeman on the street and that of the priest. *You would have no authority were it not given you from above. Jn.19:11.* Legislators will frequently be heard to say, especially when voting for some measure that is contrary to the moral law, "I have a mandate from my constituents to do so. It is they who elected me". He sees his authority as coming solely from *them*. So, for him *their will* is sovereign and he ignores any higher authority or law, and this even when he might be a Christian!

All authority is from God. In the Church it comes down from Christ to the apostles and to the bishops of today by apostolic succession. In the democratic state it also comes from God but through the people on election day in the sense, only, that they *designate* certain people for office who then rule with authority from God. Pope Leo XIII says:

> And by this choice (democratic election), in truth, the ruler is designated, but the rights of ruling are not thereby conferred. Nor is the authority delegated to him, but the person by whom it is to be exercised is determined upon. *Leo XIII, Diuturnum,; also Immortale Dei; (cf.* also John XXIII, *Pacem in Terris; CCC, #1897 ff; Compendium of the Social Doctrine of the Church, Ch. 8, sect.3, #393 ff).*

On no occasion, either on voting day or in parliament is anyone, either voter or legislator, exempt from obeying the moral law. It binds on all in conscience, which means that it is a contradiction, an insult to the Almighty, when legislators use this authority which they have from Him to legalize something forbidden by Him. This has further implications for the relationship between Church and state and therefore for priest in his preaching on such matters but which are not our direct concern here.

Pastoral Accountability

Whatever the style of leadership of the shepherd when he exercises the authority given to him - and, as we saw above it may differ from age to age or from priest to priest – each priest must bear in mind that he will be called to give an account at the end of his days of how faithfully he did this, as must all Christians in their various vocation. The parents in the family must give an account of their spiritual care of their children when they were young and still with them, so also teachers in school and rulers in government. Hence if the priest has the task of leading his flock to God then God will ask him to give an account of his stewardship. If some are lost, and it is through the negligence or scandal or false teaching of the priest, then he will have some hard questions to answer to the Lord. Padre Pio once said that a priest does not go to heaven or to hell alone; he brings many with him to whichever place. People in lay occupations cannot easily "bury their mistakes". If the architect designs a house that collapses soon after, he will be brought over the coals about it; so also, a doctor who prescribes the wrong medication causing the death of a patient has the fear that the chart at the end of the bed or a *post mortem* will show up his error. But the priest can get away with being negligent because we cannot see the state of soul of a penitent in this life as God sees it, nor do we know to what eternal destiny he/she might have been consigned after the particular judgement. Padre Pio once spoke of how the responsibility for souls frightened him, and yet he was a priest who discharged that responsibility so conscientiously.

In times past this awareness of the seriousness of accountability had the effect of begetting what was called a "zeal for souls". Correctly understood it means a genuine pastoral charity that wants very much to guide all the souls in one's care on the path to heaven. But at times it was wrongly understood and, where charity was lacking, it amounted to fanaticism and an effort to *compel* adults to practice their religion, at least externally. The line between true pastoral charity and that kind of fanaticism can be thin, and at times in the past it was crossed. Christ wept over Jerusalem because the people there would not accept Him. He had the power to compel them, but He did not do so. He provided them with the evidence they needed for His divinity and He spelt out for them what would be the consequences of their rejection of Him. But He respected their freedom of choice. Parents do have the right to command their children to say their prayers and come to Mass with them while they are young, but that too has to be a command that is given more by example and genuine care for them than by threats if it is to be fruitful. A fanatical zeal might succeed in the short term in places where the priest has immense social power but it only breeds resentment and a rejection of the faith in the longer term.

The other extreme, then, is that of the priest who has no zeal or even care for his flock and may well put a football game before a sick call and seldom give more than ten minutes to preparing a homily. He has no sense of accountability even though he will have to face being judged by his Lord on this. That this happens at times is not entirely surprising because, when I think back on my days of formation, I don't remember hearing even a single talk on this topic!

Conclusions

1. By divine will there is order in the Church for the good of the Church. Accordingly, shepherds are appointed to serve not themselves but the flock entrusted to them. The authority of the shepherds does not rival that of God, nor does it take from that of Christ the one mediator. Rather is it a participation by priests in the authority of God, as a result of their configuration to Christ by ordination, so that when they govern their flock in the name of Christ they have a likeness to God who governs all. [2]
2. All authority both in the Church and in the state is from above, from God. In the Church it comes to the leaders who have been called by God by the sacrament of holy orders. It does not come from the people. In the state, authority also comes from God, but through the people when they designate their leaders as, for example, when they vote them into office in a democracy.
3. The Church is in the world but not of the world. Therefore, she does not slavishly take up and imitate secularist models of government which too often forget that civil authority, and indeed all human authority, is from God so that neither the will of the king or the party or that of the people can ever be absolute. She takes up, purifies and transforms what she sees around her in the world. So, her form of government may indeed have notes or elements of monarchy, democracy, tribal leadership or other kinds of government, but they are recast in a distinctively Christian way in line with the form Christ gave her and reflecting His care for the flock entrusted to her.
4. Catholics who would have the Church borrow from secular models of government, of whatever kind, should first alert themselves to the weaknesses in those models as revealed by history in the abuses of authority they can lead to when rulers serve their own interests, ignore the moral law and trample on human rights
5. A model of good government in the Church is provided for us in practice by Christ Himself in the gospels and, after Him, by shepherds who are strong in faith, joyful in hope, aflame with love, humble in heart, caring for their sheep and making sacrifices for them to lead them to God with firm but gentle rule such as those mentioned above. (*cf.* Pope Benedict XVI, *Jesus of Nazareth*, Vol 1, Ch. 8).
6. The priest must bear in mind that he will be called to account at the end of his life for the way he cared for the flock entrusted to him in his parish.

Granted that authority and sacramental power come from above and are vested in the ordained, the laity too participate in the three offices of Christ. We will look at their participation in His kingly office. But we must first see how their participation relates to that of the ordained.

Chapter IV

The Kingship of the Laity and of the Ordained

History, Difference, Harmony

But you are a chosen race, a royal priesthood, a consecrated nation, a people set apart to sing the praise of God who called you out of darkness into his wonderful light. 1 Pet 2:10.

For every high priest chosen from among men is appointed to act on behalf of men in relation to God, to offer gifts and sacrifices for sins. Heb. 5:1.

Though they differ from one another in essence and not only in degree, the priesthood of the faithful and the ministerial or hierarchical priesthood are nonetheless interrelated. *Lumen Gentium, #10*

The one kingship of Christ is participated in by both the ordained pastor and by the laity but in ways that respect their essential difference from each other. In this chapter we will look at the history of these different participations to see why they are different but also why they should be in a relation of harmony with each other.

Some History

The role of the laity, it must be said, did not get much emphasis in theology in the years before Vatican II. This was due to a reaction by the Church against the over emphasis the priesthood of the laity had received from Luther at the reformation because he saw it as the only priesthood. But still, the priesthood of the laity was never lost sight of in Catholicism. For example, in Ireland long before Vatican II, it was the custom for a priest who was preaching in Irish to address his people as *A Phobail De*, which means "People of God" and to call the church building the *Teach an Phobail*, the "house of the people". Luther abolished the sacrament of holy orders and with it the ordained priesthood, emphasizing instead the one common priesthood of all the baptized. Understandably, at Trent and in the years following that council, the Church put a renewed emphasis on the priesthood of the ordained, on his authority as coming down from the apostles, not from the people, and on his standing as a man apart. She emphasized the priesthood of the ordained to counter-balance Luther's denial of it. But the counter-balance at times, in practice, became an *over* balance so that the priest was not merely set apart, as scripture says he must be, (*cf. Hebrews*) but put up on a pedestal, sometimes a pedestal that was a bit too high for his own good and the good of his people if the priest didn't have the virtue of humility. The office he holds is deserving of due respect indeed but not of adulation.

Vatican II sought to correct the imbalance, this time by taking note of the truth that Luther was upholding, that there *is* indeed a priesthood of the laity – and with it a kingship and prophetic role of the laity – arising from their baptism, and that it should have its place in the life of the Church which, numerically, is mostly made up of laity to begin with. But the council also reaffirmed the old truth of the priesthood of the ordained arising from the sacrament of holy orders which comes down by apostolic succession from Christ Himself. The challenge is to see the value of both priesthoods as different participations in the one priesthood of Christ and to co-relate them in a harmonious way that is true to scripture and tradition.

But there is a pendulum in history which never stops swinging from one side to the other, from one extreme to the other. In a mistaken effort to give effect to Vatican II, some go to the other extreme again, that of so emphasizing the priesthood/kingship of the laity that the ordained priest is pushed aside leading to such confusion of roles in the liturgy and in parish councils that there has come about what is called "a laicization of the clergy and a clericalization of the laity" with some of this being pushed by feminists who have an agenda of their own. St John Paul II commenting on the synod that preceded his publication of *Christifedeles Laici* had this to say:

> A critical judgement was voiced [at the synod]…about a too indiscriminate use of the word 'ministry', the confusion and equating of the common priesthood and the ministerial priesthood, the lack of observance of ecclesiastical laws and norms, the arbitrary interpretation of the concept of "supply", the tendency towards a "clericalization" of the lay faithful and the risk of creating, in reality, an ecclesial structure of parallel service to that founded on the sacrament of orders. *Christifedeles Laici,* #23.

<u>The Right Balance</u>

This kind of confusion can only be clarified by getting clear on fundamental principles and by priests explaining them to their people. *Lumen Gentium* provides this clarity:

> Though they differ from one another in essence and not only in degree, the priesthood of the faithful and the ministerial or hierarchical priesthood are

nonetheless interrelated. Each of them in its own special way is a participation in the one priesthood of Christ. The ministerial priest, by the sacred powers he enjoys, moulds and rules the priestly people. Acting in the person of Christ, he brings about the Eucharistic sacrifice and offers it to God in the name of all the people. For their part, the faithful join in the offering of the Eucharist by virtue of their royal priesthood. They likewise exercise that priesthood by receiving the sacraments, by prayer and thanksgiving, by the witness of a holy life, and by self-denial and active charity. *Lumen Gentium, #10.*

The two priesthoods differ essentially yet they have only one source which is the priesthood of Christ Himself:

Thus the essential difference between the common priesthood of the faithful and the ministerial priesthood is not to be found in the priesthood of Christ, which remains forever one and indivisible........this diversity exists at the mode of participation in the priesthood of Christ and is essential in the sense that while the common priesthood of the faithful is exercised by the unfolding of baptismal grace – a life of faith, hope and charity, a life according to the spirit – the ministerial priesthood is at the service of the common priesthood…and directed at the unfolding of the baptismal grace of all Christians. Consequently, the ministerial priesthood 'differs in essence from the common priesthood of the faithful because it confers a sacred power for the service of the faithful'. *Instruction on Certain Questions, #1.*

And the implications in practice for the priest should be an awareness of the complementarity of his priesthood and that of the laity:

For this reason the priest is exhorted 'to grow in awareness of the deep communion uniting him to the people of God' in order to 'awaken and deepen co-responsibility in the one common mission of salvation, with a prompt and heartfelt esteem for all the charisms and tasks which the Spirit gives believers for the building up of the church'…. *Instruction on Certain Questions, #1,* quoting also *Catechism of the Catholic Church, #1547* and *#1592* and *Pastores Dabo, # 74.* See also *Directory on the Ministry of Priests, #1-6, #18.*

This will mean that the priest will entrust the laity with certain functions of a liturgical kind and such as relate to the care of souls and instruction in the faith:

> The hierarchy entrusts the laity with certain charges more closely connected with the duties of pastors: in the teaching of Christian doctrine, for example, in certain liturgical actions in the care of souls . *Apostolicam Actuositatem,* # 24. See also *Instructions*.

But in carrying out these functions those lay people still act only under the authority and guidance of the parish priest, and if there is no priest in a particular parish then under the priest of a nearby parish designated by the bishop:

> The task exercised in virtue of supply takes its legitimacy formally and immediately from the official deputation given by pastors as well as from its concrete exercise under the guidance of ecclesiastical authority. *Instruction #2,* quoting *Christifideles Laici,* # 23.

Difference is for Harmony

The difference between the Ordained Priesthood and the Priesthood of the Laity is not for opposition or competition between the two but for harmony and collaboration:

> In effect, a collaboration of all the faithful exists in both orders of the church's mission, whether it is in the spiritual order, bringing the message of Christ and his grace to men, or in the temporal one, permeating and perfecting secular reality with the evangelical spirit. This is especially true in the primary areas of evangelisation and sanctification – it is in this sphere most of all that the lay apostolate and pastoral ministry complete each other. *Instruction on certain Questions, foreword. (cf.* also *canons 208-211).*

The priest is to positively foster this collaboration by recognizing the various charisms of the faithful and bringing them into play for the good of the Church:

> ….they (priests) understand that it is their noble duty so to shepherd the faithful and recognize their services and charismatic gifts that all according to their proper roles may cooperate in this common undertaking with one heart. *Lumen Gentium* # 30. (*cf.* also *Canon 529 #2).*

But both priest and laity need to be clear on their respective roles, which roles must be consonant with their positions in the Church arising from the sacraments they have received, those of the laity from their baptism and confirmation, that of the priest from his ordination:

> A non-ordained male religious, a female religious, a lay person may exercise administrative functions, as well as that of promoting spiritual formation. The may not, however, exercise functions which belong fully to the care of souls since such requires priestly character. They may, nevertheless, <u>supply for the ordained minister in those liturgical functions which are consonant with their canonical condition</u> and enumerated in canon 230 #3: "exercise the ministry of the word, preside over liturgical prayers, confer Baptism, and distribute Holy Communion in accordance with the prescriptions of law". Even Deacons, who cannot be equated with other members of the faithful, cannot exercise the full *cura animarum*. *The Priest Pastor and Leader,* #24.

While lay people can participate in the administrative role of the priest, under his authority, they cannot have the full care of souls. Not even a deacon, who is an ordained man, can have that. Lay people can validly confer baptism but, nonetheless, that would be in the exceptional case of a priest or deacon not being available for a long time. Again, when lay people help to distribute Holy Communion they are in the role of being *extra ordinary* ministers. But even if lay people do these things frequently or for long periods they should never see themselves reaching a point where they consider themselves as substituting for the priest so that he is no longer seen as being needed:

> However, these cannot in any way substitute the task of the pastor proper to the parish priest. The extreme cases of shortage of priests, that advise a more intense and extended collaboration of the faithful not honoured with priestly ministry, in the pastoral care of a parish, do not constitute an exception to this essential criterion for the care of souls, as is indisputably established by canonical norm. *Ibid., #5; (cf. Code of Canon Law, canon. 517, 2).*

In other words, as St John Paul explains, the exercise of such tasks does not make pastors of lay people:

> However, *the exercise of such tasks does not make Pastors of the lay faithful*: in fact, a person is not a minister simply in performing a task, but through sacramental ordination. Only the Sacrament of Orders gives the ordained minister a particular participation in the office of Christ, the Shepherd and Head, and in his Eternal Priesthood. *Christifideles Laici,* #23.

These points need to be stressed and explained by priests to their lay helpers because there are many abuses happening in these areas. I know of parishes where priests, in a pathetic effort to be so "democratic" and "all inclusive", invite the people to join in with them in saying the Eucharistic prayer. Also, in many parishes the people are invited to join in saying the doxology at the end of the Eucharistic prayer and in the *Deliver Us* prayer after the *Our Father*. I have seen Protestant ministers and presenters from hostile TV stations been invited to preach at Mass. Again it happens that a priest will have women carry the Blessed Sacrament in a *Corpus Christi* procession so as to pander to the feminists and be seen to "involve" the laity, but in a way that is irregular.[1] This fake equality and fraternity does not lead to good liturgy but only to confusion.

> This doctrine needs to be reaffirmed especially in the light of certain practices which seek to compensate for numerical shortages of ordained ministers arising in some communities. In some instances such have given rise to an idea of the common priesthood of the faithful which mistakes its specific meaning. Amongst other things, it can encourage a reduction in vocations to the ministerial priesthood ...... *Instruction, #2*.

The laity can hardly be blamed for that. But the priest, who should know better and allows that and fails to instruct them, must take the blame for the resulting chaos, loss of faith and loss of vocations. A priest who will instruct his helpers in these matters may indeed be accused of trying to safeguard a position of privilege for himself, or of clericalism, but this is not the case. The object is to conduct the life and liturgy of the Church in accordance with the divine structure given to the Church by her Founder so that she can remain truly Catholic.

> The object of this document is to outline specific directives to *ensure the effective collaboration of the non-ordained faithful* in such circumstances while safeguarding the integrity of the pastoral ministry of priests. 'It should be understood that these clarifications and distinctions do not stem from a concern to defend clerical privileges but from the need to be obedient to the will of Christ, and to respect the consultative form which he indelibly impressed on his church'... *ibid., conclusion.*

One does not play up the role of the laity by playing down role or authority of the priest. Both roles must be affirmed and *can* be affirmed provided those exercising them are clear on what precisely their respective roles allow them to do and that they stay within those limits. When all are clear on such things then good laity will be the seed-bed for good priests and good priests will form good laity in turn and the Church overall will be the winner:

> A good laity is scarcely possible without truly holy priests. Without them everything is dead - just as it is almost impossible to have a blossoming of vocations without Christian families which are domestic churches. It is therefore erroneous to emphasize the laity if this entails overlooking the ordained ministry. Such error ends by penalizing the laity and frustrating the entire mission of the Church. *Priest Pastor and Leader,* #27.

Conclusions:

1. All of God's people, by reason of their baptism into Christ and their receiving the Holy Spirit in confirmation, are a kingly, prophetic and priestly people. They exercise these offices in various ways: by receiving the sacraments, by prayer and thanksgiving, by the witness of a holy life, by self-denial and by active charity. Nonetheless, by divine ordinance, some are called from amongst God's people to exercise a special priesthood and also a kingship and prophecy, conferred by holy orders, which is different in essence from the common priesthood/kingship/prophecy of the laity. Both are a participation in the one priesthood/kingship/prophecy of Christ, but that of the ordained exists for the sake of that of the lay: to govern, teach and sanctify the latter and thus enable them to exercise their own roles all the better.
2. Both forms of the one priesthood exist for the building up of the Church and the sanctification of the world though in different ways. Consequently, there needs to be harmonious co-operation between them. But this requires a clear understanding of the underlying theological principles so that there will not be confusion or conflict of roles, neither a clericalization of the laity or a laicising of the clergy.

Priest and laity must work in harmony. Let us look next at the work of the priest in this harmony.

Chapter V

Shepherding the Flock

Priestly Duties; Visitation, Ecumenism

I will set shepherds over them who will care for them, and they shall fear no more, nor be dismayed. Jer. 23:4.

So that he may fulfil his office of pastor diligently, the parish priest is to strive to know the faithful entrusted to his care. *Code of Canon Law, Canon. 529 #1*

Now that we have discussed the kind of roles and the kind leadership that those holding office in the Church should exercise let us see more particularly in this chapter what are the principal duties of the pastor in a given parish, allowing, of course, for differences of situations and circumstances depending on the country he is in and whether he is in a rural or urban parish or whatever. We will see also that his role of shepherd will have him reach out further to people who are not of his flock.

Kingly Duties of the Parish Priest

The *Code of Canon Law* gives a very good overall summary of kingly or shepherding duties of the priest:

> He [the pastor] is therefore to visit their families, sharing in their cares and anxieties and, in a special way, their sorrows, comforting them in the Lord. If in certain matters they are found wanting, he is prudently to correct them. He is to help the sick and especially the dying in great charity, solicitously restoring them with the sacraments and commending their souls to God. He is to be especially diligent <u>in seeking out</u> the poor, the suffering, the lonely, those who are exiled from their homeland, and those burdened with special difficulties. He is to strive also to ensure that spouses and parents are sustained in the fulfilment of their proper duties, and to foster the growth of Christian life in the family. *Canon 529 #1; (cf.* also *Priest, Pastor and Leader, #22).*

There is a great sense of pastoral care and warmth in this passage whoever wrote it. It rubbishes the claim made sometimes that canon lawyers are academics or casuists aloof from parish life. Let us take it point by point.

He is to strive to know his people. That means much more than having their names on a file in his laptop. To "know" in scripture has a much wider meaning than it does in modern languages. He should try to know them personally in their various life situations: their joys and sorrows, their worries and hopes *etc*. This requires that he be in and out of their homes so much so that he even knows the names of the dogs!

House Visitation

This brings up the importance of house visitation. I would hold that a priest does not really know his parish until he has visited the last house in the parish. He will get a slightly different perspective on his parish in every house; and by the time he has visited the last house – if ever - it will be high time for him to start at the first house again! We admire the priest who has great organizing skills and can "get things going", indeed, but I would have greater admiration for the priest who might have very little of these skills but who slogs away at house visitation. Furthermore, when a priest visits a given family in their own home and talks to them by their own fire-side he will find that he has a new relationship or bond with them from there on, as compared to meeting them in a restaurant or supermarket or some other place outside the home. That is true also of visiting someone in hospital. House visitation also gives effect to what I call the "incarnational principle"- the principle by which the priest, like Christ Himself, should "go down and get stuck in" to the rough and tumble of the ordinary lives of his people. Christ was God, yet, though never losing His divine nature, *He did not cling to His equality with God (Phil.2:6)* but came among us, living in a humble home in a remote village in Israel long ago and sharing the lives of the people around Him there.

Visitation is not easy but it is rewarding. It is made difficult in terms of time because the priest is restricted by the seasons, days and hours at his disposal. In rural parishes in times past, when most people were living on the land, he could visit most afternoons, perhaps two seasons of the year or in the evenings or at night and be likely to find most of the family at home. Not so today when often both parents are out at work, away from home, and the children are not home, even after school, until they are collected from somewhere else later on. Then, when they *are* all at home there are many things to be attended to. So, it leaves the priest with only a few hours that might be suitable for visiting. Furthermore, many people are away during the Summer or are out at their gardens or engaged with other hobbies even if at home. Because of this, I usually had the practice of beginning visitation in September when people are back from holidays, schools are re-opening and the harvest is done in rural areas.

Then the priest himself is constrained by such things as meetings and funerals and other things to which he must attend which limit the number of nights available to him for visiting. And moreover, when he does go visiting, he will often find that the parents are out. In that event it is good to leave a call card under the door because there are people who like to complain that no priest ever visited them in the past ten or twenty years. That might not be true in many cases. The priest might well have called but they never came to know that. If a priest knows that he simply will not be able to get around to all the houses for a very long time he might have a "team" of religious or specially chosen lay people, perhaps some from his parish council, who might visit on his behalf. Possibly also he will have a pre-baptism team and a bereavement team who visit houses. Still, it is good if he can get round to at least some of his people himself.

As to where to begin, I think it is good to start out at the outer fringes of the parish and work in towards one's own house in the middle. This might be called the "good shepherd" approach - going out to those far off, whether geographically or socially, to bring them in, rather than be sitting in one's house and waiting for them to come. Some might come, but perhaps not those who might most need to come. Recall the passage from the *Code of Canon Law* again: "He is to be especially diligent *in seeking out* the poor, the suffering, the lonely, those who are exiled from their homeland, and those burdened with special difficulties". The good shepherd seeks out most especially those who are in any difficulty.

To make this effective I have had what I call the "four pillars" method. The people living nearest the presbytery are people that the priest is more likely to be meeting more often when going down the street or into the nearby shops, so he gets to know them easily, but he might not see those out on the periphery at all.

If we take the parish territory to be somewhat like a square or a quadrangle, I would visit a few houses at one far off corner my first week, then go to the very opposite corner the next week and so on with the other two corners. I would state in the parish newsletter that I would be going to a particular area so as to take account of the fears of people who think that a priest calls only when some bad news has to be broken to a family. Then I would work inwards during the following weeks. The advantage of this method is that it helps put the pieces of the jigsaw of the parish together more easily. One finds that Mr. White in the top left-hand corner of the parish is a first cousin of Mrs Green in the opposite corner and that her brother, whom you met at the post office one day, is married to Mary Brown in the top right-hand corner. The pieces begin to fit together. Before setting off, a priest should say a prayer to the Holy

Spirit to guide him to the house where he is most needed and to give him the right words for those who might have problems in whatever house he enters.

One will get a different kind of reception on different doorsteps but mostly positive in my experience at least. And that is more likely when word has got out in advance that the priest will be visiting a particular area.

In times past a visiting priest kept what was called a *Liber Status Animarum*, literally a note-book on the state of souls. It was a record of what sacraments those in a given family had received up to then. Whatever about the title of the note-book, a priest should try to find out what their level of practice is and make some note of that and of other things of relevance such as their marital status, the number of children they have, their occupations and other such things. Obviously, a priest does not do this by filling in some kind of a questionnaire in front of people in their sitting room. But, nonetheless, he should make some record of what he finds afterwards so that he can check it against the parish registers of baptisms, confirmations, marriages *etc.*, and have it available for himself for the next time he will be visiting or for his successor so that the latter will be somewhat informed before he comes to the door of any particular house. In filling up such a note book it is wise to know something of the civil law on data retention and on what information an individual is entitled to see should he or she come and ask to see his file.

Be Up Front

When introducing himself, it is best that a priest be up front when the door opens and that he say who he is: the new priest; and that he is here simply to get to know the people of the parish. Some parishioners will not be aware that there has been any change of priests even six months after the new priest arrives! Others will think he has come to bring bad news or to collect outstanding dues. I knew of a case where the woman of the house welcomed the new priest, brought him in, sat him down by the fireside and began chatting. But after a few minutes it was very noticeable that she was getting very anxious and agitated. So, after about twenty minutes she blurted out:

"Well, Father, tell me, is he dead?"

"And who do you mean, Ma'am?" the priest replied.

"John, my husband, he has a bad heart, you know. He is out tonight but he should be well back by now. Has he dropped dead somewhere?"

"No, Ma'am. I never knew your husband or anything about him because I am the new priest in the parish, and I am calling round to all the houses simply to get to know the people."

"Well, then, Father, if that is all it is why didn't you say that in the first place and spare me all this anxiety?!"

Or again, I have had the experience myself a few times of a crusty old man opening the door by about three inches, because he had a lock and chain on it, and, to the accompanying "music" of an Alsatian dog barking beside him, he would say "I thought I *did* pay my dues, Father, so what is this about?" To which it can be difficult to reply with the rumpus being caused by the Alsatian who is ready to jump out if the door would be opened even a few inches more. Such are some of the "joys" of visitation, and it is more "delightful" still if it is a Winter's night with the wind and the rain providing another kind of background "music" and more formidable still if it is a lone house on the side of hill facing out to sea!

While in the house one should observe and be able to make deductions from what one sees - photographs on the mantelpiece, trophies on the sideboard, the kind of books on the shelves and other such things. Those things speak in their own way even if the members of the household don't say very much beyond making small talk. [1]

As to small talk: if the conversation gets no further than that the visit may not still have been futile. If the householders are strangers to the priest, the priest should remember that he is also a stranger to them and they may be unwilling to open up to him for the present, at least. That is their perfect right. But perhaps the next time they will, when they have come to the conclusion that he is trustworthy; and if they never open up, that again is their perfect right. St Paul said he was trying to be all things to all men, but he still did not get into the hearts of some. A young priest should not presume that he can do better than St Paul.

A priest should take care never to carry stories from one house to another, much as curious people might question him so that their ears could be tickled with a bit of gossip. Such people are able to figure out that if he brings stories about their neighbours *to them*, he will very likely carry stories *from them* to the next house also; so they will not confide in him. For all his apparent friendliness he will not come across as a man of discretion or confidentiality.

How long a priest should stay on his visit will depend on what he finds in a given house. The most important house is the one the priest is in at a given moment, and, if there is a problem there that needs airing, he should give it the time it needs rather than go rushing off to the next house on the pretext of trying to "clock up" *x* number of houses each night.

Recall, then, the passage from the *Code of Canon Law* above where it says: "If in certain matters they are found wanting, he is prudently to correct them" That does not mean scolding or rapping them on the knuckles; but neither does it mean giving a green light to something that is obviously morally wrong simply to be popular with them. For example, with a couple who are cohabiting one should discuss the possibility of them putting things right before God by getting married sometime soon, and show a readiness to facilitate them in doing this. And then the *Code* talks of the support he should give even to families that seem to be doing well. We all need support at various times if we are humble enough to admit that.

Problems or no, I have found that two or, at most, three houses are enough to visit in any one night, that is if I am to sit down and give people the time they need to share their thoughts.

As for the very few houses where one might get a negative or even hostile reception that precludes all attempts at dialogue, it is best to move away quietly without provoking an argument which might only confirm them in whatever prejudices or grievances they may have against the Church. Whatever their prejudices, they will have to admit to themselves afterwards that this priest did, at least, make a move in their direction.

Permit me to say here that the pub is certainly not a place for pastoral visitation. I say this because, at times, the anti-Catholic media when doing some program on the Church like to interview a liberal priest of their own way of thinking and do so in the setting of a pub where he is seen, often in civilian clothes, "having his pint of beer with the boys" thus conveying the idea that here is a man who goes along with everything "trendy", and they will even have him sing some ballad to round off at the end. Following the incarnational principle of getting stuck in to the lives of one's people does not mean becoming "one of boys" in the pub for the amusement of those who are drinking there. The priest is still and always a man consecrated and set apart. He, like the Good Shepherd, must also reach out to all people, the good and the bad, but not in the unreal, frivolous atmosphere of the pub where he and his message are more likely to be made fun of.

Other Means of Contact

Apart from house visitation, another way of getting to know one's flock and of enabling them to get to know each other is to organize a kind of "Welcome Night" or "Come and meet us night" once a year or once every two years, possibly in September again when people are back from holidays. For this event different organizations in the parish would be invited to put up stalls or stands at a big venue and have a representative or two manning each stall so as to provide information for new comers about their respective services. There could also be a slide show or *power-point* presentation

Chapter 5: Shepherding the Flock

on things in the parish, and literature made available with more information. The Church would also have its own stand. At an event like that people can move around and meet each other and meet the priest and his team of helpers also.

If a priest finds that his predecessor has not left him any records of the houses of the parish, or if it is a parish in which there has been a lot of movement of people in and out for some years, one other thing that helps to get to know people is to distribute census forms asking simple straightforward questions about who the householders are, what occupation they have, how many children they have, if any, to what schools they are going and what sacraments they have received. Some people get suspicious about such questionnaires, and the more paranoid will see all sorts of collusion going on between the priest and the revenue or other state bodies. So, there should be a note at the end saying that filling up this form is entirely optional, that it is merely meant as a help to the new priest to get to know his people.

Then the *Code* talks about the special care the priest should give to the sick and the dying. We will see more on this in a later section on the priest in his administration of the sacraments. Suffice it here to say that the care of a soul that is about to leave this world and go before its Maker to be judged and sent on its way to an eternity, either of great happiness in heaven or of unending suffering in hell, is a most serious responsibility. To be negligent in this and say "Ah, she was a nice old lady. I'll leave her to God; the night is bad" would be a terrible wrong for which the priest himself will have to answer at the end of *his* days. Admittedly, a priest can't be on call all the time but when he cannot, he should make provisions for another priest to be available.

The *Code* then went on to talk about the additional duty of the parish priest to recognize and promote the roles of the different lay members in his parish:

> The parish priest is to recognise and promote the specific role which the lay members of Christ's faithful have in the mission of the Church, fostering their associations which have religious purposes. He is to cooperate with his proper Bishop and with the presbyterium of the diocese. Moreover, he is to endeavour to ensure that the faithful are concerned for the community of the parish, that they feel themselves to be members both of the diocese and of the universal Church, and that they take part in and sustain works which promote this community. *Canon 529 #2.*

This passage makes clear that the care of the parish cannot be a one-man-band kind of effort. Any priest who thinks otherwise would be ignoring the working of the Holy Spirit in the hearts of his people or even trying to stifle it. They too have their roles arising from their baptism and confirmation, and for the exercise of those roles they are given natural talents and supernatural charisms, gifts and graces. We touched on this already above. A priest who tries to do it all by himself will soon find himself suffering from burn out, at which point he is of no use to anyone and only becomes a burden to himself and to the diocese. Also, such an attitude devalues the willingness that good laity have to help and play their part in promoting the faith and life of the parish. Whereas, on the contrary, they should be encouraged to take responsibility with the priest and under his guidance for the well-being of the parish and especially for the faith of the young.

Practical Ecumenism in Visitation

In doing visitation, the priest will inevitably knock on the doors of people who belong to other religions or none. Such visits can have great ecumenical potential. Many non-Catholics have negative ideas about the Church due to simple ignorance as to what she teaches or due to inherited prejudices from their childhood background, such as that every pope is the anti-Christ and that most priests are money grabbers or power seekers or paedophiles or whatever. Or they might think that Catholics worship Our Lady or that Catholics claim that all non-Catholics are damned, or whatever. Cardinal Newman, though a very learned man, tells of some such prejudices that he had to overcome on becoming a Catholic. (*cf.* his *Apologia*). For such people to meet a friendly priest who will sit with them in their own sitting room and candidly answer whatever questions they might have can be a great eye-opener for them to the truth and beauty of our faith. This presupposes, of course, that the priest is clear and firm in his own faith; that he believes that Christ alone is the way to salvation, that He founded only one Church which today subsists fully and properly in the Catholic Church, that he has a clear understanding of ecumenism as an opening out by the Church to bring back in those who are separated from us recognizing whatever elements of truth he finds in other religions knowing that the other Christian religions are related to the Catholic Church by their baptism and by the truths they hold in common with us and that all religions have elements of the truth; that, by comparison, he does *not* understand ecumenism as a search for some lowest common denominator in religious truth, or as an attempt at a hotchpotch eclecticism which throws all religions into one mixed bag so as to find unity in some future globalist church with God, as the supreme architect, smiling down on all. Such ecumenism leads only to confusion, scepticism and loss of faith. True ecumenism, I believe, is better achieved by such visitation than by elaborate ecumenical services which can be somewhat contrived at times, though they too have their value.

Chapter 5: Shepherding the Flock

The priest will also meet people who will claim to have no belief *at all*, which, in fact, cannot be the case for the simple reason that the will must have *some* object perceived as good, truly or falsely; it can not latch on to *nothing*. Such a person, rejecting all religious belief will, one finds, latch on to some finite good instead such as money, pleasure, power or one's own ego as a substitute god, or to some ideology which he does not question. The challenge is to get him/her to see that the finite will never satisfy fully because we are made for communion with the Infinite.

Conclusions:

1. The kingly or shepherding office of the priest requires that he try to get to know his people in a way that is personal and caring with pastoral charity, taking account of their various situations in life. To do this is also to give effect to the incarnational principle. The aim is to seek out those who are troubled or going astray and re-affirm the faith of those who are still practicing.
2. House visitation is one basic and effective way to do this though not at all easy in urban settings in the West. But religious and lay people can help in this also.
3. Visitation makes for a simple but effective kind of ecumenism also, provided the priest knows his own faith thoroughly and is firm in it but without being condescending or offensive to those he meets of other faiths.

We saw above that the priest is to promote the involvement of the laity with their various charisms in the work of building up the Church. So that this can happen in an orderly way we will next look at the role of the laity in the exercise of their kingly function on various Church councils.

Chapter VI

Parish Pastoral Council

Purpose, Membership, Consultative Vote

Let your good spirit guide me in ways that are level and smooth. Psalm. 142.

If after consulting the council of priests, the diocesan bishop considers it opportune, a pastoral council is to be established in each parish. *Code of Canon Law, Canon. 536 #1.*

We have been looking at the general principles governing the respective roles of clergy and laity as they operate in the parish, how they differ and how they harmonize, and at the duties of the parish priest in particular. Parish councils of different kinds are an area of practical co-operation between the two and give voice to the role of the laity in a special way. In this chapter we will look at one of these councils, the pastoral council, its purpose, how it might be set up, its subject matter and mode of voting.

Purpose and Membership of Parish Councils

Parish councils and diocesan councils of various kinds are a relatively new phenomenon in the West, in one sense, not having been given much prominence until Vatican II. By comparison, the Churches of the East have a long tradition of councils and synods of various kinds at various levels. But in the West also, even in pre-conciliar times, bishops had their chapters of canons, and parish priests consulted select people when they felt the need for advice in matters that were unfamiliar or difficult or which had implications for things beyond their own usual field of competence. Also, when some major work had to be undertaken at parish level, such as the building of a new church or school, they formed committees to help with finance and in various other ways. They knew that in difficult matters "two heads are better than one", as the old saying goes, so they took counsel.

But there is a deeper reason than that for having parish councils. It is not simply that of combining what are thought to be the "best brains" in the parish for making plans. Nor is it a concession to democracy, though the predominance of democracy in civil society in the West over the past few centuries may have been an influence. The deeper and more theological reason is that God Himself is a "community" of persons and also that the Holy Spirit, being the soul of the Church, is working in the hearts of *all* the faithful with their various talents and charisms, natural and supernatural, moving them to good in various ways for the benefit of the Church overall. The parish priest leads by discerning and harnessing these gifts and co-ordinating their operation in a harmonious way. Put differently, the parish priest does not have a monopoly on the Holy Spirit or His gifts in himself. I heard of one parish priest who used to seek the advice of a young, devout, invalided girl in his parish, a girl who was suffering greatly from some chronic illness, because he believed her sanctity merited an endowment of wisdom from above due the suffering she was so patiently enduring. So, he trusted that the Holy Spirit was guiding her in a special way when he consulted her. The Eastern orthodox Churches, with their long tradition of councils have, perhaps, a better grasp of their value than we do in the West. But, then, they lack unity and coherence because they do not have Peter at the top.

In any case, Vatican II recommended the establishment of councils at diocesan and parish level. Pastoral councils were to be optional while finance councils were to be obligatory. This call for councils follows on the call for a greater and more active role for the laity in the life of the Church envisaged by the council in a number of its documents. It was also meant to beget a sense of shared responsibility for the well-being of the faith in the local Church. It is for the bishop to decide if pastoral councils should be set up:

> If after consulting the council of priests, the diocesan bishop considers it opportune, a pastoral council is to be established in each parish. If this council, which is to be presided over by the parish priest, Christ's faithful, together with those who by virtue of their office are engaged in pastoral care in the parish, give their help in fostering pastoral action. *Canon. 536 #1. (See also Instructions, Art 5 #.2).*

Referring to diocesan, pastoral councils *The Code of Canon Law* says:

> The members of Christ's faithful assigned to the pastoral council are to be selected in such a way that the council truly reflects the entire portion of the people of God which constitutes the diocese, taking account of the different regions of the diocese, of social conditions and professions, and of the part played in the apostolate by the members, whether individually or in association with others. *Canon 512 # 2.*

Chapter 6: Parish Pastoral Council

So, the diocesan pastoral council should be widely representative of the diocese, and the same can be said analogously of the pastoral council at parish level. Of those who will be members it says:

> A pastoral council is composed of members of Christ's faithful who are in full communion with the catholic church: clerics, members of institutes of consecrated life, and especially lay people. They are designated in the manner determined by the diocesan bishop. *Canon. 512 # 1; (cf. also Canon 511).*

The members should be of good faith and morals:

> Only those members of Christ's faithful who are outstanding in firm faith, high moral standards and prudence are to be assigned to the pastoral council. *Canon 512 # 3.*

It makes sense to say that, although God can use anyone as His instrument for anything, the Holy Spirit more usually works in the hearts of practicing Catholics who are morally upright and are striving to be holy. One cannot judge the inner heart, but people who are known publicly to be engaged in practices that are objectively irregular or sinful cannot be members.

Again, leaving subjective moral judgments aside, I can think of some other people whom I would not want on a pastoral council even if they are practicing Catholics in the external forum. For example, there is the feminist who resents the fact that women cannot be priests so she wants to be on the council to gain control of the parish in other ways, by obstructing or manipulating the priest or by setting the rest of the members against him. Or there is the person who campaigns publicly for some immoral, social measure clearly at odds with Church teaching. Such persons, obviously, cannot be enlisted to help advance either faith or morals.

Then there is the would-be politician. He wants to use the parish council so as to be seen and heard in public and thus make of it a stepping stone in his bid to get a seat on the city or county council. An additional problem with this individual is that he is likely to clash with someone else on the council for the simple reason that the two of them belong to opposing political parties. So, if for example, the discussion at the meeting is about the route of this year's *Corpus Christi* procession, he will insist on a rout that will go in the opposite direction to what the other proposes. An innocent pastor will wonder why so much hostility over such a simple matter, not being able to see the hidden agenda between these opponents which is all about their political affiliations and not about the procession at all, except that it is now being used as an excuse by one member to get one up on the other.

Then there is Mr. Parish-in-Person. This man thinks that he embodies the thoughts and feelings of the entire parish so much so that the pastor has only to consult *him* about everything and all will be well! And if the pastor does not consult him and have him next to him on the council then great offense will be taken.

Then there is the self-made "lord mayor" of the parish. He has wealth and property and controls a lot of things in the town so he believes he has to control the Church also and tries to make the parish priest his puppet with offers of donations to the Church.

Then there is Mr Vox. Very simply he likes to hear himself talking and will try to get on any and every council or board for just that reason. And all the while, there is the truly devout Catholic mother who has reared a good family and has the faith and great practical wisdom but is too reserved to raise her voice at a meeting, or she has learned from sad experience that when she did give her opinion in the past the feminist or Mr Vox was quick to put her down. So also, there is the devout Catholic man who too often stays too quiet and who, if he did speak up, would be denounced as a conservative – a word that is supposed to intimidate him into perpetual silence or even into apologizing for his very being. And too often the pastor, if he is a wimp, sides with these bullies for fear that he too will be denounced as a conservative.

The argument is sometimes made that non-Catholics should be members of parish councils for ecumenical or other reasons. But this is not allowed, though they might be very good-living people, because we are talking about *Catholic* parish councils. It is true that people in the other religions are related to the Catholic Church in various ways, but that still does not take from the distinctive identity of the one, true Church which subsists fully and properly only in the Catholic Church. Still, the help of such people when offered should be welcomed when various parish initiatives are being planned. I have known of such people singing in the choir and helping generously with various charitable works being organized in the parish.

Setting up a Parish Council

We must next see how a pastoral council might be set up so that the parish priest might avoid being saddled with people such as the above and have wise, good practising Catholics instead. The bishop may well set down definite rules on this or he may issue a few general guidelines leaving the rest to the discretion of the parish priest. From my own experience of such matters I would like to offer a few suggestions, basically steering a middle course between a straightforward election, on the one hand, and a hand-picked selection, on the other.

Chapter 6: Parish Pastoral Council

The straightforward election, taking place at a meeting called of all the parishioners in the parish hall, has the advantage of being representative. Those who are interested will come. But it has the disadvantage that some of the undesirables listed above will also come and will have put in place a clever, pre-planned strategy by which to get themselves elected. I have seen situations where the individual who shouts the loudest, blowing out nothing but hot air, was elected simply because other people who did not want to get elected themselves were happy to shove the burden of office over onto him or her.

I also knew of a case where the person elected as the principal member of the parish council (the so-called "chairman", a non-existent title in canon law) was a man who was not going to Mass at all and was cohabiting down the street with his girlfriend. He was well known to be a fellow of dirty tactics in many other fields. So why did the people elect *him*? The priest of that parish explained to me that those people were bringing their sporting mentality to bear on Church matters here. He said that in football or hurling (the game most played in that area) when you see that the opposing team has a big, rough, dirty player at centre field you try to see if amongst your own players you might also have a similarly dirty player. It is unlikely that either of them will be skilled as players but the thug on your team will, at least, be able to counter-act or neutralize the thug on the other team. So, bringing this thinking into the parish council the *parish priest* is seen as the "thug" on the opposing side! and, since he cannot be easily removed (or killed?!!) he can at least be neutralized by the people electing their own lay "thug" onto the council. With the priest thereby rendered ineffective, the other members can rule the parish their own way, under the leadership of their chosen thug or some other thug!!! And so, this man was, in fact, elected at an open meeting as that parish priest explained to me.

I knew of another such case where the man elected was not going to Mass and had spent time in jail for stealing tyres! He was clever and had manipulated the others on the council and was able to brow beat the parish priest, so much so that the latter cleared out after only two years. He tried the same on his successor but the latter did a divide-and-conquer job on the council and was able to break them up. He should have known that a parish council of any sort falls dead anyhow with the departure of the former parish priest which would have spared him a lot of trouble. Later, then, he put a new council together which worked much better. Only later still did one of the former members confide to him how they had been intimidated by the "big man" (the so-called "chairman") of the former council. This man had ambitions in politics and hoped that by becoming the chairman of the parish council he would have a stepping stone to a seat on the county council. He did, in fact, stand for election later but failed miserably. I don't see for the life of me why any priest should have to put up with people of that sort on any of his councils.

It is difficult when a priest of sincere intentions finds himself at odds with his parishioners because he is not willing to go along with things he knows are wrong. In the seminary, sometimes, a rather cosy picture is painted of the priest in his relation to his people. But if that is, in fact, the case - if it is all "lovey-dovey" in a given parish - it can sometimes be a sign that the priest is merely pandering to his people and flattering them for the sake of his own popularity, whereas if he was truly giving witness and preaching right and wrong it might be a different matter. The Curê D'Ars suffered greatly at the hands of his parishioners at the *beginning* of his time in Ars when he was preaching against the immoral practices he found going on there. But at the *end* of his life there he was so beloved by the same people that they were determined to hold on to his mortal remains and not let them be returned to his home village.

At times of disagreement the priest must not engage in parish politics, trying to win over a number of followers sufficiently large to outdo those opposing him, or by playing off one group against another or using the kind tactics that are often used in secular politics. But neither can he be a naïve fool. Our Lord's words are relevant here: *Be as cunning as a serpent but as innocent as a dove. Mt 10:16*. He needs to know human nature and what it is capable of, not only at its best but also at its worst. But above and beyond that, he must put his trust in the Lord. And it is here that the breviary is of such great help because so many of the psalms talk about the just man being surrounded by enemies but putting his trust in the Lord. And the Lord does indeed come to the aid of a just priest in remarkable ways. People of faith, because they have the *sensus fidei,* will support a priest whom they see is also a man of sincere faith, and, in the long run, most other fair-minded people will come to see the value of such a priest as in the case of St John Vianney above.

But then one can have the opposite problem of a priest who is heretical in doctrine or who is lazy and negligent in duty or who gives scandal but has a parish council of very good people who do not want this at all. They cannot remove him themselves but they can appeal to the bishop to do so, and canon law makes provisions for such. *(can.1740 ff)*.

So, if it is not advisable to hold a straight open election how else might a parish council be put together? The other way is for the parish priest to hand pick the entire council by himself. But this is not good either. He will be tempted to pick his own "cronies" who will be "yes men" going along with everything he proposes. I knew a parish priest who was proud of his clever strategy in this matter. He set a fixed limit on the number of members his parish council would have – let us say ten – and then he packed or rigged it so that he would always have a majority on his side for whatever he proposed. Thus, on his council there was his curate, his sacristan, his housekeeper, a retired nun who was an admirer of his and one other "fan". He told them clearly and unambiguously that they were selected specially in order to back his proposals, whatever they might be. Those five then, along with himself, assured him of the majority he needed. But the other members of such a council, and the wider parish folk, will see through that very easily and will realize that they themselves do not count. That is mere tokenism and a wasted exercise.

I would say that the best way to set up a parish council is by having a combination of election and selection. A parish meeting might be called and people asked to put forward the names of about twenty suitable candidates, with what makes for a suitable candidate as per canon law being explained first. Then, taking those twenty names the parish priest might consult with the members of the outgoing council as to their suitability. It might be good if one or two of the outgoing members were retained for the sake of continuity: and the priest should also have the liberty to select one or two entirely on his own initiative also.

Another method, somewhat similar, would be to have a ballot box and ballot papers at the door of the church on a given Sunday – with prior notice from previous Sundays – and people asked to enter the name or names of candidates they think suitable and that they also sign their own names at the bottom of the ballot papers. This would eliminate the possibility of any kind of rigging by an overly eager candidate who might try filling the box with a lot of papers with his own name on them. It would also enable the priest to ask a particular person why he/she nominated a particular candidate.

As to the number of members on a parish council, it will vary depending on the size and geographical lay out of a parish. The aim should be to have good representation between old and young, men and women, town and country or different districts. I have found that when any council is too big - more than ten or twelve persons - one will have some "dead wood" i.e., members who are present indeed but who let the "heavy lifting" to a smaller few. On the other hand, a small council, though it might be more energetic, will not be widely representative.

When a council is set up it is the parish priest who presides. Despite that, one often hears of a lay person being described as "the chairman". As said above, there is no such title in canon law and I do not know how it came to be accepted. Perhaps a parish priest who is present and fully in charge of proceedings might ask a lay person to chair the meeting if he, the priest, had a cold or was somehow unwell. There is no mention of a secretary either in canon law but it is necessary that someone keep a record of what is discussed. A parish council cannot be called or function lawfully without the consent of the parish priest. Should they attempt to act without him their decisions will be invalid.

> It is for the parish priest to preside at parochial councils. They are to be considered invalid, and hence null and void, any deliberations entered into (or decisions taken), by a parochial council which has not been presided over by the parish priest or which has assembled contrary to his wishes. *Instructions, Art 5, #3.*

Matters for Discussion

Every meeting should begin with a prayer to the Holy Spirit for His guidance.
What then should be discussed? In brief, anything that concerns the well-being of Christian life, faith and morals in the parish and even the well-being of these things outside the parish in the wider society because every parish and local Church should be outward looking towards the universal Church and not closed in on itself. The Church is universal and missionary by nature. In *Priest, Pastor and Leader* we read:

> ...the pastoral council can be a most useful aid...providing proposals and suggestions on missionary, catechetical and apostolic initiatives …. as well as on the promotion of doctrinal formation and the sacramental life of the faithful; on the assistance to be given to the pastoral work of priests in various social and territorial situations; on how better to influence public opinion *etc. #26*

The parish should also be looking in a forward direction towards the Kingdom of God of the end time and asking what part it should play in preparing the world around it for that day. (More on that later).
Many of the problems besetting a given parish will be widespread in the rest of that country, such as the fall-off of young people going to Mass or the breakdown of marriages or the isolation of the old or whatever. So also, the factors influencing these problems will be national or global such as media propaganda, peer pressure, unemployment or such like. Nonetheless, the wide dimensions of these problems need not intimidate a parish so that it loses hope of achieving anything. If even one parish council comes up with an innovative idea on what might be done at local level to deal with a particular problem it might well catch on in other parishes and wider afield. But it is of little use to the overall state of the faith in the parish if the council gives a whole meeting to discussing on which side of the front porch of the church a new yard light should be put! Or how many paper cups will be needed for the coming pre-

confirmation meeting! (Though I admit that the parents attending should not be expected to drink out of their hands!).

I knew a parish priest who, at his first pastoral council meeting in his new assignment, began by asking the members to tell him what they thought were the strengths and weakness of the parish – and he jotted down both in two columns side by side. Then he asked them for suggestions as to how the strengths could be harnessed to tackle the weaknesses. He made a note those also. He was not so foolishly ambitious as to think that there and then he could formulate a cure-all plan of action that would solve everything. He told them he would need some time to reflect on what they told him and then start with small beginnings. It was a good way to begin.

When a priest gets some good suggestions as to what things might be done, it does not follow that the pastoral council *itself* is the best organ for executing them. For example, if they tell him that there is a problem of teenage drinking in the parish it might be best for him, with their help, to approach the parents or the teachers to tackle such a problem or to revive a total abstinence association of some kind. Should they tell him that a pressing problem was a leaking roof in the church it might be best to refer that problem to the finance council because it will entail raising funds and getting a good contractor which is more the business of the latter council (as we shall see shortly) even though the matter arose at the former council.

More generally, when it comes to enlisting the co-operation of people to get things done in a parish or to get something new up and running it is well to remember that there are three classes of people: the few who *make* things happen; the many who *let* things happen but who may join in later if they think what is happening is worthwhile; and then another bigger number who have not a clue as to what is happening or who couldn't care less, unless it cuts across their own desire for comfort or pleasure or they see a gain of some sort for themselves.

Another way of categorizing possible helpers is to note first of all those who are able but not willing, e.g., the singer who does not want to join the choir – perhaps the priest can coax him/her to come along. Then there are those who are willing but who are not able – the "crow" in the church choir who wants to sing solo on Christmas night! He must be "gently dissuaded" but perhaps given another role instead. Next there are those who are not able and not willing anyhow. They won't turn up at all, not even to cause trouble! but the priest still has care of them also; and, finally, there are those who are able and willing and are waiting to be asked. The priest should look out for those people and recognize the gifts and charisms, natural and supernatural, that God has given them and enlist their help for the good of all.

A Consultative Vote

Before any election or selection the priest should explain to people that the members of a parish council have only what is called a "consultative" vote, something not always understood by people living in democracies where the vote of every member is an effective one:

> In fulfilling his duty as guide, which is his personal responsibility, the pastor will surely obtain help from the consultative bodies foreseen by canon law (cf. *Code of Canon Law*, can. 536-537); but these must remain faithful to their reality as consultative bodies. Therefore, it will be necessary to guard oneself from any form that tends *de facto* to weaken the leadership of the parish priest, because the very structure of the parish community would be distorted. *The Priest Pastor and Leader of the Parish Community, #5.*

In any civil council, say a town council or the council of a sporting club, each member has the same voting power with perhaps the chairman having a casting vote in the event of a tie. But Church councils are different. The reason is ultimately that the Church is not a democracy. It is a hierarchy ruled by clerics at different levels from the pope down. This means that if a matter being debated comes to a vote the pastor can go against the majority and follow his own path if he thinks that this is wise. To people today who are entirely familiar with the civil way of voting and know no other way, this idea of a consultative vote often comes as strange news to them and therefore might not be so easily accepted. This misunderstanding is sure to happen and will lead to a lot of friction if the pastor does not take the trouble to explain this idea of a consultative vote to his members at his first meeting and instead proceeds with the business in hand leaving them under the impression that it is the civil way of voting that holds here also. Lay people will inevitably bring with them to the parish council the knowledge and experience they have already from their involvement in other organizations. That is what they have been used to. So, if procedures in a Church council are different that needs to be explained to them.

Of course, following on this idea of consultative voting, a bull-headed pastor can proceed to steam roll over the members, regardless of their views on a debated issue and do "his own thing" anyhow. That is "tokenism" again and that kind of priest will be seen to be authoritarian in the bad sense of the word. It merely makes a joke of the members. They know they are not going to be taken seriously no matter what they say and will probably stop coming after a few meetings.

There is the other extreme then – because the pendulum is always swinging from one side to the other – of the pastor who is weak and so anxious to appear so very democratic and pleasing to everyone that he will hide behind the majority vote if some decision is taken that is problematic. If the decision turns out to be a bad one he will put up his hands innocently and say "well that is what the majority on my council wanted". He is what I would call a "democratic wimp". If he knew anything at all about human nature and democracy he should know that majorities sometimes get it very wrong, even on matters that call for a clear cut choice between good and evil, as for example when a whole parliament, or society, votes for something like abortion or euthanasia.

A wise pastor behaves in neither of these ways. He listens carefully to his council members then he goes away and prays and evaluates what he has heard and then comes to a decision which he believes is for the true good of all concerned whether that be in line with or contrary to what the majority recommended to him. A classic case of that was St Paul VI on the matter of whether or not the Church could allow artificial contraception. The majority on his commission, set up specially to examine the question, advised him that he could so allow it. But he went away, prayed about it and perhaps consulted some others and came out in the end with the opposite decision in his famous encyclical *Humanae Vitae*.

Given that a wise pastor has selected his council carefully as being made up of faithful, practising, Catholics who live morally good lives, who have experience on the ground and are genuinely concerned, along with him, for the true good of the faith in the parish then, even though their vote is only consultative, he will value their opinions and their advice and will be slow to go against it unless he sees an obvious pitfall which they are not aware of. Such people can be a wonderful source of advice and support. In other words, the phrase "a consultative vote *only*" is not be taken in a derogative sense as being a vote of little value. It is of great value if it brings good ideas to light and exposes pitfalls for the priest. The council cannot constrain or compel the priest, but when working well they can be a great help. Accordingly, we read in *Priest, Pastor and Leader*:

> The pastoral council is to be seen in relation to the context of the relationship of mutual service that exists between a parish priest and his faithful. It would therefore be senseless to consider the pastoral council as an organ replacing the parish priest in his government of the parish, or as one which, on the basis of a majority vote, materially constrains the parish priest in his direction of the parish. #26

Take the example of a new parish priest who wants to start up a youth club in the parish. He thinks it is a great idea going on his experience in other parishes. However, his council inform him that there had been a youth club in the parish up to two years previously but that it had to be shut down because of a problem of drug peddling going on there, that the peddlers were known but not convicted and would most likely infiltrate again because there was not sufficient evidence to warrant keeping them out. If, notwithstanding this advice, the parish priest still goes ahead and the problem resurfaces he has only himself to blame when parents start complaining. In that case it is the members who see the pitfall and not the priest and the priest fails to listen to them. Then, on the other hand, there can be a situation where the new priest has a new, good idea but the members simply cannot see its value due to not having had experience of such a thing before. He presses on with his idea and it proves to be a great success. I have seen such cases. In matters like this prayer to the Holy Spirit for the gift of discernment is invaluable.

As regards voting, in any of the councils of the parish it was my policy only very seldom to put matters to a vote. Voting can be divisive even if there is a clear majority on one side, and more so if there is only a small majority. If a chairman has what he thinks is a good proposal it is better that he have a good discussion on it and that he try to win full, or near to full, consensus on it, which will be forthcoming if he is really successful in presenting his idea and if the members are reasonable in assessing it. Then he is bringing his people along with him, like a shepherd leading his flock, and the chances of the success of the venture will be all the greater.

Frequency of Meetings

How often should a parish pastoral council or finance council meet? I not aware of any rule about this but there should be a happy medium between meeting very seldom and very often. If a parish priest calls meetings very rarely the other council members will conclude that he plans on doing his own thing without them anyhow and they will lose interest. If he calls meetings too often, they will very likely degenerate into mere talking shops with no action following, and this will lead to a loss of interest also. Obviously, if some big parish event is coming up, like a parish anniversary celebration or a mission or some such thing, a meeting or perhaps a number of meetings will be necessary within a short span of time. But, in the ordinary run of parish life, I would suggest a minimum set number during the year, perhaps one each quarter or so and, outside of that, whenever necessary, i.e., whenever the priest honestly feels he needs advice on some important matter, not for trivialities or for things which any experienced priest should be able to make decisions about by himself. On this matter the late Cardinal Grey of Scotland once remarked that in the days before Vatican II, when he could see that something needed to be done, he simply went ahead and got it done, enlisting the help of those he felt were the most competent, but that after

Vatican II, with the new emphasis that was put on councils for all sorts of things, he said he could no longer scarcely blow his nose without having to call some council or committee together to discuss it! Another bishop who worked in Australia, on retiring offered to help out and do supply in any of the parishes of the diocese if priests needed a break - but with one proviso: that he would not have to attend meetings. He was sick to the teeth of them from his experience of many years as bishop because he saw that many of them came to nothing.

One must bear in mind now also that with the drop in vocations and some parishes having no resident priest, and given that such parishes still want to retain their identity as separate parishes (rather than be amalgamated with those near to them), the priests who are serving them have to duplicate or triplicate their attendance at parish council meetings. So, if a given parish normally would have only three such meetings in the year, but this one priest now has three parishes to look after, it means he has to attend nine meetings of one kind of council and perhaps nine more of another kind of council and other meetings about other things again. After a while he finds he has to become a rally driver rushing around from one meeting to another and often with little visible results.

A general rule I would give about the frequency of such meetings is that they be called as often as is necessary to engender a spirit of team-work by priest and people so that all together feel they are carrying the parish forward on the path of greater faith, hope and charity towards the kingdom of God. Thus I would say that meetings should be held only when necessary but, nonetheless, not so rarely that people lose interest or that momentum is lost.

Parish councils, pastoral or financial or liturgical (as we will touch on later), should have a fixed term of three or four or perhaps five years and then be renewed, even if some few members stay on for the sake of continuity. If there is not such a fixed term there is the danger that it will be a case of the same few doing the same things all the time. It leads to staleness because it dissuades others from coming along and making their contribution so that they opt out of parish life altogether. And as to those who stay, it can lead to the belief that they have acquired an inalienable right to a place on the council or that they are indispensable.

Conclusions:

1. Two heads are better than one: it is good to take council when any difficult decision has to be made in any area of life. In the life of the Church the Holy Spirit is working in the hearts of all the faithful and parish councils are a means by which the pastor can avail of His guidance.

2. All matters relevant to the progress of the faith and the building up of the Church can be on the table for discussion.
3. The difference between a consultative vote and an executive vote needs to be explained to people who are not accustomed to the latter. It might seem to be a small technical point but it ensures the hierarchical structure of the Church in parish government, a thing not appreciated at times in a democratic age.

In addition to the parish pastoral council there is also the parish finance council which will be our next concern.

Chapter VII

Parish Finance Councils and Buildings

Purpose, Building Projects, Spirit of Poverty

In each parish there is to be a finance committee to help the parish in the administration of the goods of the parish...*Code of Canon Law, canon 532.*

The Church is divine but also human because its members are bodily creatures and not angels who have no material needs. This brings us back again to the idea of the Church as an institution and a sacrament which means that it is visible and earthly. Recall also what we said earlier about a parish being something "stably established". This, in practice means having assets which includes property of some sort even if it is only a tin-shed little church or a one room school with a thatched roof; and needing finance, which finances have to be kept in order. Hence the need for a council to see after such things.

Most of what has been said in the last chapter about the pastoral council, how it is set up *etc.*, applies to the finance council also. In this chapter we will look at this latter as to how it looks after the assets of the parish, which will also lead to a consideration of church maintenance and building projects.

Finance Council to administer parish Goods

The finance council, unlike the pastoral council, is obligatory in canon law:

> In each parish there is to be a finance committee to help the parish in the administration of the goods of the parish, without prejudice to canon 532. It is ruled by universal law and by the norms laid down by the diocesan bishop, and it is comprised of members of Christ's faithful selected according to these norms. *Canon. 537.*

Such a council is also often required by civil law in some countries; and even if it were not obligatory it is still a good thing to have. Lay people, especially those who have experience of finance in various businesses, have a lot to offer and sometimes surpass the priest with their experience in such matters. Also, it gives transparency and openness to parish finances and it takes the spotlight off the priest himself if something irregular is happening in this area. Nonetheless, canon law makes clear that the parish priest is the sole administrator of the goods of the parish. *(can 1273ff)*. If, for example, a disused church organ is to be sold off it is he who sells it but not for his own personal gain. Only he can alienate church property or finances in the daily running of the parish, though it is usually a diocesan trustee with the bishop as head that owns church buildings and lands or holds them "in trust" for the people of the parish. Consequently, it is he, the pastor, who should hold the parish cheque book or bank card. In some places where a curate has responsibility for a designated area of the parish, but under the authority of the parish priest, there may be a separate account for that area and it may be held by him, though that is more the exception than the rule. Hence, the practice in some places of the priest handing over the cheque book to a lay person is not right and often leads to problems when the priest wants it back or even wants to look at it! For this reason, in some dioceses in England, when it happens that the priest is away due, for example, to him going on holidays or to hospital, it is required that the cheque book be handed in to the diocesan office. The authorities in those places learned by hard experience that if the cheque book or bank card is not in the priest's hands but is floating around amongst members of the finance council that there can be some odd entries under the heading of "miscellaneous" which can be very large at times and very hard to trace and impossible to recuperate. But, even if the priest alone holds the cheque book, it is safer for himself if one other person is a signatory to the cheques.

Parish accounting should follow a clear system by which I mean an orderly method of documenting all incomes and expenditures. It might take the form of an advanced computer program or the old-fashioned method of two simple ledgers, one for income and one for expenditure with different headings. Once the system is set up it is then easy to add to whichever column. This point should be obvious but I make it because priests who do not have such a system, or who do have one but neglect to make entries, soon find themselves in trouble when more has been paid out after a while than they realized.

Matters of income and expenditure, of lodgements, fundraising, investments, the maintenance and repairs of existing buildings or the erecting of new ones are the kind of things to be discussed at the meetings of finance councils. So, also, when a new project has to be undertaken the members would consider who might be a good contractor for such an undertaking – one chosen for his competence and honesty and not because he is a relative or friend of one of the members. It is a good practice also, in the interest of transparency, that the parish account books be audited by a professional firm every year. Many dioceses and the civil authorities also make this obligatory.

Church Accounts and Priests' Accounts

Parishioners should be made aware of the distinction between the parish income and the priests' personal income. Some parishioners naively believe (or wish to believe) that all of church funds go straight into the priests' pockets, even if it is the case in some dioceses that priests are allowed to take some amounts from church funds for their personal use, e.g., some house-keeping costs or phone or fuel costs or for the priest's health insurance.

As regards the priest's own income, arrangements differ from one country to another. In countries like Ireland the people are expected to support their priests directly, while in other countries like Germany or Italy people of religious affiliation pay a church tax to the government from which the ministers of all recognized religions are paid a salary. The former system, though financially uncertain, does make people aware of their obligation to contribute to the support of their pastors which was one of the six commandments of the Church in the old school catechisms. Then, in a parish of two or more priests there are different systems of dividing the priests' income which I will not go into here because of their diversity. The latter system, salaries paid from church taxes, gives greater financial security than the former but it does also make the Church somewhat dependent on the state.

The services of an auditor for priests' finances as well as for church finances is also a good idea and in many dioceses is obligatory. Honesty and openness is needed here as in all financial affairs. A priest who tries to play tricks with the revenue commissioners will fall foul of them sooner or later, causing scandal to his people and incurring a heavy fine on himself, whereas revenue people can be helpful when they see they are dealing with an honest person.

As to publishing the figures of either the church or the priests' accounts in the parish website or newsletter or on the church notice board, I come across two points of view on this. On the one hand it makes for better transparency. But, on the other hand, it can give ideas to robbers as to how much they might net on a raid and as to when is a good time to strike – after which of the weekend Masses and before the priest has had time to lodge the money. Some priests fear that if the figures are too good that not only will the robbers want to raid but many parishioners will decide to stop giving! Nonetheless, transparency is to be preferred.

Buildings and Repairs

Since the business of finance councils will often be concerned with the matter of repairs and of new building projects for which fundraising will be needed, I would like to offer a few tips on such things. I do so because I have often seen priests been "taken for a ride" in such matters by some architects and contractors. I say "some" because in my dealings with such people I have come across some very honest and truly helpful people also in those professions.

As regards the planning of a new church or school or hall, it is good to consult first with other priests in other parishes who have undertaken such things already so as to learn from them. With this information it is good then to sit down with one's own finance council (or pastoral council) and try to draw up a plan. Only then should one approach an architect, (if such be necessary at all because a small job can be discussed with an honest builder). If the priest and his council do not do their homework first, they are giving the architect or builder free rein to do as he likes. He may be a man who wants to make a name for himself with some new, fancy design but which may not be fit for purpose and which may also be very costly - and the more costly the better for himself because he knows he will be getting a certain percentage of the overall cost. On the other hand, he may also be an honest and intelligent man who can see flaws in what the priest is proposing and sees how needlessly costly it might be. How fortunate to meet such a person; but it is still a better thing to have one's own homework done before meeting him/her. A retired builder who is known to be honest and practical and who will not have a vested interest in the proposed work can be also be very useful for a second opinion, or, better still if one can have such a person on one's council to begin with. Sometimes a crack in a wall or a leak in a roof simply needs a new coat of plaster or the removal of a few broken slates while the architect might be saying that the whole wall or roof needs to be taken down and replaced.

The architect will have more play if the priest is a man who most dutifully and obediently feels he has to consult him about every detail of a given job which any handyman in the parish could fix very easily. I knew of one such case where the rope from the bell in the belfry was entangled in something and needed to be freed. The very dutiful priest, so meticulous about correct procedure in everything, had to write to an architect about it even though if he had gone up into the belfry himself or sent up an altar boy or even sent up a monkey it could have been freed in two minutes! But no. There had to be a file opened and a correspondence initiated with the architect about this most "complicated" matter! I don't know if it gave the latter a good laugh or a big headache. How odd that sometimes one can have a priest who is so absolutely meticulous in material matters and yet is a careless liberal when it comes to the rules of the liturgy or the moral issues of the day!

Needless Monuments

There is also the problem – it has often happened – of a parish priest who, contrary to the advice of an honest architect and his council, wants to put up a monument to himself with the construction of some new, big building so that his name will be on a plaque on the wall at the entrance where everyone can see it. I knew of one such case of a new rectory of a most elaborate and impractical design. I asked the current parish priest why his predecessor had built such a thing. The answer I got was "Ah, my friend, you do not know what a big ego Fr X had"! As an antidote to this kind of display of pride a layman once said to me "Father, if you cannot write your name on the hearts of your parishioners by being kind to them and by helping them in their difficulties then don't seek to write it on stone plaques either."

Then there is the priest who comes home from the missions, from a country with a hot climate, to his own country which has a colder climate and who brings with him the design of a church or rectory which was very suitable in the former place but is very impractical in the latter. But he is all enthusiasm for it against everyone's advice.

At the other extreme there is the priest who has no interest in even maintaining existing buildings in his parish. It happened one time at a confirmation, as the procession was leaving the sacristy and was coming round on the outside of the church towards the main door that the bishop was throwing eyes up at the roof of the building to see if all was in good repair. He noticed a sod of earth in the eves overhead which had a crop of grass growing out of it, indicating that it was there for a long time and, of course, was blocking the drainage of water and making for a problem of dampness inside the church. The curate was walking beside the bishop and made the comment "our parish priest here forgot to mow the meadow this year". The parish priest was walking only a short distance ahead and overheard the remark. Needless to say, it made for some friction afterwards when the bishop was gone!

Another such easy-going parish priest, who left everything to the last minute, again at confirmation time, had the habit of going down the street the evening before and of rounding up a few young lads to come up and paint the front gates of the church. He would instruct them to paint only the front or outer side of the gates and not to bother with the back or inner side because the gates would be opened well back during the Mass so that only the painted side would be visible. The boys, knowing that this was the plan, would indeed paint only the outer side of the gates, as instructed; but the next day, while the confirmation ceremony was going on inside, they would come along and close *out* the gates so that the first thing the bishop saw when he came out the door of the church was their inner side, all rusted and ready to fall to pieces!

In many dioceses there is a building committee to advise the bishop when relatively major jobs are being planned that will cost more than a designated sum so that he can vet them because the cost might go well beyond what the parish is capable of coming up with by itself. But I have seen impractical and over costly plans get the approval even of the diocesan building committee in places. It raises the question of how people were selected for such committees.

Funding

As regards costs for new projects – a difficult matter – there was an old rule, which I still think holds good, that work should not begin on a new building until at least half the cost has been gathered beforehand. If there is great difficulty in gathering that much then it is unlikely that it will be possible to gather the remainder either. And in this matter, one must always allow for those hidden costs which may arise from unforeseen difficulties such as soft foundations or interruptions due to bad weather or other such things. The final cost is often higher than that calculated at first.

In many dioceses there is a central fund accumulated from a levy that is put on all the parishes and which is made available to a given parish if it has a big undertaking on hand. But basic maths teach that many parishes cannot draw on this one fund at the same time. Consequently, a certain amount of local fundraising is usually necessary as well. This requires some prior calculation also, especially if it is in a country where Mass attendance is declining and where the young wage earners will not contribute because of other payments they must make or from a simple loss of interest in the parish or the faith generally. It sometimes happens in such a situation that a priest like Fr X above will go ahead with his monument anyhow, then ask for a change of parish and leave it to his bewildered successor to finish the fundraising, a task which may go on for years, with letters coming in from the bank manager very often.

A final story in this regard is that of a parish priest whose rectory was too big and very old and so was difficult to heat and maintain. He proposed selling it off or demolishing it, and I think he had a point. But his people would not agree because they had always looked on it as part of the parish heritage, and I must admit that they too had a point: a rectory/presbytery is an icon or symbol of the faith in its own way. They appealed to the bishop and won their case. So, the parish priest then, being a bad loser, decided to take his "revenge" on them by covering the inside walls with the most costly wall paper he could buy and so use up a lot the funds which he had already earmarked for a new rectory!

I have given these various examples to bring out the point that in the very down to earth, bricks-and-mortar business of buildings and repairs there is a moral side too which the priest should not lose sight of - humility, honesty, accountability and a bit of common sense are also needed in these matters, as well as hard-headed monetary calculations.

The thought of fundraising, especially when there is a big debt to clear, can be daunting. But the effort to organize so as to clear the debt - a debt that is seen as being justified - can bring parishioners together in a unified endeavour; and if that gives rise to such things as concerts, competitions or performances of various kinds it can have a great, social, uplifting effect on the parish. That is the positive side to the debt.

On coming newly into a parish, the priest should remember that, although legally he is the sole administrator of the goods of the parish, the money already in the kitty and which is now at his disposal was put there by past and present parishioners, people who might have had to make sacrifices in order to contribute to the church and did so generously because of their faith. It is hardly honest, then, for the priest to put his hands into that kitty and splash out on works whose obvious purpose are merely to serve his own comfort or vanity.

If parish funds are used for the priest's own dwelling a general rule is that the rectory he builds or repairs should be roughly on a par with what might be considered the average kind of dwelling owned by his parishioners. Anything more is ostentatious and it also provides an excuse for begrudging, anticlerical critics who love to find fault with any priest and who can thus use this priest's excesses as an *excuse* to reject religion altogether. They will also gladly form the suspicion that he is dipping into *parish* funds also for his own pleasures or hobbies.

Parishioners of genuine faith always want their priest to live in a good house of basic comfort and to have a reliable car that will start on a bad night if he is called out to an emergency. So, they will not begrudge him prudent spending on necessary repairs; but the priest should not take advantage of that. Again, a bit of honesty and simplicity is needed here. One would hope that the finance council, even though their vote is a consultative one, would have a moderating influence on any priest who is tending towards such excesses.

A Spirit of Poverty

Even if the secular priest does not have an actual vow of poverty like religious priests, he should still have the *spirit* of poverty and live poverty analogously, in his own state, to those who do have such a vow, mindful also of the poor in his parish who have to live poverty out of *necessity* and whom he should help from any surplus personal funds he may have. That some designated amount is being given for charity from parish funds should not excuse him from giving some amount from his own pocket also. In brief, he must present Christ to his people not only by preaching and the sacraments but also in such mundane things as his dwelling and his life-style.

In all of this, in regard to finance and the spirit of poverty, I have drawn great inspiration from young German priests who ministered there immediately after World War II when everything was in ruins, including churches and rectories in many places. They were known as the *ruck-sack priests* because all their earthly belongings fitted in the ruck sacks they carried on their backs. They would set up house in what was left of the sacristy of a bombed-out church and begin from there to re-construct the church and re-organize a parish, often with little more than their two bare hands. Many missionaries, priests and religious, have often done similarly great work in other countries beginning with similarly meagre resources.

There are still parishes in third world countries which are struggling financially and could do with some help from wealthy parishes in the first world. To give such help would manifest a missionary spirit in a material way because every parish, as said before, should be outward looking to the wider world; and help could be given to some selected charities at home also. This use of parish funds and the amount to be given should be approved by the bishop and overseen by the finance council with the parishioners being informed.

When priest and people are co-operating well in the various councils and committees of the parish – despite problems and differences which are all part of life – there is a sense of achievement and fulfilment for all involved. This is felt mostly at times like Christmas or Easter Sunday and whenever some project or other has been brought to completion. It is the sense that the parish is going somewhere, like a ship making for port, and not just going round the circle of the annual routine. But what is that port? Ultimately it is the Kingdom of God which will come at the end of time. It is the goal of all Christians everywhere because they are called to prepare the world for this kingdom. How priests might prepare their people to aim at that goal will be the subject of our next chapter and later chapters.

Conclusions:

1. The rules governing the finance council are similar to those governing the pastoral council as regards its being formed, the presidency of the parish priest and the consultative vote.
2. In matters of building and repairs the advice of experts is needed, but it is wise for the priest and his council to do some home-work on their own beforehand.
3. In matters of building and finance the virtues of humility and honesty are needed as well as an ability to do prudent mathematical calculations.

Parish councils are an area of lay involvement for people in co-operation with their pastor in the life of the parish. But the role of lay people is much wider than that. In the next chapter we must look at their more distinctive role in the secular world.

Chapter VIII

The Role of the Laity in the World

Dialogue on Involvement, Living the Mysteries, Catholic Action

Let you also go into my vineyard. Mt.20:7.

...their [the laity's] own field of evangelizing activity is the vast and complicated world of politics, society and economics, as well as the world of culture, of the sciences and the arts, of international life, of the mass media. *Christifideles Laici, #23*

We have been looking at the structures of the institutional Church, in particular at the parish unit, and noted the duties of both the priest and his helpers within that unit especially as to how they co-operate on various parish councils. In this chapter we will take a wider view of the involvement of lay people in their families and work places and in all other areas of secular life, and also at the ultimate goal of that involvement, the kingdom of God.

I will begin with that much used or abused phrase "the involvement of the laity". What does it mean? For many people it means that the priest has a lot of people involved in parish work in various ways, as members of his parish councils as we saw above, as altar servers, as readers and as extraordinary ministers of Holy Communion in the sanctuary, as singers in the choir, as helpers with collections, or as helpers keeping the church grounds tidy and some other such roles. He may have some more people leading a youth club on Friday nights or an active retirement group on Monday nights. We cannot forget the "involvement" of the sacristan or the housekeeper either, (the latter more so, that is if the priest is one who never learned from his mother how to cook anything other than a boiled egg!).

Dialogue on Involvement

If we tot up the number of people involved in all these councils, ministries and other functions just mentioned, giving, let us say, a number of ten people for each of the councils, perhaps twenty or thirty for each of the ministries and the choir and so on, the total number of lay people involved in the life of the parish might come to something like a hundred or a hundred and twenty or thereabouts. But let us say that it is a parish of five thousand people: what of the "involvement" of the remainder of the people? There will, of course, be a certain number of very young and very old people who cannot be actively involved and some more who, though Catholics, are only nominally so and who don't seem to care about what is happening in the parish. When we deduct these there could still be up to or more than four thousand able bodied lay people of whose "involvement" we want to know something.

To find out we will frame a dialogue in which we ask an imaginary priest whom I will call Fr. Smart because he is smart, efficient and therefore successful, (or seems to be at any rate), in running his parish and is very proud of that. He is managing it well, a good number are coming to Mass every Sunday, the dues are rolling in, the buildings are well maintained, everyone is happy and he is popular. So, our dialogue with him might go like this:

Questioner: Fr. Smart, by all accounts you are said to be an efficient pastor and have many lay people involved in the life of the parish. Congratulations on that. But according to my figures there could still be as many as four thousand lay people who are not involved in the life of the parish. What do you say about them since we often hear you using this phrase "the involvement of the laity"?

Fr. Smart: True, they are not actively involved but many of them, perhaps near on thirty percent anyhow, do come to Mass most Sundays. That is more than the average in Western countries which is under twenty percent. And I have plans to involve more of them. I'm thinking of having more than one reader for each Sunday Mass. I could make that two and even three if I give the responsorial psalm to a third person. And then I could have five more people take a prayer of the faithful each, and then another four or six or eight people bring up gifts at the offertory. And then I could expand or even double the members in my different councils. Now that will greatly increase the involvement of my laity.

Q: But, Fr. Smart, before you go ahead and do that, let me ask you: if you increase the number of cooks in your kitchen from one to four tomorrow will your dinner then be four times better than it was yesterday?

Fr Smart: I don't think so.

Q: No indeed, and moreover the four cooks are likely to fight and spill the soup on top of yourself! And tell, if in a tennis game you have four or five players on each side of the net, taken from the spectators so as to "involve" more of them, do you think it would make for a better game of tennis?

Fr. Smart: I doubt it.

Q: No indeed. They would be clouting each other with their racquets instead of hitting the ball. And so also in a parish council; if you double the number from ten to twenty just to involve more of the laity what will happen is that, if they are interested people, they will divide because there will be too many divergent opinions on things; and if they are easy going most of them will become what is called "dead wood" because they will let most of the decisions and the tasks to a small few. As for your choir, which is pretty good as it is, if instead of doubling the number of singers you halved it and had them promote congregational singing wouldn't that be even better still? The body of people in the seats at present let all the singing to the choir precisely because it is good and they hardly open their mouths themselves even though they sing very well in the pub at night! And I will say, further, that if you did increase the number of lay people coming up into the sanctuary just to "bump up" the numbers, you would have them "bumping into" each other, going up and down the steps, the net result of which would simply be to turn the liturgy into a circus and turn off the likes of me, for one, and many others who might still have a sense of the sacred.

Fr. Smart: So, you are telling me that things are just fine as they are. Thank you for the complement.

Q: Sorry to disappoint you, Father, but I am not saying that at all.

Fr. Smart: Oh no! So, what is your criticism?

Q: Tell me, Fr Smart, when Sunday is over and Monday comes along where are most of your people?

Fr. Smart: In their work places by day and in their homes by night or in places of entertainment.

Q: And where are those work places?

Fr. Smart: Oh, I can't say for sure where most of them work or what they work at because many of them work outside the parish in places far away to which they commute. I have some idea alright of the doings of those who live and work nearby.

Q: But do you see it as your concern at all what they do in their homes and in their work places in as much as that relates to their faith?

Fr. Smart: Not really since I cannot keep tabs on all of them. But whatever their occupations I hope they are doing their work honestly and efficiently and taking good care of their families. Beyond that I think I don't have any further responsibilities, and anyhow I have enough to do to manage the church and parish activities here.

Q: But is there or should there be any relation or connection between what they celebrate at Mass on Sunday and hear in the sermon and what they are doing in their work places during the rest of the week?

Fr. Smart: as I said, I hope they are doing their work honestly and efficiently and taking good care of their families. I would see that as being Christian.

Q: Indeed. But are there not many non-Christians who do their work honestly and efficiently and take good care of their families. Is there nothing more than that to being a Christian in the work place? I would be hoping that the faith they profess and celebrate on a Sunday would throw a Christian light on the work they are doing during the week and on their married lives in their homes and that the moral teaching they hear in sermons would be given effect in those places. You don't seem to see any connection between the two beyond being honest and efficient. Not only that, but I know from hard statistics that many so-called Catholics, even if honest and efficient, do things in their work places and their homes which are totally contrary to Catholic faith and morals. Let me give you one example.

I remember a politician, a Sunday Mass goer, who said that when he would sit into his car on a Monday morning to go to the parliament that he left his religion inside the door of the church and that once inside the door of the parliament he had to vote according to the dictates of the prime minister and the wishes of his constituents, and if what they wanted didn't agree with what was preached on a Sunday, so be it. *Their* wishes came first. And he had no qualms about voting even for abortion. Indeed, in many churches what he would have heard preached on a Sunday was such timid milk-and-water stuff that it would not present him with a problem of conscience anyhow.

Chapter 8: The Role of the Laity in the World

So, Father, what do you preach on the matter of right morals and social issues and the Christian meaning of work, of the work that most of your parishioners are engaged in most of the week and for most of their lives?

Fr. Smart: Well, I think now that you are expecting me to stick my nose into people's work lives and family lives a bit too much.

Q: Is that so? And meanwhile our country and the Western world generally becomes more and more secularist and Godless and you cannot see that you might have some obligation to do something about that. God is being pushed out of the family and the workplace and indeed out of every area of life. In hospitals sterilizations, abortions and euthanasia are performed by Catholic medics; Catholic chemists sell contraceptives and the morning after pill; in schools, some of which are under Catholic management, teachers promote all kinds of woke ideology; in entertainment the erotic is promoted on the dance floor and on the screen. Catholics in the media keep on bashing their own Church; and you have no message for that world, no guidance for those who work in it as to how they can oppose such things and reclaim it and Christianize it and prepare it for the Kingdom of God!

Fr. Smart: But if I start preaching about this secularism that you are talking about, telling people engaged in different professions what they should or should not be doing, they will protest and walk out of Mass. Furthermore, the kind of preaching you are advocating would amount merely to turning the sermon into political agitation. Faith and politics should be kept entirely separate.

Q: Indeed; and your cosy, nicely-run parish enterprise and especially the collection will suffer and so also your own popularity if you preach like that. You know full well that many people like to be molly-cuddled on a Sunday when they come to Mass so that their "involvement" in the push-out of God from the world can continue without their consciences being disturbed. But don't you see the result – a world where every kind of evil is legalized and practiced even by Catholics, by the very people who should be to the forefront in opposing that kind of thing and promoting the rule of Christ in the world instead? As for interfering in politics, that is indeed the field of the politician, but have you not read *Gaudium et Spes* where it says clearly that the church "has the right to pass moral judgements, even on matters touching the political order, whenever basic personal rights and or the salvation of souls make such judgements necessary?" Along with that priests should always be instructing their flock on the basics of Catholic social teaching, what for too long has been the best kept secret of the church!

Fr. Smart: Even if a priest did start talking about things like that, he'd be hitting at many of the professional people in his parish and they would complain to the bishop and my guess is that the bishop would not like that kind of annoyance and soon tell him to shut up, to stop ruffling feathers. Anyhow, I have something else to be doing, keeping the parish in shape, besides reading Church documents.

Q: So the rot goes on and we are back to where we started – you still see no connection between the parish on a Sunday and the work place on a Monday. You also say that the percentage coming to Mass in your parish is near thirty percent. That might be high in comparison to many other parishes but it is still less than half, and it is very low compared to parishes in many parts of Africa where practice is at seventy or eighty percent. And supposing we used the statistic of the gospel which tells of ninety-nine who are in and of only the one who is out how would you fare? But even if you are right with your figure of thirty per cent attending, what about the other seventy percent who don't come at all now? Is it that they are all very bad people?

Fr. Smart: I wouldn't say so. Many of them are nice people to meet on the street and helpful in various ways.

Q: But they are gone from Mass and, I suppose, for a number of reasons which we cannot explore fully here. But one reason, I would argue, is that they see no relation between what goes on at Mass and what they are taken up with for most of the week which is more important to them, which is another way of saying that there is large gulf or split between Church and world.

<u>The Splits</u>

All through history there have been what might be called "splits" or "gulfs" in life between things that should be seen as united in ways that are complementary, but which, instead, are needlessly played off one against the other, which splits have done great harm to faith and led, in no small part, to the present secularism of the Western world. These splits are certainly not inherent defects in Christianity itself but things which have dogged it nonetheless at various times thereby clouding the true face of Christianity.

One such split is that between soul and body. Soul and body are indeed different because one is spirit and the other is matter, and the soul is the superior part of the one human person. The soul is the form of the body and *both* have been redeemed by

Christ, because the entire person has been redeemed, and, furthermore, the body too is destined to rise to glory at the end of time, joined again to the soul, and not just the soul by itself. Hence to say take care of the soul and to forget or denigrate the body, to discard it as evil (as opposed to disciplining it by true asceticism) is not true Christianity. It is, in fact, a heresy, a radical dualism that has appeared variously as Gnosticism and Manichaeism and in other guises which have often been a parasite on Christianity to its detriment.

Gaudium et Spes spoke of another split directly relevant to our dialogue above, the split between religion and earthly affairs:

> Nor, on the contrary, are they any less wide of the mark who think that religion consists in acts of worship alone and in the discharge of certain moral obligations, and who imagine they can plunge themselves into earthly affairs in such a way as to imply that these are altogether divorced from the religious life. This split between the faith which many profess and their daily lives deserves to be counted among the more serious errors of our age. #43

Many Christians do not see a connection between the mysteries which they celebrate at Mass and their ordinary work and their married lives, that is, they cannot see how in doing their work they can cooperate with the Creator and Redeemer in what He did for us long ago and what He continues to do for us in the mysteries, especially those celebrated in the Mass.

Living the Mysteries

In chapter I, when talking about the fundamental importance of the mysteries of the faith for Christian living – an importance which I argued there was greatly overlooked – I gave a few brief examples of how priest and people live out each of the mysteries in their everyday lives beginning with the Trinity and going on to the incarnation, redemption and second coming of Christ. Christian spirituality can be described as a living out of the mysteries of the faith in one's daily life so that thereby one becomes holy in the performance of one's everyday duties. Here I want to expand on that a bit more showing the relevance of this for lay people engaged in their everyday work in the secular world.

The father of the family and sometimes the mother also set out from their homes to their work places which can be very varied. They work primarily to support themselves economically, but priests should also be able to shine the light of faith on what these people are doing, and so, give it a Christian meaning. People live out the mystery of the Trinity if the kind of love they show to each other at home and then to their fellow workers and clients is that of *communio* or *koinonia* – the kind of self-giving love, which as we saw earlier, has its primary source in the inner life of the Trinity and which was brought to us here on earth when the Son, the second person of the Trinity became man in Christ.

But there is more. By their work Christians also can live out or continue the mysteries of creation, incarnation and redemption. Hence *Gaudium et Spes* says with regard to the mystery of creation:

> By work an individual ordinarily provides for self and family, is joined in fellowship to others, and renders them service; and is enabled to exercise genuine charity and be a partner in the work of bringing divine creation to perfection. *Gaudium et Spes, #67* and *Christifideles Laici, #43;* John Paul II, *Laborem Exercens; Compendium of the Social Doctrine of the Church, Ch. 6.*

The builder laying blocks can be said to complete the work of creation because God did not give men their homes and buildings ready-made. But this presumes that they develop creation and use its resources in a way that is respectful of the inherent laws of the environment and not plunder it for crude gain.

> …humanity has received from God himself the task of "dominating" the created world and "cultivating the garden" of the world. But this is a task that humanity must carry out in respect for the divine image received, and, therefore, with intelligence and with love, assuming responsibility for the gifts that God has bestowed and continues to bestow". *CL, #43; (cf.* also John XXIII, *Mater et Magistra* and *Pacem in Terris,).*

The worker is also like unto Christ at His work in the workshop of Nazareth. Christ sanctified ordinary work by his work as a carpenter and thus made of work a holy thing, a sacramental, a means of grace for those who undertake it today in the right spirit. Through work, then, the grace of Christ penetrates all of matter and all of society. Thus, do they live out the mystery of the incarnation.

By work a man or woman can share in the mystery of the redemption because of the pain inevitably incurred as a result of the Fall from the labour of work.

> Moreover, we know that through work offered to God an individual is associated with the redemptive work of Jesus Christ, whose labour with his hands at

Nazareth greatly ennobled the dignity of work… *Gaudium et Spes, #67 (cf.* also *CL, #43* and JPII, *Laborem Exercens).*

The worker can offer that labour with that of the sufferings of Christ on the cross for the redemption of the world.

But work also has a forward-looking, spiritual meaning because it can be seen as a preparation of the world for the kingdom of God of the end. St John Paul II again:

Confident and steadfast through the power of God's grace, these are the humble yet great builders of the Kingdom of God in history. *CL, #17.*

In all of this these lay workers must be animated by charity because charity is at the very core of Christian holiness. Charity in the work place will manifest itself in service of those who are at the receiving end of their work:

Through charity towards one's neighbour, the lay faithful exercise and manifest their participation in the kingship of Christ, that is, in the power of the Son of man who 'came not to be served but to serve' *(Mk. 10:45)". Ibid., #41.*

This charity is again the *koinonia* of the Trinity with which we began above because God is the beginning and the end of all that we do.

Living like this, we can say, is a closing of the split by showing ordinary work to be a *sacramental* extending the *sacrament* of the paschal mystery that is celebrated in the Mass. Work becomes a sacramental when workers see analogies or parallels between what they are doing in the work place and what God has done in the mysteries.

We can then go on to say also that the work week begins and ends with Sunday Mass. The last words of the Mass are *ita missa est* "go in peace to love and serve the Lord" which we can paraphrase as saying "go out to your places of work and family with the strength that comes from the grace you have received here at Mass and be witnesses before the world to what you have celebrated here, transforming the world so that it too will be joined to the sacrifice offered here and that *God will be all in all." 1 Cor. 15:28*. I pointed out also in chapter I that action follows on being, that one's faith as a worshipping Christian should find expression as action, as good works, in daily life in the world. Put simply, liturgy should give rise to apostolate, to the lay apostolate for most of the people who have been at Mass. We must look at this now.

The lay Apostolate

The council says that the proper field of action and therefore of evangelization of lay people is where God has put them by reason of their different occupations, in their family homes and their work places and all other places of human engagement. Their help and involvement in the parish church at weekends is indeed welcome, needed and valued and they have their rightful place there, but it is not the main locus of their involvement as Christians. As to where *that* is the council says:

> ...their own field of evangelizing activity is the vast and complicated world of politics, society and economics, as well as the world of culture, of the sciences and the arts, of international life, of the mass media. It also includes other realities which are open to evangelization, such as human love, the family, the education of children and adolescents, professional work, and suffering. *Christifideles Laici, # 23 (cf. also Evangelii Nuntiandi, #70).*

Their mandate to engage in these fields of evangelization flows from the sacraments of baptism and confirmation they have received. When they do so engage they are exercising their lay kingly, prophetic and priestly roles. This in brief is the lay apostolate as the council goes on to explain:

> The laity derive the right and duty to the apostolate from their union with Christ the head; incorporated into Christ's Mystical Body through Baptism and strengthened by the power of the Holy Spirit through Confirmation, they are assigned to the apostolate by the Lord Himself. They are consecrated for the royal priesthood and the holy people (cf. *1 Peter 2:4-10*) not only that they may offer spiritual sacrifices in everything they do but also that they may witness to Christ throughout the world. *Aposolicam Actuisitatem, #3; (cf. also Christifideles Laici).*

But the laity will not be able to carry out this, their task of evangelization, unless they are able to over come in themselves the split of the gospel from life, which split, I believe, has its origins in the prior split, mentioned above between soul and body and, underlying that again, between spirit and matter. And how is this inner split to be overcome?

> This will be possible if the lay faithful will know how to overcome in themselves the separation of the Gospel from life, to again take up in their daily

activities in family, work and society, an integrated approach to life that is fully brought about by the inspiration and strength of the Gospel. *Christifideles Laici, # 34.*

They need the help of their priests in doing so by his preaching and by giving them instruction in Catholic social teaching. As long as their priests fail to give them this lead the world of work, culture, entertainment, the family *etc.,* will continue to go off on a tangent of secularism with the added scandal of some Catholics taking leading roles on this tangent like our friend above coming out from Sunday Mass and going to parliament the next day to promote abortion there. The scandal is doubly compounded when some priests will even get on this bandwagon themselves in a pathetic bid to be popular, and the scandal is compounded even further when some of these priests will then turn around and make fun of those few lay people who *are* trying to Christianize the world, calling them "right wing conservatives". I am thinking particularly of pro-life people who have told me how their own priests would shun them or sneer at them when they were standing at church gates giving out leaflets.

Catholic Action

What I am talking about here as regards the true involvement of the laity is what has traditionally been called *Catholic Action*. It is an idea that goes back to St Pius IX and was developed further by Pope Leo XIII who wrote encyclicals on the Christian's involvement in political life and in industry (*Diuturnum; Immortale Dei; Rerum Novarum*). One can say that in the former two encyclicals he was outlining what should be the response of Christians to the emerging democracies in Europe resulting from the French Revolution, and in the latter their response to the industrial revolution in the cities of Northern Europe. St Pius X, then, developed *Catholic Action* further with his motto of "restoring all things in Christ". It gave rise to Catholic social movements of various kinds such as Christian political parties and trade unions. The ideas of *Catholic Action* received greater formulation and development at Vatican II. The council devoted not just one but *three* documents to the involvement of the laity in the secular world: *Lumen Gentium, Gaudium et Spes* and *Apostolicam Actuositatem,* to be followed later by more such encyclicals by the succeeding popes and by the *Compendium of the Social Doctrine of the Church*. But, paradoxically, it was *after* that time that the lay apostolate, as the involvement of the laity in the Christian transformation of the world, began to decline and give way to an aggressive secularism that wants to push religion, particularly the Catholic religion, aside in the name of individual freedom, pluralism and atheism.

If we are to resurrect a true involvement of the laity again, one that has them transforming the world in light of the gospel and preparing it for the kingdom of God, we need to get back to these documents again, with priests giving the lead by explaining them in their preaching and by putting on classes in Catholic social teaching.

The laity need to be well versed in the fundamental principles of Catholic social teaching, principles such as that of the dignity of the worker and of every human being as made in the image and likeness of God and redeemed by Christ; the notion of justice in its three main kinds of commutative, distributive and legal and, in the area of work, the notion of a just wage as that which takes account of the basic needs of a worker and his family. Related to this are the conditions for a just strike when there is a perceived injustice.

People also need to know that there is a right to private property but that it is not absolute because of another principle - that of the common destination of the goods of the world.

Then there are the notions of subsidiary and solidarity, the former which demands that the small unit be allowed to manage its own affairs when possible, without being consumed by any bigger unit such as the state, and the latter which extends the notion of charity to the wider society.

All of these principles serve the common good - another important principle which requires just laws that are in line with good morals defending fundamental rights so that individuals and communities can develop in ways that are truly human.

So that just laws will be enacted lay people, as citizens, need also to be instructed on their duties as voters especially with regard to electing wise and good people as legislators in various councils and chambers of government. That means they should be made aware that they themselves can be co-operators in good or in evil depending on the kind of people they elect, and that they will be judged on that. For example, to elect an openly pro-abortion candidate to office is to have a part in the deaths of those innocents who will die as a result of the kind of legislation he/she will promote. Greater still is the guilt of voting directly oneself for such measures in a referendum. Sadly, many people vote solely for the candidate whom they think will put more money in their pockets with no regard for fundamental human rights or the common good, and even many legislators who are Catholics are largely ignorant of these principles.

When lay people are instructed on these principles they will be able to take a stand on moral issues also relating to their families and their work. Christian nurses, for example, will be able to campaign for respect for life at all stages from conception to natural death in the hospital. They should campaign to oppose such practices as abortion, sterilization, *in vitro* fertilization, and euthanasia, and if they cannot stop these practices they can at least campaign for the right to conscientious objection.

Workers in other areas can campaign for just wages and healthy work conditions and know what criteria should be met. Workers in finance can campaign for low interest rates for borrowers, especially for young married couples trying to start a home.

These campaigners will have a battle on their hands because Satan never sleeps and he is increasing his efforts at present. But they must not be daunted. We are not called to win but to struggle, said Mother Theresa, and, according to Pope Leo XIII, if we do struggle to the best of our ability we can confidently hope that the Lord will bless our efforts and give the victory in His own good time.

Priests Instructors

All of this requires that these lay people have a good knowledge of Catholic social teaching. Priests, led by their bishops, must make a beginning by preaching and teaching Catholic social teaching. They must give a lead to their people in such matters because lay people look to them for a lead in all matters of faith and morals even if it is the laity themselves - because it is they who are *in* the vineyard - who will give effect to this teaching as they see fit in different circumstances. It is they who take the lead *there*. Doing this would give effect to what we described at the beginning of this study as the "social model" of the Church, the Church taking an interest in the social issues of her time so as to Christianize the solutions proposed. The council explicitly asked that some priests be specially trained to enable the lay people to live out this apostolate of theirs:

> Particular attention must be paid to the selection of priests who are capable of promoting particular forms of the apostolate of the laity and are properly trained. *Apostolicam Actuositatem, #25.*

But, in a more general way, all priests by their preaching and by putting on night classes on Catholic social teaching should be making their lay people aware of this apostolate of theirs and preparing them for it. Lay people trained in Catholic social teaching could also be enlisted to give these classes. This would engage most of those four thousand people of which we spoke about in our conversation above with Fr Smart and give effect to the truth that while, indeed, there is a rightful involvement of a limited number of the laity in the sanctuary, their primary and more urgent kind of involvement is in the vineyard of the world where they live and work so as to Christianize it, bring it under the sway of the gospel and thereby prepare it for the kingdom at Christ's second coming.

The lay apostolate in the world, we saw, begins with Sunday Mass. It ends with Sunday Mass also at the end of the week, on the following Sunday, when the laity come back *bringing their sheaves* as the psalm says. At the offertory, they bring up the bread and wine to the priest. The bread symbolizes their positive achievements during the week; the wine their labours and disappointments. But they give both to the priest who, by the action of the Holy Spirit, will soon have them transformed into the Body and Blood of Christ at the consecration and he will offer them up as joined to the perpetual sacrifice of the Son to the Father for the redemption of the world. Here we see the priesthood of the ordained and the priesthood of the laity in close interaction and so also their respective kingships because the offertory gifts which the laity bring up are the fruits of their efforts to bring the secular world under the reign of Christ the King.

Conclusions:

1. While it is true that the laity can and should help around the altar at the liturgy and in other kinds of parish activities, their proper field of activity is where the Lord has placed them in their family situations and in their places of work, politics, culture, education, *etc*. Their task is to Christianize these places so that the faith and the moral law will underpin all that goes on in these places with due respect for the religious freedom of others who might not be Christian.
2. For too long there has been a split between faith and culture, between the Church and the world so that the former has become turned in on itself and the latter has grown secularist. Instead, people should learn to see their work and family life as a daily living out of the mysteries of the faith in cooperation with the Lord.
3. The grace received at Mass should give rise to social action in the vineyard of the world. To facilitate this, instruction of the laity by their priests in the principles of Catholic social teaching is needed, beginning with the dignity of the individual and going on to those principles which serve the common good and prepare the world for the kingdom of God.

It is the laity primarily who are called to Christianize the world, but should the priest follow them there? That is our next concern.

Chapter IX

The Priest in the Vineyard of the World

Areas of Priestly Involvement, Witness to the Incarnation

Is not this the carpenter? Mk 6:3; The Word became flesh and dwelt amongst us. Jn 1.14.

It is true that those in holy orders can at times engage in secular activities, and even have a secular profession. But by reason of their particular vocation they are chiefly and professedly ordained to the sacred ministry. *Lumen Gentium, #20.*

We have seen that the primary place and role of the laity is the home and the vineyard of the secular world, Christianizing those places so as to have them permeated by the moral law and the spirit of the gospels in preparation for the Kingdom of God. We saw also that the primary place for the priest was in his parish giving guidance to his people on this enterprise by preaching the word of God to them, by sanctifying them with the sacraments and by doing all those other things which are necessary for the daily life of building up the Church in the parish. From within the parish he prepares his people for what they should be doing in the wider world inside or outside of their own parish.

But let us now pose a new question in this chapter: should the priest himself be directly involved in areas outside his church, in those secular areas of work, economics, culture, politics *etc*? The first reaction would be to say "No"; that that is not his role, that he should let that to the laity as explained above. But Church teaching and pastoral history shows that the matter is not quite so cut and dried.

Areas of Priestly Involvement

<u>In the Family</u>

As regards being involved in family life, priests of the Latin rite do not marry or have families of their own. They renounce this so as to live out more fully the spousal relationship of Christ and His bride the Church by giving themselves more fully to the people they serve. In this way they also bear witness in advance to what life will be like in the Kingdom of God after the resurrection of the dead. Priests of the Eastern rites can be married men who also care for their parishioners, and the Church respects this practice of theirs. They have the advantage of knowing and Christianizing family life "from the inside", as we might say, but they have the disadvantage of not being able to give themselves as fully to their flock, to all other families and to those who have no family for reasons of time, nor of being able to give witness to people today of the kind of life we will enjoy in the kingdom of the end.

But priests of the Latin rite can be very much involved in the families of their parish, as we saw earlier, by house visitation and by making it their business to know their people and their concerns. This, we said, was also a matter of giving effect to what I called "the incarnational principle" – that whereby God the Son entered the lives of the families of the people amongst whom He grew up and indeed of all families. By a kind of paradox we can say that the Latin rite priest, precisely because he is *not* in a family of his own is thereby more free to be involved in all of the families of his parish. Also, Christ raised marriage to the level of being a sacrament by His presence at the wedding feast of Cana. Celibacy has a value that should not be thrown away.

In the World of Work

Then, as regards the priest being involved in the wider world of work, economics, culture, health, education and so on what can we say? It should not be forgotten that priests in rural places, especially in times past, often engaged in a certain amount of farming themselves, doing that which their people around them were also doing. They did so because in those times the parochial house often had some few acres of land attached to it simply for the upkeep of the priest so that he would not be too much of a burden on the people around him who were often very poor and scarcely able to support themselves. Such priests were very much immersed in the work-life of their people and would advise them on such things as the right time to spray their potatoes against blight and other things. Accordingly, one could say that such priests also were giving effect to the incarnational principle, living the kind of life and doing the kind of work that their people were doing. On the matter of priests engaged in agriculture it must also be borne in mind how the monks of all ages (though not all of them were priests) engaged in farming and developed the countryside around them. They consecrated space by their agricultural work in the fields and time by the recitation of the divine office seven times a day in choir.

But what about priest today engaging in farming and in other professions? There are still farming orders today such as the Cistercians, and there are priests in rural places who grow gardens for their own kitchen table. It also often happens that priests engage in secular professions such as the teaching of secular subjects, doing scientific research and engaging in the administration of various kinds of organizations, usually for charitable purposes. On this matter *Lumen Gentium* says as quoted above already:

> It is true that those in holy orders can at times engage in secular activities, and even have a secular profession. But by reason of their particular vocation they are chiefly and professedly ordained to the sacred ministry. *#20.*

But let us put this in context with what it says in the *Code of Canon Law*:

> Clerics are prohibited from conducting business or trade personally or through others, for their own advantage or that of others, except with the permission of legitimate ecclesiastical authority. *Canon 286.*

I knew of an unusual case in an English diocese where a parish priest was also a gifted property developer who used to buy and renovate old houses and sell them on for a profit, which profit went to the diocese. The diocese made great use of him both for the profit he made and also for taking charge of renovations of church buildings. Unusual indeed, but he does seem to fit the requirements of *canon 286* above! Some diocese, as in Germany, own and run their own banks and other businesses which they claim they need as sources of income to fund various Church projects.

<u>In Community Development</u>

Then we can consider the many priests in many countries who did not do farming themselves, directly, in the sense explained above of the priest farming the few acres of land around his house, but who did much more when they promoted local agriculture for their people and led them in such works as draining rivers, planting trees, growing crops, founding cattle marts *etc*; and likewise priests who developed small industries and co-operatives in their own parishes because they saw what an evil unemployment is and how it drains a parish of its most able-bodied members so that after a while the priest finds himself preaching only to the very young or to the very old.

In Ireland there were two such priests in the first half of the twentieth century who did such things. One was Canon John Hayes of the Cashel diocese in the South of Ireland who founded the *Muintir na Tíre* movement in the wake of a civil war and an economic war which had divided and crippled the newly born Irish state. *Muintir na Tíre* means simply "the people of the countryside". Its philosophy was very simple: organize the people of a parish to get together to study their own besetting problems and tackle them together with (mostly) voluntary labour. It united people and promoted every kind of social enterprises from sport to drama to agriculture to small industry and more, in many parishes. It was badly needed at that time. Yet in all that time Fr. Hayes was a pastoral priest who never neglected his sacramental duties.

Another such priest was Fr. James McDyer of the rural sea-side parish of Glencolumbkille in Co. Donegal in the North West of Ireland. His parish was being drained by unemployment and emigration. So, he developed co-operatives in his parish for small industries based on local, natural resources such as knit-ware, vegetable processing and fish food processing, plus a tourist holiday village and a hotel. Again, he too was most faithful to his sacramental duties.

Then, in England, there was the Dominican priest Fr. Vincent McNabb with his *Distributist* Movement – trying to get people to move out of the big cities to the depleted county-side where they could have a more natural life-style and greater economic and political independence.

On a bigger scale then, around the same time there was the *Antigonish* co-operative movement in Nova Scotia in Canada founded by Fr. Moses Cody and there was the *Mondragon* co-operative movement in the Basque country in Spain founded by Fr. Arizmendiarrieta.

Fr. Coady began with adult education classes, instructing people on the whole idea of co-operatives. Next, he went on to found credit unions which are a co-operative kind of bank. Then he started some simple, consumer co-operatives such as a group of housewives in one place buying their groceries together at a reduced cost. And, finally, he got people on to the more difficult task of small-scale industrial production, again of a co-operative kind. Fr. Arizmendiarrieta, somewhat similarly, founded different co-ops such that one "fed into" or "led onto another" both by providing the funds for the latter and by producing things in one co-op the left-overs of which could become raw material for another. After some years it led to a network of eighty different, large co-operative industries in many countries.

One could cite many more examples of this kind by priests in mission territories developing the material conditions of their people but always with a view to the primacy of the spiritual. They did great work which often went unrecognized in the first world.

But in all of this canon law has this wise admonition:

> Clerics are to avoid those things which, although not unbecoming, are nevertheless foreign to the clerical state. *Canon 285 #2*.

For priests to promote the development of the material, indirectly or even directly when necessary, so as to put it at the service of the spiritual and the faith, I would argue, is not to engage in something foreign to the clerical state if the preaching of the faith and the administration of the sacraments are not neglected and people are shown the connection between one and the other as we were trying to do in the last chapter above.

In the Factory - the Worker Priests

A more interesting case of the involvement of priests in secular activities was that of the worker priest movement which began in the South of France in the 1940s with Fr. Jacques Lowe, O.P. Priests there could see that there was little of no connection between what they were doing in their parishes and what most workers were doing in their factories around them in city environments which had become industrialized. They knew that if they stayed in their rectories forever these workers would not come to them but would continue to pursue a way of life that was very secularist. They also knew that in the factories Marxist union leaders were having great influence on them because they seemed to be promoting the material interests of these workers, gaining pay increases for them, shorter working hours and other advantages. For these priests the only solution seemed to be to go into the factories and onto the building sites and work alongside the workers. If they, as priests, could be seen to share willingly in the lives and the work of the workers and be accepted as men standing side by side with them then, perhaps, the workers would accept them as priests also and accept their message of the gospel. To a great extent it worked. Some of these worker priests were so well accepted, and the workers had so many things to ask them, that in some factories they arranged that the priest would spend his day in a separate office where the workers could come in their turns to talk to him. And why did it work? Again, because of what I call "the incarnational principle". They, as representatives of God, were doing something like what God the Son Himself did when He took on the life of a carpenter in Nazareth for a span of thirty years, by far the greatest portion of His time on earth.

I have had some experience myself of the worker priest adventure when working on building sites in Ireland, England and America, and again in some of my parish assignments. I can remember one Summer on a building site in London, how it would happen occasionally that a worker would come to me quietly for a chat if he found me by myself. He would usually be an Irishman who still had the faith but whose life-cycle did not overlap with that of the parish. Again, that was what the French priests had found: it was simply a matter of the two life cycles, that of the priest in the parish and that of the worker in the world, not overlapping more so than any bad will towards the Church, though one found a bit of that too at times.

My first and second parishes were by the sea where many of the men were fishermen working on trawler boats in the broad Atlantic. I made a point of going out to sea with them just a few times, though not often because a day at sea was from 6.00am in the morning to 11.00pm at night so it was not easy to get that much time off from my other parish duties. Hence, usually, I did this on my day off. A day working on a trawler in high seas is rough going when one is not used to it because one is likely to be sea sick for some few hours at least.

But the experience was well worth it. It gave me a new insight into the minds of fishermen. I remember talking about this to an uncle of mine sometime later and he said to me "Do you understand now why Christ picked a group of fishermen as His first apostles and not some of the learned rabbis of Jerusalem?" It also gave *them* a new relationship to me as a priest who was prepared to share their work and the dangers that go with it because, out on the waves in the wild Atlantic, only a piece of wood an inch thick stands between a man and the bottom of the sea. Also, the sheer expanse of the ocean is a constant reminder of the Infinite, of God, and that it is He whom one must meet for judgement if one falls over board (something that did happen one day to one of those men, unfortunately).

Those fishing parishes were also places of small-scale agriculture; and, again, I had a little experience one day which again brought home to me the value of what I keep calling "the incarnational principle". I was walking down from my house one afternoon in the Summer- time and came upon some farming neighbours who were trying to save their crop of hay, something which is very much dependent on the weather, on the sun to be exact. On this occasion, as I was passing by, I saw that a group of these neighbours were frantically trying to gather up the last of the hay and put it into stacks because there was a dark cloud overhead which was threatening to pour down its contents on them and ruin their efforts. So, seeing the situation, I hopped in over the fence, grabbed a fork/pike, which they were more than willing to give me, and worked with them till we had all the hay in stacks just before the rain came down. These were people I knew well already and was meeting everyday as I went up and down through their village. But now that I had gone into the field and shared their work, as with the fishermen, I had a new relationship with them and very much for the better.

Each of these experiences convinced me of the value of the worker priest experiment which is why I tried a little of it later again on building sites in New York, but, as before, it could only be for a few weeks of my holiday time because I had to get back to my regular parish duties again. However, not all priests see the value of it. I remember talking to one fellow priest about it and he said to me, with shock: "What?

Are you suggesting that I take off my coat and pick up a shovel and start working? Not me anyhow!" – although he was strong and able-bodied.

A Difficulty

An obvious objection to what I am saying here is that it is simply not possible, in terms of manpower, for a bishop to be able to put a priest into every building site and every factory and work place, more so now, when in so many parts of the Western world there are not enough priests even to staff the parishes in the traditional way. Moreover, I might seem to be denigrating the work of the traditional priest in the traditional parish, which is by no means my intention. I would turn that objection around and say that in agricultural times the priest in the traditional parish was, in effect, a worker priest because, as I explained, he was sharing the lives of the people around him in many respects. But with the advent of the industrial revolution that was no longer possible – it was not even dreamt of then that priests would follow their people into the factories. This, in turn, was due to the fact that the industrial revolution happened first in countries which had already gone Protestant, such as England and the North of Germany, and that the monasteries, where monks *did* manual work and who might have taken up industrial work also, given more time, had been suppressed by Henry VIII. Nonetheless, where possible some priests did follow the workers into the cities and tried to set up parishes and various kinds of chaplaincies. Even so, the world of industry grew apart from the world of the faith and fast became secularist. But that need not have happened in countries like Ireland and Poland which were still Catholic at the time they came to be industrialized and where there was a surplus of priests some, at least, of whom could have been set aside for a worker-priest apostolate. Instead, they clung to the traditional model entirely and continued to maintain the attitude of my friend above: "What? Are you expecting me to take off my coat?"

Exploitation and the Marxist Solution

Working conditions in the factories of England and living conditions in the new cities rising up around those factories, soon became inhuman due to the exploitation perpetrated by greedy capitalists and because the healing balm and uplifting influence of the Catholic faith was not there. The writings of Dickens are testimony to the sufferings of those workers. See his novel *Hard Times,* for example. That also was what prompted Pope Leo XIII to write his great encyclical *Rerum Novarum* in order to assert the rights of the workers.

But around the same time another force was soon to mould the minds of the workers and promise them their rights and good wages and better conditions and that was socialism and, following it, fully fledged Marxism. Put simply, there was a vacuum caused by the secularizing effect of the reformation and the Marxists got in before the priests to fill it. The priests in the nearby parishes in the city suburbs – when allowed to function - were doing their best to ameliorate the distress and the social misery which resulted from the oppression to which the workers were being subjected. They were treating the symptoms but the Marxists were treating the cause – exploitation. Unfortunately, they were treating it with the utterly false ideology of class conflict, cashing in on the resentment of the workers, leading them on to bloody revolution and militant atheism; and the workers fell for it and fell down, literally, in great numbers at the barricades because no one offered them any other hope or vision. Later, in France, when the priests did venture into the factories and found that the Marxists had already captured the minds of the workers some of those priests tried to outdo the Marxists at their own game, by offering even better material benefits to the workers, but in doing so, some of those priests lost their sense of the spiritual and some even lost the faith and became Marxist leaders themselves. Rome, which under the supposedly strict Pius XII had allowed the worker priests movement to go ahead, heard of these defections, and, accordingly, under the supposedly liberal John XXIII put a stop to the movement, something which caused great consternation for bishops whose priests were doing a great job of winning back the workers to the faith.

Pope John is not to be criticized for stopping the movement. He had to do so if it was leading to too many defections. But a valuable two-fold lesson had been learned: a) that there was a great need for this kind of apostolate; but b) that it would be counter-productive unless selected priests were specially trained for it with a good grounding in the theology of work and in Catholic social teaching. Taking this lesson on board, Vatican II opened the way again for a renewal of the worker-priest movement. But sadly, in the decades following, priests were simply not there in sufficient numbers for it to be tried again. Nonetheless, it might be arguable that, despite the shortage, if some, perhaps only a few, priests were set aside for it with proper training beforehand and were successful in their apostolate, that the pay-off might well be that we would have more priests in the future from the sons of the workers that these priests would influence. A better prospect might be to entrust this apostolate to married deacons who work in various professions midweek or to an order of religious brothers or sisters specially trained and who could be dedicated full time to it. Not to try something like this, in some form or other, is only to let the split between the Church and the vineyard of the world grow even wider and to allow the continued rise of a secularism which is utterly godless and which reduces workers to being animals or machines with no sense of the supernatural.

Again, if something like this were to get going once more it would in no way take from the traditional work of the priest in the traditional parish which will always be needed and essential to the life of the Church. The priests in Marseilles in France saw this point and worked out a system between them whereby, in a given parish of three priests, one would go into the factory in a given week while the second stayed in the rectory on duty and the third went out and about in the parish. Then, the next week, they changed personnel around for the same tasks.

One has to face the added difficulty of deciding which are the best work places or professions to target. One cannot reach them all no matter how many priests or deacons or religious might be available. Nor should it be the aim of a worker priest movement to have priests in every work position. That is neither possible or necessary. All that is necessary is that a certain small number of priests or deacons or religious, would immerse themselves in work places here and there simply to bear witness to the incarnation and to the resulting sanctity of work by silently engaging in work in those few places. Nor should we forget the good effect of many priests who are engaged in chaplaincies of different kinds at present by being available to workers in different situations even if they don't engage directly in that work themselves, not because they are afraid to lift a shovel but because circumstances simply don't allow for it. For example, there is the priest who is chaplain to a school without being a student or teacher there himself, or the priest who is chaplain to the staff of an airport but who does not work behind a check-in desk, or to a hospital without being a medic. But, more directly, when circumstances do allow, there are those priests and nuns and brothers who do work directly in schools and hospitals, as teachers and medics and give great witness, often silently. They make Christ present to the young by conveying His teaching to them and to the sick by extending His healing ministry to them.

<u>In the World of Politics</u>

Should the priest follow his lay people into the world of politics? Does the incarnational principle require this also? One could say that down through history the popes have been very much involved in Italian and European politics especially when the pope was head of the papal states and ruled like any other monarch of the time. The pope needed to have a state of his own in times past to secure his civil independence so that this, in turn, would secure his spiritual independence. And popes did wield political power, even to anointing and deposing emperors, conquering lands and exerting political pressure on kings to have them rule their kingdoms in ways favourable to the faith. In addition, within different Catholic countries, there were men like Richelieu in France who, though a cardinal of the Church, was occupying a position in the state roughly equivalent to what we would call a prime minister today.

The gain from this was that the Church was able to use the state as its secular arm for the good of the faith, ensuring that no laws of an anti-Christian kind were passed in any land. It secured an adherence to the faith by many people who might not otherwise have come to it.

But the down side was that for far too long the Church got too much entangled in matters of state and became herself a player in the political power game, thus blurring the distinction between the two swords according to which Christ wanted His followers *to render to Caesar the things that are Caesar's and to God the things that are God's. Mk 12:17.* This led too often to the scandal of a worldly Church, a Church that was both *in* the world and *of* the world.[1] It reached disgracefully low depths when, at times, the papacy itself became a political pawn of the powerful families of Rome and was even bought and sold for money.

Whatever about these gains or losses of the past, the Church of Vatican II has renounced political or worldly means as her way of promoting the gospel. Nor does she seek any more to have privileges from the state and will even renounce some of those she might have in various places today if they come to provide a counter witness to the gospel. She seeks instead to spread the gospel by the methods of the gospel, principally by the witness of the holiness of life of her members, especially the witness of charity in daily life, and she asks of the state to be given the freedom she needs to do this:

> She, for her part, does not place her trust in the privileges offered by civil authority. She will even give up the exercise of certain rights which have been legitimately acquired, if it becomes clear that their use will cast doubt on the sincerity of her witness or that new ways of life demand new methods. *Gaudium et Spes, #76.*

But in promoting the gospel she claims the right to those earthly possessions such as church buildings, her own schools and hospitals, finances and other such things necessary for her work of evangelization.

> The Church herself makes use of temporal things insofar as her own mission requires it...It is only right, however, that at all times and in all places, the Church should have true freedom to preach the faith, to teach her social doctrine, to exercise her role freely among men. *Ibid.*

Furthermore, as said in the last chapter, the church claims the right to pass judgement on political matters in as much they affect the faith and basic human rights.

> ….. to pass moral judgment in those matters which regard public order when the fundamental rights of a person or the salvation of souls require it. In this, she should make use of all the means - but only those - which accord with the Gospel and which correspond to the general good according to the diversity of times and circumstances. *ibid.*

Because the Church is in the world, the world of money, power, politics and military might, she will always have to relate to that world with prudence but also with firmness, making pronouncements some of which, at times, will be forthright condemnations, if things evil are being advanced, but at other times giving approval when things truly conducive to advancing human rights, the common good and the faith and works of charity are happening. It will mean encouraging her people to support candidates and parties whose policies are favourable to these things and to reject others who promote evil. But this should not mean that she ties herself to any individual politician or party by such endorsement. If she does so tie herself she will lose more than she will gain and will, again, be crossing the dividing line between the two swords. She should never again descend to using the methods of the world when that means deceit but use only the methods of the gospel instead.

But we still have not confronted our question above i.e., whether priests themselves should directly engage in politics by seeking election to civic councils and parliaments or by being chairmen of political parties. We saw above, in relation to the question of clerics involved in the material development of their people, that canon law advises that they "avoid those things which, although not unbecoming, are nevertheless foreign to the clerical state". *(Canon 285 #2)*. Similarly, in relation to our present question of priests involvement in politics canon law says again:

> Clerics are forbidden to assume public offices which entail a participation in the exercise of civil power. *Ibid., #3.*

I am fully in agreement with this for the fundamental reason that Christ Himself, though He was God incarnate in the world of His time, did not enter this field. He explicitly opposed the attempt by people to make Him king after His miracle of the loaves. He explicitly stated that He was a king, indeed, but that His kingdom was not of this world. He frequently called for silence from those who proclaimed Him to be the Messiah, not thereby to deny that He was the Messiah, but because He did not want to be accepted as an *earthly* Messiah of military or political might like king David of old. Indeed, it was Christ Himself who broke down the theocracy of the Old Testament and who separated the two swords, that of God and Caesar. Despite all that, His enemies had him sentenced to death on the false charge of being a political agitator stirring up rebellion against Caesar, though they themselves hated Caesar as a foreign ruler imposed on them! Their hypocrisy in this has always astounded me.

Must we conclude from this then that what I call the incarnational principle does not hold here at all: that secular politics is a field that is not to be impregnated with the gospel or with the grace of God made present to us in Christ? No. That does not follow. Christ is king of everything. *Every knee shall bow to Him in heaven and on earth and under the earth. Phil 2:10-11.* All things must be brought under His rule, the rule of the gospel. But in this field, more than that of any other, it is the role and duty of the laity to accomplish this directly themselves. Nonetheless, their priests should be guiding them in this and instructing them by preaching, by catechetics and by classes in the principles of Catholic social teaching specifically as these apply in the field of politics. If the priest directly enters politics himself there will be a crossing of the line between the two swords again with inevitable loss for the Church because it is she who will be compromised with the world and not the world converted to her. Nonetheless, having said all that, canon law *does* leave one little window open for clerics to partake rather directly in political matters:

> They are not to have an active part in political parties and in governing labour unions unless, in the judgment of competent ecclesiastical authority, the protection of the rights of the Church or the promotion of the common good requires it. *Canon 287 #2.*

This would indeed give more vent to the incarnational principle but I would see it as applicable in very rare and exceptional cases. It has happened, at times, in history that when organized civil life broke down, endangering civilization itself, that it was the Church that saved the day by taking up and exercising some amount of civil government. The fall of the Roman empire in the West in the fifth century is an example: it was the Church which kept what might be called a semblance of an organized civil structure in place for some time afterwards. Similarly, one could imagine a situation of revolution or anarchy in a country where the only remaining stable authoritative body was the Church and she takes over civil power temporarily till the crisis was ended. As an example of that there was the case of the role played by Cardinal Sin in the Philippines at the time of the changeover of power from the Marcos regime in 1986. He forestalled what might have been a bloody revolution so that the changeover was non-violent. On a much smaller, simpler level I remember one time, when I worked in a certain parish, the chairman of the local town council – an entirely *civic* body - came to me to *tell* me (not to *ask* me!) that I was the president of that council (with no election or selection of any kind!). I told him that being president of the parish *pastoral* council was more fitting for me as a priest and that that office was enough for me anyhow. Nonetheless he persisted. His reasoning was that in the event of the town council breaking up through division or falling away through apathy it would be my task then, as president, to resurrect it again or form a new one and then to "get out of the way" again. I saw his point and I accepted. As it turned out I never had to exercise the power of my new office during the rest of my time in that parish.[2] But again, notwithstanding the above examples which are exceptional, I would still hold to the general principle that priests should not directly enter politics.

Foster Harmony

While keeping to this rule, and not entering politics directly, a priest could still cause a lot of harm by championing political or economic causes which do not impinge in any direct way on faith or morals or on the rights of the Church or on fundamental human rights. I am thinking of an example where there was a proposal to build a kind of museum of wild life, what is called an "interpretative centre," in a rural parish one time. The argument arose as to whether it should be high on the hill near to the forest where wild life roamed about which tourists would be coming to see or whether it should be down in the village nearer to the shops and restaurants with the prospect of a better financial spin off for the owners of these businesses. There were other factors also in the debate which one could argue this way or that – but none of a religious kind or which had any direct bearing on morals or on fundamental human rights – and people were divided. The priest foolishly took sides with one party much to the disgust of the other party, of course, thus making the division between the two sides all the worse and with the danger of alienating the latter side from the *Church* as a result. Such a priest (now deceased) should have read what canon law has to say on such matters:

> Most especially, clerics are always to foster the peace and harmony based on justice which are to be observed among people. *Canon 287 #1.*

Sometimes it happens that a priest who foolishly takes sides in such controversies, instead of being an instrument of peace and reconciliation, will then go silent when directly moral issues and fundamental human rights, such as the right to life, *are* being undermined for fear of being labelled as a "conservative" by the media.

If the priest *does* take a stand on those things which he is bound to defend, fundamental human rights, right morals, the salvation of souls and more generally the gospel itself, he *will* cause division, a division which is unavoidable because the Church is in the world but not *of* the world so that she will always be opposed by the world. Christ Himself, though He was the prince of peace, explicitly said that He had come to cause such division. (*Mt.10:34-36*). But the priest should avoid causing division on other purely secular matters if they do not impinge directly on the above fundamentals.

In the World of Culture

What about the priest's engagement in the world of culture? But first, what *is* culture? I pose that question because there is more hot air talked on this subject than on any other that I can think of; vain people like to be considered "cultured" and so will talk the most sophisticated nonsense about culture. Here are some examples of what I mean: in all the big cities of Europe one will have concerts with the national orchestra playing high class, classical music and ladies and gents, in their best attire, will make a point of being seen at them. But down the street from the concert hall one will often find an abortion clinic where the utmost in barbarism is being practiced daily, and these "highly cultured" people will not even bat an eye lid at it. It happened once in one of these cities, Boston, that a renowned violinist, who drew great crowds of these very cultured people to his concert one night, did an experiment on the day following his performance in the same city. He dressed in rags and stood at a street corner playing the same tunes on the same violin with his cap thrown on the ground as if he were a beggar. He saw many of the same very cultured people pass him by but they scarcely threw him a side way glance – so much for their "appreciation" of the same music the day after the concert. So also supposedly cultured people will go to an art gallery and pretend to "rave" at the beauty of a painting by Monet or Picasso, having no idea if it is genuine or only a copy and that even if it is hanging upside down on the wall![3]

Culture, materially, comprises all the arts, custom and even those multiple ways of doing little things every day that make for civilized living. Formally it is the outward expression in various art forms and in daily living of that which is deepest in man, which, consciously or subconsciously, is his relation to God from whom he came and to whom he is called at the end of life. It is that which has us look at the things of time against the back drop of eternity, which presents the mundane in the context of the divine so that we are lifted up towards the divine under the aspect of the beautiful. This does not mean that every work of art has to have an explicitly religious theme; its theme might well be the brutal or subhuman as for example the story of prisoners in a concentration camp; but even if so, in such cases, it will have the effect of telling us that man is made for something higher. The fact that there are atheists who are artists does not disprove this because the atheist is so preoccupied with denying the existence of God that he has the effect of having people wonder about God. He is capable of art in as much as he can articulate the cry of suffering man, but instead of opening our hearts to the divine for healing he tells us that we have to settle for despair. Because art should lift us up towards the divine and towards the truly human, which is man in the image and likeness of the divine, it can also be called the refinement of the natural law.

It can be seen from this that culture is closely related to religion; it is not surprising that the word "culture" is similar to the word "cult" which means worship. Culture is that which flows out in art form from our engagement with the divine which happens in cult.

Given this close relationship between religion and culture it is easy to answer the question of whether or not the priest should engage in culture. He should, and various ways are open for him to do this. The popes and under them many cardinals and bishops have been patrons of the arts down through the ages. But what about our priest in the humble parish? It might happen that he has a particular artistic talent himself such as Canon Sydney McEwan the great Scottish singer had whose rendition of that hymn to Our Lady, *Bring Flowers of the Rarest,* is truly beautiful. Or he might be a writer like the Irish parish priest Canon Patrick Sheehan of County Cork in the latter half of the 19th century, with his beautiful novels about the life and times of the people around him in the parish of Donerail, an oppressed people whom he tried to raise up.

Many more priests, who do not have such talents themselves, still have shown talent for organizing plays and concerts which also have an uplifting effect on people whether or not their themes are explicitly religious, as well as giving much needed entertainment of a morally good kind. Pope John Paul II, an actor in his young days, was convinced of the power of drama to bring faith onto the stage and to civilize and uplift a people, more so people who were labouring under a tyrannical regime as in Poland of his time.

So, yes, the pastoral priest should at least give support to such culture but not to the extent that time is taken away from his sacramental duties. Better still, he should try to promote culture in his parish in such a way that he brings out the talent which is always to be found in every parish and often in the most unassuming of his parishioners and enable them to proceed ahead by themselves with more ventures in culture and art in various kinds of drama groups or music bands or whatever so that he himself can devote himself to what is the highest art forms of all – the offering of the holy Mass and the chanting of the psalms.

Culture has come to have a wider meaning today which is roughly equivalent to what is known in German as the *Zeitgeist*, literally the spirit of the world, a spirit that is often opposed to the Holy Spirit. Today we have an ongoing battle of global proportions between the camps of those who are pro-life and pro-family and, on the other side, those who are pro-abortion and anti-family and are generally nihilistic: the culture of life *versus* the culture of death, in St John Paul's words. Needless to say, the priest should encourage those gallant lay people of the former camp, but, sadly, that does not always happen.

In Sport

Involvement in sport gives the priest valuable pastoral contact with an age group that are often remiss when it comes to attendance at church. Also, priests can see the value for virtue which is to be had from physical training and teamwork. Put simply, thugs usually don't play sport because they won't knuckle down to discipline or be willing to take defeat. That said, I have seen cases where some priests took sport far too seriously so that "to win at all costs" became the objective and the opposing team was treated as an enemy. That is counter witness. Sport then becomes sublimated warfare when it should be play and fun and thereby a form of comradeship leading to charity.

Witness to the Incarnation

The different kinds of engagements, endeavours and chaplaincies presented above should show how priests can bear witness to the incarnation in various ways. But as said in the previous chapter it is primarily the role of the *laity* to Christianize the vineyard of the world, the vineyards of family life, work, politics and culture. Should priests become too numerous in these vineyards (an unlikely scenario) they would be taking away from the role of the laity in those places. But they should enter in to them to the degree that this might be needed in different places to reach people in these places who might otherwise be gone from faith and to give a lead to the laity in those places but then to let them proceed by themselves as is their proper calling. Paradoxically, a successful worker priest movement would see the workers put the priest *back into his rectory* so that he could be *more available* to them there, now that they have become acquainted with him, or into an office in the factory as happened at times in France, as I said earlier. The last thing one would want is that priests become so immersed in secular activities or trade union agitation that they forget their mission as priests and make of it simply a means of making money. That would be a counter witness. Nor should priests become factory owners or men of property for their own gain. The priests mentioned earlier who promoted co-operative industries did so solely in order to hand them over to the workers when they were up and running and to give assistance "from the sideline" after that and continue educating workers on the Christian meaning of work. Fr. Arizmendiarrieta of the Mondragon movement was able to withdraw and retire in an apartment overlooking one of his factories.

Much fewer people are now engaged in agriculture which means that the place of peoples' residence in the parish, their domicile, on the one side and, on the other side, their places of work or culture or sport, in the office, factory, theatre or gymnasium or wherever, have become separated. Accordingly, these various chaplaincies are necessary because, unlike rural times, we cannot say now that it all happens in one's home place, in the parish. These are now new social continents, new mission fields, to be Christianized in full i.e., in ways that sanctify the full person of the worker, art lover, sportsman or whoever else along with his environment. Anything less will merely be a docetist fiction, giving these people a Christ who did not truly become man, who did not fully share their daily lives. Put differently, I am saying that, even after two thousand years, the incarnation is still largely an unpacked mystery, a mystery still waiting to be given full effect in the world, especially in the world of work.

The mission of such priests should be to give witness to the incarnation, to make Christ present in different areas of life so that the lay people engaged in those different areas will do so in such a way that their activities will be a kind of sacramental enabling them to see analogies between those activities and the mysteries of the faith thus enabling them to grow in holiness by engaging in those very activities. Priests and religious can themselves grow in holiness also, one might say in a "reflexive way", by enabling the laity to grow in holiness in those activities that are proper to them.

Of course, the Church has always taught this doctrine of the incarnation with perfect orthodoxy but its full implications for the lives of ordinary people was not preached or given full effect in their lives in the West. The incarnation was sometimes seen as a "parachute *in* and rescue *out*" kind of operation by God. Mankind was helplessly stuck in the wretchedness of sin and of so many other evils such as disease, poverty, hunger and early mortality. God became man, truly man, and died on the cross to save us from all of that, to snatch us up and out of it. True indeed, and it was a welcome doctrine when life for so many was so short and painful – "nasty, brutish and short" as Thomas Hobbes would say. So, "let's latch on to Christ who will snatch us out of this misery as fast as possible to a better world above". True again as far as it goes; but it does not give us a Christ who wants *to stay with us* in the world while we work, a Christ who is *Emmanuel*, literally God-with-us, so that we could grow holy in our work and other activities and engage in them in ways that advance the truly human in preparation for the grace He brought us and for His kingdom of the end.

There was a deeper reason also for this understanding of Christianity as something of a parachute in and rescue out effort. To see the incarnation as something that rescues us from sin is, of course, perfectly correct. That was its main purpose according to St. Thomas. But seen *entirely* as a parachute-in and rescue-out effort was at times seen as a rescue not only from sin but from the *world itself* entirely. That was a distortion of Christianity due to that radical kind of dualism which saw matter and therefore the world itself and the body as bad, ignoring the words of scripture in the first page of the Bible which tell us that God declared all that He had made to be *good* and that at the end of history the world too, matter itself, is destined to be renovated and glorified in the kingdom, not annihilated. Creation is good but spoilt in part by sin from which we do indeed need to be saved. But the world itself, simply as being God's creation, is something to be admired (though not adored, or possessed) as a reflection of the Creator, purified of sin and developed with the help of the grace of the incarnation so that it will be prepared for the glory of the kingdom when that grace will blossom in full.

The Incarnation and Divinization

There has been an old debate by theologians as to whether or not God would have become man had there been no sin. St. Thomas gave a negative answer to that question arguing that most references in scripture to the incarnation link it to God redeeming us from sin, so we should keep to that. However, another line of reasoning going back to Duns Scotus and coming down to Karl Rahner, argues that God *would* have become man even had there been no sin. God's inner life of love, of self-giving of the divine persons to each other, would have led by the logic of the same love (but not by necessity) to the Son's giving of Himself to man *ad extra* in an incarnation. It is one of those "what might have been" questions to which there is no definitive answer and on which the *magisterium* is very unlikely ever to pronounce one way or another.

But let us take the Scotus line for a moment and pose this question: what would have been the point of the incarnation had there been no sin to deal with? It could only have been to sanctify, to divinize, to make holy and elevate by grace a world already naturally good and untainted by sin. Simply put, it would have been to sanctify without the need to purify. But suppose we now take the Thomist line and ask the same question we will still find ourselves saying that the purpose of the incarnation was to sanctify but that to sanctify in *this* latter case first required purification. Grace now does the two things of cleansing from sin and then of sanctifying, of elevating and making holy what has been cleansed. The end result is the same: man is sanctified and so also is his life in the family, at work and at play and his world.

Let us now look at this debate from a slightly different angle: sanctification seen as divinization. Here in the West we talk about *sanctification* by which we mean, primarily, the effect of *created grace* in the human soul, (a grace which purifies also as said above). But the Christians of the East talk more about *divinization* by which they mean the indwelling of the entire Trinity in the human soul, what we in the West speak of as *uncreated grace*. "Divinization" is a powerful word theologically. It does not mean that the human soul is made divine *literally* but that God has come into the world - more than just into the soul - is still operative in the world and has raised the world to a sharing in His own inner, divine life so that the world is now shot through, suffused, illuminated by the presence of God from within. (It is something like Teilhard de Chardin's vision of the world as the "divine milieu"). We do not have here a conflict of theologies between East and West but a difference of emphasis, nonetheless a significant difference because the former shows us a world that is filled with God as a result of the incarnation. If the world is thus filled with God it is because God became man at a given moment in Nazareth; and by "man" we mean all of what it is to be human: the union of body and soul, human life, family, work, play, culture and whatever else engages man, and the very ground under his feet, matter itself.

With this in mind new light is shed on the meaning of Christ's family life and work in the workshop of Nazareth or, conversely, we can say that His work there illustrates the above in a literally "down-to-earth way". During those thirty years Christ was not just "playing for time" until He felt ready for His public ministry of preaching, healing and effecting the redemption. He was sanctifying family life and work "from within" by taking it on, getting "stuck into it" as we might say, and did so for the greater part of His earthly life. We can also say, with the Eastern writers, that He was *divinizing* it, making family life and work holy and, in turn, making of it a means to holiness for Christian workers coming after Him.

Even when He put down the hammer and chisel and left the workshop for His public ministry, He continued to teach the same lesson with His first public event which was His baptism at the Jordan. He entered the waters not to be cleansed of any sin of His own, nor merely to give us the example of baptism which, of course, we *do* need, but more: to make holy the waters simply by entering them so that they in turn would make us holy when poured on our heads in baptism. So here again He was divinizing - the elements in this case.

Given this emphasis that the theologians of the East put on divinization an interesting point of speculation – another "what might have been" kind of question – arises: if industrialization had come to them, the people of the East, first, instead of to the

West would the story of secularism have been different; might they have given the world the lead in a truly Christianized, because divinized, kind of industrialization?! We will never know.

Today, thanks to the improvements that have come to the lives of the workers and the general rise in living standards in the West and with some people living even to a hundred years of age, the primary emphasis need not any longer be on being "snatched up and whisked out" of this world – though man will always have to die and will always need to be freed from sin - but on sanctifying or divinizing this world, cleansing it so as to open it to the divine, during the span of life, short or long, that God will give to each of us; on preparing it for His kingdom at the end and on being sanctified oneself in the process. I see Vatican II as a council that allowed this light of divinization to shine on us from the East but sadly, even half a century after the council, it still had not penetrated the darkness of the secularism of the West or been given effect in pastoral practice.

So that this divinization might be given effect, all of this chapter has been pointing up the need for the Church to follow people from their homes to their places of work and entertainment, which are at a distance from their homes, in order to help them Christianize those places. However, the covid pandemic of 2019-2022 brought a somewhat new turn to all of this because it compelled people stay more in their own home places, not only in cities but in rural places, and work online from there to their places of work and entertainment. So, home, the workplace and the entertainment hall were coming back together again for some people at least and fining their base in the home or in the parish even if only electronically.

One would hope that the places of work and of entertainment would also, literally and physically, begin to move back out to the rural parish again as a result, and not just electronically. This would give effect to the *Distributist* movement of Fr. McNabb and give new life to all kinds of community development projects. This would also make it easy for the priest in the parish to be immersed not only in the agricultural life of his people as formerly but now in addition in their manufacturing and IT lives because they would be near to him physically. Generally, it should make for a more natural and healthy way of life on the natural level. Also, on the supernatural level it should make it much easier for the priest of the parish to be pastor and chaplain in the same place. The task of divinizing the world, now located in the parish, would still be there, but it should be somewhat easier with this move of people to the countryside. Even with this advantage there will still be a lot of work to do to bring Christ into the different new social continents of the secularist world, because, for a long time now, that world has been trying to banish God from every part of the vineyard. But we can hope.

Conclusions:

1. The secular world of work, politics and other areas of human activity is the proper field of engagement of the laity so that they can Christianize it. The priest's proper place is in the parish where he prepares his people for their engagement by good instruction in the gospel and in Catholic social teaching and by giving them the grace of the sacraments. Nonetheless, priests can enter those fields in various ways, directly as a worker or as a chaplain, so as to give witness to the incarnational principle, showing the laity how Christ first sanctified all areas of life by becoming man and by being a craftsman for most of His earthly life and how they can do the same in their own distinctive way. Deacons can do so to a greater extent if they are men who have secular professions or are married. So also can religious if properly trained for such a mission.
2. But the priest should not become directly involved in politics by seeking civil office except in very exceptional cases where the good of the Church or fundamental human rights can not be secured in other more usual ways. The division of the two swords should be upheld.
3. The aim of all this engagement by the laity primarily and their priests helping them is that the world would be purified, sanctified, divinized and prepared for the glory of the kingdom.

Good preaching and sound catechetics by priests and teachers are important in order to prepare the laity for their primary task of Christianizing the world. We will be looking at these topics in the next section of this study, the prophet section.

Part C

Prophet

We have seen already that pastoral theology has to be centered on Christ, the second person of the Blessed Trinity, who is truly God and truly man, who has the offices of king, prophet and priest. We have been looking at the pastor as he exercises his office of king or shepherd (which is what the word "pastor" means literally) as he leads his flock in the Church seen as an institution, that is, in the parish, that small, basic unit of the universal Church, being helped in doing so by his laity on different parish councils.

In this section we will be looking at the priest, conformed to Christ by the sacrament of holy orders, in his role of prophet – the words "prophet" and "herald" having much the same meaning. We saw that another model for understanding the Church was what Dulles called the "herald" model. It combines the roles of preacher, teacher and catechist. In general terms it is the role of the pastor when proclaiming the gospel all in his care.

The role of catechizing, of course, is carried out by lay people also, most often by Catholic teachers in schools at different levels. And today there are other herald/prophetic functions in addition, made possible and necessary by reason of the media, to be used by both the priest and lay people which we will also look as well even if briefly.

All of these roles or functions can be put under the heading of "evangelization" or the "ministry of the word". We will look at evangelization first in a general way so as to stress its importance and then proceed to look at the ministries of preaching and catechetics more particularly. This will also require a look at the Catholic school and its stance in relation to the state. Going outside of the church and the school we will then look at the use of the medium of radio by the priest and his lay helpers in the service of the word. The section will end with a few words on the need for a love of truth as something fundamental in all evangelization.

Chapter X

Evangelization and Preaching

Importance of Evangelization; Aim of Preaching and its Agent

"Go teach all nations, baptizing them in the name of the Father and of the Son and of the Holy Spirit, teaching them to observe all that I have taught you". Mt.28.19-20.

"Woe to me if I do not preach the gospel." 1 Cor. 9:16

We wish to confirm once more that the task of evangelizing all people constitutes the essential mission of the Church. *Pope St. Paul VI, Evangelii Nuntiandi, (EN), #14*

The word "evangelization" itself comes from two Greek words meaning "good news". Christians have good news to proclaim to mankind: that Christ, truly God and truly man, has come among us as the light of the world and that He has rescued us from the darkness of sin and death by His own death and resurrection. Hence, the subject of evangelization is principally Christ Himself and His teaching on faith and morals as that is to be found in scripture and tradition and handed on to us by the *magisterium*. Life in this world now has meaning because, thanks to Christ, its goal of perfect union with God in His Kingdom is made possible. The priest evangelizes principally by his preaching and lay people do so as catechists and when they bear witness to Christ in the secular world by trying to have the light of the gospel shine on all that happens there. In this chapter we will be looking at evangelization as effected by preaching, its importance, its sacramental nature, the opposition it is likely to meet with, its proper agent and what his objective should be.

Importance of Evangelization

Evangelization is of indispensable importance for the building up of the body of Christ, the Church, and the Church herself has always recognized this, going back to the example of Christ Himself who preached on the Mount, from the boat, along the roads and in the synagogues of Israel. The apostles, after Pentecost, began by preaching, and miracles accompanied their words as testimonies from heaven to the truth of their words. Amongst the Fathers we have famous preaches like St. John

Chrysostom – the man of the golden mouth - and St Augustine whose sermons are mines of wisdom to this day. St. John Henry Newman claimed that if we could combine the preaching of these two men we would have the best preaching possible. (Perhaps that combination was to be found in himself but that he was too humble to see that). Then in the Middle Ages there were religious orders dedicated to preaching such as the Dominicans, who are still known as the Order of Preachers. And there were many other famous preachers later still such as St Robert Bellarmine and St Francis de Sales after the council of Trent, then Lacordaire in France and Archbishop Fulton Sheen in America in more recent times and St. John Paul II to name only a few. During all this time the Church also had her schools for catechesis, from the beehive cells of the Celtic monasteries, to the universities of the Middle Ages and to the many different kinds of Church-run schools that we have today.

When we come to Vatican II and later we find Pope St. Paul VI putting great emphasis on evangelization. He even declared it to be the reason for the Church's existence, thus giving primacy of place to the prophetic role of the priest and his lay helpers:

> We wish to confirm once more that the task of evangelizing all people constitutes the essential mission of the Church. It is a task and mission which the vast and profound changes of present-day society make all the more urgent. Evangelizing is in fact the grace and vocation proper to the Church, her deepest identity. She exists in order to evangelize, that is to say, in order to preach and teach, to be the channel of the gift of grace, to reconcile sinners with God, and to perpetuate Christ's sacrifice in the Mass, which is the memorial of His death and glorious resurrection. *Evangelii Nuntiandi, #14; cf.* also *General Directory for Catechesis, 1997, #46.*

I could imagine that a neo-Lutheran theologian such as Karl Barth would be very happy with this. For him the Church is that community of people brought together by the hearing of the word. But while Pope Paul VI makes evangelization to be the essential mission of the Church, he does not stop at that but adds also the celebration of the Mass and the administration of the sacraments – evangelization being seen as a preparation for this. By her preaching the Church directs people to Christ who is to be encountered in the sacraments, especially at Mass, where we have his real presence, and in the confessional where He reconciles sinners. Word and sacrament must not be separated because even if people are called together into the Church by the word, they live in the Church by the life of grace that flows to them from the sacraments. Saying Mass for a new community of believers, while valid and of infinite value in itself

Chapter 10: Evangelization and Preaching

as the re-enactment of the sacrifice of Calvary, will still be lacking in the spiritual effect it should have in the lives of those people if they have not been instructed in what is taking place beforehand. Thus, a simple rule of pastoral action is: evangelize, catechize and sanctify.

The importance and urgency of evangelization was needlessly undermined somewhat after the council due to the recognition the Church then gave to the elements of truth or seeds of faith that are to be found in all other religions with its decrees on ecumenism, (*Unitatis Redintegratio*) and on other religions (*Nostra Aetate*). If the people of these other religions already have elements of truth (or can even be called "anonymous Christians" as Karl Rahner was claiming) then why reach out to them at all?[1] Let them follow their own paths and we ours and we will all arrive home to God. Thus, missionary activity comes to be reduced to nothing more than social action for the material betterment of third world people. But this line of argument is about as silly as to say that if there are hungry people out there who nonetheless have a few scraps of bread in their stomachs that we should not bother to feed them at all from our own baskets which are full. It latches on to St Paul's saying that *God wills all to be saved, 1Tim. 2,* but ignores St. Luke when he says that *there is no other name under heaven given to men by which we can be saved. Acts 4:12.* It ignores Christ's own words that He alone is *the way, the truth and the life. Jn.14:6.* This was a misrepresentation of the council which instead does indeed want missionaries to salvage what might be good in other traditions, but then see if that can be purified and elevated by grace so as to be taken up into the true faith, the fulness of which is to be found in Christ alone who is the head of the one true Church.[2]

If evangelization is of great importance, it follows that the priest is first of all a minister of the word of God. St John Paul II, coming later, draws this inference:

> The priest is first of all a minister of the Word of God. He is consecrated and sent forth to proclaim the Good News of the Kingdom to all, calling every person to the obedience of faith and leading believers to an ever increasing knowledge of, and communion in, the mystery of God, as revealed and communicated to us in Christ. *Pastores Dabo Vobis, #26. (cf.* also his letter *Redemptoris Missio).*

The *Code of Canon Law* spells out more exactly the task of the priest in this matter of evangelizing:

> A pastor is obliged to make provision so that the word of God is proclaimed in its entirety to those living in the parish; for this reason, he is to take care

that the lay members of the Christian faithful are instructed in the truths of the faith, especially by giving a homily on Sundays and holy days of obligation and by offering catechetical instruction. He is to foster works through which the spirit of the gospel is promoted, even in what pertains to social justice. He is to have particular care for the Catholic education of children and youth. He is to make every effort, even with the collaboration of the Christian faithful, so that the message of the gospel comes also to those who have ceased the practice of their religion or do not profess the true faith. *Canon 528 #1.*

The lay catechists extend this work of the priest in their class rooms as also do lay theologians in their research work, their writing and lecturing.

The field of evangelization today is not merely third world countries where people have not yet heard the gospel but developed countries which had been Catholic for centuries but which have now grown secularist. This latter field is the more difficult because so often one finds a willfully, closed attitude to faith there. But then, with time, the emptiness of secularism and its failure to satisfy the deepest longings of the human heart often brings such people back to opening their hearts again to the gospel.

Evangelization in Preaching

Evangelization is given effect principally in preaching. The importance of preaching was stressed at Vatican II and by the popes ever since. They were trying to redress an imbalance that had its roots in the reformation. The Protestant tradition put greater emphasis on the ministry of the word due to the importance that Luther and the reformers gave to the Bible as the only source of doctrine – *sola scriptura* – after they rejected the pope and the *magisterium*. As a result, there have been some very capable and eloquent preachers in that tradition and still to this day. One thinks of Wesley in Wales, for example, in the 1800s and Billy Graham in America in the 1900s. The strong emphasis which the reformers put on the word of God tended to have the Catholics play down preaching, somewhat, so as to play "up" the "works" of administering and receiving the sacraments, which latter the reformers had played down. Vatican II sought to redress any imbalance there might have been so as to give due importance to the word of God with its document *Dei Verbum,* though it is still true to say that in the Catholic tradition there have been some fine preachers such as those we mentioned above who came after the reformation. Nonetheless, most priests before and even after the council would say that to say Mass, hear confessions and be available for sick calls were the most important duties of a priest and might put preaching in second place. This can still be accepted as being true provided one does

Chapter 10: Evangelization and Preaching

not play off one against the other: it is not an "either/or" but a "both/and" matter for the reason mentioned already, i.e., that the word of God introduces the faithful to the presence of Christ among them in the sacraments.

But, despite the efforts of the council and the succeeding popes, preaching has not improved much in the Catholic tradition since the council. I'm not able to be strictly scientific about this due to not having carried out surveys on people's reaction to preaching, but generally speaking, the reaction I get from lay people at the receiving end of preaching is more negative than positive in many places. An American sociologist who did some research on this claimed that boring, insipid preaching turns off more people than clerical scandals even though the latter are so much publicized. An English theologian who once visited the US said that most of the sermons he heard there could be summed up as "May I suggest to you that you try to be good". A faithful Catholic layman in Ireland once told me that he goes faithfully to Mass every Sunday always hoping to come away with what he called "some little nugget of wisdom" from the sermon but that invariably he comes away disappointed.

When talking to seminarians about this I remind them of St Augustine in his young days when he was dabbling in the different philosophies of his day, Platonism and Manichaeism principally, looking for the truth. He went to this school and that in Carthage, Rome and Milan, and like our layman above, came away disappointed time and time again – until he happened to wander into the church of St Ambrose in Milan, and there he did begin getting the nuggets of gold he was so anxiously searching for. The rest is history, as the saying goes; he was on the way to conversion and to becoming one of the greatest and most influential Fathers of the Church and a great preacher also in his own turn. Then I say to my students: if there was another Augustine in your parish, a young man of intelligence and enquiring mind searching for truth, for something that would give meaning to his life in an age of pluralism, secularism, hedonism and general skepticism, would he find anything in *your* sermons that would put him on the right track, or would he too come away disappointed? The "something" need not be sensational or hard hitting or controversial but merely a well thought out exposition of some basic point of faith or morals, given with sincerity and conviction, such that it might become a stepping stone in an ongoing journey of faith for that hearer.

Another layman once said to me that most preaching is irrelevant because it is a failure to recognize the shocking inroads that moral evil had gained in his country in recent years. Instead, priests take the safer and more popular route of talking about those issues that are trendy today because they are pushed so much by media and government, issues such as climate change, homelessness, or immigration, things of importance in their own right but secondary to the issues of large-scale abortion, the breakdown of the traditional family and the general loss of faith and morals. So, the priest is largely repeating on Sunday what the presenter on TV was peddling on Saturday night. This layman claims that bishops in the West are actually telling their priests to take this "softly, softly approach" on the crucial moral issues. "Don't ruffle any feathers and we will all be happy". I can't vouch for that. But this, in fact, was, literally, the instruction a parish priest in Ireland once gave to a young Indian priest who went to do some supply in a parish there one Summer: "Keep away from any hot issues. Just keep them happy with nice stories." I knew of one black priest who still had a sense of morals and the family, as many Africans still have, who did not comply with this advice and preached against same-sex marriage but the local bishop came down hard on him.

Meanwhile the media continue relentlessly their work of undermining faith and morals so that after Mass on a Sunday the people, having heard a nice pick-me-up, sweety-sweet sermon in the church, go across the street and buy newspapers which promote the evils referred to above, but not refuted in the sermon, which, of course, cause more and more people to fall away from Church and into sinful lifestyles. But who cares: no feathers are ruffled; the collection is still fairly good – good enough to support the one priest who is left in the parish anyhow - and everyone is happy! No; not everyone is happy. Concerned, believing parents want something better for their children as they grow up so that *their* marriages in turn will have some chance of succeeding and their souls some chance of getting to heaven.

The Sacramental and unitive Nature of Preaching

In addition to the redressing of the balance between proclaiming the gospel and administering the sacraments which Vatican II sought to achieve and of countering the evils of secularism, a more fundamental point with regard to the importance of preaching is the theological truth that faith comes from hearing. Pope St Paul VI wrote:

> ... it is not superfluous to emphasize <u>the importance and necessity of preaching</u>. "And how are they to believe in him of whom they have never heard? And how are they to hear without a preacher?... So faith comes from what is heard and what is heard comes by the preaching of Christ." This law once laid down by the Apostle Paul maintains its full force today. Preaching, the verbal proclamation of a message, is indeed always indispensable. *Evangelii Nuntiandi,* # 42.

Chapter 10: Evangelization and Preaching

Faith comes from hearing not just in the natural sense that what is heard is instructive, in as much as it informs the hearer of the content of Catholic doctrine as would happen in the case of anyone listening to a lecture on anything. There is the deeper, supernatural sense that preaching is a kind of sacramental activity. Preaching is an extension of the word of God which is proclaimed when the scriptures are read, and the word of God, plus what is preached, when heard, is then, one might say, "ignited" by the sanctifying work of the Holy Spirit in the mind of the hearer - the preacher being the instrumental cause of this igniting. This produces faith as a fruit when the hearer is well disposed, or perhaps it jolts him into believing even when he is not well disposed, though he is still free to resist.

And there is still more. The faith that comes from preaching is what binds the parish community together. The theological, one might say, is the basis of the sociological. Pope Paul again:

> The faithful assembled as a Paschal Church, celebrating the feast of the Lord present in their midst, <u>expect much from this preaching</u>, and will greatly benefit from it provided that it is <u>simple, clear, direct, well-adapted, profoundly dependent on Gospel teaching and faithful to the magisterium,</u> animated by a balanced apostolic ardor coming from its own characteristic nature, full of hope, fostering belief, and productive of peace and unity. Many parochial or other communities <u>live and are held together thanks to the Sunday homily,</u> when it possesses these qualities. *Ibid.,* #43.

It is not just the local parish community that is held together by the Sunday homily, as the pope says here: that is true. But, by extension, we can say that an entire society is thus held together by the combined preaching of many priests. St Augustine defined a society as a community of people united by a common love of the same things. I would expand a little on that and say that it is a community of people who are conscious of having a common heritage from the past and who, because of that, have common aspirations for the future and love what they have in common at present. But what is the deepest element in this common love of the same things, of common heritage or aspirations and what is its deepest source? It has to be a common faith for the simple reason that religion is the deepest thing in man and religion is grounded on faith. Hence it can be seen that every civilization worthy of the name had a religion as its basis. Atheistic communism or Naziism, by comparison, were not civilizations but anti-civilizations as evidenced by their inhumanity. So also, it follows that the idea of a totally pluralist society has to be a contradiction in terms, even though a healthy civilization should be able to accommodate a certain amount of diversity and even be enriched by it. But a Catholic civilization is built up and reinforced in its fundamental beliefs, largely by the cumulative effect of devout, humble parish priests preaching to their people Sunday after Sunday in their own parishes. The people too, from their side, know this also by their sense of the faith, their *sensus fidei,* which is why the pope says above that they expect much from preaching. He also lists the properties that a sermon should have if it is to be thus effective in this twofold aim of promoting the faith and holding a community together. We will look at some of these properties shortly and the kind of preparation they call for. But first let us say something about the object and motive of preaching.

The Object and Motive of Preaching

The Object of Preaching

We saw above that the subject matter of evangelization is principally Christ and His message. But what is the aim or object of evangelization in preaching? What is the priest trying to achieve? Ultimately, as in all his efforts, he is trying to lead his people to salvation and to union with God. Specifically, as regards preaching he is trying to convey and explain the word of God to them and to exhort them to good living. St Thomas, following on St Augustine, gives us - on a scale of success - what we might call three proximate objectives of preaching: to teach, to delight, and to persuade. (*cf.* St. Thomas, *S. Th. II-II, q17, a1;* St. Augustine, *De Trinitate, xiv,1*).

The first of these objectives is to instruct in the basics of the faith. One must teach the basics of Catholic truth, mostly by appealing to reason using suitable arguments or analogies. This is a necessity. Then one delights the ear by appealing mostly to emotion, using stories and images or examples. This is a bonus. And, finally, one persuades to action, to good living, by exhortation and by providing examples such as the lives of the saints. This is to triumph. The voice range should correspond to each objective: a subdued voice for argument, a temperate voice in delighting and a higher voice in exhorting – "Come on now, let us do what that saint did". How often people will complain that a sermon is too long or boring if it goes on for more than five minutes, but if a preacher could achieve these three aims together, I, for one, would listen to him for an hour. How sad that an orator such as Hitler was able to hold his audiences for hours on end, even though what he was preaching was false ideology and hatred, and yet many Catholic preachers can scarcely hold their audiences for more than five minutes even though they have solid truths that come from God Himself!

Communicating by the spoken word is a natural talent of which some people have more than others, for example, great orators and teachers and TV presenters. In common parlance it is called "the gift of the gab". Demosthenes, the Greek orator, is still remember for the influence he had on his fellow citizens in Athens long ago even though few today could tell us what he said. St Augustine was a great preacher and had been a teacher of rhetoric prior to his conversion. St Thomas Aquinas says that Christ used preaching rather than writing because the former has the greater effect. He also said, following on St Augustine, that with preaching comes a special grace, the grace of words, something more than natural talent, which is a gift given to some for the benefit of others. *Ibid*.

But though a grace, preaching, like any art, requires hard work and some failures before it is perfected. Grace works in and through the natural. A good preacher seems to his hearers to be speaking with great ease and facility, but if he is a really good preacher and not a mere entertainer, he will have put a lot of work into his homily, work which his hearers will be unaware of. There is a saying that "art conceals itself" that it appears to be effortless when perfected, like the great violinist who can take up his instrument and, as we say, "make it talk". So also, with preaching: it too requires hard work, and prior to that, prayer to the Holy Spirit for guidance as to what *He* wants communicated to the people of God through His instrument the priest and for the continued grace of speech when doing so.

Motivation in Preaching

What then should motivate a priest in his preaching? One would hope that it would be something more than a mere cold sense of duty just because one has to "say something" because there is an obligation on him to preach on Sundays and holidays, even though a sense of duty is important at least as a minimum motivation. Nor should it be a desire for popularity as an entertainer or as a brilliant communicator, though one would hope that he can relate well to people and communicate the gospel message to them with effect. No; the real motive is that of *pastoral charity*: a love by the priest for his people because they have been entrusted to his care by Christ through the bishop, and a sincere concern for their faith in its widest sense, a concern to steer them all towards heaven, as a shepherd would steer his sheep towards the penfold at night, so that he too can follow them to heaven at the end of his days. When this is his motivation the priest will preach with conviction and heart and the question of how long or how short the homily should be will be very much secondary.

The fount of this pastoral charity is the priest's love for Christ which love begins and ends at the tabernacle. Here the words of Christ to Peter come to mind again: *Simon Peter do you love me? Yes Lord, you know that I love you. Feed my sheep. Jn. 21:17.*

Priests intimidated

But no matter how well motivated a priest might be he is not made of steel; he has his sensitivities, and can be intimidated or at least put off by certain things. Some priests can be intimidated by knowing that now some of their laity are "supposedly" educated in theology because they did a course of a few weeks online with some institute (often of doubtful orthodoxy). So, they fear that one of these people might stand up and contradict them. That more lay people should have degrees in theology is a good thing, a great gain for the Church, provided, of course, that they have been instructed in sound theology in a reputable institute, which is not always the case. If the latter is the case, if his laity have sound theology, and if the priest also knows his theology – after all he had seven years of study in formation, more than any of the laity – he should find in these lay people a good support. But should they be of the heterodox kind who would re-invent the Church in their own image and likeness, then these people, like all heretics of old, have to be put in their place. But, then, would the bishop back such a priest or would he see this also as the "ruffling of more feathers"? Some bishops would and some would not.

Another source of intimidation is the media when the priest is afraid that someone will run to some newspaper or radio station if he says something that is not politically correct. Yes, that can and does happen and it may lead to the priest being called on to explain himself on air; but that can be seen as an opportunity for the wider spread of the faith if the priest knows his theology and is prepared to defend it. We will be saying more on that later when we come to talk about the priest and the media.

Another source of intimidation for sincere priests is that of the embarrassing awareness of the scandals in the Church of past decades. That such bad things happened is an undeniable fact and is indefensible. But the numbers were exaggerated as can be seen by the differences between the numbers of allegations and the numbers of convictions, even though one case is still one too many and even one bad priest can do harm to a great number of victims. These scandals have been used to browbeat would-be good preachers into silence often by people who were not victims at all and who themselves are active in promoting other evils such as abortion, which is the ultimate in child abuse, sodomy, and the destruction of the family in various ways. But many clergy allow themselves to be brow-beaten and keep on endlessly beating their breasts and apologizing. While it is important that the Church acknowledge past wrongs, apologize and try to remedy them, it is also time to move on from there and start addressing current social evils if we are not to lose even those who are still practicing.

There is such a thing as the grace of office of the priesthood – divine help to carry out the task one has been given in a particular vocation. Priests should pray for an increase of this and put their hope in the Lord who gives it, and be courageous. There is a dire need for good preaching today. I would argue that the lack of good preaching is a considerable factor in the rise of secularism. It leaves a void which those who are opposed to the faith are quick to fill, and all the more effectively now with all the various means of communication which are at their disposal. They have the TV, the internet, the radio and the microphone available to them and they are using them effectively. Vatican II allowed for (but did not mandate) the use of the vernacular in the Mass which then led to the microphone being used in churches. This should have been a help to preaching because it allowed for speaking in a milder tone of voice which, in turn, should have allowed for greater nuance and more subtle reasoning than was possible in the days when priests had to shout from pulpits. But that advantage was not seized on. This reminds me somewhat of Chesterton's quip that "the generation which invented the microphone was the generation which had nothing to say"! I would hope that priests everywhere would strive to prove him wrong on this by making more skillful use of the microphone. There is too much at stake in the salvation of souls.

The Agent of Preaching

Who should preach? In the above I have been speaking as one taking for granted that the priest is the agent of preaching. So, this might seem to be a pointless question at first sight. But the reason for it needs to be explained because there is some dispute on the matter in some places. The priest is, indeed, the usual agent of preaching in the parish. He is that, and, of course, prior to him, the bishop is the foremost agent of preaching in his diocese. So also, is the deacon a preacher. There is a reason for this and what we have been saying about the quasi-sacramental nature of preaching gives a clue to it.

The homily is an integral part of the liturgy of the Mass (even though one can have a valid Mass without it) and the Mass is comprised of the liturgy of the word and the liturgy of the Eucharist *which, together, form one sacramental whole.* If, then, the ordained are the agents of the celebration of the Eucharist in their respective degrees it is right and proper that they, and not lay people, should engage in preaching as ordinary ministers of it. This restriction to the ordained is not at all due to a presumption that these ministers are better theologians than all of the lay people in the congregation – because, as said already, today many lay people are qualified in theology – but is due to the sacramental nature of preaching itself as just explained. Hence, we have the following rule:

> The homily, therefore, during the celebration of the Holy Eucharist, must be reserved to the sacred minister, Priest or Deacon to the exclusion of the non-ordained faithful, <u>even if these should have responsibilities as "pastoral assistants" or catechists in whatever type of community or group.</u> This exclusion is not based on the preaching ability of sacred ministers nor their theological preparation, but on that function which is reserved to them <u>in virtue of having received the Sacrament of Holy Orders.</u> For the same reason the diocesan Bishop cannot validly dispense from the canonical norm since this is not merely a disciplinary law but one which touches upon the closely <u>connected functions of teaching and sanctifying</u>. *Instructions, Art 3, #1.*

However, *Canon 766* leaves a window open for preaching by lay people in some circumstances:

> The laity may be allowed to preach in a church or oratory if in certain circumstances it is necessary, or in particular cases it would be advantageous, according to the provisions of the Episcopal Conference and without prejudice to *canon* 767 #1.

But any honest reading of this canon makes it clear that such circumstances are the exception and not the rule. It sometimes happens that a parish priest will facilitate a lay missionary who is home from abroad and who wants to tell people about his/her work there for the faith and ask for their financial support by having this person speak in church. Usually the parish priest will have this person give his talk before Mass or at the end of Mass but not after the gospel as the homily proper. Or it might happen that a foreign priest is saying Mass who is not competent in the local language so the bishop authorizes a seminarian or catechist to preach for a few Sundays – again, an exceptional situation which hopefully is shortly remedied. But despite that, I have at times seen this exception being made near to being the rule by priests who are either too lazy or too cowardly to preach themselves or who are given to a democratic type of pandering to the laity so that they invite all sorts of people to come up and preach, some of them mere entertainers with no theological training. It is basically an evasion of duty by priests of little faith. And then we have the priest who is over ecumenical in the wrong sense of the word and invites ministers of other religions to come and

Chapter 10: Evangelization and Preaching

read and preach. Far from advancing the cause of ecumenism this only causes confusion and scandal amongst the laity.

Conclusions:

1. Evangelization is of great importance for the spread of the faith. The Church exists to evangelize so as to prepare people to encounter their Lord. Preaching is the foremost part of evangelization. It is more than mere instruction. It is quasi sacramental and engenders faith.
2. Priests must not allow themselves to be intimidated in their preaching and their bishops should be supportive of them in this, assuming that their words are not openly inflammatory or insulting though the truth conveyed may well be hard to take by some.
3. Preaching is normally reserved to the ordained minister because of its sacramental character.

Having stressed the importance of preaching in the work of evangelization we will next go on to say something about how the priest should prepare for preaching.

Chapter XI

The Sources of Preaching

Scripture and Tradition; Subject Matter of Preaching

Happy indeed is the man who...ponders his law day and night. Psalm 1.

For this reason the priest himself ought first of all to develop a great personal familiarity with the word of God. *Pastores Dabo Vobis, #26.*

Good preaching is based on scripture and tradition and is faithful to tradition in its interpretation of scripture, so we must first see how scripture is to be studied with a view to preaching and go on then to speak of the need for faithfulness to the *magisterium*.

Preaching and Scripture

<u>The use of Scripture</u>

St Paul VI says above that the sermon should be "profoundly dependent on Gospel teaching". Scripture is foundational to preaching, even though the priest can also use a prayer from the liturgy of the day or a dogmatic statement from the *magisterium* as his starting point or central theme. But these latter will not be in opposition to scripture but often based on it or complementary to it because of the dialectical relation that exists between scripture and tradition. But to keep to scripture for the present: for the priest to be an effective preacher he must have at least a basic knowledge of scripture and, more than that, a love for it that is nourished by prayer and meditation. St John Paul II says:

> For this reason the priest himself ought first of all to develop a great personal familiarity with the word of God. Knowledge of its linguistic or exegetical aspects, though certainly necessary, is not enough. He needs to approach the word with a docile and prayerful heart, so that it may deeply penetrate his thoughts and feelings and bring about a new outlook in him – "the mind of Christ". *Pastores Dabo Vobis, #26.*

I remember one time being at a retreat for diocesan priests when the retreat master was an old, religious priest who had little experience of pastoral work. He began with a quote from some little-read prophet from the Old Testament, perhaps it was *Habakkuk* or *Obadiah* or some such figure, certainly not the kind of figure you would find two parish priests talking about on their way home from a football match! I settled myself down for a good snooze, saying to myself that this talk was going to be pie-in-the-sky of no relevance to priests who had to deal with the practicalities of everyday life in the parish. But how wrong I was. The old priest produced a most beautiful meditation on those few lines of scripture, which showed that not only had he a good scholarly knowledge of his text but that he had made it his own by prayer and meditation and so was able to draw out some lovely lessons from it that any priest in any kind of work could take home with him. I think he lived up to what St John Paul was saying in the quote above, and he too had that kind of familiarity with scripture.[1]

This old priest, being a contemplative, studied scripture with an eye to using it in his prayer life in his growth in holiness. An academic theologian might study the same passage with a view to a lecture he was preparing for third level students and, again, a catechist teaching primary level students might use it in yet a different way still. So, also the pastoral priest in the parish will approach a passage of scripture with a view to using it for his sermon the following Sunday. One would expect then that two such pastoral priests, when they would meet, would discuss just how they might use a particular passage for this purpose; yet I must admit I have rarely, if ever, heard two such priests discuss any such text.

I once knew two gifted carpenters who were related as brothers-in-law but were living in two different countries so that it was seldom they would meet. But when they *would* meet it was always interesting to hear them discuss how they approached certain carpentry tasks. For example, one would ask the other how he would shape a piece of mahogany so that it would be curved and suitable for the banister of a spiral stair-way; and they would share their ideas on how this might be done. But as for priests, what I have heard more often is one asking the other about an hour before a Sunday Mass what the gospel was and if he had a few points for him on it, which the latter would then scribble down on the back of a cigarette box. That might be his preparation for the main liturgical event of the week. Or he might go to a drawer, pull out a clerical magazine that had sermons for the month in it and read out whatever he found there *verbatim,* in other words, with no preparation or adaptation for a congregation of perhaps five hundred people who were unknown to the writer of the sermon in the magazine, even if in itself it might be a good sermon of general application. But I will not generalize and say that that is what happens everywhere.

Chapter 11: The Sources of Preaching

Three Approaches to Scripture

In studying scripture for the purpose of preaching there are three different but complementary approaches that I suggest one can take, what I will call a) the "over-view" approach; b) the "line-by-line" approach and c) the "consult the masters" approach. I will explain each a little further.

a) The Over-View Approach.

Here one looks at a given gospel or other book of scripture taken as a whole, noting its overall structure and main features. Thus, for example, if the gospel of Matthew might be the one for the coming liturgical year one would note how it has a structure of five discourses and five action scenes, "five" being reminiscent of the five books of the Pentateuch. Also, one would note the many quotes from the Old Testament it has because it is also a gospel that was aimed primarily at the Jews. But *through* the Jews it is also aimed at all mankind, hence the story of the Magi – three Gentile visitors - at the beginning, and the commission to the apostles to go out and teach all nations at the end. It is the gospel of Christ as the Son of David, hence the importance of the number fourteen in the genealogy. But He is also Emmanuel, a reference back to the maiden who will conceive in *Isaiah* - indeed, Matthew is sometimes portrayed as a dwarf sitting on the shoulders of Isaiah – but then, pointing forwards, He promises to be always be with His Church to the end of time. Hence there is no explicit ascension scene at the end in St Matthew's gospel.

These are only a few features of this one gospel given by way of example. One could talk about such things on the first Sunday of Advent when the new cycle of gospel readings begins and one could go further into this study perhaps with some night classes on this gospel during the following weeks of Advent or later during Lent. So, also, with the other three gospels and their different structures and features and then the *Letters* of the New Testament.

b) The Line-by-Line Approach

This approach requires simply that one get hold of a good Catholic scripture commentary and see what it says about the gospel for a given Sunday, taking it line by line. To have some knowledge of the Latin or Greek text is an advantage because of the different nuances that words can have in different languages. Some of this study will have been done in the priest's student years but it is an ongoing, lifelong task and is ever full of new surprises. It does not take too much time to read what a good bible commentary has to say on a given Sunday gospel reading.

When reading scripture, one must always bear in mind that one is dealing with a sacred text - writing that is inspired by the Holy Spirit - even though written down by men of a particular time in their own language and each with his own individual style. To treat scripture as just one other ancient set of purely human documents is to begin with a presupposition which is simply false. So, when looking at a piece of scripture one is trying to learn what God wanted to say in it as Vatican II says:

> However, since God speaks in Sacred Scripture through men in human fashion, the interpreter of Sacred Scripture, in order to see clearly what God wanted to communicate to us, should <u>carefully investigate what meaning the sacred writers really intended, and what God wanted to manifest by means of their words</u>. *Dei Verbum, #12.*

To get at the meaning the sacred writers really intended and what God was saying through them one must take account of literary forms and of the historical or literal sense of a given text. Vatican says II again:

> To search out the intention of the sacred writers, attention should be given, among other things, to "literary forms." For truth is set forth and expressed differently in texts which are variously historical, prophetic, poetic, or of other forms of discourse. The interpreter must investigate what meaning the sacred writer intended to express and actually expressed in particular circumstances by using contemporary literary forms in accordance with the situation of his own time and culture. *Ibid., #12.*

A number of different literary forms are given here: the historical is put first - an account of some event as historical or factual and which can be taken literally, as, for example that Christ was crucified on the hill of Calvary and rose three days later from a nearby tomb. The historical and literal sense is fundamental for theology because it serves as the basis for the spiritual sense and for solid doctrine. The doctrine of the redemption cannot stand if Christ did not factually die and rise again.

With prophecy then we have a promise of a future event that will happen on some condition being met or not being met by people beforehand: the people of Nineveh were told their city would be destroyed if they did not repent. They did repent and it was not destroyed.

Chapter 11: The Sources of Preaching

The next mentioned above is poetry. The Old Testament is full of poetic images: Isaiah tells us that the earth is "God's footstool", (*Isaiah 66:1*); the psalmist says that he himself, is like some "lonely bird crying on the roof". (*Ps. 102:7*). And in the New Testament we have that beautiful and most poetic image (which few scholars talk about) of Christ weeping over Jerusalem and telling the inhabitants that He wished to gather them to Himself *as a hen gathers her chickens under her wing, Lk.13:34* – how touching! We all know that the earth is not literally a footstool or that the psalmist was not stranded on some roof-top while praying, but it is easy to get the point in both cases - the solid truth of God's sovereignty over the earth and the psalmist's anguish.

Apart from the scriptures or any other kind of literature, we all use various literary forms in our everyday speech. A woman comes home from town, having done her shopping, and says to her husband that "she saw nobody in town". Were he to write that down in his diary and some historian find that diary a thousand years later he might conclude that on that particular day the town, of let us say two thousand inhabitants, was completely empty, and then he might speculate if perhaps they had all taken to the hills to avoid some impending disaster (but how then would the woman have succeeded in doing her shopping ?!). Very simply her words mean that she met none of her friends or acquaintances whom normally she would meet, or that it was a cold day and a lesser amount of people came to do their shopping. So, her words, while taking them as a literal form might be called "exaggeration" did, nonetheless, convey a factual, historical truth.

There is a danger, though, when understanding the literal forms of scripture, especially in an age of unbelief, that the student or scholar will dismiss as totally non-factual, non-historical, something he finds to be extraordinary with reference to his own experiences of life around him, which may well be very limited, dull and uneventful, or something which he presumes his hearers are unlikely to accept. Let us take an example from the Old Testament: that of the sun standing still in the sky for some hours in the book of *Joshua (Ch. 10:12)*. Is that a mere literary form telling us merely that God was on the side of Israel that day against great odds, or did it happen historically? Many scholars would opt for the former answer. But I would then ask them about a much more recent event: the miracle of the sun at Fatima at midday on October the 13th 1917 witnessed by more than sixty thousand people and documented in the newspapers of the time by reporters who were present? (Yet secular historians have dodged that story like a plague ever since). Were those newspaper accounts mere literary fictions? And if, instead, they were *factual*, what then about the story in *Joshua*? Those scholars who might want to dismiss it as a mere literary form were not there themselves; neither was I, but in light of a definite event like Fatima I would be slow to dismiss its historicity.

Or, to come to the New Testament: in the last century, there was the attempt by some scholars to describe the gospel account of Christ's miracle of the multiplication of the loaves and fishes as a mere literary form, as an exaggeration or a legend, reducing its historicity to being merely an appeal by Christ to the crowd to share what little they had in their individual lunch packs with those around them who might have forgotten to bring any, though, in fact, historically, it was a true miracle of a real multiplication of bread and fishes. Our so called "scholar", because he himself never saw such an event in his own lifetime, rules it out historically to begin with: it didn't happen in his life time so, *a priori,* it could never have happened at any time! The accounts of Christ's exorcisms, his casting out of demons, similarly have been declared by some to be a mere literary form with nothing more for a basis than a curing of epilepsy by hypnosis – an account that seems all so natural but is factually false.

Spraddling the two testaments we have the story of Jonah surviving his stay in the belly of the whale. If it is to be dismissed as mere legend – as some scholars do - then it would follow that Christ was undermining the facticity of His own coming resurrection of which it was meant to be a sign. A legend is not a good basis for a predicted fact.[2]

In an age of unbelief there is a danger of a preacher too being affected by this reductionism, so that he tailors what he finds in a scriptural passage to what he thinks people of weak or no belief are more likely to accept. He makes their unbelief to be the measure of the truth of scripture, which means that he is robbing scripture of its factual and supernatural content and is robbing his hearers of the possibility of coming to belief. In other words, he is "shortening the hand of God", setting his own limits to what God could have done in the past and therefore, by implication, to what He might do in the future. Instead of lifting his hearers up by means of the gospel, he drags the gospel down to their level of the banal.

On the other side, then, there is a kind of credulity or fideism which ignores literary forms entirely and demands a literal interpretation of every line of scripture which leads to a crude fundamentalism which is also damaging to faith: it would have God do the ridiculous such as to walk like a giant along the mountain tops, or literally sit on a material throne in the sky. An old rule in regard to both dangers, going back to St Augustine, is to go with the historical or literal as far as one can, but taking account, of course, of the literary forms in which it is couched. "As far as one can" – there are some lines in scripture which cannot have a historical or literal interpretation but only a spiritual one, as for example, when Christ is calling a reluctant would-be disciple to follow him but the latter wants to go back to bury his father first, He says to him *let the dead bury their dead. Mt. 8:22.* Literally or factually a dead man does not take up a shovel to bury another dead man. So here one goes straight to the spiritual sense.

- The Spiritual Sense

Scripture is deep and multi-layered in its meaning, not only because it is the inspired word of God but also because of the richness of its symbolism. Words signify things but things, in their turn, can also signify other things and possibly in more than one way. For example, the word "Jerusalem" literally signifies a city high on a hill in Israel. But that thing, that city, can, in turn, signify, paradise of the past, or the Church of the present, or the kingdom of heaven of the future. This takes us into the spiritual sense of scripture and into the whole field of allegory and typology. This idea of a spiritual sense goes back to Origen. But within the spiritual sense we also have what is called an "allegorical", a "moral" and an "anagogical" sense.

These different sub categories of the spiritual sense were more clearly explained in the Middle Ages though they are to be found in the Fathers and in the scriptures themselves to begin with [3]. Putting it very simply, in using the allegorical sense one relates a thing or person or event of the Old Testament to something in the New Testament, the former prefiguring the latter. Thus, Moses is an allegory for Christ, the waters of the Red Sea for the waters of baptism and the promised land for the Church. Clement of Alexandria is a great example of this use of scripture. Then there is the moral sense: Job's four sons and three daughters are seen as representing the four cardinal virtues and the three theological virtues. Pope Gregory the Great is an example of this use of scripture; and, finally, the anagogical relates something present to something future of the end time. Thus, the Jerusalem here on earth or the Church of the present time is seen as prefiguring or as pointing forward to the New Jerusalem or to the kingdom of God. St Bernard provides examples of this.

A great source in this regard is the *Catena Aurea* of St Thomas Aquinas in which he draws on the Fathers and shows the great variety of spiritual senses they were capable of giving to one and the same passage of scripture. But, at the end of the day, it is the literal sense which is foundational for developing theology.

The relevance of all of this for preaching should be becoming clear by now: it is that the priest has a variety of possible themes, based on the one text of the gospel, that he can draw on depending on the different senses of that text, so that when it comes round again and again he can still find different things to say about it. Accordingly, if the gospel is that of the good Samaritan the priest might take its literal sense one year and use it to preach against robbery and violence or to advocate charitable action. Then, on a later occasion, using the spiritual sense, he can portray Jerusalem as the early state of man's happiness in paradise. He can portray the man going down the road as mankind itself which is attacked and robbed of grace by Satan. The Samaritan is Christ who binds his wounds with the sacraments and takes him to the inn, which stands for the Church. On a later occasion again, with the same gospel, the preacher could focus in on the sacraments of baptism and penance as providing healing for the wounded soul.

A preacher who does not advert to the different senses of scripture is limiting his resources and may end up finding that he has just a few pet themes or "hobby horses" which he draws on *ad nauseam*, that is to the nausea of his listeners who will say "there he goes again, how many more times will we hear this".

As to hobby horses, there is a story about an old parish priest who could not stop talking about death, even on joyful feast days! When it came to the feast of St Joseph the Worker he proceeded as follows: "My dear People, St Joseph was a carpenter; and, as you all know, a carpenter is called upon to make many different things such as tables and chairs and window frames. But, at times, he is also called on to make a coffin!" And so, for the next half hour he was able to indulge his favorite hobby horse of death once again. He had the further advantage that St Joseph is also the patron saint of a happy death!

However, I must be fair to this priest and give him credit for talking at all about the proverbial "last things" even if he had a habit of going to extremes on them. I do so because I claim that one cause of today's secularism is the failure by priests to speak about the last things at all, except at a funeral, and even then the line taken very often will be that of assuring everyone that Grandad is now definitely in heaven smiling down at all of us and telling us not to be so sad even though Grandad may have been the biggest thug in the parish in his day.

c) The "Consult the Masters" Approach.

One other form of preparation for preaching is to consult the masters, the great preachers of the past, *them* rather than second or third rate preachers, because if one goes to these latter then one's own preaching may fall to a lower level again. Examples of the masters that come to my mind, as mentioned earlier, are St Augustine and St John Chrysostom from the Fathers, then men like St Francis de Sales, St John Vianney and St. Cardinal Newman nearer to our own time, and the sermons or addresses of St John Paul II, to name but a few. Indeed, a preacher today may well find that he has enough material in even one paragraph of a sermon of one of these masters. They usually begin with a short text of scripture and elaborate on it; so, it is a worthwhile study to see just how they elaborated on it and constructed their sermons both with a view to developing a point of faith or morals and of getting that point across effectively to their own flock. The paradox is that though they were consciously writing for a particular congregation, their own flock in their own time, they did so with such skill that what they said is of perennial value. Nonetheless, the preacher of today should not borrow slavishly from any of them because he, like them, must take account of the spiritual needs of his own flock, of their level of intelligence, level of receptivity and their general background.

The sermons of the masters, because of the way they meditated on scripture and put their reflections down on paper, are examples or instances of the Church being like *Mary pondering all these things in her heart. (Lk.2:19)*, or of what Vatican II calls the "growth in the understanding of the realities and the words which have been handed down".

> This tradition which comes from the Apostles develops in the Church with the help of the Holy Spirit. <u>For there is a growth in the understanding of the realities and the words which have been handed down.</u> This happens through the contemplation and study made by believers, who treasure these things in their hearts (see *Luke 2:19, 51*) through a penetrating understanding of the spiritual realities which they experience, and through the preaching of those who have received through Episcopal succession the sure gift of truth. For as the centuries succeed one another, the Church constantly moves forward toward the fullness of divine truth until the words of God reach their complete fulfillment in her. *Dei Verbum, #8.*

The priest has this wisdom of the ages at his disposal in the masters for his homily if he will use it rather than run to the internet and down load something written by a person a hundred miles away that might or might not have some theological value but a person who could not have known the priest's own congregation.

This pondering, this growth in understanding of scripture, happens under the supervision of the *magisterium*.

Preaching and the Magisterium

In the above we have been looking at the priest's study and use of scripture in preparation for his preaching. But the scripture commentaries he uses must be those approved by the *magisterium*, and so also the last quote above speaks of the masters as those "who have received through Episcopal succession the sure gift of truth".
Scripture and tradition are two streams of truth flowing from the one well which is Christ and they have a dialectical relationship with each other: scripture is at the basis of the doctrine of the *magisterium* but it is the latter that enables us to understand the former authentically. Therefore, preaching, if it is to be Catholic, must take account of

and be faithful to the teaching of the *magisterium*, never contradicting it or substituting some ideology of one's own liking in its place. Hence Vatican II says again:

> Sacred tradition and Sacred Scripture form one sacred deposit of the word of God, committed to the Church...<u>But the task of authentically interpreting the word of God, whether written or handed on, has been entrusted exclusively to the living teaching office of the Church, whose authority is exercised in the name of Jesus Christ</u>. This teaching office is not above the word of God, but serves it, teaching only what has been handed on, listening to it devoutly, guarding it scrupulously and explaining it faithfully in accord with a divine commission and with the help of the Holy Spirit, it draws from this one deposit of faith everything which it presents for belief as divinely revealed. *Ibid.,#10*.

It is despicable when a Catholic priest will take some text of scripture to push some pet ideology of his own, for example the text from the *Acts of the Apostles (Ch. 2:44)* which tells how the early Christians held all things in common, to advance some idea on socialism. Indeed, liberation theology of the wrong kind could be described as a misuse of the *Exodus* story to advance a disguised Marxism. It is also despicable and an abuse of scripture when a reader who is a feminist will deliberately alter the words of a reading to remove masculine pronouns when referring to God and replace them with other pronouns. When priests will not bring such readers to order they betray a great lack of reverence for the word of God - words that are sacred because inspired by the Holy Spirit - and possibly a lack of faith to begin with. But then some priests even engage in this abuse themselves. So also, some of them will even try to use a text of scripture to plug for the ordination of women. To be popular with the feminists, it would seem, is their priority above any consideration for revealed truth.[4]

Then, as regards using material from other traditions, one can indeed find some very illuminative and morally uplifting ideas and stories in other non-Catholic, Christian writings that comment on or are based on the scriptures, and sometimes they are orthodox, at least on some matters. But so very often, when it comes to a number of issues such as papal authority, justification, the Eucharist and many more, they simply cannot be relied on because these people disagree with us on these matters. Instead, the Catholic preacher has at hand T*he Catechism of the Catholic Church* as a primary resource, also the *Documents of Vatican II*, the *Code of Canon Law*, the *Enchiridion of Denzinger* as well as the many papal encyclicals. Even an old school catechism of former days can be a good source if a priest simply takes one definition from it on a given Sunday and explains it. And then there are great sources to be had in the lives of the saints and in many other Catholic spiritual writings.

The Subject Matter of Preaching

Having dealt with the sources from which to draw ideas for preaching - scripture and tradition - and how both are to be used, let us see next what, more specifically, should be the subject matter of preaching. We said already that it should be Christ Himself and His message as found in scripture and tradition and handed on by the Church. More specifically, it should be the mysteries of the faith and the norms of Christian life, or as we might say, doctrine and morals:

> Among the forms of preaching, the homily, which is part of the liturgy itself and is reserved to a priest or deacon, is preeminent; in the homily <u>the mysteries of faith</u> and the <u>norms of Christian life</u> are to be explained from the sacred text during the course of the liturgical year. *Canon 767 #1.*

This quote from canon law gives first place to preaching on the mysteries of the faith. This is needed for the sake of the mysteries themselves – that they might be explained to the people – but also as a basis for moral teaching. I touched on this in an earlier chapter but want to expand a little more on it here. I said then that there is a tendency to neglect the mysteries in preaching today because there is no controversy about them now. The debates of the early centuries are long settled and the Church has moved on. So, it is presumed, but all too easily, that people have a firm faith in the mysteries and that priests too can leave it at that and move on to the more pressing moral issues of today. This, I would argue, is a false presumption. The reason people do not engage in controversies today about the Trinity or the incarnation or the redemption is, much more likely, because they don't care a hoot about those things and are much more taken up, not even with moral issues, but with purely material things such as the cost of living, sport or health, and I believe that priests are not uninfluenced in this regard either. The following story will bring this out.

In Ireland, in the month of June when the weather is hot, people in the countryside go cutting turf, or "peat" as it is called in some countries, a kind of dense mud resulting from compressed, decayed forestry, which makes for fuel for the fire in Winter. In June one also has Trinity Sunday when the Church celebrates this first and most fundamental of the mysteries. It so happened one year that a young Catholic man from the countryside, where there was bogland, brought his new fiancé home for the weekend, a lady who happened to be a Protestant. She expressed a desire to go to Mass with him on the Sunday, more out of curiosity than anything else but also so that she might learn something about the Blessed Trinity, Catholic style. So, they went to Mass. In his homily the parish priest, to her wild surprise, talked, not about the Trinity at all but about different kinds of turf because people there would contribute some of their harvest of turf to him for his fire for the Winer. So he spoke about white fluffy turf which burns up like paper and has no heat value; black hard turf which, by comparison, has great heat value, then turf that was exposed for too long and was wet when brought in so that it would not burn, and turf that got too much sun and had crumpled to dust and was no good either. He made it clear that what he wanted from the people in their fuel contributions to him was the black, hard turf and it well dried. That was the content of the sermon on Trinity Sunday. So, on the way home the young man said to his girl-friend: "well, what did you think of the Mass?" To which she replied: "yes indeed, I learned quite a lot – about turf - but nothing at all about the Trinity even though I thought it was Trinity Sunday and that that mystery was important for you people".

Obviously, for that parish priest, the heating in his house for the coming Winter was far more important than if God might be one person, as the Unitarians believe, or three persons as Christians believe or indeed if He was there at all now so long as the turf He had created was still there after He Himself had disappeared! But, to come to his defense, had he talked about the Trinity I can well imagine how eyes would roll upwards in many heads and people would say "there he goes again, up into the clouds with his Blessed Trinity and we all taken up with the cutting of the turf. Has he any understanding of his people at all. Is he not even concerned about his own heating?" And so, we have a vicious circle: the priest won't ever talk about the Trinity, hence the people will never hear about the Trinity and its relevance in their lives is lost and instead the relevance of good, black turf takes center stage in all their lives, priest and people. Is it any "mystery" then that without any thought for the "mysteries" (pun) Christians slide into secularism and that a generation later there are very few at Mass on Trinity Sunday or indeed on any Sunday?

Morals grounded on Dogma

The mysteries need to be preached because of the truth they contain which is the basis of faith and because Christian morals have their basis in the mysteries; they flow from them. Morals follow on beliefs.[4] Take away the beliefs and soon the morals will lose their foundation and begin to fall away. This foundation has to be shown to people. For example, the self-giving love that is the inner life of the Trinity is the supreme model or analogue for the kind of love that should exist in any Christian community and especially in the family, and, we might add, between different families so that if in one family, for example, there is a widow who is not able to cut turf herself she will be sure of getting help from the other families around her. (Thus, there *can* be a link between the Trinity and the turf after all!).

So also, the spousal love and faithfulness of Christ for His Church is the supreme example for the love of husband and wife for each other and their mutual faithfulness. The divorce debates in Ireland and Malta and other Christian countries, prior to referendums or parliamentary votes in such places on such matters, teach a lesson in this regard. The indissolubility of marriage was not seen as being be grounded in the indefectible spousal relationship of Christ to His bride, the Church, because it had not been presented as such, because priests had not been preaching on this in the months prior to the referendum; and the other arguments that were mostly used, the argument from nature showing the benefit of the stable family to the common good of society, and arguments from sociology and psychology, though perfectly sound in themselves, did not prove sufficiently effective in the end to gain a rejection of this evil, even by a Catholic people.

If we keep just to preaching on morals, I can recall that in the days before Vatican II there was a prescribed rota of topics, mostly on moral matters, to be preached bi-annually or tri-annually. As a result, people were reminded periodically of the commandments and of what was commanded and forbidden by each of them. This, I believe, was a good practice and I would like to see something like it restored again, so that each commandment is dealt with when a corresponding reading from scripture is read on a given Sunday in the three-year cycle of the lectionary. The psychology behind this was, very simply, that even if people know the commandments, they will tend gradually to forget about them, to neglect the practice of them, if they are not reminded of them occasionally. Given the weakness of human nature since the Fall, we all have a tendency to backslide. A scholar and archbishop of the Middle Ages, Stephen Langton, used to make this point by taking a text from the book of *Joshua* and give it an allegorical and moral interpretation. The text refers to the priests carrying the Ark of the Covenant as they crossed the Jordan river on dry land into the Promised Land. The waters stood up on either side to let them pass. When they came up out of the river on the other side *the waters returned to their usual flow. Jos. 4:18.*

The spiritual sense given to this text by Langton was that the waters represent weak human nature in its oftentimes sinful behavior because of the Fall. But when the priests brought the Ark, containing the two slabs of the commandments, i.e., when they preached the commandments to the people, the waters stood up, i.e., the people ceased from their usual sinful ways, for a while, at least - until the priests were gone across the river to the other side. And then they returned to their old behavior again, *to their usual flow.* The moral is clear: people need to be reminded of the commandments and what is prescribed and forbidden by each of them at intervals if they are to continue to be moral though not by doing an overkill on any commandment, which is counter-productive. Otherwise, the silence of their priests will be taken as tacit consent.

How apt a lesson for our own times. Taking *any* of the articles of the *Creed* or any of commandment I could provide a long list of moral topics on which I have heard nothing whatever since Vatican II. Take perjury, for one random example, the sin of formally calling on God to back up one's lies told in court: I never heard even one sermon on that in my whole life, even though in former times it was a sin reserved to the bishop for forgiveness so as to highlight its seriousness. And we see the effects in society - sizable financial gains are made from perjury and innocent persons are convicted. Lawyers tell me that perjury is an everyday occurrence in courts today so much so that the oath has come to be seen as a joke which then leads to calls for it to be abolished entirely.

But if the commandments are not grounded in the covenant relationship of God and His people, if, very simply, they are not seen to be of *God*, then, how can they be seen to be anything more than a set of man-made rules composed by Moses and his followers in the desert long ago but of little relevance for people of the present? Hence the importance of speaking first about the mystery of God and His covenant with His people.

Without grounding morals in the mysteries of the faith one can enjoin moral teaching on people only by an appeal to authority or to predictions of negative social consequences if morals are rejected – and such appeals have their place – but, again, they will not be sufficient in the long run.

Morals will persist for some time after faith in the mysteries and the living of the mysteries in the sacraments have ceased. For example, Protestants have traditionally had a great regard for the Sabbath as the Lord's day and observed it with great strictness. Today in those countries of Northern Europe which went Protestant at the reformation one finds that religious belief and church going have largely disappeared and been replaced by a general secularism; but still some of the strict Sunday observances have persisted, for examples a ban on many sports, horse racing and pub opening, though now, in the third millennium, these restrictions are also disappearing. So, also, in those countries a good many people who do not practice a religion and who may even describe themselves as agnostics would still believe in being good neighbors in daily lives to those living near them, which is due to something of the gospel teaching of love still lingering in their mindset from past Christian times. But such good morals won't persist forever. They will fade away and be replaced by a crude selfishness and later by a new barbarity as is evidenced by the casualness with which abortion is practiced and tolerated nowadays in countries which were Christian only a few generations ago.[5]

As for the mysteries, themselves, then, they need to be presented in ways that are suitable to a given congregation in a given place or time, taking their cultural background and educational levels into account. St Patrick bending down and picking up a shamrock from the ground to try to explain the mystery of the Blessed Trinity to the pagan Irish of the fifth century, a rural people of little education, is an example for us so that we might be able to come up with examples that might be appropriate for the people of today whatever our country. It is an old rule that if you want to teach Johnny Latin of course you must know Latin but in the first place you must know Johnny.

So, I say instead to the pastor: do make sure to preach the mysteries, even the most profound of them, because they are fundamental to both faith and morals. But do so in ways that are suitable for your people, you knowing their background, the things they are familiar with and their level of understanding.

Conclusions:

1. Effective preaching requires prayer and study of both scripture and tradition. This gives the priest the foundation for preaching on the mysteries of the faith and on moral norms bearing in mind that morals are grounded in dogma.
2. Effective preaching also requires a familiar or familial knowledge of one's flock so that one can use examples suited to their background.
3. Emotion has its place in preaching because solid truths are more effectively borne in on the mind under the influence of emotion. But feelings are still not the measure of good preaching. Faithfulness to revealed truth is the real measure and the truth is often bitter. One should then use a little honey but only if that makes the jewel of truth shine even brighter.

Just what good preaching requires by way of practical preparation will be the subject of the next chapter.

Chapter XII

Preparation for Preaching

Remote, Proximate and Immediate Preparation

…always have your answer ready for people who ask you the reason for the hope that you all have. 1 Peter, 3:15.

Christian teaching is to be explained in a manner that is suited to the condition of the hearers and adapted to the circumstances of the times. *Code of Canon Law, Canon 769.*

We have looked at the two main areas of study already above: scripture and tradition, because such study is necessary for the preacher unless he is someone who is happy simply to download something from the internet and cough it up without any adaptation for his own people. I said also that effective preaching even of the highest mysteries must be adapted to the hearers by using suitable examples. Let us see now how the preacher gets down to practical preparation for good preaching.

Remote and proximate Preparation

<u>Different Approaches</u>

Preparation for preaching does not begin on a Saturday afternoon or a Friday evening either. It should have begun many *years* earlier with meditation and study of scripture and the other branches of theology, dogma, moral, canon law and more, in the seminary. We can call this "remote preparation". Knowledge of the faith does not mushroom over night; it grows slowly over time.

As to proximate preparation, different priests prefer different ways of doing this. St John Vianney, as a young priest, would spend hours writing out very long sermons and then hours more again trying to memorize what he had written. But he soon learned that that was not yielding good results because it often happened that he would be exhausted before he began at all and that he would lose his train of thought so that he would simply have to give up and come down off the pulpit embarrassed. We still have many of his sermons from the early part of his priestly life but none from his later years, the reason being that the confessional consumed so much of his time that he had no time left for writing out and rehearsing new sermons.[1] But his hearers could testify that his later sermons were simply modifications on his earlier ones, shorter because his early efforts at memorization served him well. The priest who can preach well with great fluency, going on a few points on a single page, is usually a man who had the practice of writing out his sermons carefully in earlier years. Art doesn't come easy. The man who talks "off the cuff", first time round, is usually disordered or repetitious in his thoughts though that might be camouflaged if he is a good performer or entertainer. In other words, he usually produces more flower than fruit, more heat than light.

I knew of a case where it was the turn of a student in a seminary who was a gifted wit and performer on the stage to give a practice sermon to his classmates. Naturally he was delighted with this opportunity to perform and do the showman, and he did that very well in the sense that he had the boys in stitches laughing. But the professor who was sitting at the back of the class with a long, solemn face like that of an old horse, was not impressed. When the laughter died down he said "Young man, when you are a priest your task will be the feed the sheep, not to entertain the goats"! A good lesson for priests who have lost their sense of the sacred and who don't see what difference there is between liturgy and entertainment.

A bishop I knew once told me of his way of his sermons: he would preach them into a tape recorder and play them back, correct them and rehearse them again and again until he got them right. I tried the same myself but did not find it helpful at all. Still, it did work for him and he was a great communicator. There is a saying that there are many ways to skin a cat! So also with preparing a sermon.

The method I find best is to begin at the end of the last Mass on Sunday and take a look at the readings for the following Sunday. Pray for the guidance of the Holy Spirit so that one will be preaching what is beneficial for the faith of one's flock, that is, so that one will be preaching the Lord and not oneself. Do not take to writing immediately. Allow time for ideas to come and to ferment in your mind for a few days, again under the guidance of the Holy Spirit. During that time take a look at how some of the master preachers have handled these texts and consult reliable Catholic scripture commentaries also, preferably two rather than one, an old one and a new one, because I often find that one commentary will have something which the other does not have. Start writing towards the end of the week but not as late as Saturday. I am a great believer in what I call the "overnight rule" – the value of leaving what one has written to rest on the desk (or in the lab top) overnight because, invariably, one will see the text in a somewhat different light the next day. Hence, one draft of a sermon is seldom sufficient. Sometimes two or three attempts are needed to get things right. In this regard preparing a sermon is a bit like a woman baking a cake. She has a number of different ingredients to combine in the right measure and she must have it in the oven at the right temperature for the right length of time. Sometimes she gets it just right and more times it simply flops despite her best efforts. But she learns from the flop for the next attempt. So also with a sermon: one knows when one has got it right by a kind of illative sense.

For the theme of the sermon the first reading of the Mass combined with the gospel usually gives one a good guide because often the same theme is developed allegorically from the former to the latter, and on some feast days the theme is spelt out more clearly again in the preface, for example, on the feast of Christ the King, the kind of kingdom the Church proclaims is spelt out: one of justice, truth and love. For further reinforcement, but in a way that is not slavishly repetitive, the priest can pick up the same theme again in the prayers of the faithful.

When it comes to the plan or lay out of a sermon, different approaches are again possible. One could start with a question which, it is hoped, will provoke some reflection. But one must also supply an answer to the question at some point. An old rule here is: "don't dig a trench unless you intend to fill it". Don't send people away confused or in doubt. One might also start with a story. I knew a priest who was a historian who would begin with a story from history or from the life of a saint. It was effective. The question or story might then lead on to a brief catechism statement of a defined dogma, which, in turn, might be explained by various examples, or images, or even by a little bit of humor provided this does not turn the sermon into a comedy-show, a feeding of the goats as said above, or that it does not descend to cynicism or sarcasm, things which are counter-productive anyhow because contrary to charity. There is always a gap between what is and what ought to be in life and humor seizes on that. Indeed, it is a dull fellow, a boor, according to St Thomas, that does not have a sense of humor, so why not bring that into preaching also in limited, appropriate measure when making even a serious point.

The doctrine then should lead on to a moral lesson and that to an exhortation to action. Or, one might begin with a moral and work backwards to the foundation of that moral in dogma or scripture, using images or stories or humor or whatever in the process.

<u>Knowing Johnny</u>

Why should a priest use these different approaches rather than just one? This question can be answered by posing a more fundamental one: at whom is the priest aiming his words? In any congregation there are the very bright people, those of average intelligence and the weak of intellect. There are those of different levels of education; there are the young and the old or, as the saying goes, "the long, the short and the tall, the good the bad and the ugly". Some priests recommend to aim at the bright ones because the others will follow *them* anyhow, but the others then are going to find the sermon too abstract and turn off. Again, the young are the future of the Church but are they even present at Mass? The old have the faith so do they need anything or should their faith be reinforced so that they can hand it on to the young?

Then there are those who have more heart than head, and *vice versa*. But should the priest not aim at both heart and head? The great example of that is Christ Himself with His discourse at the Last Supper, a discourse of the sweetest accents of sorrow and love in which there was deep and most sincere emotion, knowing as He did that He would soon be leaving them; but a discourse of great doctrinal content also on His oneness with Father and His Real Presence in the Eucharist, two doctrines of major importance; and then there was His moral teaching, His command of love of one another which He exemplified by His washing of the apostles' feet, which love is the ultimate solution to all of life's social problems.

In practice I have always found that every congregation, each different Church community, even within the one parish, though made up of all those different kinds of people as described above, is, nonetheless, what can be called a single "corporate person" – the phrase theology uses to refer to the Church herself as the bride of Christ. Each parish community and, even within the same parish, each sub-parish community, has a kind of personality or mentality or character of its own, a personality that has come down along over the years and which is propagated onwards to the next generation by a few influential people who might be called the local "pillars" of the community. Teachers will say similar things about the distinctive personality or character of different classes that they have taught; so also will people in entertainment when referring to different theatre audiences they have played to. The priest, if he is socially sensitive, will pick up on this mentality and form a picture of the typical or representative man or woman of his community and will aim his words at such people. He will also have picked up on this mentality if he has being doing his visitation because it is an old pastoral rule that there is a close connection between house visitation and preaching. This takes us back to the old rule about teaching Johnny Latin: to do that effectively you must, of course, know Latin but, in the first place, you must know Johnny which, for preaching purposes, means you must know his parish background also.

Chapter 12: Preparation for Preaching

<u>One Message and right Order of Points</u>

Whatever the approach a priest might take in his sermon I would insist that he try to get one core point across even if he develops it in various ways, and that the development be a logical train of thought, an orderly sequence of ideas. This simple rule, I find, is the one that is most often violated and with great loss to the homily. I once worked with a parish priest who was undoubtedly a conscientious and dutiful man who took his preaching seriously and prepared his sermons carefully. Indeed, he was over conscientious to a fault because he would try to kill too many birds with the one stone. When preparing his sermon he would have a scripture commentary on his desk and also a book of homilies and perhaps a clerical magazine with more homily points. He would find a good idea in each of them, each single idea being so good that he felt he had to use it, but the three (or more) ideas, each very good in itself, did not hang together. So, he was like a dog chasing three or four different hares. When listening to him I would find that the first point was good and so also the second point. But I would be at a loss to see how the second followed from the first or if there was any logical relation between them at all. Then he would go on to the third point, a very good point again, but I would still be trying to connect the first point and the second and would miss most of the third point in the process. So many homilies are ruined because of this defect. I find the same problem when correcting projects and papers from students, a lack of right order due to the excess of attempting to pack too many disparate ideas into one paper.

The old Greeks said much the same thing when they declared that "art is the work of the file" – a cutting away of what might be good in itself but a distraction from the work at hand. Michael Angelo once said that beauty is the cutting away of the superfluous. Cardinal Newman said much the same thing when he corresponded for some time with a student in Maynooth College in Ireland. In one letter he told him he should be ruthless with himself in selecting just one central idea for whatever he might be writing and then that he should develop that idea in an orderly way. The other ideas, little gems though they might be, could be set aside for sermons on the same gospel in future years. The dog who chases three hares usually catches none of them in the end.

When one has chosen one's central idea then one can develop it with a question, an image, a story, an argument or whatever and one may also follow on from that one idea with other related ideas provided they *do* logically follow from it.

As a help in this regard, I advise my students to take a single blank page and jot down on it whatever ideas come to mind when about to write a sermon or an essay, a word or two for each idea. Ideas, while still in the mind, are like clothes in a laundry bag: they are a jumble, and when thrown out on a table they land there in a jumble. But then one can see them objectively, as it were, and begin to sort them out – the shirts together here, the stocking together there etc. So, also, with ideas for a homily. Some, though of worth in themselves, must be cut out entirely because not capable of being harmonized with the central idea. Then the remaining ideas, if they can be harmonized, must be put in right order so that one flows from the other, and even here there may be some repetition which will require some more surgery. If the end result is that on a given Sunday the flock are fed with one core truth, with a practical moral that is driven home effectively by a right appeal to emotion, which then leads on to right action during the coming week, one will then have succeeded in the way St. Augustine described above.

Preparing for Objections

The main reason for writing out one's homily is, of course, to have a prepared, orderly, logical text to hand so that one does not have to rely on memory alone. But another reason is so that one can be accurate about one's choice of words: it makes a difference in terms of effectiveness to use the right or the wrong adjective in framing an argument or to describe a person or situation. A third reason is that, if a sermon is going to be relevant to the real lives of real people, and not mere pious bull-wash, one can take extra care to avoid using words that people who might not like what they are being told can use as ammunition with which to fire back. People *will* respond, positively or negatively, privately or publicly to any sermon that is relevant to their lives, and some who respond negatively will do so most unreasonably at times. The doctor who is doing abortions won't like a sermon on the fifth commandment; he will object and try somehow to justify his brutal business. So also, the pharmacist who sells abortifacients and contraceptives will not be willing to accept that he/she is formally co-operating in sin given the intrinsic evil of the use of such pills. So, also, people in various kinds of irregular relationships will not like a sermon on the unity or indissolubility of marriage. The businessman who is over charging will say that it is up to the customer not to buy his products if he thinks they are too dear. The pub owner who sells alcohol to youngsters will say that it is impossible for him to know the age of every customer. To come between an over indulgent person and his pleasure or between a business man and his money or a politician and his votes is like coming between a dog and the bone he is chewing. You can expect to get bitten. But there is no point in handing these people extra ammunition by using reckless or highly emotive language.

It happened in Australia in the 19th century, when there was a lot of anti-Catholic prejudice, that a priest was alleged to have said about a certain Protestant minister that he (the minister) had his (i.e., the priest's) "qualified" respect, and this was printed in a newspaper. The priest claimed he has used the word "unqualified". Nonetheless, it led to a hot dispute and made for much legal trouble for the priest. The two words differ only by one syllable in print but by much more in what they imply for a person's character. Again, there is a difference, if not in substance certainly in terms of emotions roused, between saying that the proposition "x is y" is false, on the one hand, and, on the other hand, that those who say that "x is y" are liars. A priest must beware that many people are moved more by feelings than by reason, and that is more so the case in countries where pupils are explicitly taught in school to follow their feelings rather than reason or the commandments when judging between right and wrong. But it does not follow then that a priest has to pander to the nice feelings of his congregation and ignore the often unpalatable, hard truths of Catholic moral teaching. He merely has to be careful about his choice of words.

Civil Law on Speech

In this regard a priest needs to know something of the civil law of own his country on the offenses of slander and libel. Slander refers to the spoken word which damages a person's good name, while libel refers to the written word, and the latter is more damaging because the written word endures. Insult is different again. If I say that Mr. X is an idiot – and leave it at that - that is an insult. If I say, falsely, that he pedals drugs, that is slander. Though I did not use any insulting language, I have damaged his reputation, reduced the standing he had hitherto enjoyed in society; and if I put that in print it is libel and the damage done to him is greater because a newspaper can be lying around for a long time. I have robbed him of his good name in both cases and he can appeal to the courts for compensation.

In the US the law on libel, especially of public personalities, is loose compared with the law in European countries where one can be sued even if one made a false statement in good faith, going on what one thought was reliable information. From an ecclesiastical point of view a priest offends perhaps not against justice but against charity if he names a person for wrongdoing, even if he has solid evidence for what he says. The aim of preaching should be the conversion of sinners, and naming or shaming them publicly in church is hardly going to achieve that. So also, to refer to political parties by name in preaching is usually counterproductive even if, again, what one alleges is based on solid fact. The devoted party follower, the "party hack", will not pause to consider if what the priest said about his party might well be true but instead, merely on hearing his party named in a negative way, will react emotionally immediately and accuse the priest of bias and of dabbling in politics inappropriately. But it does not follow at all then that a priest has to remain silent when evil legislation damaging to fundamental human rights is being proposed. He can and must say that *any* party which proposes, abortion, sterilization or euthanasia, for examples, or other things directly contrary to good morals is doing evil and should not be supported but instead should be opposed by people of conscience. He should point out that while it is not the duty of the civil authorities to ban all immorality they must not, nonetheless, formally legalize anything immoral because what is immoral can never be classed as a "right" and will be harmful to the common good sooner or later. Furthermore, he can point out that there is a contradiction in legislators using their God-given authority to legalize things forbidden by God.

In all of this, while evils must be confronted, one must remember that it is the sin that should be condemned and not the sinner who may be in error for various reasons, impossible to gauge, or under excessive pressure to do wrong and whose salvation is still the object of all the priest's efforts. It must also be remembered that while harsh words are needed at times in the face of great evils there is an old saying that "a spoon full of honey catches more flies than a barrel of vinegar"; also, that endless condemnation of one particular evil every Sunday becomes counter-productive eventually. On the other side then, one must not forget that there is much good being done out there also, often silently and even heroically - as when a mother goes hungry herself so as to feed her children - and priests should praise that kind of self-sacrifice and ask for help for people in such situations.

Priests must condemn and must encourage; but at the end of one's sermon the sinner should be sent away with hope. Speak of sin and hell for an hour if you wish but, if you do so, finish up speaking about heaven and present it as the dwelling place of our heavenly Father who will welcome even the greatest sinner if only he/she repents, and tell that sinner and all sinners that pardon is available at the drop of a hat in the confessional. Send them away with the hope that they too can be saved because to begin with they are loved by a God who died to atone for their sins.

Even when a conscientious priest has taken account of all of the above and has delivered a good sermon, good in the sense that it reaches people where they are at so as to instruct them in sound faith and good morals, delivered with tact and charity, he is still likely to meet opposition if he has ruffled the feathers of some people in his congregation whose wrongdoing is being exposed because they are gaining from their doings. If Fr. A is alone in the stand he is taking on various issues he is all the more a target, whereas if his fellow priests are taking the same stand on the same issues then he and all of them will be more effective and the faith itself will gain. The solution is

Chapter 12: Preparation for Preaching

for each bishop to organize his own priests so that they will all be on the same line on a given Sunday in preaching about some good that has to be promoted or some evil that has to be confronted. Then if Ms. Feminist or Mrs. Cosy-Catholic or Mr. Vote-catcher or Mr. Money-man storms out of the church in protest at what Fr. Tom has been saying he or she will soon find out that Fathers Dick and Harry and all the other priests of the diocese were preaching the same thing in the other parishes all around. It might then begin to dawn on the protester that Fr. Tom did have a point after all.

Because that common stance is not taken by all together the few who do take it are easily threatened or brow-beaten and they are tempted then to compromise and resort back to the banal and the trite as the easier line of approach. The worst scenario is when the bishop is contacted by the media and he allows himself to be used by them so as to brow-beat a priest who is thoroughly orthodox in content and duly moderate in language. The faith and the salvation of the souls of the hearers lose then – and evil wins. Hence the old saying that "evil prospers when good men stay silent".

One other reason why priests should present a united front in preaching under their bishop is that it makes for a bulwark against the effort by governments to bring in so called "hate speech" legislation. Of, course one should not preach hatred – it contradicts the gospel command to love – but this legislation is often used selectively against the Church simply to silence priests who are doing their duty in preaching against the evils of the day. It is not based on anything objective but merely on the subjective feelings of Mr. X who claims to be "offended" because his wrongdoing is being exposed. Such legislation is never used against those who advocate abortion, which is hatred of life itself at its most vulnerable. I doubt if the civil authorities will put the bishop and all the priests of one diocese in jail for the sermon they preached in unison on a given Sunday, or, if they do, their own hatred of the faith will be most obvious.

Immediate Preparation

The immediate preparation is when the preacher sits down to write his homily. A number of things must be taken into account at that point. How long should a sermon be and how is it to be presented in a way that is not mechanical or dictatorial?

As to the first question one wit said that a sermon should have a good introduction and a good conclusion and that the two should be as near to each other as possible! Another wit said that a good sermon should be like a mini skirt, short enough to be interesting but long enough to cover the point! The obsession with a short sermon comes either from people who have little interest anyhow in the faith and who are in church more from routine than from faith, or from people of true faith who are genuinely looking for further nourishment for their faith and are getting only irrelevant humbug in the sermons they are hearing. These last would gladly listen to a good preacher for an hour if they could find a priest of pastoral charity who spoke with conviction. I would gladly listen to a John Chrysostom or an Augustine or a Newman for hours if I could find one.

But here one must take account of the fact that different people have different expectations and capacities with regard to the length of sermons. In the Middle Ages, for example, a priest preaching a sermon on the passion on Good Friday would be regarded as cutting corners if he spoke for less than two hours! He would be deemed not to have gone into sufficient detail on all of the sufferings of Christ. A factor to take into account in this regard is that peoples' span of attention is limited to the degree that they are being bombarded by more and more different kinds of media during the week. An old woman in rural Ireland in the mid twentieth century would come home from Sunday Mass and at dinner recite, in full, the sermon of twenty or thirty minutes that she had just heard because during the week it was unlikely that she had seen any newspaper or even heard the radio, (which had only one station anyhow), for more than a few minutes. Compare her to her granddaughter today who is exposed to many channels of radio and TV and then to the internet, the cell phone *etc.*, with all that those things bring to her at every hour, saturating her intake capacity.

If then a priest decides on, let us say, fifteen minutes for his Sunday homily, knowing that that is about the right limit for his typical parishioner, he should stick to that and tailor his pages to that and his points to his pages so that he won't fall into the old trap of rambling on and on, going round and round, like an airplane in a fog not knowing when or where to land. He should remember also that those few minutes of preaching will probably be the only bit of religious instruction that the adults of his parish will receive for the rest of the coming week versus the anti-religious propaganda they will be getting more often over the air waves. Strictly speaking a sermon is not a catechetics talk but it must still be based on solid doctrine and, in an age when catechetics programs are so diluted of solid doctrine, some amount of instruction is all the more necessary.

With the above points taken into account the preacher, having written and perhaps rewritten his sermon, must then proceed to *internalize* it, not in the sense of memorizing it by heart, because that is too difficult, as we learned above from St John Vianney, but in the sense of him becoming so familiar with it that having the text still in front of him he is able to pick up the next sentence by a simple glance so that he appears to have no text at all and is talking directly to his congregation. Also, he should so arrange his pages so that he can slide one over onto the next unobtrusively so that his hearers are unaware he is doing this and thus are in no way distracted by the turning over of pages. He is then looking at his audience and is talking seemingly effortlessly, thus concealing the long preparation he has put into it. Hence again the old saying: "Art conceals itself."

When actually preaching the priest should sound like a man of conviction who truly believes what he is saying and wants to share that truth with others. I have mentioned this word "conviction" a number of times already. There is a saying that "nothing succeeds like success". In a similar vein we could say that "nothing convinces like conviction". This is necessary at a time when the faith of many is merely a thing of *convention* with little conviction. But to preach with conviction does not mean to try shoving the gospel down peoples' throats with a thundering zeal but simply to propose it for belief because one is genuinely convinced of the truth of the message and genuinely concerned for the salvation of the souls of one's hearers. The priest's conviction, if it is there, will come across without any theatrics. If, however, a priest is not convinced in his own faith about some dogma he should pursue the matter by prayer, study and conversation with a spiritual guide. His voice should be strong and firm but gentle and humble also because he represents the Father who cares for His children, is conformed to the Son, the Bridegroom who loves His Bride, the Church, and wants to feed her, and is an instrument of the Holy Spirit whom he believes is at work in the hearts of all in his flock even if that work will receive different responses from different members of the flock.

Humility in Preaching

Mention of humility brings up a final point I would like to make about preaching: the need for humility in the preacher. Eloquence has its place. Indeed, if properly used it is that which delights according to St Augustine as we have seen above and it makes the truth being taught all the more palatable. But if eloquence makes the homily too abstract or complex or technically theological then one should remember the old saying that Samson killed more Philistines with the jaw-bone of an ass (a rather crude implement) than many others did with finely sharpened swords. The priest, if he is successful as a preacher and delights by his eloquence and is effective in spurring his hearers on to good living, must still remember – what I said earlier - that he is merely an instrument of the Holy Spirit who is the primary Agent in all of this. It is He who enkindles faith in the heart of the hearers upon the word entering their ear. Hence the priest is not there to preach himself but the word of God. An old rule there is that, when a priest has written his homily, he should go over it with a red biro and cross out the letter "I" wherever he sees it.

Still on the matter of humility in preaching, there is a story about a young priest who was more of a performer than a preacher and thought that preaching was easy and an opportunity to wax eloquent in front of an audience. So he was looking forward to his first Mass as an opportunity to put on a display and didn't prepare his sermon very well because he felt he didn't need to anyhow. This was in the days before the microphone when to preach a priest would leave the sanctuary and climb up into a pulpit. He did that with great gusto and delighted to look down on his congregation. But after a few minutes something distracted him and, since he didn't have his sermon written out in front of him, he had some difficulty in getting back into his train of thought. He did get back for a short while - but something else distracted him again. So, he began to cough in order to gain some time so as to get back on track once more. But that didn't work, so he blushed and went red and white and a few more colours and tried a few more coughs after that. But things were only getting worse. Eventually he had to come down off the pulpit very meekly and very subdued and continue with the Mass. Afterwards, his grandmother, who had been sitting in one of the seats in front of him, said: "Fr. John, if you had gone up (into the pulpit) the way you came down you could have come down the way you went up"! She was echoing the Lord when He said h*e who humbles himself will be exalted and he who exalts himself will be humbled. Lk.18:14.* But this humility is perfectly consistent with a firm confidence in the truth of the gospel to be preached with a gentle authority that comes to the priests from God through ordination. *Fortiter in re* but *suavitur in modo* is an old rule in this regard.

Though what is said above refers primarily to the priest or deacon as the proper agents of preaching I would hope that lay people, especially catechists and Catholic lecturers will be able to take some lessons from it for their work when they exercise their own distinctive, prophetic role in the work of evangelization, be it in class or wherever.

Conclusions:

1. Effective preaching requires preparation and practice which entails hard work and a dedication that is motivated by pastoral charity for one's flock.
2. The hard work entails prayer, writing, internalizing while all the time taking the mentality and capacity of one's congregation into account.
3. Regardless of the frame of mind of those coming to church or the gravity of their sins they should be sent away with an offer of hope of being saved.
4. The priest should be humble in his preaching but confidant and gently authoritative also because the gospel he preaches is truth given to us by Him who is truth in Himself.

The parish church with the priest preaching on a Sunday is the primary *locus* of evangelization but there are other *loci* also, the home and the school being very important.

Chapter XIII

Evangelization in the Home and the School

The Catholic School, Pluralism in the Classroom, the Catholic Teacher

And you shall teach them diligently to your children, and talk of them when you sit in your house and when you walk by the way, and when you lie down and when you rise. Deut. 6:7.

Since every Christian has become a new creature by rebirth from water and the Holy Spirit, so that he may be called what he truly is, a child of God, he is entitled to a Christian education. Gra*vissimum Educationis*, (GE), #2.

Our concern in this chapter is with the work of the priest and catechists in the school, an important locus of growth in faith for most people. We will examine what is meant for a school to be Catholic and how the phenomenon of pluralism affects this, and what is required of teachers in a Catholic school. I will be drawing to a considerable extent on the Vatican II document *Gravissimum Educationis* and *The Religious Dimension of Education in a Catholic School* issued by the Vatican in the late twentieth century because I see both as having perennial relevance.

The Home, the first School

After Sunday Mass the priest will often find himself in the school on a Monday continuing the work of evangelization along with his catechists. But prior to church or school there is the home which is also of incalculable and irreplaceable importance in this regard. The example often used to bring this out is that of the three-legged stool of home, church and school. All three *loci* are important and should work in harmony with each other. Take away any one of these legs and the stool will topple.

In terms of the time-line of the child's history, and the time when the earliest and deepest impressions are made, the home comes first. One bishop used to tell how his first lesson in the faith that he could remember was when his grandmother brought him along to the church as a toddler on Good Friday and pointed up to the crucifix and said "See, Holy God is dead on the cross today but very soon He will be alive again". So simple, yet the whole of the paschal mystery was presented in those few words. How important then for parents to give time to their children teaching them the truths of faith. When it happens that both parents are out working (and some mothers *must* do so out of economic necessity, so no blame to *them*) and are home late and have a hundred-and-one things to do in the house after they come in, they are not going to have much time to spare to teach the children their prayers or their catechism. Yet it is so important that they try as best they can to give some time to this.

Worse still, many such parents, if their careers and their income have become their first priority, are more likely to imbibe their children with the same materialistic mentality and give what spare time they have with them to coaching them in secular subjects, i.e., those subjects which help one to "get on" in life. The faith is then seen as something like myth or fairytale, a thing of nice stories indeed but of no use in the rat race of life. Then one must take into account the time given to TV viewing and surfing the internet and the influence of these media on people, young and old, which is often hostile to the faith. So, the home, this leg of the stool, is not as strong now as it was in agricultural times when the family members were at home most of the time. Thus, one will often hear teachers complain that much of their time is spent trying to supplement or rather *provide* what should be done in the home, simple things like teaching children how to bless themselves or learn the most basic and familiar of Catholic prayers. But our concern in this chapter is with the school.

The Catholic School

The Divine Mandate and the Childrens' Right

I will begin by making two points which are like two sides of the same coin. The first is that the Church has a divine mission from her Lord to evangelize, which mission can be carried out in various ways and particularly through the school.

> The mission of the Church is to evangelize, for the interior transformation and the renewal of humanity. For young people, the school is one of the ways for this evangelization to take place. *The Religious Dimension of Education in a Catholic School, (Rel. Dim.), #66.*

The second point, the other side of the same coin, is that the children of Catholic parents, following on their baptism, have a need and a right to be instructed in a full and proper way in the truths of the faith. The educational process must take account of this:

Chapter 13: Evangelization in the Home and the School

> Since every Christian has become a new creature by rebirth from water and the Holy Spirit, so that he may be called what he truly is, a child of God, he is entitled to a Christian education. *Gravissimum Educationis, (GE), #2.*

It follows from the divine mission given to her that the Church has a right to have her own schools. This is required for practical reasons also because parents don't always have the time or ability to accomplish the formation in faith of the young entirely by themselves without any further help. Thus, the Church says that:

> …this sacred synod proclaims anew…the church's right freely to establish and to run schools of every kind and at every level. *Ibid., #8.*

Such schools will be under the authority and guidance of the bishop even though the day-to-day management and running of the school will be mostly in the hands of lay people. The *Code of Canon Law* says:

> The Catholic religious instruction and education which are imparted in any schools whatsoever or are provided through the various instruments of social communication are subject to the authority of the Church. It is for the conference of bishops to issue general norms about this field of action and for the diocesan bishop to regulate and watch over it. *Canon 804 #1*

For parents to bring their children along for baptism and then to neglect their Catholic education and formation in the home and then in the school is a most serious omission when a Catholic school of orthodox teaching is near at hand. When such a school is not near, parents must still try to supply this formation in other ways as best they can. Canon law says on this matter:

> Parents are to entrust their children to those schools which provide a Catholic education. If they are unable to do this, they are obliged to take care that suitable Catholic education is provided for their children outside the schools. *Canon 798, (cf. also Canons 796-806).*

Sometimes parents are prevented from doing this. Indeed, in countries of persecution where the teaching of the faith is entirely forbidden in all schools the home has then to be the sole *locus* of education in the faith.

But today we sometimes have the phenomenon of supposedly Catholic parents deliberately by-passing Catholic schools which are available to them so as to enroll their children in multi-denominational or even in non-denominational schools. The underlying thinking in regard to multi-denominational schools is that all religions are more or less the same, like the washing powder one finds in boxes of different brands, so that it makes little difference if the school is a mix of many religions. Or, if real differences *are* acknowledged, the thinking then is that the more children are exposed to all and every kind of religion the more "enlightened" and "broadminded" they will be and so be better able to choose whatever religion they like for themselves individually, later, which might be some kind of hotch-potch of three or four different religions. Or, more likely, it might also have them reject all religion due to being confused so that they become skeptical and lose the faith entirely.

Then, as regards non-denominational schools, the thinking by some parents, even Catholic parents is: give us *any* school so long as it is *not* Catholic! It is an attitude of sheer prejudice, somewhat reminiscent of that of the Jacobins of the French revolution, because it is not based on any rational argument which purports to show what it is that is false or harmful in Catholic doctrine. One even sees Catholics, nominal or lapsed Catholics, occupying positions as managers and head principals in such non-Catholic schools!

To call for a Catholic education for children is not merely to ask that knowledge of the faith be "tacked on" for good measure as a kind of "added extra", just as one might call for an added art or music class, which would not be a core subject. No; the faith is not an added-extra to human formation, like a bit of icing on a cake such that the cake might be pretty good anyhow even without this top layer. At stake here is the Catholic, Christian understanding of the human person.

Christian Anthropology

The human person has come from God, because the human soul is created and infused by God at the moment of conception. The body too comes from God because all matter is created by Him. He or she is in the image and likeness of God because of having an intellect. All through life he/she is sustained in being by God in his natural life. When baptized he receives the grace of Christ, is sanctified by the Holy Spirit and receives the infused gifts of faith, hope and charity. His destiny is to return to God again at the end of his earthly life.

That is Christian anthropology and requires a corresponding education, a nurturing of faith, hope and charity, if the child is to reach his/her destination of union with God. Accordingly, children who are not given this kind of education are somewhat like a car which has been started and sent off down the street but with no destination, or like a boat, well-built materially perhaps, but having no compass so that

Chapter 13: Evangelization in the Home and the School

it is blown about on the high seas. The faith is at the beginning and end of life for the Christian and permeates every aspect of it to enrich, enlighten and perfect it.

> The educational process is not simply a human activity; it is a genuine Christian journey toward perfection. *The Religious Dimension of Education in a Catholic School,* #47.

Or, again, faith is not something on the side of life, never interacting with it, or in some realm above life but with no influence on it, like oil above water in a jar. It is more like wine and water; wine representing the divine, coming into water representing the human, coloring, purifying and enriching it. So, the same document says:

> The world of human culture and the world of religion are not like two parallel lines that never meet; points of contact are established within the human person. For a believer is both human and a person of faith, the protagonist of culture and the subject of religion. *Ibid., #51.*

Both priests and the school staff, from their respective angles, can and should help parents to see the importance of a Catholic education for their children. The priest can do so in preaching and at pre-baptism talks, and the school staff can do so at teacher-parent meetings:

> The first and primary educators of children are their parents. The school is aware of this fact but, unfortunately, the same is not always true of the families themselves; it is the school's responsibility to give them this awareness. Every school should initiate meetings and other programmes which will make the parents more conscious of their role, and help to establish a partnership; it is impossible to do too much along these lines. *Ibid., #43.*

When this is done the three legs of the stool of the faith are helping each other to stand firm and the Christian pupils gains humanly and spiritually.

<u>The Catholic School and the Gospel Spirit</u>

Granted the right of the Church to have her own schools, we must see now what kind of institution such a school should be, what characterizes it, what kind of ethos it should have. Materially, of course, it is a building with classrooms, a time table for lessons and other events, with qualified teachers in charge – just like any other school. It teaches subjects such as mathematics, languages, history, geography, science and more, again, like any other school. But it is different formally as the Vatican document explains:

> While the Catholic school is like any other school in this complex variety of events that make up the life of the school, there is one essential difference: it draws its inspiration and its strength from the Gospel in which it is rooted. *Ibid., #47; (cf. also General Directory, #73).*

The Catholic school develops the natural talents of the pupils and instructs them in reading and writing, in the arts and sciences, and in everything else that they need to learn as rounded people. But, following on what we have been saying above, a "rounded" person is one who is developed not only at the natural level but also at the supernatural level because grace builds on nature and nature is a rather impoverished entity without grace. So, a Catholic school consciously and deliberately unites the natural and the supernatural in its pupils. To suggest that doing so will inhibit the natural talents of the pupils or stifle their development in any way is utterly false. The opposite, in fact, is the case: grace purifies, elevates and perfects nature so that nature prospers all the more under the influence of grace. The light of intellect receives the guidance of the higher light of faith. The will is strengthened in doing good and in resisting sin and the entire person is set on his/her path towards God, the final end of all of us. Our document explains this further:

> The catholic school pursues cultural goals and the natural development of youth to the same degree as any other school. What makes the catholic school distinctive is its attempt to generate a community spirit in the school that is permeated by the gospel spirit of freedom and love. It tries to develop the adolescent in such a way that personality development goes hand in hand with the development of the 'new creature' that each one has become through baptism. It tries to relate all of human culture to the good news of salvation so that the light of faith will illumine everything that the students will gradually come to learn about the world, about life, and about the human person. *Gravissimum Educationis, #8; (quoted also in Rel. Dim., Introduction).*

In practice, this requires that catechetics gets a frequent, regular and prominent slot in the school time-table, that it will not be stuck into the last slot on a Friday evening when the school busses are lining up outside the gate and the students are tired and

Chapter 13: Evangelization in the Home and the School

anxious to get away. And the lure of the bus will be even greater, of course, if attendance at the religion class is optional. This downgrades the quality of religious instruction and undermines interest in it. St John Paul II puts it as follows in his letter on catechesis:

> The special character of the Catholic school, the underlying reason for it, the reason why Catholic parents should prefer it, is precisely the quality of the religious instruction integrated into the education of the pupils. *Catechesi Tradendae, #6*

The quality of religious instruction should be good and its place in the time-table should be central. We can then imagine the religion class to be like a light shining out from the middle of the curriculum to light up the glass ball of all the other subjects being taught all around d it. So, for example, if the teacher is talking about the formation of the continents in the geography class she will refer back to the religion class in which she had been talking about the *Genesis* account of creation. If she is talking about the history of Europe she will show how central a role the Church, and in particular the popes, have had in that history. When talking about evolution she will make the point that it is a theory, not as yet accepted as a proven fact by some scientists, and that, even if it is ever proven to be fact, the soul of the first man and woman and of every child since then is not something that evolved from any previous matter, living or inanimate, but is something that was created and infused by God at the moment of conception. This, in turn should serve as a basis for instruction on the sanctity of human life in classes on morals and civics so that the utter wrong of direct abortion or of euthanasia will be made clear. The faith will be as a leaven in the dough in the cake of knowledge that is forming in the minds of the pupils. It will be the wine in the water purifying and enriching it.

And, in addition to the strictly academic side of things, such a school will be a place of welcome and of friendliness where pupils sense immediately that they are cherished as persons of value – their value arising from their being, each one of them uniquely, in the image and likeness of God and more so His adopted children by baptism. They will also be taught to value the dignity of each other, to respect the authority of the teachers as being *in loco parentis,* (in the place of their parents), for the school day, which also means that they will have to accept being disciplined so that any beginning of vice in them will be rooted out and that virtue will be promoted, especially the four cardinal moral virtues of prudence, justice, fortitude and temperance - and then the crowning virtue of charity. Good discipline says "No" to children doing wrong but then goes further and teaches them how to say "No" to themselves, to their own selfish desires, and thus how to grow in character and in Christian self-denial, things not popular in a permissive society but greatly needed nonetheless not only for religious living but for any kind of civilized living.

This is how it should be in a Catholic school; and the harmonizing of faith and reason is readily accepted by pupils because it gives an overall, unified vision to their education. It is complete because it takes account of God and the supernatural. However, problems can arise when the Catholic school accepts pupils of non-practicing Catholic parents and pupils of other religions and none. Such parents will often send their children to a Catholic school because, perhaps, it is the nearest one available but also often because they will be aware of the fine reputation that Catholic schools have had almost everywhere for producing well-formed students of high academic standards. Nonetheless, knowing this and taking advantage of it for purely secularist reasons, some have the audacity to object to the Catholic teaching which is at the core of such fine education, and such people may object also to holy pictures, or statues or crucifixes on the walls of the school, calling these "harrowing" or "gruesome". They will say that time spent in preparation for the sacraments is so much waste and that it entails discrimination against non-Catholic pupils when they do not participate in that preparation. But they will not object at all when sports day comes along or when the school puts on dramas or concerts or goes on tours - things which also take time away from the core subjects. Nor will they object to immoral sex-education programs.

Lapsed Catholic parents, now calling themselves humanists or agnostics, who protest over these things should not be given a moment's hearing from a Catholic school board or from Catholic teachers or parents. They know what a Catholic school is as distinct from other kinds of schools, and if they don't like that then they are free to ask the government to set up godless schools for themselves or set up such schools on their own. Catholic school boards, teachers and parents will stand firm in this regard if they are committed Catholics themselves but, sadly, that does not always happen. One finds Catholic school boards only too willing to accommodate these humanists in some places by downsizing the place of Catholic teaching in the curriculum or even by agreeing to divest the school of Catholic management entirely.

The Phenomenon of Pluralism

<u>Pluralism in Society</u>

This brings us to the matter of the phenomenon of pluralism in the classroom and how the school board should deal with it. The pluralist classroom is a microcosm of the wider, pluralist society of the West today. It has many causes: the greater facility of travel and the ever restlessness of the human spirit which always has people on the move; war and famine in some countries causing migration to other countries; the low birth rate in the West due to contraception creating a vacuum which is being filled with people coming from countries with a higher birth rate, and so on. There are deeper ideological reasons also, going back in history, such as the breakup of the Catholic world-view which began with the Protestant revolt and which ushered in the idea of private interpretation. That was followed by the liberalism of the Enlightenment which rejected the certainty that comes from faith so that tolerance of every idea, even contradictory ideas, became the supreme virtue. "You might be wrong and I might be wrong but I will defend your right to be wrong even though I think you are crazy"- this is a paraphrase of the thinking of men like Voltaire in France before the revolution and is still with us.

Then today there is a false kind of ecumenism which claims that one religion is as good as another and that it is very impolite for any one religion, such as the Catholic, to claim to have the fullness of truth given to us by Christ. The supreme virtue then is tolerance. Nonetheless, I can't help noticing how this kind of pluralism and tolerance, supposedly open to everything, falls short of showing respect for Catholic dogma, as was the case with Voltaire and is the case today again with liberal media presenters and journalists. "We will listen to anything you say provided it is not Catholic".

Pluralism then is a phenomenon of our time and, because it is such, the deduction is simplistically made that it has to be good inherently and so must be welcomed and fostered *for its own sake* uncritically. Hence, one sometimes hears Catholic school principals saying that they welcome diversity for its own sake when enrolling pupils of all faiths and none. How naive and simplistic!

I would like to put a few points for critical reflection before such people. The first is that there is some benefit in pluralism of a limited kind and that tolerance is a good thing, again within limits and when properly understood. Diversity can enrich. It brings new ideas and ways of doing things to a society from which they can pick and choose so as to assimilate them into their own thinking and way of life. Thus, for example, the immigration of Polish people into Ireland at the end of the twentieth century was positive and enriching even though their language was different. The example that can be used here is that of the human organism taking in different foods for its nourishment. That is good and strengthening. But if the person takes in poison or bad food or even foods that are good but to which he/she has an allergy then his organism will reject them or else he will become very sick and possibly die. So also with a society: it will be enriched depending on how close to its own beliefs and values are the beliefs and values it takes on board from foreigners. But if it tries to take in people with beliefs and values directly contrary to its own there must needs be conflict, disharmony and eventually the demise of one or other community. Put differently, the concept of a pluralist society, if pushed to its limits, is contradictory; if taken too far in practice, it will lead to disruption, violence and the dissolution of a given society. Ultimately a society can have only one soul. If it has two or more it will be schizoid, divided or eventually soulless, anarchic and will perish.

A society is not a collection of individuals juxtaposed to each other like stones in a heap, no matter how many of them are there. It is, instead, an organism, a living collective person, a community of people who are naturally social beings, bonded together by a heritage of common beliefs from the past and aspiring towards common goals for the future. Instead of stones we have people with hearts and minds held together by what they hold dear. (Recall our reference to St Augustine in this matter when talking about the uniting power of the Sunday sermon in a previous chapter). If, then, there is introduced into their society what is contradictory to what they hold dear, to what is central in their hearts and minds, there will be conflict, and that society simply will not hold together. The glue will disappear. Crime, violence, homelessness, loneliness, mental illness, addiction and even suicide will be ever more common.

To "cure" such maladies more money will have to be spent on policing and governments will need to use more force so that the coherence resulting after a while will be that of a harsh totalitarianism, the very opposite of the promised freedom supposed to result from the imagined pluralism which naive people, the successors of Voltaire, were welcoming a generation earlier. Or, the opposing communities might move apart geographically into different ghettos for security. But such a ghetto is not at all pluralist and is therefore proof of the point I am making. Or the conflicting communities may agree to keep all beliefs out of the public square and settle for a very permissive, because minimal, level of morality in their state legislation. But this only leads to more violence and lawlessness. For example, when the killing of the unborn is legalized, the killing of the old soon follows and the murder rate in the streets goes up. The "cure will even be worse than the disease", as the old saying has it.

A wise immigration policy then would allow foreigners to come in in proportion as their beliefs are close to those of the host community, or, at least, that they respect those beliefs which will, at root, be religious for the simple reason that religion is the deepest thing in man; and that is so because, as said already, man is made by God, in the image and likeness of God and has God as his ultimate lawgiver and final destiny. That is true even of the atheist who spends his life denying the existence of God, making such a fuss about something that is supposedly non-existent! (*cf. CCC, #2241*).

Those who are fixated on the Voltairean type of pluralist ideology and who dream of a paradise of freedom in which everyone can disagree with everyone and live happily nonetheless will see my idea of selected immigration as discrimination. To that I would reply: would such people absorb all kinds of foods regardless of whether they were good or bad for their health?

Pluralism, in theory at least, claims to respect the conscience of each and every individual and therefore to allow all people their freedom to profess their beliefs and follow them in their respective ways of life. Again, I say: good as far as it goes. Conscience is sacred and should not be coerced, and sadly it was often coerced in times past. But conscience needs to be informed by a knowledge of the truth about God and human nature and it needs to be informed of the existence of an objective moral law and of the exigencies of the common good, which latter cannot be promoted without regard for the moral law. Otherwise, to grant freedom of conscience is simply to grant license to unfettered desire, to gross selfishness. And when that becomes the norm, might becomes right, the weak and the poor are oppressed, and again we have a state of affairs the very opposite of the pluralist dream.

St John Paul was one of the principal architects of the Vatican II document on religious freedom, *Dignitatis Humanae*. Due to his experience of oppression in his native Poland as a young man under communism - the ideology that promised paradise to the workers - he was a strong advocate of religious freedom. But a number of times in that document the phrase occurs of "subject to the moral law". That has been largely forgotten by those who use that document to promote the ideology of pluralism. He often in his talks made the point that the common good of society, of all in society regardless of creed, cannot be safeguarded if the objective moral law is violated by evil legislation and if fundamental human rights are ignored. (*cf. Centesimus Annus*).

Is this then intolerance from the Catholic side? A distinction needs to be made here between persons and practices. Persons should be tolerated, and not only that but cherished and loved with Christian charity. But false beliefs and immoral practices should always be opposed. Where there is true respect and love for persons, some of whom profess false beliefs and engage in immoral practices, the host people will oppose them patiently and charitably with honest, respectful debate and try to correct them by giving them instruction in the truth and in good morals, pointing out the relation of these things to the common good. Where there is a blatant unwillingness to refrain from practices directly harmful to the common good then the civil law must be enforced for the good of all, including the good of the offender also.

The best argument that Catholics can present to reasonable people of other beliefs is the example of their own lives lived fully according to Catholic principles. But sadly, that is where things most often fall down. As Pope St. Pius V once put it: most of the troubles of society are caused by lukewarm Catholics.

Pluralism in the Classroom

How do these more general principles on pluralism apply to the classroom of the Catholic school? The naïve management board which welcomes diversity uncritically will sometimes adopt a policy of watering down the content of catechetics in class so as not to offend supposedly sensitive pupils who might run home and tell their parents that the teacher was talking about sin or hell or obligations in school. Or, what comes to much the same thing, they might try to present a catechetics program which is so vague in content that pretty well anyone and everyone could say "yes" to it because it amounts to little more than a handbook of civic politeness. Worse still, in the area of morals, they might present a parallel program to the Catholic program which makes mutual consent to be the only and the supreme moral principal. Hence if the girl is willing the boy can do just about anything he likes with her and she can then choose abortion if things "go wrong". That such a policy would prevail in a supposedly Catholic school is simply a sellout, a betrayal and a disgrace.

So, what policy should a Catholic school board adopt if the school has pupils of other religions and no religion also on its roll book? St John Paul has good advice on that:

> While Catholic establishments should respect freedom of conscience, that is to say, avoid burdening consciences from without by exerting physical or moral pressure, especially in the case of the religious activity of adolescents, they still have a grave duty to offer a religious training suited to the often widely varying religious situations of the pupils. They also have a duty to make them understand that, although God's call to serve Him in spirit and truth, in accordance with the Commandments of God and the precepts of the Church, does not apply constraint, it is nevertheless binding in conscience. *Catechesi Tradendae, #6*

St John Paul had a simpler formula which he often used to express the same thing: the Catholic school "must propose but not impose" the faith. The faith must be taught *undiluted in its entirety* to all who are willing to stay in the class room. In some schools there may be a provision for non-Catholic pupils to leave the class room in accordance with the wishes of their parents and do some other studies in another room. The obligations which flow from professing the faith should also be clearly pointed out, such as that of going to Mass on Sundays and keeping the commandments, but compulsion should not be used. There should be no head count on a Monday morning of those who were at Mass on Sunday or penalties for those who stayed away. But Catholic truth and the moral law should be proposed in a clear and attractive way simply because it is truth and because the moral law is binding on everyone in conscience.

Ironically, it was my experience as an examiner of religion in Catholic schools which had an enrolment of many non-Catholic pupils that often these non-Catholics, some of whom were not even baptized but who nonetheless remained present in the religion class, were far better at answering the questions I put to them and did so with greater interest and even with more enthusiasm than many of their fellow Catholics! And I found examples of the converse also: pupils from supposedly Catholic families who not only showed no interest but who were openly hostile to their own faith and to the pope and to the Church. This I saw as a reflection on the homes they came from – the "anything but Catholic", irrational kind.

Good Teachers

If Catholic truth is thus to be proposed in undiluted form it follows that teachers in Catholic schools should themselves be well versed in the faith and should be seen to practice it with upright lives. I heard of a teacher in a Catholic school with religion as one of his subjects - supposedly the *core* subject - boasting to his friends in the pub at night that he was an atheist! So also, there are teachers who see nothing wrong with cohabiting publicly and see no discrepancy between doing that and teaching the pupils about the sixth commandment. What kind of instruction do they give? Furthermore, if they are called to order over such behavior their trade unions will back them against the school board. Evidently such people have no regard for the faith and morals of their pupils but only for their own careers and pay cheques. They seem to be unaware of what canon law says on this matter:

> The local ordinary is to be concerned that those who are designated teachers of religious instruction in schools, even in non-Catholic ones, are outstanding in correct doctrine, the witness of a Christian life, and teaching skill. *Canon 804 #2.*

This concern must result in practical steps when it comes to employment:

> For his own diocese, the local ordinary has the right to appoint or approve teachers of religion and even to remove them or demand that they be removed if a reason of religion or morals requires it. *Canon 805.*

Since attendance at Sunday Mass is obligatory for all able-bodied Catholics,

Catholic teachers should be expected to show an example in this regard to their pupils, especially if they live in the parish in which the school is also located, allowing for the possibility, of course, that for various reasons, such as going on holidays or sickness, a teacher might not be able to attend every Sunday. Failure in this regard I would see as a "reason of religion" for a teacher to be reprimanded or removed according to the above quote; so also, if the teacher fails to implement the religion program in total in an orthodox way, giving it its designated hours in the time table.

A "reason of morals", then, regards the public behaviour of the teacher, that he/she be of upright, moral behaviour as per the commandments. Because teachers' unions will nonetheless often back the teacher of bad morals, calling his/her behaviour a "private matter" - even though it is publicly visible to the children and to all in the parish – it makes it difficult at times for the bishop to act. Nonetheless, I am not suggesting that teachers be under surveillance in their free time. The presumption should be that they are people of sound faith and good morals if employed in a Catholic school to begin with, the school having done all that is reasonably possible to ensure this by obtaining good references from their institutes of training, their places of former employment and from their pastors. To be fair and open with candidates from the beginning, their contracts of employment should be of such a kind as to make it crystal clear that good behaviour in accordance with the ten commandments is expected of teachers and that behaviour of a contrary kind, when publicly noticeable so as to be a matter of scandal for young people, being contrary to what is taught in the catechetics program, will be grounds for dismissal, and that such agreements have legal standing. If a candidate is going to teach in a Catholic school then it is perfectly reasonable to expect that he/she will uphold the Catholic ethos of the school or, at the least, not undermine it. If religious freedom is guaranteed in the constitution of a given country then the feasibility of having such contracts should follow as a consequence.

Hence, I cannot understand the argument of some candidates who are not believing Catholics that they are being discriminated against in the work place when they are refused a position in a Catholic school. I have never heard them make this complaint when refused a position in a Protestant or Muslim or Jewish school? Furthermore, in a free country they are free to seek employment in some other kind of school whose ethos is more to their own liking.

Moreover, how strange that when society makes such noise about the physical abuse of children that doctrinal falsehood and moral corruption by a minority of teachers, whose very profession demands that they give good example, is not seen to be another kind of abuse, one of a spiritual kind, one which is not only not objected to but is even supported by unions, the media and legislators! Yet this spiritual kind of abuse is all the more damaging because the young accept so readily what they are taught by their teachers and are influenced by their example, especially in matters of morals.

School, a homely Place

When the Catholic school lives up to its distinctive ethos, with good teachers in *loco parentis,* the school itself then becomes a kind of second home or extension of the home with school and home cooperating for the good of the pupils.

> Many of the students will attend a Catholic school - often the same school - from the time they are very young children until they are nearly adults. It is only natural that they should come to think of the school as an extension of their own homes, and therefore a "school-home" ought to have some of the amenities which can create a pleasant and happy family atmosphere. When this is missing from the home, the school can often do a great deal to make up for it. *The Religious Dimension of Education in a Catholic School,* #27.

And to give it this character of being "a home from home" the school should give a special place to Mary by having her represented with statues or pictures before which prayers will be said at certain times.

> An awareness of Mary's presence can be a great help toward making the school into a "home". Mary, Mother and Teacher of the Church, accompanied her Son as he grew in wisdom and grace; from its earliest days, she has accompanied the Church in its mission of salvation. *ibid.,* #29.

Conclusions:

1. Because Christ commissioned His apostles to go forth and evangelize all peoples, and because the human being has need of the gospel to reach his/her goal of everlasting life with God, the Church has the right and the duty to establish schools of her own as means of evangelization. The local ordinary has the task of ensuring that the school is truly Catholic in educational content, in ethos and in the moral character of its teachers.
2. Catholic children have a right to a formation in the faith following on their being baptized so that their education will be complete because formation in the faith is not a mere optional added-extra to their education in secular

subjects. It is that which guides them to their complete fulfilment and their final goal which is union with God in heaven.
3. If the young are to be evangelized successfully, the home, the school and the Church must work together and reinforce each other. The parents are the primary educators of their children and have an obligation to try to secure a Catholic education for them by sending them to Catholic schools when possible.
4. The Catholic school is permeated with the gospel spirit of freedom and love. It is an extension of the home. Religious instruction there is like a leaven that sheds the light of faith on all other subjects. Mary's motherly care is experienced there. The pupils are brought to full development not only as to their natural powers but also, and more so, as they grow in grace towards union with God.
5. The fact of pluralism in the classroom should not lead to a diluting of the content of religious instruction. But the faith should be proposed rather than imposed. In doing so the school is being missionary in its own way.

If faith is the light at the centre of life in the Catholic school, we should next look at the teaching of the faith – catechetics.

Chapter XIV

The School and Catechetics

Content and Method in Catechetics, Inculturation

Take care about what you do and what you teach; always do this, and in this way you will save both yourself and those who listen to you. 1 Tim.4:16.

Catechesis is an education of children, young people and adults in the faith, which includes especially the teaching of Christian doctrine imparted, generally speaking, in an organic and systematic way… *Catechesi Tradendae, #18.*

Having tried to give a picture of the Catholic school as an institution that presents the teaching of the faith as a light at the centre of the curriculum which illuminates all other subjects and activities in the school, it is fitting that we now look at the teaching of the faith itself more closely which means that we examine what catechetics is and then say what its content and method should be. We will end with some general points on pedagogy and inculturation so that the divine origin of Christian doctrine will be highlighted and how this is manifested in educational practice.

Catechetics

First let us say what catechetics is as compared to other forms of evangelization. Let us go to St John Paul II and his letter *Catechesi Tradendae*:

> Catechesis is an education of children, young people and adults in the faith, which includes especially the teaching of Christian doctrine imparted, generally speaking, in an organic and systematic way, with a view to initiating the hearers into the fullness of Christian life, community, and apostolic and missionary witness. *#18.*

He is describing catechetics here in a way that is familiar and traditional: it is instruction in the faith so as to prepare young and old for the sacraments and Christian life in its widest sense of living in a morally upright way and in bearing witness to the faith in society. It is closely related to other forms of evangelization such as kerygma, apologetics or, we might say, to general religious instruction that might be given to any interested group of people:

> Accordingly, while not being formally identified with them, catechesis is built on a certain number of elements of the Church's pastoral mission that have a catechetical aspect, that prepare for catechesis, or that spring from it. These elements are: the initial proclamation of the Gospel or missionary preaching through the kerygma to arouse faith, apologetics or examination of the reasons for belief, experience of Christian living, celebration of the sacraments, integration into the ecclesial community, and apostolic and missionary witness. *Ibid., #18.*

The word "kerygma" evokes the picture of St John the Baptist standing at the Jordan and shouting to the people to "repent and believe" for the kingdom of God is close at hand, or of St Peter in Jerusalem telling the people that this Jesus whom they crucified, God has risen from the dead, or St Paul coming into places like Corinth or Athens and shouting out the message that Christ crucified is the power and wisdom of God. Today we might describe such proclamation as "sound bites" or "catch phrases" as one often gets from a public figure on radio or TV when launching some campaign or other . In the Church it is a core message that gets to the heart of the faith in a few words.

Apologetics, then, presents arguments for the faith so as to meet the objections of non-believers.

More generally still, a parish priest might put on night classes during Lent which for some, be they believers or non-believers, would be general instruction in the faith, but it might incorporate elements of catechetics also for some in the class who are preparing for a sacrament or it might incorporate some apologetics also for others who are already committed lay Catholics but who seek to be able to discuss the faith with others who might not be practicing.

The State of Catechetics at the beginning of the third Millenium

My interest here is in catechetics taken as the kind of evangelization that takes place in the religion class in the school. I should not have to waste time looking at this because one should be able to take it for granted that instruction in the faith would be more or less of uniform content and standard in all Catholic schools in all parts of the world so that we could expect that, for example, six year old pupils or ten year olds or twelve year olds, or whatever age group one chooses to examine, would have much the same basic knowledge of the fundamentals of the faith, appropriate for their age, wherever they lived. That was mostly the case in times prior to Vatican II but, unfortunately, it has not been the case since then. As a person teaching theology at third level, one rule I have had to keep in mind going in the door of the classroom every day is "presume nothing". I cannot presume that, even at post graduate level, the students will all have a common, uniform knowledge of the faith, even of the most basic elements of the faith, of things which in former days every pupil had off by heart for confirmation before they even left primary school. Some will and some will not have these basics depending on where they come from and the kind of programs being used in the schools in their respective countries.

Once when teaching catechetics, I gave one student from Australia the exercise of comparing three different catechetics programs that were being used for ten year olds in different countries: in his native Australia, in the US and in Ireland. His findings were that the US program was the best, followed by the Australian program, followed in third place, very far down the line, by the Irish program which he described as "trash - little better than a comic"! Yet I can distinctly remember how that same program, when it was being introduced into the schools in Ireland, was hailed as being wonderful, so "user friendly", so "child centred" and given other such accolades by catechists and teachers who themselves were the products of other, prior, defective programs and who therefore were in little position to judge. Then, some years later, when that program was being replaced, after thousands of children had been fed on this "trash", it was deemed to be not so good after all by the same catechists and teachers and the next program was again welcomed uncritically!

Should anyone think I am being a bit harsh on catechetics programs of recent years I would say to him to go and question some children that you know and ask them some very basic questions. For example, ask them to list the ten commandments and say what is commanded and forbidden by each, or perhaps one could begin by asking them to name the three persons of the Blessed Trinity. Expect to hear that there are three "people" in the Trinity! Ask them about the Eucharist and expect to be told that it is "holy bread because it is blessed by the priest"! Ask them about mortal sin and the teacher may well intrude and say that "we don't talk at all about such negative things nowadays". Nor can there be mention of purgatory or indulgence and certainly not of hell, lest these things "frighten" the children! One could also look at the many surveys, done on this matter in many countries, showing the great lack of knowledge of the basics of the faith by youngsters today. One could also go to the document of St. John Paul II, *Catechesi Tradendae,* and see there a long list of doctrines conspicuous by their very absence from catechetics books. I will quote;

What kind of catechesis would it be that failed to give their full place to man's creation and sin; to God's plan of redemption and its long, loving preparation and realization; to the incarnation of the Son of God; to Mary, the Immaculate One, the Mother of God, ever Virgin, raised body and soul to the glory of heaven, and to her role in the mystery of salvation; to the mystery of lawlessness at work in our lives and the power of God freeing us from it; to the need for penance and asceticism; to the sacramental and liturgical actions; to the reality of the Eucharistic Presence; to participation in divine life here and hereafter, and so on? Thus, no true catechist can lawfully, on his own initiative, make a selection of what he considers important in the deposit of faith as opposed to what he considers unimportant, so as to teach the one and reject the other. *#30.*

The list results from complaints made to the Vatican by concerned parents and teachers who still had the faith when they were getting deaf ears from bishops in their own countries. But that was not true of all bishops by any means.

A Frenchman described this demolition of catechetics to me by using the example of a shoebox the inside of which is mostly taken up by the pair of shoes it contains plus a little bit of paper packaging around them. But with the next purchase one finds that the space inside the same sized box, which is taken up by the shoes, is much less and that the packaging is much more, and so on with the next purchase until after a while what one gets is mostly packaging and one has to strain one's eyes to see the shoes. The shoes in this example stand for solid doctrine and the packaging stands for all the gimmickry that goes on now in many religion classes from drama to painting to playing pop songs or whatever - all supposed to help the transmission of the faith. These latter activities can, indeed, be of some value in *enhancing* the transmission of the faith, but that presupposes that the *essential doctrines* of the faith are being taught in the first place, which is not always the case.

In brief, what we now have in the area of catechetics in many countries is a thorough mess, a disaster scene. And it raises the question of how this happened. That is still a mystery to me because I do not remember either parents or teachers complaining about the traditional question-and-answer style of catechetics of the past which was accompanied by Bible stories and stories from the lives of the saints and with hymns and prayers. The old rule of "let well alone" and "if something ain't broke don't fix it" was not followed in this matter.

Head or Heart

Somewhere or other some new "experts" popped up who declared that what we had traditionally in catechetics was a "thing of the head only" and not of the heart, that it was too abstract, that children were learning off big words which they never understood, that, instead, catechetics should be a thing of feelings and be child-centred and simpler, with topics like sin and hell best avoided. I remember once listening to a nun catechist saying such things, and I put up my hand and asked her if then Our Lady at Fatima was a bad catechist, breaking all the rules, when she told the three very young children about the many souls who were going to hell and even showed them a vision of hell? The "expert" replied as I expected: she waffled and blew a lot of hot air. But because she was supposed to be an expert and "modern" she got a round of applause from an audience of priests at the end.

Catechetics is not a matter of head *versus* heart for the simple reason that the human being has both intellect and emotions and other powers also. Good teachers in the past took account of that. They catered for the "head" by imparting sound doctrine which the pupils learned off by heart but which those teachers explained also by using various examples appropriate to the age and background of the pupils. Inadequate teachers, by comparison, people who were misfits in their profession or lacking in faith (and unfortunately there were always some) simply made the pupils learn off the catechism answers without explaining them so that they would pass the test when examined for admission to the sacraments when the diocesan examiner came round. But even with that minimum, those pupils did, at the least, imbibe the doctrinal content, which content they came to understand a bit better by themselves in later years. The good teachers catered for the "heart" also, along with the head, because of the care they took to explain the doctrine with stories that appealed to emotion, stories from the Bible which were full of beautiful emotion and stories from the lives of the saints. They catered for the heart additionally because so many of them, especially the women teachers, were caring, motherly people (those of them who were lay teachers often being mothers themselves to begin with) who truly had faith and hope and above all a charity that radiated tender love to the pupils, a love that was willing to listen to their little problems and meet their needs; often they would give their own lunch to children of poor or broken families who came to school hungry. Will the "experts" still tell me that there was something wrong with that, that it was all head and no heart?!!

Readers will note a certain anger in the above, the reason being that what we are talking about with bad catechetics is not simply a deficiency in educational content or methods but the potential loss of souls, which is very likely if young people grow up not knowing truth from falsehood in matters of doctrine or right from wrong in matters of morals. But catechists who see little importance in the doctrine of hell will probably laugh at my concerns. However, it is of some consolation to know that, as a reaction to this, there *are* some individuals and institutes who are trying to produce good programs suitable for our times even if they are getting little hearing. It should also be said that in places there are good teachers using good programs but still having little effect because they are not getting cooperation from the parents at home.

Having thus exposed some of the fundamental errors in many of today's catechetics programs let us proceed to say a few things about right content and correct method in catechetics, continuing to keep to St. John Paul as our guide.

Content in Catechetics

As regards content the pope says:

> It must be systematic, not improvised but programmed to reach a precise goal. It must deal with essentials, without any claim to tackle all disputed questions or to transform itself into theological research or scientific exegesis. It must nevertheless be sufficiently complete, not stopping short at the initial proclamation of the Christian mystery such as we have in the kerygma. It must be an integral Christian initiation, open to all the other factors of Christian life. *CT.*, *#21; (cf.* also *General Directory of Catechetics, 1997, #112, #149-154).*

A catechetics course must be systematic. Its content must not depend on what happens to be on the teacher's mind today but must be structured to cover a definite course of instruction and reach a definite goal by the end of the year. It must deal with essentials, with the principal mysteries of the faith, the seven sacraments and the commandments of the old and new testaments, and with prayer. These are the four pillars of the *Catechism of the Catholic Church* which is now the basic handbook from which all other catechetics books should be derived. A school program cannot hope to be so comprehensive as to cover all aspects of theology, especially when children are the recipients, but nonetheless it must be sufficiently complete and go beyond the "sound bites" of an initial kerygma.

When presenting the mysteries of the faith the order of the hierarchy of truths is to be followed. This means that some truths are more foundational than others, such as the Trinity and then the Incarnation and redemption following it. It does not mean that other truths, for example, the Immaculate Conception of Mary or her Assumption into heaven, because they are less foundational, and therefore lower in the hierarchy,

Chapter 14: The School and Catechetics

can be discarded. Certainly not. But their place and relevance is to be seen in relation to the former, higher truths. So the pope says again:

> This message transmitted by catechetics has a "comprehensive hierarchical character", which constitutes a coherent and vital synthesis of the faith. This is organized around the mystery of the Most Holy Trinity, in a Christocentric perspective, because this is "the source of all the other mysteries of faith, the light that enlightens them". Starting with this point, the harmony of the overall message requires a "hierarchy of truths", in so far as the connection between each one of these and the foundation of the faith differs. Nevertheless, this hierarchy "does not mean that some truths pertain to Faith itself less than others, but rather that some truths are based on others as of a higher priority and are illumined by them". *Ibid., #114; (cf.* also *Gen. Dir. Cat., #114).*

The mysteries are in hierarchical order of importance, one above the other. But they are also in an organic relationship with each other because all are interrelated like the seamless robe of Christ on Calvary so that to omit or distort the presentation of any one of them will do injustice to all of them.

As regards the sacraments, pupils need to know the basics of what each signifies, who can administer and receive them validly, with special attention being given to the Mass.

As regards the teaching of morals, especially the ten commandments, it is not enough to have the pupils learn them off by heart if they do not also learn what is commanded and what is forbidden by each commandment. I have known teenagers who know nothing of the obligation to attend Sunday Mass or who were binge drinkers but had no idea that such behavior is contrary to the fifth commandment. One such teenager told me that it was wrong indeed to get drunk *solely* because of the hangover one has the next morning! Again, many do not know the difference between fornication and adultery and think that such things are "acceptable" (the new word that replaces "morally right") if there is mutual consent. Or if, per chance, they do know what fornication is they will claim that it is not mentioned in any of the commandments. There are catechist who will say that all one need to do is to "show love" and somehow all such things then become "acceptable". It is not much different from the consent theory of humanists.

As regards prayer, pupils need to know those fundamental prayers such as the *Our Father, Hail Mary,* and the *Glory* – the essentials of the rosary; the prayers needed for those sacraments which are more frequently attended such as the Mass and confession; morning and night prayers, and prayers they will need at times of difficulty such as the

Memorare. I would argue that many a suicide might have been prevented if young people knew that prayer and said it frequently. The Psalms too are and have always been a great source of prayer. Pupils could be encouraged to memorize a few of them at least.

Language in Catechetics

In all of the above, correct language is important for the sake of clarity and accuracy so that mistaken ideas can be avoided. In the case of the commandments, I recommend keeping to the words of scripture when they are being learned off. Pope John Paul again:

> In catechesis as in theology, there is no doubt that the question of language is of the first order. But there is good reason for recalling here that catechesis cannot admit any language that would result in altering the substance of the content of the Creed, under any pretext whatever, even a pretended scientific one. Deceitful or beguiling language is no better. On the contrary, the supreme rule is that the great advances in the science of language must be capable of being placed at the service of catechesis so as to enable it really to 'tell' or 'communicate' to the child, the adolescent, the young people and adults of today the whole content of doctrine without distortion. *ibid.*, #59 (*cf. Gen. Dir. Cat.*, #208).

Hence to speak of three "people" in God or of the Eucharist as "holy bread" is not correct because it conveys ideas which are plainly heretical. There has also been a trend in catechetics to avoid supposedly "big" words like "incarnation" or "redemption" on the supposition that such terms will somehow frighten off the pupils. Yet in other subjects, such as maths or geography or science or whatever, there is no hesitation about using difficult technical terms and demanding that the pupils know what they mean. This is another example of that "child centred thinking," wrongly understood, which wants to reduce revelation and mystery to the level of what the child knows already (which is very little) instead of trying to raise the child up to higher things.
Ideology is to be kept out of catechetics. If the teacher is a feminist she must not use the religion class to push her claim that the Church supposedly discriminates against women on the grounds that they cannot be ordained as priests. Or if the teacher is a Darwinian he cannot use his ideas about evolution to push the idea that the Bible account of creation is a fairy tale.

Method in Catechetics

What is the starting point of catechetics? A catechetics program can begin with the life experiences of the pupils and then present the pupils with the truths of revelation as that which gives meaning to their lives in this world and gives them the hope of eternal life in the next. To take that approach is to have catechetics be "child-centred" in the true and proper meaning of that term. That is simply to apply the old rule of first knowing Johnny if one is to teach him Latin later. Or, conversely, one can begin with revelation, explain it, and then show how it provides answers to deepest questions and longings of the human soul. But in taking this approach one must *not* then reduce or tailor the contents of the faith to what the children have experienced already in their own homes and environments, because that suggests that our faith is nothing beyond the natural which is verging on the heresy of modernism and makes for a false understanding of the term "child-centered". Hence, as to method, Pope John Paul says:

> It is also quite useless to campaign for the abandonment of serious and orderly study of the message of Christ in the name of a method concentrating on life experience. "No one can arrive at the whole truth on the basis solely of some simple private experience, that is to say, without an adequate explanation of the message of Christ, who is `the way, and the truth, and the life' *Jn. 14:6. Ibid., #22.*

This needs a little further explanation.

The principal object of the study of the faith, of theology, is not man but God and all other things then - the world, man, history or whatever - as related to God. It is what God has revealed about Himself to man and what man then can know about himself and his world as seen in the light of that revelation. To say that it is "man-centred" or "child-centred" in the sense that it is a *product* of human consciousness or experience and that it arises from man's feelings of dependence on God (Schleiermacher) is false. From this it would follow that religion can never be about the Christian mysteries because human knowing cannot arrive at the great mysteries, such as the Trinity, the incarnation, the redemption and others, by itself. If that were the case, then, revelation would be unnecessary to begin with or, if accepted at all, would be so tapered down as to fit what human experience can arrive at or be comfortable with, given the time, place and circumstances of the hearers, so that doctrine would be forever changing, former doctrines being discarded to be replaced by new ones as history moves on and brings us new experiences in new circumstances. Again, this is modernism.

Yet I have found that sometimes the mysteries of the faith are presented to pupils in a curtailed or over simplified fashion since the council, which smacks of modernism. Once when I was asking children in school some questions about Christ Himself I was being told that he was a "nice guy", a "pal", a "buddy", going around with his twelve friends and having a meal with them at the end. This would fit with *their* experience of friendship and going to parties. When I tried to make the point that He was also God, the teacher intruded and said "No, we don't talk about that at this stage. They will hear about that later on". So, they were to be fed on Arianism for their first few years at school: a Christ who was human but not divine because that seemed to fit better with their experiences!

When talking to children in another school during Holy Week about the sufferings of Christ in His passion the teacher interjected and said "No, we don't talk about such things at all because they are a bit too 'gory', it might 'put them off'"!! It didn't fit with the nice, comfortable, middle-class backgrounds of those children. If then they were not to be taught about what happened on Calvary how could they learn about the Mass as that which makes the sacrifice of Calvary present again; and if they didn't know about this relation of Calvary to the Mass, our central act of worship, is it any surprise that most of those children stopped going to Mass as soon as they left school!

Human consciousness or experience might be said to be the starting point of faith in the sense that a person begins his journey by asking questions about God: whether or not He exists at all or what attributes He might have, and we know that such an inquirer can indeed arrive at some amount of true knowledge of God. The pagan philosophers made some – though limited – progress taking this approach. Still, this does not allow us to say that faith is merely a product of human experience or of philosophical inquiry. But the philosophers could not know what God is in Himself in His inner life or His plan for salvation by their own unaided reason. This knowledge comes to us from God Himself by revelation. Proving first that He exists or discovering that the Church is His credible voice in the world is what is called the "*preambula* of faith", a clearing of the ground by reason, as it were, so that we can trustfully open ourselves to God and what He has revealed when we encounter Him in His Church's teaching and assent to it. When we do assent to this revelation by faith we can then proceed to delve ever deeper into the mysteries it contains by using our reason, though never exhausting them. In this sense there will always be development of doctrine, that is, growth in our understanding of the same eternal truths. But this growth or development is entirely different from the ever changing coming and going of doctrines which is modernism. The former is an expanding on what has been revealed and is constant; the latter is a rolling wave of endless novelty arising from human experience, with doctrine amounting to nothing more than formulas which give expression to that experience, which experience, to begin with, is merely the product of history and ever-changing circumstances and the feelings they arouse.

So, as regards method in catechetics, as said already, the teacher can begin from above with an explanation of the revealed truths of the faith and show how they give meaning to the lives of the pupils here below and answer their deepest longings, or she can begin with these latter questions and show how the true answers are to be found in what God has revealed, with those truths being presented in full and never tapered or diluted. So, St. John Paul says:

> Nor is any opposition to be set up between a catechesis taking life as its point of departure and a traditional doctrinal and systematic catechesis. Authentic catechesis is always an orderly and systematic initiation into the revelation that God has given of Himself to humanity in Christ Jesus, a revelation stored in the depths of the Church's memory and in Sacred Scripture, and constantly communicated from one generation to the next by a living, active *traditio*. This revelation is not however isolated from life or artificially juxtaposed to it. It is concerned with the ultimate meaning of life and it illumines the whole of life with the light of the Gospel, to inspire it or to question it" *CT.*, #22. (*cf.* also *General Directory for Catechesis, #151).*

Chesterton used to talk about the faith as being like a key and human life as being like a lock. Good catechetics presents the pupils with the key that opens the lock even if the key still remains a mystery and so also the lock.

Memorization in Catechesis

Another point in regard to method in catechesis is the importance of memorization: making use of the *tabula rasa* of the young mind while memory is fresh and receptive. Our religion itself is very much a thing of memory – *do this in memory of me*. In the Mass we remember and make present the great events of our salvation. The vigil of Holy Saturday night, with its many readings, makes this point very forcefully, beginning as they do with the account of creation and coming up along to Christ. When she teaches, the universal Church, like the wise scribe, brings out of her store house of memory "things new and old". So also in the classroom, when teaching young pupils, memorization is very important in the double sense of bringing to the minds of the pupils the great events recorded in scripture and the doctrines defined by the

Church in her two thousand year history and then having the pupils commit to memory short summaries of those things. Pope John Paul says:

> At a time when, in non–religious teaching in certain countries, more and more complaints are being made about the unfortunate consequences of disregarding the human faculty of memory, should we not attempt to put this faculty back into use in an intelligent and even an original way in catechesis, all the more since the celebration or "memorial" of the great events of the history of salvation require a precise knowledge of them? A certain memorization of the words of Jesus, of important Bible passages, of the Ten Commandments, of the formulas of profession of the faith, of the liturgical texts, of the essential prayers, of key doctrinal ideas, etc., far from being opposed to the dignity of young Christians, or constituting an obstacle to personal dialogue with the Lord, is a real need, as the synod fathers forcefully recalled. We must be realists. The blossoms, if we may call them that, of faith and piety do not grow in the desert places of a memory–less catechesis. What is essential is that the texts that are memorized must at the same time be taken in and gradually understood in depth, in order to become a source of Christian life on the personal level and the community level. *ibid.,* #55.

One can see here that, again, the pope is responding to the many complaints coming into him about the discarding of memorization in catechetics which became part of the agenda of the new catechetics after the council. The pupils, supposedly, were being overburdened with big words and long answers. But, as said already, the maths teacher continued to insist on the pupils learning their tables and difficult mathematical formulas, the language teacher continued to insist on they learning how to spell some big words, the geography teacher continued to have them learn the names of the rivers of China, and the science teacher continued to have them learn off the chemical formulas of the different substances, and all this memorization in these other subjects didn't seem to cause any problems!

It should be "remembered" also that much of ancient culture, often of a highly developed kind, was passed on from generation to generation mostly by memorization. It had to be so in times when most people were illiterate but still intellectually capable and well formed. Down as far as my parents' time there were people who could "reel off" even hundreds of lines of poetry or drama which they had learned in their youth. I often remember coming home from school and telling my father about a new poem that we had to learn. He would say: "Give me the first two lines of it" and then he would continue to recite the next twenty lines at his ease. Of course, today we can store ten times more knowledge in our laptops or even on a pin drive the size of a cent, but if all that knowledge merely stays on the pin drive and is not assimilated, even in small amounts, in the mind, it is of little value.

The value of memorization was brought home to me most forcefully one time that I was bringing the sacraments to two old men, two brothers, one of whom had been badly disabled by a stroke, so much so that he could not talk at all and seemed confused also. I wanted to give him the sacrament of penance but the healthy man told me it was no use. Nonetheless, I asked the man with the stroke if he wanted confession and he nodded affirmatively. Of course, he could not tell his sins; but then, from habit, I asked him to say his act of contrition, forgetting that I was asking what would be the impossible in his case. To my surprise he recited it perfectly, despite the brain damage resulting from his stroke. He had learned that prayer as a child, when memory was fresh and it was still there, well bedded into the "disc" of his memory so that he could still recall it, word for word, despite the damage to his brain cells.

In the difficulties of life we need to be able to call on the Lord, Our Lady, the angels and the saints, and in old age, when powers of concentration and learning are gone and death is drawing near, what has anyone to hold on to then except the prayers they learned when they were young? How wrong then to send young people out into the broad field of life without such fortifications stored in memory. Yet that is how many Catholics live and die today.

Pedagogy and Inculturation of the Faith

A final point in relation to method is what the pope calls the "pedagogy of faith". In simpler language it is called the "need to know" principle - that one does not throw the full content of the faith at the pupils all at once but that one brings them along by the hand from the known to the unknown, from the visible to the invisible that is already revealed but which needs to be elucidated by means of the visible. It is the method of God Himself when teaching His people from Abraham to Christ and afterwards when His Holy Spirit was guiding the Church in the development of her doctrine. I am arguing that it should be our method too in unfolding the mystery of Christ to people today. Here we will quote from the *General Directory of Catechetics*:

> [This is] the *integral* presentation of the Gospel message, without ignoring certain fundamental elements, or without operating a selectivity with regard to the deposit of faith. Catechesis, on the contrary, "must take diligent care faithfully to present the entire treasure of the Christian message". This is accomplished, gradually, by following the example of the divine pedagogy with

<u>which God revealed himself progressively and gradually.</u> Integrity must also be accompanied by adaptation. Consequently, catechesis starts out with a simple proposition of the integral structure of the Christian message, and proceeds to explain it in a manner adapted to the capacity of those being catechized. Without restricting itself to this initial exposition, it gradually and increasingly proposes the Christian message more amply and with greater explicitness, in accordance with the capacity of those being catechized and with the proper character of catechesis. *#112.*

One could also call this the development of knowledge of doctrine according as God has revealed it and as the hearers are able to take it in. However, this emphatically does *not* mean that we give the pupils only part of a particular doctrine first and the other part later, for example, that in teaching them about the mystery of God we speak only of His unity and make no mention of Him being a Trinity or that when speaking of Christ we talk only about His humanity apart from His divinity, leaving that to later (if ever), as we saw happen earlier. Again, later, in the study of comparative religions in higher classes, Christ is not to be reduced merely to being another holy man or wise guru or founder of religion like Confucius, Mohammed or Buddha. He is also God.

> ...care should be taken not to reduce Christ to His humanity alone or His message to a no more than earthly dimension, but that He should be recognized as the Son of God, the Mediator giving us in the Spirit free access to the Father. *Catechesi Tradendae., #29.*

We must give the pupils the "entirety" of the faith as said in the quote above but obviously not be throwing the full content of the *Catechism of the Catholic Church* at toddlers on their first day at school. We begin the first day by teaching them about the one God in three persons, the Trinity, and we do so simply by taking the child's right hand and getting him/her to bless himself in the name of the Father, Son and Holy Spirit. So also, we tell them that Jesus was "Holy God" from day one, that is, both God and man, that He died and rose again to make up for sin even though a life-time of study will not exhaust the full content of such mysteries.

<u>The Faith in new Clothing</u>

Another aspect of pedagogy is the recognition that our faith, though it is something revealed from above, was nonetheless "clothed" in the cultural *humus* of Judaism first, that then it was clothed in Western garb and that now it is being clothed in the cultures of Africa and the East, that it purifies, enriches and elevates all of these cultures while they, in turn, give it new modes of expression.

> ... to recognize a cultural dimension in the Gospel itself, while affirming, on the one hand, that this does not spring from some human cultural *humus,* and recognizing, on the other, that the Gospel cannot be isolated from the cultures in which it was initially inserted and in which it has found expression through the centuries. *Gen. Dir. Cat.,* #203

Revelation, coming from above, is "clothed" in different cultures: it is not the *product* of any culture, which again would be modernism. As to this clothing in different cultures, the important thing here is that one does not try to bypass or jump over any stage of this clothing, this development, in a rush to a later one, or try to go back simplistically to a former one. Thus, to try to erase the medieval period of the faith and try to get to a new faith suitable for today by trying to return simplistically to apostolic times is not right, even though what happened in apostolic times will be normative for all times. Or to try to erase the Greek or Latin stage of the faith for a new African stage is not right. The new African stage will be rich and diverse and beautiful only if it takes up and transforms those earlier stages - all as directed by the *magisterium*. All of that history of inculturation of the faith is also a seamless robe woven from the time of Christ to the present.

The end result to be hoped for is that the pupils in a given place today will make of their environment a new *humus*, in which to cloth the traditional faith with new art forms, customs and other expressions. Thus, African children will depict the Holy Family as being black in skin and Asian children will depict them with yellow skin and the features of those people.

Some funny things can emerge when children pick things up wrongly in all innocence and try to give them expression in their own *humus*. For example, there is the story of the young lad from the inner city who never saw a cow in his life and did not know what a *calf* might be. When asked by a visiting priest to write out the story of the prodigal son in his own words he said that the father was delighted and told the servants to kill the fatted *duck*!!! He knew from TV what a duck was but not a calf so, being of practical mind and limited experience, he concluded that it was surely a duck which the father must have killed for the celebration. Then there was the other young lad who was asked to write out the story of Mary Magdalene and called her Mary Mag Dillon!!

But regardless of these innocent mistakes one would hope that the faith expressed by these children will be that which has had a rich history because it has been richly clothed in Catholic tradition, in the *humus* of different philosophies and cultures down through the entire two thousand years of the history of the Church. The teacher will draw on this history in order to better explain the perennial mysteries to the children so that they can make their own of them. They love when the teacher/scribe draws out these things new and old, especially by means of stories from the scriptures and the lives of the saints. They will take all this to head and to heart and make it their own.

Conclusions:

1. Catechetics is a part of the overall development of faith and good living in the Christian. While not being a detailed theological study it must nonetheless be full and integral in its content, recognizing the hierarchy of truths centred on the Trinity, the incarnation and redemption.
2. Dogmas and moral principles must be presented in formulas that are clear and accurate and suitable for memorization by young minds. These truths should also be conveyed with stories from the Bible and from the lives of the saints so that both head and heart are catered for.
3. In its method, catechetics must recognize that religious truth is revealed from above by a divine pedagogy over a long period of time which culminated in Christ. Accordingly, it is not a mere product of human experience, but it must strive to relate that truth meaningfully to human experience, taking account of the varying cultural backgrounds of the pupils so that those backgrounds will then become a new *humus* for the perennial faith.

Teaching catechetics includes instruction on the sacrament of marriage and the sixth commandment which in turn requires instruction in chaste living. This will be our concern in the next chapter.

Chapter XV

Education for Chastity

Changed Context; Content and Method, Chastity explained, the Priest and the School

Your bodies, you know, are temples of the Holy Spirit who is in you since you received Him from God. 1 Cor.6:19.

Chastity is the joyous affirmation of someone who knows how to live self-giving, free from any form of self-centred slavery. *Truth and Meaning of Human Sexuality, (TMHS), #17.*

We have been studying the school and catechetics within the school in the previous two chapters. Within catechetics we saw that according to the *Catechism of the Catholic Church* the four pillars or general fields of subject matter are faith, liturgy, morals and prayer. Here I want to focus on the field of morals, more particularly on what might be called "education for chaste living" or "Christian love" or what is more commonly called "Relationship and Sexuality Education", (RSE) in secular language. It relates to the other areas of catechetics because marriage is a sacrament, a symbol of Christ's love for His Church, and, as such, is celebrated in the liturgy which, in turn, takes us back to faith and doctrine, particularly the doctrine of the incarnation. Education for chastity, or RSE, also brings up again the question of the right relationship of the home and the school in this area of education.

Changed Context of Education for Chastity

In times past not much attention was given to Education for Chastity (RSE) in many Catholic communities, sometimes out of a certain reluctance on the part of some parents to talk about the origins of human life with their children. This was not entirely a negative attitude but due mostly to a sense of modesty in the face of a topic which is sacred and sensitive. In societies where this modesty prevailed, young people did eventually learn of the mysteries of human life in ways that were moral and Christian from various good people around them and also because negative sources of information on such matters such as the television, as we have it today, and the internet were not there to mislead them.

That scene has changed. That modesty is largely gone, and instead of what should be called "education for chastity" " or "education in the mysteries of human life" what is presented instead might well be called "crude sex", immoral and often pornographic, and is easily had online. In light of that, it is necessary for priests, parents and teachers to deal with this matter in a direct, positive and Christian way because it is a problematic area today and often one of controversy when the state tries to impose programs in schools which are not in accord with Catholic teaching. The Church has given us clear principles on this. I will be quoting below mostly from the Vatican documents *Educational Guidance in Human Love* and *The Truth and Meaning of Human Sexuality*.[1]

In the Home or the School

In the years immediately after the council the Church took the line, quite rightly, that sex education is entirely a matter for parents in the home on a one-to-one basis with their own children, fathers talking to their sons and mothers to their daughters:

> Parents in particular have the duty to let their children know about the *mysteries of human life,* because the family 'is, in fact, the best environment to accomplish the obligation of securing a gradual education in sexual life. The family has an affective dignity which is suited to making acceptable without trauma the most delicate realities and to integrating them harmoniously in a balanced and rich personality. *Educational Guidance in Human Love, #48.*

The reason for this is simply that the parents know their own children the best and can best judge what is suitable for each of them and at what precise time:

> Each child is a unique and unrepeatable person and must receive individualized formation. Since parents know, understand and love each of their children in their uniqueness, they are in the best position to decide what the appropriate time is for providing a variety of information, according to their children's physical and spiritual growth. No one can take this capacity for discernment away from conscientious parents. *Truth and Meaning of Human Sexuality, #65.*

But, before imparting any knowledge formally to their children, the first prerequisite of good sex education in the home is that the parents themselves are living out their own marriages in accordance with the Church's teaching, that they love each other in

Chapter 15: Education for Chastity

a generous, self-giving way and that they observe the Church's teaching on family planning. The children will see their parents loving each other in this self-giving, self-sacrificing way and it will make deep impressions on them; and even before they come to learn anything about family planning they will be benefiting from the kind of generous, self-disciplined love that it entails. Hence the document says:

> Parental respect for life and the mystery of procreation will spare the child or young person from the false idea <u>that the two dimensions of the conjugal act, unitive and procreative, can be separated at will.</u> Thus the family comes to be recognized as an inseparable part of the vocation to marriage. *TMHS., #32*

As a principle, it still holds true that the parents are the primary and proper persons to instruct their own children on this matter. However, this presupposes that both parents are there in the home and are able and willing to discharge this delicate duty. This is the ideal and should be given priority. But it soon became clear in the succeeding years, when there was a lot of social upheaval due to the sexual revolution of the 60s, that this was not always the case. So, the Church began to allow a role to the school in this regard but always in co-operation with the parents so that they have the first and final say in what is presented in the school.

> As we have recalled, this primary task of the family includes the parents' right that their children should not be obliged to attend courses in school on this subject which are not in harmony with their religious and moral convictions. The school's task is not to substitute for the family, rather it is 'assisting and completing the work of parents, furnishing children and adolescents with an evaluation of sexuality as value and task of the whole person, created male and female in the image of God'. *Educational Guidance in Human Love, #48.*

So, the parents are still to be seen as the primary educators in this matter of sex education and the school as helping them to fulfil their duties. This means that the traditional principle of subsidiarity is being brought into play here;

> Sex education, which is a basic right and duty of parents, must always be carried out under their attentive guidance, whether at home or in educational centres chosen and controlled by them. In this regard, the <u>Church reaffirms the law of subsidiarity</u>, which the school is bound to observe when it cooperates in sex education, by entering into the same spirit that animates the parents. *Familiaris Consortio, #37, (quoted also in TMHS., #43).*

Parents should be informed in advance if the school will be giving instruction on sex education and should be made fully aware of the content of what will be presented. Parents should be able to meet with the presenters of the instruction.

> Parents who are not always prepared to face up to the problematic side of education for love can take part in meetings with their children, guided by expert persons who are worthy of trust, for example, doctors, priests, educators. In some cases, in the interest of greater freedom of expression, meetings where only daughters or sons are present seem preferable. *TMHS., #131.*

Parents should also be allowed to sit in on such classes and perhaps dialogue with the presenters during it, if such is feasible. Boys and girls should get separate instruction from the teachers of the school or from outsiders who may be invited in who are good practicing Catholics with expertise in such matters.

Content and Method of RSE

Christian Content, different Methods

A good program of sex education should, for its content, present the mystery of human life in the context of God's creation of our first parents and the commands He gave them to remain in an indissoluble union and to increase and multiply. *(cf. Gen. 1:27-28)*. Such a program should also be presented in the context of the sacrament of marriage because the act of intercourse, in Catholic teaching, is exclusively for a man and woman who are validly married to each other, which marriage is also a sacrament in the case of two Christians. Again, it should be presented in the context of the sixth commandment which tells us what is commanded and forbidden in love relations so that we can live chaste lives. More precisely, as to what a program might or might not contain and at to what age group it should be given, the document on the *Truth and Meaning of Human Sexuality* gives the following guideline:

> Before adolescence, the immoral nature of *abortion,* surgical or chemical, can be gradually explained in terms of Catholic morality and reverence for human life. As regards *sterilization and contraception,* these should not be discussed before adolescence and only in conformity with the teaching of the Catholic Church. *#137.*

As to method, there can be different approaches. In one school of which I was a board chairman, we had the practice of having a Catholic nurse or doctor of sound morals visit on a particular day and give instruction on the more physical aspects of reproduction – boys and girls taken separately - and then the priest would come the next day and follow up with the more religious and moral aspects and answer any questions the pupils might still have. The parents would be fully informed of this and welcomed to sit in on the class if they so choose.

In another school I prepared material in the form of a short, simple, easy to read booklet on the mystery of human life which a ten or twelve-year old could read, or which parents even of very low levels literacy could also read. I would give it to the parents at a meeting at the start of school year to take home and read. They could then discuss its contents with their children, or, if they felt uncomfortable about doing that, they could simply hand it to the children or (individual child) and let them read it for themselves. Then I would ask for the return of the booklet by a certain date - perhaps early December - accompanied by a note informing me if they had shared it with their children. When I knew that they had done so I knew then that I could speak more freely to the children about such matters in class or on such matters as the Immaculate Conception of Mary (which feast day would be coming shortly on the 8th of December). Some parents would report back to me and say that the booklet was very suitable, others that it was too much for their particular child at his/her present age or that it was suitable for one of their children but not for the other. I would then take account of such findings when talking in class later about the matters involved.

Whichever method is used, the guiding principle is that the content be Catholic, the parents be well informed and that their rights as the primary educators be respected:

> In the case where parents are helped by others in educating their own children for love, it is recommended that <u>they keep themselves precisely informed on the content and methodology with which such supplementary education is imparted.</u> No one can bind children or young people to secrecy about the content and method of instruction provided outside the family. *ibid., #115.*

Bad Programs

If there are good programs there can also be bad programs of sex education, and it is important to be clear on the difference because controversy in this whole area arises due to the government in some countries trying to impose programs which are contrary to Catholic morals. Let there be no mistake about it: these government programs are backed by large, multi-national abortion companies whose goal is money derived from the sale of contraceptives and from the killing of babies. The programs are readily taken on by government education departments which have uncritically swallowed the ideology of secularism, peddled to them by the media, and have the idyllic vision of a society of unrestrained freedom which takes no account of the moral law. Although the big companies that promote bad programs, to promote contraception and abortion, are capitalist, it is left wing governments that mostly promote this anti-life agenda. Some governments will even use their peoples' taxes to fund abortion, even if they know that many of those taxpayers are pro-life. Moreover, the abortion companies have plenty resources to promote their deathly programs and even to give governments back-hands for pushing them in schools. Such companies, and the governments which go along with them, will use fake scares such as that of over-population or the danger of venereal diseases to promote their wares, or they will make fake promises such as that the number of unwanted pregnancies will be reduced and that women will have greater freedom over their own bodies when this liberal kind of ideology is adopted; and thus the fears of parents and the false hopes of young people are played on so that they will succumb. But the Church says:

> ...parents must reject <u>secularized and anti-natalist sex education</u>, which puts God at the margin of life and regards the birth of a child as a threat. This sex education is spread by large organizations and international associations that promote abortion, sterilization and contraception. These organizations want to impose a false lifestyle against the truth of human sexuality. Working at national or state levels, these organizations try to arouse the fear of the 'threat of over-population' among children and young people to promote the contraceptive mentality, that is, the 'anti-life' mentality. They spread false ideas about the 'reproductive health' and 'sexual and reproductive rights' of young people. Furthermore, some anti-natalist organizations maintain those clinics which, violating the rights of parents, provide abortion and contraception for young people, thus promoting promiscuity and consequently an increase in teenage pregnancies. *Ibid., #136.*

<u>Tactics</u>

The *Truth and Meaning of Human Sexuality* document goes on to explain some of the tactics used in these programs:

> One widely-used, but possibly harmful, approach goes by the name of 'values clarification'. Young people are encouraged to reflect upon, to clarify and to decide upon moral issues with the greatest degree of 'autonomy', <u>ignoring the objective reality of the moral law in general</u> and disregarding the formation of consciences on the specific Christian moral precepts, as affirmed by the *Magisterium* of the Church. Young people are given the idea that a moral code is something which they create themselves, as if man were the source and norm of morality..., #140.

The trick here – I deliberately use the word "trick" because we are dealing with deceit – is to win consensus in a discussion by pupils in class for positions on social issues which are clearly immoral, as if moral principles depended on majority opinion for their validity. So, the pupils are given the example of a seemingly difficult but utterly far-fetched social problem such as that of a lifeboat at sea with ten survivors on board but having only a limited supply of drinking water. The survivors are various individuals such as a brilliant engineer but who is now in his nineties, or a strong young man but he is arrogant, or a young mother but she has terminal cancer, and others with varying positive or negative credentials. Since the water is likely to run out long before the boat makes land, the question is posed as to which one of these people it would be best to throw over board so as to save the others. The unexamined presumption is, of course, that *there is nothing wrong* with throwing someone over board when a seemingly good end is proposed. The only question is: who? The discussion proceeds and really it does not matter who the class decide to throw overboard; the point has been sold that it is right in some cases to directly kill an innocent person. So, the notions of objective morality and intrinsic evil are subtly undermined and the notion of direct, intentional killing is installed.

The next discussion then will show how this kind of reasoning is applied to a hard case scenario of a sixteen-year-old girl who comes home and tells her Mom that she has *discovered* that she is pregnant (seemingly she doesn't know how that might have happened!!!). But Dad has a bad heart and might get another heart attack and die if he hears this but the family still need him because there are other, younger children in the family to be provided for. So, the class must decide which would be better – more compassionate !!– a quick, early abortion or putting Dad's life at risk. Put in those terms most of class will vote for the abortion. One or two pupils from good Catholic homes will hold out and say "no, that is wrong". But they will be marginalized and branded as conservatives and as being against "progress". A morality of relativism or situationism based again on consensus has won the day in that class room, - the ground having been prepared already by the life-boat story - and abortion in certain hard cases is deemed acceptable. The next step, abortion on demand, will come soon inevitably.

But these anti-life forces need to promote promiscuity first, which is achieved by promoting contraception of all kinds, especially the use of condoms by teenagers. The lie used here is that of so called "safe sex", that by using condoms venereal diseases and unwanted pregnancies will be avoided. It is about as silly as suggesting that two ten-year olds can be given a box of "safety matches" and told that they can go and play in the hay barn or at a petrol station with no fear of fire. Statistics in abundance show that condoms lead to promiscuous behaviour with unwanted pregnancies resulting, and then, of course, abortions follow as the fall-back solution. Yet this lie has been sold all across the world. But the Church teaches:

> ... parents must also reject the promotion of so-called "safe sex" or "safer sex", a dangerous and immoral policy based on the deluded theory that the condom can provide adequate protection against AIDS. Parents must insist on continence outside marriage and fidelity in marriage as the only true and secure education for the prevention of this contagious disease. *Ibid., #139.*

Erotic material and erotic actions are used to further this drive towards promiscuity, supposedly to better explain the marriage act. Sometimes the *double* trick is used of showing the pupils some pornography under the pretext of teaching them to *avoid* pornography but with the end result of encouraging them to seek more pornography themselves after class. But the Church warns again:

> No material of an erotic nature should be presented to children or young people of any age, individually or in a group. *Ibid., #126.*

Of course, young people should be warned against pornography but done by simple instruction in the immorality of debasing the human body which is created good and a temple of the Holy Spirit because of baptism. So also simple, non-erotic diagrams can be used to explain the functions of the organs of the body. Once, on a national TV station, I saw a *mixed* class of second level students being instructed on how to put on condoms, using wooden models for the male organ. It caused no protest at all! But again the Church teaches:

> No one should ever be invited, let alone obliged, to act in any way that could objectively offend against modesty or which could subjectively offend against his or her own delicacy or sense of privacy. *Ibid., #127.*

Chapter 15: Education for Chastity

The aim here is to get the youngsters to be sexually desensitized in class under the pretext of being "educated" in life matters so that they will become sexually active outside of school.

A Morality of Feelings

A another very subtle trick in this drive to promote promiscuity was the introduction of "so called" child abuse prevention programs whose basic message to the pupils was that whatever gives you a "yes" feeling is good and whatever gives you a "no" feeling is bad. If a stranger or anybody gives you a "no" feeling then run away from him and tell your parents or your teacher. Such a person is likely to be a molester. But such instruction is utterly subjective and irrational. It does not begin with explaining what is objectively wrong with molestation and why it should then, rightly, give one a bad feeling because to give such an explanation would entail instruction in right morals, in the sixth commandment in particular. But that would not be consistent with the new secularist morality which says that all kinds of sexual behaviour, even what was traditionally considered unnatural and downright perverted, are fine so long as the two participants are consenting and enjoying it. This implies that molestation would be right also if the child were a few years older and could give consent or would get a "yes" feeling from cooperating. Furthermore, the molester, having learned that this is the way children are being instructed, can resort to the trick of convincing the child that all the other children around find this behaviour enjoyable because they all say that it gives them a "yes" feeling.

And outside of the area of sexuality, let us take other areas of behaviour: two young lads get hold of a bottle of vodka at home while mother is out and begin drinking it and find that it gives them a hilarious "yes" feeling. Does that mean, then, that doing this is "right" and that they should finish the bottle between them! Or if a little lad is watching a great cowboy film on TV and his Dad tells him to turn it off and do his lessons, will he not say "Dad, you are giving me a 'no' feeling and the teacher in school told us that we should report any such person?" What then becomes of discipline in the home with this kind of training at school? What protection will such children have against drug peddlers if the latter can tell them of the great, "high" feeling the drug will give them?

The fundamental point over looked in all of this is that morality, right and wrong, is not based on feelings, which are purely subjective, but on the moral law which is objective because based on nature, the nature of the human being as that is designed by God and known by reason. And if people have difficulty reading this law as they find it in nature around them, then God Himself comes to their aid with His ten commandments which explicates the natural law, and if this were not enough the Church then explicates, even more clearly, on what is commanded and forbidden by each of the commandments in her teaching.

Because the moral law is from God and written in nature it is objective: certain actions are morally right and others morally wrong no matter how many in the class say otherwise or what feelings are experienced. Accordingly, one way of describing moral formation is to say that it tries to ensure that it is reason and will, man's two highest powers, which will be in command in the human person, and not his/her feelings; that feelings and desires have to be brought into submission under reason and will in accordance with the objective moral law. A morally upright person, then, is not someone who is devoid of all desires, feelings or emotions but one whose emotions are in harmony with the dictates of right reason because this, in turn, is in harmony with the moral law. Hence, such a person will have feelings of peace and wellbeing precisely when he/she is doing what is objectively right. A child will feel bad about doing anything impure with anyone else, younger or older, because he/she has been instructed in the sixth commandment and sees its reasonableness. He will feel good about being pure and chaste even if that calls for will-power and self-denial at times.

So also with the young person's observance of the other commandments: as he/she grows up he will feel good about paying his debts, for example, because he knows that doing so is in accord with what is objectively morally good. He will feel bad if, on coming out of the shop, he has got more change than is right and will go back in and gladly return the excess money. The dishonest youngster, by comparison, one who has no training in the seventh commandment, will have a great "yes" feeling whenever he succeeds in cheating the shopkeeper. The respective feelings follow on moral formation based on objective moral principles. But to start with feelings and make *them* the guide to morality is to turn moral formation upside down. It is to set young people on the downward spiral to hedonism and sheer selfishness.

Yet many parents, genuinely concerned for the safety of their children, fell for these seductive kinds of so-called child prevention programs which are based solely on feelings because the media were blasting their supposed merits at them day and night and because so many clergy said nothing, or even fell for them themselves also in some cases, despite years of training in moral theology in their student days.

I was once asked by some concerned parents to come and give a talk on this matter. Apart from those few concerned parents who invited me, most of the others, mostly Catholics, were arguing for these kinds of programs for the simple reason that the government and the media were advocating them – so they must then be good! About half an hour into the discussion a Protestant lady came in who introduced herself as the head principal of a nearby Protestant primary school. She listened only for about twenty minutes and then got up and said: "Thank you Father. You have made it so clear and simple", and went out. Meanwhile so many others of the remaining Catholic parents and teachers kept on arguing that these programs must be good if the government and the TV say so. I thought of Abraham Lincoln and what he once said about fooling some of the people all of the time. It seems an easy thing to do in some places at any rate.

Prone to Manipulation

Programs that base morality on feelings, on the subjective, have their effects in later life, when the pupils who were at the receiving end of these programs become the next generation of adults. Such adults are easily manipulated by totalitarian governments who will know how to play and prey on their feelings, and they will also have to contend with their own children rebelling against themselves.

One way of doing that kind of manipulation, is to create some kind of scare – play on their feeling of fear – by using false propaganda. As we saw above already, one can persuade parents that their children will be vulnerable in some way or other if they are not subjected to these false programs. The myth of over-population is another such scare, with more condoms and abortion proposed as the solution despite the blatant fact that the Western world has now gone below the birth-replacement rate with the many problems that that, in turn, poses for everyone in society. It even points to the eventual extinction of the human race. Another way to manipulate people is to work on their feelings of fear and sympathy by presenting some "heart-wrenching, sob-sob" cases: the young boy who will commit suicide if he is not allowed a sex change; the old man in great pain crying out to be euthanized. Then, using the mega phone of the media, get legislators or the people themselves to vote for measures that are blatantly at variance with the moral law.

Akin to these tactics is another one of using terms such as "inclusiveness", "equality", "compassion" and "non-discrimination" to justify things morally wrong. These terms do have a basis in Christianity but they have come to be distorted in their meaning and used to promote things *contrary* to Christianity, things immoral such as same-sex marriage, transgenderism and euthanasia. Everyone will agree that bullying in school is wrong and parents are genuinely anxious that their children would not be bullied. So, the trick this time is to introduce a program supposedly to combat all bullying which includes bullying of students who might claim to be "gay" – and I for one would not want to see such students bullied no more than any others - but the ulterior aim, indirectly advanced, is to win acceptance for so-called "gay" behaviour and then for so-called "gay" marriage. Traditional marriage and immoral marriage, good and evil, are put on a par as being equal, alternative life styles, and a person is labelled as "discriminatory and lacking in compassion" and even as "inciting to hatred" if he/she takes a stand against such things. Once again, objectivity is cast aside and feelings are made to rule, and, so often, the parents are deceived and unable to see the ulterior aim here. Students of such inclinations should not be bullied but gently corrected by being given objective, moral teaching, suitably explained, and by being helped onto the path of normal, emotional development.

The final step in undermining the morals of young people is to try to say that the moral law should not be the basis of legislation at all, because morality has now been reduced to feelings, to mutual consent and to the enjoyment of maximum freedom for each and every individual, which takes us down the road of mere subjectivism, relativism and anarchy because my freedom and desires are soon going to bring me into conflict with your freedom and your desires. Catholicism, in this scenario, is presented as a religion of gloom because of its moral code, by which is meant that its many supposedly burdensome prohibitions prevent me from enjoying myself. Hence the best way to universal happiness is to get rid of that religion. That comes near to Voltaire's way of thinking again, a man who continued to believe in God but was soon followed by many socialists and nihilists who took the ultimate step of atheism. Lenin, a rabid atheist, the first leader of communist Russia, once said that debauched people who are led by their feelings are the most useful in the cause of the revolution. They can be easily manipulated and thus persuaded to do just about anything they are told and even to die at the barricades for that cause. A people thus deceived are "sitting ducks" for a totalitarian leader. And such was Stalin – Lenin's successor – who made of Russia a totalitarian prison camp for the most of the remainder of the twentieth century.

As to the question of whether or not we would be happier without the ten commandments the answer I would give is: yes, indeed we would, but it would be the happiness of the animals, of the pig, of the debauched human being. Indeed, it would be a happiness that goes even lower than that of the animals because they, at least, follow their God-given instincts and observe times and seasons for mating.

Perhaps in this undermining of morals we should give the last word to another Russian, to Dostoyevsky, who foresaw the coming of communism and who put is so well when he said that when God is gone everything is permitted.

<u>Taking a Stand</u>

The Catholic school board, with its limited power and resources, and faithful Catholic parents, have to try to stand against this onslaught. What makes their stand even

Chapter 15: Education for Chastity

more difficult is that some parents, even supposedly Catholic parents, are deluded by media propaganda into thinking that such programs are good simply because they are now the "in thing". It is made very difficult in some countries like Germany where governments impose such programs on schools even if they are under Catholic management. In some other countries the priest, if he is the school-board chairman or a member of the board or a chaplain to the school, can play an important role in informing the parents and teachers about the dangers of such programs so that the parents can exercise their rights as the primary educators of their children and block them. The priest, in turn, needs to act in unison with his fellow priests in giving this support to parents, and all priests, in unison, need the backing of their bishop. When that uniformity is not there it is easy to see how the individual priest who might want to take a stand can easily be browbeaten into silence.

In any case, it is most painful for those Catholic parents who can see through the evil of these programs and the harm they will do to their children's morals when they are left so isolated and helpless in combating them. They are martyrs of an unbloody kind today. It is not surprising that some of them take to home schooling in desperation, (that is, if the government of their country will allow such a thing), even though it is a difficult thing to organize.

Chastity: Negative and Positive Ideas

<u>Negative Idea</u>

Discussions, such as those above, lead us to a consideration of a more fundamental kind on what chastity or purity rightly entails. Too often in the past chastity amounted to a negative understanding of the body and then of sex as being bad or dirty and therefore to be avoided as much as possible or allowed only in as much as the continuation of the species required it. It led at times to some extreme forms of self-discipline harmful to both mind and body. It led to problems in marriage where sex can, of course, be lawfully enjoyed if the husband or, more likely, the bride has been brought up to believe that such pleasures are always sinful. It has led to what the philosopher Jacques Maritain once called "angelic suicide" which does not mean that angels can commit suicide – an impossible idea given their entirely spiritual nature – but, instead, the idea of humans trying to deny the bodily side of their nature, with its desires and emotions which have been implanted in it by God, so as to live like angels who don't have bodies at all as part of their nature. Hence, it amounts to an attempt at the suicide of one's human nature so as to live as creatures who have natures which are above our level. The result of such an attempt is usually not only certain failure to reach this higher level of being but is exactly the opposite: it has people descend to a level that is *below* that of their own nature, to debauchery of a crudely animal kind because their human nature is trying in a pathological way to compensate for the deprivation imposed on it and, so, goes to excesses which are grossly immoral.

This attempt at angelic suicide has its source in a theological "virus" that has often attached itself to Christianity in different forms down through the ages, as mentioned in earlier chapters. It goes back even to times prior to Christianity to Zoroaster in ancient Persia with his radical dualism of good and evil. It appears again with the Platonists in Europe: the soul was entrapped in the body because of some kind of fall and should seek to be liberated from it as fast as possible. Then when we come into Christian times we find something similar again in Gnosticism, Manichaeism, Albigensianism and Jansenism. It should be easy to see that when this kind of thinking is taken over into Christianity how it will lead to a rejection of the body and especially of sex as being evil.

To come to the Fathers of the Church, just to take the example of St Augustine: he had a background of Platonism in philosophy and dabbled in Manichaeism for a while. He also had his own personal experience of living in sin because of being captivated by lust, a battle which he fought for many years and eventually won due largely to the prayers of his saintly mother, St Monica, who obtained for him the grace he needed to win. Understandably, it led him to a mistrust of human nature in its fallen state and to a greater love for the things of the spirit. But on becoming a Catholic he fully embraced the biblical teaching that the body is good, because God saw all that He had made and declared it to be good as we see in the earliest pages of *Genesis*. He also believed in the resurrection of the body at the end of time when it will be glorified and beautiful and completely free of concupiscence. But he was realistic in seeing that in this life our human nature, though good as created, has been wounded by original sin so that its effects are still in us even after being baptised. The wound, to be precise, is in the will so that it has not full control over our desires and emotions, which latter, all too often, carry us off into sin. The catechism of Trent used to say:

> Because of original sin our will is weakened, our intellect is darkened and our emotions often lead us into sin. (*From the school catechism of my young days which I still remember*).

Hence the need for self-discipline and self-denial and for avoiding the occasions of sin. But this is not because the body in itself is bad or the desires implanted in it by God but because we are weak and need to take precautions and exercise self-control which can often be difficult. A bottle of vodka is something good in itself. It is a drink made from good crops which grow in the good ground and is meant for relaxation which is also good and necessary. But we say to the alcoholic that it is "bad" for him, not bad *in itself*, but for *him* and that because of *his excessive desire* for it which is bad and, if not controlled but indulged in, will lead him to drunkenness which is sinful and to damaging his own health which is also sinful. But vodka is good in itself as a created thing.

However, it would happen in time that later theologians of smaller minds would use St. Augustine to promote a negative, narrow kind of Christianity which still despised the body and sex as evil giving us a rehash of Gnosticism and Manichaeism. Calvinism was such a thing in the Protestant tradition and this then took the form of Jansenism in the Catholic tradition. The virus was never fully shaken off. What happened then is that the modern world, tired of being scolded for being bad, rebelled and shook off not just Jansenism (which would have been a good result) but true Christianity as well, confusing the latter with the former, and then over reacted by going to the other extreme of sheer licentiousness and promiscuity so that now we are at the stage where behaviour of such a kind is legalized and considered good, and we even have pressure being put on the Church to give its blessings to such behaviour.

Evil, then, is taking on the mantle of good and good that of evil. Following on that, we have an attempt at a spirituality which has no cross, no sin, no self-denial or no hell. But people cannot rise to union with God while steeped in any sin and are unwilling to break from it. Like St Augustine, they too, each and all, must make a break from their sins. These people need sound instruction from their priest on the commandments, and he should lead by practicing self-denial in his own life for the sake of his own soul and also to obtain the graces needed for holy living in his people.

<u>A Positive Idea of Chastity</u>

The solution is to get back to a true Christian understanding of creation, matter, the body, desire, emotion and sex as being good because put there by God. But it means also accepting the fact of the Fall and being realistic about the weakness of human nature ever since. So, in practice, in instructing the young, it means that we tell them that they should exercise self-control in regard to the body not because the body is bad but precisely for the opposite reason - because it is good, in fact, sacred - it being the dwelling of an immortal soul which has the image and likeness of God stamped on it; it being also a temple of the Holy Spirit since baptism, and, finally, because it is destined to rise in beauty and glory at the resurrection of the dead at the end of time. Such instruction makes clear that sex is good, a way of expressing the total commitment that two people make to each other when getting married, but that for that very reason it must be reserved strictly to those who are validly married and exercised with moderation and the kind of chastity that pertains to married people.

Following St Augustine, we should see in the beauty of the body not a thing to be lusted after but a thing to be admired as giving us a foretaste of the even greater beauty it will have in the kingdom of God at the end. But only the one who has struggled to overcome concupiscence in himself will be able to see things in this light. At the end of the day this is a call for self-control and self-denial, as good pastors have always prescribed, but its meaning and its implementation in practice will be different when seen no longer in a negative Manichean way but in light of true Christian teaching. Self-denial then, though still difficult, even becomes joyous.

In light of the above what then is chastity? It is the fruit of the ongoing struggle that restores in us that original harmony of the person when the body is made subject to the soul, and within the soul, when its lower powers are made subject to its higher powers. It is the harmony which results from the subjection of desire to will when the intellect is instructed in sound teaching on the commandments.

The struggle needed to restore this harmony might be difficult at times, depending on the weakness of the will or the strength of an excessive desire which might even have some underlying genetic causes. But the struggle is not negative in the sense of being a *destructive* exercise. No; it is positive. To use the example of the gardener and his hedge: he does not try to cut down the hedge to nothing because then he will have no hedge at all (obviously). Instead, he tries to trim and cut back the excess growths on the hedge so that it will be in its proper shape according to his design for it and grow with ever greater health and vigour. Or it is like the athlete in training. He is not trying to exhaust himself when training but to subdue his body as his sport requires so that he can run all the faster to his goal. Still, he won't try to run as fast as the hare or fly like a bird, things beyond his nature as a man. His training requires self-discipline, difficult indeed but positive in its results. The Christian who succeeds will have harmony in his soul and inner peace in his mind. The challenge is to communicate that vision of chastity to our young people. So, we can say, following Church teaching, that harmony is another name for chastity:

> Chastity is the joyous affirmation of someone who knows how to live self-giving, free from any form of self-centred slavery. This presupposes that the person has learnt how to accept other people, to relate with them, while respecting their dignity in diversity. The chaste person is not self-centred, not involved in selfish relationships with other people. <u>Chastity makes the personality harmonious.</u> It matures it and fills it with inner peace. *TMHS.*, *#17*.

Individuals of such inner harmony relates well, then, to other persons. They do not love less, as is the case of those whose form of self-denial amounts to self-torture, but love all the more, and more truly, because they are no longer self-centred. They can see the other human being, the attractive young girl, for example, as a person, also in the image and likeness of God, with hopes and fears and needs and longings and not just as an object of pleasure to be shunned as a danger, as Jansenist would do, or taken hold of for self-gratification as promiscuous people will do.

But because of human weakness the precautions mentioned in the foregoing will still not be enough. There is also required the help of grace from above; and what better way to avail of this than to turn to Mary, the one who is *full of grace* and who never experienced lust, never sinned, and to ask her to ask her Son to give us this grace. Hence the need for prayer and the frequent use of the sacrament of penance. The person of self-denial is not one who hates everything around him as evil but on the contrary one who loves all things with a purer eye because he sees the handiwork of God in them and can envision what they will be like at the eschaton. Yet he is wise enough to see that there is a lot of evil in the world due to the disharmony that men of evil desires have brought about and he must try to avoid that. He has all the desires of a natural human being but, with self-discipline and the help of grace, has them in their proper place, under control, so that he is truly free and what can be described as "noble" and thus able to walk like a prince.

The Priest and the School

<u>Priest and Pupils</u>

As an addendum to what we have been saying about the Catholic school and what is taught in it, I would like to say a little about the priest's role in the school as a support to the work of evangelization there. That, in turn, will depend to some extent on his official position in the school which might be that of chairman of the board of management, or a member of that board, or a religion teacher or a chaplain with or without a teaching function; and the brief of each of these positions could vary from country to country or even from one kind of school to another within the same country. He might have no role in the school itself but simply be the parish priest of the place in which the school is situated. It will not be possible here to examine each possible role in detail because, as said, these roles can be very different in their briefs. So a few general comments must suffice.

Obviously if the priest is the chairman of the school board he can have a strong say in the appointment of good practicing Catholic teachers and in matters of school policy. He will have less of a say in the other positions mentioned above. But even if he has no position at all within the school still, as a priest in the parish, he may come to be informed by concerned parents of programs of an unsuitable kind being introduced and he can alert people to that in his sermons or by calling meetings of the parents and helping them to organize against such things. He might be able to set up a watch-dog group of parents and teachers, or possibly find some retired teachers who might have more time on their hands who could examine all new books proposed for the school curriculum. The school might not be in Catholic management at all but might still have Catholic pupils on the rolls whose souls are still his concern as indeed are the souls of all other pupils if they are being put in danger.

If the priest is simply a chaplain but has access to the classroom, his role is of great importance there for the faith of the pupils, especially those at primary level. To go in and talk to them regularly, giving them instruction in a way that is suited to their age and background, is of great benefit. In doing so, he should also make time to listen to their questions, so that he can know what their line of thinking is, and answer questions on things which might be problematic for them. Later, in their teenage years, it may well happen that these pupils will go through a rebellious phase when they want to throw the faith aside, which may be due to peer pressure or to the influence of agnostic teachers who like to take pot shots at the church, or to the media; but, even if they do fall away for a while, it is my experience that the early influence of a priest who took an interest in them and gave them sound doctrine and a love for the faith in their younger years will win out eventually over this later negativity.

Priest and Teachers

But there is more to the school than the pupils. His visit to the classroom gives support to the teachers also in their work if he expands on what they are teaching. He can direct them to sources of further reading such as the *Catechism of the Catholic Church* if they need to go deeper into some topic. He should remember that teachers often have to pick up on problems of an emotional kind which pupils bring with them from their homes if there is trouble in the home. Also, it sometimes happens that teachers themselves have their own problems in their own marriages and families and need support. In other words, the priest should be like a team coach encouraging them in the work of handing on the faith and helping them with their other problems also.

The staff room at break time is another place where the priest can witness to the faith and provide support for the teachers when there is a discussion going on over a cup of coffee. It can also be a situation where some anti-clerical teacher will make snide remarks about the Church when the priest is present. That fellow has to be answered one way or another, depending on what is motivating him to begin with. It may be just crude cynicism or he may have had some genuinely bad experience of the Church in the past, or he may be an immature fellow simply wanting to get a laugh from the others. With some patience the cause will eventually reveal itself and can then be dealt with. But what is deplorable is when a wimpy priest will go along with the snide jokes of such a teacher simply because the others are laughing and he wants to be popular and part of the fun. Such a priest should know that the popularity he gains in that manner is utterly shallow and that those who are laughing are not laughing *with* him but *at* him and are secretly despising him as a man who stands for nothing only his own ego.

That aside, the priest who takes an interest in the school is bearing witness to the incarnation simply by going in the door of the school: he brings Christ into the vineyard of education; and inside the door he is doing an important work of evangelization. By teaching the pupils about chastity he is responding to the warning given by Our Lady at Fatima when she said that many souls go to hell because of sins of the flesh. How important it is to steer even one soul towards heaven.

Conclusions:

1. As with the education of the young generally, but more so in the area of education for chastity, the parents are the primary educators by natural right. However, it is permissible, and sometimes necessary, for the school or other chosen persons outside the family, to help the parents in discharging this responsibility. But this must be done according to the subsidiarity principle. These others must share the beliefs of the parents in this regard and be of good character.
2. The instruction given should be based on a Christian view of the person and marriage and follow sound moral principles. It should take account of the age, intelligence and maturity of the children and allow for the difference of gender between boys and girls. The example of Catholic parents living their own marriages according to Catholic principles is of great importance in this.
3. Parents, teachers and pastors need to be vigilant about secularist sex education programmes being introduced into schools which see sex merely in biological terms, detached from the objective moral law, and which offer instead a purely relativist, subjectivist morality founded on a hedonism that promises unrestrained pleasure without consequences.

4. The priest or catechist in the school should be a person who exemplifies the gospel in his/her life, giving sound teaching in class but also providing support and encouragement for the school staff in their various needs.

The school as an institution can be the *locus* of complex relations between Church and state. We will look briefly at this in the next chapter.

Chapter XVI

The School and the State

Good Catholics make good Citizens; Catholic Schools undermined; Lessons from History

God wants you to be good citizens so as to silence what fools are saying in their ignorance. You are slaves of no one except God, so behave like free men and never use your freedom as an excuse for wickedness. Have respect for everyone and love for our community; fear God and honour the emperor. 1 Peter 2:15-17.

A Christian education must promote respect for the State and its representatives, the observance of just laws, and a search for the common good. *Religious Dimension of Catholic Education in a Catholic School, (Rel. Dim.), #45.*

The problems aired in the last chapter regarding immoral programs being imposed on Catholic schools by governments raises the wider question of what should be the proper relation between the Catholic school and the state. Both Church and state meet in the school, and the classroom is often a microcosm of the wider society. The Catholic school is an institution of the Church for the handing on of the faith and for the overall development of the pupils, natural and supernatural. The bishop or a religious superior is often the chairman of a board of trustees which owns the school or holds it in trust for the parish. He can be the patron even when the school is owned by the state. The priest is sometimes the chairman of the school board or a member of the board.

The school is also an institution of the state under the government's department of education which, in many countries, pays the teachers, sets the curriculum for most of the subjects taught, and makes rules and regulations on various matters pertaining to education so that the school is subject to state authority in these matters. Hence the school can be a place of harmony and cooperation between Church and state or a battle ground between the two. In this chapter we will set out some principles that will make for harmony and cooperation between the two.

Good Catholics make good Citizens

The pupils, on leaving the Catholic school, if they have been properly formed according to Catholic teaching and example, will be good members of the Church in this world and heirs to the kingdom of heaven in the next for the greater glory of God. They will also be good citizens of the state contributing to its wellbeing with the knowledge and skills they have acquired in being educated and more so because of the moral virtues in which they have been formed: natural virtues acquired in the home and developed further in the school and the supernatural virtues which were infused into them at their baptism, which latter can bear all the more fruit by building on the former. Let us hear what the Church says in regard to the benefits which the school gives to the state:

> A Christian education must promote respect for the State and its representatives, the observance of just laws, and a search for the common good. Therefore, traditional civic values such as freedom, justice, the nobility of work and the need to pursue social progress are all included among the school goals, and the life of the school gives witness to them. The national anniversaries and other important civic events are commemorated and celebrated in appropriate ways in the schools of each country. *Rel. Dim., #45*.

If, for example, the pupils have been instructed in the fourth commandment they will know that all authority comes from God and will respect all lawful authority in the land, not only that of their parents at home but those of their employers at work later on and those of the state, provided these latter do not contradict the law of God with sinful instructions or immoral legislation. That should make for right order and peace in the state so that government can be respected and rule with a gentle hand.

If they have been taught the meaning of the fifth commandment then one would expect a much lower level of violence in society, with no threat to the unborn or to the old. Policing and security costs, then, will also be less.

If they have been given a truly Catholic education in chastity in accordance with the sixth commandment then they are more likely to enter stable, faithful marriages so that the state will not have to spend much in welfare payments for the fallout that results from marriage breakdown. More positively: solid, stable, happy families are the building-blocks of a state that will also be solid, stable, protective of the weak and providing for the common good with a resulting greater happiness for a greater number of people as far as that might be possible in our fallen world. Children from stable families are more secure and mature in themselves and less likely to become delinquent and rebellious.

If they have been taught basic honesty in accordance with the seventh commandment the entire economy will benefit because there will be less robberies or on-going "leaks" of state money resulting from fraud and embezzlement.

Again, if they have been taught the eight commandment there won't be the huge losses resulting from wrongful payments made in the courts when large sums are procured by perjury and miscarriages of justice.

More generally, if they have been taught the priority of the moral law over civil law, as the former is to be read from nature and from divine revelation, they will then be alert to block any civil legislation that might seek to undermine the moral law and so be better able to promote the common good, because immoral legislation will, as said already, undermine the common good sooner or later.

Catholic schools, paradoxically, are schools of true patriotism, producing citizens that are devoted to their homeland even though their teaching on faith and morals comes from the Church, a universal – that is, "Catholic" body - and ultimately, of course, from God. By applying Catholic social teaching in all areas of life the graduates of Catholic schools confer the maximum benefits on their own country so that they love their country, its history and culture, and will even sacrifice their lives for it. Put simply, not only is there no contradiction between being a good patriot and a good Catholic but being a person of the latter actually reinforces the former.

This is not mere speculation. There have been many instances of rulers in countries which are predominantly non-Catholic deliberately surrounding themselves with ministers and civil servants who were educated in Catholic schools because the competence and trustworthiness of such people was well known and, so, was greatly sought after for the good of the state. Such rulers have been known even to send their own children to such schools even if they are not allowed to convert to the faith.

Catholics undermining the Catholic School

But conversely it also happens that in countries which have been Catholic for centuries, such as Ireland or Belgium, one will see government leaders and other well-healed parents who were educated in Catholic schools try to undermine Catholic education and work against Church bodies and against the religious orders which run Catholic schools. Such people might scarcely have been able to write their own names were it not for the dedication of many religious orders of bothers or nuns who provided education at minimum costs in the past, often by sacrificing their own salaries in order to subsidise their schools. These people seek to undermine or weaken Catholic education in the name of a supposed pluralism that pretends to be concerned not to offend a minority of pupils of other religions or none who might also be attending these schools. Their real agenda, of course, is to oppose formation in Catholic virtue - even though they see the benefit to the state that such a formation gives - because they themselves are not willing to live up to the demands of such formation in their own lives. They fail to see that, as leading citizens of the state, they are pulling the rug from under their own state because they are allowing a society to develop which will be guided by no other moral principle than that of the absolute freedom of the individual – a sure recipe for anarchy, which, in turn eventually leads to tyranny because people cannot live with anarchy for very long.

It often happens, on investigation, that the government ministers or the parents of these supposedly non-Catholic pupils, who might call themselves humanists or socialists or whatever are, in fact, lapsed Catholics who are turning round to bite the hand that fed them. Moslem or Hindu or Buddhist or Protestant parents, whose pupils are sometimes enrolled in Catholic schools, and are always made welcome there, are often found to be much more respectful towards Catholic education because, in valuing their own traditions, they understand how sincere Catholics value theirs also. These don't usually have that "chips on their shoulders" which lapsed Catholics have. Paradoxically, though these latter will claim to be "enlightened" and "broad minded" and "tolerant" of all view-points, one finds that they are usually gullible, uncritical recipients of what the secularist media are peddling to them every day with the result that they are no longer open to the Catholic view point.

The first and most obvious way that a secularist state proceeds to undermine Catholic education is by cutting funding from Church-run schools. The argument is made that peoples' taxes should not be used to fund any particular denominational school because some of those taxpayers do not belong to any religion. This argument is all the stronger when there is a total separation of Church and state in a given country such as the US or France. With funding cut from denominational schools it is then up to the churches and ultimately to the parents to find money for the building and then for the running of such schools. That puts an enormous financial burden on most Catholic parents.

This argument conveniently forgets, as said above, that the pupils who belong to these different denominations are also future citizens of the state who will be contributing to the welfare of the state because of the education they will have received in these schools.

As for the argument from the separation of Church and state, it could still be possible for the state to give vouchers to the parents to be spent as they see fit by sending their children to whatever school is their choice or to engage in home-schooling if they so choose. In the US, where this principle of the separation of Church and state is so often invoked, it is noticeable that the federal government there had no problem of giving millions directly to the Catholic bishops every year so that the latter could finance programs for helping migrants, many of whom are illegal. If these strategies or deals can be done in a country with a radical separation of Church and state why cannot something similar be done in all countries for the worthy cause of denominational education?

Church and state are separate anyhow as to their authority structures in most countries, except perhaps in some predominantly Protestant countries where there is an established Church - and no one objects to that, or where the monarch is head of both Church and state and, again, nobody objects! But in the classroom, Church and state cannot be separated because each Catholic pupil is both a member of the Church and a citizen of the state (unless we somehow split each student down the middle!).

Another way that some governments have of undermining the faith in Catholic schools, supposedly again in the name of pluralism, is to have the faith taught but in so diluted a way, in both doctrine and morals, that in practice it amounts to little more than instruction on a vague, nebulous notion of Christianity with no solid doctrines, and, for morals, a civic politeness or an etiquette of "niceness" that tells the pupils that they should smile all the time and be sure to always help old ladies cross the street with their message bags!– as if God the Son became man and died on the cross merely to tell us to do such things. Those who argue for this strategy claim that non-Catholic children (or even Catholic children in some cases) would find certain topics in Catholic teaching, such as hell for example, too frightening or abstract or offensive so that it is better that it be watered down in this fashion.

One can understand how this kind of religion would be taught in non-denominational schools where religion is only a poor relation of the other subjects, but one expects something more substantial than that in a *Catholic* school.

Another tactic by some governments is to allow a Catholic religion program be taught indeed but only as an optional subject and have it slotted for 3.00pm on a Friday evening when the school busses are pulling up outside the school gate. Needless to say, a good many pupils will choose the school bus over the religion class simply to get out early.

One other tactic used by some governments is to make religion a state exam subject but ensuring that what is taught is merely a course on comparative religions in which Christianity is just one belief system alongside Islam, Hinduism and Buddhism and in which Catholicism specifically gets little mention. The aim in all these strategies is to so dilute or displace the Catholic faith that it is reduced almost to nothing.

Worse still in this banishing of the faith from education are schools which are supposedly Catholic which not only present a watered-down version of the faith but which welcome programs of a thoroughly evil kind, such as we dealt with in an earlier chapter, and even *give over some of the religion time to these programs* with government approval! That presents a major problem for good Catholic parents. They are left with the only other option of home schooling- if allowed by the state - which is difficult to set up but something which, nonetheless, is proving to be very successful in some countries, especially in the US.

Not all blame lies with government. Often it is "supposedly" Catholic teachers and parents who are pushing for the secularization of education and will even agree to their school being divested or detached from Catholic management and given over to non-Catholic management. "Let's throw out this religious superstition stuff so that we all become pagans in practice, very 'skilled' in the ways of the world, and there will be no more problems about the place of religion in the school" – is the thinking. We mentioned this already in a previous chapter.

Priests' Support of Parents

Priests in their parishes should support and organize parents who sincerely do want a proper Catholic education for their children. They should remind all parents of the sacrifices made by former generations of parents so that we could have truly Catholic schools today. Staying silent or being "nice" so as not to offend those who want to banish religion is a betrayal. Sadly, some priests will not even visit the Catholic schools in their own parishes and will even favour the idea of religion being taken out of the school entirely, thus playing directly into the hands of the humanists. In some countries, where religious education has already been taken out of the schools and given over to the parishes with their Sunday schools, the percentage of pupils who do come on a Sunday is very small because the percentage of their parents who are Mass-going is small to begin with. What then of the many other children who never get any exposure to the faith? How will they be evangelized?

In any case, the very notion of a Catholic school *not* being allowed to give full and proper instruction in the faith and preparation for the sacraments *in* the school contradicts the very idea of a Catholic school as we presented that already above wherein the faith is at the centre of everything there. The Church is the one voice which can and must oppose this irrational push for secularism.

Lessons from History

A government which wants good economy, right order and peace should be very favourable to Catholic education. It often happened in the past that regimes which were totalitarian, and which tried to control the Church also, did so, not with a view to wiping out the faith but with a view to using the Church and its schools to make the people law-abiding and submissive to civil rulers. This was the case in France and in some other European countries during the age of the absolute monarchs just prior to the French revolution. The revolution then turned against the Church and tried to impose a new religion on the people, the worship of the goddess of reason or the Supreme Being as with the Jacobins and as with Robespierre who tried to make himself the high priest of one of these cults. His legacy was a reign of terror from which no one benefitted, not even Robespierre himself, because, fortunately for everyone in Paris at the time, he too was sent to the guillotine.

After the revolution, when Napoleon took control, there resulted a concordat between state and Church. Napoleon had more regard for power than for faith – though a Catholic in his youth – but the determined resistance of the people of the Vendé taught him how resilient a thing the Catholic faith is and how necessary it is in the lives of ordinary people simply for right order. He is supposed to have said that better a parish priest in each village than an army captain to keep order amongst the people. So, he realized that it would benefit his own rule if he gave it some guaranteed place in the life of the country and proceeded to make a concordat with Rome. A later French government abolished the concordat so as to make of France a thoroughly secularist state.

Again in Russia, in the early part of the twentieth century, Stalin tried at first to wipe out the orthodox faith (though he was once a student for the priesthood himself!) but soon saw that that was impossible, so he then tried to use it for his own greater control of the people, even using its priests as informers, a role which some of them, sadly, were willing to play.

I am not suggesting for a moment that the proper relation of state and Church and therefore of state and the Catholic school should follow the model of any of those regimes – the Church being used by the state for its own security - because the Church has a divine right to run her own schools in her own way. I'm simply making the point that these dictators, though they had little or nothing of the faith in their own hearts, still had a better grasp of its social usefulness and the usefulness of Catholic education than many rulers and many parents in some Western countries who cannot even see *that much* of its value and who think we will have a utopia as soon as the last vestige of the faith is got rid of. Voltaire, the liberal cynic of France of the days prior to the revolution, who saw the faith as something to be swept away, has a lot of likeminded followers in many Western countries today. But they should also know that the same man died crying out for a priest – yes, for one of those priests whom he had spent his life mocking - so as to obtain forgiveness. But the nurse who witnessed his death said he died in utter despair. (*cf.* the account of his death by St John Vianney in one of his sermons).

The correct Relationship

The correct relationship between the Catholic school and the state is presented as follows by a Church document we have quoted already:

> That Catholic schools help to form good citizens is a fact apparent to everyone. Both government policy and public opinion should, therefore, recognize the work these schools do as a real service to society. It is unjust to accept the service and ignore or fight against its source. Fortunately, a good number of countries seem to have a growing understanding of and sympathy for the Catholic school. A recent survey conducted by the Congregation demonstrates that a new age may be dawning. *Rel. Dim., #46*

This document is somewhat hopeful. Very simply, the state should help and foster Catholic schools as kings did the new universities in the Middle Ages. So, the state should not hesitate to finance such schools to a greater or lesser degree depending on the nature of ownership of the school as being entirely public or entirely private or some combination of both. The state should, in fact, see this as a wise investment for the good of the state.

The state may also set up totally non-denominational schools to facilitate those parents who want to have their children learn nothing of the true faith (oblivious to the loss which that entails for those children). But Catholic school boards should not bow to any pressure from the state or from any other body that wants the faith to be diluted in or abolished from Catholic schools.

When the Church promotes loyalty to a state that takes account of the existence of God and His moral law, and when the state from its side recognizes the value of Catholic education as something that leads to the worship of God and to the good of the state, everyone gains in both Church and state because both are willed by God and therefore are meant to relate to each other harmoniously. True Catholics must be vigilant in protecting their schools so as to enjoy this harmony and its fruits and they need a lead from their priests in this.

Conclusions:

1. The Catholic school helps form new members for the Church and for the kingdom of God and also good citizens for the state by reason of the knowledge it imparts and the training in virtue which it gives. Loyalty to the state and respect for civil authority is encouraged in the Catholic school when that does not conflict with the law of God. The state should recognize this contribution and support Catholic schools financially and in other ways.
2. Catholic priests, parents and teachers and all who are concerned for the handing on of the faith must be always vigilant to secure the place of the faith in the classroom because anti-Catholic regimes always try to eradicate it from there.
3. "Parents must possess a true freedom in choosing schools; therefore, the Christian faithful must be concerned that civil society recognizes this freedom for parents and even supports it with subsidies; distributive justice is to be observed". *Canon. 797*
4. "The Christian faithful are to strive so that in civil society the laws which regulate the formation of youth also provide for their religious and moral education in the schools themselves, according to the conscience of the parents". *Canon. 799*

There is yet another field of evangelization which reaches out beyond the boundaries of the parish, that of the various mass media of communication. These too can and should be used profitably in the spread of the faith. We will look at these next.

Chapter XVII

The Church, the Priest and the Media

Media and Morals; going on air; Media Vigilance

How beautiful on the mountains are the feet of him who brings good news. Isaiah 52:7.

It is the duty of Pastors to instruct and guide the faithful so that they, with the help of these same media, may further the salvation and perfection of themselves and of the entire human family. *Inter Mirifica, #3.*

So far, in this section on the prophetic role of the priest, we have been looking at him evangelizing by preaching at Mass, talking to the children in the school and supporting the school effort in various ways. We saw too that in this last activity his work is shared by parents and teachers also. All of this happens within the parish using well-known means of communication such as the microphone, the newsletter, the text book and computer programs.

But developments in electronics have given us ever more advanced means of communication and therefore have greatly enlarged the field of evangelization. Radio and television have been with us for some time but we now have the internet and various kinds of media platforms, unheard of before, which enable the priest and Catholic lay people to reach literally to the ends of the earth. We have come a long way in communication from the days of Guttenberg and his printing press of 1480. In this chapter we must see how the priest and his lay helpers can make positive use of the various kinds of media for the good of the faith.

The Church and the Media

<u>Making use of the Media</u>

Luther and the reformers were quick to see the usefulness of the printing press to popularize various translations of the Bible but not to spread the teaching of the *magisterium* which, instead, they rejected. But soon the Catholics also became aware of its usefulness both for good and for bad. They saw, for example, how Marat, a pamphleteer in Paris, fanned the flames of the French revolution which had turned against the

Church; and soon after the revolution we find Consalvi, the secretary of state of Pope Pius VII, worrying that the newly emerging democracies would be controlled by anonymous liberals using the new print media for evil.[1] Then, when we come to the early twentieth century, we hear Pope Pius X calling for a Catholic press, and later we find Vatican II extending that call and the use of all other available media also for the promotion of the faith.

> It is, therefore, an inherent right of the Church to have at its disposal and to employ any of these media insofar as they are necessary or useful for the instruction of Christians and all its efforts for the welfare of souls. It is the duty of Pastors to instruct and guide the faithful so that they, with the help of these same media, may further the salvation and perfection of themselves and of the entire human family. In addition, the laity especially must strive to instil a human and Christian spirit into these media, so that they may fully measure up to the great expectations of mankind and to God's design". *Inter Mirifica, (IM)*, #3. (*cf. Gen. Dir. Cat., 1997, #160-162*).

The media, whatever their form, no matter how advanced, are still only instruments, technical gadgets, which in themselves are neither morally good or evil, but powerful in influence nonetheless whichever way they are used. In times past, in many a rural village there was the old woman who was an idle gossip and had no other way of getting attention than by peddling bad stories about some neighbour – especially about someone who did not give her the attention she pathetically craved – and yet she was feared because of the harm she could do simply with her tongue; how much more, then, is the harm that the person who has today's social media at his/her fingertips can do when he can send information round the globe in an instant. Revolutionaries of all kinds give testimony to its power because when they stage a *coup* they immediately grab the radio and TV stations. The media empower the people using them so that they can do good or evil extensively. But such power carries great moral responsibility with it. Vatican II says in this regard:

> The Church recognizes that these media, if properly utilized, can be of great service to mankind, since they greatly contribute to men's entertainment and instruction as well as to the spread and support of the Kingdom of God. The Church recognizes, too, that men can employ these media contrary to the plan of the Creator and to their own loss. Indeed, the Church experiences maternal grief at the harm all too often done to society by their evil use. *IM., #2.*

In order that the media be properly used in the service of the faith the Church calls for an orderly setting up of training institutes for future media people:

> Importantly, laymen ought to be afforded technical, doctrinal and moral training. For this purpose, the number of school faculties and institutes should be increased, where newsmen, writers for screen, radio and television and all other interested parties can obtain a sound training that is imbued with the Christian spirit, especially with respect to the social teaching of the Church. *ibid #15*.

By *Catholic* media is not meant outlets which will report only on Church news, even though that has its importance. Nor does it mean having presenters in secular outlets who can be trusted to put a "spin" on controversial issues in ways that will always be favourable to the Church. It means media that will report on all events of the day, from world news, to finance, to sport or whatever, but doing so from a Christian Catholic perspective. It means looking objectively on what is happening in the world, that is, reporting on things truthfully and with completeness, but analysing them in line with Catholic teaching, particularly Catholic social teaching.

<u>The Media and Morals</u>

This leads on to the question of what moral criteria govern media reporting and presenting because all deliberate human action is subject to the moral law. That might seem to be an obvious truism not needing to be stated but, as regards the use of the media, it still needs to be stated, the reason being that many media people claim a freedom that often tries to be absolute, independent of all control by either Church or state, and ignoring the moral law. Hence the phrase "the freedom of the press" is so often used to justify even the most blatant falsehoods and acts of defamation. Yes, indeed, there is such a thing as freedom of the press – and it a valuable thing - but not in disregard of the moral law which is binding on everyone. To get recognition for this truth is difficult now when the moral law itself is no longer accepted as being an objective measure of human behaviour and its commands are being side-lined, treated as mere subjective opinions, in favour of individual choice which now is so often made into an absolute.

As regards the moral norms and the use of the media Vatican II had this to say:

> For the proper use of these media it is most necessary that all who employ them be acquainted with the norms of morality and conscientiously put them

into practice in this area. They must look, then, to the nature of what is communicated, given the special character of each of these media. *Ibid., #4.*

Truthfulness in information is the first moral requirement. The information broadcasted should be true and complete – half truths can sometimes be as damaging as falsehoods – and justice and charity are also needed:

> The first question has to do with "information," as it is called, or the search for and reporting of the news. Now clearly this has become most useful and very often necessary for the progress of contemporary society and for achieving closer links among men… The proper exercise of this right demands, however, that the news itself that is communicated should always be true and complete, within the bounds of justice and charity. *Ibid., #5.*

These requirements are all the more necessary when issues affecting the common good of society are being aired. In the run up to an election, for example, a combined, monolithic media can put their weight behind a candidate or party of immoral policies and have them elected and stir up an outcry against people of other parties who might be trying to promote morally good policies.

The morals of a people, and, again, the common good, can also be undermined by the kind of entertainment presented over the airwaves if it is immoral. But sometimes the media will try to justify this in the name of art. On this Vatican II continues:

> The second question deals with the relationship between the rights, as they are called, of art and the norms of morality. Since the mounting controversies in this area frequently take their rise from false teachings about ethics and aesthetics, the Council proclaims that all must hold to the absolute primacy of the objective moral order. *Ibid., #6.*

Art is indeed a good. But it is meant to uplift, not to debase, so that the obscene or the vulgar, passing itself off as art, cannot be justified.

The Watchdogs

But how can the media be controlled so as to be made to serve good morals and the common good? Since it is the responsibility of government primarily (but not exclusively) to promote the common good it is those in power who have the right to exercise this control by making laws on what constitutes good entertainment, fair broadcasting, libel *etc*. Vatican II again:

> The public authority, in these matters, is bound by special responsibilities in view of the common good, to which these media are ordered. The same authority has, in virtue of its office, the duty of protecting and safeguarding true and just freedom of information, a freedom that is totally necessary for the welfare of contemporary society, especially when it is a question of freedom of the press…….legitimately concerns itself with the health of the citizenry, is obliged, through the promulgation and careful enforcement of laws, to exercise a fitting and careful watch lest grave damage befall public morals and the welfare of society through the base use of these media. Such vigilance in no wise restricts the freedom of individuals or groups, especially where there is a lack of adequate precaution on the part of those who are professionally engaged in using these media. *Ibid., #12.*

Of course, if the government is too strict in exercising control one can have a situation where objective, honest reporting is prevented and those media which are allowed to use the airwaves simply become organs or megaphones of government; and if the government is corrupt and cannot be challenged by any journalist or presenters then one has a situation like that which exists in communist countries. "Pravda", a word which means "truth" was the name of a newspaper in Russia in soviet days but what it printed was seldom the truth but communist propaganda for the enslavement of the people. In brief, media and government have watchdog roles with respect to each other but to the extent that both are willing to abide by the moral law that should not lead to conflict of any serious kind.

When, instead, the media where it is still free, show little regard for the moral law or when governments do the same as often happens, it means that neither body sees its respective role in relation to the common good but, instead, in relation to the grabbing of power over people's minds, each for its own benefit. In that scenario both bodies will also look on the Church as another power institution and as nothing supernatural but merely as one other corporation seeking control over people as they themselves are doing, so that they strive to control or restrict it or, if possible, to eliminate it altogether so that it will no longer compete with them in having influence over people. Accordingly, it happens at times that, while media and government will fight each other over various issues, all for power, they will both readily set their differences aside when it comes to the Church and join together in attacking *it*. Wrongdoings of any kind in the Church are, therefore, grist for both their mills. They will set themselves up as champions of victims of various sorts, especially those wronged by the Church, but they themselves will then promote evils such as abortion, divorce or euthanasia which also victimize innocent people and do irreparable harm to the common good. It is a bit rich, then, when they demand transparency from the Church and claim the right to call the Church to order when they themselves not only promote the evils just mentioned but will engage in a brainwashing process that has people come to believe that these things are not evil at all but good, civil rights to be enjoyed by all. It annoys them that Church teaching still stands, saying that such things are evil, and they ignore surveys which keep on showing the negative effects of these things on society. These double standards need to be exposed by the Church but too often her leaders are too timid in doing so.

Preach the Moral Law for the common Good

The solution is that priests repeatedly preach on the moral law and on the duties of both legislators and media personnel to serve the common good and for them to show that the Church's aim, when preaching in this way, is that of promoting the common good and the salvation of souls and not any kind of power grab for herself. Of course, the Church wants to influence people – as does anyone who speaks publicly on anything – but to influence people for the good of their souls is very different from a mere power grab for oneself.

The Church herself, then, will also gain from such preaching when her true interests are seen. There will still be some tensions between all three institutions from time to time, given the human failings of the agents involved, but when all three have the same aim of promoting the common good and accept that the moral law is necessary to secure it, then this common aim will outweigh the differences caused by occasional quarrels, which latter will then turn out to be healthy tensions, more about means than ends.

"Transparency" is a word often heard today on the lips of media people and government leaders. It goes so far as to say in some countries that Church leaders have no right to a lock and key for their own filing cabinets but must be ready to throw them open to the police or to media people at any time. I often wonder how willing these people who call for transparency would be if they themselves were asked to hand over the keys of their own filing cabinets! Is it really the case that none of these people have any skeletons at all in their own cupboards? So, if instead the Church were to turn the tables round and start calling on *them* to account for *their* wrong doings I wonder what their reaction would be? Or, if the Church stood firm and said it would refuse to co-operate with the state in dealing with any wrongdoing until the state first made a commitment to eradicate those evils I mentioned above, I wonder what the reaction would be again! The old rule: *Let him who is without sin throw the first stone (Jn. 8:7-19)* could be applied here also.

In making these criticisms of the media I am mindful of those very honest outlets which are favourable to the Church, not as whitewashing or watering down the wrongdoings of some of her members but simply as trying to be fair and objective and of people in those outlets who are made to suffer in various ways for doing just that.

That said, there have indeed been wrongdoings in the Church at various levels at various times by some of her leaders. So, the Church, from her side, has to put her own house in order. Indeed, I must admit that much of Church wrongdoing might never have been checked were it not for the secular media putting the spotlight on it, even if their motive in doing so was mostly to discredit the Church rather than to help any victims. Had canon law been followed strictly in the decades after the council many cases of wrong-doing would have been prevented or nipped in the bud.

When wrongdoings happen in the Church, and they are likely to happen again also, given the fallen state of human nature, the first and most important thing for the Church authorities to do is to put a stop to them *immediately* by following the provisions of its own canon law so that no further harm is done, either to victims directly affected or to the faithful by the scandal caused. If that is not done in a way that is swift and effective then they, the Church authorities, have only themselves to blame when the secular media come in on such cases and use them as battering rams against the Church. The secular media are then performing necessary though painful surgery on the Church because of the resulting scandal, even if they do so for negative motives. Thus, good comes out of it all in the long run though at great cost.

The Priest and the Media

Giving Witness

The above are general points on relations between Church, state and media. I want now to say a few things about the priest in his use of the media and his dealings with media personnel. This field of evangelization has the priest reach people outside of the church or the school, though I would continue to hold that the priest preaching to his own people on a Sunday is the most important and effective medium of all. The few points I want to make should be of help to lay people also in using the media for evangelization.

Priests at parish level use various media of communication since they are useful instruments of evangelization. Thus, priests make use of simple things like the parish newsletter for conveying information on parish events but also for conveying little bits on doctrine. Some priests and, of course, teachers are skilful in using various internet programs and social media as tools for catechetics in their schools and in other places and some use these things to broadcast church services to people who cannot be present. Of course, using all of these media will achieve nothing if there is no substance in the content broadcast, which takes us back again to the need for prayer and study as a preparation, as dealt with already in an earlier chapter.

Going wider than the parish and the school, the priest or a lay person can be called on at times to defend the faith in other media also such as radio, television, media platforms or newspapers when, in scripture language, he must *give reasons for the hope that is in him. 1Pt.3:15.*

It is not every day that a priest is called on to go on the airwaves to discuss or debate some point of religion; but, when he is so called upon, he should be ready and able. The bishop, however, might well reserve all discussion on religious topics to himself or to a spokesperson specially designated by him, and the priest should adhere to *canons 822, 832* and *321* on these matters. This last of these says:

> It is for the bishops' conference to lay down norms determining the requirements for clerics and members of religious institutes to take part in radio and television programmes which concern catholic doctrine or morals. *Canon 321 #2.*

But assuming that the priest is left to his own discretion as to whether or not he will go on air, it often happens that he is reluctant to do so. I have known many priests who were scared of such an encounter. This can be due perhaps to a lack of training in the seminary in what might be called "media combat" though today many seminarians do receive such training. But even when they don't, there might still be a tradition of holding debates in a seminary with questions and even heckling (hopefully of a constructive kind) allowed from the floor. That too is good training for media engagement.

The priest's reluctance might also be due to defective theological instruction in his seminary. Or it might be that that instruction was good but that the student-priest merely crammed what was taught to him for exam purposes without making much of an effort to comprehend it or see how it might be of use to him in the future. In any case, the priest has had six or seven years of study and training in the seminary, a privilege that most other people, including most media people, do not have. The radio or TV presenter usually knows very little theology and is relying mostly on a few pages of notes researched for him by the producer a few days before. If then, even with this advantage, the priest shies away from an interview or debate on the airwaves an opportunity is lost for the presentation or defence of the faith.

Media Discretion

When called upon to go on air, although it is an opportunity to promote the faith, as just said, a priest should not necessarily always jump into the fray on each and every topic proposed to him. "Discretion is the better part of valour", after all, provided discretion is not used as an excuse for sheer cowardice so that the priest becomes the hireling shepherd fleeing before the wolf. A priest should try to pick his own battles as far as possible. By that I mean that he should not rush in to comment on some area of theology in which he is not competent. A priest might be very competent, let us say in knowledge of the Old Testament, but have only a basic knowledge of canon law so that he would not be competent to talk, for example, on the intricacies of appeals processes in marriage annulment cases. In such an event it is better that he pass that topic on to a canon lawyer. Or a priest might be very competent in canon law but have merely a scant knowledge of Church history so that he would not be able to give a detailed account of what happened, for example, during the Monothelite controversy. Let that to the church historian of the diocese. "Shoemaker stick to your last" is an old saying. But in most radio or TV discussions the subject matter is usually not of a very specialized kind but instead more general in order to appeal to a wider audience; hence, any priest with a good basic seminary formation should be able to handle it.

Again, the topic for discussion might be, for example, a dispute in a Catholic school in a neighbouring parish between a teacher and the school board. The matter is already being handled by the school manager or by the diocese which has its own spokesman, in which case a neighbouring priest commenting will only confuse matters and perhaps do harm to reputations. Even in one's own parish it is not wise to go on air about particular issues involving particular individuals who will be mentioned by name.

Or again, it can happen that a radio presenter will use a religious topic, about which he does not give a hoot himself to play off one priest against another priest or a priest against his bishop. To divide and conquer, to provide a dog fight for the rabble and drive up the tam ratings of the program is the object here. A priest should not jump to that kind of bait.

Background Preparation

But if or when he decides to go on air a priest, or lay person, should prepare by praying for the guidance of the Holy Spirit and by ensuring that he is in a state of grace (as far as anyone can judge that) so that the inspirations of the Holy Spirit won't meet with obstacles in his soul. He should then look up Church documents on the topic to be discussed so as to refresh his mind on them and bring them with them to the microphone so as to be able to quote from them accurately. Having done that much, he should not get too preoccupied about what he might be asked or how he might handle this or that objection. One could spend the night worrying about such things and then find that the discussion takes quite a different turn on the day. That is where the help of the Holy Spirit comes in again as Christ advised His followers when facing cross examination and persecution: *it will be given to you on that hour what to say. Mt.10:19.*

It is also useful for the priest to know something of the mentality or ethos of the media station and of the presenter before going on air and to ask who else will be in the discussion. If he knows that it is an anti-Catholic station or if he learns that there will be two or more people lined up against him then he knows that this is likely to be a rigged discussion and that he will get a rough ride. Sometimes a hostile station will actually invite a faithful priest to come on air to give the impression that it is open and balanced and tolerant of all viewpoints when in fact the aim is to have his argument torn to pieces precisely because he is known to be faithful, and thus make him sound like a fool. When it comes to phone-ins at the end of a program it is an old trick – as I learned from *inside* one media station – to select which comments to read out. Thus, if five favourable comments have come in and five unfavourable comments, the producer in the background will give the presenter, perhaps, one or the former and four of the latter to read out. If none of the unfavourable kind has come in then the producer himself or a colleague might phone in from a room up the hall, pretending to be "Jo from London" or "Kate from Canada" with the needed negative comment.

A woman of intelligence who was able to see through these tricks said to me one time about going on air in a certain media station that it was like going to law with the devil in a court held in hell! She was right indeed from my experience of the same station. Nonetheless, I often did take up invitations to go on air on that station because I have seen that such media bias usually goes overboard so that listeners of any intelligence are able to see what is happening and where the truth lies, because truth has a "ring" about it so that it speaks for itself. Thus, when the priest knows what the aim of a given station is he can prepare for it accordingly and he can expose the unbalance to the listeners while on air.

Media people fair and unfair

Media people come "in all shapes and sizes" with different agendas. The media is the voice of the world, a world in which Satan, the prince of this world, has great influence, so that it is a voice which is mostly hostile to life, family, faith, morals and the Church. Then there is the presenter who simply does not have a sense of sin or a perception of objective moral standards so that he/she fails to see that there is an infinite metaphysical gap between what is objectively right and what is wrong. That kind of presenter, in chairing a discussion on something like abortion or euthanasia, will try to do what he thinks is a balancing act between two things which he imagines to be of equal moral value – or which he thinks have no moral value at all - because everything for him boils down to mere personal opinion anyhow, with individual freedom of choice being the only value. So, in this kind of debate he will see the pro-life and the pro-death positions, for example, as two things like pepper and salt, or tea and coffee and he does not really mind which side comes out on top no more than he cares whether the person next to him at lunch time later is drinking tea or coffee. All he wants is a good dog fight for the listeners and for the tam ratings. Instead of the categories of objective right and wrong, such a person usually thinks in terms of conservative and liberal or of right and left without ever defining what these terms mean. These terms belong in the realm of politics, not in the realm of religion.

Because conservative and liberal, right or left, are relative terms, to have any meaning at all there must be some measuring-rod in the middle. But who or what is this measuring-rod? Is it the supposed "average man or woman in the street"? But then who is he or she? The presenter himself often thinks of himself as being that person or as representing some anonymous crowd out there who hold this middle position, even though he never consulted them for their opinion, nor have they – even if they ever existed - elected or deputized him to represent them. Once a faithful Catholic can be labelled as "conservative" or as "right wing" then it seems he can be mocked and dismissed as little more than a fool trying to hold back the tide of what is deemed to be "progress". Rational, objective debate now gives way to the argument *ad hominem.*

In sum, your media man is sometimes a mere peddler of opinions, the word "opinions" being the operative word here because opinions are subjective and shifting like quicksand. But, though claiming to be open to all opinions, he is still consistently opposed to what is Catholic. He is a disciple of Voltaire without realizing it, though the latter, anti-Catholic and anti-dogma as he was, did, at least, believe in God.

But in advancing these cautions one must be careful not to make sweeping over generalizations so that all media people are tarred with the same negative brush. There are media people who are very Catholic and are just waiting for an opportunity to interview a priest of sound faith so that the gospel can be spread in an unbelieving world. There are media people who are not Catholic but are genuinely open minded and interested in getting at the truth of things. G.K. Chesterton, the Englishman, was one such journalist. He refused to be taken in by the anti-Catholic propaganda of his time in the early twentieth century and wanted to get at the truth about the Catholic Church for himself. He noticed how this Church alone was accused of contrary faults, for example, some criticizing her for favouring the rich to the point of being capitalist and others for favouring the poor to the point of being socialist. This made him curious to get at the truth of things, and his investigations led him to see that the Church was in the right position, not in some imaginary halfway position between these contraries but in line with objective truth about God and man. He too has his disciples today even if they never heard his name. They are sincere, honest media people whose sole aim is to present the truth objectively but who are browbeaten by editorial boards whose aims are partisan and of obvious anti-Catholic bias. I also wish to acknowledge the service to justice that some investigative journalists have given when they took up the cases of priests who were wrongly accused and abandoned by their bishops and fellow clergy due to a fear of being tarnished also.

Then, also, on the other side, it is sadly not possible to credit all priests who are willing to go on air or into print with orthodoxy. Some are mavericks kicking against the Church's teaching on all of the hot issues of the day, usually issues of sexual morality, so as to be popular with the media or with a rabble who are destructive of everything decent. More pathetic still is the priest whose god is his own ego and likes to be on air and have his photo in the front page of the paper, so much so that he will rush to any encounter that will have him in front of a camera or a microphone. Flattery, ambiguity and what is politically correct are his usual armoury. He does not stand for or against anything except that which will gain him a name. He is a disciple of the sophists of ancient Greece as compared with someone like Socrates who had a thirst for truth. It often happens that such a fellow eventually gets more of the media than he bargained for in the beginning. He sees himself as their darling boy, and the media will use him for a while, for as long as he is useful for their purposes; but, once he slips or says anything that is politically incorrect, the same media will pull the rug from under his feet very fast and leave him flat on his tail on the ground.

Thus, with his home work done on a point of discussion and with some knowledge of the people he will be dealing with, favourable or unfavourable, the priest or Catholic lay person should be prepared to go on air.

Chapter 17: The Church, the Priest and the Media

Going on Air

Prior to going on air a priest or lay person is likely to be contacted by the presenter or his producer to get some idea as to what he is likely to say on the topic to be discussed. Or he may be contacted by a journalist for a newspaper for a story which the latter wants to print. In the former case it is best not to show one's hand fully at first – the soldier doesn't fire all his shots at the first go. In the case of the latter, it is better to ask for time to prepare a statement, preferably over a span of twenty-four hours, because something one reviews the next morning will be seen to need some adjustments before being sent off; and one must remember that the written word, once published, stands for ever. In either case a priest/lay person needs to be on guard against the over friendly presenter or journalist who feigns familiarity and will try to engage him, the interviewee, in a casual conversation in which the latter leaves his guard down. The media person may say, for example, "surely you remember me, we met at such a place and I knew your brother at school. Now tell me, between the two of us, what do you think of that new school policy by Bishop X? Many people think it is stupid. What do you think? And, by the way, this is off the record." So, the priest, now taken off his guard, says "Yes, I think it is a bit stupid myself also". And then, next morning on the front page of the paper: "Priest Lashes Bishop's School Policy as Stupid".

As one goes on air the interviewee must be clear as to his/her role or position relative to the interviewing presenter. Often the interviewee is fearful because he sees himself in the role of an accused person in the dock in front of a judge with authority over him so that he has to answer all the questions put to him and be sure to answer them well or pay the price of being condemned to ridicule. But that need not be the situation at all. The interviewee is a guest who has agreed to come on air to enter into a discussion of his own choosing and who is free to answer or not to answer whichever question he chooses, or to throw questions back at the presenter if he so desires. We have Christ doing that in the gospels when asked by what authority He cast out demons and he replied: *By what authority do your own leaders cast them out? Mt.12:27*. A Catholic defending the faith is in the superior position of being in possession of divinely revealed, objective truth as compared to the presenter who, as I said already, is often merely an agnostic peddling opinions prepared for him by his producer.

When on air the priest must be calm and restrained. There is such a thing as a justified anger in the face of evil which makes clear that one does not tolerate certain things, but it must still be restrained in mode because an interviewee losing his self-control is likely to say rash things damaging to his own cause and damaging to the good name of others. The rule there is expressed in the old Latin tag we had already:

fortiter in re, suavitur in modo - be strong in your principles but suave or gentle or diplomatic in the way you present them. He needs restraint also so that he can see one step ahead and foresee where a line of questioning is likely to lead and anticipate how to respond. He needs also to foresee the double-edged question of such a kind that he is trapped whatever way he answers it. The classic example of this - when it is a married man that is being interviewed - is: "Is it true that you have stopped beating your wife"!

Presenters often have great sport when interrogating their interviewees or when setting one interviewee off against another for a dog-fight for the entertainment of the listeners. But, when one of the interviewees turns the tables back on the *presenter* with a question about *his* presuppositions or his public behaviour, the latter can be seen to get very agitated all of a sudden. "How dare you question me like that" is the attitude, which reveals how haughty such people can be at times. They are not indeed judges in a court of law but often think they are. If at that point the interviewee tells the presenter that *he*, the presenter, is now "losing *his* cool," and that he is being very unprofessional in doing so, the tables are then fully turned round and the listeners have even greater entertainment!

But if the interviewee sees that a discussion is blatantly loaded against him then it is a good tactic (when he *is* allowed to speak) to address the *listeners* directly and point out to them that he is well aware that this program is unbalanced and biased and that he hopes they can see that also. He could then threaten to walk off the program very soon as a protest if some balance is not restored. Presenters don't like blanks in the airwaves.

Media and Vigilance

A priest who has some experience of how the media operate should then instruct his people on how to take a critical look at what is presented to them by the media and they, in turn, especially if they are parents or teachers, should form the minds of the young to be likewise critical. This is necessary because it is simply a fact that ordinary people *are* influenced by what is being beamed into their sitting rooms by the various media and also by what is called "social media". A mother is ironing clothes or cooking meals in her own kitchen with the radio turned on beside her for perhaps two or more hours each day. It is inevitable that she will be influenced and swayed by what she hears if she is not already well grounded in her faith and in moral principles. So, also, will her husband be influenced as he drives to work in his car with the radio on, and both of them may be largely unaware of this influence.

When Hitler was embarking on his propaganda mission of brainwashing the German people - an advanced people most of whom had at least a primary education -

with his ideology of the super race and his antisemitism, he formed a commission of sociologists and psychologists and charged them with the task of ascertaining what percentage of the people could be persuaded by his propaganda, using the media available at that time which were, simply, radio, newspapers and cinema reels. They reported back saying that, if skilfully used, about eighty-five per cent of the people could be won over. As things turned out the figure was nearer to ninety or perhaps ninety five percent. If that was the success that *he* had at a time when most people in Germany were attending church, and the outlets of mass media were so limited, what now is the likely level of success that social manipulators can expect to have given the deterioration in catechetics and the increase in media outlets? There is now the added newcomer to media which is artificial intelligence. It can fabricate images and information all so easily and therefore all the more deceptively. And this influence is even more forceful when, in a country like Ireland, nearly all media are monolithic in singing the same secularist, anti-life, anti-family, anti-Catholic song. The outcome of referenda on most social/moral issues in Ireland since the 1970s is evidence.

Pope Pius XI courageously alerted people of Germany to the danger of Naziism with his encyclical *Mit Brenner Sorg,* written in German and smuggled up into Germany and read out at all Sunday Masses there when Hitler was on the rise in the 1930s. So also did Bishop Von Galen in Germany and, in the Protestant tradition, there was the philosopher Dietrich Bonhoffer who paid the price of his life for his opposition. But, shamefully, there was another bishop who supported Hitler. So also today, when the media becomes monolithic in its opposition to the faith in a given country or in a whole continent, it falls to the Church again to be a voice for independence, free thought, human rights, faith, morals and, generally speaking, for truth and civilization.

This points up the importance of the role of the priest at parish level if he cares for his flock and wants them to remain Catholic. He must speak out himself, indeed, but he must also enable his flock to be vigilant and discerning. Vatican II called for discernment, moderation and self-control in the use of the media, especially by the young with their parents and teachers guiding them:

> Those who make use of the media of communications, especially the young, should take steps to accustom themselves to moderation and self-control in their regard. They should, moreover, endeavour to deepen their understanding of what they see, hear or read. They should discuss these matters with their teachers and experts, and learn to pass sound judgements on them. Parents should remember that they have a most serious duty to guard carefully lest shows, publications and other things of this sort, which may be morally

harmful, enter their homes or affect their children under other circumstances. *Inter Mirifica., #10.*

The priest can give a unifying lead to parents and teachers in this role of guidance of the young and indeed to all his people on how to respond to what is presented to them over the airwaves. For the priest simply to engage in bashing the media is not the answer because the media are a fact of life today just as they always were in some form or other in the past, even if less powerful due to the absence of the technology we have today. To bash indiscriminately would also be an injustice to those good media people I mentioned above. No; the priest must lead his people in discernment in how to respond. He need not devote every Sunday sermon to commenting on a chat show that was on TV on Saturday night, but he could and should preach on the doctrinal truths and the moral principles which are so often undermined by media and, instead, provide his people with the Catholic position on these things. Sadly, what often happens is that he gives a banal, pious sermon, lifted from some clerical magazine, that does not relate to any such issues – for fear of giving offense – and then his people go out and across the road to the shop where they spend their money on newspapers which relentlessly attack the Church and its teaching. It is an appalling contradiction – Catholics swallowing what is poison to their faith and financing more of the same for the week ahead! To prevent this, the priest could adopt the old "boycott" tactic simply by telling his people not to support any paper or channel that is anti-Catholic and instead to spend their money and their viewing time on those that are supportive of the faith. He need not mention the name of any such paper or channel explicitly (better not to for legal reasons) but by instructing them on what is true and false, right and wrong make it abundantly clear to his people what they should support or reject. Sadly, I have never yet heard even one sermon on that topic of discernment and critical media awareness.

Conclusions:

1. Advances in technology have given increase to the power and influence of the mass media. In itself the media are mere instruments, morally neutral, but in the hands of those who use them they can be used for great good or great evil. So, the Church and the priest and his helpers should use them for good. It is an important form of evangelization today.
2. The media need to be free but that freedom is not absolute because the moral law binds on all. The common good of society and individual human rights are at stake if the media are not used in a morally good way. Some media people

have been great defenders of truth and justice even at the risk of losing their jobs and even their lives.
3. Priests and Catholic lay people need to be trained for media engagement. Priests also need to make people critically aware of what is being presented to them on the airwaves.

The above can be described as helps towards witnessing to the truth. But that brings up the underlying question of what truth is to begin with. We will look at that next.

Chapter XVIII

A Love for Truth

Truth and Realism;
Truth undermined and reinstated; bearing Witness

And what is truth? Jn. 18:38.

Truth is the adequation of the mind with reality. *St Thomas Aquinas. I Sentences d.19, q.5.*

In all of this section on the pastor as prophet or teacher an underlying principle or presupposition should be that he would have a love of truth. Good advice on preaching, catechetics and media engagement will effect little if the priest or the catechist or the Catholic media person does not have a love for truth for its own sake as it is revealed to us by God and then a passion to bear witness to it when he/she speaks. The one who does not have this love and passion is somewhat like the sophists in ancient Greece, intelligent fellows, indeed, capable of arguing any point or its contrary, be it true or false, according to whoever might hire them, so as to make money and appear clever before the crowd. The lover of truth, by comparison, has his predecessors in Socrates, Plato and Aristotle, but most of all in Him who came on earth and proclaimed Himself as *The Truth* because He is the One through whom all things came to be and so is their measure, because their arch-types - their *forms* in Plato's language - are in Him as in the Divine Essence. He stated that His very mission was *to bear witness to the truth. Jn.18:37*. He did that at the cost of His human life, being condemned by Pilate, the judge who could not recognize Truth even when it was standing in front of him. Socrates, too, had already paid the price of his life for truth, being forced to drink the hemlock, and, following on Christ, there was St Stephen, then St Justin and many, many more witnesses, martyrs, down through the Christian centuries.

Truth is often denied. That has always been the case. But today there is the deeper problem that the very concept of truth itself is being undermined, that its very possibility is being questioned and replaced by sheer scepticism or by a notion of truth that makes it to be ever changing and malleable.

In this chapter we will say briefly what truth is, see how it has come to be undermined in philosophy and theology and then seek to lay out some principles for its restoration.

The Objectivity of Truth

Truth is the adequation of the mind with reality, which means that truth is not a product of the human mind but the faithfulness and fruitfulness of the mind when it judges correctly as to what is there in reality. Were it otherwise, reality would be a malleable plastic shaped by the mind. No; the real is what *is*, what exists out there objectively, independently of one's mind. If I hit my toe against a stone then, regardless of my feelings or my wishful thinking that that stone might never have existed, it does, in fact, exist and so does the injury to my foot; and when I know the stone my mind is squaring up to, recognizing, what, in fact, *is*, not inventing it or negating it to comply with my wishes one way or the other.

It is indeed a principle of St. Thomas, oft repeated by him, that whatever is received is received in the mode of the receiver, which means that whatever is known is grasped by the knowing mind in a way that is adapted to that mind. (*cf. S. Th. I, q84 ff*). Thus we humans grasp the essences of things through the avenues of the five senses, whereas an angel needs know such help. For example, we know what grass is firstly through its colour of green, perceived by the eye, whereas an angel knows it first hand through a concept implanted in his mind from his beginning. But this granted, it still does not follow that either the human or the angel makes grass to be what it is. That is an act of God.

If man's mind produced reality man would then be the creator of what exists. No; God is the creator of what exists, through the Son in the Holy Spirit, so that it is *His* mind, the *Logos*, (not ours) which is the cause and measure of all that exists. When we judge correctly as to what exists our minds adequate with reality as it is, and, because we know that the things of nature come from God as their Creator we then accept that these things "adequate" with the mind of God to begin with. We can indeed alter and give shape to the material God has given us when we work on it, and we do so in accordance with designs conceived in our minds. Thus, the artist carves a piece of rock into a statue and the builder arranges stones into a house according to a preconceived idea/plan in his mind. When doing so he imitates the creativity of God in a minor way. But it is God who gave him the matter upon which to work and the mind to conceive his designs, which one way or another are borrowed from what already exists and so, come from God as their ultimate source no matter how "creative" the artist might be. Man is a creator only analogously, not absolutely.

God has revealed Himself in nature, in the things He has made, and they all speak of Him and sing His praise simply by obeying the laws of their nature implanted in them by Him. But God has also revealed Himself in a more special way to His chosen people and He taught them when He was forming them in the desert, speaking through Moses and later through the prophets when they came into the land He had promised them. It was a gradual revelation in accordance with the people's ability to absorb it, a divine pedagogy. It was not an evolution of teaching in such a way that the earlier teaching changed into something different as time went on. It was, instead, a greater drawing out and fulfilling of what was earlier in what came later and additional teaching also. He revealed Himself most fully in His Son, the *Logos*, when He came on earth as man with a teaching that was inseparable from His own being. This teaching He gave as a deposit to His apostles in the Church which He founded so that they would hand it on to succeeding generations and preach it to all nations, they being guided by the Holy Spirit after He had ascended to the Father. It is the objective truth of God about Himself and how believers should relate to Him. Yet this understanding of Catholic truth is not always accepted today even by some in the Church.

Truth undermined

Ockham and Luther

The great coherent system of St Thomas (1225-1274) its harmony of philosophy and theology, was undermined by the criticisms of Duns Scotus (d 1308) and more so by the nominalism of Ockham (1287-1347). This paved the way for the major challenge to the objectivity of truth which came at the reformation with Luther (1517 *ff*). He rejected the teaching of St Thomas because it made use of the philosophy of Aristotle, a work of mere reason which was untrustworthy according to Luther because man was so hopelessly corrupt due to the Fall. Moreover, Aristotle was a pagan. So, he rejected this help which faith had previously enjoyed from reason. For him theology was faith alone, *sola fide,* in scripture alone, *sola scriptura* (that is, in what *he* declared to be scripture) interpreted by the individual's private judgement (which in the ensuing debates had to be *his* private judgement against that of all others). In thus interpreting scripture one is "supposedly" guided by the Holy Spirit, who "supposedly" would lead all readers of the Bible to Luther's interpretation which was based on *his* theory of justification.

But, if one is allowed to reason at all, it should be easy to see that if Tom, Dick and Harry read the same passage of scripture but come up with three different and contradictory interpretations of it, each claiming the guidance of the Holy Spirit, that one is straight away on the road to pluralism in doctrine and relativism as to what is true, so that the objectivity of truth has to give way to mere opinion. "Well, this is my opinion and it is as good as yours (though contradicting it!) so we must respect each other's opinions and all opinions." It doesn't take much to see that this soon leads to endless division, so that by now there are many thousands of Protestant sects, which, in turn, leads to scepticism in matters of faith and eventually to loss of faith entirely.

As to scepticism in the natural realm, the British empiricists, Lock, Berkley and Hume, all Protestants, pushed philosophy further down this road of scepticism by limiting what can be known to sense impressions and, then, Kant in Germany, influenced by these empiricists, claimed that natural reason cannot know God, though He should still be "postulated" as a guarantor of morality. Kant, also a Protestant, went on to say that mind *constructs* reality in the sense of imposing its *a priori* categories on these impressions it receives through the senses. (*cf.* his *Critiques of Pure reason* and *Practical Reason*).

To say that the mind constructs reality by imposing its innate categories on sense impressions is to be only one step away from saying that reality *is* mind, which leads to the philosophy of idealism as taught by Hegel and his school in Germany. In the case of the individual, the subjective is now taking over from the objective. But since my subjectivity is different to yours it is easy to see that certainty as to what is objectively "out there" must soon give way to relativism and scepticism. Indeed, the next step is to say that what is "out there" is only what mind *puts there*, not by knowing objectively but by trying to objectify its own inner experiences, which experiences will result from ever changing circumstances or from action. With this line of thought in philosophy we come to Marx who was an atheist. For him truth is praxis; the philosopher does not seek to understand the world but to change it by revolutionary action. In theology this line of thought brings us to modernism.

Modernism

We touched on modernism already when talking about catechetics in an earlier chapter. To recall, it is the theory that there is no revealed truth to begin with in the sense of God speaking from above to man and giving him truths which he could never have attained by himself. Instead, the starting point is man's consciousness of himself as a being dependent on some higher being which some might call "God", or it is man's consciousness of some inner being of some sort, a kind of world-soul within him. Then this consciousness is formulated into propositions by theologians which are called "dogmas" and these dogmas then shape the mind of a people for a while. But with the passing of time and the changing of experiences due to the changing of

Chapter 18: A Love for Truth

circumstances - material, economic, social and political - these dogmas are changed into "better" ones, i.e., more suitable to the new circumstances, so that the former dogmas are discarded or they undergo an evolution and new ones take their place for another while. And so, on it goes, so that what our ancestors in the faith believed is, in time, changed beyond recognition and discarded in favour of new dogmas. But that too leads to relativism and scepticism and eventually to loss of faith. Why should I adhere firmly to something as true today which might well be declared false tomorrow?

Paradoxically change is then becoming an absolute even by people who don't believe in absolutes! The world came to be seen in historical, dynamic, evolutionary terms, all of which was deemed to be unstoppable progress. Philosophers such as Hegel and Marx and then Darwin, with his theory of evolution, underpinned this new dynamic world view.

It should be easy to see what happens when one transposes this kind of thinking into theology. Revelation, in the sense of an objective, divine teaching from above, is replaced by man's consciousness or mere feeling, that is, by the subjective. Doctrine or dogma, in the sense of the Church's formulations of what God has revealed, is replaced by dogma understood as man's formulation of his own inner experiences. Faith, then, in the traditional sense of assent to a divine deposit of truth - which truth is *not* a product of the human intellect but can be understood to lesser or greater degree by the human intellect - is gone and is replaced by feeling and sentiment, things that are ever changing like the clouds floating across the sky.

The word "dogma", in the *traditional* sense, is detested by modernists. "You are being dogmatic, or fundamentalist" is a slur that will be thrown at any faithful Catholic of definite beliefs. When Pope Benedict XVI was visiting England in 2010 the atheists got alarmed and wanted to put up advertisements on the sides of busses saying "God does not exist". But someone pointed out to them that doing this was also being dogmatic though, this time, in an *anti*-religious sense. So, they changed their add to read "God *probably* does not exist" which means they were admitting the possibility that He *might* exist after all! Anti-dogmatism had backfired on itself. In the end, for the modernist, religion becomes a spirituality of one's own making as one goes along worshipping a god who is not distinguishable from the world, or the world-spirit (whatever that might be) or the ideology of the day (the *Zeitgeist*) or from one's own ego.

When the foundation of theology is not that which is revealed from above, held by faith and understood by reasoning minds, that have the real for their object, it has only the mere shifting sand of scepticism below as its basis which leads to eventual unbelief because if dogma is mere ideology or theological fashion what does it leave me with to hold on to? In brief, modernism is theology without faith, relying on a philosophy of endless flux. (*cf.* Pope Pius X, *Pascendi Gregis*).[1]

Truth reinstated

Truth, Objectivity, Certainty and Development of Doctrine

In Philosophy

Beginning with natural reason and philosophy, and given that many philosophers have fallen into various errors, how does one reinstate truth, objectivity and certainty? One need not resort to philosophy at all with its subtle arguments when an appeal to common sense will suffice by posing a few simple questions. I would simply ask the sceptic if it is *true* that there is no such thing as *truth*? And since his answer, either way, will compels him to admit of truth I would then ask him if he is *certain* that there is no such thing as *certainty*? And again his answer, even if in the negative, will have him at least admit the possibility of certainty. Again, I would ask him to explain the term "relative" if its very meaning is other than that of being measured against something absolute.

As to objectivity I would ask him if two euros plus two euros could possibly be made to equal twenty two euros for a man who was very short of money? If he disputed the fact that two and two make four, regardless of one's needs, I would take him back to a simpler proposition: that one and one makes two; and if he disputed *that* then I would have to say good bye to him as one out of touch with reality because then one is rejecting some of the most elemental principles of thought which are innate in us and cannot be proved but must be accepted if we are to reason at all, which is what common sense does, a thing that is available even to the illiterate (and perhaps in greater amount than to the over educated)!

Catholic philosophy accepts that there is truth and objectivity because it insists on the minds ability to know the real, that which is extra mental, because that is the mind's very object, just as food is the object of sense appetite, and colour the object of sight, and sound the object of hearing, and in knowing the real the mind naturally attains to truth and does so in the case of every sane man and woman.

As to certainty, Catholic philosophy admits that certainty in truth can often be difficult to attain especially in things abstract and spiritual due to the weakness, laziness and the fallen condition of our minds, but it insists that it can still arrive at certainty, even in those difficult matters, with effort and the help of the light of faith. In ordinary, everyday matters it arrives at certainty with ease, like the woman who knows exactly how long to leave a cake of bread in the oven. (*cf.* St. Thomas, *Summa Contra Gentiles* Bk. I, Ch. 3).

As to whether reality is permanent or always changing Catholic philosophy is happy with Aristotle's theory of matter and form, the two elements of substance, and with his theory of potency and act as an explanation for change. A given substance is in potency to achieving full act by a process of change but still in accordance with its form or nature which stays the same. If some change causes it to lose its natural form, as when fire burns wood, then we have a new, a different substance resulting.

If these principles of philosophy are so elemental, as elemental as common sense, why were they ever challenged by philosophers during the second half of the second millennium beginning with Descartes (1596-1650) and his doubt? Because the division of faith caused by the reformation shortly prior to him made for scepticism not only in religion but in philosophy and other areas of academia also because the bedrock of the true faith, which underpins *everything* in life, had been split. Doubt began to reign everywhere henceforth.

Faith itself was then split off from reason and reason then, in turn, soon became powerless to assent to anything beyond sense impressions until the Church reaffirmed its power to know being and the Being of God with Vatican I. (*cf. Denzinger, #1789 ff*). Academia today is a fragmented area of life because it has lost the unifying powers of faith and metaphysics, leaving us with a plurality of mere opinions in place of wisdom and leaving open a vacuum that is being filled with ideology, that of a global Marxism that despises all religion and leaves us only with atheism for religion and the outcome of praxis for truth.

<u>In Theology</u>

Thus, when we move into the field of theology, the Church teaches that our realism about the objective world, perceived by sense, understood and judged to be true by intellect leads logically to objective knowledge of God and not to any mere projection of our minds. The truths He has revealed are grasped by faith and understood, at least partially, by reason and, furthermore, that faith is supported by various signs such as miracles, the enduring survival of the Church and the goodness of the lives of her saints, things that can also be observed by the senses and studied by reason.

As to the permanence or mutability of her teaching, there is a definite deposit of faith revealed by God and handed on by Christ to the Church. But it is developing all the time in the minds of contemplatives and faithful theologians and in the devout faithful by reason of their *sensus fidei*. *Mary kept all these things and pondered them in her heart. Lk.2:19*. And it finds definite formulation in Church dogmas. St Vincent of Lerins, in the early centuries, and St John Henry Newman, in more recent times, set out the laws of this development showing that it is a deepening and enlarging of the original revelation which is going on and not an innovation such that something of a different nature might come from what was first given.

To give an example: the little acorn develops into the stout trunk of a big oak tree and that into the branches and the twigs and the leaves, each different in shape and size from what went before but still of the same nature: it is an *oak* that is developing all the time from that first little acorn planted in the ground until it becomes a tree seventy feet high forty years later. That is normal development. But, if at some point, an *ash* branch were to emerge from the trunk of this oak tree then we would have something strange and unnatural.

The truth we have today in the scriptures and in the dogmas of the Church is that which has come down to us from Christ Himself, unchanged in substance, but well developed through the centuries especially in contests with the various heresies which emerged from time to time. This failure to distinguish between faithful development of what is unchanging in substance and evolving alteration of one teaching into something different is at the root of the confusion which is modernism. There must be faithful continuity with the original deposit of faith. When talking about catechetics we were making the point that the contents of revelation is from above, from God and unchanging as to its substance though developing as just explained here, but that it must relate meaningfully to life situations here below which are always changing.

In sum, the Church does not split faith off from reason as Luther did but uses reason, first as a *preambula* to faith, to prove the existence of God and establish the credentials of the Church as His authorized organ of teaching in the world, then to explain the contents of faith once believed as far as that is possible for the human intellect. She uses the perennial philosophy of St Thomas (which is a refinement of Aristotle in light of the faith) in doing this. It is a philosophy of realism, of objectivity and respect for the natures of things created and it is put at the service of faith to explicate its contents ever further. And she gives us faith then, which, from its side, is presented as a superior light which guides reason in its enquiries to lead us ever deeper into truth. It does not rob reason of its rightful autonomy but acts as a negative corrective to make sure it stays on the right path and, positively, it supplies insights which reason would not attain to by itself.[2] In St John Paul's words, faith and reason are two wings enabling man to rise to God.

Bearing Witness to Truth

The priest of today must bear witness to revealed truth in his preaching and in his life. He too, like his Master and the martyrs, will pay a price if he bears this witness because, as the old saying goes, "the truth is often bitter". Christ warned us of this when He said *if the world hates you remember that it hated me before you. Jn.15:18*. This hatred does not always come from atheists or agnostics outside the Church but often from cosy Catholics within the Church who expect to be pandered to and made comfortable when they go to Mass so that they can *feel* religious but continue with their selfish, sinful lifestyles. But there have been many bishops and priests in history who spoke the truth and paid a price for doing so. One thinks again of Bishop von Galen in Germany at the time of the Nazis, mentioned above, and Bishop Oscar Romero in San Salvador, and it has happened at times that some such bishops did not always get the support from their priests that they needed. But truth wins out in the long run because He who bore witness to the truth on the cross will never abandon His Church. Indeed, it might be argued that the witness of the martyrs surpasses all arguments of reason that can be made in defence of the faith.

The suffering which follows on bearing witness to the truth is, in a word, the carrying of the cross. We saw in our section on the pastor as king/shepherd that this can call for a laying down of one's life for the flock. Being a pastor as prophet/teacher leads to the same at times. Both offices are roads to Jerusalem to go on the cross in imitation of Christ in His sacrifice there. In our next section on the pastor as priest we will see more on this when talking about the Mass. But the cross led Christ to the resurrection on Easter Sunday morning and it leads His Church, His mystical body, to the kingdom of God at the end of history.

Conclusions:

1. A concept in one's mind is true when it conforms to what really exists outside the mind. Prior to that, the things we see in the world around us are true of themselves because their natures conform to their original designs in the mind of God. God's knowledge of natural things is the cause and model of those things.
2. Accordingly, another name for truth is "realism", a recognition that the mind can know the world as it is and with certainty so that the real is not a fabrication of either the human mind or of human action or of the forces of history. The mind can also rise from a knowledge of things visible to things invisible such as the existence of God and some of His attributes. But God Himself has taught much more about Himself in revelation, that He is a Trinity of persons and came on earth in His Son to redeem us *etc*. We hold to these truths by faith.
3. Modernism would have us believe that dogma is merely a formulated expression of some inner feeling so that it can change as circumstances change and give rise to new feelings and new expressions of them in supposed dogmas,

thus rendering former dogmas obsolete. It is religion based on the humanly subjective and not on objective revelation held by faith and understood by reason in as much as reason can do so.

4. The priest and catechist, if sincere, are people who have a love for truth and are willing to make sacrifices for it. To bear witness is to carry the cross.

We have been looking at the work of the priest and his lay helpers when extending the kingly and prophetic offices of Christ in the Church. We will see in the next section how they extend His priestly office in their different though complementary ways.

Part D

Priest

Introduction

We have been looking at the pastor as he builds up the Church by exercising his offices of king and prophet which he has from Christ to whom he is conformed or configured by the sacrament of holy orders. As king or shepherd he leads his flock in the parish which is a small unit of the institutional Church and which needs guidance in spiritual things as well as administration in material things. As prophet or teacher he proclaims the word of God to his flock so that they have a common faith in what God has revealed to them in Christ, a common hope of eternal life in His kingdom and a common commitment to charity in what they say and do. This proclaiming of the word prepares the flock for the graces they receive in the Mass and the other sacraments. It introduces them to Christ who becomes present in their midst in the liturgy. With this celebration of the Mass and the other sacraments and the *sacramentals* the pastor exercises his priestly office.

In this section of our work we will be looking at this exercise of the pastor's priestly office, his work of leading his people in worship and in sanctifying them by the power of the Holy Spirit. In the exercise of all three offices we take note of how he is helped in various ways by lay people according to their different ministries.

In this undertaking it is not my intention to present anything like a comprehensive study of the liturgy or the sacraments or even a summary of such things because that has been done many times already and can be had from such sources as the Church's documents on the liturgy, in particular *Sacrosanctum Consilium (SC)*, and the many commentaries that have been made on them. It can be had also in the *Catechism of the Catholic Church (CCC)*, in the *Code of Canon Law (CIC)*, and in many other works on the administration of the sacraments. Presuming these sources, but drawing on them as needed, I will confine myself simply to highlighting what I think, from my own limited experience, are some important points more of a directly pastoral nature, but sometimes overlooked, that the pastor needs to take account of in his daily work of sanctifying.

The structure of this section will simply be that of the seven sacraments looked at one by one as they are listed in traditional order: baptism, confirmation, Eucharist, penance, anointing of the sick and holy orders. But before we begin with the sacrament of baptism we will look first at the context in which all the sacraments are celebrated today in the West, the context of a secularist world.

Chapter XIX

The Sacraments in a Secularist World

Decline of the Sacred, Sacraments and Liturgy, the overall Unity of the Sacraments

Grace and truth have come through Jesus Christs. John 1:17.

The liturgy then is rightly seen as an exercise of the priestly office of Jesus Christ. *Sacrosanctum Consilium, (SC), 7, #2*

The Western world has become secularist in great part, by which I mean that reality is reduced to the visible, the measurable, the pleasurable and the useful, this last being often viewed in monetary terms. In such a world the spiritual, because it is invisible and therefore not measurable, is relegated to the margins if not outrightly denied, so that God Himself is often denied or at least forgotten in daily life. To a hard-headed secularist in that kind of world what meaning does a sacrament have? What does he think if, perchance, he wanders into a church and sees water being poured on a baby's head by a priest with some accompanying words? The baby doesn't seem to look anything different afterwards. Or what does he think if he sees a priest rushing into the emergency ward of an hospital to anoint a man who has just been brought in after a car accident? That dab of oil which the priest puts on the man's forehead with some accompanying words: what is that supposed to do? He might see it simply as an intrusion on the work of the medics, hindering them. To him the sacraments are merely rituals or gimmicks (if he is a bit cynical) unrelated to the world of his experience and unrelated to each other, which are performed randomly here and there by priests. He may well conclude that this is so much mumbo jumbo or superstition still lingering on from the Middle Ages, an antiquated fad to which some pious people still cling for whatever kind of comfort it might bring them.

Our secularist might be excused somewhat if he is someone who has had little or no experience of organized religion because of his upbringing. But it often happens now, as I know from my work in parishes in countries where the majority are still Catholic (at least in name) that Catholics will often delay baptism for months on end and will stay away from Sunday Mass for long periods; and even in the event of an accident or sudden illness they will call a doctor or an ambulance immediately but might not even think about calling the priest, whereas prior generations would have seen to baptism early, gone to Mass regularly and, in an emergency, have definitely called for both the priest and the doctor, and in that order.

More than that, it seems to me also that sometimes the sacraments mean little even to some of the very priests who celebrates them. I can remember visiting a friend in hospital one day when the priest came in to give Holy Communion to some people in the ward. He flew in like a swallow that had come in through an open window, shoved the sacred Host in the patients' mouths and flew out again as if his tail-end was on fire. A few minutes later a nurse came in giving out tablets to the same patients, but she did so at a much slower pace and spent time with each patient to make sure they had got the right medicines and to say a few kind words to them. Again, often the priest will begin Mass by saying "The Lord be with you", as prescribed in the liturgy, but will then add "Good Morning everybody"- a purely secularist greeting which eclipses the previous sacred greeting but, of course, makes the priest a popular guy with all present. Indeed, sometimes when I go to a funeral Mass or a wedding Mass I wonder if I am at a sacred liturgy at all or at a theatre show or at a cabaree or some other kind of circus.

In this chapter we will examine some reasons for this decline in the sense of the sacredness of the sacraments and offer a reply by situating the sacraments in the context of the liturgy, as high moments in the life of the Church, organically connected to each other and having a common objective. I will also be suggesting that we need new *sacramentals* for the age we live in.

The Decline of the Sacred

The Reformation

The question is a serious one as to why the sacraments now mean nothing to secularist people and rather little also to many (so called) Catholics. This loss of meaning did not happen overnight. There is a history behind it. If we go back to the Catholic Middle Ages – an age that comes in for ridicule by the secularists of our universities today – we will learn how people in those times, being mostly agricultural people, saw signs of God everywhere in nature around them, in the fields, the flowers, the animals, the mountains, the sea and so forth. The world of created things, and man more so, were seen as various reflections of God. One thinks of St Francis Assisi's love of nature and St Thomas Aquinas' scale of being, in which each thing is a reflection of and participation in the very Being of God. Furthermore, people then tended to believe in many sacraments, even more than the correct number of seven with which we are familiar today. One count puts the number of rituals held to be sacraments by some people at eighteen, another puts it as high as thirty. For example, in those times most people would have seen the coronation of a king as a sacrament, it being so splendid a liturgy, yet it was only a sacramental. St Thomas Aquinas had indeed listed the number of sacraments as seven at that time but it was only at Trent, in response to the reformers, that the Church made it definitive once and for all that the number of these rituals which could properly be called "sacraments" was seven, they alone being effective *ex opere operato* i.e., by the very working of the ritual itself.

The reformers had a pessimistic view of the world and of man who, they claimed, had lost his likeness to God by sin and had tarnished the world so that, as one writer put it, it now reflected more the *sneer* of Satan rather than the beauty of God. *(Adriano Tilgher, Work Through the Ages Ch. XXI).* They reduced the number of the sacraments to two, baptism and the Eucharist, but even these were seen more as *tokens* of faith rather than as effective signs of grace which work *ex opere operato* as the Church teaches.

At Trent the Church responded to the reformers' denial by affirming the number of sacraments as seven and making clear that they were efficacious signs. Thus they were good works in contradistinction to Luther's exclusive emphasis on faith. This was necessary; but there was a downside to this also. Precisely because so much emphasis was then put on these seven special rituals or works as sacraments there tended with time to be a loss of the sense of the sacramentality of created things in the world around us. Of, course the Church retained her many ritual sacramentals such as the blessing of water, homes, vehicles, animals etc., as well as her consecrations of altars, exorcisms, religious profession and processions *etc.* These latter, even if they did not confer grace *ex opere operato,* did *dispose* people for grace and made things holy by the efficacy of the prayers of the Church *ex opere operantis.* But people began to lose the sense of the wider sacramentality of other, natural everyday things even though, according to Catholic teaching, the right use of nearly all material things can become matter for sacramentals, which things are then seen as reflecting some aspect of the divine and thus can become sacred signs which can also dispose people for grace. (*cf. The Catechism of the Catholic Church, #1667-77*).

This phrase *ex opere operato,* gave Catholics the assurance that by reason of the "work" or action of the minister this sign of grace conferred grace with certainty, regardless of the moral state of the minister, presuming that he had the right intention, said the right words and performed the right actions and that the recipient was not putting any obstacles in the way. But this certainty, with the great assurance it gave to the recipients, which was good, could also lead to a kind of carelessness or irreverence by some priests who did not have much of a sense of the sacred. "Be sure to say those central, minimal words necessary for validity and all is fine" was the thinking by some at times. Hence the Sunday Mass that was rushed because of a football match was still valid because the minimum words were said. There can indeed be emergency situations such as car accidents where the priest simply does not have time allowed him to say all the accompanying prayers of the ritual of the sacrament of the sick because the injured person is being whisked away in an ambulance in a genuine hurry; but Sunday Mass on the day of a football game is not such a situation. A rushed liturgy is inevitably lacking in solemnity and it implies that the impending football match is of much greater importance.

Still, the rushed Mass was valid because the necessary words were said. But, then, with the advent of the vernacular came the showman priest (few in number I wish to believe) who takes the liberty of tampering with the very words, even those necessary for validity. Liturgy then is reduced to entertainment. That Mass might not even be valid and all sense of the sacred is lost. I am not saying that because of the vernacular the liturgy is now turned into entertainment everywhere; not at all. Many priests celebrate Mass very respectfully. (And it must be remembered also that in the days of the Latin Mass there were some priests who rushed through the liturgy in indecent haste taking advantage of the fact that there were no microphones and that the majority of people in the pews did not understand Latin anyhow, even if they did hear the priest).

The Enlightenment and the industrial Revolution

After the Protestant revolt, with its reduction of the sacraments in number and in meaning and its negative view of nature, there next came the Enlightenment which had a more positive view of human nature, so much so that the supernatural in general and grace in particular was no longer deemed to be needed. God was indeed retained (by *some* of these philosophers) but seen as an outside architect or clock-maker of the universe who didn't intervene in history. And, so, He was not to be elicited or called upon by rituals such as the sacraments which then, more and more, came to be seen as superstitious practices left over from the Middle Ages, comforting indeed for simple, credulous country folk in rural France but not for the *intelligentia* of the saloons of Paris.

The next event of significance in this regard was the industrial revolution, roughly in the mid 1700s, which happened in countries already gone Protestant such as England and North Germany. This brought the steam engine, the train, mining, the big factories and the slum cities of England with their subhuman living conditions which Dickens so aptly described in his novels. Now nature was being covered over with concrete and steel and the skies were being blotted out with smoke and smog so that nature was no longer even visible to city dwellers and so was less likely to be seen as a sign of God for them. The concrete and steel and the new technology offered no such signification. The Church, of course, continued to preach and administer her seven sacraments and her ritual sacramentals and to put great emphasis on them as a counter balance to the secularism of the emerging secularist world. But, paradoxically, by putting all of the spotlight on these rituals, it was if there was no spotlight left for the many new things of the emerging industrial world so that they too might be seen in a Christian light and be made into *new* sacramentals.

So, for these different reasons: the under-emphasis on the sacraments by the reformers, the exclusive emphasis on the seven special sacraments by Catholics, the rejection of the supernatural by the Enlightenment thinkers and the new, steely face of the industrial world, new sacramentals which would give religious meaning to the new things of that world were not being developed, even though, of course, the Church never abandoned the use of her ritual sacramentals, her blessings *etc*. This meant that the new industrial world developed in a non-sacramental or secularist way. That world has continued to change its face even more with the coming of electricity, electronics, intelligence technology (IT), space exploration *etc.*, which makes it even more alien today in relation to faith. One might say that it is pushing ahead too fast for us to see it as matter for new sacramentals appropriate for our age. And because we are lagging behind in this, today's world continues to be largely secularist.

The net result of the foregoing developments is a world grown secularist and materialist with the sacraments seen as out-dated rituals, disconnected from life and from each other so as to be seen as superstitions by some and as gimmicks by others even though all things material come from God and could or should come to be seen as signs of Him.

As a corrective to this mentality, it is necessary that we set forth a few basic points about the liturgy and the sacraments drawing on what the Church has set forth in her documents. But even after doing that there will still remain the challenge in the future of coming up with new sacramentals for this new age so that the new things now available to us can come to be seen as gifts given to us by God due to man's inventiveness and as materials to be used for our sanctification.

The Sacraments in the Context of the Liturgy

Actions of Christ and the Church

The priest's work of administering the sacraments has to be set in the context of the liturgy and the life of the Church. But a consideration of the liturgy must have its beginning – and its end - in God Himself, in the mystery of the Trinity. The liturgy is man's participation in the work of the Father who saves us through His Son, made man in Christ, and all by the power of the Holy Spirit. Christ saved us principally through His death and resurrection, His paschal mystery, when, as priest and victim in one, He offered Himself for us to the Father and won for us the forgiveness and the graces we need when we are sanctified by the Holy Spirit. So, the liturgy can also be called the work of Christ the High Priest, along with His mystical body, who acts in the liturgy so that it is also the work of the whole Church. Using the image of the Church as the bride of Christ one can also say that liturgy is a dialogue between Christ and His bride in the Holy Spirit.

> Christ indeed always associates the Church with Himself in this great work wherein God is perfectly glorified and men are sanctified. The Church is His beloved Bride who calls to her Lord, and through Him offers worship to the Eternal Father. *Sacrosanctum Consilium, (SC), # 7*

In the Church some, the ordained ministers, are designated to represent Christ the Head in this work. So, the liturgy is the work of the priest principally but also of the laity, whom he leads in worship especially in the offering of the Mass, and also when they play their respective, rightful parts in receiving and administering the other sacraments as the Church allots their different roles to them with her laws. *Sacrosanctum Consilium* says again:

> The liturgy then is rightly seen as an exercise of the priestly office of Jesus Christ. It involves the presentation of man's sanctification under the guise of signs perceptible by the senses and its accomplishment in ways appropriate to each of these signs. In it full public worship is performed by the Mystical Body of Jesus Christ, that is, by the Head and his members. From this it follows that every liturgical celebration, because it is an action of Christ the priest and of his Body which is the Church, is a sacred action surpassing all others. No other action of the Church can equal its efficacy by the same title and to the same degree. # 7

And again:

> For it is in the liturgy, especially in the divine sacrifice of the Eucharist, that "the work of our redemption is accomplished," and it is through the liturgy especially that the faithful are enabled to express in their lives and manifest to others the mystery of Christ and the real nature of the true Church. *SC., #2*

The object of the liturgy is to proclaim the faith, give worship to God and sanctify His people and, in doing so, to build up the body of Christ the Church. It proclaims the faith by its preaching and by the signs it uses which point to things divine. For this reason, the word of God is an integral part of the liturgy which makes for a close bond between the prophetic and priestly work of Christ and therefore of his ministers also. The liturgy gives worship to God because of His infinite goodness and is a response to what He has done for us in Christ. It sanctifies His people by the working of the Holy Spirit so that the Church is built up because the sacraments are ecclesial actions which confer the grace of Christ the Head on the members, which grace is the inner life of the Christian community.

The Three Directions of the Liturgy

The liturgy looks or points in three temporal directions: back to the historical event of the paschal mystery of two thousand years ago which took place on Calvary. It makes what happened in Christ "pass over" into the sacraments because the same Christ who is now in heaven is exercising a sanctifying causality in the sacraments of today. So, the liturgy is also a thing of the present: it is effective by its signs in making grace present in souls today. And, though a thing of the present, it participates in the eternal liturgy of heaven, in the liturgy of the Lamb who is interceding for us before the throne of the Father. It makes that liturgy present on earth every day wherever Mass is said; and, finally, it looks to the future because it is an anticipation of the kingdom of the end when we will be able to participate directly in that heavenly liturgy, no longer needing signs, but immediately, when enjoying the beatific vision. For that reason, the liturgy on earth should always reflect the splendour of the heavenly liturgy, by which I do not mean that it should be exuberant or lavish, but that it should be solemn and decorous even if it is Mass said with a small congregation in a tin-shed church in a lonely valley in a poor country. St John Vianney, the Cure D'Ars, was a poor priest in a small church in a poor parish in the South of France but it is said of him that when he went into Lyons to buy altar cloths or vessels or whatever for the sanctuary that he would try to purchase the best available within his means, so great was his sense of the sacredness of the liturgy as an anticipation of the banquet feast of heaven of the end.

The internal Unity of the Sacraments

Origin in God, Pulse-Beats of the Church

As said above, for the secularist the sacraments are disjointed, unconnected rituals because he does not see who or what is their origin or goal or who it is who operates in them. In reply, we must explain to him that their origin is in the Trinity, the second person of whom became man in Christ who then can be seen as the sacrament of God who, in turn, founded the Church which can then be called the "sacrament of Christ".

Historically the Son, having come on earth in Christ, is the one who instituted all of the sacraments and works in them as said in the foregoing quotes.

Christians who rely solely on the Bible will object and say that in the gospels we see Christ instituting only two sacraments, baptism and Eucharist, and then that we have St James instituting the sacrament of the anointing of the sick later on – that is if they accept his letter at all. But, as scripture itself testifies, not everything Christ said and did is recorded in scripture. Hence it can be argued that, since the sacraments confer grace, which is a participation in the divine life, only the Divinity can be their authoritative source which is Christ Himself, He being truly God. He it was who instituted all seven even if that is not explicitly stated in scripture in the case of some of the sacraments. The sacraments also have a source of unity in the fact that it is Christ Himself, the high priest, who works in all of them as we saw above and as *Sacrosanctum Concilium* makes clear again when it says:

> ….. Christ is always present in His Church, especially in her liturgical celebrations. He is present in the sacrifice of the Mass, not only in the person of His minister, "the same now offering, through the ministry of priests, who formerly offered himself on the cross", but especially under the Eucharistic species. By His power He is present in the sacraments, so that when a man baptizes it is really Christ Himself who baptizes. He is present in His word, since it is He Himself who speaks when the holy scriptures are read in the Church. He is present, lastly, when the Church prays and sings, for He promised: "Where two or three are gathered together in my name, there am I in the midst of them. *(Mt. 18:20). SC., #7*

The liturgy is also the work of the Holy Spirit who is always present and operative when men are sanctified.

As a work of the entire Church, one could say that the celebration of the sacraments are the high moments of her self-actualization, the celebration of the Mass being the highest. Karl Rahner puts it as follows:

> …when the church in her official, organized, public capacity precisely as the source of redemptive grace meets the individual in the actual ultimate accomplishment of her nature, there we have the sacraments in the proper sense, and they can be seen to be the essential functions that bring into activity the very essence of the church herself. For in them she attains the highest degree of actualization of what she always is: the presence of redemptive grace for men, historically visibly and manifest as the signs of the eschatologically victorious grace of God in the world. *The Church and the Sacraments, p.22*

Perhaps we could use the image of the sacraments as pulse beats of this great mystical body with the Mass corresponding to the heart at the centre, making the paschal mystery present again. The other sacraments, then, can be seen as channels bringing the graces and merits of the sacrifice of Calvary to people in different ways by different signs in their different life situations. Hence, far from being disjointed unrelated actions, all the sacraments are moment in the life of that one sacrament which is the Church and of Christ as head and high priest of the Church.

Christ is central to all the sacraments, their inner source of union, and His paschal mystery is central to all that He did. One could say that all the sacraments are internally united or are interrelated in that they flow from His wounded side. The blood and water are traditionally taken to represent all the sacraments. Hence, one can say that the redemption He won for us on the cross is channeled to us in diverse ways through the different sacraments because of their different signs and the different existential situations in our lives which they address. Thus, even if a priest is administering the last rites to a lone Christian who is dying in a small cottage on a remote hillside, with no one else present, that is not theologically an isolated or disconnected event: the liturgy of the Church is being celebrated there also and the effects of Christ's sacrifice on Calvary are being made present.

<u>Parallels of Nature and Grace</u>

By continuing to use different images, the internal unity of the sacraments can also be illustrated by making analogies between the growth we see in living things in the world of nature and the growth in grace which the sacraments effect in the life of

Christians. There is new life in the natural order when a seed is planted or a baby is born, and so also, on the higher level, there is new life in the supernatural order when baptism is conferred. That new life is nourished by food in the natural order and similarly by the Eucharist in the supernatural order. It comes to full flower or adulthood in the natural order at late teens, and similarly there is the sacrament of confirmation in the supernatural order. But all growing things in the natural order are subject to set-backs and weakness and, so also, there are the sacraments of penance and anointing of the sick in the supernatural order.

These sacraments, just mentioned, refer to people who are recipients as individuals, but we are social beings also; and so, there is the sacrament of holy orders which provides the Church with men in leadership roles who will prepare people for the other sacraments, administer them and keeping order in the Christian community. And, finally, there is marriage, both a natural institution providing new citizens for society and, when these are baptized, new members for the Church and new heirs to the kingdom of heaven also.

The sacraments are united in their final purpose which is to free us from sin and bring us into ever closer union with Christ by the working of the Holy Spirit, until we are fully united with Him in heaven and see the Father though Him, the Word, in the beatific vision.

When the priest is aware of these things his sense of the sacred will be strong also and will influence the way he administers the sacraments; and that, in turn, will be noticed by the people, and their sense of the sacred will be strengthened also and their participation in the liturgy will be all the richer and give greater glory to God.

New Sacramentals

We said above that new sacramentals are needed to counteract the secularism of this age of high technology. That will take time because we are too close to these new developments to be able to stand back and re-envisage them in the light of faith. But a start must be made. For example, big machinery used to excavate minerals from the earth, or to manufacture goods of all kinds from those minerals, can be seen as an instrument giving us more power to fill the earth and subdue it as God commanded us to do at the beginning. It need not then be seen as an iron monster distracting us from God and defacing the world, assuming that the work is done in a morally upright way and respectful of the environment. Or, again, a complex scan machine in a hospital can be seen as an instrument enabling us to extend Christ's work of healing in our world of today. A food processing plant can be seen as an instrument in feeding the hungry. The television and internet can be seen as instruments of evangelization and of union providing us with a material, electronic basis for our supernatural union by grace in the world-wide Church, but again, if used in a morally good way. People need to be helped to see these things around them in this new light.

Conclusions:

1. The sacraments are special actions of Christ the high priest and of the Church, His mystical body. They elicit the divine and make it present unfailingly, *ex opere operato*, in distinctive ways according to the different signs used in each of the sacraments.
2. In response to the secularism of our time the sacraments need to be seen in their internal unity as coming from God, instituted by Christ, and leading to the beatific vision of the end. They are the different high moments of the liturgy whereby the one Church actualizes herself in her liturgy.
3. The sacramen*tals* are also important because they dispose people for the grace of the sacraments and confer grace by the intercession of the church *ex opere operantis*. The sacramentals enable us to see many and varied things in the world around us as signs of things divine and are greatly needed in a secularist world which is lacking in such signs.
4. Given their relation to the divine, the sacraments and the sacramentals need to be celebrated with great dignity by ministers who have a true sense of the sacred.

With this introduction to the meaning and context of the sacraments we will now proceed to say something about the sacraments individually, beginning with baptism, and treating of them in the traditional order.

Chapter XX

The Sacrament of Baptism

Matter, Form, Effects, Minister, Recipients, Catholic Upbringing

Go teach all nations baptizing them in the name of the Father and the Son and the Holy Spirit. Mt.28.

Holy Baptism is the basis of the whole Christian life, the gateway to life in the Spirit (*vitae spiritualis ianua*), and the door which gives access to the other sacraments. Through Baptism we are freed from sin and reborn as sons of God; we become members of Christ, are incorporated into the Church and made sharers in her mission: "Baptism is the sacrament of regeneration through water in the word." *Catechism of the Catholic Church. (CCC), #1213*

Baptism is always listed as the first of the seven sacraments because none of the others can be received validly without it. This needs to be borne in mind when ecumenical dialogue might leads to requests for some of the other sacraments by non-Christians.[1]

In this chapter we will say a little about the matter and form of this sacrament, the minister and recipient, the time and place of baptism and some related pastoral matters such as giving hope to parents of infants who die before baptism; and, finally, we will say a little about the duty of parents to follow up on baptism with a Catholic upbringing.

Matter and Form

From the event of Christ's own baptism in the river Jordan and from His institution of baptism before He ascended into heaven we learn clearly that water has to be the matter of this sacrament and that the form is *N, I baptize you in the name of the Father and of the Son and of the Holy Spirit.*[2] There is no need to add anything else to that formula by way of piety or for any other reason. These terms "matter and form" are not used in the *Catechism of the Catholic Church*, perhaps taking account that they come from Aristotelian metaphysics which few people have knowledge of today. Even so, they do help for clarity and exactness of meaning in understanding the signification of the sacraments because it is precisely by signifying that the sacraments are causal:

significando causant, as the Latin phrase goes. The pouring of water, the proximate matter, if taken by itself, could have different meanings but the words of the formula, the form, specify the meaning exactly: it is a *baptism* that is going on, a cleansing from sin and a conferring of grace, and not any ordinary washing or watering.

Baptism is a cleansing of the recipient from original sin and from all actual sins if he/she has reached the age of reason. It also takes away all temporal punishment due to sin, confers sanctifying grace and makes us children of God and members of the Church. It also imprints a spiritual mark, a character, on the soul which is permanent.

The pouring on of water on the person's head brings out the point of a cleansing from sin. But the signification of baptism is deeper than that if we consider that it was first administered by immersion in a pool or river as with Christ Himself and with most of the early Christians. St Paul points out the significance of this as a symbolic entering into the tomb with Christ – into death because one can drown in water – so as to emerge to the new life of the resurrection, because water is also a symbol of life: nothing lives without it. So, to be baptized is to undergo or participate in Christ's own paschal mystery by water. Or, we might say that it is the paschal mystery brought forward in a particular way to the candidate by his immersion in the water.

Minister and Recipient

The minister of baptism can be anyone, even a non-Catholic, who has the right intention of doing what the Church does when she baptizes; and that holds good even if the minister's knowledge of the theology of baptism is minimal. But, apart from situations of emergency, it is the norm for baptism to be administered by a priest or deacon because these are ministers representing the Church into which the candidate is now being formally admitted. That too is why the baptism should take place in a church building, the house of God and before the Christian community even if only a small group of family members are present. That the minister can be anyone with the right intention and that water, a common and plentiful element in most parts of the world, is the prescribed matter shows us that God intends that baptism be easily available, which points up its importance for salvation and His will that all would be saved.

The candidate is someone who, if being of the age of reason, has the intention to receive baptism even if, again, his/her knowledge is minimal but that, of course, is no excuse for omitting a proper preparation if there is time for that. Properly, the preparation of an adult takes place during Lent leading up to the baptism itself on Holy Saturday night. The RCIA program structures this preparation. When the recipient is a small child the intention of the parents will suffice. When it is a situation of a miscarriage one should baptize if the baby is thought to be still alive, and a second time, conditionally, in case of twins when what is born is not clearly distinguishable - the old rule being that whatever is born of woman (however conceived) is to be considered human.

The Non-Baptized

When the baby is clearly born dead, or is born alive and dies unexpectedly without baptism, there arises the old and difficult question of what happens to the souls of such infants. This problem has greater point now than in former ages when we see that the vast majority of the world's population is non-Christian and also because of the large number killed by abortion. When trying to respond to that problem one finds that there is little or nothing explicitly to be had in scripture or, consequently, in tradition. Nearly all references to baptism in the New Testament relate to adults, except for odd references such as that of Cornelius and his household being baptized as recounted in the *Act of the Apostles. (Ch.10:34 – 48)*. The household might have included small children also.

What we *do* find in scripture is a clear statement that God wills that all would be saved. *(1 Timothy 2:4)*. So, one would expect that God's will would be effective unless a person deliberately puts an obstacle in the way, something a small baby cannot do. But we also have it stated that baptism is necessary for salvation. *Unless a man is born again of water and the Holy Spirit he cannot enter the kingdom of God. Jn 3:5.* This raises the further question of how necessary is "necessary"; is it an *absolute* necessity? Some Fathers of the Church took stern positions on this, varying from saying bluntly that all unbaptized children were damned outright, to saying that they were damned in the lesser sense of being shut out from the beatific vision but not suffering the sense pains we usually associate with hell. Then, in time, came the theological construct of limbo – a place of natural happiness but without the beatific vision.

But whatever way one approaches this problem there are difficulties. To say that all such children go to hell goes flat against the goodness and mercy of God. It also says that the incarnation and redemption won by Christ had no bearing on these children at all. The old practice of refusing Christian burial to such children was also very harsh on parents who were grieving enough already because of the loss of their child. But, then, taking the opposite approach and saying that all such children are saved automatically is making little of the necessity of faith and baptism. Limbo, as a compromise theological construct, has problems with it also. If the vision of God, of the Infinite One, who alone can satisfy our infinite longing, cannot be had by the unbaptized for all eternity then will the finite happiness of limbo not lead to eternal boredom and non-fulfilment after a while?

This problem is a kind of theological knot which becomes ever more entangled when one tries to unravel it. Yet it is not just an academic problem but a very real and frequent pastoral problem. The *International Theological Commission* went into great depths on this problem at the end of the 20th century and after producing a lengthy document concluded tersely by saying simply that "we may hope" that such children can be saved.

The sacraments are the normal means prescribed by God for people to receive His grace and so they should be availed of whenever possible. But God is not tied to His own sacraments and can communicate His grace, the grace of Christ and the Church, in virtue of Christ's paschal mystery to people who cannot access the sacraments through no fault of their own, so that those who are not formally visible members of the Church can be saved. But if or when they are saved it is still by the grace of Christ and His Church because He is the only savior. We may hope that such a thing happens in the case of the unbaptized also, but that still does not allow us to say with certainty that Baby A is definitely gone to heaven and enjoys the beatific vision.

The Church now has a liturgy of commendation for unbaptized infants, so, if we let the *lex orandi* give the lead here to the *lex credendi* we can say to the parents of such children that if God allowed this miscarriage or mishap to happen in His all-seeing providence, and given that He is a God of mercy and love, we can take it that He is now taking care of this infant in His own way. But to go on from there to say that that taking care *must* be happening in heaven or limbo or wherever else is to go beyond the limits of what we are allowed to say, given what we know of His ways from revelation.

There is a humbling lesson in this particular problem for the minister also. It is that he cannot claim to know everything about God's ways even though he is ordained to speak on His behalf, less still, then, can he presume to pontificate about what exactly God is doing in many sad and difficult situations. God is infinite mystery. He revealed so much to us in scripture and in His Son when He came on earth and spoke to us; but there is immensely more that still remains mystery which even the angels cannot fully fathom. That is so because faith is a constant challenge for us to go beyond what seems appropriate to us in our limited vision so that we will continue to follow with an attitude of childlike trust in our heavenly Father.

Time and Place of Baptism

Assuming the normal birth of a healthy baby the question arises as to what is the appropriate time and place for the baptism? It often happened in the past that the baby was baptized on the very day of his/her birth in the place of birth or in a nearby church very soon after. (If in the church, it meant then that the mother was often, unfortunately, not able to be present). There was this haste because parents saw an urgency in conferring baptism lest anything might happen to the child if there was a delay.

Today we recommend that the mother, and, of course, the father be present so that they can be made aware of the obligation that is on them to follow up on the baptism with a solid Catholic upbringing for the child. That can mean a delay of a few days or more before the baptism takes place. That is tolerable, but now one often finds baptisms being delayed for months on end. The excuse might be that they are waiting until Dad's brother, Uncle Jim, or Mom's sister, Auntie Kate, is home on holidays so that they can plan a big meal in the hotel for a celebration. But that might not be for another six months. The point is completely overlooked that in the meantime the baby could take suddenly ill and die, as happens at times, and the more serious point that the longer the baby is without the grace of the sacrament the more of an opening that is left to Satan to move in and do his mischief, something people in former times were aware of but which is not taken at all seriously now in a time of waning belief and increasing secularism. Parents should be made aware that in the prayers of a baptism ceremony there is included an exorcism prior to the pouring on of the water. This does not mean at all that every baby, prior to being baptized, is inevitably possessed by Satan. But it does mean that such a thing *can* happen and that the baby is vulnerable. If children and adults who *are* baptized can still be possessed or harmed in various ways by the Evil One, the unbaptized are all the more open and vulnerable. Canon law does not set a specific time frame for a baptism because circumstances can vary from place to place but it does say "within the first few weeks". *Canon 867 #1*

Then we have some Catholic parents who, though they supposedly have the faith, advance the argument that children should not be baptized as infants or even as children but left till they are adults so that they can then decide for themselves if they want to be baptized. How strange: these parents will want to give their children the best in terms of nutrition, health-care and education from their earliest years, and will pay for them to have swimming lessons and art and music lessons *etc.*, but will still deprive them of the most important treasure of all which parents can give to them, namely the gift of the grace of baptism and the infused virtues of faith, hope and charity which come with baptism. They fail utterly to see that if they themselves have been given the gift of faith and have been blessed by God with children, that it is God's plan that these children will come to the faith by these parents bringing them along for baptism and then giving them a proper, Catholic upbringing. There are indeed some very inspiring stories of adult conversions to the faith by people who grew up without being baptized, but they are few in most societies, and particularly in the secular West. Instead, most Catholics come to the faith by reason of infant baptism and that is in keeping with the providence of God. To do otherwise is to let them to their own devices or caprice and to leave them a prey to the *roaring lion who prowls about seeking the ruin of souls. 1 Peter 5:8-9.*

Catholic Upbringing

This brings us to the matter of a proper Catholic upbringing as the necessary follow up on the sacrament of baptism. Vatican II teaches:

> It is particularly in the Christian family, enriched by the grace and office of the sacrament of matrimony, that from their earliest years children should be taught, according to the faith received in baptism, to have a knowledge of God, to worship Him, and to love their neighbour. Here, too, they gain their first experience of wholesome human companionship and of the church. *Gravissimum Educationis, #3.*

At the pre-baptismal talk and again at the start of the ceremony the point is forcefully made that the parents, in asking for baptism, are undertaking to bring the child up in the practice of the faith, helped by the God-parents. I always make that the topic of my brief homily in the baptism ceremony. They are asked if they clearly understand this and are expected to answer affirmatively. The seed of new life is been planted in the soul of the child with the pouring on of the baptismal water, but if that is not followed up with a definite Catholic upbringing then, while the character imprinted will endure forever and the grace will endure at least for some time, the sacrament will go largely to waste because the grace received will be lost and the child will be allowed to fall into sinful ways from an early age.

A Catholic upbringing requires first of all the simple presence of the parents (or guardians) in the home. Without any words being spoken, the very presence of both father and mother in the home, available there to support and comfort the children in their difficulties, in ways that are distinctive of the father and the mother respectively, ensures the healthy emotional development of the children and forestalls the many forms of deviancy which can develop when such support is lacking. During the early years the presence of the mother in the home is invaluable and irreplaceable. Small children need their mother. "Where is Mom?" they will say so often, especially when they come in from school. I am allowing, of course, for situations where one parent dies young, as when a mother dies in childbirth, or a father must work far away from home for reasons of economic necessity. If such things happen in God's providence, and the parents trust in that providence, then they can hope that the Lord will supply in other ways.

Then, a Catholic upbringing requires that the parents teach their children their prayers, especially those to be said "every morning and every night and in all dangers, temptations and afflictions" as the old catechism teaches; that they teach them their catechism; that they be brought to Mass regularly and faithfully, at least on Sundays, and to the other sacraments; that they give them tender affection combined with firm discipline according to clear rules about what is right and what is wrong; that they give them good example, first, by the way they treat each other as husband and wife, that is, with respect, kindness and with a willingness to forgive and make sacrifices for each other, and, second, in the way they treat the children themselves. It is from their earthly father at home that children get their first impression of God their Father in heaven and of His provident care for all of us, and it is from their earthly mother that they get their first impressions of their heavenly mother Mary and of the Church.

The ultimate goal of baptism and of the consequent Christian upbringing is that the children will become citizens of heaven for eternity. Parents, of course, hope that their children will be successful in school and in their careers here on earth, happy in their marriages and have sufficient wealth and good healt; but I always pose the question to them of what use all of this would be if in the end they miss out on the happiness of heaven, and I add the question: Do you think you would be admitted to heaven yourselves, if their loss was directly due to your neglect? Such points as these should be conveyed at pre-baptism talks and possibly again, briefly, in the baptism homily.

If at a pre-baptism talk parents indicate to the priest that they are not practicing Catholics and do not intend to be and that they want baptism for their child simply to please Granny who is still practicing, or as a pass-card to a Catholic school which produces good results academically, or for the celebration meal that would follow as a big family event, then I think the priest should challenge them to think seriously about their true stance in respect of the faith. If it is only nominal and if the baptism is requested for purely secular reasons then what is the point of the baptism at all? Why not challenge them by having them face the consequences of the total apostasy of this whole family? Hopefully the challenge might have them do a re-think for the better so that a sincere request for the sacrament would be the end result. Canon law advises a delay rather than a total refusal in such cases. (*Can. 868 #2*).

There is, then, the further difficulty when two parents in an irregular union bring along a child for baptism, or worse still, when they are two parents of the same gender. In the former case one has a situation of ongoing fornication or adultery and in the latter one of ongoing sodomy sacrilegiously dressed up as "marriage". They and the priest want baptism for the good of the child, but the priest, in admitting such parents, is giving recognition to unions that are objectively sinful and clearly not in accord with what the Church calls "marriage".

The Church does not compromise with sin but is willing to forgive sin at the drop of a hat when there is sincere repentance and purpose of amendment. If the priest sees that in such a union it is unlikely that the child will get a Catholic upbringing then he should refuse to do the baptism, at least for the time being, until things might be put right. The example of parents in irregular unions, especially same-gender unions, militates against a full and proper Catholic upbringing because the children will learn about true marriage in school and then see something different being practiced at home. Or the priest might admit the child if brought along by two practicing God-parents, sponsors, one of each gender, and is reasonably sure that they will take an active part in the child's Catholic upbringing. But how likely is that? He should also take account of the religious character of the wider environment: it might be a small community, still very Catholic in practice, so that the child could pick up some of the faith from neighbours and from school. In any case, there should be definite guidelines from bishops' conferences on such matters so that we won't have the situation of a conscientious priest doing one thing and then Fr Popularity doing the opposite in the next parish.

<u>The God-Parents</u>

The parents are the primary educators of their children in the faith, a point made already in the prophet section of this work, but the God-parents are important also, especially when a parent is dead or absent for a long time or when there is a problem in regard to the parents even if present. At the baptism ceremony they are asked if they are willing to help the parents in the Catholic upbringing of the children. In countries that have been traditionally Catholic, such that the children were growing up in a Catholic environment because their own family and the other families around them were Catholic - and so also the school and the entire parish - the role of the God-parents, while always important, was not of crucial importance. In such a society that role was often a somewhat honorary one: "we must ask Uncle Jim to be the God-father because he is Dad's only brother, or Auntie Kate to be the God-mother because she is so seldom at home and it would be a nice honour for her when she does come again in the Summer. But if Uncle Jim is not going to Mass and is partnered with his girl-friend how can he be considered a suitable God-father? Canon law requires of a sponsor that he/she:

> ...be a Catholic who has been confirmed and has already received the most holy sacrament of the Eucharist and who leads a life of faith in keeping with the function to be taken on... *Canon 872 #3.*

And if Auntie Kate is living and settled two thousand miles away, of what practical use is she if she is needed to take up the role of instructing the child in the faith, even if she is practicing the faith where she is? It is time that we looked on this role as more than a merely honorary thing, that is if we are truly serious about the importance of a Catholic upbringing. Some Italian bishops have had to deal with the problem of mafia members imposing themselves on families as God-parents for purely secular reasons. In some cases the bishops simply forbid having any God-parents at all to try to convey the point that a God-parent, properly, should be simply and solely a help for the growth in the faith of the child. But the day of the baptism itself is not a suitable time for the priest to begin raising objections if he sees Uncle Jim turning up. A good practice is to use the Sunday sermon on a day like the feast of the Baptism of Our Lord to make clear to all present what is required of a good sponsor.

Accurate Documenting

A final pastoral point on the sacrament of baptism, which indeed has application for some of the other sacraments also, is the importance of recording the baptism speedily and accurately.

> The pastor of the place where the baptism is celebrated must carefully and without any delay record in the baptismal register the names of the baptized, with mention made of the minister, parents, sponsors, witnesses, if any, the place and date of the conferral of the baptism, and the date and place of birth. *Canon 877 #1.*

If a priest or his secretary forgets to write in the details of a baptism for more than twenty four hours then he is even more likely to forget doing so for another day and perhaps forever. Also, if the details are inaccurate, for example, if there is a discrepancy between the way the child's name is recorded here and then in the civil certificate, it will cause problems; they should be in accord. Even if a little letter such as the "O" is omitted in the case of a child by the name of O'Sullivan or O'Brien it can lead to complications later on that may even require court orders to put right, because such records can not to be altered at will later. It is very wrong for the priest to be the cause of such confusion and trouble to people by his negligence. There may also be a difficulty when registering the name of the father of a child of an unmarried mother or when the child is adopted. (cf. *Can 877 #2*).

Conclusions:

1. Many saints have seen the day of their baptism as the most important day of their lives because baptism cleansed them from original sin and brought them the life of grace for the first time and admitted them into the family of God in the Church. It should be administered within a few weeks of birth.
2. The sacrament of baptism needs to be followed up with a truly Catholic upbringing for which the example of the parents and the help of the God-parents are important. The role of the God-parent is more than an honorary one, so the requirements of canon law should be adhered to in this regard.
3. There is a difficult theological problem surrounding the case of children who die before baptism. Nonetheless we can believe that the all-merciful God takes care of them also and we may hope that somehow His grace, necessary for salvation, might reach them in other ways. Their parents need this assurance.

After the sacrament of baptism, the sacrament of confirmation follows next in the traditional order.

Chapter XXI

The Sacrament of Confirmation

History, Doctrine, a big Day, the Fall Off, Solutions

And they were all filled with the Holy Spirit and began to speak in other tongues. Acts 2:4

Baptism, the Eucharist, and the sacrament of Confirmation together constitute the "sacraments of Christian initiation," whose unity must be safeguarded. It must be explained to the faithful that the reception of the sacrament of Confirmation is necessary for the completion of baptismal grace. For "by the sacrament of Confirmation, [the baptized] are more perfectly bound to the Church and are enriched with a special strength of the Holy Spirit. Hence they are, as true witnesses of Christ, more strictly obliged to spread and defend the faith by word and deed. *Catechism of the Catholic Church, #1285*

In pastoral practice it is penance that follows on baptism in the West when the latter sacrament has been conferred in infancy but, in the case of adult baptism, confirmation follows immediately because, theologically, there is a close link between these two sacraments. In this chapter we will say a little about the history and theology of the sacrament but more on some of the pastoral problems that surround it today, particularly the sad phenomenon of the big "drop off" from practice of so many young people just after confirmation.

History and Doctrine of Confirmation

Scripture shows the close link between baptism and confirmation as, for example, when we see Christ being baptized in the Jordan and the Holy Spirit descending on Him in the form of a dove (though Christ had the Holy Spirit from the very start of His earthly life). Again, because most of the early Christians in apostolic times were baptized as adults, they were also confirmed in the same ceremony and admitted to the Eucharist. This is still the practice today with newly baptized Christians in the West; and in the East, even in the case of infants, confirmation is administered along with baptism. But given this close link between the two sacraments they are still distinct and always were, even if the clear distinction between the two was not clarified finally and definitively until Trent. Even in scripture we find sources for the distinction there is between these two sacraments: Pentecost was the event of the coming of the Holy Spirit without any baptism taking place, and we find in *The Acts of the Apostles (19:1-6)* that some Christians in Samaria had been baptized but had not received the Holy Spirit and had not even heard of Him!

Given this little bit of historical background we can say that confirmation is the sacrament of Christian adulthood when the confirmed persons receive the Holy Spirit and take on their role as public witnesses of the faith. It brings to full flowering the seed of new life that was planted in baptism. Vatican II teaches:

> Bound more intimately to the Church by the sacrament of confirmation, they are endowed by the Holy Spirit with special strength. Hence, they are more strictly obliged to spread and defend the faith both by word and by deed as true witnesses of Christ. *Lumen Gentium, #12.*

So, it is the sacrament of Christian completion or perfection, not in the sense that the candidate is now deemed to have reached the heights of sanctity, but to have come of age spiritually. It is for this reason that St Thomas argued that it was most fitting that the bishop confer it because he is the perfector of spiritual growth (even if, as St Thomas freely admits, he might not himself be a very holy man). But a priest can be the minister in the case of a baptised child being in danger of death or if he is the priest who has been the spiritual guide of a catechumen about to be baptised. There are still other cases where the bishop might delegate a priest to confer this sacrament. (*cf. can 884 ff*). The recipient, then, must have been baptised and be properly disposed if over the age of reason.

The form of this sacrament is *N, be sealed with the gift of the Holy Spirit* and the matter is olive oil and balsam blessed by the bishop at the Chrism Mass on Holy Thursday. The oil symbolises strength in this case – the strength needed for giving witness - and the balsam, being a kind of perfume, symbolizes an adornment of the one stepping into adult society. This sacrament is not repeated because it confers a character, as does baptism, a spiritual mark on the soul binding the recipient more closely to Christ so as to be able to represent Him in society.

A Big Day in the Parish

For the priest(s) of the parish, the *confirmandi* and their families, and indeed for the entire parish, confirmation is a big day, a day on which the parish wants "to put its best foot forward". So, it requires a lot of preparation on the part of the priest, of the catechists who are often the teachers in a Catholic school, of the people in the choir and sacristy, and of those who look after the church grounds. The preparations need to begin a long time in advance especially that of ensuring that the *confirmandi* have a good understanding of this sacrament and of what they are receiving. But, sadly, I find at times that they don't, due either to faulty catechetics programs or to teachers who have no interest in the faith or to negligent parents who will not give support to good teachers who are trying to do their best in the school.

When there are *confirmandi* from two or more schools there needs to be a meeting in advance to sort out which students will take which parts in the ceremony. I have seen this cause trouble when there are teachers who see the ceremony primarily as an occasion on which to "show off" the talent they have in their respective schools. There can also be the opposite problem of little of no preparation because teachers are intimidated by non-practicing Catholic parents who see the time given to confirmation catechesis and to practices in the church as wasted, as taking from what *they* consider to be the more important studies i.e. the purely secular subjects. Then there is the added problem when some of the pupils are from non-denominational schools or multi denominational schools where little or perhaps no provision is made for sacramental preparation. There are no easy answers to such problems and they have to be resolved pragmatically at local level.

There are also the problems that can occur when the ceremony is over and the meal for the bishop and the visiting priests is about to begin. It can happen that if the pastor has enlisted the help of a second cook she might be resented by the regular cook and the two might have a disagreement in the kitchen ten minutes before the soup is served!! For all these reasons the pastor can often be heard breathing a sigh of relief when at last the bishop's car drives away. I remember once standing beside such a pastor when the bishop's car was departing and he was saying "I wonder do bishops ever realize how glad we priests are to see the tail end of their cars going out the gate after confirmation". The irony of it was that, soon after, the same man became a bishop himself in another diocese and was not all that well received there, he being an outsider, so that a good many other priests would soon to be saying similar things as *his* car pulled off!

But, regardless of the problems and difficulties before and after the ceremony, the liturgy of confirmation itself is something splendid when those in charge - priests, parents and teachers - give it their best. I have always found that the moment of the singing of the *Veni Creator* is a great one, an experience of the Holy Spirit Himself at work, the One who comes in a special way in this sacrament and who sanctifies in every other sacrament also.

The Big Fall Off

But the biggest problem that follows in the weeks and months after confirmation in the countries of the West is the sad one of many of those who have been confirmed, far from becoming adult witnesses of the faith, take the very opposite course and fall away from nearly all practice of the faith. There is the sad joke about the parish priest who had the problem of crows coming into his church through a top window which was too high up for him to reach. When he asked another priest how he might get rid of them the latter said cynically "Why don't you confirm them and then they will exit fast"! Happily, in the Far East and in many African countries the situation is much healthier.

This phenomenon of many young people, newly confirmed, falling away from the practice of the faith raises a lot of questions for which I have not seen satisfactory answers so far, and points to serious underlying problems. It raises the question also as to whether or not the age of ten or twelve years, at the end of primary school, is the right time. Is it too young to expect of these children to begin playing the role of adult witnesses of the faith in society? But, then, in centuries past, many children left school about that age, or at fourteen at most, and had to go out into the "big, bad world" and take their part in adult society, often far from home, and often marrying in their mid-teens. In more recent times we have pushed that age of adulthood up to sixteen or eighteen. So, should confirmation be deferred till then? The plus is to say that then they will be more mature about their new role and that their age of natural adulthood and spiritual adulthood will coincide. But the minus is that many of them will not come forward at that point because their peers will have been telling them prior to that that it is not "cool" to be going near a church at all. Because, then, they might never be confirmed we bring it forward so as to "catch them" while they are still in primary school and get them confirmed anyhow – even if for some it means nothing more than a big day with a big meal and photos afterwards.

A solution which I have seen in dioceses in mainland Europe is to take confirmation and preparation for confirmation out of the school entirely and locate it in the parish. But then the number being confirmed can often be as small as six or eight even in highly populated inner-city parishes. They are the children of parents who have been bringing them to Mass faithfully on Sundays. But what of their other classmates most of whom are also baptized Catholics? They, or some of them, get confirmed as adults when they come along to get married. But some others will not marry and some of those who do will marry in registry offices. Hence the likelihood is that many will not be confirmed at all unless on their death bed, if, at that point, they have the desire or the opportunity to receive any sacraments. In many countries now, even nominally Catholic countries, the primary school is not always under Catholic management thus making it more difficult to locate sacramental preparation in the school. But in a country like Ireland where most primary schools are still in Catholic management many people, and even some priests, will still argue that sacramental preparation should, likewise, be taken out of the school and located entirely in the parish due to the problem, mentioned above already, of their being other pupils in the school who are non-Catholic or are non-practicing Catholics. But to my mind this is a capitulation, another instance of the ongoing sell out or cave in of the Church to the world that should not be allowed to happen – a Catholic school no longer able to do what is Catholic in its own classrooms! If a school is Catholic then preparation for the sacraments should have a big place in it regardless of the objections of those who cannot or will not recognize the value of sacramental preparation, even though they still want the academic benefits of a Catholic school.

The Causes of the Fall off

Different solutions are taken up by different bishops in different places to the above difficulties and it is not for me to prescribe any one-for-all solution. Whatever be the solution adopted in a given diocese the underlying question still remains: why is it that many of those confirmed in the West not only will *not* take up an adult role of witnessing to the faith in the wider society but will stop practicing the faith almost entirely and fall away? This question is an instance of the wider question of why there is an ongoing apostasy in the Western world; and I don't claim to have a simple answer or solution to it because many factors are at work, some of which have a long history going back to the break-up of faith which happened at the reformation.

That break-up of faith led to relativism in matters of doctrine and morals so that instead of their being one pope at the top, recognized by all as a final arbitrator in such matters, everyone became his/her own pope even when one person was contradicting another as was inevitable. Tolerance, even of such contradictions, with each one's belief being given the same truth value, became the supreme virtue so that religious truth was reduced to mere opinion, which in turn leads to skepticism and unbelief. We touched on this already at the end of the *prophet* section of this work. Nonetheless, Catholic truth was still holding ground in many countries in the midst of all this relativism and skepticism until the aftermath of Vatican II when things began to fall apart though not as a result of what the council taught but as a result of how some chose to interpret its documents and use them to promote various ideologies of their own. In Holland, for example, Catholics were a minority since the reformation. But they were a solid, faithful minority until after the council when the faith collapsed there and Catholics went liberal in the extreme. But, to keep to our particular question of the why the young fall away now in so many families in the West even where parents are practicing, I can only hazard a few ideas.

In the providence of God most people come to the faith because their parents bring them along to the church for baptism. There are indeed some rare conversion stories of young people coming to the faith from other religions or none, but normally, as said before, it is God's plan that the parents, who hand on natural life and other natural goods to their children in the family setting, would hand on the faith and the life of grace to them also. This is what happened in most Catholic families in the past. But now it is as if a kind of wedge has been driven in between parents and children, preventing that from happening. Obviously, if the parents themselves are not practicing, then, this handing on will not happen (but that merely pushes the same question back one generation). But what is especially distressing is to see how in some families, where the parents are devout Catholics and practicing faithfully, that, nonetheless, the children fall away and begin to cohabit or marry invalidly in civil ceremonies or profess themselves to be agnostics or even atheists. When they, in turn, become parents they sometimes do not even bother to bring their own children along for baptism. The anguish of the grandparents then is all the greater in proportion to their love of the faith and their grandchildren because they have good reason to fear the loss of their souls.

The handing on of the faith from one generation to another is like the adding of links to a chain. If one generation lapses it can happen that the grandparents might still be able to "bridge the gap" and hand on the faith to the grandchildren. The loss of one link may not be unsurmountable. But when two successive generations turn away then the outlook for the future of the faith in such families is bleak. Perhaps the influence of good teachers with good catechetic programs in the school might supply in part. But it is not fair to expect such teachers to take on full responsibility for the faith of such children if the parents and the priests are not doing their part as well. The three-legged stool, which we saw earlier, is of little use if even one leg is missing.

Different Wedges

But what is that wedge that is splitting off one generation from the other? It is multiple in its make-up. If the faith is handed on primarily from parents to children in the normal course of things this then requires that parents are with their children a lot of the time, especially that the mother can be with them in the home when they are very young and when they come in from school; and the father's presence also is needed as much as is possible. But that does not happen in many cases due to both parents being out working, the flip side of which is that the children are thrown into creches from morning to evening from a very young age. When the parents cannot spend time, daily, with their children then, of course, they cannot hand on much to them and they try to compensate for this by heaping material things on them as presents, things which entertain and distract for a while but which are no substitute for parental presence and care.

Then there is the wedge of defective catechetics programs of which I have spoken already. The object of faith is primarily the person of Christ but Christ cannot be separated from His teaching, which teachings are the doctrines of faith and morals. One cannot have Catholic belief, even in Christ Himself, unless one is clear that He is truly God and truly man in one person and that He is truly present in the Eucharist; but many are vague on such things. So also with morals – so many pupils today do not know what is right or wrong according to the most basic understanding of the commandments. Faith cannot be reduced to generalities nor can morals be reduced to sentiments and feelings about love if solid doctrine is left aside. This deficiency in catechetics raises further questions about the kind of formation teachers now get in their training colleges.

Then there is the wedge of defective preaching about which I have also spoken. If parents hear little more than banal platitudes every Sunday about how we should be "nice" to everyone then they will not have much to hand on to their children. This raises further questions about the seminary formation of priests.

Then there is the wedge of the media which is mostly anti-Catholic in the West and which has great influence due to the multiple kinds of social media which exist now and which are ever in the hands of young people. It divides and isolates family members from each other. I heard of a man who took his wife and family to Spain for a holiday one time. He made a rule that while they were there together there was to be no intrusion from cell phones or ipads or ipods or smart phones or any such things. He found that the children simply could not do without such things and that when they were not allowed them, such as at meal times, they could only bicker and fight with each other.

The Influence of Music

The media also present the kind of music and entertainment that young are enjoying - if they really *are* enjoying it - or rather should I say, are "being saturated" with, which is not good. That kind of music and entertainment is a continuing fruit of the sexual revolution of the 1960's and is grossly erotic. It is loud, coarse and vulgar. It is based more on beat than on pitch and sometimes repeats dangerous and even

Satanic mantras subliminally. It is no surprise that some of the rock bands which pedal that kind of music, or should I say that "noise", have the picture of a well-known Satanist on the covers of their albums. It goes without saying that such entertainment is most conducive to promiscuous behavior and that young minds, saturated with that kind of thing, simply have no taste whatever for the spiritual.

This raises a fundamental topic seldom discussed today: that of the influence of music on the soul. Plato was aware of it and so were all ancient cultures. He even went so far as to say that when a city changes its music it will soon change its laws also, meaning that the influence of music will change the minds of the people so much that their laws, which are an expression of their minds, will change also. Man is not just an intellect capable of abstraction, nor, at the other extreme, is he a mere bodily machine capable of diverse movements. He is also a being with emotions, those springs of the soul that move the body to action. Now, just as abstract truth can supply the intellect's longing for truth and as food can supply the body's physical needs, so also music can stir and feed the emotions. An obvious example is the piper playing a rousing march as he leads a platoon of soldiers into battle. Good music will lift the emotions upwards towards what is good and noble and beautiful. Plato saw it as making for harmony between the different powers of the soul. (*cf.* Plato, *The Republic*). If it raises the soul to what is good and noble it will thereby prepare the soul for the spiritual. St Augustine spoke of the effect of the Church's music on him (*cf. The Confessions*). So also, going in the opposite direction, coarse, vulgar music, which uses strong beat to arose the erotic, leads the listener down to what is base and sinful. These two kinds of music are diametrically opposed.

The people in the entertainment business either are not aware of this, of the damage they are doing to the young with this kind of music, or don't care so long as it draws the crowds to discos and rock concerts and that that brings in money. Add to that the greater influence today when young people are wired up to this kind of thing for many hours of the day with their wi-fi gadgets.

Then add the influence of pornography, alcohol and drugs – all of which are easily accessible even in country villages - and one is really down in the depths. It is difficult for good priests or parents or teachers to combat that kind of influence; but it must be done. If drug barons can be tracked down with some success why not the producers of porn also?

In the past, prior to the 1960s, in all Western countries there was folk music and folk dancing and songs which evoked ideas of generous love, patriotism and neighborly co-operation. In the East also people sang and danced in ways that were expressive of what was good in their different cultures. But the sexual revolution of the 60s happened rather suddenly and foisted a different culture on young people. [1]

In the past also priests were very alert to the kind of entertainment that the young enjoyed, trying to ensure that it was morally good and helping to promote what was good in our heritage. Sadly, however, there were some priests of a Puritan or Jansenist mindset who sought to ban all kinds of dancing at a time when it was mostly morally upright, when music was uplifting, evoking noble emotions, and dancing was a graceful art. They begot a reaction of an opposite kind – the unending swing of the pendulum again - so that priests today utter not a word when entertainment has changed from being healthy and joyful to being erotic and Satanic, with the result that souls are being led to ruin. One can even find that children who have made their first communion or have been confirmed in the morning will sometimes be treated to a rock disco in the evening – and priests, teachers and parents fail to see the contradiction: they have been confirmed as "strong and perfect Christians" in the church and shortly afterwards they are to be found jumping around in a darkened hall with psychedelic lighting like wild animals just out of a cage! What a descent this is from the *Veni Creator* in the morning to that kind of vulgarity in the evening!

The young must enjoy themselves; they are not going to sit down twiddling their thumbs at home. But their entertainment needs to be structured by their seniors in a way that is morally and aesthetically good, because left to themselves they will simply imitate what they see on the screen in front of them. My own experience with young people is that when they are introduced to a good type of dancing, such as folk dancing or the waltz, they take to it very well and enjoy it. If they are not introduced to this they will go for the animal kind of dance for the simple reason that their peers are doing so and because they know no better.

Youth Clubs

In the 1970's there began the youth club movement in England and other countries and then in Ireland. It had the aim of providing structured entertainment of a good kind for young people of teenage years at weekends. It was "specialized" in the sense that it made young people to be a special group or club by themselves with youth leaders in charge who were only a few years older than the others in the club. It was very popular in those years and had its successes. But I remember an old priest making the point that to make a special category of the young, made up of teenagers mostly, was to cut them off from the older generations and therefore from the steadying influence and the good, moral example which the latter could pass on to them if they were integrated with them. Looking back on it I think he had a point. Since then there has been the added problem of drug peddlers infiltrating youth clubs in places, also promoters of sodomy, and even of governments providing free condoms to youth.

Prior to the 1970's, in rural Ireland and many parts of Europe, there were organizations which promoted drama, dancing, variety concerts, quizzes, outings *etc.*, which involved all generations, young and old, so that the old were able to exert a moderating influence on the young and pass on their culture and values to them. There were also temperance movements aimed mostly at curbing the abuse of alcohol which had all kinds of social activities for young and old and which invoked the help of the Sacred Heart for the grace needed to be sober and self-controlled. The leaders had enough faith and wisdom to know that education alone is not sufficient to combat addictions because of the weakness of the will resulting from original sin but that the grace of God is needed also, which is obtained by such devotions. Sadly, when the youth clubs became the fashion they drew young people away from these other organizations so that the latter faded out in many places, which was a great moral and cultural loss in my opinion.

No Sense of Purpose

One other cause I would identify for the fall off in the practice of the faith after confirmation relates to the very goal of the sacrament itself which is to make of those confirmed to be adult Christians ready to take their part in society as witnesses of the faith. The question must be asked: what in practice does this mean? One answer is that, from confirmation day onwards, those newly confirmed would take part in the liturgy as readers at Mass or as singers in the choir or as Eucharistic ministers. Good indeed. But the total number involved in such things will still be relatively small. There are the much wider fields of life, which include business, industry, farming, politics, culture, health, education, *etc.*, indeed the whole of life in society when the world is seen as a field to be cultivated in preparation for the kingdom of God. We touched on this already in our King section when talking about the role of the laity as being principally that of preparing the world for the Kingdom of God by Christianizing it, by making the law of God and the values of the gospel to be the major influence in society, and we will return to it again later at the end of this study. Here I am saying that we should be directing our newly confirmed to this goal. If they are confirmed at, let us say, the age of twelve or thirteen and if they are still in school, at second level, for another four or five years, they will not be free to engage in the wider society directly, immediately on being confirmed, but *we should be preparing them to do so* and be instructing them on social issues, and on the Church's principles in relation to those issues. In sum, we should be training them in the basic principles of Catholic social teaching while still at school so that when they do go out into society they can start giving effect to those principles in the world around them and be well fortified against the ideologies which will be pedaled to them by the media.

Confirmation, at present, is like a sacrament of completion of initiation which does not have a goal afterwards. To use an example: it is as if a class of trainee pilots got only a vague training on what flight is all about but nonetheless got their wings in an elaborate ceremony and had no idea of what to do next. They do not even know where the airport is or how to start an airplane. What then is the point of giving them the wings in the first place? So also, with a class of young Christian who have only a general and often faulty knowledge of the faith and know nothing about Catholic social teaching: they see no definite, or tangible purpose to the sacrament after being confirmed. Instead, what we see in so many countries of the West now is young people being completely taken in by the ideologies of "choice" or feminism, of humanism and Marxism (disguised in various ways) so that when they leave school they become counter witnesses: they campaign and vote for things utterly contrary to the moral law and become willing agents in the preparing of the world for the kingdom – not of Christ – but instead of the anti-Christ.

Possible Solutions

To counter this problem of the fall off from the faith of so many young people after confirmation many things are needed seeing that the causes of the problem are multiple and can not be exhaustively covered here. Parents need to be made aware of their responsibility to practice the faith by being faithful to Sunday Mass and by trying to keep the commandments. But for parents to pass on the faith to their children they need to be able to be with their children in the home, especially the mother while the children are very young. Many mothers cannot do this because they have to take jobs outside the home due to economic necessity. If the state would give them salaries as home makers and give grants for the building of homes that facilitate relatively large families it would be a great help in this regard because I would argue that the mother in the home is the most important person of all in society. She would then have time with her own children and be able to pass on the faith to them. The support she gives to the children in the home, sound instruction, tender affection and good discipline, would forestall many social problems later on which cost the state millions.

Teachers, next, need to be properly trained and made aware of the urgency of good catechetics. They need to be alerted to the Marxist influence in the trade unions that claim to represent them.

To counteract the bad influence of the rock culture (or rather anti-culture) entertainers need to be made aware of the moral effects of good and bad music and dance. Young people themselves need to be made aware of how debased they become when they engage in entertainments of an erotic kind. The early Christians provide a lesson here: they would not go to the theatres or circuses of their times, knowing what brutality was displayed in these shows, they being aware of their own new dignity as followers of Christ. Christians today have the same dignity and are in a similar social position but don't seem to realize it.

Organizations of a multi-generational kind, such as those described above, should be resurrected even if in somewhat different forms taking account of changing times.

To remedy the lack of social purpose following the reception of confirmation, training in Catholic social teaching is needed. In practice this would require that our young people would first be well informed in the basics of the Catholic faith by sound catechetics and then that they be formed in the principles of Catholic social teaching. Formation in the basics of the faith should continue till about the age of fifteen and formation in Catholic social teaching begin then for the remaining years of second level schooling (and hopefully into third level as well and perhaps as night classes for young, post-school adults). It would be convenient then if confirmation was about the age of fifteen. But even if it were to remain at twelve or thirteen some elements of Catholic social teaching could begin to be introduced along with the basics of the faith as soon as they entered second-level school.

The priest could be pivotal in promoting these solutions and the moral and cultural renewal which is so badly needed, both with his preaching and by organizing parents to provide something better for their young. Thus, along with pointing out the immorality of what is presented to the young at present, they, the priests, would also be proposing positive alternatives.

Youth is naturally idealistic and hopeful. Proof of that can be seen in the way they get involved in all kinds of causes, some noble and some base, though they sometimes fail to recognize which is which because of the strong influence of ideology. Youth is uncertain, insecure and therefore easily manipulated by bad people but also easily led to good by good people. So why not the Church get in first and instruct them in the truth and beauty of Catholic social teaching so that their natural idealism will be guided by the principles of that teaching thereby enabling them to tackle the problems of society with that as their weapon and have the vision of the kingdom of God as their goal? Confirmation will then become the springboard towards great action by these new disciples of Christ for the glory of Father with the grace and fire of the Holy Spirit moving them.

Conclusions:

1. Confirmation is the sacrament of Christian adulthood. It makes the baptized to be strong and perfect Christians. They receive the Holy Spirit and His gifts. It enables them to take an adult part in the Church and to bear witness to Christ in the world exercising their kingly, prophetic and priestly roles as lay people.
2. Confirmation is a special day in the parish so the ceremony should be well prepared in advance with sound catechetical instruction and rehearsals in the church. It may also require meetings between the different schools to decide what parts the different candidates will play in the sacrament.
3. Priests, parents, teachers, entertainers and all who have care of the young should work to create a culture of entertainment that is conducive to good morals.
4. Confirmation for young people should be followed up by more advanced catechesis and by instruction in Catholic social teaching so that they can make the gospel effective in the world around them.

Eucharist is next in the traditional list of the seven sacraments, being also their high point. We will look at that next.

Chapter XXII

The Sacrament of Eucharist

Real Presence, Mass, Sacrament and Sacrifice

This is my body which will be given for you; do this as a memorial of me. Lk 22:19.

The Eucharist is "the source and summit of the Christian life. The other sacraments, and indeed all ecclesiastical ministries and works of the apostolate, are bound up with the Eucharist and are oriented toward it. For in the blessed Eucharist is contained the whole spiritual good of the Church, namely Christ himself, our Pasch." *Catechism of the Catholic Church, #1324*

We said earlier that the sacraments are like the seven pulse moments in the life of the Church. The Eucharist is the central and highest of these because the other sacraments flow from the Eucharist. It is like an apex in relation to them. Going further, we can see that there is a reciprocal relationship between the Eucharist and the Church: it is in the Church, at Mass, that the Eucharist comes to be by the working of the Holy Spirit when the words of consecration are said by the priest. But it is also true that the Church herself exists only because of the Eucharist, she flows from the Eucharist, so much so that a Christian communion which does not have a valid Eucharist (because lacking a validly ordained priesthood) cannot properly be called "Church". By a further extension of this reciprocal relationship we can say that the entire treasure of the Church is to be found in the Eucharist.

The sacrament of the Eucharist is traditionally listed after those of baptism and confirmation because it nourishes the new life of grace begun in baptism and brought to adulthood in confirmation. It is special because it not only confers the grace of Christ but gives us Christ Himself in His real presence in His body and blood in His paschal mystery. The sacraments are often depicted by the blood and water flowing out from His wounded side as He hung upon the cross. They would have no meaning apart from the paschal mystery. Baptism, for example, an immersion in or a pouring on of water, is described by St Paul as a symbolic dying and rising with Christ but a symbol which is effective in our souls of what happened at Christ's death and resurrection. Also, conversely, Christ Himself referred to His coming passion as a baptism with which He was to be baptised. (*Lk. 12:49-56*). The sacrament of marriage symbolizes Christ's marriage to His bride the Church, a marriage He consummated by His death on the cross.

Again, as with the other sacraments, I am not attempting to be comprehensive on a topic on which so much has already been written but merely to pick out a few things which I believe are important pastorally for these times. I will begin by speaking of the real presence of Christ in the sacred Host and in the precious Blood and then go on to speak of the Mass as that which makes His sacrifice on Calvary present again; who can receive it, its effects in the soul and consider some pastoral points relating to this. In the next chapter we will say more about these pastoral considerations.

The Real Presence

The catechism of Vatican II, following on the Councils of Trent and Lateran IV, summarizes Catholic faith in the Eucharist by declaring:

> Because Christ our Redeemer said that it was truly his body that he was offering under the species of bread, it has always been the conviction of the Church of God, and this holy Council now declares again, that by the consecration of the bread and wine there takes place a change of the whole substance of the bread into the substance of the body of Christ our Lord and of the whole substance of the wine into the substance of his blood. This change the holy Catholic Church has fittingly and properly called "transubstantiation." *CCC, #1376*

This most central truth is often denied, not surprisingly because it seems to go against the evidence of the senses which see only what appears to be bread and wine. It requires faith. Down through history one can see that many heretics baulked at this doctrine even if their main bone of contention happened to be some other doctrine taught by the Church. They would usually opt instead for what they would call a merely "symbolic" or "spiritual" or "mystical" interpretation – and these words do indeed have their place in talking about the Eucharist because this and all the other sacraments are symbols or signs of things that are spiritual – but when challenged to say if they would genuflect in adoration before the sacred Host, as containing the Body of Christ substantially present, they refuse and some would even say that it is idolatry to do so. In more recent times one survey carried out in the US found that 70% of Catholics there would only go as far as to say that the Eucharist is a "symbol" of Christ. My own experience of interviewing candidates for teaching posts in primary schools revealed to me how very hazy and vague were many of them on this matter of the real presence,

Chapter 22: The Sacrament of the Eucharist

yet all of them were Catholics who had gone through a Catholic school system and had been trained in Catholic teacher-training colleges. Imagine then what their pupils would learn of the Eucharist if these candidates were appointed as teachers. However, I was somewhat consoled to learn that a survey of Catholics in the Philippines showed that well over 90% there *did* believe in the real presence.

Transubstantiation

The technical word which the Church has been using since the fourth Lateran council of 1215 to express this great truth of the real presence is "transubstantiation", a word borrowed from Aristotelian metaphysics and promoted further by St Thomas Aquinas.

> …Jesus Christ, whose Body and blood are truly contained in the sacrament of the altar under the species of bread and wine; the bread (changed) into His body by the divine power of transubstantiation and the wine into the blood… *Lateran IV, Denzinger 430.*

"Trans" means "across" which should be an easy concept to grasp. But "substance" in metaphysics means more than something material like stone or wood (or cocaine for many today!). It means something that exists, or subsists, by itself, be it something visible such as a rock, an apple or a man, or invisible, such as an angel or even God. Substance stands in contrast to the word "accident" in philosophy and to the word "species" in many Church documents. For people today "accident" means a mishap or an unforeseen event, for example, a collision of two cars or a fall from a bicycle or some such happening. But in metaphysics it refers to something that is real indeed but not with its own independent act of existence, for example the size (quantity) of a rock or the colour (quality) of an apple. If the apple were to cease to exist as an apple on being eaten so also would its green colour. But the colour might change from green to red with the ripening of the apple yet the apple continues to exist in substance. The word "properties" today or perhaps "characteristics" might come closer to what in philosophy is meant by accidents.

In the Mass the substance of the bread is changed into the substance of the Body of Christ. It is a *change* that takes place, not a creation of something totally new from nothing. By a "change" is meant that one pre-existing thing is transformed into another so that it gives way to a new reality but in such a way that something of what had been of the first reality persists. In the case of a log of wood being burned in the fire the wood ceases to be and a heap of ash comes to be instead but something has carried over from the wood to the ash, what is called "prime matter". The form of wood has gone and the form of ash has come but the underlying prime matter makes for the carry-on link between the two substances. Now, in the case of the Eucharist, an even more radical transformation takes place: the substance (not just the form) of the bread is changed into the substance of the Body of Christ, but because it is a change and not a totally new creation there has to be some connecting reality between the two. That reality is the accidents of what was the bread. Hence, though the new reality of the Body of Christ has come to be from what had been bread, what we still see when we look at the sacred Host are the properties, the quantity and qualities, i.e., the accidents, of what had been the bread: a round shape, a white colour and a soft touch.

The Body of Christ on the altar after the consecration is the Body of the same Christ who is now in heaven as a result of His ascension. So, it is His *live, risen* body in a glorified state, as it is now in heaven, which we have on the altar, not His dead Body as it once lay lifeless in the tomb. Because it is living it has a soul as any living man must have, and further, in His unique case, it is also conjoined to His divinity. So, we can say that, as a result of the consecration, the Body of Christ comes to be present in the Host and so also does His soul and divinity come to be present by "natural concomitance", that is by a natural accompaniment, so that the entire Christ is present.

As a child of six years of age in school the nun who prepared us for our first communion put all of the above very simply by making us learn off the following short little formula: "the Blessed Sacrament looks like bread and tastes like bread but it is not bread, it is really and truly the Body of Christ".

Yet I have scarcely ever heard a sermon on the real presence, neither one that would explain the meaning of transubstantiation in simple language or at least present the substance of that term as the good nun had done. Perhaps the reason is again, as in the case of the mystery of the Blessed Trinity which I spoke of earlier, that priests presume a solid and orthodox faith in the Eucharist in all their people so that there is no need to say any more on it. Or, it could be that they are adhering to an unwritten law which says that Mr and Mrs Cosy Catholics should not be "burdened" or "disturbed" at Sunday Mass by having such "high-flung abstractions" like transubstantiation imposed on them but that, instead, they should be "soothed" and "comforted" by banal, simplistic talk about Jesus' love for us when He shared Himself so generously with His friends at the last supper regardless of whether that sharing was merely a symbolic gesture or a true giving of Himself in His real presence. But when the same Mr and Mrs Cosy Catholic go home and begin doing their tax returns or arranging their business or legal or medical affairs they are quite capable of handling the difficult technical terms and formulas that are required. They prove to be adults in such matters on weekdays but are treated as infants in matters of the faith on Sundays.

And so, infants they remain and are thereby subject to the wind of every heresy that blows their way on social media.

The nun who gave us that simple formula above taught us the same thing by having us genuflect when she brought us to the church and pointed up to the tabernacle and to the red light beside it indicating the presence of Him who was in the tabernacle. A German priest was telling me how he too once brought his first communion class to the church in his country to point out the same things to them. But soon he could see that it was the first time for many of them being inside a church building– due to the negligence of their parents - because they behaved there as if they were in a basketball court. He had an uphill task to instill in them the respect they should have for sacred places and things. However, it is my experience that that sense of respect for the sacred is something they *do* take on board once it is explained to them what they are in the presence of and when words are accompanied by little gestures such as genuflection and the joining of one's hands, and all in an atmosphere of reverential silence.

As an example of that I can recall a priest who worked in London one time telling me how he had a secretary who was a non-believer but who was interested in the faith and who asked him for some catechetical instruction which he gave her. But it seemed to produce no fruit of faith in her for some time until one day she told him that she had come to believe what he had been telling her about the real presence. When he asked her what had brought her to believing she said she had watched him saying Mass and noticed how carefully he cleared off every particle of the remains of the sacred Host into the chalice, taking great care that no particle would be lost. She concluded that he would not have taken such care only that he really believed in the real presence. Gestures along with sound doctrine instruct, which is why all religious and civilized people value custom.

Communion in the Hand

What then of the practice of communion in the hand which came into vogue in Holland some years after Vatican II and has spread everywhere since, even though there was no basis whatever for it in any of the documents of that council and was forbidden by Pope Paul VI when it did begin? It has a basis in the gospels because Christ told His apostles to "take and eat" at the last supper and the early Christians followed sooth, even though some scholars claim that the practice was that of the communicants coming forward with a little white towel or handkerchief in their hands on which the priest placed the Host and which the communicants then raised up to their mouths to receive it. As time went by and the Church came to enjoy and era of peace, the number of Christians increased, but with that rise in numbers came an inevitable lowering of respect – what spreads wide also spreads thin – so the Church introduced the practice of receiving only in the mouth, a custom which persisted until the reformation. The reformers introduced reception in the hand as a way of making little of Catholic teaching on transubstantiation which they all rejected in favour of some kind of symbolic or spiritual presence about which they divided endlessly among themselves. Luther came up with the very ambiguous term "consubstantiation" which I fail to understand because it suggests to me some kind of mix of bread and the Body of Christ, an impossible notion to my mind. Taking this desire to reject transubstantiation a step further, in more recent times a Swiss priest told me of an evangelical pastor in that country who, at the end of his communion service on a Sunday would make a point of giving the left-over communion breads to the hens which were in a coop at the back of the church! It was his way of saying most emphatically that what Catholics claimed for the real presence of Christ in the sacred Host was nonsense. I do not know what were the motives of those who first introduced communion in the hand in Holland in the latter part of the 20th century; I just hope they were not the same as those of the reformers or of this pastor.

If then Catholics are now receiving in the hand and get very little by way of straight doctrine on transubstantiation, what is likely to be the net effect on their faith in the real presence? I cannot judge any individual on this and I must admit that most of the time most people who come up to receive when I am saying Mass do so reverently. I must also concede that at a time of an epidemic which can have infection spread from people's breath there can be a case for communion in the hand (though some medics would say otherwise and I defer to their judgment). But all in all, I think it was a bad thing to introduce communion in the hand and more so in this age when black masses and Satanic rituals are on the increase and consecrated Hosts can so easily be taken away for such evil purposes. Also, church cleaners will often report finding discarded Hosts under the seats after Mass. Furthermore, at big, open-air Masses, with large crowds in attendance, some horrible abuses happen when communion is given on the hand: Tom getting the Host from the priest and handing it back to Dick who, in turn hands it back to Harry or lets it fall in the mud and be trampled on. I cannot for the life of me see how such abuses can be justified by an appeal to the "fuller participation in the Mass" advocated by the council, that is if the Host is truly the real presence of Christ, the Son, the second person of the Trinity through whom all things were made and who came on earth to redeem us by His death on the cross; nor do I believe that this is a correct understanding of the intention of the council.

That such abuses are allowed to go on raises more questions about the faith of those in authority in the Church than about the faith of the laity who take a lead from them: do the former believe in the real presence to begin with? Further still, the practice of communion in the hand for children receiving for the first time makes it more difficult to square that with sound doctrine on the real presence of Christ in the Eucharist (assuming that they receive that doctrine at all to begin with). After all, to them it is like going up and getting a biscuit or candy into their hands. To mitigate that difficulty somewhat, I had the practice of having all my first communion children receive in the mouth and I used to encourage their parents to have them continue doing that at least until after confirmation, and then to instruct them carefully on how to receive respectfully in the hand if that was the parents' wish. That, and repeated sound instruction on the Eucharist, helps somewhat to safeguard some degree of respect while communion in the hand continues to be allowed. But I hope this practice will be reversed someday.

The Mass, Sacrament and Sacrifice

The real presence of Christ comes to be in the context of the Mass and only there. It is utterly wrong to consecrate either bread or wine outside of the Mass or one without the other even within the Mass.

I want next to say a little about this the greatest of liturgical celebrations, a little because I am not attempting to be comprehensive on a topic which is mystery to begin with and on which so much has already been written. But some basic explanation is necessary if people are to believe in it and if priests are to celebrate it worthily, i.e., in a way that expresses that belief, because a mature faith calls for at least some understanding, and today some Catholics seem to have a poor understanding in places, as the figures given above show. The nun that I referred to above gave us a short, simple formula for this also taken from the school catechism we were using at that time which was based on the *Roman Catechism* that followed on Trent. It said simply: The Mass is the sacrament and sacrifice of Christ's death on the cross.

The *Catechism of the Catholic Church* today says more fully:

> The sacrifice of Christ and the sacrifice of the Eucharist are one single sacrifice: "The victim is one and the same: the same now offers through the ministry of priests, who then offered himself on the cross; only the manner of offering is different." "In this divine sacrifice which is celebrated in the Mass, the same Christ who offered himself once in a bloody manner on the altar of the cross is contained and is offered in an unbloody manner." *CCC, #1367*

A sacrament is an effective sign, a sign that signifies what it effects and effects what it signifies. Hence the sign which is the Mass, if it signifies Christ's death and resurrection, must make it present also, and that death was a sacrifice offered by Christ to the Father to atone for the sins of the world. That sacrifice of Calvary was offered for each and all of us so that we could be saved from our sins, but it took place once and for all about two thousand years ago in one particular place, Jerusalem, which made it impossible for most people of other times and places to be present. Put simply, most people missed out on it. Left at that, we could not have appropriated it for ourselves tangibly as individuals or as whole communities. But Christ did not leave it at that; He devised a means by which it could be brought to us, made present to us, so that we could benefit from it directly. The means He devised was the Mass, a ritual that has the format of a meal, a supper with bread and wine, something very natural and familiar to all of us, but now being taken over for a supernatural purpose. Thus, the Mass makes Calvary present, which means the Mass is also a sacrifice, not one that is new or different to the sacrifice on Calvary except that Calvary was bloody and the Mass is unbloody. Let us hear Pope Pius XII on this:

> Likewise, the victim is the same, namely, our divine Redeemer in His human nature with His true body and blood. The manner, however, in which Christ is offered is different. On the cross He completely offered Himself and all His sufferings to God, and the immolation of the victim was brought about by the bloody death, which He underwent of His free will. But on the altar, by reason of the glorified state of His human nature, "death shall have no more dominion over Him" and so the shedding of His blood is impossible; still, according to the plan of divine wisdom, the sacrifice of our Redeemer is shown forth in an admirable manner by external signs which are the symbols of His death. *Mediator Dei, #70*.

When by transubstantiation, as we saw above, the bread is changed into the Body of Christ in the Mass it is His *glorified* body that comes to be present on the altar which, of course, is His *living* body as said already. Nonetheless the sacrifice, which necessitated His *death*, is made present also. As to how this can be so we will hear Pius XII again:

> For by the "transubstantiation" of bread into the body of Christ and of wine into His blood, His body and blood are both really present: now the eucharistic species under which He is present symbolize the actual separation of His Body and Blood. Thus, the commemorative representation of

> His death, which actually took place on Calvary, is repeated in every sacrifice of the altar, seeing that Jesus Christ is symbolically shown by separate symbols to be in a state of victimhood". *Ibid., #70*

Christ died on the cross when, at a precise moment, foreordained from all eternity, He gave up His spirit. Death is the separation of the soul from the body. He had then consummated His sacrifice and also His marriage with His bride the Church. That He was indeed truly dead was confirmed when the centurion opened His side with a lance and *there flowed out blood and water. Jn 19:35*. The water came last after His blood which was now mostly on the ground beneath Him. We can say of anyone whose body and blood are separated, or who has lost too much blood, that he is truly dead (hence the importance of blood transfusion today when there is a car accident).

Christ's body and blood were separated, which indicated that His soul was separated from His body. But His soul, when thus separated from His body, was still united to His divinity. With His soul He descended to the underworld to free those just people there who had died before His time and who were waiting for Him to free them: people like Abraham, Moses, the prophets and His foster-father St Joseph, since we can rely on the tradition that Joseph had died before Mary who was a widow thereafter. And His Body, when thus separated from His soul, was also still united to His divinity even when placed in the tomb later on Good Friday evening so that if, perchance, a disciple was passing that tomb that evening He would be right to genuflect because he would be in the presence of the divine.

But in the Mass today Christ, the one and only Christ, is alive and glorified both in His body and His blood, which means that we have Him present, living and glorified, on the patten and in the chalice. Because He is *living* in both, then His body there on the patten must have His blood, soul and divinity there with it also by what is called "natural concomitance" or, as we might also say, by natural accompaniment; and so also His Blood there in the chalice must have His body, soul and divinity there with it also by this same natural concomitance. As to *sign*, His body and blood are separate on our altars but as to natural concomitance His body, blood, soul and divinity are present on both the patten and in the chalice, in every particle of the sacred Host and in every drop of the precious blood.

I will clarify a bit further the difference between the presence of a thing in sign and by natural concomitance. If I tell to my pupils in class that in a few minutes time the *head* of our college will come in to visit us and that I want them to show him respect what do I mean? I do *not* mean that soon the door will open and that the *head* of Fr X will be brought in on a plate! I mean that a full blooded, living man, Fr X, soul and body, blood and bones will come in, which means that, indeed, his head will come in but firmly placed on his shoulders and on the rest of his healthy, living body! Nonetheless, I am correct in referring to him solely as "the head", singling out that one part of his body, because as to *sign*, he is indeed the *head* of the college, the person with highest authority in it and not the vice rector who might then be called his "right hand".

So also in the Mass: as to *sign* it is the Body of Christ we have on the patten and His Blood in the chalice, but as to natural concomitance the full living Christ is present in both. But let us keep to the meaning of sign for a moment: because Christ is present in His body, separate from His blood, then His death is also made present as to sign, for the reason explained above, that when a man's body and blood are separated he is truly dead. But recall that the sign we are talking about here is a sacrament, an effective sign, which means that this signified representation of Christ's death also makes His death really present, albeit now in an unbloody form. So, it is a commemoration of His death in a way that makes it truly present and not just as a looking back to a past event like looking at the death of someone in a film.

But that death was a sacrifice offered by Christ of Himself to the Father, hence it follows that the Mass is, as that simple catechism answer says above, the sacrament *and* sacrifice of Christ's death on the cross. Put simply, to be at Mass on Sunday or at any time, in your local church or in mine, be it a big cathedral or a small thatched oratory in the wilds, is the same in import as to be standing at the foot of the cross on Calvary with Our Lady, the other holy women and St John that first Good Friday afternoon. How sad then that so many Catholics see no point in going to Mass.

The Mass: Calvary past, present and future

The Mass makes the sacrifice of Calvary, an event of two thousand years ago, to be present in the here and now. This leads on to some further comment on the temporal aspect of all of this which we touched on already in our earlier chapter above on the sacraments and the liturgy.

We say that the Mass "commemorates" Calvary as making it present. This is not an entirely forced understanding of what it means to commemorate. For example, a wife who has lost her husband in some tragedy will, we say, "re-live" the events of the terrible day on his anniversary and recount every detail of how the accident happened to those who come to console her, though, of course, as we all know, that re-living does not make those events to be *truly* present again. But in the Mass there is more: the event is truly made present. Anniversaries make time to be a wheel, as it were, bringing events round again even if not literally. But the anniversary which is Good Friday goes further. It is the one day in the year when Mass is *not* said but, instead, we have a commemoration or celebration of the passion by readings and prayers as if to say that when the event comes round in time there is no need to make it present again in the sign which is the sacrament of the Mass.

Speaking of the Mass in its time-relation to Calvary, as we have been doing, is to have the time's arrow point back to the past, lay hold of the death of Christ and bring it forward to the present. But the arrow also points upwards to the heavenly liturgy where Christ, in his risen and glorified body, is eternally in a posture of sacrifice before the Father interceding for us. Cardinal Ratzinger, later Pope Benedict XVI, describes it as follows:

> ...the glorified Christ stands in a continuous posture of self-giving to his Father. Indeed, he is that self-giving. The paschal sacrifice abides in him as an enduring presence. For this reason, heaven, as our becoming one with Christ, takes on the nature of adoration. All cult prefigures it, in it comes to completion. Christ is the temple of the final age; he is heaven, the new Jerusalem, he is the cultic space for God. *Eschatology: death and eternal life, P. 234.*

It is not the case that there is one liturgy, one sacrifice, going on in heaven eternally and another one going on down here in the Mass. No: it is the one sacrifice, that of Calvary, eternalized in heaven, because the Priest is eternal, being truly God as well as man. But it is made present to us here below every time Mass is said.

And there is still a third time-arrow to this liturgy, this time pointing forward to the Eschaton, to the end time when the New Jerusalem will have come down from above and we below will have been gathered up into it. The liturgy of heaven and the liturgy of the Mass here on earth will be like two lines that will converge in the banquet feast of the Lamb. That is why Ratzinger says above that "all cult prefigures it, in it comes to completion". That cult of the end time will be splendid, beyond our imagining at present, because all the faithful along with the angels will be gathered round the throne of the Lamb. (*cf.* Raphael's painting of this in the Vatican).

Our expectation of this banquet should have us make our liturgy here to be splendid, not in any exotic or bombastic sense, but in a way that humbly anticipates the glory of the liturgy of the end. In practice it means that Sunday Mass should be the kind of ceremony that "lifts up" ordinary, hardworking, burdened people and gives them a taste of the heavenly so that it gives them hope in their trials for the week ahead. Indeed, as St Thomas teaches in regard to the beatitudes, to have such hope is to have an initial possession of the things of the end already. (cf. *Summa Theologiae I-II, q. 69).*

This splendour of our liturgy here should be proportionate to the wealth and living standards of the faithful who contribute to the support of the church. One does not try to build a cathedral-size church in a poverty stricken, county district (though, as said in an earlier chapter, I have seen such things attempted, not for the glory of God but for the glory of the pastor). I have had the experience, when taking visitors on tours of the Vatican Basilica, of seeing them, at first, express their amazement of the splendour of that building – not surprisingly because it *is* splendid – but then, sometimes one individual will object and say how excessive, how wasteful all this splendour is and ask why the money could not have been given to the poor (echoing a certain individual in the gospel who raised the same kind of objection with Our Lord on one occasion). I reply to him/her that the splendour of the Vatican was within the means of the people of that time because all of the Catholic world contributed over a long period of time and that it was intended that the finished basilica would be seen as an anticipation of the splendour of the liturgy of the new Jerusalem.

The effects of this sacrament

The effects of this sacrament are that we receive Christ Himself, truly and sacramentally, and the entire Trinity by concomitance. We gain a cleansing of the soul from venial sin and the mitigation of some, at least, of the temporal punishment due to sins already forgiven. We gain an increase of sanctifying grace with an accompanying increase in charity and a lessening of selfish desire.

Calvary was a sacrifice offered in atonement for sin. At Mass, immediately prior to the consecration, the priest extends his hands over the bread and wine, a sign that recalls *Leviticus 16* when the Jewish priest put his hands over the head of the goat while he spoke the sins of the people into the ear of the goat who would then be driven away into the wilderness carrying those sins with him. Hence the term "scape goat" down to this day and so also in the case of Christ, about to come on the altar: He will be the "scape Lamb", or as St John the Baptist puts it *The Lamb of God who takes away the sins of the world. Jn.1:36*. Pope St John XXIII used to say that all of Christian living is sacrifice, but such a statement wears thin in an age of materialism and consumption when people have little of sacrifice in their lives. Conversely, I would argue that Christians living under persecution make great sacrifices to attend Mass because the sacrifices they make in their own lives gives them an appreciation of the sacrifice of the Mass. At a deeper level I would see the problem as amounting to the fact that Western man sees no need to be saved from sin or from anything but, instead, has a craving for immediate self-fulfilment. (See *CCC #912* ff for more on this).

Given these effects of the Eucharist it would be good to revive the old tradition of the recipient spending at least fifteen minutes in silent prayer after receiving communion so that they could speak to the very special Guest who has come to make His home with them.

Celebrants and Recipients of the Eucharist

The celebrant of the Mass is the bishop or priest, not the deacon. The deacon assists. The recipients are baptised Catholics who are not under a penalty, are not conscious of mortal sin, have the right dispositions and are fasting for at least one hour. *Canon 915* says that "those who obstinately persist in manifest grave sin are not to be admitted to holy communion." A politician publicly promoting abortion would be an obvious example. Yet in many places such people are being given holy communion, which makes it clear that such bishops or priests put cheap politics and their own popularity with the powers that be ahead of the sacredness of the Host and the right to life of the unborn. They seem to be utterly unaware of the scandal they are causing by doing this. We should welcome Christ in our hearts by preparing them with the diligence with which Mary prepared the manger in the crib in Bethlehem, by cleansing them of sin; and after receiving Him we should spend some bit of time in conversion with this special guest by private prayer after Mass.

Conclusions:

1. The sacred Host looks like bread and tastes like bread, but it is not bread. It is really, truly, substantially, the Body of Christ; likewise with the precious Blood. The name for this change is "transubstantiation".
2. The Mass is the sacrament and sacrifice of Christ's death on the cross, a true though unbloody sacrifice made present again and offered to the Father in atonement for sin.
3. Silent prayer before the Blessed Sacrament and especially after receiving communion are venerable traditions that need to be revived, so also Benediction and Holy Hours.

From these mostly theological considerations of the Eucharist we will next turn to some more pastoral consideration.

Chapter XXIII

Eucharist

Pastoral Considerations, Decline in Mass Attendance and Solutions

Come to me all you who labour and are overburdened. Mt. 11:28

On Sundays and other holy days of obligation the faithful are bound to participate in the Mass. CCC, #2192.

Even a minimal explanation of the Mass such as was presented in the last chapter, should convey to any thinking mind what a wonderful mystery is contained in it. Yet so many of people who are supposedly Catholics react to it with cold indifference and outright negligence as manifested in the poor attendance at Mass in most Western countries in the third millennium. It is this problem and what might be its cause and its solution that we will look at in this chapter.

Indifference and Decline in Mass Attendance

Spiritual authors have written at length on the sufferings of Christ, physical and mental; but with regard to the latter there is one particular suffering they seldom mention and it is His foreknowledge that, despite all He would undergo, even to literally shedding the last drop of His Blood, thousands of future Christians would simply shrug their shoulders and say "so what? I couldn't care less". A priest who was a school chaplain once told of how he was recounting the sufferings of Christ to his pupils one day and one young man grunted "He needn't have bothered as far as I am concerned"! At the *Reproaches,* which are sung on Good Friday during the veneration of the cross, Christ says *My people, what have I done to you, how have I aggrieved you? Answer me.* He tells them what He has done for them by His saving actions and how they, in return, have treated Him with the sufferings they inflicted on Him. Good Friday, in that respect, is now an everyday phenomenon in many places.

This cold indifference leads inevitably to a decline in Mass attendance. In many European countries, and in much of America North and South, even in countries that were mostly Catholic in the second millennium attendance is down to 20% or lower in the third millennium and often down to 2% in the cities. In the previous chapter on confirmation I dealt with a number of factors which I believe lead to a falling away from Church of the young people who have just been confirmed, and the things that drive a wedge between one generation who are practicing parents and the next generation, their own children, who do not follow that example. Those same factors have effect most obviously in the decline in Mass attendance because Mass attendance is one barometer of practice of the faith. So, there is no need to recount them here again. Instead, I want to mention some more factors which I believe are directly related to Mass attendance: loss of the sense of sin, of the sense of obligation and changes in the liturgy.

Loss of the Sense of Sin and of Obligation

If Christ's sacrifice on the cross was offered in atonement for sin then it follows that people who have a sense of the evil which is sin will have an appreciation of the value of the Mass as a sacrifice - as that which rescues us from our sins and puts us at rights with God again. But when this sense of sin is lacking, when there is such a lowering of individual and social morals that evil is promoted as good and good is condemned as evil then there will be little value put on the Mass. "Why do I need the Mass, I'm doing nothing wrong" will be a question from people whose lives are no different in practice from that of non-believers. But we will see more on this in the next chapter when considering the sacrament of penance.

Along with the loss of the sense of sin there is also a loss of the sense of the serious obligation there is on Catholics to attend Sunday Mass. I found it amusing that, when the covid epidemic hit the world in 2019, Church leaders told people, rightly, that the obligation to attend Sunday Mass did not hold in these circumstances; but for a whole generation of young people it was news to them that such an obligation ever existed in the first place! And, even with the passing of covid, very little was said about the reintroduction of the obligation. Indeed, in some countries the bishops made it policy *not* to use the word "obligation" even then, but at the same time they began to lament the fact that so many had not returned to Mass!

Covid apart; for some strange reason it is not the "done thing" to even mention the word "obligation" in the area of religion today, even though in all other areas of life people accept fully that they are bound by various obligations.

One answer often given is that there is more to religion than going to Mass, that the important thing is to love one another as the Lord Himself commanded. True; but it is not a matter of either/or. The Lord commanded the former also when He said "do this in memory of me" and it makes sense to say that one who neglects Sunday Mass will fail to receive the grace and encouragement he needs to love his neighbour in a truly Christian way.

Another answer is to say that to speak of obligations is to make of religion a thing of fear and of rules instead of it being a thing of joy and love so that it becomes a Phariseism, a saving of oneself by keeping all the rules out of fear of being damned. If that is so, then obligations should be removed from all other areas of life also and so also all penalties for failing in them. But we don't do that: we demand that people live up to their obligations in all of these other areas.

<u>Abuses in the Liturgy</u>

Abuses in the Liturgy is another factor that turns away people of faith who have a sense of the sacred. The Church lays down precise rules for the celebration of Mass. She does so to safeguard and enhance the liturgy as a sacred thing, as something we have from God and not a concoction of our own. Thus, she makes clear that no priest has the right to change what is in the missal by himself. But many priests do take liberties with the missal in pathetic attempts to be supposedly "creative" or to make it more "acceptable" to the people when so often the result is banality or distortion, if not sheer clown-acting; and people of faith can see that. Others, who have no clue as to what is happening in any sacrament will go along with it for the entertainment but only for a while.

Again, if one priest places the missal in the middle of the altar and another priest places it at this side or at the other side that too sends out a message, one of a lack of unison even though it may seem a small matter where any book is placed. What may seem to be small matters on the altar are big matters for faith because of the power of the symbol.

When readers or Eucharistic ministers come up in shabby, raggy attire – because that is "trendy" – that shows a greater desire to be "in the fashion" than to show reverence for the Lord. Then there is the reader with a feminist agenda who will distort the pronouns of the reading. I spoke of that already in an earlier chapter. Again, an unprepared sermon sends out a message of carelessness, that the faith is not much of a thing to talk about anyhow.

When we come to the Eucharistic prayer some priests will improvise words which are not in the text and some will even *ad lib at the words of consecration* which, of course, raises the question of the validity of such Masses at all. And that raises the further question of the morality of taking stipends for such Masses?

Then, at the sign of peace, the Mass sometimes turns into a circus because of the clown-acting which so often goes on amongst the people. Indeed, it often begins with the priest who takes flight down the church to shake hands with the people in the top seats or further down, which means that he is leaving the Blessed Sacrament, newly present, unattended on the altar. But the message is clear: being popular with Tom, Dick and Harry and with Joan, Jill and Gemma in the front seat is more important than staying with the Sacred Species until they are consumed. Popularity again – how important is the ego! When the priest gives the sign of peace to a newly-wed couple they are usually within the sanctuary which is tolerable. Pope Benedict XVI was considering having this gesture moved to a more appropriate part of the Mass, perhaps after the *I Confess* or before the offertory, but never got round to giving it effect.

At the end of Mass, if it is a funeral Mass, it is now common to have a lay person come up to the ambo (from where the word of God was proclaimed) and give a eulogy. This is *not* a part of the liturgy at all. I will say more on this later when talking about the sacrament of the sick.

Another abuse is the playing of secular music and songs in the liturgy of a wedding Mass or a funeral Mass. If the music and song is not in line with the mystery being celebrated on the altar then it is an abuse, regardless of the preferences of the bride or of the late granddad. And then the big applause after the eulogy or the secular song as if we are being transposed from a church into a concert hall; and, to make matters worse, the celebrant will often join in in the applause himself, the shepherd following the sheep, or rather the goats in this case.

We speak of Holy week as the high point of the liturgical year when the paschal mystery is re-lived in a most solemn way. One would then expect that there would be *some* practice before each of the ceremonies, indeed a lot; and happily there is in many places. Yet I have been present as a concelebrant for such liturgies when the practice was merely a few brief confusing instructions to a few bewildered altar servers about ten minutes beforehand. On one occasion, at an Easter vigil, the celebrant did not even know where the Easter fire was set. The sacristan had hid it under his chair! He did not miss it until the gospel because it was at *that* time he had planned on lighting it, not at the beginning as per the missal, because he was following some self-appointed liturgist in some other part of the country who introduced that innovation by himself, and got away with it, and was followed by sheepish shepherds in many other places. Imagine the message that that sent down the church and out into the parish.

I am pointing out these errors not to condemn anybody but to make the point that one very necessary way of bringing back good attendance at Mass is to have the Mass celebrated in a way that "elicits the sacred and makes it present" in the words of Cardinal Newman, in a way that will bring God to people and lift them up towards God, in a way that will bring consolation to weary souls at the end of one week and recharge them for the difficulties of the week ahead.

Changes in the Liturgy and Church Settings

As well as abuses in the liturgy even *changes* in the liturgy and in church settings will be seen by some people as abuses also, or at least as *disruptions* to their traditional practice of the faith and their piety in ways that they find hard to take, and this may cause them to walk away. I will give some examples.

After the council (but, again, not because of it) there began a craze for the vandalizing of sanctuaries, the side-lining of tabernacles, the removal of altar rails, statues and tapestries *etc.*, all of which things were material expressions and supports of the faith of sincerely believing Catholics. "Change for sake of change" suddenly came to be the new motto in architecture and liturgy in many places. With these props to faith pulled away suddenly, is it any wonder then that there was a resulting loss of faith and a decline in Mass attendance?

Ironically, many churches which abolished altar rails in this fit of vandalism have had to restore them again, at least in the form of movable posts with ropes between them. This is especially the case in churches in tourist towns due to non-believing visitors wandering in, trampling all over the place and even going up into the sanctuary, (thereby giving effect to the old saying that when a goat enters the temple he won't stop till he reaches the altar!).

I came to a particular parish one time as the new priest, where the church had been renovated about the time of the council, nearly thirty years previously. Soon a number of elderly people began asking me where was the tapestry that "always" hung on the back wall of the sanctuary; did I know where it had gone and would I put it back? It depicted some scene from the gospels which must have been very beautiful and was a great help to the faith of these people. Sadly, I saw no trace of it so I could not put it back. In its place was a monotonous, grey brick wall with a gaping space in the middle because the tabernacle had been pushed over to a side altar out of sight of people coming in the main door. But that was the "design" of some architect or parish priest or liturgist but certainly not the wish of the people. The significant point of that story is that, even thirty odd years after the removal of the tapestry, people still missed it, so much was it a support to their faith.

Something similar had happened in another church that I served in: a little Lourdes grotto in one corner of the church had been removed and replaced by a bronze statue of Our Lady in a side sanctuary with *two* children at her side!! I was told that one was of Christ and that the other represented you and me. But I seldom saw people praying in front of it. In another church the old tabernacle was replaced by a new one which was round and blue, set above a stone pedestal and which, in the mind of the parish priest, was meant to represent the Host elevated above the chalice, but the people referred to it as the "oil tank"!

I am aware that an objection could be made that if one takes this line of reasoning too far then there can be no changes of any sort in the liturgy or in the structure of any church. Not even simple repairs to church buildings could be carried out as evidenced one time when a priest I know was renovating the church porch so as to conserve heat. It meant the removal of a *stool* that was "always" inside the door on which three or four old men "always" sat, and they were upset and objected at its removal! So also, there is the devout old lady who will complain to the bishop that Fr X moved the picture of Padre Pio from the left wall of the church, where it had "always" been, over to the right. At that point one is dealing with the ridiculous. Church leaders need a prudence and discernment that steers between a conservatism that sees the Church as utterly static, on the one hand, fixed in one form for ever, be it of liturgy or of church design, and, on the other hand, a recklessness that wants novelty for the sake of novelty and which violently discards all the inherited treasures handed down from the past, replacing them with the banal or the grotesque.

The new Rite of Mass

A major cause of controversy with direct impact on faith was the *novus ordo* of the Mass. The new rite of Mass, introduced after the second Vatican council, is blamed by some for the decline in Mass attendance. The priest was thenceforth saying Mass in a new rite, in vernacular languages and facing the people. Some argue that that was the best thing that happened to the liturgy, making the Mass simpler, more direct and more easily intelligible for ordinary folk, and more so with the use of the microphone, thus giving them a greater participation in it rather than having them sitting in their seats saying their rosaries or looking at their watches. They also welcomed the variety of having four Eucharistic prayers, three more in addition to the one already in use, but this last simplified a little in its rubrics. They will say that it is more ecumenical also to have the vernacular since the other Christian denominations have had that since the reformation. Such people will argue that this new order came just in time; that otherwise Mass attendance would have dropped even further by now.

Others will claim that it was an unnecessary novelty because Mass attendance was high anyhow prior to the council, despite being in Latin, so why change what was going well? They will claim that it was disaster for the faith and for morals and that the drop in attendance and the neo pagan life style of so many people now in what used to be Christian countries is proof of that, because liturgy gives the lead to all other areas of Christian living: *lex orandi lex credenda* and *lex moralis* they would add. They will argue that the sense of mystery or mystique which was conveyed with the Latin language has been lost, being replaced by the banal and the commonplace and by downright desecration when the priest happens to be a showman entertaining "the fans", a thing greatly facilitated by having him facing the people and having a microphone - something that would be less likely if he were facing East, symbol of the risen Christ, and using a sacred language. They will argue that the ecumenical value of the new rite is minimal, that being so similar to Protestant services it merely leads to confusion between the two religions and to an attitude of indifference which has people think that one religion is as good as another. As a final blow these people will claim (truly of falsely?) that it was a freemason in the Vatican who devised the new Roman missal, one who would hardly have had the good of the faith in mind. They will also claim that more and more people are turning to the Latin Mass, some of them elderly and therefore perhaps for reasons of nostalgia, but many of them young people also who were born long after the council and who had no prior tie to the old Mass, but that they find it more enriching for their faith in every way.

And so, on goes the debate. It is not my intention to take sides because I can see some validity in all the pros and cons of both sides. As an altar boy I used to serve the old Mass, and as a priest I have been saying the new Mass for many years and have a love for both. But there are some lessons I would like to draw from it, lessons which I believe have been ignored and which may go further towards explaining the fall off in Mass attendance and hence what might be done about it. Later below I will propose what I think would be a good solution to this difficulty based on theological principles.

<u>Lessons on Change</u>

The first lesson is to move slowly and with clear explanations when changes have to be made of any sort. Church leaders, in the aftermath of the council, did not take serious account of the importance of tradition in the lives of the faithful - tradition here meaning the totality of objects and practices which give support and expression to faith such that when one takes away these things one damages faith and causes great hurt and anger. I gave examples of reactions to the removal of objects above. Here I will give some examples of reactions to changes in the liturgy. They might appear ridiculous to the academic theologian but they teach a lesson of pastoral value nonetheless.

The Summer of 1978 was particularly wet in Ireland. I remember it because I was trying to help my father to save hay that year and it was well neigh an impossible task because it was seldom we got more than two dry days together which is not enough if one is to bale one's hay. Farmers were throwing up their eyes to heaven and asking why all this rain. Then one old man exclaimed "what else would you expect when they tampered with the Latin Mass!" The "new" Mass had come in a few years before and he found that to be so strange, such an up-scuttling of his Catholic way of life, which was centred on the Mass, something that had been as much a part of that life as the coming and going of the seasons every year, that to change it in any way at all had, *for him*, to have what we might call drastic, *cosmic* consequences – and the unending rain of that Summer for him was such! Now I am not trying to argue at all for some seismic or cosmic connecting between the weather and any particular rite of the Mass, but I *am* arguing that to people who are not theologians but who are often intelligent and of simple but solid, faith, a faith learned from their parents at home and from a simple but solid catechism at school, a faith which gave them a coherent, unified world-view that provided them with a pathway of meaning through the mystery of life with all its ups and downs, that to such people a change in something that was central to their faith is a major disruption and has the effect of pulling the foundations from under their world. Priests need to be sensitive to this.

Even to tamper with a small part of the Mass has its effects on the faith of such people. About ten or fifteen years after the introduction of the vernacular, the words of the *Gloria* in English translation were changed a little. An old parish priest – a man who *did* have a sense of the sacred and a sense of the effects of the liturgy on the faith of the people - said to me then that there was a downside to such changes, minor though they might be. At that time in Ireland the back of the church would be crowded with men standing during Sunday Mass, though not always with great attention to what was happening at the altar, (but I do not wish to judge their faith, often they stood at the back so as to give the seats up front to the women). The old priest said to me "do you see those guys down at the back? They wouldn't be able to say the *Gloria* at all if asked, nor would they know one version of it from another. *But they do know that someone has tampered with it with these new changes and they don't like that*". Quite simply, you don't tamper with the sacred - this was his point - because to do so is to tamper with faith also. Soon after, those men were no longer to be seen in any part of the church building (though I am not arguing that their disappearance was due *solely* to those changes in the *Gloria*). They are gone.[1]

Pastoral Solutions

Sundays and holy Days: Obligation

What might be done to halt or reverse the decline in Mass attendance? I would draw attention to an old principle in this regard is that "it all begins in the home".

Parents need go to Mass regularly and faithfully themselves and bring the children with them while they are young. Even if later, in their teenage years, they come under those negative influences which, as we saw, act like wedges that are driven between practicing parents and their children, so that the latter fall away for a while, there is still hope that the early influence of going to Mass will prevail again at some later stage, possibly when they become parents themselves and discover that they need to turn to God for help with many of the problems that raising a family can bring.

Faith is supported by knowledge because God gave us the natural gift of intelligence. Hence, if ignorance of what the Mass is causes the decline then obviously an improvement in preaching and in catechetics is called for – clear teaching on what the Mass is, tailored to the age and education levels of the hearers. But instruction needs the support of good example, in this case of parents and teachers going to Mass themselves.

This brings us to the matter of the obligation again so that we can respond to the objections raised against it. There is need for a renewed emphasis on the obligation, that is, on able-bodied Catholics of attending Mass on Sundays and holy days because the Mass is the high point of the Christian week. The *Catechism of the Catholic Church* says:

> The Church obliges the faithful "to take part in the Divine Liturgy on Sundays and feast days" and, prepared by the sacrament of Reconciliation, to receive the Eucharist at least once a year, if possible during the Easter season…*#1389*

It is an obligation which goes back to the early centuries and which theologians have spoken of as binding under pain of mortal sin, unless, of course, illness, or distance or some emergency makes it impossible to attend. So, it is not optional. Canon law tells pastors to remind people of the obligations that relate to the Eucharist. *(cf. #898)*.

As to the objection that making attendance at Sunday Mass an obligation makes religion to be a thing of fear rather than of love and a new kind of pharisaism we can point out that, along with religion, in all areas of human life, there are obligations of various sorts. All contracts carry obligations with them. Even in sport, the would-be player is told that he *has* to turn up for training perhaps two or three evenings a week if he is to get his place on the team; and he complies. It is not an exaggeration to say that life is largely the fulfilling of the obligations that follow from one's place in the family or from one's occupation; for example, parents in old age look forward to enjoying a bit of rest because they have fulfilled their obligations towards their children, when they have seen their children "done for", i.e., settled in their own families and careers. A great priest writer in my country, Canon Patrick Sheehan, used to say that there are two stars which guide the life of the Christian: the star of duty and the star of love – obligations fulfilled in a spirit of love, justice informed by charity. So why then will priests (or teachers or parents) not speak about the obligations that follow on baptism, one of which is to go to Sunday Mass? I knew of one parish priest in a city parish in Ireland who was informed that there was only a 2% attendance at Mass there and he replied "That's no problem. We can hope that they are spiritual in their own way!" Another parish priest in a provincial town, when again asked about the majority that no longer attend, said simply "Ah that's fine, that's their choice and we must accept it".

Another reason for the Sunday obligation is that the Church, like her Lord, "knows what is in man". Morality is not just about doing the right thing but about doing the right thing for the right reason. A robber refrains from raiding the bank while the policeman is nearby – good - but that does not make him to be an honest man. Ideally, all Christians should indeed *want* to go the Mass on all occasions out of love for Him whose sacrifice, offered for them, is being made present; and we can presume that many have this motivation at times, at least, or that they are motivated by some genuine need such as to pray for a loved one who is sick; or they may simply wish to meet their friends after Mass, which is still a good motive even if not the highest. If we are honest, we will admit that we do not all *always* do the right things for the *highest* motives – would the good student who might like his subject still study as hard if there was no exam? Hence, we need a pinch or jab of some sort to make sure we do what is right because, at times, our motives are a bit slack – that we will get up for Mass on a cold Winter's morning as well as on a sunny Summer's morning. Hence the need for obligations. But the hope is that from attending Mass, perhaps from a motive of mere obligation at first, or from merely being brought along by our parents, or from a desire to meet our friends that we will come to an ever greater appreciation of what is going on there – the Son of God sacrificing Himself out of love for us - and so continue to attend henceforth from the high motive of making a return of that love, obligation or no.

I have known priests who were indeed concerned about Mass attendance, but for fear of talking about obligations tried instead to "coax" or "attract" people to Mass, resorting to things like folk Masses or other kinds of "performances" which they think young people would like, i.e., would find entertaining. There can indeed be good folk Masses if the songs are truly hymns expressive of what is happening on the altar, and such things do draw some young people for a while at least. But if the "name of the game" is entertainment, simply because young people like to be entertained, then that priest is playing the "wrong game" to begin with for the obvious reason that the Mass is not about entertainment and certainly not a "game". Young people may enjoy the entertainment and come along for a while but, even if they have very little knowledge of what the Mass is, some of them may still have some vague, implicit sense of the sacred and will know that entertainment is a different thing to liturgy and, thus, is more appropriate for a different place like the discotec where they can have much more of it.

There is then the priest, with the same concern, who wants to draw the parents to Mass and does so by having the children do art at school, coming up to some special time like Christmas or Easter or first communion or confirmation, and have them put up their drawings on the walls of the church, his strategy being that this will draw in the parents on Sunday who will come to look at the drawings of their children. Again, as with the entertainment strategy, it might draw some for a while but not with a dedication that is constant and long lived.

Such a strategy reminds me of my young days when to catch birds we would set up a crib, an upturned basket on the ground, propped up at one end by a peg from which a long string came out to us the captors. Then we would put crumbs along the ground out along from the crib, making a pathway of them which, we hoped, the bird would follow in along until he was under the crib, when we would then pull the peg and have our prey caught underneath.

Yes, it is nice to see the religious art work of children displayed in the church at times. But parents are not birds to be enticed into the church with stunts of any kind. They are adults and should be treated as adults; that is, they should have the mystery of the Mass and the obligation of attending explained to them at intervals and the consequences for their souls, if they do or do not respond, spelt out to them – and also the responsibility they have before God for the souls of their children in all of this. That means spelling out the two ultimate possibilities that lie before all of us once we reach the age of reason and free choice which is that of an eternity of happiness in heaven or an eternity of suffering in hell. It is their responsibility then. But, then, heaven and hell have also become two other taboo subjects ever since Marx objected that religion was a distraction from our commitment to this world with its supposed promise of pie-in-the-sky in the next world, an objection which too many clergy took on board uncritically.

Devout Celebration

To make attendance at Mass to be more than a thing of mere obligation, to make it appealing to people of faith, not in the sense of being "entertaining" but as giving expression to the faith they have since their baptism and lift them up, a number of things might be suggested.

In the first place abuses in the liturgy have to be stopped. Bishops and priests have a responsibility to see to this (*cf. canon 528 #2*). It amounts simply to following the words and rubrics of the lectionary and the missal faithfully. The *Code of Canon Law* and the *Girm* contain valuable directives on the celebration of the Mass which I fully endorse and which it is not necessary for me to spell out here. But these directives, even when followed correctly, will be merely mechanical if the celebrant does not have a true sense of the sacred born of genuine faith in the mystery being celebrated. This sense of the sacred, if it is there, will come through to the people in a devout celebration of the Mass regardless of the rite being used, be it Eastern or Latin, or within the latter, traditional or *novus ordo*.

When the Mass is brought to people of other cultures, devout celebration will be enhanced or destroyed depending on how appropriately the task of inculturation is accomplished in these places. That was brought home to me by sheer chance as a young man one day mid-week, when I was coming home from a football match in my own country and happened to be passing a church and saw a lot cars parked outside it. It was in the early years after the council. Because it was not a Sunday I got curious and went in to see what was going on. It so happened that a Czech priest who had spent his life working in India was celebrating the *novus ordo* Mass but adapted to Indian culture. He himself was dressed somewhat like an Indian guru. Ladies with beautiful safari dresses brought up the gifts with graceful gestures. There was a single drone bagpipe playing in the background during the Eucharistic prayer up to the consecration. The entire tone or air or ethos of the whole liturgy was so beautiful and holy and sacred that the memory of it has stayed with me ever sense. I said to myself afterwards that even if I were an atheist I would have been brought to my knees in adoration and then lifted to heaven by such an experience of the sacred. I then began pondering if my own ancient Celtic, cultural tradition could likewise be used as "swaddling clothes" for the Mass in my country. But I never saw such a thing attempted, except that on St Patrick's day some priests would have jigs and reels played during Mass and even folk dancing in the sanctuary, thereby turning the liturgy into a disgusting jamboree.

Yet I want to sound a note of caution here too. What I have just described is what I would call a good example of inculturation of liturgy, though it is not for me to pronounce authoritatively on such things. Inculturation can be taken to excess if symbols or gestures or hymns or prayers from other religions are incorporated uncritically in ways that cannot be harmonized with what is truly Catholic. Keeping to the Indian scene, one cannot simply take over Hindu prayers or chants or their use of incense - things which are used in *their* worship of *their* gods - supposedly in the name of ecumenism. If one does so one will have an eclecticism which destroys the sacred and what is truly Catholic. The Hindus themselves would object and call this "poaching" by Catholics. When talking about structures of authority in the Church in the King section of this work I made the point that the Church takes over things she finds at hand to use them in the service of the faith. But, in doing so, she discerns if they can be used at all in the first place and, if they can be used, how they might be purified, transformed and elevated under the influence of grace. The same applies with inculturation of the liturgy. It is for the Church authorities in Rome to vet such things and not for any individual priest.

Different but complementary Rites

Let's now deal with the objection that the change of rite in the Mass from the Tridentine Latin Mass to the "new" Mass was responsible for the decline in attendance. A wider view of things will show that as well as these two rites there have been, and still are, many other valid rites all within the one Catholic Church (and then those others in the orthodox Churches which are also valid). One thinks of the Ambrosian rite in Milan, the Armenian rite in Syria, the Syro-Malabar rite in India and others. They are different but valid, each with a beauty of its own, and they all have a place in the one Church. So, to play off these two other rites, the Tridentine Mass and the *novus ordo*, against each other as if they were the only two, is a narrow way of thinking. Even if they were the only two, why could they not co-exist side by side anyhow provided they did not clash as to the times and places of celebration or give rise to an elitism on the part of those who prefer the old rite or a sense of being "trendy" on the part of those who prefer the new?

Hence, the debate need not be one of diametrically opposed positions, old *versus* new being understood simplistically as good *versus* bad, with a line drawn between the two historically at the council. The old Mass was *not* abolished at the council but incorporated in the new *ordo* as the first of four Eucharistic prayers we have now. So, it still links us with tradition. The supposedly "new" second Eucharistic prayer is even older than the "old" Mass because its roots go back to Hippolytus, (and is very suitable for priests who are sick or in prison because of its brevity). And then there are the third and fourth Eucharistic prayers, which though "new" in composition are faithful theologically to tradition and have a distinctive beauty of their own.

The perceived opposition might have been much less if Church leaders after the council had read the document on the liturgy and saw that it did *not* make the vernacular *obligatory*, nor did it command that the priest would face the people all the time, all of which means that a bit of sensitivity and a gradualness of change could have produced less opposition and better results.

A theological Solution

In the early 2020s there was a row in India with regard to the orientation of the priest at Mass in the Syro-Malabar tradition. Some wanted to go back to pre-conciliar days when the priest faced East while others had got used to the post conciliar stance of the priest facing the people. But then one bishop wanted to revert to the old tradition again and this led to a division amongst priests and people. Two solutions were proposed both of which were called "50/50 solutions" though in different respects. One such solution was to allow some priests to face the East for the entire Mass, as was the custom before the council, and have other priests face the people for the entire Mass as became the custom after the council, perhaps in different dioceses or even in the same diocese in different churches. The other solution, what was also called a "50/50", was to have the priest face the people for the first "half" of the Mass, i.e., the liturgy of the word, and then have him face the East for the second "half", i.e., the liturgy of the Eucharist. Both solutions were basically compromises so that most people might be pleased.

Now, though I have argued above for tolerance of different rites, assuming that all are valid, each with its own richness, nonetheless I want to say also that in sacred matters such as the liturgy it is not proper to decide things merely on the basis of compromise or on the basis of mathematical proportions such as 50/50 so as to keep most people "happy" because we are not talking now about material things such as wood and stone in a house, or water and wine in a glass - things which can be had in different quantitative proportions - but, instead, of things spiritual and sacred and relating to the divine. Nor is it the object of liturgy to keep "the fans happy" so that they won't riot (as they *were* doing in India, proof once again of how dangerous it is to tamper with what people regard as their traditions). The right solution should be one that is based on some sound theological principle regardless of mathematical proportions.

And what might that theological principle be? Very simply it is that the priest is a mediator because he shares in the mediation of Christ the high priest by reason of his ordination which configures him to Christ. He represents God to the people and he represents the people to God. So there are two "directions" to his mediation.

Let us go back to the Old Testament, to Moses at Mount Sinai, for an example. He is a man called by God from the priestly tribe of Levi. So he goes up the mountain when called by God and, facing God, he pleads for his people who are down below behind him. He receives the ten commandments on the mountain and then he comes down from God to the people below in front of him with the two slabs of stone in his hands. Those are the two directions of his mediation. Again, in the New Testament,

Christ is one who is sent by the Father to mankind. He faces them and instructs them with His sermon on the Mount but He also pleads for them and offers Himself to the Father for them on the cross. Thus, we have the two directions of mediation again.

So also with the priest as a mediator sharing in the mediatorship of Christ because called to do so and is given authority to do so by his ordination, (and not on his own initiative): there are the same two directions to his mediating also. He represents God to the people and the people to God. Of the two, the first has priority, theologically, precisely because he is one called by God and not one chosen by the people as would be in the case of a civil democracy when elected by the voters, a point we dealt with already in the *King* section of this work when establishing the source of the authority of the priest. Let us go to Pope Pius XII with his encyclical *Mediator Dei* again which we quoted then. There the pope says that the priest is a representative between God and mankind:

> Only to the apostles, and thenceforth to those on whom their successors have imposed hands, is granted the power of the priesthood, in virtue of which they represent the person of Jesus Christ before their people, acting at the same time as representatives of their people before God. This priesthood is not transmitted by heredity or human descent. It does not emanate from the Christian community. It is not a delegation from the people. *Mediator Dei, #40.*

As to which direction has priority the pope says in the same place:

> <u>Prior to acting as representative of the community</u> before the throne of God, <u>the priest is the ambassador of the divine Redeemer</u>. He is God's vice-regent in the midst of his flock precisely because Jesus Christ is Head of that body of which Christians are the members. *Ibid.*

But the question of which direction is prior is not our primary concern here. It is simply that there *are* these two directions to the priest's mediation and *I am arguing that that should find expression in the Mass, his most central action, and that it will happen if the priest is facing the people at one part of the Mass and facing the East at another part.* If his mediation in the Mass does find expression in this way it will also give effect to the principle enunciated by Pope Leo the Great that what Christ did in his mysteries has passed over into the sacraments. *(cf. Sermon 2, On the Ascension 1-4).*

If, in implementing the liturgy reforms of the council, both postures of the priest had been implemented it would have been more accurate theologically than either that of the pre-council posture which had him nearly always facing East or the post council posture which has him always facing the people. For the liturgy of the word he would be facing his people and for the liturgy of the Eucharist he would be facing East. It would have lessened the gap between the two *ordos* and provided less material for an acrimony that has been divisive at times. But instead, would-be liturgical reformers, i.e., clergy at all levels, some of whom had no knowledge of liturgy beyond the rubrics they had learned off in the seminary, rushed in and thought that everything of the old had to be "scrapped" of necessity and replaced with what was called "creativity" but which, in practice, was often banal and sometimes plain silly. It would have helped even more and made for more continuity if the vernacular was used for the liturgy of the word and that Latin was retained for the Eucharistic prayers, on some occasions at least, with good translations handed out to the people.

Solemn Music

Where there is a truly solemn liturgy, whatever the rite, one finds that the music and song gives expression to the mystery being celebrated. I touched on this already above when talking about secular songs at weddings and funerals. As to what kind of music that might be, we find a prime example in Gregorian chant, which is not to say that that is the only kind of music to be allowed. It is merely to say that this kind of music best accords with the spirit of Catholic liturgy because it is profound, though simple, and gives expression to those great sentiments of contrition, adoration, petition and thanksgiving when the human heart is pouring itself out before God. Only a heart of stone would not be touched, softened and uplifted by the music of the *Missa de Angelis* or the *Adoro Te*.

Sometimes hymns from other traditions that are near to Catholic, and which give orthodox expression in their words to what we are celebrating, can be admitted or adapted for admission. Again, it is for the Church authorities to decide what is most suitable in such matters. One rule I got from a bishop one time was that a tune which is well known in secular circles, though very solemn, should not be used if it would carry the minds of the hearers in the direction of the secular theme.[2] I can give one rather amusing example of that: in years past in our seminary we often sang the *Tantum Ergo* to the air of the German national anthem without even realizing that it was the German national anthem! It was very solemn and beautiful and very suitable for that particular hymn. But one evening there was a visiting student from Germany beside me at benediction and when he heard it he gave me a nudge and said "This is my national anthem. I'm supposed to stand up for this even if the rest of you are kneeling down"! However, he did restrain himself and stayed on his knees. But so often what one gets is vulgar and degrading in a pathetic attempt to entertain or draw the young. That fails and merely drags everything down.

There is a lesson to be had from St Augustine on this: he tells in his *Confessions* of how the Church's music of his time was a big factor in drawing him to the faith. It drew tears to his eyes. So also today, music that is solemn and truly Catholic will help to draw people and improve Mass attendance.

The radiating Effect of Liturgy

What happens in the sanctuary has its effects further out beyond the walls of the church building into the wider parish and that not only in relation to Mass attendance but in relation to other happenings also. I will use the example of the hub at the centre of a wheel. The parish church is to the parish territory, theologically speaking, like the hub to the wheel (even if the church is not geographically at the centre of the parish). Within the church, then, the sanctuary is the most central place – the axel within the hub, we might say. It should follow then, and it does follow in practice, that what happens in the sanctuary will have its repercussions in the church itself and out along to the borders of the parish. So, if things are thrown about in a sloppy or careless way in the sanctuary, that will send out a message to the perimeter – that the house of God need no longer to be seen as a very holy place. If the priest comes late or rushes through the Mass to get away early, that sends out a message: that for him there are more important things than the Mass. One will find also in such a parish that other parish events, and even secular events, meetings *etc.*, will start late. How the priest is vested sends a message: one priest with a chasuble, another with only a stole (though he is the main celebrant) or another with something round his neck which is neither one or the other, and finally the abomination of a priest wearing a stole with the colours of the rainbow, knowing well what that signifies. His very personality will have its effects on people also, whether he be truly saintly or a mere performer or manager or whatever.

The Church is a living organism growing through the centuries but always faithful to her own nature and constitution as given to her by Christ and the Holy Spirit. She is the bride of Christ. She is a queen as Mary is, and she walks through history, led by the Holy Spirit, but with a gait that shows that she is always faithful to Her Lord and to what He has revealed to her. So, there will indeed be change in liturgy and in other areas of the life of the Church but it must be change that is in continuity with what has gone before. Thus, in implementing change another simple rule for the priest is never to disturb faith whenever one finds it but try to build on it, develop it in line with tradition and bring people along gently.

A Note of Hope

On our specific pastoral problem of Mass attendance we need not despair but can hope for improvement if the things advocated above are given effect. Furthermore, there is the consolation of knowing that there is a *rise* in attendance in other parts of the world apart from the West. The West is not the whole world. At the synod on youth held in Rome in 2020 a bishop from the Cameroon reminded the other bishops present of this fact and said that *his* problem was that of trying to accommodate all the young people in his diocese that were coming to Mass, that priests would be found debating which wall of the church building they would have to knock down so as to make more room! Nigeria, in the mid 2020s had a 97% rate of practice, a country where the Church was also suffering persecution. So also the Philippines have a high practice rate. Western clergy would do well to have a talk with those clergy so that they might learn something from them.

Conclusions:

1. "It all begins in the home". Attendance at Mass is fostered by prayer and good example in the home, by sound catechetics in the school and by good preaching from the altar. It is also fostered by liturgy that is celebrated in a sacred way.
2. The object of the liturgy is the worship of God and the sanctification of His people. Whatever the rite, it should be celebrated by a believing priest in a way that engenders a sense of the sacred and draws people nearer to God.
3. It is not for the priest or any lay people to alter the words or rubrics of the liturgy. This is the prerogative of Church authorities.
4. In implementing change a simple rule is "never disturb faith whenever one finds it" but build on it in continuity with tradition and bring people along gently.

The Eucharist nourishes us as we grow in the Christian life but we fail, we sin and fall backwards. But the Lord has come to our aid with two more sacraments, those of penance and the sacrament of the sick. To avail of these helps we need first to have a sense of sin and know something of its divisions. That will be our next area of study.

Chapter XXIV

The Loss of the Sense of Sin

Causes, Solutions, the Demonic

… their empty minds were darkened. Rm. 1:21.

…the sin of the century is the loss of the sense of sin. *Reconciliatio et Penitentia, (RP), #18.*

To be sunk in sin is a great misfortune for the Christian because then grace is lost and his/her eternal happiness with God is in danger of being lost. Nonetheless, if a person is aware of being in such a state and seeks forgiveness with a contrite heart, resolving to amend one's life, it is freely available from the all-merciful God. But when a person is not even aware of being in a sinful state then his/her plight is all the more serious. Sadly, today in much of the Western world this awareness seems to be disappearing. Gone are the days of the long queues on Saturday nights for confession. So often now the confessional is a convenient place for storing the brushes and buckets that are used for cleaning the church or for storing the figures of the crib. The sacrament itself seems to have become superfluous. Sin is no longer seen as a reality in many people's lives: no sin, so why confession? In this chapter we will examine the reasons for this loss of the sense of sin and suggest some solutions. We will take secularism as the first reason for this loss.

Causes of the Loss of the Sense of Sin

Secularism:

St John Paul II quoted Pope Pius XII where the latter had said "…the sin of the [20th] century is the loss of the sense of sin". *RP #18*. Pope Pius had lived through two world wars when one might say that sin abounded on a big scale. His successor, St John XXIII, told of his days in the Italian army as a young man during World War I and said that the immorality practiced by many of the soldiers made it difficult for any soldier with a conscience to stay on course morally. It was during that time that Our Lady at Fatima had told the children that many were going to hell due to sins of the flesh. Yet the cinema was only beginning then and was morally clean for most part and the TV and internet, with the pornography and blasphemy they often portray today, were still a long way down the road. So, what we find is that, as sin was increasing during the 20th century and on into the 21st century, the *sense* of sin has been decreasing, which, by a downward spiral, leads to even more sin. And where does that lead eventually? Our Lady provided the answer to that question also, for those who want to hear it, and predicted terrible things to come both in this world and in the next for those who ignored her message.

This change, this loss of the sense of sin, accelerated in the relatively short span of the half century that followed Vatican II. It went hand in hand with the loss of the sense of God Himself which is the root meaning of secularism, a world-view that shuts out God and everything supernatural as well. St John Paul II could see this:

> ….secularism cannot but undermine the sense of sin. At the very most, sin will be reduced to what offends man. But it is precisely here that we are faced with the bitter experience which I already alluded to in my first Encyclical, namely, that man can build a world without God but this world will end by turning against him. *RP, #18.*

His successor, Pope Benedict XVI, described that world-view as a kind of "bunker" mentality, as if the world was a large concrete box with no opening for the sunlight of grace or faith to shine through from God.

We have here a kind of dilemma as to which is the cause or which is the effect, like the question of the hen and the egg once again. St. John Paul above says that secularism undermines the sense of sin, so also Dostoyevsky had said before him, very simply, that when God is gone everything is permitted. But prior to both of them St Paul saw sinful living, the succumbing to passion, as something which leads to a blotting out of the sense of God - *their empty minds were darkened. Rm 1:21.* I think it is fair to say that there is a reciprocal causality going on here leading society in a downward spiral to a new barbarism.

From this position of secularism or practical atheism, then, a certain perverse logic develops: instead of God, it is man by himself who becomes his own source of morality and aspires to an independence that tends to be absolute. Or, if he still has some kind of moral code, it is only that which happens to be imposed by general consensus at a given time. St John Paul again:

> …from a rejection of any reference to the transcendent, in the name of the individual's aspiration to personal independence; from acceptance of ethical

models imposed by general consensus and behaviour, even when condemned by the individual conscience. *ibid..,* #18.

The pope is exposing a contradiction in the mind of secularist man here: he chooses to do whatever he likes or what society around him is doing, but inside him conscience is still protesting. But then, when that man-made consensus gets the approval of civil law, and that law is at variance with natural law, even more harm is done because law does not merely regulate behaviour but reinforces it. In effect, then, many people will believe simplistically (or some dishonestly) that because something is legal it is morally good, and the protest of individual conscience is silenced all the more.

The secularist or atheist may still agree that one "should not do to others what one would not like to have done to oneself". He sees the need for some kind of moral code if total barbarism is to be avoided. But, if pushed on this, his answer cannot have any solid foundation because whatever dignity he might accord to the individual will not arise from him/her being seen in the image and likeness of God but only in his being seen as another animal, at most an animal who is only one grade above the ape. Accordingly, his moral code will soon become that of the jungle where might is right and the weak go to the wall. We have had the lesson of Nazism on this already.

<u>Relativism</u>

If we take the rise of secularism as a general or universal cause of the loss of the sense of sin then, following on that, we can see how Pope John Paul identifies other more particular causes such as the relativizing of moral norms, the denial of their objectivity and the denial of intrinsic evil. He says:

> The sense of sin also easily declines as a result of a system of ethics deriving from a certain historical relativism. This may take the form of an ethical system which <u>relativizes the moral norm, denying its absolute and unconditional value,</u> and as a consequence denying that there can be intrinsically illicit acts, independent of the circumstances in which they are performed by the subject. *ibid.,* #18.

Pope Benedict, going further, frequently spoke of a "dictatorship of relativism". It is a kind of contradictory mentality which imposes the *relativity* of morals on everyone with an arrogance that is *absolute*! But, to keep to Pope John Paul, morality is objective and cannot be reduced to the relative or the subjective even if it *does* have a subjective and personalist aspect to it because moral norms need to be internalized and issue from the person's free will when he/she acts. The moral law, which we find within us in the sanctuary of conscience, is something which comes from some source outside of us. It is a measure which stands above us, just as the ruler with which I measure the length of a table is no part of the table, though laid on top of the table when I am measuring, but something above it. Conscience is not the product of my wishes or feelings or even of my intellect or will or social influence. It comes from some higher source. For Cardinal Newman this experience of conscience was a proof of God's existence: this law that we find within us must come from a supreme Law Giver outside us or above us. According to this law, conscience tells us that some actions are morally right and others morally wrong regardless of one's desires or circumstances. Deny this and objective morality is soon reduced to total subjectivism or to historical relativism, a cousin of modernism, which would have moral norms dependent on the consensus of people in a given place at a given time, due to the social or economic conditions prevailing at that place or time, and not on the law that we experience within us as coming from above us or that we learn from a study of our own nature or the revealed word of God.

The idea of objective morality leads on to an understanding of the idea of intrinsic evil. Because human nature is objective, as something designed by God, and does not change in its essence, even though it is dynamic in the life of the individual, then it follows that actions directly contrary to the good of human nature as individuals or as social beings are intrinsically wrong: they are wrong in themselves even if the end aimed at is morally good. Thus, to regulate the size of one's family by sterilization is morally wrong because it involves the destruction of healthy human organs: the end here, perhaps to have more resources for the children already born, does not justify the means. If we try to rationalize and justify such means as right, then right becomes whatever one desires as useful to an end, even though the end might still be good. The idea of intrinsic wrong, wrong in itself, is lost. If the idea of wrong is retained at all then it is reduced to being merely that which the audience in a TV chat show is saying is "unacceptable" today. In time, even *bad* ends will be sought as good. Thus abortion now is presented as "reproductive health". This granted, it should be easy to see how an entirely subjectivist morality leads to a loss of the sense of sin and soon to anarchy in society.

Though morality might be relativized like this, conscience, the voice of an objective rule within, still speaks. So, to get away from objective morality and to silence conscience, the aid of psychology, false psychology, is sought. In brief, guilt feelings have to eliminated, or, if that cannot be done - because conscience won't stay entirely silent – blame has to be shifted elsewhere, onto society or its structures or onto anything, and for this the help of sociology also is enlisted. So Pope John Paul says again:

> Thus, on the basis of certain affirmations of psychology, <u>concern to avoid creating feelings of guilt or to place limits on freedom</u> leads to a refusal ever to admit any shortcoming. Through an undue extrapolation of the criteria of the science of sociology, it finally happens as I have already said that all failings are blamed upon society, and the individual is declared innocent of them. Again, a certain cultural anthropology so emphasizes the undeniable environmental and historical conditioning and influences which act upon man, that it reduces his responsibility to the point of not acknowledging his ability to perform truly human acts and therefore his ability to sin. *ibid.*, #18.

In a normal person, i.e., one who is not a psychopath, guilt is an unpleasant feeling because it registers the judgment of conscience in the emotions as explained above. The judgement is objective but the feeling of guilt is subjective - it is something experienced as painful. So, a "quick fix" for the sufferer - but one that is false, because contradicting the objective, - is to get rid of this painful feeling and replace it with a happy feeling. This is achieved by false counselling. So, the man who has walked out on his wife for a younger woman can walk out from the psychologist with a happy feeling after being told by the latter that society today has made marriage to be a transient thing, which development was not *his* doing, and that anyhow his individual fulfilment, his feeling well, is more important than his marriage. So also the habitual thief can be persuaded that he has greater need of the money he stole from his boss than the latter has because inequality, he is told, is endemic in our capitalist society, and he is happy to believe it – at least until his conscience starts picking at him again. In other words, this kind of counselling says "blame *them* (whoever *they* might be) or blame the system or society but don't blame yourself". In brief this means that social sin is acknowledged but not personal sin. It is Jean Jacques Rousseau come alive again. The latter blamed all ills on the structures of society and made feeling the measure of right and wrong. So also today we have school programs that make feelings to be the measure of morals.

<u>Neo-Gnostic Preaching</u>

One other cause of the loss of the sense of sin today is to be found in the way sin was preached in the days before the council by some priests. It provides us with one more example of what I call the swing of the pendulum of history: things going from one extreme to the other. St John Paul puts it well as follows:

> ....from <u>seeing sin everywhere they (preachers) pass to not recognizing it anywhere</u>; from too much emphasis on the fear of eternal punishment they pass to preaching a love of God that excludes any punishment deserved by sin; from severity in trying to correct erroneous consciences they pass to a kind of respect for conscience which excludes the duty of telling the truth. *ibid.,* #18.

There were, indeed, some preachers in times past who were obsessed with the idea of sin, especially with sins against the sixth commandment, which they denounced relentlessly. This was due, possibly, to a kind of training in moral theology that was tainted by a smattering of Gnosticism or Manichaeism or Jansenism which saw the body and therefore marriage and sex as bad rather than being based on an understanding of the body as good in itself because created by God, though a possible object of lust due to concupiscence resulting from the Fall. So, this kind of preaching was due to a negative understanding of chastity rather than to a positive understanding such as we outlined already when talking about sex education in an earlier chapter. Or they may have been emotionally malformed themselves and had problems with living celibacy.

It could even be argued that this very negative attitude to sexuality by some, a minority, in the Church contributed somewhat, perhaps indirectly, to the sexual revolution of the 1960s, in this much at least, that if one is constantly bashing the flesh as being bad then, in time, the flesh will revolt and protest its right to exist and to be considered good and to be enjoyed. But when a pendulum swings at all it can swing very far so that the revolt, then, will rush ahead to a throwing off of all moral restraint and to pursuing pleasure for its own sake, which leads to crude hedonism and sheer promiscuity. There is a kind of double paradox if not a contradiction in this neo-Gnosticism. The body, at first declared by the preacher to be bad, revolts and demands to be celebrated as good, indeed as a new idol to be adored and given maximum freedom to indulge itself. But this indulgence, soon going to extreme, given the force of lust, then leads on to the body being used or sold for cheap pleasure, thus being desecrated and debased and rendered worthless, bad. It is an example of "too far East is West". In any case, this exaltation and subsequent debasing of the body leads to an ever greater amount of corruption and an ever greater loss of the sense of sin.

Those preachers, then, had inadvertently added fuel to the sexual revolution, which revolution their successors could not (or would not) quench. Furthermore, these latter were embarrassed at the excesses of these few former preachers and went silent not knowing how to respond with a more positive understanding of chastity. But this silence came to be seen by society as tacit consent so that the fire became a blaze out of control, with immorality being practiced increasingly, and then legalized and declared to be a civil right, thereby fuelling the revolution all the more. Priests then became blind to the evils around them and began preaching what is called "cheap grace": that God loves and forgives everyone regardless of their lifestyle because all will end up in heaven anyhow as is now a common theme in funeral homilies. Some priests then went even further along this path by condoning or even trying to put a "blessing" on kinds of behaviour which are blatantly immoral. Thus, we have some priests even being openly supportive of the so called "gay" culture and celebrating what are called "gay Masses"! "If you can't beat them then join them" became the new policy. At that point, in these priests, one must say that the Church is caving into the world.

When this kind of thinking gets a place in seminary formation – as happens in places - and then in preaching and then in the confessional one can imagine the confusion it causes in the minds of the faithful with the consequent abandonment of morals and loss of the sense of sin. The perennial moral principles such as explained above come to be challenged and undermined. Hence, Pope John Paul again:

> And should it not be added <u>that the confusion caused in the consciences of many of the faithful by differences of opinions and teachings in theology,</u> preaching, catechesis and spiritual direction on serious and delicate questions of Christian morals ends by diminishing the true sense of sin, almost to the point of eliminating it altogether?" *ibid.,* #18.

Prior to the council seminarians were taught by professors using the manuals of moral theology which were uniform in all seminaries throughout the Catholic world. But after the council (and not at all by command of the council) the manuals were cast aside as being supposedly "narrow" or "limited" as if the perennial moral principles contained in them, which are based on the unchanging truths of divine law and natural law, could be declared obsolete overnight. What replaced those manuals, then, was the individual professor concocting his own moral teaching, sometimes still in accord with what he had learned himself in the manuals but, at other times, in accord with what he found in some periodical written by some supposedly "rising star" in theology who was gone off track. The students had that diet as the basis of their preaching and it also percolated down into the catechetic books which the teachers were using in their schools. The same confusion reigned in the confessional: a penitent would tell how one priest told him that a certain action was wrong while another told him that the same thing was right so long as he performed it "with love". The end result is that the penitent comes away and "does his own thing" and stops going to confession altogether. In every age Satan tries to blind people to the evil of their sins[1].

Solutions

Update the Manuals

In the preparations for the second Vatican council a draft document on moral theology was prepared but it never got to the floor of the council. That may have accounted somewhat for the reckless explosion in moral theology which happened in seminaries just after the council, the bad effects of which are still being felt. But, to fill that lacuna, St John Paul II issued his *Veritatis Splendor; Riconciliatio et Penetentia* and *Evangelium Vitae* documents which tried to clear up the confusion. At the risk of over simplification, *Veritatis Splendor* says that the end does not justify the means if the latter are intrinsically wrong. It also presents a correct understanding of the subjective or personalist aspect of morality.

What then is the solution? How can the sense of sin be restored, a healthy sense of sin that does not see evil everywhere, but which will not shy away either from calling it out and naming it where it visibly manifests itself? I would suggest a new set of manuals, standardized and approved by the Vatican, taking account of *Veritatis Splendor* and those other documents of Pope John Paul and of the Congregation for the Doctrine and the Faith of his time which would continue to uphold the perennial principles which were to be found in the old manuals but which would still leave room for new applications of those principles to the new problems which have arisen in different regions today. The old manuals were limited, from our perspective today, in the sense that they did not – because they could not – address moral problems which were not there or were not prominent in the days before the council, problems such as the morality of nuclear war or cloning or other issues in bio-ethics that have become prominent today. Indeed, every manual on any subject has to be limited to some degree in as much as no one book is ever going to say the last word on anything. But the manuals had the perennial, unchangeable principles, which principles can be developed further and given fresh application to new problems. When consistently and uniformly preached and applied, this should help restore a balanced and healthy sense of sin, as Pope John Paul says in another of his letters:

> But the sense of sin can only be restored through <u>a clear reminder of the unchangeable principles of reason and faith which the moral teaching of the Church</u> has always upheld. *ibid.,* #18.

Chapter 24: The Loss of the Sense of Sin

In presenting the principles of morality it is necessary to affirm the objective nature of the moral law, as we have said already above: that right and wrong are not a matter of individual choice or taste, that there is a law outside of us and above us because it is from God, but which is also planted within us in our conscience. Also, the notion of intrinsic evil needs to be reaffirmed.

> ...some sins are intrinsically grave and mortal by reason of their matter. That is, there exist acts which per se and in themselves, independently of circumstances, are always seriously wrong by reason of their object. *ibid.., #17*

When a civilization begins to decay morally this is the first principle to suffer: people may continue, for a while at least, to pursue good ends but will do so by evil means and see nothing wrong with that – the end justifying means that are evil. Hence some will claim that one can have such things as nude road races or strip shows to raise funds for a worthy cause such as cancer research.

One may never do evil directly and intentionally to achieve good. But this principle must be accompanied by an explanation of the principle of the two effects: that a person may perform an action whose first or direct and intended effect is morally good even though it is foreseen that it may have a second or side effect which is bad. This is important in the world-wide, pro-life, anti-abortion debates and, of course, in medical practice because sometimes the pro-abortion people will accuse the pro-life people of putting mothers' lives at risk by not allowing *any* medical procedures at all such as the giving of chemotherapy to an expectant mother who is suffering from cancer. The mother *may* receive chemotherapy notwithstanding the foreseen risk to the baby, if this is the normal and most likely beneficial treatment in her case. But the baby may *not* be *directly* aborted so that doctors can get on with giving chemotherapy to the mother. It should be said that many gallant mothers in that situation freely refused chemotherapy until the baby had first been born, even though they knew that such a choice might well cost them their own lives.

One other moral principle, needing emphasis, is that there is an *infinite* metaphysical difference between good and evil so that no one action can be right and wrong at the same time and in the same respect. A corollary of this is that Christians must not compromise with evil though they may have to tolerate it if their hands are tied or if uprooting a particular evil might cause even greater evil in the longer term. Governments should not legalize any evil because that is to give it approval as good. This is important at a time when people are being told that various contrary kinds of behaviour, good and evil, must all be "cherished" in the name of "equality", for the sake of "inclusiveness", so as not to be "discriminatory". People who sin should indeed be cherished as *persons* with a view to their correction and salvation but not their errors especially when those errors undermine faith, morals and the common good.

Knowing the different Categories of Sin

As well as speaking about the fundamental principles one must also speak about the different categories of sin: original sin, actual sin and social sin because they are basic and yet so much ignored today. It is not my intention here to give anything like a comprehensive treatment of these things but merely to focus on some aspects of them that have more direct pastoral relevance.

First, let us take original sin. It is a sin that is passed down from Adam to all of us – with the exception of Our Lady – and, even though it is taken away by baptism, it leaves our nature enfeebled so that, as Trent tells us, our will is weakened, our intellect is darkened, and our passions incline us to sin. Hence there is a rebellion within us of our lower powers against our higher ones.

The question as to just *how* enfeebled our nature has become due to the Fall has been answered in different ways down through history, giving us another example of the swing of the pendulum from one extreme to the other. The Pelagians saw only a little weakening of our nature so that a bit of good example and some asceticism is all we need, whereas the Gnostics and Manicheans saw it as greatly weakened – matter, hence the body and especially sex are evil; and we see St Augustine trying to find a path between the two with his theology of grace. Later, we see the theologians and mystics of the Rhineland and later still the reformers going very much to the negative side – the will can only choose evil, and concupiscence in itself is sinful. Even grace cannot cleanse or renew nature, but God covers over its sinfulness by imputing justification, legally, to the sinner on account of the death of Christ.

By reaction to this, the renaissance writers were much more optimistic, but it was the optimism of the classical Greek pagans restored, and, then, leading up to the French revolution, we have Rousseau telling us that man is born good by nature but made bad by the structures of society. This is a naturalism that has no need of grace. The horrors unleashed by the revolution soon after still did not dispel this naïve optimism from later generations. Half a century later we have Darwin with his theory of evolution giving us a world-view in which everything is progressing upwards from the lower to the higher, from good to better. It is easy to see how a doctrine like original sin would get little or no innings in that kind of world-view despite the evidence of the two world wars and the two atom bombs that were soon to follow in the 20th century. Today, in many bookshops, we have a section with all kinds of self-help books telling us how we can be very healthy, successful and happy by our own efforts, thus giving Pelagius and Rousseau a second run.

But revelation teaches that there was, in fact, a Fall at the beginning of our race due to an act of disobedience, motivated by pride, by our first parents. As to how enfeebled our nature has become as a result, we get a balanced answer from St Thomas Aquinas who gives us a positive view of human nature as a thing created by God but a realistic assessment of the damage done to it by the Fall: the will has been weakened but its object is still the good, and concupiscence, while it does indeed incline us to sin, is not sinful in itself until we consent to the evil that is desired. The will can aim at natural good but it needs the help of grace to do the good that will save us and bring us to God.

G.K. Chesterton once caused a surprise when he said that the good news of the gospel was the news of original sin! How could sin be good news at all? – one may ask. He was trying to be forceful in saying that only the man who is aware of his illness to begin with will take heed and seek help from the doctor and take the precautions he needs to get better. The man who knows he has a bad heart won't go running up the stairs to the top floor. He will take his medicines and follow his doctor's orders (and use the lift if there is one) and thereby will have a good chance of living a healthy life. But his colleague of the same age with the same condition, but not knowing his condition, or not heeding the doctor, will run up the stairs and get a heart attack on the way. If priests would preach original sin but with this balance it might bring the pendulum back near to the middle again.

In such preaching the advice of the old spiritual writers is still relevant: to avoid occasions of sin, be they persons or places or certain kinds of entertainment, and today there is need to add the danger posed by pornography, youth binge-drinking and drugs because these things are so easily available now, as compared to former times. Yet I have seldom heard a sermon on such things. Schools do indeed have various programs dealing with these evils but they are often entirely secularist, not presented in the context of God or His commandments and omitting any mention of the need for grace. The assumption is that information alone will suffice to make pupils moral, but this ignores the fact that the wound of original sin is principally in the will and that it needs asceticism and grace to be healed.

Actual Sin

Because of original sin we are inclined to commit actual, personal sins of our own, which inclination continues even after baptism has taken away the guilt of original sin. Actual sins can be of "thought, word, deed or omission", as we say at the start of Mass, and they can be of mortal or venial gravity. After the council some theologians began talking about "grave" sins as a new and separate category of sin, supposedly more serious than the traditional two categories of mortal and venial sin. A grave sin, in their account, would be something like a formal renunciation of one's faith or a formal declaration of atheism or a deliberate act of blasphemy, things which (until recently anyhow) were relatively rare. The problem with creating this new, "top" category of sin is that it relativizes those sins which traditionally were classed as mortal – fornication, adultery, perjury, large theft *etc.*, - these latter, then, coming to be seen as being of lesser seriousness and then, after a while, as not being serious at all, when, in fact, the very word "mortal," - a word with its roots in scripture – means literally a sin that kills *(cf. 1 Jn.16)*. It kills, not the soul itself (which is immortal) but the life of grace in the soul and, so, puts one on the path to eternal loss. True indeed, the sin of a formal denial of God is more serious than, let's say, fornication, but both are deadly. Both can still be called "grave" or "mortal". Hence distinguishing them as two formally different categories of sin is about as silly as asking if drowning a man in twenty feet of water is more serious than drowning him in ten feet of water. But this categorization did lead to confusion and to a lessening of the sense of sin.

Coming down a step further, there is the traditional distinction between mortal and venial sin, the former requiring the concurrence of serious matter, clear knowledge and full consent. But, again, some priests have clouded this distinction. I'm not sure how much credence I give to stories of near-death experiences – I suppose I can say that some, at least, are genuine – such as perhaps the following: a lady called Gloria Paola of South America relates how she had such an experience after being hit by lightning in 1995. She claimed she experienced being judged by God and would have been sent to hell were it not for the prayers of a saintly old man who interceded for her recovery. As to why her life was judged to be so sinful as to warrant hell she said it was due to a sermon in which the priest said there was no longer any need of the old distinction between mortal and venial sin, from which *she* drew the conclusion that all those sins which she had been told were mortal in her youth were nothing more than venial. So, she gladly set about committing many of them and was enjoying herself doing that until the day she was hit by this freak flash of lightning as she walked down the street. I just wonder how many other young people that priest had led down that path with that kind of preaching. Traditional teaching, with its basis in scripture, maintains the distinction between these two levels of sin and adds also that the habitual committing of venial sins leads on to mortal sin sooner or later. This too needs to be affirmed again today as St John Paul did in his day:

The Synod in fact not only reaffirmed the teaching of the Council of Trent concerning the existence and nature of mortal and venial sins, but it also recalled that mortal sin is sin whose object is grave matter and which is also committed with full knowledge and deliberate consent……there is no middle way between life and death. *RP, #17.*

Social Sin

We saw above that resorting to "society" in the abstract can be a way of evading personal responsibility for one's own actual sins: "that's the way things are. Don't blame me". There are, indeed, unjust structures in society. Rousseau did have a point when he claimed that it is society that makes men bad. There is a partial truth in it. One can imagine a young married couple, who need some place of their own to live, going to the bank to borrow money for a modest sized house but find that the very high interest rates will make their repayments impossible. So, they ask the lady at the bank why these rates are so high and she tells them, with a shrug of her shoulders: "well that's just the way things are. It's not my fault, sorry, I can do nothing about it". They might press her further by asking, whose fault it is or who it is that might be able to do something about it and simply get another shrug of her shoulders. "The powers that be, I suppose. I don't know. Speak to the manager if you wish or try any other bank if you like but you will find that it's the same everywhere." Since there is no "face" to this social sin, such evil structures can endure for ages as we can see from history: the persistence of slavery for centuries in times past and the persistence of corrupt regimes for decades in more recent times.

But Pope John Paul insists that *there is a face* and indeed many faces of individual people behind this kind of sin and that *they* carry the burden of the guilt of the resulting evil:

> …cases of social sin are the result of the accumulation and concentration of many personal sins. It is a case of the very personal sins of those who cause or support evil or who exploit it… The real responsibility, then, lies with individuals. *ibid., #16.*

Hence the social sins, or the sinful structures, come back and land on the desks of the few, who are usually in high places and are often unknown to the many in the street who are the victims; for these few they are personal, actual sins for which they will have to give account some day. History tells of brave, lone individuals who tried to call them to account but who often had to pay for doing so with their very lives.

The demonic Roots of Sin

Actual sin today can be traced back to the original sin of Adam. But it has an origin that is even prior to that, at a level higher than man, in the revolt of the angels - spirits of much higher intellect than man who knew from the moment of their being created that their true good lay in obeying their Creator who alone would give them glory as their final end. But some of these chose themselves instead of God and sought happiness by their own unaided powers. Hence, one might call them the precursors of the Pelagians. Given their much higher level of intellect, it is all the more difficult to understand why they would make such a choice. It brings out the nature of sin as something irrational or mysteriously dark. Then Satan, the leader of the rebellious angels, successfully tempted our first parents to sin and, along with his demons, continues to promote sin in the world with all its terrible consequences for mankind. Again, we find the irrational or incomprehensible here: why would Adam, with his high intelligence, his gifts of infused knowledge and enlightening grace fall so easily? And in sin today that dark mystery is still to be seen but is so difficult to understand because of its sheer irrationality. Thus, there is the mystery of evil at work in history with great effect because the forces of evil have their roots not merely at the human level but in the demonic; and within the human individual we have this irrationality again, so well expressed by St Paul when he spoke of being unable at times to do the good he would like to do and doing instead the very things he knew to be wrong *(cf. Rm.7:21-23)*. Psychologists of more recent times take us down into the dark recesses of the subconscious to try to analyze this dichotomy between human freedom and sinful compulsion. St John Paul put it well in the following:

> If we read the passage in the Bible on the City and Tower of Babel in the new light offered by the Gospel, and if we compare it with the other passage on the fall of our first parents, we can draw from it valuable elements for an understanding of the mystery of sin. This expression, which echoes what Saint Paul writes concerning the mystery of evil, helps us to grasp the obscure and intangible element hidden in sin. Clearly, sin is a product of man's freedom. But deep within its human reality there are factors at work which place it beyond the merely human, in the border-area where man's conscience, will and sensitivity are in contact with the dark forces which, according to Saint Paul, are <u>active in the world almost to the point of ruling it</u>. *ibid., #14.*

In a world gone secularist, where belief in anything higher than man is fading, it is difficult, but therefore all the more necessary, to make people aware of this dark irrational area of the demonic – without, of course, going to the extreme of imagining the devil to be around every corner, because much sin is simply stupidity, carelessness and plain selfishness. But this task is not impossible because secularism will never captivate men totally because a good many people still have some awareness of the spiritual above or some fear of occult below, however faint. Proof of that was to be had many years ago when the film *The Exorcist* was first released and was a box office sell-out, with people queuing up to see it who rarely came to church. But if they did come to church would they ever hear a sermon on the devil or the occult to give them true teaching on all of this? I, for one, never heard any such sermon in the past forty years.

The resurgence of Satanism in the form of black Masses *etc.*, is another indication of the workings of evil in today's world. How strange that there are people in those cults who *do* believe in the real presence of Christ in the Blessed Sacrament because they make a point of stealing *consecrated* Hosts from churches, while at the same time there are regular Mass goers who do *not* believe in the real presence and will say that the sacred Host is only a *symbol* of Christ's presence! And one will find atheists, such as Karl Marx in the past, who refuse to believe in God but who will engage in Satan worship[2].

Despite the loss of the sense of sin Pope John Paul was, nonetheless, optimistic about its return in a balanced way, because conscience will never be fully stifled and the very success of the forces of evil in causing misery in the world will have some people, at least, turn back from evil, having learned their lesson the hard way. But honest, hard, truthful preaching will also be necessary. So, he says:

> There are good grounds for hoping that a healthy sense of sin will once again flourish, especially in the Christian world and in the Church. This will be aided by sound catechetics, illuminated by the biblical theology of the Covenant, by an attentive listening and trustful openness to the Magisterium of the Church, which never ceases to enlighten consciences, and by an ever more careful practice of the Sacrament of Penance. *ibid.,* #18.

A healthy sense of sin points us on to good. Sin is to be seen in the context of grace because evil, no matter how formidable, is still only a privation of good. Hence, it is only a parasite on good: fire cannot burn down the house unless there is a house in existence to begin with. That is how things are in the natural order. But in the supernatural order sin is to be seen in the context of the grace that Christ gives to each and all of us to overcome sin in our own lives. *Where sin abounds, there grace does more abound* as the apostle says *Rm. 5:20-21*. But Christ won that grace for us by His most agonizing death on the cross which cost Him His last drop of blood. Thus, the idea of "cheap grace", the idea that sin is no big deal, that God's loves everyone regardless of sin, so that He forgives everyone even before they come to confession at all, is cheap in itself; it is a mockery of the divine benevolence and the sacrifice it entailed. Yes, indeed, God does love all of His creatures with an eternal love, but if that love was manifested by a most cruel death on the cross, offered to make up for our sins, then sin must be a great evil, and the response from our side should be a detestation of our sins and a resolve never to commit them again. That is why all of the saints, without exception, had the practice of meditating on the sufferings of Christ as shown to us in the gospels and on the crucifix. When they, in their response to that love, strove to keep the commandments and the other observances of the Church to their best ability they were not being Pharisaical, parading their virtue before God so as to be able to demand their salvation from Him as a right. They were, instead, responding, as all true lovers do, by seeking to avoid all offense to the Beloved and to return love for love. But the last time I heard any sermon making these points was before Vatican II.

Conclusions:

1. The sense of sin is lessened and in danger of being lost due to multiple factors, principally due to secularism, to ignorance of perennial moral principles, to a wrong understanding of chastity, and to contradictory preaching and teaching.
2. There is original, actual and social sin. One can sin in thought, word, deed and by omission; and as to gravity, sin can be mortal or venial.
3. The sense of sin can never be fully lost because of conscience which is the voice of God in the sanctuary of the soul. It can be restored by good catechesis and sound preaching and the witness of holy lives of people who are mature, joyful and truly chaste. The beauty of a truly Christian kind of life shows up the evil of sin and gives hope of conversion to those who are in sin.

With this understanding of the loss of the sense of sin and the basic divisions of sin we can now turn to a study of the sacrament of penance.

Chapter XXV

The Sacrament of Penance

Nature, Parts, Effects, Seal, Children's Confessions

Whose sins you forgive they are forgiven, whose sins you retain they are retained.   Jn. 20:23.

Those who approach the sacrament of Penance obtain pardon from God's mercy for the offense committed against him, and are, at the same time, reconciled with the Church which they have wounded by their sins and which by charity, by example, and by prayer labours for their conversion. *Catechism of the Catholic Church, #1422*

Baptism plants the seed of new life in the soul, the life of grace, a life that will grow if aided by a good Catholic upbringing and it will receive completion, as we have seen, in the sacrament of confirmation. But the sacrament of baptism is also closely related to the sacrament penance because the growing plant of Christian life can receive setbacks and fail, even die. The spiritual life of the Christian is dynamic in the sense that it is either progressing or regressing; it does not stay stationary on a plateau. When the Christian fails in a serious way, in a way that is deadly, by committing a sin that is mortal, there is need of this second sacrament, penance, to pick him/her up again. The early Fathers referred to it as a "second plank after the shipwreck" of mortal sin committed after baptism. And, even if the sin is not mortal, this sacrament is a remedy for venial sins also, the sins that dim or weaken the life of grace without actually destroying it, even though such sins can be forgiven in other ways. In the West, in pastoral practice, penance is the sacrament which comes next after baptism.

In this chapter we will say something about its nature and parts and then look at some related pastoral problems.

Nature of Penance

<u>Institution, Form and Matter</u>

The opening scripture quote above shows us Christ instituting this sacrament. It was on Easter Sunday evening, which means that peace and the forgiveness of sins were His first gifts to us after He rose from the dead. *(Jn. 20:20-24).*

The form of this sacrament is the words of absolution: *I absolve you from your sins in the name of the Father and of the Son and of the Holy Spirit*. What the matter is has caused some debate. It would be inappropriate to say that the penitent's sins, something evil, should be the matter of a "sacrament" which word literally means a "sacred" thing. Better to say that the matter is the acts of the penitent in confessing his/her sins, in being sorry for them and doing penance for them. So, putting all the "parts" together we have contrition, confession, satisfaction and absolution. We can see then that the word "penance" has two meanings: it can be understood as a sacrament, this sacrament taken as a whole, but it can also be understood as a virtue, that by which one is sorry for sin and does something in reparation for it, which means that penance in the second meaning is a part - the penitent's part - of penance in the first meaning of the word.

In the order of grace in the new covenant, the sacrament of penance and the virtue of penance are intimately connected. Since the acts of sorrow/contrition, confession and satisfaction/atonement (or at least the *will* to do these acts), which appertain to the nature of the sacrament of penance, are applications of the virtue of penance, the *sacrament* of penance cannot, in fact, be accomplished without the *virtue* of penance.

The acts of the virtue of penance, by themselves, cannot bring a Christian in mortal sin to justification if they are not associated at least with the desire for the sacrament of penance and with a sorrow that is motivated by the love of God.

The sacrament of penance, then, is that in which the sinner who repents of his/her sins, committed since baptism, confesses them integrally and sincerely and has the will to make satisfaction/atonement for them has them forgiven by the words of absolution pronounced by the priest. The priest, saying these words, is here an instrument of Christ channelling to the penitent the grace of forgiveness which Christ won for us by His paschal mystery. The sacrament of penance makes no sense and has no effect apart from the paschal mystery, which was Christ's most perfect sacrifice offered on the cross in expiation for all sin. This sacrament has the format of a tribunal, a tribunal of mercy surpassing justice in the sense that instead of being condemned, though guilty, we are forgiven and renewed.

Let us look a little closer at the parts of this sacrament.

Parts of Penance

<u>Contrition</u>

It should be easy to see that a person coming to confession with no sense of sorrow for sin cannot be forgiven. Yet, it can happen though rarely, that a person will enter the confessional with this frame of mind in a strange effort to try to have the priest justify what he, the penitent, knows deep down is morally wrong. There was a case, one time, of Satan coming to Padre Pio in confession in the guise of a talented, clever young man, confessing the most heinous of sins and then trying to persuade the saint to agree that what he was doing was right. Padre Pio was given an inner light to see what was afoot and dismissed him.

Contrition is imperfect when a person's sorrow for sin is motivated by a fear of hell or of the ugliness of sin. Such contrition, more accurately called "attrition", is still a fruit of grace and is adequate in the sacrament of penance for the forgiveness of mortal sins there. There is also *perfect* contrition which is sorrow for sin motivated by love of God because of His infinite goodness and the love He has shown us by the terrible sufferings He endured on the cross as a sacrifice offered for our sins. This sorrow is sufficient to obtain the forgiveness of mortal sin even outside of confession when the penitent is unable to get to the sacrament but desires to do so and hopes to do so later when that becomes possible. There is another kind of sorrow, or what might be better called "regret" or "remorse" as when the robber must spend six months in jail and is feeling sorry for himself as he looks out through the prison bars and firmly resolves that the next time he sets out to rob a bank he will make sure he has the right code for turning off the alarm!! He is not likely to come to confession to begin with.

Conclusions:

1. Sorry for one's sins requires an understanding of the wrong involved and a firm purpose of amendment so as to try, with the help of grace, not to sin again.
2. Contrition is sorrow motivated by the love of God and the offense that sin has caused Him. Attrition is sorrow arising from a lesser motive such as the fear of hell or the ugliness of sin but it still suffices in confession.

Confession

There is the requirement that a penitent confess his/her mortal sins as to their kind and number, not wilfully concealing any. Hence if Hitler had a notion to go to confession it would not suffice for him to say that he had "ruffed up a few prisoners in the concentration camps". In other words, a confession must be integral; and if it is not, if some serious sin is deliberately hidden, then one has what is called a "bad" confession, the end result of which is that none of one's sins are forgiven either, and one comes away with the added sin of a deliberately dishonest confession. The *Catechism* says:

> All mortal sins of which penitents after a diligent self-examination are conscious must be recounted by them in confession, even if they are most secret and have been committed against the last two precepts of the Decalogue; for these sins sometimes wound the soul more grievously and are more dangerous than those which are committed openly....
> When Christ's faithful strive to confess all the sins that they can remember, they undoubtedly place all of them before the divine mercy for pardon. But those who fail to do so and knowingly withhold some, place nothing before the divine goodness for remission through the mediation of the priest, "for if the sick person is too ashamed to show his wound to the doctor, the medicine cannot heal what it does not know. *#1456*

This requirement of an integral confession has been made to suffer in recent years because in some places, in a pathetic effort to draw people to confession at parish missions, some priests have resorted to telling people that it is sufficient if penitents will simply confess one or two sins which they can take to be "representative" of all their other sins. It does not take much to see how such a practice leads to many bad confessions.

Coupled with that bad practice, some such priests have also tried to introduce another one of administering this sacrament by standing at the sanctuary steps and having the penitents come up to them in single file as they would to communion, with just a space of a few feet left between the first penitent and the next. Again, it does not take much to see that a penitent with complex or embarrassing matter to confess or discuss is not likely to do so in an open setting such as that but will satisfy himself instead with confessing only trivialities. The thinking behind this practice is that grown adults are "afraid" or are somehow "intimidated" by the traditional confession box - an utter fiction.

Confession of a truly honest, integral kind is a necessary part of this sacrament because the sacrament has the format of a tribunal, as said already, and in any tribunal the judge needs to hear the evidence. Yet one finds people objecting: "why should I confess my sins to another man who might be as sinful as myself?" Yet such people will willingly go to a psychiatrist and pay him a large fee per session to "confess" some very personal things to *him*. They do so and find it therapeutic. But, if it is buried guilt they confess, he, though he may be skilled in analysing the root problem, will not be able to absolve it. There is a story of a troubled woman going to Freud, the famous psychiatrist, with a problem of buried guilt which he was able to uncover for her. She went away happy then that the problem was brought to light, but only for a while. Three weeks later she was back to him again and still troubled even though she now knew the cause of her trouble. He, though an atheist, asked her if she were a Catholic. When she said she was, he told her, very honestly, that his expertise lay in *uncovering* guilt by psycho analysis, as he had done in her case, but that to be *absolved* she should go to a priest for confession.

The penitent will sometimes need help in making a good confession. Hence, the priest will need to ask him/her some questions so that a clear picture of his sins will emerge and an awareness of their gravity. Some who try to knock this sacrament will say that this is interrogation or intimidation with the purpose of condemnation, that, instead, the priest – and indeed everyone in every role of counselling – should be "non-judgemental," even with regard to things that are clearly and definitely wrong. All deliberate actions of people over the age of reason carry moral import: they are either morally good or bad. We can all judge the *actions* of others externally- we can rightly say that a man running out of the bank with a bag of money is engaged in an act of robbery – but we still cannot judge his state of soul as he stands before God: he may be doing so under great compulsion because his wife and family are being held captive for ransom. But if in the confessional a penitent also discloses his motives the priest can then tell him if he is on a path towards God or towards damnation. Saints like John Vianney and Padre Pio had no qualms about telling some penitents that they were on course for hell.

Keeping to external actions alone, the priest has to judge what is confessed because the doctor must be told of the ailment if he is to heal it and also to assess its moral gravity, because sometimes a scrupulous person will confess something that might indeed be wrong but which is slight as to its gravity and, *vice versa*, a person might confess something as trivial which in fact is serious, and, in the latter case, the priest needs to alert the person to the possible peril of eternal loss in which he has put his soul. This can be done with a firmness that is still kindly and merciful.

Strangely, I have often noticed how some people, who insist that everyone should be non-judgemental, even with regard to the most heinous actions of other people, can still be very judgemental themselves when an allegation, even if unproven, is made against a priest, calling him a "demon" who should be sent to "hell" *etc*.

Before asking any questions of the penitent a simple rule is to "let him tell his own story first" and don't react until he has done that. The penitent begins by saying how long it has been since his last confession. Should he say that this is a very long time, and the priest react immediately with shock or scorn, then it is possible that the penitent will become hesitant and conclude that if he is open with this priest and tells him all of his sins truthfully that he, the priest, will likely flare up and give him "hell here on earth before sending him to the hell down below"! So, he runs away or, worse still, stays and makes a bad confession. When the penitent is first allowed to tell his own story the priest will be better able to assess the person's state of soul. He may also be able to see that there may be other matters closely related to what the person has just confessed but which he might be omitting. For example, a person who confesses a long absence from Sunday Mass very likely has greatly neglected daily prayer also but has not mentioned that, so the priest can bring that to his attention.

In asking questions the ten commandments, and what is commanded and forbidden by each, can be used as a framework, or the seven deadly sins, or the cardinal virtues; but discretion has to be used by taking such things as the gender, age, maturity and understanding of the penitent into account. The aim is to help the penitent to make a good and thorough confession so as to put him/her right before God again and regain the state of grace and peace of mind. And experience has taught me that penitents are thankful when they receive this help.

The joy and relief that penitents, who were once bowed down with the weight of their sins, will nearly always experience on coming away from confession is proof in itself of the value of an integral confession and the power of Christ's forgiveness, mediated through the words of the priest. Indeed, where a penitent does *not* experience this joy one is dealing with a serious psychological problem, (which problem, I would argue, is a key to understanding the mind and hence the theology of Martin Luther). Pope St John Paul II once said that, without this sacrament, the weight of one's sins would drive one to despair. (*cf. Reconciliatio et Penitentia, #31*).

One is obliged to confess one's mortal sins at least once a year, preferably during Lent or Easter, what is traditionally known as one's Easter duty, but every spiritual writer would recommend more frequent confession. I have always recommended that a penitent not delay at all once conscious of mortal sin, no more than one would delay over a newly discovered tumour in the case of one's physical health. The confessing of venial sins, while not obligatory, is nonetheless recommended by all spiritual writers. Otherwise, a person can be on the slippery slope that will soon lead to mortal sin. Regardless of mortal sin, it is good to recommend to people that they make the big feasts of the Church's calendar occasions for going to confession, times like Advent in preparation for Christmas and Lent in preparation for Easter, or during Easter for Pentecost. Then, because Ordinary time lasts for about thirty four weeks across the Summer and into Autumn I advise picking some feast in early Autumn such as the Assumption of Mary as another time for confession; then November so as to gain indulgences for the Holy Souls, which then brings one round to Advent again.

Conclusion:

> One must confess all mortal sins as to their number and kind once a year. The nature of the sacrament of penance as a tribunal of mercy requires this. But more frequent confession is highly recommended.

Satisfaction

This third act of the penitent is concerned with repairing the damage done by sins already forgiven. The *Catechism* again explains clearly:

> Many sins wrong our neighbour. One must do what is possible in order to repair the harm (e.g., return stolen goods, restore the reputation of someone slandered, pay compensation for injuries). Simple justice requires as much. But sin also injures and weakens the sinner himself, as well as his relationships with God and neighbour. Absolution takes away sin, but it does not remedy all the disorders sin has caused.[62] Raised up from sin, the sinner must still recover his full spiritual health by doing something more to make amends for the sin: he must "make satisfaction for" or "expiate" his sins. This satisfaction is also called "penance." *#1459*

When talking to young people I like to use the example of the doctor removing a piece of glass from a person's hand. The glass (the sin) is gone and thrown away (forgiven) but a wound remains that needs healing. In the case of the penitent that wound can go deep in the soul, spiritually, and psychologically it can go down into the dark areas of the subconscious. We share in Christ's work of atonement. St John Paul II clarifies further:

> They [the acts of penance] are a sign of the personal commitment that the Christian has made to God, in the sacrament, to begin a new life (and therefore they should not be reduced to mere formulas to be recited, but should consist of acts of worship, charity, mercy or reparation).
>
> They include the idea that the pardoned sinner is able to join his own physical and spiritual mortification -which has been sought after or at least accepted- to the passion of Jesus, who has obtained the forgiveness for him. They remind us that even after absolution there remains in the Christian a dark area due to the wound of sin, to the imperfection of love in repentance, to the

weakening of the spiritual faculties. It is an area in which there still operates an infectious source of sin which must always be fought with mortification and penance. This is the meaning of the humble but sincere act of satisfaction. *RP, #31.*

The penance needs to be in some way proportionate to the sins forgiven and serve as healing therapy for them. Over the centuries the severe and lengthy physical penances of the early centuries were commuted to the saying of a few *Hail Mary's* as in more recent times. That is perfectly permissible and very suitable for people who might not be able-bodied. But it can have the downside of trivializing what might be serious sin. Accordingly, taking the age and health of the penitent into account a penance comprised of some acts of therapy or reparation or charity can be more appropriate at times. I remember hearing a student tell of how he went to confession one time and confessed the sin of laziness, saying that he found it hard to get out of bed early in the mornings. For his penance the priest told him that he was to set his clock for 6.00 am every morning for the next week and to be sure to have his big toe out on the floor at the first sound of the alarm! It was an appropriate penance for that sin, but there is a "tail to this tale" which is that the student declared to everyone that he would never again go back to that particular priest for confession!! On the prescribing of penance the *Catechism* says:

> The penance the confessor imposes must take into account the penitent's personal situation and must seek his spiritual good. It must correspond as far as possible with the gravity and nature of the sins committed. It can consist of prayer, an offering, works of mercy, service of neighbour, voluntary self-denial, sacrifices, and above all the patient acceptance of the cross we must bear. <u>Such penances help configure us to Christ, who alone expiated our sins once for all.</u> They allow us to become co-heirs with the risen Christ, "provided we suffer with him." *#1460*

I underlined the last point in the above because it tells us of the particular way in which this sacrament conforms us to Christ in His paschal mystery. All of the seven sacraments do that, each in its own distinctive way. Baptism, for example, conforms us by having us die with Christ on entering the water – a symbol of death because one can drown in it, and also it has us rise to new life with Him when we come up out of the water – water now a symbol of life because all living things need water. By making satisfaction, by taking on a penance of some sort given to us by the priest, we are, as it were carrying a share of the cross which Christ is giving us in this sacrament so that we become somewhat like Simon of Cyrene following behind Christ on the road to Calvary taking some of His cross on ourselves.

A Lutheran would object and say that doing such penances, good works, are of no avail and superfluous anyhow because Christ's once-and-for-all sacrifice on the cross was perfect and more than sufficient to make up for all sins, that for the penitent to take on any penance is to imply that he, and not Christ, is making the expiation that sin requires. The *Catechism* takes full account of this, quoting Trent, with the following:

> The satisfaction that we make for our sins, however, is not so much ours as though it were not done through Jesus Christ. We who can do nothing ourselves, as if just by ourselves, can do all things with the cooperation of "him who strengthens" us. Thus man has nothing of which to boast, but all our boasting is in Christ…in whom we make satisfaction by bringing forth "fruits that befit repentance." These fruits have their efficacy from him, by him they are offered to the Father, and through him they are accepted by the Father. *ibid., #1460.*

Apart from the penance given to us in confession the many other sufferings and set-backs that come to us in the course of a day can also be "offered up" as penance for sin, our own sins or those of the souls in purgatory. This takes account of the possibility that the penance given in confession might not atone fully for our sins – a debt we cannot measure from this side of the grave - so that otherwise it will have to be paid in purgatory. I think this is a point that needs to be made in preaching today at a time when the hedonism of a secularist age sees no value in suffering at all and fails even to see that sin has any consequences to begin with.

If there is temporal punishment still to be expiated in the next life, in purgatory, the faithful on earth can help by gaining indulgences for the souls there and for themselves. The Church "dips into" the spiritual "treasury" of the merits of Christ, Our Lady and the saints and applies them to the holy souls to shorten their sufferings when the faithful on earth say certain prescribed prayers and perform certain prescribed actions, such as visiting a cemetery. By doing so they can gain a full remittance of such punishment (a plenary indulgence) or a partial remittance (a partial indulgence). This is a doctrine that needs to be preached again especially in the lead up to the month of November when we pray specially for the Holy Souls. Padre Pio often spoke of those souls calling for our help. They cannot help themselves but we can help them. To grant them this help is to have them praying for us with gratitude when they get to heaven when we, by then, might be in purgatory. I cannot remember when I last heard a sermon on this topic, even during November. It would seem as if many priests have followed Luther, instead of the Church, on this matter and stopped believing in indulgences altogether. It doesn't seem to occur to them that if they themselves stay silent on this topic those coming after them won't even think to pray for *them* because they will know nothing about such matters to begin with.

Conclusions:

1. All temporal punishment for sin is not always remitted by God with the guilt of sin and the eternal punishment. *(de fide)*. *Denzinger,* 807, 840, 904, 925.
2. The priest has the right and the duty, according to the nature of the sins and the ability of the penitent, to impose salutary and appropriate works of satisfaction. *(de fide)*. D 905.
3. Extra-sacramental penitential works, such as the performance of voluntary penitential practices and the patient bearing of trials sent by God, possess satisfactory value. *(de fide)*. D., 923, 906.

Absolution

In the three parts of the sacrament of penance dealt with above we have what in Thomist language is called its "matter". The form, then, is the formula of the words of absolution pronounced by the priest:

> *God, the Father of mercies, through the death and the resurrection of his Son has reconciled the world to himself and sent the Holy Spirit among us for the forgiveness of sins; through the ministry of the Church may God give you pardon and peace, and I absolve you from your sins ✝ in the name of the Father, and of the Son and of the Holy Spirit.*

On hearing these words the penitent can have the assurance that his/her sins are truly forgiven. Accordingly, St John Paul II says:

> …with regard to the substance of the sacrament there has always remained firm and unchanged in the consciousness of the church the certainty that, by the will of Christ, forgiveness is offered to each individual by means of sacramental absolution given by the ministers of penance. *RP, #30.*

Many priests can tell stories of troubled penitents, who might have been many years away from the sacraments, coming to confession and going away with tears of joy because of the assurance and comfort they found when the words of absolution were pronounced. G.K. Chesterton said that one reason why he had to become a Catholic and remain in that Church was because there he could be know for sure that his sins were forgiven.

I mentioned above how the sufferings or trials of daily life can be offered up for one's sins in addition to the penance given in the sacrament itself. In the Tridentine rite the following prayer was added whereby the merits of Christ and the saints as well as one's own trials patiently borne would help towards the remission of any remaining temporal punishment. Some priests still use it:

Passio Domini nostri Jesu Christ, merita beatae Mariæ Virginis, et omnium Sanctorum, quidquid boni feceris, et mali sustinueris, sint tibi in remissionem peccatorum, augmentum gratiae, et praemium vitae aeternae. Amen.

Since Vatican II we have had three rites of penance. That which we have been describing here is rite one, the traditional or, we might say, the individual rite – one penitent confessing individually to the priest, usually in a confessional or some other withdrawn place. Then there is the second rite which is that of a penitential service of readings and prayers followed by individual confession. It has the benefit of bringing out the "horizontal" side of sin and reconciliation because sin not only offends God but also one's neighbour and indeed the whole Church. That, nowadays, usually takes place in the lead up to Christmas or during Holy week. And then there is the third rite, general absolution, to be used in times of emergency or when it is foreseen that it will be impossible for a small number of priests to hear the confessions of a huge number of penitents individually. Examples would be those of ship sinking or a lone priest in mission lands who simply cannot get round to all the villages in his care for a very long time. But this third rite requires that the penitents have the resolve to confess their mortal sins individually afterwards as soon as they can. A large crowd turning up at a Marian shrine on one Sunday would not suffice as an occasion for the third rite. Despite these provisos one will, at times, hear priests calling for this rite as a first resort in place of the other two. I can see nothing more in such a call than lack of faith or sheer laziness by the priest.

Conclusions:

1. The form of the sacrament of penance consists in the words of absolution. *(de fide)* D, 896, 699.
2. Absolution, in association with the acts of the penitent, effects the forgiveness of sins. *(de fide)* D, 919.

Minister and Recipient

The Minister of this sacrament

The minister is a bishop or a priest who has faculties, but in an emergency any priest, even a laicized priest can absolve. Hopefully he will be a man of sensitivity and be well prepared. St John Paul, a great confessor himself, was aware of the difficulty and sensitiveness of hearing confessions but also its rewarding greatness:

> This is undoubtedly the most difficult and sensitive, the most exhausting and demanding ministry of the priest, but also one of the most beautiful and consoling. Precisely for this reason and with awareness also of the strong recommendation of the Synod, I will never grow weary of exhorting my brothers, the Bishops and priests, to the faithful and diligent performance of this ministry. Before the consciences of the faithful, who open up to him with a mixture of fear and trust, the confessor is called to a lofty task which is one of service to penance and human reconciliation. *RP, #29*

So the priest needs to have certain human qualities first of all:

> For the effective performance of this ministry, the confessor must necessarily have human qualities of prudence, discretion, discernment and a firmness tempered by gentleness and kindness. *ibid., #29*

I would venture to say that if a candidate for the secular priesthood does not have these qualities, or is a person who is likely to be bored or impatient with this work, it is possibly a sign that he does not have a vocation at all to this life. He would be like a doctor who has "no patience with his patients"!

More than having these qualities, the would-be confessor needs to be adequately prepared by his study of moral theology and canon law. It should hardly be necessary to say this for the obvious reason that anyone in any profession should know his subject, but I feel the need to say it because since Vatican II – though not because of it – there has been a kind of disparaging of moral theology and especially of canon law. To study and seek to adhere to the principles of these sciences is to be considered "rigid" or "legalistic" or "casuistic" - stuck in the "letter of the law" instead of following the "spirit of the council" whatever that is supposed to be. In practice, it usually turns out to be "doing your own thing" by following your feelings. Imagine then the advice such a confessor would give to a person troubled over something

Chapter 25: The Sacrament of Penance

he/she knows full well is sinful! Yes indeed, there can be a such a thing as a narrow legalism which only leads to scrupulosity, but are we then to throw away all the principles of moral theology and all the practical wisdom to be found in canon law which resulted from deliberation by great minds on difficult problems over the centuries? The following is how St John Paul says the confessor should be prepared:

> He must likewise have a serious and careful preparation, not fragmentary but complete and harmonious, in the different branches of theology, pedagogy and psychology, in the methodology of dialogue, and above all in a living and communicable knowledge of the word of God. *ibid., #29.*

But being well versed in the *theory* of moral theology is still not enough: the priest needs to give effect to theory in his own life by living morally himself:

> But it is even more necessary that he should live an intense and genuine spiritual life. <u>In order to lead others along the path of Christian perfection the minister of Penance himself must travel this path.</u> More by actions than by long speeches he must give proof of real experience of lived prayer, the practice of the theological and moral virtues of the Gospel, faithful obedience to the will of God, love of the Church and docility to her Magisterium. *ibid., #29.*

He must lead by example not only in upright moral living in his everyday life but also in this particular practice of going to confession himself. So, again, the pope says:

> ...the whole <u>of his priestly existence, suffers an inexorable decline if by negligence or for some other reason he fails to receive the Sacrament of Penance</u> at regular intervals and in a spirit of genuine faith and devotion. If a priest were no longer to go to confession or properly confess his sins, his priestly being and his priestly action would feel its effects very soon, <u>and this would also be noticed by the community of which he was the pastor.</u> *ibid., #31.*

The last sentence here is revealing: it says that the priest's neglect of this sacrament in his own life will reveal itself in the defects that will show up soon in his ministry, which defects will be noticed by the people. How interesting: they have no way of knowing by observation of his movements whether or not he goes to confession, yet his failure to do so will show itself in his ministry! I would see that as a peculiar example of the *sensus fidelium* at work.

The recipient of this sacrament

The recipient can be any baptised person who, after baptism, has committed a grievous or a venial sin. *(de fide)*. D 911, 917. Penitents are presumed to be baptized Catholics, although there can be exceptions when baptized people of other religions ask for this sacrament of their own accord and show a correct faith in it. (See *CIC, 844 # 3 and 4, || CCEO, 671 # 3 and 4)*.

Conclusions:

1. The sole possessors of the Church's power of absolution are the bishops and priests. *(de fide)*. D 920, *cf.* 670, 753. Priests must have faculties to do so. Superiors of religious houses should not normally be confessors to their own subjects. In an emergency situation all priests have faculties.
2. Absolution given by deacons or laymen is not sacramental absolution. *(de fide)*.

The Effects of this Sacrament

Fourfold reconciliation

St John Paul explains that this sacrament effects a four-fold reconciliation:

> ...the four reconciliations which repair the four fundamental rifts: reconciliation of man with God, with self, with the brethren and with the whole of creation. *RP, #26*.

That is why this sacrament of penance is also called the "sacrament of reconciliation", the reconciliation being effected by the working of the Holy Spirit who sanctifies in every sacrament, and in this sacrament by the words of absolution and by the carrying out of the penance given as satisfaction for sin. We might use the example of a wheel whose hub – the penitent – is off centre due to sin and needs to be put back in its right position again. Baptism does this for the new Christian without any remaining debt of temporal punishment so that no penance is required, but in the sacrament of reconciliation some temporal punishment usually remains which must be carried out in this life or in the next, in purgatory, as we saw above.

Chapter 25: The Sacrament of Penance

Conclusions:

1. 1 The principal effect of the sacrament of penance is the reconciliation of the sinner with God. (*de fide*). D 896. It usually has the psychological effect of peace of soul and a settled conscience.
2. 2 It revives the merits due to good works performed in the state of grace which have been rendered null by grievous sins, that is, made inefficacious. They now revive. (*sent. communis*).
3. 3 Past sins, once forgiven, do not revive.

The Seal of Confession.

The seal of confession, secrecy in regard to what has been confessed, must be maintained by the confessor and by any eavesdroppers or translator. This is absolute and unconditional. The seal regards what was discussed in the sacramental rite, even if the confession was only begun and not concluded, or was sacrilegious.

The seal regards *whatever* was discussed, even if it was not directly connected to sins and absolution. Even under oath, the confessor must state that he knows nothing or has heard nothing, since he has no communicable knowledge (*cf.* Thomas Aquinas, *Summa Theologiae, Suppl.*, q.11, art.1 ad 1). A few brief point on this:

- Outside confession the priest may not lawfully speak to the penitent about a confessional matter without receiving first the free, express, and certain consent of the penitent.
- The confessor may never use knowledge acquired from confession to the detriment of the penitent, and thus, a priest in authority cannot use such knowledge in his external governance that would reveal directly or indirectly what transpired in the sacrament.
- The seal binds the confessor and all who overhear a confession (bystanders, translators). The seal does not bind the penitent.

This protection of the seal is not just a matter of Church law but also of natural law. It is fundamental because without it a sinner, ladened with mortal sin, would not be able to confess if he thought there was some possibility of his matter being disclosed, which means that there would be a real danger of him dying in that state and losing his soul. Many priests have spent long years in jail and suffered torture and even gave their lives rather than break the seal. Even renegade priests have upheld it. The fundamental, absolute and unconditional character of the seal was recognized in the civil law of most jurisdictions in most ages apart from utterly tyrannous regimes. Despite that, it is necessary to reaffirm it again because today governments in some jurisdictions are passing laws that seek to compel priests to disclose cases of child abuse that come to their knowledge in the confessional. This is as unnecessary as it is hypocritical. It is unnecessary because a child penitent is perfectly free to go to the civil authorities himself and report such abuse regardless of having confessed it to a priest. It is hypocritical because the same jurisdictions that are making this demand on priests see no problem with legalizing abortion which is the very ultimate in child abuse, which means that they put themselves up on high moral ground pretending to be defenders of those who may (in some cases at least) have been genuinely abused, but, in reality, are using those victims to undermine the Church by undermining this most necessary sacrament. In other words, the victims are being abused on the double.

Taken further, some states want priests to disclose any matter that the state might consider to be treasonable, a sure hallmark of encroaching totalitarianism.

The response of the church to any such demands by the state has to be an unequivocal, resounding "NO" without any further discussion, regardless of the consequences for priests.

Conclusions:

1. Always protect the identity of the penitent, bearing in mind that the disclosure of a sin, even without naming the penitent, can still betray the penitent if there is something particular or unusual about the circumstances of the sin. Give no information, directly or indirectly, by word or any other sign, that would enable a third party to connect a particular sinner with a particular sin.
2. Maintain the same ignorance after hearing confessions as you had before. *(St. Augustine)*.
3. The seal is absolute and totally non-negotiable.

Children's Confessions

Confession and Communion

From the moment of conception, when a new human soul is created by God and infused, the baby has the powers of intellect and will in that soul – the will being the appetite of the intellect. But due to the underdeveloped state of the brain the child will not be able to properly use those powers until about the age of five or six, what is traditionally called "the age of reason" and which also, therefore, could be called "the age of will," which means that the child can then choose between good and evil. This, in turn, means that a child can sin if his/her choice is for some evil, though at the age of five or six that is not going to be anything major for most part (though on rare occasions one does hear even of children doing sensationally bad things). I say this to counter the simplistic idea that all children are so totally innocent that, as the saying goes, "sugar would not melt in their mouths". Indeed, children are innocent to the degree that they are not corrupted by bad instruction or bad example and are well brought up, and their innocence, then, is something truly delightful, proof of that being the joy that Our Lord had in welcoming them, and His harsh words for those who would lead them astray. *(Mt.19:14)*. But they can and do sin. It is not without cause that parents will be heard shouting such things as "you little brat" or "you little monkey" at times at their children or that they reach for the wooden spoon; and the little culprit knows why, and *does* have a sense of guilt. Children can be cruel to each other also. And even if most children don't sin mortally for the most part but only venially, all spiritual writers recommend to all penitents, children included, that they confess their venial sins also, regularly, as a preventative from sliding gradually into mortal sin; all of which raises the question of what age might be the most suitable for children's confessions.

We saw, when dealing with confirmation, that there can be different views on what is the best time to administer that sacrament and there can be such differences about most of the other sacraments also. Prior to the 20th century first communion was usually administered around the age of ten or twelve or even fourteen in places, the thinking being that only then would the young people have a sufficiently mature grasp of the idea of the real presence so that they would receive it all the more worthily. But then St. Pius X brought the age down to six or seven at the start of the 20th century, the thinking this time being that it was better that they receive while still the more innocent provided they also had the idea of the real presence explained them in a way that suited their level of understanding. Yet, once again, around the end of that century the age of receiving was moved up a little to eight for a little more maturity.

I mention these difference in the ages of receiving first communion because they are relevant to the age of making one's first confession. However, some people, latching on in an excessive way to the idea of the innocence of little children, have tried to suggest that, while first communion could indeed be received at the age of six or seven or eight, first confession could be deferred until the age of ten or twelve or even later, arguing that only then do they have any idea of serious sin. That is deceptive and spiritually harmful. As I argued above already, children do have a sense of sin as soon as they reach the age of reason and do sin with varying degrees of seriousness so that they do experience guilt. To suggest then that they make their first communion early and their first confession much later is, in fact, to encourage sacrilegious communions and indeed to so dissociates the idea of confession from communion as to make the former almost irrelevant, which, in turn, then, encourages the idea of living continuously in a state of serious sin as they grow older and proceed to live their own independent lives.

There is, of course, the other extreme of some people thinking that they have to go to confession prior to every receiving of communion. Some people still have this idea arising from the practice that existed before Vatican II of receiving only two or three times a year or once a month at most, and of going to confession prior to receiving on those occasions. But the pastoral connection between these two sacraments is, very simply, that one can receive often, even daily, provided only that one is not conscious of being in a state of mortal sin, that otherwise one is adding sacrilege to sin as St Paul had warned long ago *(1 Cor 11:29)*. Hence, with young children, I would argue for keeping a relatively close timing of the reception of these two sacraments. If, in some places, first communion is going to be as late as eight years of age, then first confession could still be made at seven or even at six years of age followed by the practice of monthly or quarterly confessions until it comes to first communion time. Then, a week or a few days before first communion there should be a special confession ceremony with the parents present also. After first communion this practice of regular confession should not then be dropped but maintained with some degree of regularity though, of course, never with compulsion of any sort. I had the practice of offering confessions to children both at primary and secondary level once a term, before Christmas, before Easter and before the Summer break.

<u>Children and the Confessional</u>

Another false idea regarding children's confessions is that the confessional is a frightening, "spooky" place for them because it is enclosed and dark; that, therefore, we should defer first confessions till much, much later or have confessions up at the altar rails, facing the penitents, as practiced by some missioners and by the secular priests who ape them, as I mentioned already. All of this is merely a cheap ploy to keep children away from this sacrament for as long as possible, till they forget about it altogether due to not having been introduced to the habit of frequenting it earlier. Yet I notice that the kind of people who raise these objections seldom object to bad programs of erotic material being introduced into schools! In all my years as a priest in parish work, I never, ever, even once, came across a single child, even one as young as six years of age, who was afraid of the confessional. I had the practice of bringing them to the church before-hand and letting them open the confessional for themselves, go

Chapter 25: The Sacrament of Penance 383

in and open and close the shutters. Not only were they never afraid but they seemed to enjoy doing this.

For the special occasion of the children's first confession, it is possible to have this ceremony in the sanctuary, though certainly not with the priest standing at the altar steps facing the children, but seated in a chair further in and more secluded with a kneeler behind or beside him for the child to use. It is also a suitable occasion for a simple version of rite two of the sacrament of penance so that the individual confessions are preceded with some readings, prayers and a simple examination of conscience.

With this sacrament, as with baptism, confirmation and first communion, the parents have the primary responsibility of seeing to it that their children receive them and are prepared. But many parents are totally negligent in this regard, in particular with regard to confession. It was for that reason that I had the practice of hearing the confessions of children in their schools about once a term. But the downside of this was that some parents, then, felt there was no need for *them* to give any encouragement to their children to frequent this sacrament, taking it for granted that the priest was looking after that duty for them so that when the children left school they gave up the practice for want of encouragement from the parents. The best solution I can give for this is for the priest to talk to the children in class about the value of regular confession and to the parents in homilies. I used to give them the example of the gardener taking good care of his garden (the soul) and regularly plucking up any weeds (vices) he sees appearing.

Confessions in the school requires the cooperation of the school board and the teachers which cannot be presumed in all places, not even in some schools which are supposedly under Catholic management, because some parents, for example, self-styled humanists who are often simply lapsed Catholics, will object that time given to any of the sacraments is wasted. It amazes me how such minorities are allowed to have so much of a say, supposedly in the name of tolerance and pluralism, but to the detriment of the faith of the children.

When actually hearing confessions in a school setting, neither priest or penitent will have the protection of the grill of the confessional, so he needs to pick a place such as a large, empty room leaving the door open so that both priest and penitent are in full view of people in the hallway but also in such a way that people will not be able to hear what is being confessed.

For a prudent timing of the age at which children receive the two sacraments of confession and holy communion the overall aim should be to instil the lesson that people should be in a state of grace when receiving holy communion and the further lesson of always taking care of one's soul so that one tries to keep the white robe of baptism, as unsoiled as possible, till we come to life's end when grace blossoms into glory.

Conclusions:

1. In the sacrament of penance actual sins, committed since baptism, are forgiven, and people are reconciled to God and neighbour. It has four parts: contrition, confession, satisfaction and absolution. The former three being the matter and the last being the form of this sacrament.
2. In the confessional the priest is both judge and healer who welcomes sinners and makes God's forgiveness available to them. His own study of sound moral theology and his own personal devotion to this sacrament will make his ministry all the more fruitful in this regard.
3. *Where sin abounds grace does more abound. Rm.5:20-21.* We need not despair of our sins because of what Christ did for us on the cross but neither must we be presumptuous and take such love for granted.

The sacrament of penance remits mortal sin and venial sin but sin leaves the soul and, at times, the body in a weakened condition. Hence closely related to this sacrament is the sacrament of the sick which strengthens the weakened soul and may also heal the body and prepares one for the next life if the end is near. We will turn to this soon but by way of preparation we will look first at the Christian meaning of suffering.

Chapter XXVI

The Pastoral Care of the Sick

The Psychosomatic, Christ as the Meaning of Suffering and Death

Ours were the sufferings he bore. Isaiah 53:4.

It makes me happy to suffer for you, as I am suffering now, and in my own body to do what I can to make up all that has still to be undergone by Christ for the sake of his body the church. Colossians 1:24

Yes, it seems to be part of the very essence of Christ's redemptive suffering that this suffering requires to be unceasingly completed. *Salvifici Doloris, #20.*

In the natural order creatures are born, grow, are nourished and come to maturity. But they can fail also, suffer from various ailments and eventually they will decline as they approach their end. So also in the life of grace, after the sacraments of initiation and penance we come to the sacrament that sustains people in sickness and old age and strengthens them in the face of death so that dying, for them, will be a passing over into an even fuller life in Christ. Having lived "in Christ" in this life, carrying the cross with Him, they die with Him and rise with Him again to glory in the next life. The sacrament which sustains them as they come near the end, or when they must carry some potentially life-threatening illness for a long time prior to death, is that of the anointing of the sick. This is our next concern.

But for a better understanding of the context of this sacrament I will begin by saying something in this chapter about suffering and death, first in the secularist and then in the Christian understandings of these things. Put simply, I will be posing the question of what it is a priest-chaplain or spiritual counselor can say to a patient to give him or her meaning and hope of a Christian kind in his or her suffering. To do this I will draw much on the apostolic letter *Salvifici Doloris* of St John Paul II, the first pope to devote an entire document to this topic, notwithstanding how longstanding and all pervasive a thing suffering is for most people. Then, in the next chapter, we will look at the sacrament of anointing itself and then at some related pastoral and medical problems.

Suffering and the Psychosomatic

Suffering and death have been the lot of man since the Fall because they are consequences of the disobedience of our first parents: their revolt against God led to an inner revolt in their own nature whereby the soul no longer had full command over the body to preserve it in union with itself. Suffering and death provoke much soul-searching because suffering is something that goes against human well-being, and death is something from which we naturally recoil because of a healthy instinct in us that wants life to go on for ever. (*cf. Gaudium et Spes #18*). It is a fundamental axiom of metaphysics that all things desire to stay in being. It would be contradictory for anything to desire its own annihilation. The sad fact of suicide does not gainsay this, because suicide is simply an extreme attempt to escape from a situation deemed to be unbearable so as to attain some kind of peace in some other state.

Perhaps the first thing to point out is that suffering is not solely a physical or bodily phenomenon. It can be mental or spiritual also, and whether bodily or mental it engages the whole person.

> Man suffers in different ways, ways not always considered by medicine, not even in its most advanced specializations. John Paul II, *Salvifici Doloris, #5*

This should be borne in mind in a secularist age when everything is reduced to the material and when some medical people see themselves merely as technicians of the "machine" which is the body. They are aware, of course, that living people – as distinct from corpses – have minds but they will try to reduce mind to being a mere epiphenomenon of the body, somewhat like the electric currents in a laptop which is otherwise a thing of various metals and plastics. To back up their claim they will point out how psychiatry can bring about cures, formerly unheard of, simply by administering certain drugs. These people are taking us back to the position of the ancient Ionian philosophers who had basically a monist, materialistic understanding of man. The Christian position is very different, teaching, as it does, that the soul is the form of the body, a thing created and infused by God at the moment of conception and destined to return to God at the end, which means that it can subsist by itself even when the body is in the grave.

Soul and Body, Matter and Form

The teaching that the soul is the form of the body is of great importance for the care of the sick because it means that these two components of the human person are not juxtaposed accidentally as Plato would say so that the soul, one separate entity, is a kind of prisoner in the body, another separate entity, waiting to be set free and be rid of this burden. Nor is it like a ghost in a machine, to use an example from Descartes many centuries later, but, again, a very dualist one. The soul, being the form of the body, communicates its own act of existence to the body so that the body exists by reason of the life it has from the soul and would only be a corpse on the way to decay without the soul. But, unlike the souls of lower animals, the human soul continues to exist by itself, to subsist, even when it has departed the body. Nonetheless, the idea that the soul is the form of the body, and that the body is the matter that is individuated by a given soul, means that the two components, soul and body, belong to each other by nature, so much so that the Christian doctrine of the resurrection of the body from the dust, though a miraculous work of God at the end of time, is not at all alien to Christian anthropology but is in accord with it and a thing of great hope.

For pastoral practice, understanding the soul as the form of the body means viewing man in what today is called a "holistic" or "psychosomatic" way, which means that a physical suffering can have a mental origin; - worry, for example, which is a thing of the mind, can have its effects in the body as well. And *vice versa*; a suffering which originates in the body - let us say a simple tooth ache - if it is ongoing, will have a negative effect on the mind also. Hence it is not surprising that a moral fault, if it is not dealt with but instead is buried, will have an effect in the body also, assuming that the person has a conscience. Thus, St John Paul says:

> In fact one cannot deny that moral sufferings have a "physical" or somatic element, and that they are often reflected in the state of the entire organism".
> *ibid., #6.*

I knew a doctor who "seemed" to be wasting time with each of his patients (to the annoyance of those still in the waiting room) by chatting to them about home, family, work, past history *etc.*, but he told me that domestic and social factors in the patient's background were often the root explanation of many of the physical ailment he had to deal with in the surgery. When the factor turns out to be buried guilt, what the patient sometimes needs is not a prescription for another medicine but simply to be told to go and make a good confession. And the relief that some such people experience on doing just that bears this out because their health often improves thereafter.

From the above it follows that a priest and other councillors of the sick should have some basic knowledge of psychology and physiology, of the different powers of soul and body and of the more common ailments of both.

As regards the mind or soul, chaplains and medics should adopt the Thomist understanding which presents the intellect and the will as man's two superior powers which should govern his lower powers: the emotions and the desires which give rise to the emotions, and the senses, both the five external and the four internal senses, which present him with objects of desire or aversion. They should be made aware of the difficulty the higher powers have in governing the lower powers due to the damage done to our nature by original sin. As regards the body, they should know the basics of its composition and how external circumstances impinge on its well-being, which, in turn, will impinge on the well-being of the soul.

A frequent ailment of the mind is neurosis when a person is, indeed, still in touch with reality but not able to cope well with it, thus giving rise to a chronic emotion of fear which defies the control of intellect and will. Then there are the various psychoses when the person is not rightly in touch with reality, and there is paranoia when the person sees grounds for suspicion everywhere. Fairly common also are the various kinds of depression which can have an internal cause due to a lack of some chemical like serotonin or an external cause as when a person is too much isolated or overworked.

As regards the body, those caring for the sick need a basic understanding of anatomy, the muscle and bone structure, the organs, *etc*, and again, the ailments that can affect the well- being of any of these. A patient is told that he must have his spleen removed and doesn't even know what or where it is in the body and then when, in addition, he is told he has only *one* spleen is worried as to how anyone can manage without it. The doctor has already left the patient because he is in a hurry and presumes that his patient has some knowledge of physiology. Then enter the chaplain. A simple explanation from him, if he has some basic knowledge of physiology, will put the patient at ease in a few minutes.

With this knowledge it is not a matter of the priest or carer trying to play the role of the psychiatrist or doctor but of him being able to make a right assessment of the condition of the patient so as to be able to give the correct advice or consolation or whatever might be needed by way of pastoral help. Patients are anxious when awaiting the result of an x-ray or a biopsy. In some cases it may be an over sensitive or nervous patient being unduly worried about a matter which is nor serious, while in another case the matter might be very serious or fatal and the patient is oblivious to the real import of the situation.

Tact and Empathy

It should hardly need saying that tact and empathy are required in these situations but, just as we saw that in matters of liturgy a sense of the sacred is not always forthcoming there, so also in medical matters tact and empathy are not always forthcoming either, even from some people who are supposedly professionals in this field. I heard of a nurse in charge of ward, who on being told by the consultant that patient X had a terminal illness, opened a drawer, took out a printed page and gave it to the said patient to read saying briskly: " Here, read that; it contains five points on how to prepare for death"! But I must add that in my own experience of medical people at all levels I found the vast majority of them to be very understanding and so also the chaplains. Tact, like the sense of the sacred, is something that some people have and some others simply do not and it is often difficult to instil it in these latter.

Empathy, like sympathy, means being able to share in the sufferings of others, to appreciate what they are going through and to walk that road with them. But in the case of the Christian chaplain more is expected: he should be the good Samaritan bending down over the wounded man so as to lift him up not only naturally with good counselling but also with the supernatural offer of faith and hope and the help of the sacraments and, in doing so, be a person of practical charity also.

In all of this a basic rule is to take the patient where you find him/her in his existential situation which can vary greatly from one person to another, even though they are all trying to cope with suffering and with the possibility of death, near or remote.

This brings us to the deeper question of the *meaning* of suffering and death.

The Meaning of Suffering

This question has often been treated of in philosophy and in theology in a theoretical way but it becomes a very concrete existential question when the priest enters a hospital ward and finds there a young man or woman who has had an active, healthy life up until recently but is now struck down by some malady or accident. The patient's question is: "Why has this happened to me?" If he/she is a person of entirely secularist mind he will try to say to himself: "Well, so much bad luck. Pleasure and material success, seemingly, must give way to pain and restriction in my life for the near future at least if not for the longer term". He may accept his lot despairingly or rebel against it angrily and declare life to be absurd anyhow. For the secularist life is largely a balance of pleasure and pain, pleasure and only a little pain in the first half of life and then the balance tipping more and more the other way in the second half of life until death finally sweeps everything away into a black hole. For him, to spare himself the increase of pain and to shorten the wait for the black hole, euthanasia is a solution he may consider. Suffering is sheer waste and death is final disaster better not dwelt on.

But it is also possible that the self-styled secularist has his non-belief challenged by his malady so that he begins to ask himself if there is, after all, more to life than a mere balance of pleasure and pain, or mere luck, good or bad, or if there might not, after all, be some unseen hand governing all these seemingly haphazard events and if, perhaps, something of himself might survive the grave. Is the chaplain able to meet him at this point, pick up on these questions and take him further in his search? I have never yet come across a fully convinced atheist who could calmly answer "no" definitively to these questions. Hence, being hit by adversity can be the opening of a door for him to new horizons to be pondered on, at least, and perhaps the first ray of light to a hope that goes beyond this life.

If the patient is a Christian, the self-questioning provoked by the malady will put him a few steps ahead of the non-believer but perhaps not much further ahead if he is a lukewarm or non-practicing Christian. So, he may be asking if God is punishing him with this affliction. That is most likely to be his first question. He might not be able to see what connection there could be between what he is suffering now and what Christ suffered on the cross - it might not even have entered his mind at all as of yet, even though he knows from his school days that Christ did suffer and die on the cross and that it was somehow for our salvation. But again, the chaplain needs to be able to pick up on him at the point he is at so as to take him further and enable him to see this connection.

Suffering and Sin

There *is* a connection between suffering and sin. Nearly every religious tradition has believed in that connection. In the Christian tradition it arises from the fact that our first parents sinned, and because Adam was the head of the entire human race, his sin was handed down and has had repercussions on all who came after him. We were all contained or represented in him, as it were, somewhat like the way an entire tribe might be represented in its chief, because of our physical descent from Adam. Like him, we lost sanctifying grace, our nature was disordered and our relation to God above and the world around us was also disordered. Though baptism restores grace, the disorder continues even if mitigated somewhat. This disorder impinges on all of us in different ways, with sickness of mind and body, with accidents, with an environment that is hostile at times, and with many other afflictions. Because these misfortunes go against the good we would naturally will for ourselves they are called "sufferings".

One might say that this describes what might be called a "general" connection between sin and suffering because all people are affected by Adam's revolt one way or another. But can we go on from there to judge that the particular suffering of a particular individual is the direct result of a moral fault of that individual or his parents or spouse? We can not. If Mr. Smith has a broken hand today we may not conclude that it is a punishment for his action of stealing money with that very hand yesterday, even if it transpires that he did, in fact, steal money yesterday. It might or it might not. Were we to hastily conclude that he must have done something wrong recently then we would also have to say that great saints who had great sufferings, like Padre Pio, for example, must have been great sinners in their spare time! It could well be that the patient is a very good living, holy person and that, from the divine perspective, his suffering is a trial from God (permitted by God and happening, perhaps, by the agency of Satan) to make him an even better person. St John Paul (also a man of great suffering) makes this clear referring to the example of Job in the Bible:

> While it is true that suffering has a meaning as punishment, when it is connected with a fault, it is not true that all suffering is a consequence of a fault and has the nature of a punishment. The figure of the just man Job is a special proof of this in the Old Testament. *Salvifici Doloris, #11.*

This quote makes clear that suffering may be a punishment for sin in a particular case though not necessarily so. It is important to repeat this at a time when priests are not supposed to use the words "sin" or "punishment" at all in their preaching. Much (though not all) preaching since the council (but not due to the council) has become a sickening lovey-dovey, sugar-and-candy kind of talk, giving us what some call "a religion of nice": "Jesus loves you so all is rosy in the garden" sort of thing. Also, priests who fall for this kind of thing know full well that if they do suggest that there could be "punishment for sin" at all they will be asked to specify which sins, which means treading on the toes of those committing those sins and having to take the inevitable backlash. Hence, to get back to the hospital situation, it can happen that the sick man is convinced that his affliction is, indeed, a punishment for some sin or sins or for a whole life of sin of which he is perfectly cognisant. And he may well be right, although the chaplain would need a special revelation from above to be assured of that beyond all doubt. If then the chaplain tries to convince the sick man that God is so loving that He never punishes at all and that he, the sick man, did not sin at all or never could have, he is going directly against the man's own testimony and also the evidence of salvation history as spelt out in the Bible where punishment often does follow on sin.

So the chaplain, then, is simply trying to bring the patient down the path of the rosy garden where everything is "nice", but the patient himself sees this as fake compassion.

We see clearly in every second page of the Old Testament that God calls His people to repentance from sin through the prophets and threatens them with chastisement if they do not respond – and usually they don't respond – but when they do, He forgives them and sheds many blessings on them. So also in the New Testament: Christ cures the invalid who had been waiting thirty eight years beside the pool but could never get into the pool in time when the waters were disturbed. *(Jn.5)*. Christ cures him but warns him to turn away from his life of sin lest something worse befall him. That suggests that *his* sufferings, in this one case, were directly linked to his particular sin. And now he is cured. But we cannot still argue from one such particular case to that of all others who are suffering.

The important point here is that God *does* at times and in some cases send afflictions as punishments and at other times not. But even when He does send them as punishment the purpose is not to *down* a person but instead to correct, to recall, to restore. It is meant to be therapeutic, not destructive. Again, St John Paul says:

> ….in the sufferings inflicted by God upon the Chosen people there is included an invitation of his mercy, which corrects in order to lead to conversion…
> *ibid.,* #12.

Only the sufferings of the damned are entirely punitive and that because of their total refusal to repent. (But, of course, priests may not mention hell or damnation either if they want to continue practicing in the church of "nice"). God is not a cruel tyrant delighting in punishment. He is most definitely a God of love, and that precisely because He corrects His beloved children whom He sees going astray so as to bring them back to what is good and to union with Himself in a love that will be eternal if they remain faithful. Responsible parents do the same with their children, that is if their love is genuine and not mere sentiment. The danger with the patient in the sick bed, who is perfectly aware of his sinfulness, is that he might despair and think that God is putting him down definitively with this affliction; so the chaplain must not try to fool him into thinking that his wrongdoings are not sins at all but assure him that with this suffering God is, in fact, loving him in an unexpected way and trying to bring him forward and upwards to a better life, a life of true holiness which, hopefully, will lead to new health in this life or to perfect happiness in the next in union with God, if that be God's will for him.

But then there are cases where the sick man or woman is a good and innocent person (in as much as anyone can be so in this world of imperfections). Such a person also might be tempted to despair on account of his sufferings precisely because he is *not* conscious of grave sin. "Why then this affliction", he will ask. In the Old Testament the classic case is that of Job, mentioned already above – a prototype of Christ - who keeps protesting his innocence in the face of his three friends who keep rigidly to the sin-punishment line. We see that in *his* case it was a trial so that his steadfastness might be demonstrated to Satan who was permitted to be the agent of the affliction and that he, Job, might grow in virtue; and then in the New Testament we have the incident of the cure of the man born blind (*Jn. 9*) where, again, the Jews keep to the same sin-punishment line, but Christ makes it clear that sin was not the reason for the man's affliction but that *the works of God might be revealed* as they certainly were with the miraculous cure that followed. The profound truth being conveyed here is that God does indeed allow evil at times but only in order to bring even greater good out of it than would have been the case otherwise. So, trial for growth in virtue and consequent gain in merit is a second message of consolation and strength that the priest/chaplain can give to the patient and that God is always working for good for those who trust in Him.

Suffering and Expiation

But there is even more to the meaning of suffering: if we move on through the Old Testament we come to the figure of the innocent Suffering Servant in Isaiah. I say "figure" because he "prefigures" Christ Himself, which is why we have this reading in the liturgy of Good Friday. He, by his suffering, is taking the sins of others on himself and atoning for them. *Ours were the sufferings he bore. Is. 53:4*. So here we have the idea of vicarious suffering: the sufferings of innocent people in one place atoning for the sins of bad people in other places. This is a most enriching insight and an offer of hope for the patient because his sufferings, when offered up with those of Christ on the cross, are a source of great power for good in the world.

This idea of "offering up" one's sufferings for the sins of the world is an old one and has been handed down by the old to the young in every generation. Yet I feel the need to spend a little time on it because I find today that many young people do not have this concept at all. I even met a seminarian once for whom it was an entirely new idea.

I remember as a young man working on a building site carrying concrete blocks up a ramp to a builder who could not be supplied fast enough. This was in the days when conveyor belts and teleporters were not very common. I was sweating in the heat of a Summer day. Two elderly carpenters, who were also working on the site, were having their lunch at the time. One of them, watching me sweating and labouring, shouted over to me: "young man, for whose sins are you doing all that labour, your own or those of the Holy Souls?" There was no such thought on my mind, only the thought of how to get these blocks up the ramp in time. But it was a great lesson: suffering is not at all a waste – contrary to what the secularist would say – it is most valuable; therefore a Christian should let no suffering go to waste. One should offer it up with those of Christ for one's own sins or for those of others or for the souls in purgatory and also for the conversion of sinners as requested by Our Lady at Fatima.

Years later, as a priest, I once had a young man come to me very upset because his sister, who was an invalid, was suffering greatly. The same young man was making money by going around the town in a white van renting pornographic videos. I asked him if it ever occurred to him that his good sister might well be an innocent soul, specially called by God to be a "victim soul", that is, someone specially chosen by God to be given a share in Christ's passion for the saving of sinners, of people who are sinning themselves and leading others into sin. He seemed not to get the point at all and went away quickly. Perhaps again, it is the case that a generation unfamiliar with the idea of sacrifice or of making sacrifices find such questions to be strange. But, nonetheless, I must say that I did not see so much of the white van around the town from there on.

What God is doing in our lives, by means of the sufferings He allows to come upon us, is a question that takes us into mystery. The question of why this particular suffering befell Tom and a different one Dick and a different one again on Harry is as difficult to answer as to why Tom has been given brown eyes, Dick blue eyes and Harry grey eyes; and, when we know of their different ailments, the question arises as to what God is doing in their individual lives by means of each of these different ailments. Is it a therapeutic punishment in Tom's case, or a trial for an increase in virtue in Dick's case or is Harry being asked to suffer vicariously for the sins of others? Each is possible. When the patient is an innocent little child the question becomes more difficult still. And then there is the even more ponderous question as to why some people will respond positively to the grace that God offers to all in their sufferings - because He wills all to be saved and tries no one beyond his/her limits - and why others will rebel and persist in their rebellion and perhaps be lost? Here we are dealing with the mystery of election and predestination from God's side and of the mystery of iniquity and the response of the will from man's side.

But while we cannot provide a simple answer to such questions, they are pastorally important because the priest, at times, has to deal with people who are in rebellion because of what God has allowed to befall them. This rebellion is all the more likely when there is so much talk about peoples' rights (and so little about peoples' obligations) so that every desire, be it moral or immoral, is hailed as a right. God, in that kind of thinking, should have no right to frustrate the patient's right to health!

Job is famed for his patience: "the patience of Job" is a hackneyed phrase, but anyone who takes the trouble to read that book will find that Job is protesting quite a lot at times to God about the afflictions that have befallen him – and they were indeed great – but if one continues to the end of the book there one will see God replying by asking Job if he (Job) was there when He (God) was putting the stars their place in the sky and setting out the foundations of the earth at the beginning of things, to which Job has to answer "No", of course. The point being that Job, as a mere mortal, knows very little about the ways of providence, so little that he has no grounds for asserting any rights over against God, that the best thing he can do is to bow his head in humble submission and trust that God *does* know what He is doing, not only in creating things but also in governing things and in even in permitting bad things to happen to good people, and that what He is doing in our lives is for a good purpose no matter how great the sufferings. Hence also with the chaplain: it is better that he not pry too deeply into the ways of God but that he encourage his patients to trust in His will, to call out to Him in humble prayer for His grace, for forgiveness and for the strength they will need to get through their suffering.

Christ as the Meaning of Suffering

These different meanings of suffering find their clearest answer in Christ and His cross which is why Job and the Suffering Servant are His prototypes. Apart from Christ, our sufferings are indeed a waste in the long run, though, in the short run, they may make for an increase in the natural virtue of endurance which may be of use to the patient on his recovery (if he does recover). But Christ, by reason of His divinity, gives suffering and death an infinite value and ours also if offered up and endured in union with His.

Soteriology is the study of how Christ saved us from sin and damnation by His suffering and death. What happened on the cross is described in different ways in scripture and then in tradition building on scripture. St Augustine saw it as a sacrifice making for union between us and God *(cf. City of God, Bk. X, 6)*. Later St Anselm and then St Thomas saw it as a meriting, a liberation, a redemption and as a sacrifice of atonement or reparation *(cf. S. Th. III, q46-50)*. One finds these ways of thinking in the scriptures, especially in the words of institution of the Eucharist which speak of Christ's body as being "given up" for people, *(Lk.22:19)* and they are to be found in the liturgy also as a result.

The idea of justice is fundamental here: sin is an offense of infinite magnitude because the One offended is the infinite God. Accordingly, justice required an appropriate act of recompense which was beyond the capability of man, the offender. But God Himself came to the rescue out of love for man by sending His Son to die on the cross to make the required atonement.

This soteriology of atonement fell somewhat out of favour during the second half of the twentieth century which I believe was due to a prior, distorted understanding of justice which had over emphasized the idea of justice to the detriment of the idea of love in the act of redemption. The idea of justice had been so exalted by some theologians that it became something like one of the forms of Plato standing high and aloof, even above God, so that God would have to conform to it to satisfy it, which then led to God Himself being seen as cold and even blood-thirsty, somewhat like a pagan god of pre-Christian times, a god always demanding his "pound of flesh" from sinful man. This caricature of the redemption begot an opposite reaction whereby the emphasis was then put on God's love, but this time at the expense of His justice – the pendulum then going too far the other way – so that God was depicted as loving but without any regard for justice. This, when taken too far, leads to the sloppy "Jesus loves you" kind of thing, "sin or no sin, it doesn't matter; and even if you do sin there is no need even to be sorry, God forgives you anyhow". It is "cheap love" as mentioned earlier. Indeed, it is no love at all because it is unreal, because it takes no account of the evil which is sin or the offense it causes – even when sin is seen to abound in the world around us - or of the need that something be done to put things right.

Love in God does trump over strict justice, otherwise we would all be damned; but, nonetheless, both love and justice are infinite in God and neither can be cast aside for sake of the other. Furthermore, justice is not some Platonic abstraction standing above God to which He has to comply. Justice is in God, and it is in Him not as an accidental addition to His being but as one with His very being (because there are no accidents in God). Hence in being just, God is in fact being true to Himself. But because He is also love – it is His very definition - He took our debt of justice on Himself by loading it onto His own Son on the cross. Because God is both the offended One and the judge at the same time, He could indeed have waved all atonement aside. That He did not do so, but sent His Son to die for us, was not due to Him being constrained by something outside of or above Himself but so that we would learn of the great love He has for us which had him endure such terrible sufferings by way of sacrifice for us and learn also what an evil thing is sin when seen against the backdrop of such goodness. This should have us be ever more thankful to Him for having saved us in this way, more so than if He had waived all requirements of atonement aside. The result should be a great return of love for Him from our side, a love that would abhor sin, the kind of love one finds in the lives of the saints, a love that had them embrace the sufferings that came their way so as to make an offering of them to God in union with those of Christ and even had them take on penances for the sins of the world, apart from any sickness that might befall them in addition, a love which is very different from the cheap, candy-floss love so often peddled today.

The soteriology of Pope Benedict XVI is not based primarily on the idea of justice and atonement but neither is it one of cheap love. For him God's love in Christ was powerful enough to consume or burn or purge the world of sin and Christ's great agony in the garden was due to Him, the sinless One, taking all this evil on Himself. (*cf. Jesus of Nazareth, Vol II*).

I have made this brief excursus into soteriology because I am making the claim that the cheap love which is being peddled today, which takes no account of the evil of sin, in a pathetic desire to win people back to Church, is not only not working but is even counter-productive. It is about as pathetic and futile as an incompetent teacher trying to curry favour with her pupils by telling them that they need not do any lessons or make any corrections. The pupils themselves see through this. So also those sinning today know that this cheap-love stuff, peddled by so many preachers, is merely a fear of mentioning sin and what needs to be done about it and, in general, an indication of spiritual bankruptcy. The result is that sinners continue in their sin, laugh at the Church and walk away. I am also making this excursus because, to get back to the man or woman in the sick bed, only a well-thought-out soteriology can truly take account of his/her sufferings and more so when death seems close. Cheap-love talk is soon exploded if the patient replies "Well if God is all that loving, as you say He is, why doesn't He cure me now of this illness".

Soteriology is not kids' stuff because the world, the real world, is not a kids' playground. It is often a battle field between good and evil, with evil descending to some terrible depths, as we all saw at Auschwitz and in many more instances. The great strength of Christianity and a proof of its genuineness is that it faces all evil head on with its proclamation of the cross: God taking all that evil on Himself in His Son and overcoming it by His resurrection, all by His power as God and His love for us.

The priest or chaplain should know his soteriology, but that does not mean that he should come to the patient's bedside and bombard him/her with a heavy theology lecture, no more than the cariologist will come and bombard him with a lecture on the chambers, valves and arteries of the heart. Both should know their subject but be able to take account of the patient's age, intelligence, level of education, receptivity or lack of it due to pain and the medication he is on and then, proceeding on a need-to-know basis, be able to advise or encourage or console as is necessary and, in the case of the chaplain, be able to provide credible meaning for what the patient is going through.

Colossians as the Answer

To this end St John Paul in his letter *Savifici Doloris* goes back to scripture and makes much use of St Paul in *Colossians 1:24*. *I make up in my own body what is lacking of the sufferings of Christ*. It is not that there was anything defective in Christ's sacrifice on the cross. It was a perfect sacrifice because He was divine and also because, as man, He was a perfect mediator. But Christ is both head and mystical body, and His body is still growing in His members, and in each of those members He is still living out the paschal mystery and thus completing that mystery in the lives, sufferings and deaths of those people. St John Paul again:

> Christ achieved the Redemption completely and to the very limit; but at the same time he did not bring it to a close. In this redemptive suffering, through which the Redemption of the world was accomplished, Christ opened himself from the beginning to every human suffering and constantly does so. Yes, it seems to be part of the very essence of Christ's redemptive suffering that this suffering requires to be unceasingly completed". *SD, #20.*

Hence there is an invitation in those words to everyone who suffers to give, offer up, hand over those sufferings to Christ so that Christ can unite them with His sacrifice of the cross in the Mass for the merit, liberation, redemption and atonement they will then accomplish through Him and which they could never accomplish on their own. These sufferings, when given over to Christ, will bear these good fruits for the patient him/herself and for others also be they sinners in need of conversion in this world or souls in purgatory waiting to be freed.

We hand over our sufferings to Christ, but there is a reciprocal aspect to this also in that Christ hands over various parts of His sufferings to *us* in accordance with, or by means of, the sufferings sent us by providence. Christ suffered physically and mentally, and in diverse ways in each, and He gives different people different shares in those diverse sufferings. One man, for example, may be given a share in Christ's physical sufferings if he is burdened, let's say, from chronic arthritis. A mother may be given a share in His agony in Getsemany because of her worries about the loss of faith of her children, and a priest in a communist country, locked away and forgotten in jail for years for his faith, is given a share in His abandonment. We see this more clearly in the lives of many saints: those who were called to be victim souls by a life of illness which may confine them to bed for many years, those who were given the stigmata and those who have had to endure the dark night of the soul perhaps for a long time.

For the secularist such things make no sense, but these saints feel privileged to be given this share in Christ's passion, and it is a source of joy to them to know the good that they achieve when they offer their sufferings with Him. In prayer they meditated on the passion; and on their death beds they would hold the crucifix in their hands and focus their loving gaze on it as so many other faithful Christians have been doing through the ages. That enables them to die with a great resignation and peace and with a firm hope of sharing also in Christ's resurrection.

Conclusions:

1. The priest/chaplain has, as his model, the good Samaritan bending down in pity over suffering humanity in the patient, having at hand the words of scripture, the doctrines of the faith and the sacraments to bring him/her consolation and healing. One could also say that he is one who is living the prayer of St Francis of Assisi by being an instrument of peace, light and hope for the sick.
2. The priest/chaplain must take the patient where he finds him/her existentially, taking account of his age, faith, intelligence, education, family background and, of course, his illness so as to be able to help him find meaning in his sufferings. He needs a basic knowledge of psychology and physiology to do this effectively but more so a good knowledge of soteriology.
3. Ultimately it is only in Christ and His cross that we can find full meaning for suffering and death even if in the end we are dealing with mystery.

Having looked at the Christian meaning of suffering above we can now turn to a study of the sacrament of the sick itself.

Chapter XXVII

The Sacrament of the Sick

The Sacrament Itself, Moral and Medical Problems, the Patient's Family

Is any among you sick? Let him call for the elders of the church, and let them pray over him, anointing him with oil in the name of the Lord…. James 5:14.

By the sacred anointing of the sick and the prayer of the priests the whole Church commends those who are ill to the suffering and glorified Lord, that he may raise them up and save them. and indeed she exhorts them to contribute to the good of the People of God by freely uniting themselves to the Passion and death of Christ. *Catechism of the Catholic Church, #1499*

In this chapter we will look at the sacrament of the sick itself from a pastoral view point, but not as substituting for a more complete study as is to be had in the manuals of the administration of the sacraments or in the *Code of Canon Law*. Then we will look at a few of the more frequent problems of medical ethics and problems of a social kind that the chaplain can encounter, but again, not as a substitute for a more thorough academic study of such things.

This sacrament is given to us by Christ as a special help for those who are suffering and in a possible danger of death. Like all the sacraments, it was instituted by Christ because He is the author of the grace of the sacraments, even though the gospels do not give us an explicit account of Him doing this. In the gospel of Mark we have Christ sending the twelve out on mission and we are told that *they anointed many sick people with oil and cured them. Mk. 6:13.* But the above quote from St James is the usual one cited as the locus of this sacrament.

The Sacrament Itself

Form and Matter

The faith which has the Christian die with Christ in the hope of rising with Him again finds expression in the form of the sacrament of the sick which is as follows:

Through this holy anointing may the Lord in His love and mercy help you with the grace of the Holy Spirit. May the Lord who frees you from sin save you and raise you up.

The matter is the oil of any plant but blessed by the bishop (or by a priest in a case of necessity). This is necessary for validity. The above words in the form speak of the sick person being "saved and raised up" by Christ. Oil indicates healing and strength. This sacrament, like all the others, channels Our Lord's paschal mystery to us in its own distinctive way so that we can participate in it and receive its fruits in the ways indicated by the signs employed in its administration, i.e., by being healed or strengthened.

Its first effect is a gift of the Holy Spirit bringing strength, peace and courage to the person that is suffering. If his/her sufferings will be long-term it sustains him in that struggle and, in the end, it prepares him for his exit from this life to the next. In this regard St Thomas Aquinas speaks of it as the "sacrament of glory" claiming that it takes away any remaining weaknesses of soul and also most, if not all, of any temporal punishment still due to sins already forgiven so that the person is ready for the glory of heaven, (*cf. Summa Contra Gentiles, Bk. IV, Ch. 73*) even though the *Catechism* does not mention this last effect today.

The *Catechism* lists this sacrament as one of those given to us for the forgiveness of sins even though its direct object is not the forgiveness of mortal sin. Nonetheless, it will effect this, one might say indirectly, should it happen that the sick person is burdened with a mortal sin that he/she is completely unaware of due to lapse of time or memory. If the sick person is conscious, the priest will first offer him the possibility of confessing before anointing him, thereby providing him with the proper means of being cleansed of mortal sin. If he is unconscious the priest should say the act of sorrow into his ear and give him absolution if it can be assumed that he would have accepted the sacraments were he conscious. No sacrament is to be given to one who is clearly dead. The sacrament of the sick can bring bodily healing also, if this is the will of God for the good of the person's soul, and priests can tell of remarkable cases where this sacrament made for a definite turn-about in someone's illness. *(cf. The Catechism of the Catholic Church, #1520 on this).*

Today we no longer see this sacrament exclusively as being for those at the very end of life, which is why we now no longer call it "extreme unction" but instead by its new name. Indeed, even in times past it was permitted to administer this sacrament about every six weeks to a person in a long, continuous illness, or even in a long continuous state of debility and more often in the case of a person who became dangerously ill all of a sudden - as for example due to a heart attack - and who recovered seemingly well but suffered another attack again soon after. Nonetheless, this sacrament has always been associated in people's mind with the danger of death. Now, since the council, due to the change of emphasis signified by the renaming of this sacrament, it is also administered on special occasions such as the world day of the sick on February the 11th every year in parish churches, and at places of devotion such as Marian shrines. Nonetheless, the sacrament does, or should, still have some relation to life's end, at least in the sense that the patient's illness, even if long term, does still have a life-threatening element to it, perhaps remote but there nonetheless. (*cf. Code of Canon Law, can. 1004*). There can be a danger of abuse if the meaning of this sacrament is completely dissociated from any relation to the danger of death as when people with only minor ailments go up to receive it. Indeed, some people will go up simply because "something is being given out" scarcely knowing what it is. I suggest that there be some norms to prevent this, that perhaps people be asked to show some kind of green card from their doctor stating simply that this person is suffering from a condition that is potentially dangerous without specifying the ailment so as to safeguard privacy.

When this sacrament is followed by Holy Communion, when a person is near death, the latter is called "viaticum" which means "strength for the road" to the next life.

A bishop or priest can administer the sacrament of the sick, not a deacon or lay person, and the recipient must be a baptized person who has reached the use of reason and is thus capable of sinning. It would be an abuse of the sacrament to administer it to non-baptized people who might come to hear that it can have the effect of sometimes bringing physical healing.

Some Pastoral Points

<u>Move promptly to the right Place</u>

The following are a few simple basic, but I think, important points which I have learned from my own pastoral experience.

It should not be necessary to point out that when a priest is called out on a "sick call" he should go immediately. Most people do not call a priest frivolously, or, if they do, it is because they misread the symptoms of the sick person and get unduly alarmed. But I still do emphasize the point of making no delay because I have heard of priests not responding immediately, proceeding instead to go out for a meal with some friends as planned or see the finish of a football match on TV. This is a callous neglect of souls and raises questions about the faith of such a priest. It is the special duty, in justice, of the parish priest to take care of his flock when they are about to leave this world and go before God for judgement. He must do so himself or see to it that another priest is on call to do so. It is a duty in charity of any other priest who might be in the area, but I see that distinction as academic because, very simply, it is an urgent matter which no priest who happens to be nearby can ignore. A laicized priest can also validly administer the last rites in an emergency.

It might also seem needless to point out that when a priest is called out on a "sick call" that he should know where he is going. Yet I feel it is necessary to emphasize this, especially if it is a call in the middle of the night in a strange territory, because to get the address, or postcode wrong when most people are in bed can mean a waste of valuable time in getting to a person who might be in dire spiritual need of the sacraments and near to death. If one puts down the phone without getting the caller's phone number one might find oneself asking oneself a few minutes later: "did he say Roselawn Drive or Roselawn Avenue or Roselawn Terrace and if it was Roselawn *Drive* was it number 8 or was it number 18 or 80"? In a country place one might find oneself asking if it was the first turn right after the bridge and then the second left up the hill or was it the other way round.

It can happen that on the way out on a sick call some sinister things will begin happening. Old priests can tell strange stories about such things: simple things like the keys of the car not being in their usual place or a breakdown in a relatively new car or a flat tire, or more dangerous things like a near miss with a car crash. Satan does not want that priest to get to this particular man or woman who is dying. Prayer to one's angel guardian and holy water are good helps in this regard. On the other side, it is also wonderful at times how a priest can be found most unexpectedly when he is needed in an emergency, as if providence placed him in the right place at just the right time to help save a soul. Such graces are more likely to be effective when a priest is wearing his clerical garb, for the obvious reason that he is then more easily identified.

A priest can be called out to some horrible scenes especially if it is a car accident or a suicide or a burning or drowning. I knew of one case where a young priest was called out to anoint a man who was in the back of a van and had been decapitated. When the priest went to anoint him the trunk, minus the head, sat up straight in front of him. The priest panicked and got a breakdown. One must prepare oneself mentally for such things by simply telling oneself to expect something horrible. Then the reality will not appear to be quite so bad. In Northern Ireland, during the years of conflict there in the second half of the 20th century, some priests claimed that some scenes to which they were called - horrible mutilations for example - convinced them that the Satanic was the only explanation, working, of course, through human agents.

When the priest arrives at a nasty scene, or indeed at any sick bed, he must bring with him the calm and reassurance of Christ when He calmed the storm and cured many people who were greatly troubled. I have often been impressed in this regard by old priests who were genuinely holy men. One could see that for them it was more than a case of "having seen all this before" and thus being unmoved. It was, instead, the case of a devout man bringing the peace of Christ, a peace this world cannot give, to a troubled situation because he was a man close to Christ in the first place by time spent in prayer.

At the Scene

When he arrives at the house or scene, the priest should briefly greet those present but go immediately to the sick person. The time prior to administering the sacraments is not one for chatter. After hearing the sick person's confession it is good to gather the family round the sick bed while the sacraments of the sick and viaticum are being administered. This can be a salutary moment for young people who might not have had any previous near contact with death, so that they learn of the Church's care for the dying and learn that death, though a penalty on all of us due to the Fall, has become a passage way to new life, due to Christ having taken it on Himself, so that it need no longer be a thing of dread. The prayers of the parents, mingling with the sobs of the grandchildren when a grandparent is dying, surely touch the heart of Christ, just as the tears of Martha and Mary did so long ago. So also, a decade of the rosary at that time, each *Hail Mary* finishing with the words *pray for us sinners now and at the hour of our death* will have Mary present for what might just be the moment of the particular judgement of the person who has died so that she can intercede for him or her and keep the Evil One away. It is good then to talk to the family for a few minutes to comfort them; but one must remember that they will want to get on with contacting other people in the event of the sick person having just passed away.

The priest should remember that he is again in the role of the Good Samaritan bending down in pity over the sick, bringing them the help of the sacraments in the inn which is the Church. He and the medics can also be seen as another Simon of Cyrene or Veronica bringing whatever help or consolation they can.

Moral and Medical Problems

Medical Problems: Euthanasia, Painkillers

The hospital, like the school, is increasingly becoming an arena of conflict between Christian and secularist values in the Western world and between Church and state if legislation in this area of health is contrary to the moral law. The priest/chaplain is very much in the middle of this. This is most obvious when state hospitals perform abortions and demand that medical people who are Catholics take part also by direct, formal cooperation, something that can in no way be justified. So also, it is immoral to co-operate directly and formally with sterilizations on healthy reproductive organs as a way to regulate the size of a family or on innocent people. St John Paul once again:

> Except when performed for strictly therapeutic medical reasons, directly intended amputations, mutilations, and sterilizations performed on innocent persons are against the moral law." *CCC, #2298, cf.* also *DS, 3722.*

But our concern here is with the care of the sick and the evil of euthanasia being presented as an instance of "care". This happens sooner or later in countries where abortion has already been accepted: if innocent life can be cut short at one end of the life spectrum why not at the other on the utterly false pretext that it is "in the patient's best interest" when, more often than not, it is in the selfish interest of relatives who do not want to be bothered with the care of the old (or who are greedily waiting to inherit their money) or in the interests of a health board that wants to cut costs. The *Catechism* says on this:

> .... an act or omission which, of itself or by intention, causes death in order to eliminate suffering constitutes a murder gravely contrary to the dignity of the human person and to the respect due to the living God, his Creator...*CCC, #2277.*

That a patient might have no relatives to care for him/her and is in pain and feels desolate and is calling for euthanasia does not change the morality of what the *Catechism* says here because neither the patient or anyone else has that kind of authority over innocent human life, a thing that is God-given and God-taken when God alone decides. The right to life of the innocent is inalienable.

Closely related to this is the question of the morality of administering painkillers when these might be very strong such that they can reduce a person's life expectancy.

Here the principle of two effects comes into play. To administer, let's say, morphine, which can be severe on the heart, to lessen pain is justifiable if otherwise the patient would die all the sooner from excessive pain. The goal directly intended is morally good, the relief of pain with the hope that this will give some greater extension of life free of pain. But there has to be a proportion such that the life expectancy of the patient, one hopes, will be greater, or at least more bearable, if the morphine is administered than if it is not administered. By comparison, to administer the painkiller with the primary aim of killing the patient all the sooner is morally wrong, even though this will, obviously, have the secondary effect also of lessening pain. One may not do evil directly and intentionally to bring about good; that is a fundamental moral principle.

If painkillers, administered near the end of life, will have the effect of making the patient continuously drowsy, care must be taken that he/she has first had an opportunity to receive the sacraments, especially the sacrament of penance, with a clear mind and has also had an opportunity to settle any other affairs such as those of a legal kind that might still be outstanding.

Given this rightful understanding of means and ends in caring for the patient near the end of life there is, nonetheless, a kind of care that is over zealous in a way that is wrong. The *Catechism* says on this:

> Discontinuing medical procedures that are burdensome, dangerous, extraordinary, or disproportionate to the expected outcome can be legitimate; it is the refusal of over zealous treatment. Here one does not will to cause death; one's inability to impede it is merely accepted. The decision should be made by the patient if he is competent and able or, if not by those legally entitled to act for the patient, whose reasonable will and legitimate interests must always be respected". *ibid., #2278.*

A distinction needs to be made here between what is extraordinary and what is artificial. To perform a heart by-pass operation on a patient of ninety years of age which might gain him another month of life (if he survived the operation at all) would be extraordinary, and so, is not obligatory. By comparison, to feed a patient who cannot swallow liquids by using a tube or by a peg in the stomach is artificial; nonetheless it is *not* extraordinary though such techniques may have seemed extraordinary when first introduced, as also were such things as pacemakers and blood transfusions. To withhold the use of such things if death is not imminent would then be wrong.

There can be problems for the priest/chaplain if a patient asks for measures that violate the moral law, for example if he/she is drawing up a living will that specifies that he be euthanized merely because of a loss of memory or speech or limb power, though there is no imminent danger of death and his overall health be otherwise fairly good. The chaplain cannot cooperate with such a request nor can any other medic cooperate with its being given effect because this is not a situation of them being no longer able to impede the close and inevitable onset of natural death.

The Congregation for the Doctrine of the Faith in 1980 stated that:

No one is permitted to ask for this act of killing, either for himself or herself or for another person entrusted to his or her care, nor can he or she consent to it, either explicitly or implicitly, nor can any authority legitimately recommend or permit such an action. *Declaration on Euthanasia.*

Life Supports

Such considerations lead on to the question of the morality of turning off a life support machine when the monitor "seems" to say that the patient is "brain dead". One monitor may indeed show a blank screen, but that because it is only able to record brain activity that is on the outer edges of the brain while another monitor, of a more sensitive kind, will be able to detect brain activity at a deeper level; and there are numerous cases of patients in comas, declared to be brain dead according to the monitor, who have recovered after long periods - weeks or even months later - and some who came round to normal life even after the life support machine had been turned off.

This problem raises the deeper question of what is death? and whether or not it is the medical scientist or the philosopher should have the last say on it. For the medical scientist death is now often taken to mean the cessation of brain activity, going on the presupposition that the brain is the control organ of the entire body. But if the heart and lungs are still functioning, albeit with the help of a machine, what does the medical scientist say? That such functioning is now useless and irrelevant because totally dependent on the machine; so, it is better to turn off the machine! And, he will say further that if, perhaps, the patient might live without the help of the machine for a while he would only have a vegetative existence, so he recommends that it is better to withdraw all sustenance, such as water or liquid foods, that are being administered by drips.

Chapter 27: The Sacrament of the Sick

An added consideration that comes into play then is the need for organ harvesting to save the lives of other patients in dire need of transplants, and then there is a further consideration of crude money-making when such harvested organs are sold. The best time to harvest an organ is while the patient is still "living" on a life support machine.

But this is where the philosophical aspect comes into play – if this aspect is allowed consideration at all in a secularist age. Is the person with the "supposed" irreparable brain damage dead or still living? This question poses the more fundamental question: what is death? Is it merely the quiet condition of a patient when the monitor screen shows blank though he is still breathing with the help of the machine? If we say "Yes" to that we are left with the problem of explaining how a person can be dead as to his brain but alive as to the rest of his body. The scientist will reply by saying that the rest of his body is not alive but merely functioning artificially. That answer is scientifically false because anyone at all who has ever had to administer artificial respiration will know that a dead man will not respond actively to any input of air from outside. All that will happen is that his lungs will exhale the air just as an inflated balloon will do when let go. But when the patient is *co-operating* with the machine it must mean that his heart and lungs are functioning actively, which means in addition that they have life in them though they are being helped artificially to function and might not function without that help. That idea is as easy to grasp as that of an old man who cannot walk at all by himself but who is able to do so with the aid of a walking stick. We do not say of *him* that his legs are dead or that they should be amputated.

Here is the rightful place of the philosopher to come into the debate and explain that the human soul is *one* entity only and that it is whole in every part of the body; that death is the separation of the soul from the body, so that if the body is functioning at all, even if doing so *visibly* only in one part and with artificial help, that we must say that the soul is still present, and if so, that it is immoral to do anything intentionally and directly, either by act or omission, that will cause it to separate from the body before nature has taken its course and the dying process has begun.

There have been anthropologies which taught that there are a number of souls in man, a vegetative, animal and rational soul, each of which came and departed in succession, and that after a serious brain injury only the vegetative soul is remaining. Hence the oft used phrase "We turned off the machine because he was only a vegetable. The man we knew was not there anymore". But this is not consistent with Catholic philosophy which teaches that there is only one soul, the source of all these powers in one, which comes to be in full at the moment of conception, is present in every part of the body, and departs as one substantive entity at the moment of death when, henceforth, it is no longer "informing" the body but subsisting apart from it when gone to the next world.

The Moment of Death

So when does the soul depart? When is the actual moment of death? This is difficult to determine with exactness for the obvious reason that the soul is spiritual and therefore invisible and so cannot be seen departing, which means that all we have to go on are the visible or external signs of life. Traditionally they have always been taken to be heartbeat and breathing. When these are no longer detectable for a period of time then the person is presumed to be dead. Common sense always told people this, and then science, prior to the invention of brain monitors, confirmed this by telling us that without an intake of air and a functioning heart to pump the blood around the body that all cells will be starved of oxygen, including, of course, the cells of the brain, even the deepest cells, whether that can be measured clinically or not. In brief, I am claiming that the older symptoms of death are a surer guide than those provided by monitors today.

But what period of time must elapse for a safe presumption of death? In the days before science people had (and still have) the custom of "waking the dead". It was not only a time for mourning but also as a time of trial to make sure of the onset of death. Priests in olden times used the rule of thumb that in the case of a person who had been suffering from a long illness the soul might stay with the body for about half an hour after all signs of life had ceased, whereas in the case of a young person, who dies suddenly as a result of some accident, the time span might be as much as three hours or even more. The underlying philosophy here is that the soul, being the form of the body, has a natural union with the body (as compared to dualist philosophies which see the soul as trapped in a body and wanting to escape) and so, will try to stay with the body if there is any likelihood of the body becoming functional again. Accordingly, we have stories of people who came near to being drowned describing how they found themselves outside of and up above their bodies, looking down on them, while the medics were trying to resuscitate them, and then describing how they woke up as if nothing had happened, perhaps in the ambulance on the way to hospital (or to the morgue!).

For the administration of the sacraments a priest would do well to err on the side of allowing too much time rather than too little, that is of allowing for the possibility that the soul might still be present even if he is not sure how many hours have passed since the last signs of life were noticed by relatives. This is the situation when a priest is called to a person who died some time during the night but was discovered only in the morning. But in the case of someone who has been missing for some days and is then taken dead from a river, one does not administer any sacraments but, instead, reads some prayers for the dead.

The desire to save another patient who is in need of a transplant is indeed laudable, but one must never do evil directly and intentionally to bring about good; hence to rip out the heart or lungs of a person still alive, because still responding to life support, is to directly kill an innocent person, and that is intrinsically wrong. Put simply, one may not kill Peter to save Paul though Paul be in great need of a transplant.

Hopefully, new developments in the transplanting of animal organs and tissues will provide a better solution. For a long time pig insulin has been used by diabetics. Or, artificial hearts may come to be invented, a kind of follow-on to the pacemaker. The guiding principle here is that one may not transplant anything from an animal that would compromise the genuine humanity of the recipient patient. So, for example, a transplant of brain matter that would render the recipient no longer capable of reasoning, willing or of relating emotionally in a human way would be immoral.

In relation to all of this I would like to caution chaplains against agreeing to what is called the "apnea test" if this goes on for more than a few minutes as often happens. This is deceptive. It purports to see if the patient can live by his own resources for some time without the support of the machine, usually a half an hour, and if he cannot, then he is presumed dead. The deception here is that a patient in need of life support will most likely die of asphyxiation if air is cut off from him for that length of time. So, it is not a matter of the test "showing" that he is dead but of the test actually killing him.

There is an added wrong when a woman who is pregnant is presumed to be dead because the monitor says she is brain dead and the machine is turned off, thus killing the baby as well if the baby is below the age of viability. I have seen it happen, the excuse being used that to keep the woman alive – even though she is, in fact, alive – would be "extraordinary or disproportionate to the expected outcome". Yet the expected outcome in this case is the delivery of a healthy baby with a whole life in front of him/her and, who knows, perhaps the recovery of the mother also if given enough time.

When a point is reached that all medical treatment or medications cease to be of any use and death is imminent the patient is still not to be abandoned but given whatever ordinary care and support may make him/her as comfortable as is possible at that stage. The *Catechism* says:

> Even if death is thought imminent, the ordinary care owed to a sick person cannot be legitimately interrupted. *CCC, #2279*.

It is certainly not a time to willfully shorten life, for example by withholding water or air, even if these can only be received artificially but still successfully. Yet this does happen in many hospitals once the anti-life mentality that follows on abortion creeps in. When the patient can no longer absorb any such sustenance, when it might even cause suffocation if protracted, then indeed it can be withdrawn.

The treatment of the morality of medical problems given above is by no means complete. I have merely touched briefly on some of the more prominent problems with the aim of highlighting the need for the chaplain to be well versed in the study of medical ethics.

The chaplain has one other function, in light of these problems which is to try to organize hospital staff so that they can put a stop to immoral practices or at least secure the right to conscientious objection so they will not have to cooperate.

Patient's Family

The patient in the bed is not the only one who needs the chaplain's attention; his/her relatives will also be distressed at his suffering and in need of encouragement and consolation. The bed-side scene can become complicated in an age of family break down when, for example, the patient's present "partner" and his former wife call to see him at the same time and the chaplain gets "caught in the cross fire". In addition, there can be all kinds of inheritance problems complicating things further when the children of both unions have an eye to Dad's money. I don't have simple answers to such situations because they are multiple and can be complex. Tact and honesty are needed so that one is not used by being pulled into one camp against the other, and by remembering that very likely it is the lawyers who will end up handling these problems and carrying off a good portion of Dad's inheritance for themselves!

There are also problems when the patient or his relatives are accusing the hospital of neglect or maltreatment and want the chaplain to take their side. Discernment is needed here to distinguish between the chronic grumbler, on the one hand, but also, on the other hand, the case where the hospital is in fact trying to starve the patient to death or otherwise hasten his demise. When the latter is evident to the chaplain he has a duty to act in defense of the patient-victim.

Post Mortem

After the moment of death it is an old custom to leave the body undisturbed for some time, allowing for the possibility that the soul might now be facing judgement. So it is good to light candles, have holy water available and to say the rosary so as to counter any possible last assaults of the Evil One. The very sound of the prayers of the rosary at that time can provide great consolation.

The funeral Mass should be carried out strictly according to the prescribed rituals of the Missal. The readings should be, of course, from scripture and nowhere else. The homily should *not* be a eulogy even if some truly edifying practices of the dead person can be briefly alluded to so as to provide good example for those listening. But this cannot be over-done because if Dad was non-practicing or living in sin or indeed a prime blackguard as known to the people, what then can the priest say? And if he says nothing about Dad then this omission will be noticed. The homily should focus on the Christian meaning of death and the centrality of Christ as the One who is our answer to death with His resurrection.

Nor do I recommend eulogies or speeches by relatives in church. It is God who judges and he will have done so already immediately after the death of a person. There is also the danger with eulogies, if there is a family row simmering in the background, that the eulogist will say something defamatory about those on the other side of the quarrel, in which case the priest who allowed the eulogy to begin with could face legal action. This kind of thing more than anything reveals how liturgy, now, no longer has God for its object but man; how worship is turned into circus, with the result that faithful Catholics are turned off for good.

Even when nothing offensive is said, the eulogy or often times the eulogies will go on too long in a way that is totally disproportionate to the rest of the liturgy. I knew of one case where the speaker, an anti-Catholic writer, continued speaking for longer than the length of the Mass itself, and another where as many as *fourteen* people came up to tell us about the great man in the box, with a bishop present who did nothing to stop it then or try to rule out such abuses later! At the end of the eulogy there is the big applause even though most people are bored to tears with all this silly sentiment. The graveside, after the Mass, at the end of the burial prayers, was traditionally the place for speech making and that was a good practice; "the graveside oration" as it was called.

One might argue that the bereaved family would like that a member would go up to the ambo at the beginning of Mass to welcome people who have come to sympathize with them. But why could not the priest do that briefly on behalf of the family? Also, it is argued that the family would like to thank those people who helped the dead man/woman in his last illness. But this could be very easily fitted into one of the prayers of the faithful which would be read by a relative.

I made some of these points already in previous chapters but I feel the need to repeat them here because these abuses go on unchecked due to of the failure of those in charge of the liturgy to face up to the responsibility they have to safeguard the sacred. I find myself avoiding funeral Masses as much as possible now, unless someone very close to me is dead, because of the clown-acting I'm likely to have to endure if I attend. But I have to be fair to some, at least, of my fellow priests who do try to safeguard the sacredness of the liturgy but are complained to higher authority when they refuse some outlandish requests from family members who, most likely, hardly ever attend church apart from such events. It can happen then, at times, that the bishop, if he is a popularity seeker, will back such people against his own priest. And then he wonders why there are so few new vocations!

Another solution to this problem is to have a religious ceremony, such as Mass, first, and then a separate civic ceremony, perhaps an hour later in a hall or community centre, where various people can come up and give testimonies about their experiences with the dead person and where his favorite songs can be sung. This would be all the more appropriate when the dead person was a notable political, cultural or sporting figure. The religious ceremony could then be truly and properly sacred and carried out in strict accord with liturgical rules.

Finally, the cemetery should a place that is well kept, not just out of respect for the dead, or to make of it a place of quiet for prayer for relatives but also because it is what in Celtic spirituality is called the "fód an aiseirí" the sod, the dust, from which the bodies of those lying there will rise again when the soul of each returns to take the body up into union with itself at the resurrection of the dead at the last day. The faithful need to be made aware of this in preaching.

Cremation is permitted when it does not express any anti-Christian sentiment and when factors of finance (long distance from home) or lack of burial ground (big cities) or contagion in an epidemic come into play. But the ashes should be buried in whole in consecrated ground to express belief in the resurrection of the body. (I must say that personally the "hot" idea of cremation gives me the shivers!).

Conclusions:

1. The chaplain, like a good Samaritan, applies the holy oils of the sacrament of the sick to heal both spiritual wounds and also bodily ailments (if God so wills) when this sacrament is administered.
2. Caring for the sick does not mean doing whatever makes the patient comfortable or happy in any secularist sense of the word but in giving them the hope and consolation which is in keeping with true faith and the moral law, because true charity cannot bypass these. That said, all good natural care is to be provided even when there is no hope of recovery.

3. In medical practice one must never intentionally and directly do anything that is intrinsically wrong even for a seemingly good purpose. Life is to be supported by ordinary means, even if these are artificial, until natural death is imminent and unpreventable.
4. The priest/chaplain, a carer of others, must make sure that he does not become exhausted in his work. Who will care for the carer? He has needs also. He needs time off especially if he is often on call for night duty. He needs to recharge with prayer before the Blessed Sacrament and have time for good clean fun with others who care sincerely about him.

The foregoing sacraments are directed towards the sanctification of the individual. But the individual belongs to the communities of Church and society. There are two more sacraments which are directed towards the good of these which we will look at next.

Chapter XXVIII

The Sacrament of Holy Orders

Origin, Nature, Decline in Vocations

You are a priest forever like Melchisedek of old. Psalm 109.

Do this in memory of me. Luke 22:19.

The ministerial priesthood differs in essence from the common priesthood of the faithful because it confers a sacred power for the service of the faithful. The ordained ministers exercise their service for the People of God by teaching (*munus docendi*), divine worship (*munus liturgicum*) and pastoral governance (*munus regendi*). *Catechism of the Catholic Church, #1592*

The sacraments we have dealt with up to this concern the beginning, growth and maturity of grace in the faithful and also with the failure which is sin and the decline and demise brought by sickness and old age. But, because man is a social being, the recipients of these sacraments belong to the community of the Church and that of civil society. They are born into civil society through the basic community of the family, and, if the family is already Christian, the parents will bring them into the community of the Church, in the usual run of things, when they bring them along for baptism. Thus, we see that the family is fundamental for both Church and civil society. The remaining two sacraments which we need to look at, holy orders and marriage, are concerned with the wellbeing of the two communities of Church and family. In the traditional list of the seven sacraments holy orders comes before marriage which is last on the list, so we will look at them in that order.

The sacrament of holy orders is administered by the bishop, though priests join with him in the laying on of hands in an ordination liturgy. The newly ordained priest lives out his ordination when he guides and teaches his people and sanctifies them by the administration of the other sacraments. He also makes his people aware of their lay priesthood, their sharing in that of Christ by reason of their baptism and confirmation, recognizing and eliciting their various charisms and showing them how they can be of service to the building up of the body of Christ in daily life by using these charisms. He has also a responsibility to promote vocations to the priesthood and the religious life so that there will be more shepherds to succeed him in the future.

He grows in grace himself by doing these things, helped by the special grace of his office. I have spoken of the mutual relationship of the two priesthoods, that of the ordained and that of the laity, already in the *King* section of this work so I will concentrate mostly on the priesthood of the ordained in what follows, though the two cannot be separated.

In this chapter I will deal with the sacrament itself, its origin and nature, its matter and form and who can receive it and about the fostering of vocations. As with the other sacraments what is said in the *Catechism of the Catholic Church* and in the *Code of Canon Law* is presumed. This is not meant to be another commentary on either of these but, again, a highlighting of some pastoral aspects which are sometimes overlooked in the commentaries but which experience tells me are important. In the next chapter we will look at the spirituality of the diocesan priest.

Origin and Nature of the Priesthood

The Catholic priesthood has to be seen in the context of the Old Testament priesthood which, in turn, is to be seen in the context of Israel as a holy nation, a consecrated people specially chosen by God in preparation for the coming of the promised Messiah. At first the head of each family performed priestly functions for his own family, but after the golden calf incident a particular tribe, that of Levi, was set apart to perform such functions for the whole people. From there on we have the idea of the priest as a man apart though taken from among the people and being always close to them in his care of them. The essential priestly function is that of offering sacrifice. Thus, bread and wine were offered and animals were killed and offered, the idea being that the object sacrificed was put out of earthly use – destroyed – so as to be given over or given up completely to God. This giving-up symbolized, gave external expression, to the giving up of the priest himself and his people to God to be united with Him and to appease Him for having offended Him with their sins and to seek His help in the future. The priest also sometimes had the function of teaching or guiding, though in the Old Testament these three roles were usually divided out amongst different persons. Sometime the king also offered sacrifice or the prophet ruled as well as taught (e.g., Moses).

The Old Testament priesthood prefigured that of Christ and the New Testament priesthood which latter fulfilled the former, but the line of development is not entirely straight because Christ was not of the tribe of Levi but of Judah, and what He offered was His own body on the cross, not any animals. Also, He combined the three offices of priest, prophet and king in Himself. He did not refer to Himself as a priest explicitly when on earth but His actions such as those of forgiving sins, making regulations for

Chapter 28: The Sacrament of Holy Orders

the Sabbath and His words of consecration at the Last Supper were priestly. Later, the *Letter to the Hebrews* becomes explicit in referring to Him as a priest, a priest of the order of Melchizedek to emphasize the eternity of His priesthood because it would endure for ever and be shared in in various ways by His ordained minsters and by the new Christian laity until He would come again at the end of time.

Because Christ's sacrifice of Himself on Calvary is made present to us in the Mass, and because He gave us the Mass for this purpose at the Last Supper, and because of the intrinsic connection between sacrifice and priesthood, it is to be understood that the moment of institution of the sacrament of holy orders was at the Last Supper with the words *Do this in memory of me*.

Matter and Form

Today the sacrament of holy orders in its three grades of fullness, which are those of bishop, priest and deacon, is conferred by the laying on of hands and by the prayer of consecration which is different for each grade of the sacrament, indicating their different, respective meanings, even though the sacrament itself is one. In every sacrament the words of the form are added to the matter to further specify the meaning of each particular sacrament. (Otherwise, it would be impossible to distinguish the difference of meaning there is, for example, between the anointing that is performed at confirmation and that which is performed at the sacrament of the sick). Prior to Pope Pius XII and going back to St Thomas Aquinas it was held that the handing over of the instruments – the paten and chalice - was the matter of this sacrament but that pope decided it was the laying on of hands.

The ordaining bishop must be in a direct line of apostolic succession, and both he and the man being ordained must have the right intention. Because of that the Church does not recognize the validity of Anglican orders – the line of apostolic succession was broken at the reformation because the ordaining bishops, who were Catholic up to that time, did not use a correct form or have the intention of doing what the Church does when ordaining. Pope Leo XIII made this clear with his encyclical *Apostolicae Curae* of 1896. It is not the case that Anglican orders became invalid at that time of the encyclical, *viz* 1896: the line had been broken three hundred years previously. I mention this with no intention of denigrating the pastoral care which Anglican ministers give to their flock but because many Catholics today, due to a wrong understanding of ecumenism, assume that anyone in any religion wearing vestments has the same powers of consecration as any other. Also, with greater convergence between Anglicans and Catholics in some areas of theology some people think that this can somehow validate Anglican orders as a result. That this can not be so is shown by the

Church's continual practice of having Anglican ministers, who convert and ask to become Catholic priests, undergo a Catholic ordination.

The Recipient of Orders

Only a baptized man can be the recipient of this sacrament for validity and he should also be of right intention as one responding generously to a divine call, be of sound faith and be suitably formed in knowledge and virtue. It is for his seminary formators to judge if he shows signs of a true vocation and has these qualities. *No one takes this honour on himself. Heb. 5:4.*

In light of this, those calling today for the ordination of women are not to be heeded. We touched on this already in the *King* section of this study. Scripture, two thousand years of tradition and recent popes make it clear that only men can be ordained. Pope Paul VI has given us a lengthy summary of the reasons why women cannot be ordained in his letter *Intersignores* of 1976. Following him Pope John Paul II in another letter *Ordinatio Sacerdotalis* of 1994 says "that the Church has no authority whatsoever to confer priestly ordination on women and that this judgement is to be definitively held by all the Church's faithful".

I see this prohibition as applying to the ordination of women as deacons also because the deaconate is one grade of the one sacrament of holy orders. Furthermore, the scripture references to deaconesses do not speak of a sacramental rite for their commissioning and, in any case, something which did not exist at all during two thousand years of tradition cannot pop up and come into tradition all of a sudden on the mere demand of some feminists.

Having a male priesthood is not a thing of mere "cultural conditioning" coming from a "patriarchal society" of the past such that it can be declared obsolete in present-day, democratic, egalitarian society wherein feminism is a dominant ideology. In ancient patriarchal societies of the Middle East there were women priests in some of the surrounding pagan religions, but the Judeo-Christian tradition never adopted this. There were also queens ruling in some civil societies. There is also the fact of the spousal nature of the Church, as we saw in our *King* section, with Christ as the bridegroom and His people as the bride which requires that Christ be represented by a man in that function which is most central to the life of the Church, namely the celebration of Mass. Otherwise the Church would have a same-sex spousal structure (but many today see no problem with such a monstrosity). The Church in knowing her own nature is not aware of having authority from Christ to ordain women. Very simply, the Church insists on a male hierarchy in order to remain faithful to Christ and His design for the Church. It is not then a matter of discrimination at all.

In light of the above why then do some people, mostly feminists, keep calling for the ordination of women? Given that the matter has been definitively closed by scripture, tradition and two recent popes what we have here is a shift to a new question: that of why some people cannot accept what has been settled with teaching which is equivalent to being infallible even if that word is not actually used in the two letters mentioned above.[1] Some are naïve adherents of the French revolution slogans of liberty and equality as if these ideas should be guiding principles for the Church also. By shouting words like "equality" and "discrimination" they think that anything they desire can be justified because to say otherwise would be deemed to be *unjust* or discriminatory. Others think, again naively, that to ordain women will draw people back to Church as a simple "fix" for the fall-off we are seeing at present. They have not learned anything from those other Christian religions which have already gone down this road. Others are in the grip of modernism without even knowing what that is - the idea that the Church herself in her institutions and her dogmas and moral teaching are like plasticene which can be molded or remolded at will so as to be in line with the *Zeit Geist*, the fad or fashion of the day. Others, of more sinister intent, know that any such a reshaping of Church structure - not willed by her Founder - will destroy her, because it will change her *essential* structure. But what is most reprehensible is to see some priests, and even some bishops, jumping onto this bandwagon simply to be popular with the feminists whom they are afraid to confront with honest, Catholic truth.

There is then an effort to promote women to high, non-ordained positions in the Church to make the hoped-for jump to ordination easier or to compensate them for the perceived "injustice" of being delayed this jump while the supposedly "reactionary, conservative" male hierarchy is dragging its feet on this. Women can indeed be given, and are delegated some positions in the Church's administration and teaching, and in exercising such roles they are of great help to the ordained. But in doing so they cannot arrogate those roles to themselves in such a way that the ordained priest is no longer allowed to exercises them in his parish or that they can exercise these roles independently of his authority. Were that to happen it would mean that the kingly and prophetic roles of the ordained man were severed from his priestly role, which cannot be allowed because all three roles (*munera*) are one in Christ and the ordained priest is configured to Christ by the one sacrament of holy orders. Put simply, the priest has the power to guide and teach, as well as to sanctify, as flowing from Christ to him through the bishop by ordination. In practice this means that one cannot allow a situation where a woman (or even a lay man) has full authority in the administration of a parish or has the care of souls in such a way that the priest is merely slotted in as a sacramental functionary to the say the words of consecration at *her* discretion or that she is allowed to preach or teach independently of him or perform those sacramental actions which are strictly priestly.

Faithful Catholic women do indeed give wonderful advice in pastoral councils and they do wonderful work in the area of catechesis, especially in schools, and they help in so many other ways in the life of the parish; but the over emphasis that is being put on their "empowerment" in the running of the Church tends to subvert the proper, divinely-ordered structure of authority of the Church. It also takes away from women's most valuable contribution of all which is that of marrying (should they chose to do so) and having and forming their own children in their own homes in sound faith and good morals, or the contribution they can make as spiritual mothers in religious life, as so many did in the past. It is those women who, above all, promote the Church's future well-being. But today's obsession with empowerment obscures this. Hence to depict the Church's refusal to ordain women as an attempt by men to hold on to their clerical privileges is simply to miss the point.

It is noticeable also that truly great Catholic women such as St Catherine of Sienna, St Theresa of Avila, Mother Teresa and St Gianna Molla, to name but a few, never had any of these ambitions to govern the Church or become priests, even though some of them were advisers to popes. For *them* authority was for service, not power, and the Christ they wanted to serve was the One who washed His disciples' feet. Meanwhile, as this needless debate goes on, convents are emptying, which shows scant regard for the wonderful service which these dedicated women have given over the centuries and still do in some remaining places.

The Decline in Vocations

Ordaining new priests raises the hope of more vocations in the future. Looked at globally, world population has been rising since the second world war and vocations have been rising globally since 1976. But that increase has been mostly in Asia and Africa, whereas in the West population is now falling below replacement rate and so also are vocations. Countries that formerly were hothouses of vocations, sending priests out to the missions, now cannot even supply the home parishes.

One can take it for granted that as the Lord has promised to stay with His Church to the end of time that He will also provide for her with new shepherds, men who will share in His own priesthood in order to care for the flock and to perpetuate His sacrifice of Himself to the Father in the Mass. That means that at any given moment the Lord is calling men, young and not so young, to come follow Him in sufficient numbers. But, nonetheless, this does not mean that all of those being called will respond and follow. Due to free will and the many things that can pull people this way and that, men can turn away like the rich young man in the gospel. That has always been the case.

Fatalism

Prior to Vatican II vocations were at their highest in the West and it was presumed that the council would give a boost to the faith and therefore that we would see an even greater increase in vocations. So strong was that expectations that many seminaries began building on extensions so as to be ready to accommodate the predicted increase. But, alas, the very opposite happened, so that most of those seminaries are closed now and the remaining seminarians could be accommodated in very small living quarters. On the pastoral scene, parishes and even diocese are being amalgamated, rectories are being sold off, churches are being closed up, and even demolished in places. There is now instead the same blind certainty of a reverse kind: that vocations are going to keep on falling, and even the belief by some that this is good!! Plans are being made to cope with this decline which I think are fatalistic and self-destructive because they do not get down to analysing the root cause of the decline or try to propose a remedy, which hesitancy indicates not an attitude of faith but of despair.

It is argued that the fall in vocations is only imaginary because it is seen as relative to a situation of too many vocations in the past. But what is too many and what is too few? That depends on many factors: area of territory to be covered, density of population, modes of communication and travel *etc*. A lone priest today in the countryside can serve a larger territory than a priest of a hundred years ago because he has a car and a cell phone. A priest in a small area of inner city, traversable by foot, may, indeed, be over worked if there is a high practice rate there but might have little to do there if practice is low. It can also be assumed that in the days of high numbers of vocations some candidates joined up for less than the right reason and that this did more harm than good. It is no loss if their likes are not coming forward now. Granted all of that, it is still alarming when churches are being sold off and huge areas are now being served by lone priests in their seventies. One cannot say that that is good. Instead, one must ask why this is happening.

Because the lone priest has now to enlist lay people in ever greater numbers to do many things in the parish, done by priests in the past, it is presumed that that is the way to go: less priests, more lay people and all will be well. Hence we get the endlessly repeated mantra of "the involvement of the laity". The laity will come in from the long grass, take over, and all will be well. It reminds me of that passage in the Old Testament where the people are living sinful lives but endlessly chanting *the temple of the Lord, the temple of the Lord, this is the temple of the Lord. Jeremiah 7:4*. Because they had the Temple and went up there now and then to offer sacrifices, they presumed they could continue to sin at their hearts content and that all would be fine. But the prophet tells them bluntly that they are fooling only themselves with this kind of talk and not the Lord.

And who are these laity that are going to jump in and take over and solve everything? In the *King* section of this work I already gave descriptions of the kind of laity that often push themselves forward, not just to help but to take over for ulterior purposes of their own. In my experience some were dubious people who could hardly say the *Hail Mary* and had less than worthy motives for coming forward. Others, who had good intentions indeed, had little or no knowledge of theology and had erroneous ideas of what their roles should be. Some had no idea of the real presence or of the Mass as being anything more than a jamboree with some relation to religion. There are others then who do have the faith and at least a basic knowledge of it from the study of sound catechisms in their school days. They would like very much to help but they will already have had the label of "right wing conservatives" pinned on them by the others, and the remaining few priests won't invite them to help lest they too have that label pinned on themselves. [O dear, what a tragedy that would be for the popular Fr. X if he were to be called a "conservative"!!!][2] So, the parish can fall into the hands of liberals, feminists, humanists and every other kind of "woke" parishioner and with it the faith of the next generation (that is if there will be a next generation at all).

Confusion of Structures and Roles
=================================

Realistically, I ask my readers, would any young man of true faith and even minimum intelligence, even if he did think he had a vocation, come forward to be ordained when he sees priests before him being pushed around in parishes which are "run" or "hijacked" by such people, being slotted in only at their command to say the words of consecration now and then?

Even if the Church were to be mostly run by good, well-informed lay people in the future that is still simply not the design of the Lord for His Church. Indeed, in situations of persecution, when the existing priests are imprisoned, then lay people have had to take over as best they can and they have been truly wonderful in such situations as history shows. But those are exceptional situations because priests simply cannot function then. If that were to become the *norm* it would mean that the Catholic Church had become Methodist or Congregationalist or Presbyterian or something like that. It would simply cease to exist as Catholic.

When lay people do help in the running of a parish, something needed and welcome, their administrative functions have to be delegated to them by the parish priest of that parish or, if there is none in that parish, by the parish priest of a nearby parish

Chapter 28: The Sacrament of Holy Orders

designated by the bishop to look after both parishes. I will quote from St John Paul again:

> A non-ordained male religious, a female religious, a lay person may exercise administrative functions, as well as that of promoting spiritual formation. The may not, however, exercise functions which belong fully to the care of souls since such requires priestly character. They may, nevertheless, *supply for the ordained minister in those liturgical functions which are consonant with their canonical condition"* and enumerated in canon 230 #3: "exercise the ministry of the word, preside over liturgical prayers, confer Baptism, and distribute Holy Communion in accordance with the prescriptions of law". Even Deacons, who cannot be equated with other members of the faithful, cannot exercise the full *cura animarum. The Priest Pastor and Leader,* #24.

He goes on to explain that even the "extreme" shortage of priests does not lead to this divinely constituted structure of the church being changed:

> However, these [roles of lay helpers] cannot in any way substitute the task of the pastor proper to the parish priest. The extreme cases of shortage of priests, that advise a more intense and extended collaboration of the faithful not honoured with priestly ministry, in the pastoral care of a parish, do not constitute an exception to this essential criterion for the care of souls, as is indisputably established by canonical norm (cf. *Code of Canon Law,* can. 517, 2). In this controversial sector, the interdicasterial Exhortation *Ecclesiae de Mysterio,* (*Instruction*) that I approved in a specific way, is a sure guide to follow". *ibid.,* #5.

The reader can refer back again to the *King* section for more quotations on this. The point I am trying to make here is that all this talk about the magical fix-all solution of the "involvement of the laity" is not only wishful thinking, it is theologically false and amounts to a self-fulfilling prophecy of despair. It is the drowning men of the clergy, who know they have failed to keep the Church afloat, clutching onto this straw of the involvement of the laity, envisioned now as something that will save everything, but, as explained above, if the laity did come along (*per impossibile*) and do this it would be a self-defeating remedy because then the priest would become obsolete contrary to the design of Christ for His Church.

The laity have their rightful role due to their own rightful participation in the priesthood of Christ flowing from their baptism and confirmation. This is a truth always held by the Church but neglected somewhat in theology (but always there "on the ground") until Luther brought it to the fore with his one priesthood of all the faithful. But he did so at the expense of the priesthood of the ordained, which he denied. Then with the swing of the pendulum, by a reaction to Luther, Catholics put great stress on the priesthood of the ordained, putting him up on the proverbial pedestal at times. Vatican II, then, sought to get the balance right again with *its correct affirmation of both priesthoods* with their one source in Christ, but affirming also the essential difference between them and therefore their different roles in the life of the Church. But pendulums don't stop swinging, and now, by an over-reaction going the other way again: Catholics are in danger of going back to the position of Luther with this over-emphasis on the involvement of the laity and the consequent damage to vocations, a cure that is turning out to be worse than the disease. The Church must have both priesthoods – good laity giving us more priests and good priests giving us ever better laity - so it is a sign of a healthy Church when both are blossoming and in good co-operation with each other. Should that lead to a surplus of priests again in some places – priests of right intention this time - then recall that the harvest is great because the mission fields are many. There will never be too many and a surplus in one place can redistributed to other places still in need.

Enough on that point because I am repeating what I said already in the *King* section. There are still other things hampering the flowering of vocations which I will enumerate briefly.

Other Causes of the Decline

A vocation is from God but the family is the seed bed of vocations, the first seminary as it were. This being granted, the breakdown of the family must inevitably lead to a decrease in vocations. That breakdown begins with the practice of artificial contraception. This reduces the number of boys that will be born in a given district so that the pool of possible vocations is smaller to begin with. It also turns Christian love, the love of self-giving and self-sacrifice, into lust, a love of pleasure for pleasure's sake, with no reference to life. But the priest is expected to be a model of the former kind of love. There is the added factor of both parents being outside the home most of the time due to their work and other commitments, which means that they have less time for handing on the faith to the young who are more influenced by their childminders or their teachers, many of whom have no interest in the faith, or by what they see on their ipads and smart phones.

If in school the children are subjected to inadequate catechetics programs and are taught by teachers who themselves have only a poor grasp of the faith, and that even in schools under Catholic management, their faith will get little doctrinal nourishment.

If a young lad has only a vague idea of what the Mass or the Blessed Sacrament is, it makes it less likely that he will commit himself to a life of service of the Eucharist.

The easy availability of pornography on the internet is another obstacle to vocations because such viewing destroys all taste for the spiritual. Add to that the many forms of entertainment that teenagers are presented with, which we touched on in our chapter on confirmation, and we see how a divine call is easily blocked out. There is then the contradiction of Church leaders claiming to stamp out the scandal of clerical child abuse while at the same time promoting sodomy, ignoring the connection between the two as when the abuser is "gay" and targets boys (which does *not* mean that *all* homosexuals do this). When young men of any intelligence see bishops allowing "gay" Masses and "gay" material in Catholic RSE programs (supposedly under the guise of inclusiveness, tolerance or respect *etc.*,) they know that "something is rotten in the state of Denmark" - to take a line from Shakespeare. It is like a football team passing the ball to the opposition and kicking in own-goals. No new player with any sense of right and wrong wants to join such a team.

If, despite all this, some young men of sound faith and good morals from good families do come forward to study for the priesthood they could find themselves rejected in some seminaries precisely because they are of these good dispositions. I can remember one very good parish priest of certainly sound faith telling me how he had sent three young men from good homes forward to his diocese as possible candidates but that they were rejected for reasons that he never understood. So, he stopped encouraging vocations in his parish. Again, when seminary rectors invite noted pro-abortion or pro-sodomy politicians to major functions in seminaries, that sends out a message that is totally destructive of would-be vocations.

From the above one can see that the shortage of vocations is certainly not due to any failure on the part of the Holy Spirit – God is always providing - but to the influence of the secularist environment of much of the Western world and more so to obstacles from within the Church itself. There is a vicious circle going on here: secularism from outside the Church is having its impact within, and wrong solutions from within are leading to more secularism in the surrounding world.

In sum, the decline in vocations is but a symptom of the deeper decline in faith in the Western world, and until that is tackled then quick fixes like the involvement of more laity to the point of take-over, or the ordination of women or married men or the importing of priests from third world countries will not solve the problem. The Western missionaries of centuries past who went out to third world countries to evangelize were going to peoples who were *open* to the new message of the gospel. These latter were receptive, nature being open to grace in those countries, but, in the reverse direction, the priests who now come from those countries to the West are like salt being put on meat that is already in decay. Nature has had a cover of secularism and materialism put over it so that the light of faith and the grace of Christ is kept out.

Solutions

<u>Prayer, Preaching, Family</u>

We can begin with the presumption that the Lord is always with His Church and is providing for her needs. So, we can also presume that He is calling young men and women to the priesthood and religious life today but that in doing so He respects the freedom of those being called. Thus, so that the response will be positive, the first thing is for the Christian community to pray for vocations as the Lord Himself prescribed. *(cf. Mt. 9:38)*. It is noticeable that in dioceses and parishes where there is adoration of the Blessed Sacrament for this cause that vocations do emerge. But prayer must also be accompanied by the example of good Christian living by both people and priests in the parish. The next is to strengthen the traditional Christian family founded on a valid marriage in every way – by organizing people to oppose anti-life, anti-family legislation as soon as it is proposed and by promoting good legislation and good social conditions for the family. The family, as said already, is the first and the most formative seminary. The next is sound preaching on the basics of faith and morals in the Church - that too is one other way of promoting the family - followed up then by sound teaching in schools and in seminaries. Faith comes from hearing but hearing what? Something more challenging than "Jesus loves you so you can continue in your sin, because sin is out of date anyhow" is needed.

I knew of one bishop who fired the entire staff of his seminary and replaced them with others as the only way of getting it back to orthodoxy. He knew that there comes a point in any institution that is corrupting when the rot can only be stopped by a complete restart. To quote another old saying "desperate diseases are by desperate remedies cured". It is also noticeable that where there is a bishop who takes a stand on social-moral issues, especially issues that relate to life and the family, and is prepared for the back-lash that will come inevitably, that vocations flourish in his diocese. Very simply, young men who have true vocations are always idealistic, are ready for a challenge, and will flock to a leader who will give them a lead. By comparison, others who see the priesthood as an easy ride, will go to other diocese where there is a weak bishop. However, not all blame can be thrown onto all bishops in this regard; it happens at times that a good bishop who *does* want to take a stand on some issue of faith and morals, is not supported by his own clergy, some of whom will even go so far as to undermine him by lending themselves to be used by the secularist media against him.

Chapter 28: The Sacrament of Holy Orders

The priest and individual lay people, who are observant of signs of the Holy Spirit at work, can foster vocations by acting as vehicles of external grace when they suggest to a young man or girl of good morals that perhaps the Lord is calling him/her to follow Him in the priesthood or religious life.

There is no need to be fatalistic. The Holy Spirit is still at work in the Church, and man is free to cooperate with Him. Trends in vocation, going up or going down, are not fixed like railway tracks. They are going up in other places like Africa and Asia and there are still some mustard seeds in the West which are planted in good ground, in faithful families, and they will bear fruit in time. Indeed, I heard a Dutch bishop describe his own country as the most secularist in the world but I also heard him say that there are now pockets of young people who are finding that such secularism does not satisfy and are looking for a new spirituality. Or, as a Dutch student once put it to me, having gone down into the dark depths of godlessness some are beginning to realize that the only hope is to start climbing back up to the light of faith again.

Conclusions:

1. The newly ordained is configured to Christ the Head by the sacrament of holy orders and receives a share in His three offices of king, prophet and priest for the service of the Church. It is the bishop who confers this sacrament on men by the laying on of hands and the prayer of ordination.
2. If we love Christ we will love His Church as He structured it by His divine authority. We will not try to alter it in ways that suit the spirit of the times but will seek the legitimate development of what He has given us in a hermeneutic of continuity with scripture and tradition.
3. Because a vocation is a charism of the Holy Spirit, who "blows where He wills", we should not be making fatalistic predictions about vocations or resorting to quick-fix solutions that are theologically unsound. If we pray for vocations, and are doing what we should be doing in our respective vocations, as priests or lay people – witnessing to the faith in word and deed, in season and out of season – we can trust the Holy Spirit to do the rest.
4. With vocations it is not a matter of priests *versus* lay people - having more of one by having less of the other – it is a matter of both/and: good lay people giving us more good priests and *vice versa*.

Whether the number of priests be high or low at a given time one would hope that each priest would be a man of holiness of life. This leads us to the matter of priestly spirituality.

Chapter XXIX

The Spirituality of the Secular Priest

Configuration to Christ, a distinctive Spirituality, Stages in spiritual Growth, The Evangelical Counsels, An underlying Metaphysics

Be holy in all you do since it is the Holy One who has called you and scripture says: Be holy for I am holy. 1 Pet.1:15 -16.

Holiness does much for priests in carrying on a fruitful ministry. *Presbyterorum Ordinis*, #12

The effect of the sacrament of holy orders is to impress a character on the soul of the newly ordained man, a spiritual mark or stamp which says that he now belongs to Christ the Head, publicly, as shepherd, teacher and sanctifier of His people, and it enables him to act in His name. (Whether that character is impressed on the whole soul or only on one of its powers, such as the intellect, is something I will not go into here)[1]. In any case it conforms or configures the recipient to Christ in a way that is different from the way a newly baptized person is conformed to Him. Then follows the grace of the sacrament and the grace of office if the priest has not put the obstacle of mortal sin in the way.

This change, an ontological and permanent change, in the soul of the new priest happens in an instant by the working of the Holy Spirit and it marks the culmination of his years of preparation. But in another sense, it is just a beginning because he now has the challenge of conforming or configuring his mind and heart, his desires and deeds, to those of Christ whom he will be following as His representative for the rest of his life so that people who observe him in his ministry will be able to see in him a duplicate of Christ and be drawn to him and thereby to Christ, and through Christ to the Father, again by the help of the grace of the Holy Spirit. (Indeed, this conforming should have been well prepared for already in his seminary training). This second kind of conformity might be called an "existential conformity" or more simply "growth in holiness". It is what priestly spirituality is all about, and it is fitting that we say something about it here, attempting to identify what is distinctive in the spirituality of the secular priest and examine the stages and requirements of its growth.

Existential Configuration to Christ

Too often in seminaries in the past spirituality was tacked on at the end of the moral theology course, if there was any time left for it at all. Or it was dealt with in talks outside of the theology class-time proper. It was like icing that might or might not be put on the cake of Christian living. I would argue instead that it should have a much more central place. If the priest is not a holy man, his administration of the sacraments will indeed be still valid if he has the right intention and carries out the rituals properly, because God can use a bad instrument to sanctify His people (or even dispense with all instruments if He so chooses). But it makes more sense to say that He desires to work through good instruments, through devout priests who are seeking to be always united to Him. Vatican II has this to say about the value of holiness:

> Holiness does much for priests in carrying on a fruitful ministry. Although divine grace could use unworthy ministers to effect the work of salvation, yet for the most part God chooses, to show forth his wonders, in those who are more open to the power and direction of the Holy Spirit, and who can by reason of their close union with Christ and their holiness of life say with St. Paul: "And yet I am alive; or rather, not I; it is Christ that lives in me" (*Gal 2:20*). Vatican II, *Presbyterorum Ordinis, (PO), #12*

A splendid example of this was St John Vianney, the Curé D'Ars. He brought thousands to God by his labours in the confessional not just because he had the gift of reading souls, but also because he was truly a holy man.

We touched on this earlier in the first part of this work when speaking of the principal mysteries of faith, the Trinity, the incarnation and the redemption, because, as I explained then, spirituality, all Christian living, can be described as a living out of those mysteries in one's own life which is especially true in the case of the priest whose life is in great part given to preaching the mysteries and the administration of the sacraments which make those mysteries present for everyone.

If Christ calls on all His followers to be perfect this must surely apply to the priest in a special way if he is to lead others to holiness. How can a priest lead his people to God if he is not walking towards God himself? What Christ is by nature – the Son of God – priests, and indeed all Christians, are called to be by grace, and the priest in his distinctive way. The truly spiritual priest is not someone who is up in the clouds, so divine that he cannot relate to the human scene. That would indicate a false spirituality to begin with which gives us the supposedly pious priest who is cold and humourless and unable to empathize with people in their difficulties. If he is divine, in the sense of being by grace what Christ is by nature, he will be all the more *truly human* precisely because the working of that grace in him should purify, elevate and transform him so that his people will see Christ in him and be drawn to him and thereby to Christ for that very reason. The Holy Spirit, the One who sanctifies, will then be drawing priest and people closer together in Christ.

We live in or by the Holy Spirit when we allow ourselves to be led by Him, to be moved by His promptings in all our decisions. A spiritual life is a life lived in the Spirit just as Christ was led by the Spirit many times in the gospels. (*cf. Lk. 4:1*). The priest should always be trying to discern the workings of the Holy Spirit in the events of his times and in the lives of his people so that he can guide and console them all the better in their everyday situations and also have the longer view of the times and see what is coming. He is a watchman on the tower of life reading the "signs of the times".

Spirituality as pertaining specifically to the secular priest, I claim, has had a poor innings for many years, so much so that many priests didn't bother with it at all and even stopped reading the breviary even though to read it is obligatory. In its absence many turned to pass-times and interests and enjoyments which sometimes were less than edifying and at other times were even a source of scandal. Why did this happen? I believe that history provides some answers.

Spirituality and History

The early Christians of Roman times lived as small groups of followers of "the Way" in the cities of the empire, united around the Eucharist, suffering martyrdom at times - depending on the whim of the current emperor - and looking forward to the second coming of Christ at the eschaton.

Freedom of practice came with the edict of Milan in 313 AD; and then we see a move from the city to the desert, from red martyrdom to white martyrdom and from the group in the city to the solitary in the desert with the beginning of monasticism. These monks lived in their little beehive cells though they never lost their sense of being small communities in the one big community of the universal Church. They gave priority to the soul over the body and took on severe fasts and penances. In doing this they still did not see the body as bad, though some did in some extreme cases.

Underlying this spirituality was the dominating philosophy of Platonism which gave priority to the world of the Ideas/forms "up above" over the world of shadowy matter "down below". There were also the Fathers of the Church who were also grounded in Platonism and who had great influence in the Church of their time and long after. I am thinking in particular of St Augustine. So, the spirituality of the monks and the Fathers, (and some Fathers were also monks) one might say, was more vertical than horizontal and individualistic rather than social, though they did not lose sight of these other dimensions. But their aim was mostly individual perfection, renouncing the world so as to reach union with God.

Monasticism began in places like Egypt and Syria, and spread from there Westwards to the South of France and to Ireland. But it had another beginning also in Italy with St Benedict (480-547); and both streams mingled with each other and later flowed Northwards and Eastwards to give rise to that that great Christian civilization of the Middle Ages which was known as Christendom. This was an era which saw the flourishing of the great religious orders such as the Dominicans, Franciscans, Benedictines and Cistercians, and of the great works of architecture such as the cathedrals of Cologne, Paris and Chartres, and great works of art and scholarship. These monks farmed the land and preached to the people and played a great part in giving Europe its Catholic soul.

Each of these religious orders had its own distinctive spirituality; one thinks for example of the witness to poverty of the Franciscans, the combination of prayer and farm work of the Benedictines and Cistercians and the love of learning and preaching of the Dominicans. The Dominicans came into possession of the newly rediscovered philosophy of Aristotle, brought back from the East, which gave a more positive metaphysical value to the things we perceive with our senses because one could say that he "brought down" the Ideas of Plato and made them the forms of the substances we see in the world around us. At the hands of a man like St Thomas Aquinas this kind of metaphysics served as a basis for that great biblical truth that God declared all that He had made to be "good". The spirituality, then, of the new religious orders was more positive because supported by a more realist metaphysics even though the members of these orders still lived in communities that were mostly monastic. But the Albigensians were there also in the South of France at this time with their very negative spirituality which did not see the body as good.

Where was our local parish priest in all of this development? He was in the rural village in the middle of his people, setting a few rows of vegetables behind his little cottage and keeping a few sheep in the field nearby? As regards spirituality or theology, he does not figure much at all. What he had of these things he got from the priest before him to whom he was "apprenticed" or from the monks if there was a monastery somewhere nearby. Hence, even though he was not a monk, nonetheless, if he was to be spiritual at all he was expected to be somewhat *like* a monk, a monk out in a parish, so great was the influence of monastic spirituality. Jordan Aumann expressed it as follows:

> The fact that the monastic life was held up to the ordinary faithful as the ideal demonstrates that in these early centuries there was only one spirituality for all Christians: the authentic *vita apostolica*, and it constituted the perfection of the Christian life. For Basil and for some of the Fathers the monastic life was the logical consequence of the commitment made by the Christian at baptism. Jordan Aumann, *Christian Spirituality in the Christian Tradition, p. 38.*

We can see from Aumann here that the monastic model of spirituality was held up as the ideal for the ordinary faithful as well as for the priest; and as to what in practice that entailed David Bohr, an American secular priest, tells us:

> Being spiritual now referred to performing individual ascetical practices in order to arrive at perfection of virtue rather than living in the Holy Spirit and sharing in a koinonia with the Risen Lord and one another.... David Bohr, *The Diocesan Priest, P. 50.*

After the more positive theology and spirituality of St Thomas Aquinas (1225–1274), there came a swing back again to an Augustinianism of a narrow, negative kind with the Rhineland mystics.[2] The 1300s saw the emergence of that great spiritual classic *The Imitation of Christ* allegedly written by Thomas A Kempis, a book of great wisdom and consolation for any age, but very other-worldly in its spirituality. Yet it was the handbook of spirituality used in seminaries right up to Vatican II.

The year 1517 is usually given as the date for the start of the reformation when Luther nailed his ninety five theses to the door of a cathedral in Germany. Then, after the reformation, there was also what might be called the inflow of reformation/Protestant thinking into Catholic spirituality in the form of Jansenism, which like Protestantism, was very negative towards human nature and the body and marriage *etc.*, though these were things which the secular priest has to deal with every day in the care of his flock. That certainly did not help the development of a distinctive spirituality for *him*. His spirituality and spirituality generally continued to be mostly other-worldly, *rightly* indeed upholding the priority of the "things above" but doing this so often at the *expense* of the "things below", deemed too often to be bad even though these too came from God.

Sadly, after Vatican II, but not in a way that was faithful to Vatican II, there came an inevitable reaction in seminaries against the excessive other-worldly character of the monastic type of spirituality that had so long been the norm. The pendulum swung to the other extreme, so that some seminaries - such as the one I studied in – from being monastic-type, military barracks with very strict rules became what I would call "free-for-all holiday camps where everything goes". I raise a lot of eyebrows whenever I describe some of those "goings" but I will refrain from doing so here. Suffice it to say that that certainly is not spirituality either.

The distinctive Spirituality of the Secular Priest

Roughly a century after Luther's revolt, in refreshing contrast to the gloom of the reformers, and long before Vatican II, St Francis de Sales (1567-1622) exposed the folly of a one-size-fits-all spirituality, i.e., a monastic, other-worldly kind of spirituality, in his classic the *Introduction to the Devout Life*. There he pointed out that the spirituality of the bishop has to be different from that of the monk and that that of married people has to be different again from either of those, that otherwise only chaos will result. I will quote him:

> The practice of devotion must differ for the gentleman and the artisan, the servant and the prince, for widow, young girl or wife. Further, it must be adapted to their particular strength, circumstances and duties. Is the solitary life of a Carthusian suited to a bishop? Should those who are married practice the poverty of a Capuchin? If workmen spent as much time in church as religious, if religious were exposed to the same pastoral calls as a bishop, such devotion would be ridiculous and cause intolerable disorder. Yet this foolish mistake is often made. *Introduction to the Devout Life, Part I, Ch. 3.*

So also, we can conclude from this that the spirituality of the secular priest in the parish is also distinctive in its own way, even if the priest can learn many lessons from both the monk and the layman and can take certain things on board from both of their lives. He cannot be in choir seven times a day like the monk but he can and must read the Liturgy of the Hours at suitable times, a rich legacy he has from the monks. He does not have a family of his own but he has to care for the flock in a fatherly way. The secular priest is not a monk sent out into the parish, nor is the monk a secular priest who confines himself in a monastery, and the lay man is different again. If his way of life has him dealing with people in their marriages and their everyday work then he needs a spirituality which gives their right value to such things.

Certain things are common to all spiritualities because, at bottom, there is really only one spirituality, that of responding to God's call in whatever is one's walk in life and, with the help of His grace, turning away from sin so as to move forward to union with Him, a union which will be perfect only in the beatific vision of the next life. But within this commonality there should be room for the distinctively different spiritualities also.

Stages in spiritual Growth

There are three classical stages in this movement towards God which is the spiritual life. The first is the turning away from sin which is described in spirituality books as the "purgative stage". The stock example given here is that of the boat which cannot sail out of the harbour and head for its destination across the sea if it is tied by even one rope. That one, last rope must be cut. So also, the Christian cannot journey towards union with God if he is held by even one wrong attachment. The priest too must cut all wrong attachments. He must be a man of self-denial and self-control, bringing his lower faculties, desires and emotions into subjection under his intellect and will for that harmony which is chastity which we saw earlier in the *Prophet* section of this work. More than that, he must be a man of self-sacrifice also if he is to make the Lord's sacrifice, the sacrifice he celebrates in the Mass, real in his own life every day.

The second stage is what is called the "illuminative". Here the Christian tries, again with the help of grace, to make progress in knowledge and virtue. As to knowledge, hopefully the priest's seminary studies will have been basically sufficient; but still he will need to follow this up with a life-long commitment to good reading. He should be a man of continuing learning not just because he needs to be able to comment intelligently on the events of his time but also because good reading is fuel for prayer and preaching. The reservoir of ideas he will have from his studies in the seminary will run dry in a few years, so that he finds himself repeating himself, much to the boredom of his parishioners, unless he keeps on reading in his spare time. The scriptures, the dogmas of the Church, sound manuals on moral theology, the history of the Church, the great spiritual masters and the lives of the saints are highly to be recommended. One thinks of the published "lives" of great pastoral saints like St John Vianney, mentioned above, or St Francis de Sales, St John Bosco, St John Paul II or many more such shepherds. The priest of today cannot imitate each of these in the details of their lives because their circumstances were different, but he can imitate them in the universal lessons they teach which will always be valid and he can pass on those lessons to his people.

As to virtue in the priest *Presbyterum Ordinis* says:

> Among the virtues that priests must possess for their sacred ministry none is so important as a frame of mind and soul whereby they are always ready to know and do the will of him who sent them and not their own will. *#15*.

But he also needs those virtues which will also help him in relating to his people. *Optatum Totius* of Vatican II says:

> They are to be formed in strength of character, and, in general, they are to learn to esteem those virtues which are held in high regard by men and which recommend a minister of Christ. Such virtues are sincerity of mind, a constant concern for justice, fidelity to one's promises, refinement in manners, modesty in speech coupled with charity. *#11*.

Then, of course, he will need the three theological virtues of faith hope, and charity and the gifts of the Holy Spirit.

The final stage, when one gets closer to the goal of union with God, as far as that is possible in this life, is called the "unitive" sage. In this life it means being close to Christ in the Eucharist and in prayer be it vocal, meditative or contemplative.

In all of this, charity is the supreme law, the supreme virtue, because, as St Paul pointed out, if one were to give away all his possessions and even give up his body to be burned and still did not have charity it would be all a waste of time. (*1Cor13:1-4*). As helps towards living charity there are the three evangelical counsels of poverty, chastity and obedience.

Given these basics, if we are to get away from a one-size-fits-all spirituality of monasticism we must ask how these things are to find expression and be lived out in the lives of different Christians in their different callings. But that assumes that we are clear on what is distinctive about each of those different callings and, in our case, about the calling of the secular priest.

Traditionally, the Church teaches that religious life, a life of contemplation, virginity and asceticism, is the highest because it most closely resembles that of Christ and makes it more easy for a person to follow Him more perfectly. This is true and it means that the religious will always have an indispensable place in the life of the Church and will always be an example of holiness for all others. But it still does not follow from this that the secular priest is some kind of trimmed down monk at a lower level of the pyramid of sanctity or that a lay person is some kind of trimmed down priest lower again, and that these latter should try to re-shape their own callings to be as much like that of the religious as possible.

Chapter 29: The Spirituality of the Secular Priest

The desert fathers left the cities to go out to lonely places and they reached great heights of holiness which benefitted the whole Church. That is how *they* practiced poverty and asceticism. But what about those whose very calling is to live in the cities? They too are called to holiness according to *Lumen Gentium*. To dismiss them or to tell them to become some kind of religious in their homes or their workplaces, which somehow should then become domestic monasteries, is about as sensible as having everyone in town squeeze his or her foot into the shoe of the lord mayor. Yet this mistake was made and for far too long, the mistake to which St Francis de Sales alerts us above. As a result of this mistake the secular priest often had no distinctive spirituality of his own and the end result, in a lot of cases, is that he had no spirituality at all. If the lord mayor's shoe does not fit my foot, am I, perhaps, not better off going barefoot? Hence, we get the secular priest whose first priority is not the Lord or His flock but football or golf or money (if not perhaps even more base priorities completely antithetical to his calling but filling that void in his life which is there in everybody's life).

The religious are there to give all of us lessons in holiness but to take the lesson on board does not mean becoming holy in exactly the way a monk does unless, of course, one is called to be a monk. To take the lesson on board is to see how it should be given application in the respective callings of all the other people in the Church, callings which they have from God by reason of His providence when He puts them where they are – the mother in the home, the father on the building site, the single girl in the office or whatever – and to do so in ways which do not do violence to these other callings but instead purifies, sanctifies and elevates them to God because of the fundamental rule that grace builds on nature.

The religious give all of us an example in holiness but it is not all a one-way influence because all the different vocations in the Church are complementary to each other, because organically related to each other, because the Church is a living organism. They help each other and lessons can also be learned in reciprocal directions: the priest can learn from the monk but he can also learn from lay people in many ways, and they from him.

<u>Complementarity in Difference</u>

To see further how all this works out in practice, let us begin, as *Lumen Gentium* does, and ask of whom, numerically, is the Church made up? It is mostly made up of the laity, ordinary men and women in their families following their various professions, going about their daily lives in the city or the countryside. If *they* did not exist the priesthood would have no meaning because the purpose of the latter is to serve the laity so as to steer them towards the Lord and His kingdom; neither would the monks – or religious of any kind - exist because they serve the laity also in various ways, contemplative and active, and by being beacons of light for them of the kingdom ahead.

And what are the laity meant to be doing most of the time? Not running up into the sanctuary on a Sunday to take over the liturgy from the priest or running the parish instead of him, even though they do have a rightful involvement in these areas which is needed and welcomed. The laity, at the natural level, are mostly trying to raise their families, do their work, make ends meet and enjoy some bit of leisure. But at the supernatural level, while engaged in these very natural activities, and not in spite of them, they are trying to live the mysteries of the faith in their own homes and work places and they do so by keeping the commandments, practicing charity, allowing themselves to be led by the Holy Spirit and by preparing the world around them for the coming of the Lord. The task of the priest is to help them to do this, to enable them to unfold the lay priesthood of their baptism and confirmation by leading them in their communities, by preaching and teaching the true faith to them and by sanctifying them with the sacraments, especially the Mass. Thus, he enables them to bring their achievements and sufferings of the week to the church, i.e., the fruits of their efforts to prepare the world for the kingdom, and, through his hands, makes of them an offering joined to Christ's own sacrifice of Himself, the sacrifice of Calvary now made present again on the altar. And just as the laity will grow in holiness by what *they* do in their homes and in their work places so also *the secular priest will grow in holiness precisely by helping them in this, by exercising his functions of king, prophet and priest in respect of them, so that they can exercise their own rightful kingly, prophetic and priestly offices as laypeople.*

We could say that his holiness is a *reflexive* holiness in the sense that he, in *his very work of helping his people* to grow in their distinctive path of holiness, grows in holiness himself in *his* distinctive path of being a priest. So he grows in holiness by those very ordinary acts of getting out into his car on a wet night to go on a sick call; by chairing that school board meeting in which he may have to face criticism from angry parents; by organizing concerts to pay for church repairs; by patiently waiting in the confessional even if very few penitents come along; by looking up that scripture commentary to prepare his next sermon; above all by celebrating Mass for his people and by a hundred and one other deeds with all their attendant pains at times, which make up the cross for him, but all done with pastoral charity for the good of the flock entrusted to him so as to lead them to God.

A false spirituality of the secular priest, one modelled entirely on that of the monk, would say that the priest grows in holiness *in spite of doing these things* as if they were distractions from the contemplative life which should be his first priority as it is for the monk. That would be the case if the secular priest was, in fact, a monk on leave from his monastery to help in a parish and who was trying to combine monastic life and parish life. If the secular priest tries being a full-time contemplative in his rectory and takes on sever penances like a monk, he may indeed impress some people with his piety but he will be neglecting those many other tasks such as those mentioned above so that he will not grow in that holiness which is distinctive of *his* calling

At the other extreme, the priest might be very enthusiastic about his parish duties but might try to perform them without the support of prayer, relying only on his own efforts and get carried away in doing so like a workaholic, all for his own sense of achievement until soon he burns out. But that is not spirituality either, but merely the heresy of activism, doing the work of the Lord while forgetting the Lord of the work, love for whom should be his primary motivation. It is simply pride at root. He must make time for prayer and must practice self-denial but in ways that are suited to his distinctive calling. *He* makes sacrifices and does penance not just for his own sins but for the conversion of sinners in his parish.

The two callings, that of the secular priest and the monk, are different. But they are complementary. The priest is obliged to say the liturgy of the hours and spend time in private prayer each day. And in his prayer he will be bringing the needs of his people before God as well as his own personal needs. He should also make time to visit a monastery for a few days of retreat occasionally to benefit from the wisdom of the monks, from the fruit of their study and contemplation and the example of their asceticism and see how *he* then might be ascetical, though differently, in his own life. The monastery is a light on the hill calling the priest and his people forward towards the kingdom of God even if his own calling is to serve the people down in the valley which is the parish. And when the monks are in choir singing the psalms at early hours they are supplying the entire Church with its much needed "fuel supply" of prayer.

Again, the vocation of the priest is also complemented by that of the lay people he serves. Priestly vocations come from the families of lay people even though a vocation is firsts of all a call, a charism from above, from God. The laity support the priest materially and also emotionally with kindly gestures of encouragement. From them he can learn how husbands care for their wives, how fathers provide for their families and the sacrifices that both parents make for each other and for their children, spending nights up with them when they are sick and even sacrificing their own food to give it to them when times are tough. He sees their love for each other which is truly Christian because it is a giving of self, and there are lessons for him in this. Yet his love for them, though it is also a giving of self, has to be different, because non-physical, because of his vow of celibacy.

They too have to grow in holiness by taking the first step of purgation, which demands that they try to see their own faults and overcome them, that they forgive and give way to each other when they hurt each other but in ways that are different from that of the monk or the priest; and then they take the second step of the illuminative stage, though the virtues they mostly need will be different to those of the priest and different again to those of the monk. The secular priest will need those virtues primarily which will serve him in his relations with people as we saw above.

Finally, they too must go on to the unitive stage of growth which requires time spent in prayer. A mother of five young children cannot spend an hour in meditation in the early morning as a cloistered nun might do if the children have to be got up and fed and put out to school. To do so would be a gross neglect of duty on her part. But perhaps when they are gone out to school, she can make some time for prayer, and at night she can have them kneel down with her and her husband to say the rosary. She grows in holiness precisely by means of her efforts at getting those children ready for school in the morning and perhaps by her suffering of having missed her night's sleep if one of them was sick, by doing her shopping, cooking meals, cleaning the house and doing all those other duties which the secular world might see only as chores but which she does out of love for the children God has given her.

The Evangelical Counsels

Poverty, Chastity, Obedience

So also, the evangelical councils of poverty, chastity and obedience will be practiced analogously differently in the three vocations. As to poverty, the family might have property and a bank account but the account might be over drawn so that poverty is imposed on them rather than being something chosen. Or they might run a lucrative business, but, if so, then going with that, is an obligation to help the poor. The lone Capuchin does not have a bank account from which to help the poor but his order does. Finally, the secular priest might handle big sums of money if he has cheque books for the church, the rectory and the school, but only that amount is for his own pocket which is permitted by diocesan regulations. His standard of living should be roughly in line with what might be considered the average of people in his district. Critics of the Church like to be able to point to the materially minded priest as an excuse for them to say that the Church is all about money and nothing else.

Again, chastity is different for all three. The married couple live chastity with a love that is physical by observing Church teaching on that matter so that their actions accord with the natural law at a minimum and are performed in a spirit of true self-giving. For the monk and the priest chastity entails a love that has to be genuinely affectionate, emotionally sensitive, kindly, but still non-physical. The monk has the company of his community around him as close friends but the secular priest is often alone in his rectory, yet dealing with many lay people who can't all be close friends and some of whom may pose temptations for him. Still, he too needs a circle of friends, better perhaps if they are outside the parish.

Obedience then is also analogously different. The married couple obey each other by taking account of each other's needs and desires, and, if they are in employment, by taking account of the boss's commands, assuming that those commands are not sinful. The monk has his daily duties assigned to him by the abbot. The secular priest might only get one command from a bishop who is fifty miles away: to go and take charge of St John's parish; but once he does this he has a whole lot of decisions to make every day by himself on the running of the parish.

These evangelical counsels, analogously lived, different in each of the different ways of life, should foster charity, as said above; that is their root purpose. In the case of the lay, married couple it is family charity in the home and work-mate charity in their places of employment. In the case of the monk, it is community fraternity, and, in the case of the priest, it is pastoral charity, his self-sacrificing love for the sheep entrusted to him by Christ because of his prior love for Christ Himself to whom he turns in prayer before the tabernacle every day and whose self-sacrifice on the cross he is imitating, as his own share in the cross, when he cares for flock and makes their crosses to be his own. He must also be in union in charity with his bishop and fellow priests even if he cannot meet them very often.

Models of Balance in different Callings

Were I to use models to illustrate the three different kinds of spirituality outlined above and the balance needed in each, then for the lay couple I would use three concentric circles, the inner most being that of the domestic Church in the home, the next being that of the work-place and the outermost being that of the parish or the wider society. The aim there is that the family would so influence the parish that the latter would become a family of families and then that the wider society would become what St John Paul called a "civilization of love".

For the monk I would use the model of the crucifix with the vertical beam pointing upwards to the heavens to indicate prayer and downwards to the earth to indicate manual work, then the horizontal beam to indicate study at one end and recreation at the other. There is balance in this but with the cross at the centre.

Finally, for the secular priest I would use the model of the pendulum that swings too and frow between the tabernacle and the parish to illustrate the priest going out from his Lord in the Eucharist to his care of the flock in the parish and returning again bringing their ups and downs back with him to present them to the Lord at night. This going to and frow is indicated in the gospels where it says that Christ called the twelve *to be with Him and to be sent. Mk.3*. But he too will need time for study, for friends and some enjoyment, for some kind of hobby provided the hobby does not become his main interest. The aim here again is balance, because man is a complex being of body and soul (unlike the angels who are pure spirit), balance in his human nature, but a nature that is being purified and elevated by grace and by a healthy asceticism, i.e., one that prunes nature by counteracting those excesses of desire which result from original sin but without damaging it because human nature itself is good and a gift from God.

An underlying Metaphysics

To continue trying to specify what the secular priest should be doing about this or that in relation to religious or lay people would be an endless task leading only to casuistry if one is not guided by the underlying principles involved. We have seen already that all vocations are complimentary to each other and at the service of each other, because the Church is organic and because spirituality, at root, is one: progress to union with God in Christ through the guidance of the Holy Spirit by frequenting the sacraments, keeping the commandments, practicing the virtues and carrying one's cross *etc*. But given that much, we saw also that each vocation is distinctive because people must try to reach God in the place and calling in which He, by His providence, has put them.

Where God has put lay people can very simply be called "the world" and that by reason of the fundamental fact of them having bodies. We are embodied persons whose habitat is the world because we walk on the earth, eat food taken from the earth and go back into the earth when we die. We can also call the world the "created" or the "natural", all that which comes from God, which is totally dependent on God but is still *not* God (lest we fall into pantheism).

But a difficult question in metaphysics arises if we grant that God is infinite in every way with every perfection and then we ask how can anything "more" can exist "outside" of God? How can you add the finite to the infinite if God "takes up" all the "metaphysical room" there is? If one thinks in material, spatial terms like this, then there is only one way to answer this question: that it cannot be done unless we "play down" the created so that we can "play up" the Creator and thereby secure His glory and transcendence. Platonist metaphysics does that with its emphasis on the world of the Ideas/forms *at the expense* of the world of things down here which are declared to be mere shadows (*cf.* Plato's parable of the cave in his *Republic*). Quite a lot of spirituality did something similar: denigrate the world as a wretched thing in order to play up heaven and the next life – and I am not denying that the world has been a wretched place for many people at various times. Think for example of what it must have been like to live in Europe during the Black Death of the fourteenth century or during the two world wars of the twentieth century. So also with the human being: the strategy of negative metaphysics has often been used to denigrate the body in order to play up the soul – and I am not denying that the soul is the greater part and that all our bodies will get sick and decrepit with age. Once again with marriage: denigrate marriage and sex to play up religious life and chastity – and again I am not denying the fact that many marriages are unhappy and that lust leads to sinful actions. Denigrate every created thing as being evil or at least quasi evil in itself so as to play up the Lord and His glory. There has been a lot of this.

A negative Spirituality

When this kind of metaphysics become the basis of spirituality one falls into the heresies of Gnosticism, or Manichaeism, Lutheranism, Calvinism or Jansenism. These are all derivatives of that ancient heresy of Persian Zoroastrianism which, like a virus, has plagued the Church throughout its history. Zoroaster even believed that there are two radically opposed principles operating in the universe, that of a good God and an evil god. We touched on this already in the *Prophet* section when taking about chastity.

The monk is then seen as one who flees the world and scourges the body because it is evil, who despises woman because she is but an inducement to sin, who endures work only as a necessity in order to live but more so as a penance for sin. Then the secular priest and the laity are supposed to try to follow the monk in thinking and living like this as far as possible. The end result, in the case of some priests who think like this, is that they become men of gloomy faces and cold hearts, with no emotion, joy or humour in their lives so that they come near to being Jansenists. But by a reaction to all that gloom it can also produce the profligate priest who indulges himself in every way he can to compensate for all the deprivations inflicted on him by this his distorted view of Christianity.

In both cases we see a misunderstanding of the nature and purpose of celibacy. Given a negative, Platonist or Jansenist metaphysics, celibacy is seen as hatred of the body and of all desires which have to be "mortified". That word has often been misunderstood as a literal "putting to death" of the body and its natural desires by long fasts, scourging and other kinds of self-imposed torments. The Albigensians made no secret of their desire for eventual suicide by such means. The opposite extreme, by way of reaction to this, scoffs at celibacy and tries to justify every kind of self-indulgence. It goes some way to explaining the scandals of past decades. On a wider plane, going outside of the ranks of the clergy, it goes someway to explaining the sexual revolution of the 60s and the pervasive promiscuity of the West since then.

A positive Spirituality

The solution is to restore the metaphysics of St Thomas Aquinas, a metaphysics which avoids the trap of trying to accommodate the infinite to the finite by understanding, instead, that God is not a material, spatial or extended being to begin with from which something might be added or subtracted; that He is infinite spirit and thus infinite goodness and generosity because He is love as scripture says (*1 Jn.*) and freely wants to share His own goodness with new being outside of Himself, each created thing being given its own act of finite existence even though totally dependent on Himself by participation. St Thomas firmly taught the goodness of creation, of every spiritual and material thing, and the goodness of the body as against the Albigensians of his time. Yet he was aware of sin and analysed it in detail and spoke of it as an excessive attachment to material things, the excessive *attachment* being that which is bad while the things desired are still *good in themselves* as created things. He spoke of the body and marriage as good, the latter being a source of grace, an idea that was contested in his time. Yet he was aware of the damage done to our nature by original sin and was able to analyse concupiscence thoroughly. (*cf.* his *Summa Theologiae, I-II, q71-89*).

Just prior to St Thomas there was St Francis of Assisi with his love of creation, the sun, moon earth *etc.*, as good, yet with an insistence on radical poverty. Created things are to be loved as reflections of the beauty of God but not possessed out of selfish desire. With these saints there was metaphysical accuracy and spiritual balance. Nature is good because made by God. Grace then builds on nature and elevates it to heights otherwise impossible, but in doing so it must first purify it because, though good as coming from the Creator, it has been tarnished by sin though not so badly as to destroy the divine likeness in things or the divine image in man or prevent his entrance into glory, given the help of grace.

When seen in the light of these principles the spirituality of the secular priest and indeed all spiritualities take on a different and much healthier meaning. The monk who flees the world is not doing so out of hatred for the world but to love it in an even more perfect way, proof of which is the wonderful work accomplished by the monks in reclaiming and working the land and mastering so many arts. The lay man is not simply saving his own soul individually with no regard for the sinful body or a world deemed to be "going to the dogs" but is trying to bring himself *along with* his family, and the world around him, to God because that is their destiny if they do not deliberately put sin in the way. He also looks forward to the resurrection of the body at the eschaton. The secular priest then is helping the layman and his family and work-mates reach this goal.

Celibacy then presupposes chastity, but the latter is not seen as a negative thing but as a development of the human being in body and soul in such a way that the former is in harmonious subjection to the latter, retaining all its desires but purified in such a way that one loves with emotions that are controlled, sincere, tender and joyful and in such a way that the person in question is a forerunner of and pointer to the kind of love we hope to enjoy in the kingdom of God of the future.

Mortification also can have a positive meaning. It is not the killing of what is natural but the pruning of the natural of the contagion of selfishness, contracted by original sin, still remaining after baptism. And there is more: there is a lesson to be learned here from St John Vianney, the patron of parish priests. Good preaching and the administration of the sacraments, and all those things a priest does for his people are what we might call "external graces" for them in the sense that the priest brings them to the people in the external visible signs of the sacraments. But more is needed: the grace thus brought to people must take effect internally in their souls by the working of the Holy Spirit. That grace is won for his people by a priest who is prepared to make sacrifices, do penances and take on vigils of prayer and fasting for them though with a moderation that does not harm his health. That is a demanding challenge from which some priests shy away. St. John Vianney is a great example for them in this.[3]

Priestly spirituality, then, is the priest conforming himself to Christ in mind and heart by prayer and sacrifice so that he can be like a new Moses leading his flock to the promised land of the kingdom, showing them how they can prepare their families and the world around them for the second coming of Christ and growing in holiness himself every day by doing all this.

Conclusions:

1. The priest is configured to Christ the Head by the sacrament of holy orders but he must configure himself in heart and mind by a life of holiness so that his people will be led to Christ through him and to the Father by the sanctifying power of the Holy Spirit. All spirituality tries to break with sin and progress towards union with God but, that said, each calling in life has its own distinctive spirituality, complementing and serving the others in various ways. That

of the secular priest has *him* grow in holiness precisely in his work of helping the laity to grow in the holiness that is proper to *them*.
2. The above requires that the three stages of the spiritual life, the purgative, illuminative and unite be lived in analogously different ways by religious, secular priests and lay people; so also, the way they live the evangelical counsels of poverty, chastity and obedience.
3. All of this presupposes a metaphysics of earthly things which does not see things as bad or as being in competition with the Creator but as good in themselves with their own finite but real value as fruits of the generosity of God. But it also requires that the priest take a realistic account of the damage done to our nature by original sin.

In the list of the seven sacraments marriage comes last and is the second of those concerned with the social, with the building up of the Church and in the case of marriage with the building up of society also. We will turn to that presently.

Chapter XXX

The Sacrament of Marriage

Definitions, Properties, Ends, Goods, Effects, pastoral Care

Therefore, a man leaves his father and his mother and cleaves to his wife, and they become one flesh. Gen. 2:24.

This mystery has many implications; but I am saying it applies to Christ and the church. Eph. 5:32.

Sacred Scripture begins with the creation of man and woman in the image and likeness of God and concludes with a vision of "the wedding-feast of the Lamb." Scripture speaks throughout of marriage and its "mystery," its institution and the meaning God has given it, its origin and its end, its various realizations throughout the history of salvation, the difficulties arising from sin and its renewal "in the Lord" in the New Covenant of Christ and the Church. *Catechism of the Catholic Church, #1602*

The firsts five sacraments, we saw, are directed towards the individual as he/she is spiritually born, grows strong, fails and declines. All of this happens in the context of the Church, the people of God, who prepare the individual for these events and come together to celebrate them. We saw how holy orders exists for the ordering and building up of the Church in which the word of God is proclaimed and people are guided and sanctified. The last remaining sacrament, that of marriage, has a social character also in that it is concerned with the wellbeing of the family, which is the fundamental unit of the Church, so that it is called the "domestic Church", and of civil society also. This will be our concern in this chapter: looking at its nature, properties, ends *etc.*, and saying something about the pastoral care it needs.

Today, in pastoral work, much of the energy of the priest and of his helpers is taken up with the care of the family because it is under attack from many sides and is broken down in many cases. The defense and care of marriage and the family is of fundamental importance because it is the fundamental building block of society, and the good things of civilization, all the treasures of the heritage of a given people, natural and supernatural, are passed on from one generation to the next largely through the family. As the blocks are to the wall so is the family to society. Hence in the documents of Vatican II we read:

> The well-being of the individual person and of human and Christian society is intimately linked with the healthy condition of that community produced by marriage and family. *Gaudium et Spes, #47.*

But if the blocks are weakened by dissolving the cement that holds the gravel in them together soon the wall will come tumbling down, which is happening in great part today with respect to the family. Thus there is a great urgency about the care of the family and thus a great importance attaches to the study of the sacrament of marriage.

Definitions of Marriage

I will begin by offering some definitions of marriage and the family because it is fashionable today to define it in ways that are very loose or to redefine it in ways that are blatantly at odds with scripture and tradition, indeed with nature itself, and that redefining is being done not just by non-Christians but even by some clergy.

In pagan Roman law we find this definition:

> Marriage is a union between a man and a woman, an association for the whole of life, in which both are under the same law, divine and human. *Modestinus, lib I, Regularum (*taken from *Casti Conubii).*

Bearing in mind that these pagans did not have the advantage of either the scriptures or the *magisterium* and that divorce and many perversions of marriage existed in Roman society, it was nonetheless a pretty good definition. It insisted on a union of one man and one woman of a permanent kind and saw that union as bound not only by human/civil law but by divine law also, even though their ideas about the divine were rather confused given the polytheism of that society. Compare that with some of the very unchristian definitions of marriage being proffered today, even by people calling themselves Catholics, despite them having the teaching of the Church available to them.

If we come up to the 1917 *Code of Canon Law* and the manuals following them, marriage was usually defined as a *contract* between a man and a woman whereby they exchanged exclusive, perpetual rights to each other's bodies for "acts apt for the generation of offspring". (*cf.* the *Manuals of Moral Theology* based on *Can. 1013* of the *1917 Code).* It was a minimalist definition and somewhat cold with a word like "contract" being used and reference being made only to the spouses' bodies. But it was accurate from the point of view of canonists who had the task of determining whether a given marriage was valid or not in doubtful cases.

Chapter 30: The Sacrament of Marriage

When we come to 1930 and the encyclical *Casti Conubii* of Pope Pius XI we find a more complete and more personalist definition:

> Marriage, before being a union of bodies, is first and foremost intimately a union and harmony of minds, brought about not by any passing affection of sense or heart but by a deliberate and resolute decision of the will; and from this cementing of minds, by God's decree, there arises a sacred and inviolable bond. #7.

Words like "intimacy" and "harmony of minds" give us a more personalist description even if such things are not easily measurable by canonists concerned with determining validity; and the stress put on the commitment of will as being more important than "any passing affection" is to be noted because it rules out the ridiculous idea which floated for a while in the last century of "no love no marriage", *viz*, that when a couple cease to be "in love" so also does the marriage cease to exist! The pope's definition talks also of "a sacred and inviolable bond" being brought into being in a valid marriage. This is more than a thing of sentiment that might depend on the level of infatuation of the couple; it is an ontological reality even though not of the same kind as the character that comes into being with the three sacraments of baptism, confirmation and holy orders.

Then with Vatican II we have still more of personalist language and the use of the term "covenant":

> The intimate partnership of married life and love has been established by the Creator and qualified by his laws. It is rooted in the conjugal <u>covenant</u> of irrevocable personal consent. *Gaudium et Spes, #48.*

"Covenant" is a scriptural word and more personalist than the word "contract". But it should be remembered that in biblical times a covenant was usually between unequal parties: a powerful king on one side and a neighbouring king of lesser strength on the other side, the former guaranteeing to defend the latter but the latter having to supply the former with man-power for his army. This does not agree so well with the idea of equality in marriage that is so much in vogue today but I still think it is more personal than the word "contract".

The essential properties of marriage

- <u>Unity and Indissolubility</u>

The essential properties of marriage have traditionally been listed as unity and indissolubility. Marriage is a life-long, exclusive union of one man and one woman both of whom were free to marry in the first place. The two become one in an intimacy of mind and body of a most profound kind which excludes all other persons even if the two of them continue to have many other friends and business partners. And this union is for life. Accordingly, there can be no such thing as a same-sex marriage or a temporary marriage if the word "marriage" is to retain its true meaning. Hence it follows that should a couple intend only a provisional marriage, subject to things going well, it would not be valid to begin with. A valid marriage of two Christians which has been consummated in a properly human way is for life and is dissoluble only with the death of one of the spouses.

It should be pointed out, especially in a divorce culture where many Christians divorce civilly and then form second unions which they then regard as "second marriages", that such is a misnomer. The second union in a registry office cannot be called a "marriage" if the first union was, and therefore still is, a valid marriage in the eyes of God and His Church. If the state insists that it is a "civil marriage" then the state is pitting itself against God and in a contradictory way because the authority of the state is from God to begin with. Again, there are many who do not realize this and think that a civil divorce breaks the bond of their first, true, valid marriage. If there are reasons to think that the first union was not a valid marriage then the possibility of a Church annulment could be investigated. Yet many couples do not know this and proceed into a second union regardless of how they stand with the Church.

It can happen that a couple are living in a country where divorce is prevalent all around them and is accepted by most people as being "normal" but, nonetheless, this particular couple firmly intend that their own marriage will be for life: in their case they have a right intention as regards the essential properties of marriage – unity and indissolubility. Without that intention the marriage would *not* be valid from the beginning.

It is for the priest or his lay helpers to explain these things to intending couples in pre-marriage talks. He needs to explain the differences between a dissolution of the bond as understood by the Church, and an annulment and a separation; and then the equivalent of those terms in civil law. One cannot presume very much in the case of most intending couples when preparing such a talk due to the inadequacy of catechetics and preaching and the confusion caused by the media in people's minds in such matters.

So also a same-sex union does not have that complementarity willed by the Creator which is necessary for a true marriage. It does not even have a remote, analogous similarity to true marriage. This holds true even when a whole society tries to legalize same-sex marriage in a referendum. (*cf. CCC, # 2357*).

These are *essential* properties, and when something lacks an essential property it simply is not that thing, just as a creature with two legs and feathers can not be called a bird if it still lacks wings because having wings is essential to being a bird.

For a priest or his pre marriage team to fail to explain such things in basic outline is for them to be responsible for some marriages being invalid due to ignorance and wrong intentions. I have never heard even one Sunday sermon in which these things were explained, even when the gospel reading on a Sunday was about Christ's prohibition of divorce?! To say that the Sunday sermon is not the proper place to explain such things, at least in simple outline, is something I do not accept because there is little other opportunity for doing so once people leave school, and often they are not explained in school either. The priest himself, or his pre-marriage team, should know their canon law in these matters, something that requires considerable study and which I am presuming here because it is too extensive to be covered fully here and which is covered adequately in any case in the various commentaries on the canon law of marriage.

The Ends of Marriage

Procreation and Mutual Love

Marriage, like everything else willed by God, has its ends or purposes. The ends of marriage have been traditionally listed as, 1) the procreation and education of offspring, (these two always put together as one because the child has an intellect needing long term formation especially in the faith); 2) the mutual support of the spouses, and 3) a remedy for concupiscence, though this last seldom appears in more recent documents. Should a couple attempt to enter marriage explicitly ruling out offspring then that marriage would be invalid. If the woman is elderly, children will not result but in that case it is nature that is ruling out children and not the couple by a deliberate choice.

Mutual aid is a wide term referring to the love, loyalty and the day by day help a couple can give each other in all their undertakings and, hopefully, with a love that is generous and self- sacrificing, each having the well-being of the other in mind. This continues even when the children are up and gone and is all the more necessary when old age brings its infirmities and loneliness.

The term "remedy for concupiscence" denotes an orderly, institutionalized way of regulating the sex drive in people which, being so very strong as a result of the Fall, would lead to unrestrained lust and endless quarrelling if it were not so regulated.

In the history of the theology of marriage one can see at times some altering of the primacy of the ends of marriage. For example, St John Chrysostom in his writings is usually very strong on chastity as the primary end of marriage though at other times he stresses mutual aid and procreation, and he varies at times in the order in which he mentions these different ends. (*cf.* his *Sermon on Marriage* and *How to Choose a Wife*). St Augustine stressed procreation and had problems at times with the morality of the marriage act when not used for that purpose. (*cf. On the Goods of Marriage, Ch. 6*). So also in more recent times, prior to Vatican II, the primary purpose was still procreation (and education of offspring) with mutual aid and the remedy for concupiscence added on in second and third places respectively. But post Vatican II, with the influence of personalism in philosophy and the rise of urbanization, which sees the emergence of the nuclear family, when more and more couples are constrained to living in small apartments in big cities, one saw a new emphasis being put on the secondary end, that of mutual aid between the spouses, and so much so that it seemed to be competing with procreation for first place. The love relationship between husband and wife came to be seen as all important. This jostling for first place is reflected in the *magisterium* as we read, for example, in paragraph 49 of *Gaudium et Spes* which is a lengthy paragraph on the importance of mutual love; but then, immediately, the next paragraph goes on to say that "Marriage and conjugal love are by their nature ordained toward the begetting and educating of children".

So which end is primary? One cannot do a dodge on this by saying that both procreation and mutual aid are primary, as we might do in sport when we cannot tell which athlete crossed the finishing line first, and we give "first" prize to both. Traditionally procreation has been put first in most ages for the simple reason that there are many kinds of partnerships of love and mutual aid but that which is distinctive of marriage is that it has the founding of a family as its aim when nature allows for that.

In answering this question the important thing is that we do not fall into the old trap of "making the good to be the enemy of the better". Yet this often happened in the case of the ends of marriage in the past and is still happening today. Too often in the past, as for example in the case of royalty, when the king was obsessed with having a male heir for the throne, or in the case of landed people when a farmer was obsessed with having a son who would inherit the farm and carry on the family name, the queen or the wife, respectively, was sometimes seen merely as a conduit for the hoped-for son to whom she would give birth and then be a nurse of his biological needs. Her standing as an equal party in the marriage and her own needs for affection and tenderness *etc.*, sometimes got scant attention from her husband whom she had to reverence as her "Lord" so that "mutual aid" was often far from being mutual but very one sided instead.

Then, by a pendulum swing, due to the influence of feminism and the easy availability of contraception, mutual aid can take priority to the point of seeing children as a burden or nuisance, so that the traditional, primary end is lost sight of almost entirely. If the love of husband and wife were to be absolutized to the detriment of procreation as an end, then something essential to marriage would be wilfully discarded thereby rendering such marriages invalid, as said above. It would also lead psychologically to an "over heating" of the one relationship, that between husband and wife, as compared to the extended family of agricultural times when a family was a household of three generations and many children and thus constituted a complexity of many different relationships. It would also inevitably lead to a kind of love that would soon become mostly contraceptive and which would fast degenerate into lust. No. One end must not be played off against the other. Both are very important and necessary even if procreation is ultimately primary. Accordingly, *Gaudium et Spes* is balanced when it says:

> Hence while not making the other purposes of matrimony to be of less account, the true practice of conjugal love, and the whole meaning of the family life which results from it, have this aim: that the couple be ready with stout hearts to co-operate with the love of the Creator and Saviour, who through them will enlarge and enrich His own family day by day. *Gaudium et Spes, #49*

Procreation is primary in the terms of ends, but children should result from a truly *loving* relationship of husband and wife, which relationship has a causal priority in terms of agency.

The Goods of Marriage

<u>Offspring, Fidelity and Sacrament</u>

Traditionally, in addition to the essential properties and the ends of marriage there was also listed what were called "the goods of marriage" and they were given as children, fidelity and the sacrament.

That children should be a good or benefit flowing from marriage should be easily understood if procreation is the primary end of marriage; and indeed, in most ancient societies in which agriculture by manual labour was the principal way of making a living, children were welcomed so as to help with work on the land. Many children died young and needed to be replaced. But children were not *always* welcomed even in agricultural times. When, for example, a farmer of poor means had to provide a dowry for each of his daughters so as to "marry them off" to other men who had land there was a temptation to abort or kill the new-born girls. That is still a problem in India today. Then, in the Western world of today, where there is affluence, there is still a high abortion rate due to families being cramped into small apartments in big cities; and, even amongst the wealthy, some couples see children as simply a nuisance because a hindrance to a high life style. These difficulties present us with the question of whether we are going to allow economics to dictate the future design of marriage and the family (as Marxists would do) or endeavour to have economics serve the well-being of the family as it was designed by God. To put it very simply: will we have the family redesigned to fit the house or will we see to it that the house is redesigned to fit the family as God has instituted it and as nature would have it?

Fidelity as a "good" of marriage has a more positive meaning than simply refraining from having affairs with third persons. It signifies that mutual dedication to each other of the spouses in a deep friendship, rising above all other friendships, which has each of them put the interest of the other first.

"Sacrament" is traditionally listed as the third "good" of marriage. Even in pagan societies, as we saw earlier, marriage was seen as a symbol of something higher than itself, of something above the natural, of something divine; and then with Christianity that something higher is explicitly named as the union of Christ and His Church, His bride. (*cf. Eph. 5*). That sense of the sacrament as being sacred helped keep it intact in times of difficulty but is being steadily being lost in societies growing ever more secularist today.

Vatican II tells us explicitly that marriage between Christians has been raised to the dignity of a sacrament by Christ. St Thomas Aquinas taught this also though it was not universally accepted in the Middle Ages. But Trent listed marriage definitively as one of the seven sacraments. The two people themselves are the ministers of this sacrament, not the priest who is a witness on behalf of the Church. (In the Orthodox Churches the minister is the priest). When the man and the woman exchange consent, they make a contract and also confer the sacrament on each other at the same moment. Some Catholic couples, not understanding this and who attempt to marry in a registry office come to the priest afterwards to "put a blessing" on their marriage thinking that that puts everything right and that it will somehow make it a sacrament (assuming that they even know what a sacrament is). It does not. Such a union (if there was no impediment) may be put right by a canonical process called a *sanatio*, not be a simple blessing.

The usual locus in scripture cited for the elevation of marriage to being a sacrament is the wedding feast of Cana even if the gospel does not explicitly give an account of Christ raising marriage to the level of a sacrament on that occasion. We can take it, in any case, that Christ did institute this sacrament as with the others because – as explained earlier – a sacrament confers grace, which is a participation in the divine life, and which therefore only someone who is God can institute. But another locus, cited by St Thomas, for the sacramentality of marriage is *Ephesians 5* where St Paul says:

> *For this reason a man shall leave his father and mother and be joined to his wife, and the two shall become one flesh. This mystery is a profound one, and I am saying that it refers to Christ and the church. Eph. 5:32-33.*

Effects
―――――

The first effect of marriage is the bond which it creates between the two people. This comes into being in every valid marriage but, in Christian marriage, sanctifying grace follows upon it unless the couple are in a state of sin when contracting their marriage. The bond still comes into being but the grace will not follow until they remove the obstacle of sin by a good confession. This is of relevance at a time when many couples come to the altar to get married from the same house where they have been cohabiting. Because of this it is a good thing if the priest recommends to them that they live apart in preparation for their wedding and go to confession beforehand.

Christian marriage, then, we can say, when in place and is being lived by the couple, is a small-scale image of the great sacrament of Christ and His bride the Church. We can also say that a Christian marriage lived out by a couple in a state of grace is an *instance or actualizing* in their own home of that higher marriage of Christ and His Church. Their natural love is purified and elevated by His grace so that they can overcome selfishness and become truly a couple of mutual self-giving. Their love then becomes a sharing in the inner life of the Trinity itself, which is one of self-giving love of the three persons to each other. This grace is given on the day of their wedding but it is not a once-off kind of thing: it is available to them all the days of their marriage if they stir it up and nourish it by family prayer. Otherwise, it is somewhat like a cheque in one's pocket that is never cashed. A very suitable prayer for this stirring up of the grace of marriage is the rosary said by all the family together. It is good for the priest to remind them of this grace to give them hope in facing the difficulties which will be sure to come along on the road of their married life.

Drawing on the above, then, and returning to the definition of marriage we began with above, we can flesh out that definition somewhat more and say that marriage is a divine institution giving rise to a life-long, unbreakable union of mind and body between one man and one woman, both of whom are free to marry, which binds them together for the purpose of begetting children in a context of self-giving love (when nature allows for children) and for the mutual support they can give each other even if there are no children. It is the basic unit of civil society. Moving up to the supernatural plane we can say that it is a sacrament, a reflection of Christ's union with His bride the Church and a source of grace for the couple, enabling them to live up to their obligations and to love each other in the way Christ loves his Church. We can go further then and say, by implication, that the family is also the basic unit of the Church, that it is the Church in the home, the domestic Church.

True pastoral Care

I believe that it is important to be clear and accurate in defining marriage and the family, especially today, when other definitions are being put forward which are clearly at variance not only with Catholic teaching but with nature itself: cohabitation or civil unions, second unions, so called "same-sex marriages", "incestuous marriages", "trisoms," "polygamous unions", and who knows what next! I have heard of three women celebrities in the US each of whom each attempted to marry just *herself* alone! I also heard of an old lady wanting marry her *cat* so that she could bequeath her fortune to the cat, tax free, so that the cat would have an abundance of cat food for years to come after she was gone!!! To compound matters further and give fuel to such irregularities one will hear some bishops and priests, with a warped sense of pastoral charity, saying that we must be more open and flexible in defining what we mean by "marriage" so as to be "inclusive" of the many unions one finds today so that the Church can embrace and bless them all and even admit such people to the sacraments. How strange that people who demand accuracy and clarity in most other areas of life, finance, sport, medicine *etc.*, are willing to be so lose and vague on what constitutes the primary building block of society! Of course, in an analogous sense, any grouping of people with a common origin or with common objectives can be called a "family"- the members of a sporting club, the past pupils of a particular school, a religious community, even the human race itself – but where there are analogies there must be one primary analogate with a precise and definite meaning and, in the case of the family, that is the small unit of society resulting from a life-long union of one man and one woman as explained above.

The objection will be made that now I am being exclusive and discriminatory, elitist and disdainful of the many people who are simply trying to find happiness in ways that in the past were deemed unconventional but which society today deems to be more acceptable, that I don't have much pastoral charity for such people, that I see things as simplistically black and white when life is mostly grey *etc.* I will be told that, instead, the priest today must "accompany" (a new "in" word) such people on the road of life in their quest for fulfilment and never be "judgemental" (another "in" word). But if there is an absolute metaphysical difference between what is right and what is sinful and if all of such relationships are objectively irregular - and often subjectively sinful also if the couples knowingly persist in them - then is it really pastoral charity to accompany such people as they persist in such relationships as if all were fine morally? To use a simple example, if I see a couple walking along a road which leads to the edge of a cliff a hundred yards further on and I accompany them, all smiles, as if all was safe and well, because I do not want to offend them by pointing out the danger they are in, can that be called "charity or care of any sort"?! I would call it something like "assisted suicide". If a doctor sees that the scan just taken shows his patient has a large tumour in his lung but "accompanies" him with painkillers and gives him nice assurances that all is fine, lest otherwise he upset him, can that be called "medical care"? So also if the priest has true pastoral care for couples in irregular unions he should not reject them or avoid them; on the contrary he should seek them out in his visitation of houses and "accompany" them by speaking to them of the true state of danger of their souls. But if they persist in a firm attitude of defiance, then he has to take them at their word, leave them to their own devices and simply commend them to Our Lady for the grace of conversion.

Conclusions:

1. Marriage is a life-long union of one man and one woman instituted by God when He created Adam and Eve and put them together as husband and wife at the beginning of history.
2. The essential properties of marriage are unity and indissolubility.
3. The ends of marriage are procreation and education of children, and mutual love.
4. The goods of marriage are offspring, fidelity and sacrament.
5. When God is recognized as the author of marriage and His plan for marriage is then accepted by accepting also the laws of marriage that follow, everything is clear, even if married life will still have its difficulties and some marriages

will still fail. But when God is left out of the picture, then as Dostoyevsky said "when God is gone everything is permitted".

This is the plan of marriage as instituted by God and raised to being a sacrament by Christ but we don't find this plan realized everywhere, not even in supposedly Christian countries. Let us see next how it is often undermined today.

Chapter XXXI

Marriage Undermined

Causes, the Church's Position, the great Let Down

He who divorces his wife and marries another commits adultery. Lk.16:18.

Yet the excellence of this institution is not everywhere reflected with equal brilliance, since polygamy, the plague of divorce, so-called free love and other disfigurements have an obscuring effect. *Gaudium et Spes, #47.*

The Church's teaching on marriage, as we have briefly outlined it above, is very consistent and beautiful, but, due to the Fall, those who try to give it effect in their lives have the weakness of human nature to contend with, even when they are Christians living in the state of grace: the weaknesses of pride, selfishness, lust, hard-heartedness *etc*. More than that, couples today are living in a society which has inherited a legacy of ideologies and legislation which expressly militate against marriage and the family as God intended it. In this chapter we will look at some of those ideologies and also at artificial contraception which I hold is a practice of great harm to marriage and to society generally, and then we will look at the Church's position on these things.

Undermining Causes

<u>False Ideologies</u>

At the reformation marriage was no longer seen as a sacrament. The way was open then for it to be seen as a purely civil contract and, as such, came to be placed under the jurisdiction of the state and no longer of the Church. This became more explicit at the French revolution: the state claimed the right to regulate all marriages including those of Christians. Not surprisingly divorce was allowed then as a normal request for whoever wanted it. In the two centuries since the revolution we have seen the ideologies of socialism, humanism, nihilism, feminism, globalism and sheer atheism come to the fore which are still exercising influence.

Rather than try to give a detailed account of each of these ideologies, if we simply take the three slogans of the revolution: liberty, equality and fraternity, they will provide us with some keys to understanding some of them.

Liberty has come to be understood as the absolute freedom of the individual in disregard of the ten commandments; *equality* as a common levelling which ignores our filial relation of dependence on God and the natural differences there are between man and woman but excludes the baby in the womb, boy or girl, who is degraded to being a mere object to be discarded at will; and *fraternity,* a counterfeit of charity based on a common, global citizenship with nothing of the supernatural about it. It is now coming to be understood as "sisterhood", which exalts the choice of the woman above that of the man thereby contradicting the revolutions own slogan of equality!

Finally, with Marx and communism, marriage and the family were seen to be closely related to private property which was anathema to the advocates of socialism and of state ownership of all the means of production. It is no secret that Marx and the Bolsheviks studied the enlightenment philosophers of the time prior to the French revolution and admired the "achievements" of the revolution itself.

These false ideologies have being pushed by the media ever since the French revolution and are becoming easily accepted by people today and, I claim, are the general cause of this breakdown of marriage and the family. Thus, abortion was legalized in Russia in the mid1930s and contraception in the West shortly after, leading to abortion there also in the second half of the century. Divorce had been legalized in most Western countries by the end of the 20th century, then same-sex marriage, euthanasia, infanticide and more. One evil followed on another in general practice, hence at Vatican II we find the following list of the resulting problems of marriage:

> The well-being of the individual person and of human and Christian society is intimately linked with the healthy condition of that community produced by marriage and family......Yet the excellence of this institution is not everywhere reflected with equal brilliance, since polygamy, the plague of divorce, so-called free love and other disfigurements have an obscuring effect. In addition, married love is too often profaned by excessive self-love, the worship of pleasure and illicit practices against human generation. Moreover, serious disturbances are caused in families by modern economic conditions, by influences at once social and psychological, and by the demands of civil society. Finally, in certain parts of the world problems resulting from population growth are generating concern. *Gaudium et Spes, #47.*

I have known housing estates in Ireland, England and Germany of twenty or thirty houses in which one finds that only in one or two houses are the original two spouses still together as husband and wife after ten or only five years of marriage. In the other houses one finds couples in various kinds of irregular unions or single, abandoned parents.

Contraception

These ideologies take from God and give to man the right to redesign and regulate marriage according to the whim of the latter. But the more particular cause, I would argue, is the easy availability of contraception since the middle of the twentieth century. It is the root cause of the many other problems listed above in the quote from *Gaudium et Spes* and helps give effect to the ideologies just mentioned. It should be easy to see how this is so: with contraceptives being made easily available promiscuity outside of marriage and infidelity within marriage will follow quickly. Both evils will then give rise to abortion as back up for failed contraception. Infidelity, in turn, gives rise to divorce which becomes more easily available to the point that the marriage bond is seen as a mere piece of paper that is easily torn up. Abortion, furthermore, gives rise to infanticide and euthanasia and to trafficking in human organs. These things, moreover, give rise to new definitions of marriage such as same sex-marriage, trisoms and even incestuous marriages. God and His design for marriage are soon pushed aside and their place is taken by anything that the mind of depraved man can conjure up.

Even though this sequence of destruction, flowing from contraception is easy to grasp, I feel it still needs to be emphasized because so many clergy today of all ranks refuse to face up to it. As evidence of that, I have not heard a single sermon on contraception since the days immediately following the publication of *Humanae Vitae* in 1968 when a minority of clergy did make some effort at supporting Pope Paul VI on this matter. On one occasion I heard a priest on radio on what was supposed to be a religion program say, as regards contraception, that "the train had left the station on that matter". As if to say, "forget about that debate. It has been lost long ago; contraception is in and accepted by more than eighty per cent of Catholics. So don't disturb them". Worse still, some marriage advisory councils which come under the name of being "Catholic" will even propose methods of artificial contraception of various kinds along with natural family planning (which is only briefly mentioned, if at all). If there was ever a case of the Church shooting herself in the foot this surely is one.

By refusing to face up to the evil of contraception priests are assuming that their people can grow in holiness while living in sin, this despite the teaching of all schools of spirituality, going back to the very gospels themselves, that the first step in holiness is to repent, to turn away from sin. This helps understand why St John Chrysostom put chastity high on his list of the ends of marriage. Nonetheless, the appalling rise in abortions, promiscuity and marriage breakdown and the resulting loss of faith, all the bad fruits which have come from this tree of contraception, is still not enough to convince many priests of what a bad tree this really is.

Effects of Contraception and attempted Justifications

Then, if one looks at the demographic results of a half century of contraception one sees again how bad they are. The birth rate has gone below replacement rate in most countries in the West so that society there is now top heavy with old people. This means that the middle-aged group has to support both old and young with their time and their taxes. A young, Chinese girl told me that, as a result of their one-child policy of the early 21st century, she had no brothers or sisters or any aunts or uncles, and that, were she to marry, she would have about four or perhaps five old people, between parents, grandparents and some grandaunts and granduncles, to look after plus the one or two children she might have herself – a burden she said she would find impossible. And if many other young people like her refuse to marry at all, because of this burden, what then of the future of their country? Nothing but despair. China and some other countries are now trying to reverse their restrictive policy but without great success because young people have got used to lives of free sex with no responsibilities and want to continue enjoying this. Pope Paul VI predicted many of these bad fruits in his encyclical but was dismissed by many as a prophet of doom. Now we see how right he was, even though many still refuse to see the evidence that is staring them in the face.

One other effect of artificial contraception, wherever it is introduced, is the decline in vocations. As the former goes up the latter go down. This is because contraceptive love usually degenerates into lust - sex for mere gratification with no reference to new life. That kind of love is inimical to the kind of love which is at the centre of Christian living: the love of self-giving and self-sacrifice. According to St John Paul, as we saw earlier, small children can detect this deficiency in their parents' love even if they know nothing about contraception or even the facts of life. Yet that on-going loss of vocations still does not alert many priests to contraception as one of its root causes!

Even if one could argue for some positive results from contraception, such as that of a higher standard of living for those who are allowed to be conceived - the privileged few - it still remains true that something intrinsically wrong can never be justified. Yet attempts are made to justify it with all sorts of moral gymnastics which boil down to situation ethics and a moral relativism which reject the objectiveness of the moral law and the notion of intrinsic evil. One example of such moral gymnastics was the appeal to the right to privacy by the civil courts when contraception was first

Chapter 31: Marriage Undermined

being legalized in some countries. Of course there is such a thing as a right to privacy, a very valuable right indeed, but it does not then follow that everything done in private is morally good, otherwise a man murdering his wife in the "privacy" of their bedroom (which happens at times) should be deemed to be good! Another argument was that times had changed and with them economic and social conditions and that morality had to follow sooth. This is only thinly disguised Marxism: the teaching that morals and all things cultural arise from below, from what is called the "infra structure of society" and not from above, from God speaking through nature and revelation. In theology this same argument is made by modernists saying again that morals are a product of man's feelings and not of God's decree, not from His design for man revealed in nature. The teaching of situation ethics is similar: that while moral principles are fine as ideals, one must take account of differing situations, so much so that what is intrinsically wrong can somehow become right in this instance and then in that and then in another and soon pretty well everywhere.

Another argument, to be expected in a democracy for the legalizing of practices intrinsically immoral is that supposedly arising from figures spun out from opinion polls: "the polls say that they are all doing x so it cannot be wrong for me then". The idea here is that mere numbers make for morals or for a truthful expression of the sense of the faith of the people, of the *sensus fidei*. But to this claim Pope John Paul II replies:

> Following Christ, <u>the church seeks the truth, which is not always the same as the majority opinion</u>. She listens to conscience and not to power and in this way she defends the poor and the down trodden. The church values historical research when it proves helpful in understanding the historical context in which pastoral action has to be developed and when it leads to a better understanding of the truth. Such research alone, however, is not to be considered in itself an expression of the sense of the faith. *Familiaris Consortio, #5.*

One can use numbers or statistics for just about anything one wants to propagate – just as a tottering drunk will latch onto any lamppost to hold him up. But even this argument is often found to be weak if one honestly looks at the statistics. For example, it is little known and quiet forgotten now that when the legalizing of contraception was being debated in Ireland in the 1970s one laywoman alone, whom I knew, was able to gather *seventy thousand signatures of married people* who were opposed to contraception! She presented them to the government of the day - which conveniently put them in the nearest waste bin. Again, the first divorce referendum in Ireland in 1986 was defeated by a ratio of 3 to 1. But instead of accepting that as a clear sign that the Irish people still valued natural, life-long marriage, so that the government would then proceed to give even more support to marriage, the anti-family lobby and their media allies redoubled their efforts at selling the idea of divorce to the people and were able to persuade another government to try another referendum nine years later which saw divorce passed by a narrow margin. How conveniently that the statistics of the seventy thousand anti-contraception signatures and those of that first divorce referendum were ignored and not seen as an expression of the *sensus fidei* but that statistics supposedly advocating the opposite *were* taken on board.

The Church's Position

<u>Reply to the Ideologies</u>

In reply to the ideologies the Church gives us a view of man as made in the image and likeness of God, subject to His laws, and a humanism that is centred on Christ as the one who not only reveals God to man but reveals man to himself. *Its* "globalism" is a universalism of all people of faith gathered into the mystical body of Christ marching towards the kingdom of God of the end. In reply to the slogans of the French revolution the Church has been pointing out that these were merely distortions or caricatures of Christian doctrines prevalent for centuries prior. It is as if these doctrines were plants pulled up out of the Christian soil on which they had grown and distorted. Hence Christian liberty is not unbridled license but the exercise of the power of will when its object is the good as presented to it by the intellect, informed by true teaching. The fundamental liberty for the Christian is that won for us by Christ when He broke the power of Satan on the cross and *freed* us from sin – very different from the revolution-type liberty which is license to *indulge* in sin.

The Church does affirm the equality of all men and women because all – including the unborn - are made in the image and likeness of God, and the destiny of all to return to God. It is this likeness which gives all people their dignity. But it takes realistic account of the natural differences there are between men and women, rulers and ruled and the different talents of people. It does not reduce all to a base commonality as communism does (all equal in the misery of the mire except the party elite!).

Fraternity, if the word is to have any meaning, must mean that we have a common Father in God above and are brothers and sisters in Christ, something abhorred by communists, humanists and, of course, atheists. By comparison, it is difficult to see what basis their comradeship can have when God is left aside.

Reply to Contraception

How the Church responds to contraception is spelt out clearly in the encyclicals of *Casti Conubii,* 1930, by Pope Pius XI; in the encyclical *Humanae Vitae,* 1968, by Pope Paul VI and later again in the exhortation *Familiaris Consortio* by Pope John Paul II. Here I will merely present a few quotes from those documents that provide good summaries of the Church's arguments and add a few comments.

> Just as man does not have unlimited dominion over his body in general, so also, and with more particular reason, he has no such dominion over his specific sexual faculties, for these are concerned by their very nature with the generation of life, of which God is the source. *Humanae Vitae, #13.*

Here we have a truth which is forgotten in an age of secularism: that man does not have either the first or the last word in matters pertaining to the generation of human life. Only God does. Hence the oft quoted saying, by both men and women, that "this is my own body and I can do what I like with it" is false. We don't have absolute ownership over our bodies but only stewardship, and we must remember that the soul of the new baby does not come from the bodies of the parents but from God by direct creation and infusion at the moment of conception.

God is the principal agent in the begetting of new life but He gives to the couple the privilege of cooperating with Him in this noble work as St John Paul explains:

> In its most profound reality, love is essentially a gift; and conjugal love, while leading the spouses to reciprocal "knowledge" which makes them "one flesh" does not end with the couple, because it makes them capable of the greatest gift by which they become co-operators with God for giving life to a new human person. *Familiaris Consortio, #14.*

But just as God has a design for human nature so also He has a design, a law, for the actions that transmit human life so that the act of intercourse can have its natural effect of leading to new life when the woman is fertile. Hence, other ways of engaging in sex are morally wrong:

> Similarly excluded is any action, which either before, at the moment of, or after sexual intercourse, is specifically intended to prevent procreation – whether as an end or as a means. *Humanae Vitae, #14.*

Here we have the crunch line in *Humanae Vitae* which caused all the uproar, mostly by people who did not read the encyclical at all. But Pope Paul added a clarification:

> But the church in no way regards as unlawful <u>therapeutic means considered necessary to cure organic diseases,</u> even though they also have a contraceptive effect, and this is foreseen – provided that this contraceptive effect is not directly intended or for any motive whatsoever. *ibid., #15.*

Here we have an instance of the principle of two effects. If the primary effect intended is the curing of some illness or the regularizing of a woman's problematic cycles, a doctor may prescribe a pill for that purpose even though he knows it will also prevent conception as a secondary effect. Also, a married woman may cooperate *passively* in a contraceptive act, if she is under compulsion such that to refuse could put the unity of her marriage and the well-being of her family at risk. That woman is more sinned against than sinning. A girl who is abducted and knows that she is likely to be raped may take a contraceptive if it is her only defense against a man who is an attacker making advances against her that are totally unwanted. These examples are not exceptions changing wrong to right all of a sudden. In such cases there is no willing of an evil object as a means to an end. What is objectively, intrinsically wrong can not be willed as a means even to a good end. The next quote explains why:

> ….it is never lawful, even for the gravest reasons, to do evil that good may come of it – in other words to intend positively something which intrinsically contradicts the moral order, and which therefore must be considered unworthy of man, even though the intention is to protect or promote the welfare of an individual, of a family or of society in general. Consequently, it is a serious error to think that a whole married life of otherwise normal relations can justify sexual intercourse which is deliberately contraceptive and so intrinsically wrong… *ibid., #14.*

The old principle of the end not justifying the means, if the latter are intrinsically wrong, is spelt out here again. As said earlier, when morality is weakening in any society that is the first principle to disappear: people may still seek good ends but will take moral short cuts in achieving them. Later, then, even the ends sought will also be immoral. The *meaning* of intrinsic wrong is also spelt out above again: it is something which is directly contrary to the moral order because it violates the good of human nature as constituted by God. The quote is also replying to an objection that was often raised during the contraception debate *viz* that if couples do engage in natural sex for most of their married life that that will justify them engaging in contraceptive sex on some occasions. No; each action has its own separate moral value, right or wrong, by itself.

There are indeed many situations, medical, environmental and social, which make it difficult for couples to observe what the Church teaches in the matter of family planning. Hence Pope John Paul's use of the phrase "ascetical practices" as being needed in marriage at times. Indeed, he even speaks of married couples needing *heroic* asceticism at times. That such a phrase might be used at all today in relation to married people will sound strange to many; today's society associates asceticism exclusively with monks or religious and sees no place for it in marriage. But that is simply an indicator of how hedonistic our society has become because of secularism. Nonetheless, such people will find no problem in accepting that ascetic practices are necessary for success in all other areas of life: finance, business, sport or health for examples. Indeed, they will practice great asceticism when the doctor tells them to give up some delicacy in food or when a sport's coach tells them to take on some difficult bodily exercises, yet when it comes to marriage the expectation is that it must be a thing of uninterrupted pleasure, and this even before or outside of marriage. Chastity, with the asceticism it requires, is necessary in both religious life, married life and single life but analogously different in each. That said, there can indeed e some circumstances which make marital chastity very difficult and the Church is aware of this and has always been very understanding of it. So *Familiaris Consortio* says:

> As mother, the church is close to the many married couples who find themselves in difficulty over this important point of the moral life: she knows well their situation which is often very arduous and at times truly tormented by difficulties of every kind……even in understanding its inherent values. *#33.*

The Church, being a mother, comes to the aid of couples with the wisdom of her teaching, the example of her saints and the grace of her sacraments – and there is a grace of office for every calling in life. But she does not pander to every desire of her children if they seek things which are opposed to the law of God and the dignity of human nature, a thing she holds in high regard because of the image and likeness of God in each person. And if they fall, as many will do at some time or other due to the weakness in our nature resulting from the effects of original sin, she is ever ready to extend her forgiveness. The world, by comparison, promises the false happiness that comes from self-indulgence and too often both media and government will serve as the megaphones of these promises, but when people fall in matters the *world* deems to be wrong these agencies will *not* be forgiving, ever.

The Church, while in the world, is not *of* the world and has often to be counter cultural. The Anglican communion gave up its opposition to artificial contraception with the Lambeth conference of 1930. At the same time the Catholic Church held firm on this matter with the encyclical *Casti Conubii* of Pope Pius XI and then again later with Pope Pius XII in his addresses and Pope Paul VI with his encyclical *Humanae Vitae*. What the Anglicans had done was a u-turn while the Catholic Church stayed consistently firm. Yet the former are praised for their u-turn and the latter is criticized though remaining consistent!

Arguments from Natural Law and from Personalist Philosophy

How a contraceptive act is a violation of the good of human nature can be looked at from a natural law perspective and from a personalist perspective. From the former we see that such acts artificially separate the procreative and the unitive purposes of the marriage act. This takes us back again to the ends of marriage. It should be patently obvious to anyone who has any understanding of sexuality that one and the same act naturally leads to the begetting of new life (given fertility) and naturally unites the couple with each other. I do not see how I can make this clearer. Just because we can now separate the two ends by using condoms or pills or coils it does not follow that it is morally right to do so, no more than it is morally right to drive a car through town at top speed just because we can now install engines in them which can do high speeds. What is technically or scientifically possible is not always what is morally right, and what is morally wrong will have bad effects on the common good, sooner or later.

When we do separate the two ends artificially we can have procreation without human love as for example when babies are conceived in test tubes in laboratories by *in vitro* fertilization. Take that to the extreme and what we get is Huxley's fiction, *Brave New World*, becoming reality. It is happening already, even to the point of human-animal hybrids being generated in laboratories to be killed off later for trafficking in body parts. Surely such a monstrous fruit suggests something wrong with the original principle. Then again, conversely, when the two ends are separated a couple can make what they think is "love" in a way that has no reference to new life because conception is deliberately blocked. This, then, leads on easily to the idea of same-sex love (sodomy) and then to such relationships being given the title of "marriage". Again, such an outcome says clearly that there is something very wrong with the original idea of artificially separating the two ends of the marriage act. This may be called the "naturalist" argument.

Chapter 31: Marriage Undermined

From the personalist perspective, then, we can see that the existential meaning of the marriage act, as an act of total, mutual self-giving, is falsified or contradicted by contraception. Pope John Paul is the best exponent of this argument:

> The total physical self-giving would be a lie if it were not the sign and fruit of a total personal self-giving, in which the whole person, including the temporal dimension, is present… *ibid., #11.*

With the act of intercourse the couple are saying to each other with their bodies what they said with their words at the altar on their wedding day: "I am giving myself totally and exclusively to you". "Intimacy" is another word for that kind of self-giving, and of its nature, psychologically, it has to be total and exclusive – a man does not promise his wife half of his heart for half of his life if he is sincere in his love for her. So also, with the wife from her side: she is giving of herself totally to him. The marriage act expresses all of this. But when performed in a contraceptive way it contradicts all of this by saying in one breath: "I do and I don't give myself totally to you". Thus, St John Paul says:

> …the innate language that expresses the total reciprocal self-giving of husband and wife <u>is overlaid, through contraception, by a contradictory language</u>, namely, that of <u>not giving</u> oneself totally to the other. This leads not only to a positive refusal to be open to life but also to a falsification on the inner truth of conjugal love, which is called upon to give itself in personal totality. *Ibid., #32.*

It is obvious how using a condom does this. But one might object that taking a pill does not because it allows for the uninterrupted performance of the marriage act so that it can be classed as a total self-giving. However, this is to forget that the act of intercourse finds its completion in the begetting of new life – assuming fertility – but the pill cuts this completion short artificially: it prevents the meeting of sperm and ovum or kills what might have resulted from their meeting. Hence that too is only a "half giving" at best.

Instead, the Church urges couples to use natural methods of family planning, methods which predict and make us of those cycles of the woman when she is naturally infertile.

> The choice of the natural rhythms involves accepting the cycle of the person, that is, the woman, and thereby accepting dialogue, reciprocal respect, shared responsibility and self-control. *Ibid., #32.*

It calls for respect by the husband for his wife and the maturity to be able to dialogue with her about the right time for making love. Many men are unprepared for such dialogue because they have inherited an attitude to sex from their fathers which sees it as a kind of pleasure-commodity to be enjoyed at will. These natural methods will require of both husband and wife that they discuss these matters in a way that shows a greater concern for the other spouse than for one's own immediate pleasure, and that they come to agreement as to when they will or will not have intercourse. Showing such respect and such willingness to forego one's own immediate pleasure is much more an example of love, true Christian love - because of the element of self-denial and self-sacrifice it entails - than the world's understanding of love which is selfish and often amounts to mere lust. If man is to rise above the animal and conquer his own nature, weakened as it has been by the Fall, he has to practice self-control. Christian living in general has self-sacrifice at the heart of it for the simple reason that it has the cross at the centre, and in the particular area of marriage this calls for periodic continence.

Our will was weakened by the Fall so that our bodily desires incline us to actions which exceed the measure required by virtue, and our higher nature then becomes a slave to our lower nature. Addictions of any kind are extreme examples of this. Hence it follows that only people of restraint can truly love and properly enjoy themselves. That is why the pope is so right in saying that periodic continence in marriage not only does not harm married love but actually strengthens and enhances it. Natural family planning makes this love possible. Sadly, many young men have no understanding of this at all.

An objection: is not the end aimed at here, when the naturally infertile period is used, just as "contraceptive" as when artificial methods are used? Do not both amount to the wilful prevention of new life? This is an objection that is sometimes raised against natural family planning so as to justify artificial planning. No: natural family planning is the responsible spacing of a family by availing of those times, the infertile days, when, by nature, the possibility of new life is not there to begin with to be interrupted. To say otherwise would be to suggest that a couple are bound to use the marriage act always or only for procreation. The very fact that nature has made some times of the month to be infertile answers that objection. By using those times they are co-operating with God's design for human sexuality.

I remember one time explaining these moral and psychological advantages of natural family planning to a class of students in Rome when a young English priest objected and said I was asking too much of couples and that natural family planning was not reliable anyhow. He gave the example of a couple who tried using it with the intention of having only two children and they ended up having six. But immediately a small nun from Shri Lanka put up her hand and objected to *him* by telling us that in her country she and her fellow sisters go around on bicycles to the homes of poor couples, most of whom are illiterate, and explain the different methods of natural family planning to them. Her finding was that they took to them gladly and found them very effective in most cases.

I say "in most cases" because there will never be a method of family planning, artificial or natural, which will be one hundred per cent effective in preventing all possible conception. I believe that this is God's way of reminding couples that it is He who will always have the last say in all this matter because He is the primary originator and goal of human life. But even if a couple *could* use natural methods with one hundred per cent effectiveness, so that they were able to avoid having *any* children at all, they would then be denying the primary end of marriage entirely; and if such was their intention at the time of their marriage it would nullify that marriage from the beginning.

The great Betrayal

Institutions that failed

Given the importance of the family for both Church and society one would expect that every institution in society and their agents: government, legislators, media, health agencies, social workers, clergy and married people themselves – everyone - would try to defend and promote it and the bond of marriage on which it is founded. Yet we find that since the French revolution there has been a continuous attack on the family, an attack *led* by many of these agents.

I can remember when, as a youngster going to school, a fellow student would occasionally come in to class and boast of having found a bird's nest in the hedge in some field out the road. He would claim the nest as his own even though he would do nothing more with it than look at it. However, it would sometimes happen, though very rarely, that another boy of mischievous mind would go and wreck that nest and boast of his destructive deed. But his boast would always be condemned by the others in the class and he would be put to shame as one who had destroyed the home of a little bird and her young ones. His act of destruction was a wrong that was targeting only mere birds. How much more malicious then when, at the human level, the very agencies whose duty, supposedly, is to promote the common good of society will use their energies to *undermine the family* at every turn though knowing full well the fundamental importance of the family for the overall common good?

Pope John Paul, on his visit to Ireland in 1979 said that divorce, wherever legalized, spreads "like a plague". Nonetheless, after he had left, successive Irish governments pressed ahead with legalizing it, helped by the media, and the people eventually voted for it. They rejected it in a first referendum but passed it in a second one as noted already above. It was legalized with the proviso (or supposed safeguard) of a prior four year separation period by the couple but, still, it did spread "like a plague" and the four year proviso was later whittled down to two years. It is as if people are somehow mesmerized by evil once it is legalized at all and, even though they see its bad effects, they want more of it! The abortion story in every country is similar: a little first and then the flood gates opened. Of course, the pro-divorce and pro-abortion lobbies claimed they were being "compassionate" towards individuals trapped in disastrous marriages or towards women who were over burdened by unforeseen pregnancies. In other words, they hijacked what is a Christian virtue, i.e., compassion, to serve unchristian and unnatural practices and did so even though they had been warned that the cure would prove to be worse than the disease.

There are other helps for people in such difficult situations that still stay within the bounds of the moral law. There will always be some amount of unwanted pregnancies and of marriages that will break down, but the aim of all agencies of social care should be to minimize those numbers, to bring them down to as near to zero as possible and to provide help and support then for the remainder. To break down the institution of marriage and repeal the very laws that protect life, morals and family, on the pretext of showing compassion for hard cases, only makes matters worse. It is an old saying that "hard cases make for bad law".

Priests and the Betrayal

Of the agents mentioned above which should be defending life, morals, marriage and the family one would expect that priests would be to the forefront and that they would have come out strongly in support of Pope Paul VI when he made his stand in 1968 with his encyclical *Humanae Vitae*. That pope called for this support and so also did Pope John Paul II later, making it clear that only by presenting people with the truth about human nature could priests be said to truly care for their people:

Chapter 31: Marriage Undermined

> To diminish in no way the saving teaching of Christ constitutes an eminent form of charity for souls. *Familiaris Consortio, #33*, (quoting *HV, #29*).

Obviously, theologians also would have a key role to play in presenting the Church's teaching on contraception faithfully, hence the invitation of Pope John Paul to theologians to do this:

> ... asking them to unite their efforts…with the magisterium…. to the task of illustrating ever more clearly the biblical foundations, the ethical grounds and the personalistic reasons behind this doctrine. *Ibid., #13*.

Some priests and theologians did respond positively and also some lay theologians such as Janet E Smith in the US.[1] Then there were those gallant lay couples who formed organizations for the teaching of methods of natural family to other couples, as for example, those of the *Couple to Couple* league. But, sadly, many priests did the opposite. Even though they presented themselves as living celibacy, they set themselves up as champions of the desires of lay people whom they assumed all wanted sex at all times and seasons. They were ignorant of the fact that a husband who truly loves his wife does not see in her a mere object for his pleasure but cherishes her as his life-long companion and the mother of their children, and that sex for him is not *mere* gratification – pleasurable though it be and rightly so – but an expression of his self-giving love for her. Furthermore, while claiming to abstain totally themselves, these clergy did not have the courage to ask of lay people to abstain even periodically during the naturally fertile times. It showed a scant regard for the self-control which lay people are indeed capable of with the help of grace and it raised questions in the minds of lay people as to how committed those priests were to their own vows. But they gained popularity from those others who liked being told that it was alright to follow all their desires at all times.

Then there were the many more priests who did what one might call a "nod and a wink" to papal teaching. They said only very little or nothing about it, or, if they spoke at all, presented it as an "ideal" that was attainable only by a few. Sadder still, there were whole conferences of bishops in some countries who left the popes down with statements which, if they did not outrightly reject the encyclicals, so diluted their content, by throwing everything over onto the conscience of the individual, that their content was toothless and provided no barrier for other immoral practices soon to come on stream. In England, when Cardinal Heenan was dying, he admitted that had the British clergy been united against contraception after the publication of *Humanae Vitae* they would then have been in a much stronger position to resist the onslaught of abortion in their country.

It was a great betrayal for which the Western world is now paying the price with the evils that have followed. It shows that when one instance of intrinsic evil is allowed or connived at other such evils will be sure to follow, just as with children - if one can persuade a child to steal one euro one can get him to steal ten, and then to lie so as to cover up his stealing. Then, with the "demographic Winter" of society, the West is on a path of self-destruction. Migrants from non-Western countries, mostly Muslim, see this and are rushing in to fill the empty space. Satan sure did find the Achilles heel of Western society with artificial contraception and he used it with maximum effect to destroy human life, the family, morals and virtue - things without which no civilization can survive for very long.

There are other things which contribute to the undermining of the family such as cramped or over costly housing, addictions of all sorts, unemployment, over work, the separation of work from the home, dire poverty and excessive wealth and especially pornography and more. But I focused on artificial contraception as a root cause, as the "Achilles heel" as said above.

<u>Conclusions:</u>

1. Marriage and the family are undermined by false ideologies and many other things, with artificial contraception being a major cause. Priests, legislators and all other agencies should be working to uphold this institution given its divine origin and its fundamental importance.
2. The Church's stance on artificial contraception, divorce and other things is not be seen as negativity, as a long list of prohibitions framed to kill all pleasure. It should rather be seen as her concern to safeguard the dignity of marriage, the body, the family and the common good of society because of the high value she puts on these things as coming to us from God for our good.

From looking at things that undermine marriage and the family let us now see how the priest and his pastoral team and all others can support them.

Chapter XXXII

Marriage Supported

Preparation, Ongoing Care of the Family, Different Situations

Come to the wedding. Mt. 22:5.

It devolves on priests duly trained about family matters to mature the vocation of spouses by a variety of pastoral means, by preaching God's word, by liturgical worship, and by other spiritual aids to conjugal and family life....
Gaudium et Spes, #52.

Because marriage, as the life-long union of one man and one woman, is natural and has God's blessing, even in the case of non-sacramental, valid marriages, it will endure despite all attacks. But, precisely because of the attacks, it needs to be defended and helped by everyone. In this chapter we will look at that help in terms of preparation prior to the wedding ceremony and then afterwards as provided by families themselves, by the priest and his co-workers in the parish.

Preparation for Marriage

<u>Remote Preparation</u>

Preparation for marriage begins in the home, in the earliest years of the children when their parents teach them their prayers, give them sound instruction in the Christian understanding of marriage, in the sixth commandment and in the virtues of chastity, modesty and self-giving love. Sound instruction is helped by good catechetics programs in the school, but formation in virtue comes largely from good example and moderate discipline: primarily from seeing their parents share, help, forgive and love each other in ways that show concern, that is by seeing each spouse put the other before him/herself. Good marriages are unions of virtuous people, of couples each of whom is capable of hard work, is honest, trustworthy, sincere, humble and caring, in other words, they are unions of people of character. Character endures, whereas pleasure and utility are short term. We might call this the remote preparation for marriage.

It should be obvious that, to be successful, this preparation requires the presence of both parents in the home as much as is possible, especially the presence of the mother while the children are very young. This is not to deny the right of married women to work outside the home, and sometimes a mother *has* to do this if her husband is unemployed, deceased or gone. Sometimes also she feels compelled to work to have her own money because, in a divorce culture, she lives in fear of her husband abandoning her and the family and leaving them financially destitute. No blame to such women. But children do need their mother, not just so that their biological needs can be met, such as being fed and clothed, but also so that their emotional needs for security, correction and affection can be met. The father, of course, has his part, his distinctive and inestimable part, to play in supplying those needs in a different and complementary way. Young boys who do not have the role model of a good father may take some gang leader as their model and become delinquent. But while the children are very young it is their mother they need most. A simple proof of this is that when a toddler is crying it is Mom who knows best what is wrong and later, at school going age, when the child comes home in the evening his/her first question will be "where is Mom?" Even if the house at that moment is full of other people the child will still look for Mom. When parents (or perhaps some substitutes such as aunts or uncles or grandparents) are not present, there is a danger that the emotional growth of the children will be stunted which can then lead to a development that will be deviant in different ways.

A false feminism gives priority to careering over home making for women as if the latter was something restricting or dehumanizing, as if to beget, nurture and mould the bodies and minds of one's own children was something base, and that, instead, to climb the career ladder in some company was more important. Only an ideology which has lost the true understanding of the feminine could advocate that. [1]

Yet many women have great talents for work in occupations outside the home which talents should be put to use. But why then not re-arrange work hours and practices to suit the mother who *wants* to take care of her children rather than compel her to neglect her family if she must earn money outside the home? In agricultural countries there are many farm tasks which allow the mother to have her children near her while she does them. Why not, in industrial countries, have places of work where small children of pre-school age can also be nearby, partially cared for by child-minders but still with the mother very nearby? Or why not arrange the working hours of the mother so that she can be mostly available to her children at those times when they need her most, as for example when they come in from school? Or, again, why not arrange that women with qualifications in various kinds of work can cease from those occupations for the years that the children are young and then resume them again by doing a refresher course when the children are at second level school age? It is again the old question of whether the economy is going to be reshaped to suit the normal, natural family or *vice versa*: family life stunted to suit the economy, or the company, which latter will not give a hoot if the children grow up as angry deviants with stunted emotional development. Marxism hates the family and wants the mother torn away from her own children as much as possible so that they can then be put in creches controlled by the state, thereby making it easy to indoctrinate them.

<u>Intermediate Preparation</u>

The next stage of marriage preparation might be called the "intermediate" which will continue to be a time of formation in prayer and virtue in the home and in sound catechetics in the school. Here it is necessary for parents, guided by their priests, to be vigilant against secularist programs introduced into the schools which derive the norms of morality from the consensus of the class so that objective moral standards and the notion of intrinsic evil are cast aside and replaced instead with the idea of "herd rule" or of individual feelings as the new norms. I spoke of this earlier in the *Prophet* Section above.

But to be vigilant against bad programs is not enough unless there is put in place good programs on the Catholic understanding of marriage, the virtues, especially those of modesty and chastity, and on the sixth commandment. Sadly, many supposedly Catholic programs are deficient because they water down what is Catholic in a pathetic effort to somehow go half way towards meeting the secularist way of thinking so as to suit non-Catholic pupils.

Young boys need to be taught to respect girls because, due to their immaturity, they often see nothing more in sex than the pleasure it gives, with little or no understanding of what nine months of pregnancy and childbirth entails for the girl. But the corollary of that is that girls need to be taught to respect themselves in the first place, especially in the way they dress, which is where modesty comes in, so that they don't make mere sex objects of themselves in front of boys whose emotions are strong and whose self-control is weak in those young years. For girls to reply, again, that it is their choice and that they can do what they like with their own bodies is nothing more than a correlative immaturity from their side. It is, of course, always morally wrong when a boy takes advantage of a girl, but girls too have a responsibility from their side to protect themselves.

There is also need to provide morally uplifting entertainment and sports for young people, especially for teenagers, which respect the difference of their genders. I spoke of this already also in relation to the sacrament of confirmation. Erotic music will lead to erotic behaviour, as will pornography. It is noticeable that, even with the deluge of loud, vulgar, heavy metal, rock music (so called), when a sweet song of refined taste does come on air once in a while young people take to it immediately. More than that, it has happened a few times that when monks and nuns in enclosed orders have brought out CDs of Gregorian chant that they have been great hits.

It goes without saying that anything that leads to addiction is bad as a preparation for marriage: drugs and the excesses of alcohol. I see drugs as being not just a medical or social problem but, at a deeper level, a spiritual problem, a pathetic attempt to fill the void that is in everyone when God is gone. With alcohol in some countries such as in Ireland, it is not merely a matter of some young people going to excess unintentionally but of them deliberately engaging in what is called "binge drinking" when they compete with each other as to how much they can consume in a single bout – all of this in a country which, in the first half of the twentieth century, had a strong total abstinence movement. Experience shows that such behaviour in one's teenage years will lead to addiction even in one's early twenties and is obviously not a way to prepare for marriage.

In times past girls were seldom seen in pubs or consumed alcohol at all. They were warned by their parents of the danger of being taken advantage of when their self-control was weakened by alcohol. To give the same advice today is to be accused by feminists of restricting women's freedom and of discrimination – back to the old argument again that "it is my body and I can do what I like with it". In reply, I would say to such people to go and talk to some girl who was raped, (or possibly gang raped), because brutes of men, grossly lacking in self-control, took advantage of her because she was so drunk that she scarcely knew what was happening. My reply is not based on rights or equality – I accept that people have rights and that all are equal as human beings - but on prudence, given the weakness of human nature since the Fall and the special vulnerability of women when confronted with the crude lust of some men. Given this prudence, it is indeed possible for a woman to enjoy drink in moderation in suitable company in suitable places.

A former abstinence movement, known as the *Pioneers*, had devotion to the Sacred Heart as its motivation and provided healthy kinds of entertainment for its members. Today some schools do try using educational programs to counteract alcohol abuse but, being without any religious underpinning, they have much less effectiveness, which proves the old truth that education alone does not make for virtue. Grace and example are needed also.

Proximate Preparation

The final stage of marriage preparation is the proximate stage, when a couple come to the priest to arrange for their wedding. He will direct them to do a Catholic pre-marriage course, fill up their pre-nuptial marriage form, and explain the liturgy of the wedding ceremony to them.

The pre-marriage course will need to live up to its name as "Catholic" and explain the morality of natural family planning as against the immorality of artificial methods. In that course also one would hope that experienced advisers, who are in stable marriages themselves, would be able to spot problems ahead of time as for instance when there are signs of addiction, insanity, gross immaturity, deviancy, a lack of freedom on the part of one party, or personality traits that will make for bad relations. Such traits might be impulsiveness, uncontrolled anger, or an unwillingness to forgive or compromise on the part of one person who has to be always right or is domineering. It is a sad fact, for example, that a man who is a psychopath can be very intelligent and charming, knowing how to win over his fiancé; and how she can be blind to his condition because of her infatuation, not realizing that he is so emotionally unbalanced that his delight will be in manipulating her and even in torturing her later when they are married – a marriage that will most likely be invalid to begin with depending on the severity of his condition.

Apart from such an extreme case, the marriage advisers should also look out for cases of potential incompatibility even in two people who are reasonably balanced in most other cases. For example, if a committed Catholic is going to marry a committed Muslim, both of good character and of good intentions, there is still a likelihood of trouble ahead, especially in such matters as the upbringing of the children. The Church can and sometimes does give a dispensation from disparity of cult to facilitate such marriages – so I am not suggesting that they always be prohibited from marrying – but there is a potential for trouble there which should, at least, be pointed out. Again, one can have two people of the same faith but of very unequal intelligence or of very different backgrounds so that there is a potential for trouble there also. Or again, one can have a couple one of whom is of high academic intelligence but of low emotional development and the opposite in the other party. They might complement each other, each supplying what the other lacks, but they might also be incompatible.

The very success of some people in their own careers can sometimes become obstacles in their marriages if they are not made aware of such pit falls. For example, the very efficient business man who will treat his wife as another secretary (and possibly treat his secretary as a girlfriend on the side!), or the army captain who thinks his family are soldiers under his orders, or the teacher who thinks the others in the family, husband included, are children to be put in their place and dictated to, or the politician who, in his climb to power, will trample over his family, or the man or woman whose work is going to have him/her away from home too much.

The pre-marriage course will look at the different areas of married life, medical, psychological, financial *etc.*, and also the religious. This last must underpin the others so that the couple are made to see that, ultimately, the success or failure of a marriage will depend on their recognition of God as the author of marriage, so that His laws for marriage – unity, indissolubility, fidelity *etc.*, will be taken on board by them, and of their need of His help to overcome life's problems, which help is to be had from daily prayer by the family together.

Though the marriage course might be comprehensive and sound, the priest (or his pre-marriage team) should, nonetheless, try to arrange that they come to him for a few visits so that he can get to know them better and explain the theology of marriage to them more thoroughly, those things which we have covered above on the essential properties of marriage, its ends and goods *etc*. It is not safe to assume this knowledge in most couples today. It is more prudent to assume that they are, instead, influenced in their understanding by the divorce culture they see around them. The questions in the pre-nuptial enquiry-form can serve as a format for this instruction. Very reprehensible is the practice of some priests who simply hand the form to the couple and tell them to go away and fill it in themselves. A great opportunity for much needed instruction is then lost.

The priest has to gauge the intentions and level of faith of each of the two people in the sacrament when they come to him to arrange their marriage. They are adults and should therefore have a right intention, which means that they understand that marriage was instituted by God and raised to being a sacrament by Christ and accept it as such. But, due to poor formation, they might be lacking or deficient in this regard. Pope John Paul gives the following advice:

> In fact, the faith of the person asking the church for marriage can exist in different degrees and it is the primary duty of pastors to bring about a rediscovery of this faith and to nourish it and bring it to maturity. But pastors must also <u>understand the reasons that lead the church also to admit to the celebration of marriage those who are imperfectly disposed.</u> *Familiaris Consortio, #68*

They might be hazy in their understanding or weak in their faith and may have a variety of motives for seeking a Church wedding, such as to please a parent who is a devout Catholic, but, nonetheless, positive faith is seen to be there to some degree at least, a faith which can be built on later by the help of the grace of the sacrament and by their future ongoing contact with the priest. So, the pope also says:

Chapter 32: Marriage Supported

> ...the decision of a man and a woman to marry in accordance with this divine plan...really involves, even if not in a fully conscious way, an attitude of profound obedience to the will of God, an attitude which cannot exist without God's grace. *ibid., #68.*

Take them as they are and build on that. Don't expect perfection all at once. But he also warns of situations when the priest finds the attitude of one or both to be bluntly negative:

> However, when in spite of all efforts engaged couples show that they reject explicitly and formally what the church intends to do when the marriage of baptized persons is celebrated, the pastor of souls cannot admit them to the sacrament of marriage. *ibid., #68.*

The Wedding Ceremony

When the time of the wedding draws near it is good to have a practice session in the church one or two evenings prior. It puts everyone at ease when each person knows his/her part and is clear on such simple things as when to stand or kneel or come up to read or whatever. It is, again, a good opportunity for some catechesis on this sacrament. It is also a time to remind them to avail of confession so that their marriage will not merely be valid but an occasion of grace also.

As to music, what is sung and played should be religious. The church is not a place for pop songs or secular music. I keep to this strictly because experience has taught me that to give an inch in this matter means having to give a mile very soon. I have also found that couples who, at first, seemed disappointed at being kept to this rule often said to me after the ceremony that they were glad I did so, that it made the ceremony solemn and sacred, something they appreciated.

A wedding is, of course, a thing of joy and celebration when relatives and friends who have not met for some time come together. So, there is an air of light-heartedness, which is perfectly understandable, and the priest will inevitably share in this mood. But he is nonetheless the person in charge of what is happening, and what is being celebrated is a sacrament, two sacraments, in fact, if the wedding is in the context of the Mass. It is his duty, therefore, so to order things and to preside in a way that safeguards the sacred with the solemnity that is due to the sacraments being celebrated. So, while one would hope that he will be friendly and welcoming and accommodating, he must not allow the ceremony to become jocular and flippant, which can happen if some of the guests are people who have no regard for the sacred. In this matter he also must see to it that those taking photos or making videos or arranging flowers do not take over the sanctuary as if it were merely the stage of a theatre. In my experience most of these people are respectful and compliant, but one does meet the occasional person who will tell the priest that he/she is employed by the couple and will do whatever he thinks fit. In can happen then, for example, that, a photographer (though rarely) will have lights and equipment erected obtrusively in the sanctuary and will jump around there with about the same decorum as a monkey jumping from one tree to another. His contribution to the ceremony is nothing but a distraction for everybody. Such people have to be put in their place. One way to do so is to forward their names to the bishop's office so that they will be banned from operating in all churches of that diocese in future, at least for a while.

The priest is the person in charge and should not relinquish his responsibility of maintaining order and the sense of the sacred merely for the sake of being "nice" and jovial. So also, his homily, while it might have some notes of light-heartedness, with some humorous anecdotes, should also convey some solid truths on the Christian understanding of marriage which many of those present might need to hear, especially at a time when marriage is being undermined so much. I had the practice of beginning by pointing out that we were gathered in a church because John and Mary understand that marriage is from God and that it should be lived in accordance with His design so that, at the end of their life together, they will bring each other, hand in hand, back to God from whom they came.

The Ongoing Care of the Family

The wedding day is a new beginning for the couple. There may be a long road ahead till they reach their goal of the wedding feast of the Lamb in heaven, and the priest must accompany them along that road. Each stage of their lives will have its joys but its difficulties also. The early years bring the difficulty of them adjusting to each other, a difficulty which can be greater in proportion as the couple are more advanced in years because, though they are richer in the experience of life, they are also more set in their ways. Habits are well formed by one's mid thirties so that the mutual adjustment can be difficult for a while. Then children, as they come along, or the absence of children if for some reason they cannot come along, bring their own challenges for adjustment. In the former case, love is then a triangle of relationships and no longer simply a two-way thing. Then there are the many other things that life can throw at people, what Shakespeare called "the slings and arrows of outrageous fortune", anything from sickness to unemployment to misunderstandings and more. They may want to turn to the priest for support in any of these situations or to counselling services provided by the Church. I recall a married man in a parish in the US one time who had a solid friend in his parish priest, over a long span of time. He said of him that "he was a rock in my life". Lay people also, especially those who are married, can provide great help to newly married couples and indeed to all other couples who might be struggling. When that help is organized in some structured way in a parish it can make for a very valuable apostolate.

Marriage Counselling

It is impossible here to cover the topic of counselling comprehensively. I will just mention a few things which cause problems beyond those mentioned already above and a few principles that might help in solving them.

One problem is that of high or unrealistic expectations by one or both spouses. That can be due to them having to "come down" from the "high life" they had as single persons. The difficulty can be greater if, perhaps, they were well qualified in their respective professions and used to travelling a lot and spending freely, and now have to adjust to the humdrum of being tied down by family commitments and having mortgage payments to meet. Unrealistic expectations arise also due to the influence of television where they see the lives of celebrities being presented as glamourous and full of sunshine in many films. They know full well that this is only TV fiction but, nonetheless, it has its influence, mostly subconsciously, of causing discontent: "and here am I cooped up in this small apartment with a heap of clothes to iron and listening to children crying"!

Another problem is that of an uneven intellectual or emotional level of development between the two spouses. I had a sixteen-year old girl come to me one time crying because her boyfriend, whom she "loved so much" had just got a new motor bike and he now had no interest in her. He preferred his motor bike! *He* was still at the level of a "love" of mere physical pleasure whereas *she* was at a level of emotional infatuation. But her love, being mere infatuation, rendered her immature also. Neither had got to the level of a love that was controlled by reason and will. Fortunately, they had not yet got married. Intellectual development and emotional development are different things. Sometimes a man of high intellect will marry a girl supposedly of low intellect so that he can control her and use her as a servant, or *vice versa*. But it can happen also that the person of supposedly low IQ (as measured academically) can be very emotionally mature, more practical and "down to earth", much more so than the person of supposedly high IQ who is "up in the clouds".

I remember a case of a wife who was a very mature and balanced woman emotionally and of good intelligence also. She had married a man of very high intellect in matters such as mathematics and especially finance, but emotionally he was a delinquent of only fourteen years of age and still enjoyed playing the kind of pranks that such young lads play. That marriage was more like a mother and child relationship. The wife was able to control him like a child and he was happy to have her make decisions for him. The problem there is that such a woman is likely to get tired of "mothering" such a child after a few years and may throw him over for a more mature man.

Emotional development never really ends so that people of immature emotions can grow in time due to life's experiences in most cases, though that did not happen in this particular case. Thus, in the natural course of development, we see the daft teenager become a solid responsible person in a few years, or the deviant person become more normal. Same-sex attraction, for example, is mostly a matter of arrested emotional development, but the individual *can* be brought on from there to a fuller development and to more healthy attractions directed to persons of the opposite sex.

Another problem is that of two people who have inherited wrong, subconscious, pre-set ideas of what marriage is all about. I once heard the famous English marriage counsellor, Jack Dominian, tell the story of a couple who came to him with the "major" problem that they could not agree on whether the window of their bedroom should be open or closed at night! The disagreement began the very first night of their marriage and continued each night after that and had them near to killing each other by the time they came to him for counselling. She wanted the window closed because her Mom said that that was best, but he wanted the window open because the room was small and they needed air, and such was always the way in *his* home. Mr. Dominian startled them both when he told them that the window was *not* the problem at all even though they had both agreed that it was, and had made that clear to him. So, they asked him what then it might be. He proceeded to ask them what marriage was about: was it about who would dominate whom or was it about caring and sharing? They agreed reluctantly that it was about the latter. Then he pointed out to them that they each had come from a family in which one parent was dominant, the mother in the case of the girl, the father in the case of the man, and that they were each going to prolong this domination in this their new marriage. In other words, they were each determined that their new marriage was going to begin as a battle of wills to establish from the outset just who was going to be the boss in their home. But, should they manage to change their attitudes and agree instead that it should be about caring and sharing and making sacrifices, each for the good of the other, then they might be able to take a very different approach to what they thought was their "major" problem. The end of that story is that on their next night in bed the girl was insisting that the window stay open to please *him* and he was insisting that the window stay closed to please *her*! And, may we assume that, as they old saying goes, "they lived happily ever after"!²

Unravelling the Problem

When there is a problem, it is usually the wife who will make the first approach to the priest or the counsellor to look for help. She usually has a greater sense of the need to hold the family together, especially when there are young children. She comes along with a story of neglect or abuse or addiction at the hands of her husband. But there is another old saying that "there are two sides to every story" so that the counsellor should not take just one side uncritically. He should try to meet both parties and get a fuller picture. Sometimes it happens that the husband is immature and unable to face up to the responsibilities of a new family. He is a "brave" man when in the company of his "buddies" in the pub or at a football match and is weak and irresponsible when he no longer has their company around him. He does not know how to relate to his new wife at a level deeper than the physical and runs back to the pup or the club for the support he can have there. When a new child comes along, the wife, if she is also immature, gives all her affection to the child and may even expect the same in return from the child! The husband sees this and decides that she has no affection for *him* any more, and may even see the child as a rival for his affection. This, then, drives him more definitely again towards the pup and to drinking more, which, in turn puts a strain on the family finances and reinforces the wife's belief that he is a bad husband. A downward spiral of immaturity is now pulling that marriage down to near breaking point. So, the counsellor must help them to see this.

Getting a person or a couple to see their problem can be difficult. Take the case of the man whose problem is uncontrolled anger. Just tell him that such is his problem and he will fly into a rage – proof in itself of the problem though he still may not admit it. Direct talking is sometimes the only way to spell out what the problem is, but it is better if people can be brought, by discussion and pointed observations, to see the problem for themselves. That is what Jack Dominian succeeded in doing in the story above.

So, we can say then that the first rule in marriage counselling is to listen and, as one counsellor told me, the second rule is to listen even more and the third rule is to listen more again! The idea is that they, in talking, will unearth the problem, when probed by pertinent questions from the counsellor. They may well know what it is subconsciously but might be unable to articulate it. If the counsellor blurts out his diagnosis or his solution after a short few minutes of a chat – because he might well be able to see the problem speedily and clearly from his long experience – they will indeed hear his words but may still not "see" or "get" the point. Instead, one spouse will more likely turn to the other and say: "do you hear what the counsellor is telling you - just what I was trying to tell you all along" but without seeing his own contribution to the problem at all.

There are parallels between the spiritual and the material. When the doctor sees a surface injury such as an open wound he can prescribe or treat it immediately. But if it is an *internal* problem it will mean questioning and examination, and the solution may not be a simple prescription but a long-term treatment plan of diet or exercises. With marriage problems it is more like the latter. The counsellor does not usually have a ready prescription up his/her sleeve. He diagnoses in a way that enables the couple to see the problem for themselves and then enables them to see what changes or adjustments they themselves must make if their marriage is to get back on a good footing. One could say that he "elicits" both the problem and the solution from the couple. But if the solution that either of them "arrives at" is clearly morally wrong then the counsellor must point that out even though he cannot *compel* them to follow a morally good solution.

It can happen at times, unfortunately, that after the wife has made contact with the counsellor, and the counsellor, then, has a session with both spouses, that the husband indicates that he has no further interest in the marriage and is not willing to try any solution. This is bad news because, just as a marriage is brought into being by the will of the two people, so also its continued success requires the committed will of the two.

Violence in a relationship is, of course, another bad sign. But there are certain categories of people, often people of very low literacy rates, where the "physical" is the "order of the day". They sort out their differences with violence but, then, they can also be very physical when showing affection shortly after. Nonetheless, violence is never to be *condoned* between spouses or even regarded as good at all, even if it is "normal" with some people.

When a husband or indeed a wife decides that a marriage is not worth saving there can be a number of reasons at root. It can be a case of sheer pig-headedness or selfishness by one spouse. It can also be a case of a spouse declaring that he or she is no longer finding "fulfilment" in the marriage, as if the personal fulfilment of the individual were the sole purpose or criterion of marriage, in total disregard of the other spouse or the children. Yet this happens in countries that have become secularist. It is very difficult for the counsellor to deal with this because such a problem takes us to the meaning of marriage as being not just a social or psychological institution but as something religious at root. Put differently, marriage counselling is not a therapy that any counsellor can practice totally independent of religious belief. This is because dedication to marriage, as a life-long commitment, poses the question as to *why* an individual should continue with such a commitment if he/she is no longer deriving a high amount of material gain or bodily pleasure or some other kind of worldly benefit from it. It is religion alone that can provide an answer to that: God has willed it so, and one's commitment to one's spouse is part of one's deeper commitment to God and to what He asks of people in marriage. This may sometimes be very rewarding, indeed, in worldly terms but at other times it may be very difficult and thus demanding of great sacrifice by each for the other. The sacrifices they will need to make can be made fruitful and even joyful if seen in light of Christ's sacrifice for His bride, the Church, on the cross and are offered to Him in the Mass. That said, there are situations nonetheless where a separation, for a while at least, is necessary though the bond still remains.

In all of this the counsellor cannot put his Catholic moral principles to one side and pretend to be non-judgemental when the root of so many marriage problems are religious and moral one way or another. To say otherwise is one other attempt to push God out of one more area of life, this time out of marriage. Also, most of his clients will have some moral background to begin with so that advice along moral lines will not come as a surprise to them.

Counselling and Psychology

Counsellors are sometimes people of little formal training but nonetheless are intelligent, have insight and are good-living in their own lives and marriages; and because of their intuition and practical experience they can be very good at helping other couples. I knew of one Cistercian lay brother who had never been married himself but who had a talent or charism for marriage counselling, and, though he lived in an enclosed monastery, would often be sought out by couples for his advice. Nonetheless, some formal training is to be recommended.

That training would have the would-be counsellor go to some school of counselling which usually follows the teaching of some well-known psychologist: Freud or Jung or Adler or whoever. There are advantages in this but disadvantages also and dangers. Freud, for example, drew new attention to the whole area of the subconscious which, in turn, gave rise to great advances in psychotherapy when counsellors learned how to unearth traumas and injuries which were buried in the subconscious and were still causing problems in the patient's conscious mind until brought to light. But Freud was an atheist, so he did not see man as a being in the image and likeness of God nor, therefore, would he see conscience as the voice of God in the innermost sanctuary of the soul indicating sin, or sin as an offense against God. He saw man as a bundle of drives seeking satisfaction, the sex drive being the most prominent, and the super ego – which for him was much the same as social conditioning - as that which kept the various drives in control so that they would not become destructive. There is an underlying philosophy of man here, an anthropology, which is not properly Christian. So, yes, there is a certain amount to be learned in such a school of counselling, especially as regards the power of the subconscious, but it must be evaluated against the teaching of a school of psychology that gives a full and true account of man that is properly Christian, which school must have a true philosophy or anthropology as its basis.

If the school of psychology is that of Adler and his theory of the "will to power" as being fundamental one could say that, in the case of the couple above who were quarrelling over whether the window should be open or closed, a counsellor steeped in this psychology might insist that this was a battle of wills which could only be resolved by one party being the complete victor over the other, which would then, of course, be destructive of a *true* marriage relationship; or, perhaps, he might see this and counsel against it as Jack Dominian did in the story. But in that case would the councillor be contradicting his own school of psychology?

Thomism provides the best psychological basis because its philosophical anthropology is true to begin with. It sees man as made in the image and likeness of God with a soul that is rational and therefore on a higher level than that of the other animals so that intellect and will can or should rule over the desires and emotions and make for a harmony in human life. It sees conscience as the voice of God in the sanctuary of the heart, something that can be misinformed indeed, but which rises above mere social conditioning. It also takes account of the fact of an original Fall which has disrupted this harmony so that man needs self-discipline and, more than that, the help of grace from above, so as to live a balanced life and thus be prepared for union with God in glory in the next life. With Christ's way of loving as its model, it sees that it is in self-giving rather than in self-indulgence that true happiness is to be found even though, of course, refined pleasure is necessary in the lives of emotional beings, such as we humans are, and a source of joy.

The Care of Families in different Situations

<u>Mixed Marriages</u>

Because man comes from God, is in the image and likeness of God, and is called to return to God at the end of life, religion is the deepest thing in him. This is true whether people want to admit to it or not. Indeed, the very obsession that atheists have with denying the existence of God strongly suggests that God, their non-existent God, *does* exist after all; otherwise why would He be such a great problem for them?! Put differently, if God does not exist, atheists should not exist either! If, then, people are divided on the ground of religion by holding conflicting doctrines, the division will be serious, more so than divisions of race, culture, nationality or other things which also arouse emotions. In a mixed marriage there are some differences, large or little, depending on how close or far the religion of the non-Catholic party is in relation to the Catholic religion. Accordingly, mixed marriages can be troublesome or they can be very happy and successful, depending on how these differences are handled. Problems can arise in the matter of the baptism of the children or the Church they will attend on a Sunday. The Catholic party is asked to do all in his/her power to bring up *all* the children in the Catholic faith, and the reaction of the other party is to be sought. Sometimes the reaction is positive before the marriage but negative afterwards and then there can be serious quarrels. To settle the matter by having the boys brought up in one religion and the girls in the other is for the Catholic party to say that he/she is *content* that some of the children will *not* be brought up in the true faith. That is difficult and painful for a sincere Catholic and the Church does not accept this compromise.

To avoid any quarrels over religion the couple will sometimes take refuge in a false kind of ecumenism which pretends that there are no doctrinal or moral differences, anyhow, between the many religions that we find around us today, that sincerity is the all-important thing, so that differences of doctrine do not matter. But this implies that Christ did *not* found only *one* Church and hence that there is no obligation on anyone to seek the one, true Church or to stay in it when found. This is the ecumenism of indifferentism which soon leads to loss of faith, agnosticism and secularism, if not in the parents themselves then, more likely, in the children later on. The priest is not to encourage anything of the sort. Instead, St John Paul says:

> It is of the greatest importance that, through the support of the community, the catholic party should be strengthened in faith and positively helped to mature in understanding and practicing that faith, so as to become a credible witness within the family through his or her own life and through the quality of love shown to the other spouse and the children… the contribution they can make to the ecumenical movement. *Familiaris Consortio, #78.*

The priest should try to strengthen the Catholic party in his/her faith so that he will practice it with a maturity that will provide a credible witness to the other party of the truth and beauty of the faith, all done with respect and charity and never with arrogance or compulsion. The pope does not go on from there even to suggest that such a Catholic should impose his/her faith on the other party. He was a great defender of religious freedom and, in matters such as this, his method was "to propose but not to impose", (as we saw earlier with catechetics) to propose by the good example that flows from sincere faith in true doctrine rather than to try to force conscience in any way. If the other party is a Christian of any denomination it is likely that he/she will have a fondness for scripture and will enrich the faith of the children by reading Bible stories to them. But an indiscriminate hopping back and forth between Catholic Mass and other church services of other religions on different Sundays is not to be recommended even though ecumenical gatherings are.

Free Unions or Cohabitants

Today, with the breakdown of the family and of morals, free unions of couples have increased and, sadly, some priests accept this as a new kind of "normal" so that at funeral Masses, for example, they will openly refer to the dead person's "partner" as if cohabitation is a state of life now officially recognized by the Church as a morally right way of living. Indeed, not to do so is seen as a snub or a kind of discrimination. Then there is the recommendation that priests should "accompany" such couples on their life's journey as if all is fine. But if objectively they are living in a state of ongoing fornication, that can hardly be said to be "fine", as we saw earlier above. This was not the line of pastoral approach of St John Paul II:

> The pastors and the ecclesial community should take care to become acquainted with such situations (as free unions) and their actual causes, case by case. They should make tactful and respectful contact with the couples concerned, and enlighten them patiently, correct them charitably and show them the witness of Christian family life, in such a way as to smooth the path for them to regularize their situation. The people of God should also make approaches to the public authorities..........to try to ensure that public opinion is not led to undervalue the institutional importance of marriage and the family. *ibid., #81.*

The other extreme is to berate or scold or publicly humiliate such couples. It is clear from the above that neither was this the approach of the pope. They should be tactfully brought back onto the path of upright, moral living by separating or by marrying soon and be assured of the continuing support of the Church.

Those Divorced or in Second Unions

Due to the confusion arising from improper catechesis it happens, at times, that a woman civilly divorced may think she is barred from receiving Communion or even that she is excommunicated while, in fact, she is still living in faithfulness to a marriage which is still valid in the eyes of God but broken down. She may even have been divorced and abandoned against her will. Pope John-John Paul says the following to pastors and all others as to how they should treat such people:

> I earnestly call upon pastors and the whole community of the faithful to help the divorced, and with solicitous care to make sure that they do not consider themselves as separated from the church, for as baptized persons they can, and indeed must, share in her life. They should be encouraged to listen to the word of God and to attend the sacrifice of the mass, to persevere in prayer, to contribute to works of charity and to community efforts in favour of justice, to bring up their children in the Christian faith, to cultivate the spirit and practice of penance and thus implore day by day, God's grace. Let the church pray for them, encourage them and show herself a merciful mother, and thus sustain them in faith and hope. *ibid., #84.*

Sometimes a civilly divorced person is one who has found out that his/her marriage is invalid in the eyes of God on some ground or other and gets a Church annulment but cannot get a civil annulment on those same grounds due to the civil law of that country. So, his/her only way to rectify the situation is to get a civil divorce knowing that this is not the dissolution of a marriage bond valid in the eyes of God (because the union was not a valid marriage to begin with) but the dissolution of a civil union, recognized by the state indeed, in order to be civilly free to marry validly in a second union which will also be valid in the eyes of God.

Some people, when civilly divorced, enter a second union which they call a "marriage" even though in the eyes of God their first marriage is still valid. The Church cares for those people also and encourages them to continue coming to Mass and to engage in various parish activities. But she does not allow them to receive Communion unless they can live as brother and sister. The pope explains why:

> However, the church re-affirms her practice, which is based upon sacred scripture, of not admitting to Eucharistic Communion divorced persons who have remarried. They are unable to be admitted thereto from the fact that their state and condition of life objectively contradict the union of love between

Christ and the Church which is signified and effected by the Eucharist. Besides this, there is another special pastoral reason: if these people were admitted to the Eucharist, the faithful would be led into error and confusion regarding the church's teaching about the indissolubility of marriage. *ibid., #84.*

Note that in saying this the pope refrains from commenting on their subjective state of soul before God; such people are sometimes unaware of the irregularity of their situation, not knowing the difference between Church and civil law on marriage. But when the priest in a friendly, private conversation explains the difference to them and the irregularity of their situation the question of their subjective guilt does arise if they continue to live and engage with each other as a married couple. Though final judgement on the state of anyone's soul lies with God, this does still not allow the couple themselves to have the final say on whether or not to approach the altar for Communion. It is the duty of the priest to uphold the discipline of the Church on this matter.

To suggest that such couples can be admitted to the sacraments is to make for a rupture, a discontinuity, with Church tradition, a tradition which we can see from the quote above has its basis in scripture (*1 Cor. 11:27*). Couples openly known to be in so called "same-sex marriages" cannot, likewise, be admitted to Communion. There can be no analogy at all between their relationship and that of Christian marriage and what the latter signifies. But they too need the ongoing care of the Church, again, a care which points out to them the irregularity of their situation and helps steer them to a life of chastity and, hopefully, to normal relations with people of the opposite sex so that heterosexual marriage may become a real possibility for them if they should choose that.

It is a good thing for a priest to organize a Mass once a year for validly married couples who are celebrating a significant anniversary, for those who are five or ten or twenty or more years married, and to have a function afterwards at which they can share experiences, or to put on talks or refresher days for couples at significant stages.

One last category of people who must not be forgotten when talking of marriage are those who remain unmarried throughout their lives for one reason or another. The pope wants them too to find a welcome in the great family of the Church:

There are others who for various reasons have been left alone in the world…for those who have no natural family the doors of the great family which is the church…must be opened ever wider". *ibid., #85.*

Priestly celibacy has a number of different meanings. One of those is that it is a sign of the availability of the priest, and hence of the Church which he represents, for those who are alone and perhaps are marginalized or have few relations of their own to care for them. One thinks here of the old and the bereaved. When they come to the priest they should know that he is fully available for them because he does not have the commitments of a natural family of his own and can see in them members of the family of God in the Church, the bride of Christ, in this parish entrusted to his care.

Conclusions:

1. Remote preparation for marriage begins in the home when children, future spouses, are brought up with sincere affection, gentle discipline, and sound instruction by parents who can love each other in a Christian, self-giving way to begin with. Intermediate preparation takes place in the home also and in the school with good catechesis, growth in virtue and wholesome entertainment. Proximate preparation takes place in the lead up to the marriage ceremony which can also be a time for further catechesis on marriage as a sacrament and the kind of commitment it entails.
2. Physical attraction and emotional fulfilment have their place in bringing a couple together and in bringing joy to their marriage afterwards but virtue and character in both spouses is of paramount importance, that they be loyal, honest, hardworking, willing to forgive and make sacrifices for each other and their children. *Eros* then leads on to *agape*.
3. After the wedding in the church, the priest and his pastoral marriage team have an important role in bringing couples along in their journey towards the wedding feast of the Lamb but they must do so by trying to have them take account of the marriage laws of the Church especially when dealing with situations that are irregular.

The care of marriage has an objective that lies beyond this life because it should lead the couple to the wedding feast of the Lamb in the next life. We will next see what things will help achieve this goal.

Chapter XXXIII

Marriage in the Wider View

Bring God back, Housing, Media, Legislation, The Way Forward, Spirituality

The marriage of the Lamb has come and his bride has made herself ready. Rev 19:7.

Do not tolerate any legislation which would introduce into the family practices which are opposed to the natural and divine law – for the family is the primary unit of the state. *Humanae Vitae, #23.*

What we have said above on the ongoing care of marriage and the family could be described as "particular" in the sense that it deals with the priest and his team of counsellors in their care of particular couples at particular stages of their lives: the preparation stages before marriage and then in their different situations of joy or difficulty afterwards. But all who are concerned for marriage, given its foundational importance for the wellbeing of society and of the Church as a whole, should stand back and see the wider picture so as to be able to evaluate the deeper causes underlying the problems we have mentioned already, thus enabling them to promote the deeper solutions, because it is an institution of such fundamental importance. Not to do that is to like a doctor curing this illness and that in a given patient but not seeing to the overall or underlying conditions bearing on the health of the patient: his living conditions, his work situation, his general lifestyle and the many other influences to which he is subject so as to be able to decide if some deeper, overall change is needed in his life. This chapter will try to get to some of these deeper causes and propose some solutions.

God absent and restored

<u>Restore God</u>

We have posited the advance of secularism as the root cause of the undermining of the family, which secularism amounts to atheism whether official, as in communist countries, or practical as in much of the Western world. When God is pushed aside, then, just about any new reconfiguration of marriage is possible or its reduction to any and every kind of promiscuous relationships or its elimination entirely. The solution then, obviously, is to put God back into the picture again, and give Him back His rightful place in society, law, culture, education *etc.*, and in the family. Otherwise, the priest, like the doctor above, is only tinkering around with a crumbling institution, trying to patch it up here and there as he comes across broken or disjointed families in his visitation of homes. That is a tall order in today's world given the many influences at work to push God aside. God, who never abandons His people, will indeed reassert Himself in His own way in His own good time but He invites our cooperation in His plan of salvation. To put God back must mean a call to people to return to His Church also because there we find His authoritative voice on earth. So where do we begin? There are various steps to be taken in doing this, one might say steps that reverse or counter the false steps the West has been taking for a long time now. To do so does not mean attempting to return to some imagined golden age long gone, be it that of the Middle Ages or apostolic times; no, it means to draw principles and truths from the heritage of Judaism and Catholicism and give them fresh application in the world of today, somewhat like the scribe in the gospels drawing out things new and old from his storehouse.

I would say to start with straightforward preaching and renewed catechetics: the priest and the teacher telling the world that God exists and that His design for the family is the best design and thus the only design that will bring peace, stability and happiness - as far as that is attainable in this life. They have to hold up that design of one man married to one woman in a life-long, exclusive relationship as the goal to aim at, not just as an ideal for the perfect but as something achievable for all with the help of the grace of God. That was God's design at the beginning and it is still His design now and will be until the end. To propose anything less is to settle for some kind of compromise that will not work, a state of affairs for which we have evidence in abundance by now.

Christian Families witnessing to God

As to God's very existence we can and should come forward with philosophical proofs which are valid for people of open, reasoning minds. But according to Pope John Paul, one of the most compelling proofs for God is the lives of the saints – and he was one himself – and especially the witness of the martyrs. They gambled *all* on their convictions about God. So also, following on this line, since this chapter is all about the family, I would argue that another great "advertisement" for God is the example of the truly Christian family, of even a small few families who are living in accordance with God's plan for the family as that is to be found in the teaching of His

Church. A Catholic couple with a relatively large-sized family in which all the members pray, care, share and make sacrifices for each other is a beautiful thing, a divine thing, because it is the domestic Church, the Church in the home. There is always life and fun, as well as problems and tears, in such a family. There is never a dull moment. But they trust in providence and bring their joys and sorrows to God in prayer. This is most evident when they kneel down together at night round the fireside to say the rosary. Then the hearthstone becomes their altar, the fire lighting on it becomes the symbol of their daily sacrifices, the smoke going up, the symbol of their prayer, with the parents taking the place of the priests and the children being the congregation. (*cf. Lumen Gentium*, St John Chrysostom and St Augustine on this). More than being a *symbol* of the Church, we can say that such a family *is* the Church itself alive in this its smallest unit. It is evident again when they all march out to Sunday Mass together.

It is my strong claim that such families, even if small in number to begin with, *are the best antidote to the cold, selfish, impersonal secularism of our time, that, speaking more positively, they are a great witness to the truth of the Church's teaching on the family and a proof for the existence of God Himself as the one who instituted the Christian family because it is His goodness which is reflected in a good family*. Each such family is a miniature of the universal Church in the home and a light to set ablaze again what St John Paul used to refer to as a "civilization of love".

But such families need the teaching and pastoral support of their priests and, in providing them with that, priests can point to the example of the early Christians and, after them, they can make use of the writings of great preachers such as St John Chrysostom and St Augustine amongst the Fathers. The writings of Chrysostom are so relevant and contemporary that one would think he was writing only yesterday. The writings of Augustine show forcefully the power of concupiscence due to his own life experience of sin and hence the need for the help of grace. In more recent times, then, we have the encyclicals, mentioned in the previous chapter, of popes such as Pius XI, St Paul VI and St John Paul II who wrote so much on marriage especially in his *Theology of The Body*, a series of catechetical talks he gave in his Wednesday audiences in 1981.

But still more is needed by way of practical support if we are to have such Christian families giving such witness of God and the beauty of the family as God designed it. In reversing the steps which the West has been taking for more than two centuries certain institutions or agents, which hitherto have been undermining the family, need to be redirected to supporting the family. Intellectually the ideologies of today need to be purified and restored to their Christian roots. This is a task for preachers and the institutions of learning. This we have seen already when talking about the slogans of the French revolution. But there are other agents also: the state has responsibility for things like suitable housing, home-based work and legislation based on the natural law.

The media also have a great influence in all of this. We will look first at things the state can do and later the media.

The State and the Family

Suitable Housing

It should be obvious that the living conditions of a married couple are important; will they be stuffed into a small apartment in a block of high-rise flats in the centre of a big city or will they be able to afford a modest-size house in a suburban or rural area with a little ground surrounding it in which children can play and be safe? From time immemorial people, especially young people, have tended to gravitate towards the big city in the hope of finding adventure, better opportunities and more money there. Some achieve these things – and we hear of their great successes - but many also go to the wall there of whom we hear little until they do something drastic. It is also a fact that all social problems – including loneliness, paradoxically, – are greater in the big city. Then, there is the anomaly of huge cities that sprawl outwards for miles and miles while all around there is ground that is unpopulated for the want of a water supply. One could argue that the big city is one of the worst of all social developments in history.

To counter act these trends the *Distributist Movement* arose, founded by a Dominican priest, Fr Vincent McNabb in England in the early twentieth century, which tries to break down the big city into smaller units or take people out of the city and resettle them in simple, affordable housing in rural villages spread around in the countryside. I fully support such a movement as something which, I believe is of benefit to the family.[1] I would like to see the state give more support to this movement.

Work and the Home

Another phenomenon, causally linked to this concentration of people in the big city, which has had a negative impact on marriage and the family, is the divorce we have today between work and home, something that has been happening since the industrial revolution. In agricultural times husband, wife and children were together most of the time working on the land or around the house with a division of labour that gave each member his/her task: the man looked after the crops, the animals and the machinery and the woman looked after the house, the meals and the hens, and both helped with the milking of the cows and the saving of the hay. The children also helped with these jobs as befitted the boys and the girls respectively. There was also small-scale, home or cottage industry such as hand-powered looms for making garments from wool which was collected from one's own sheep in the fields nearby.

But then, with the industrial revolution, came big technology, such as looms powered by water or steam, which had to be located in big factories which, in turn had to be located in big cities. This led to a split between home and the work-place. Today some commute from the country to the city every day, but, even when the whole family migrates to the city, home and work are still two different places and often husband and wife work in different locations away from each other for long hours. The children then are put into creches or put on school busses so that the family see very little of each other in the course of the day. The cost of buying or renting an apartment in or near the bit city, an apartment which is empty for most of the day, necessitates that both parents have to go out to work. As a solution to this Pope John Paul says:

> … a renewed "theology of work" can shed light upon and study the in depth meaning of work in the Christian life and determine the fundamental bond between work and the family, and therefore the original and irreplaceable meaning of work in the home and in rearing children. Therefore, the church can and should help modern society by tirelessly insisting that the work of women in the home be recognized and respected by all in its irreplaceable value…that wives and mothers are not in practice compelled to work outside the home and that their families can live and prosper in a dignified way even when they themselves devote their full time to their own family. *Familiaris Consortio, #23*.

Now that the industrial revolution is giving way to the IT revolution and technology can be made smaller, even as it becomes more complex, and people can communicate remotely by internet, the idea of work coming back into the home again is emerging as a real possibility so that the family can be together again. The covid pandemic of 2019 -2022 made this a reality in many places at least for a while. This too is something I fully support. There could also be a kind of hybrid arrangement between the factory and the cottage if the factory is nearby so that mothers could bring their children with them to work or so that they could work lesser hours which would enable them to be home with their children more of the time as said in the previous chapter.

One other help would be to give the mother in the home a wage so that she will not have to leave the house for work for economic reasons. It would also mean that the state was recognizing the value of what she is doing in the home for the common good by raising children who will be all the more secure, mature, balanced, formed in virtue and generally happy for having had the advantage of being close to their mother in their earliest years. Instead of that, and most foolishly, some governments give this money to parents to pay for *out-of-home child care*, the aim here again being to separate mother from child so that the child will be in state run creches where they can be indoctrinated, socialist style, from their earliest years.

Legislation and the Family

Then there is the support which the family can receive from good legislation. Here again, laws do not only regulate behaviour but influence it as well because, when we legalize something, we are saying that we approve of it as being conducive to the common good and so as good in itself.

It is not the function of civil law to ban every evil or to enforce every good because to attempt such would be impossible. But, nonetheless, law should not, at the very least, militate *against* good morals and or make virtue impossible. It should not legalize what is immoral. Civil law might not be able to effectively ban some evil practices which are harmful to the common good – prostitution is the usual example – without provoking greater evils in the process. But such things should never be positively approved of by legislation.

There is also the situation where good legislators who want to ban a certain evil completely – abortion for example – are only able to achieve a reduction for the time being. They can vote for this reduction or restriction as the best deal available to them for the present while making clear their total opposition to the said evil. (*cf.* John Paul II, *Evangelium Vitae*). But for the state to positively legalize any behaviour which is intrinsically immoral is for it to use the authority it has from God to give approval to something *forbidden* by God – a contradiction but one still not admitted by many legislators. The state is then also defeating its own purpose of promoting the common good because the latter is never served by immoral legislation because such legislation contradicts the truth about man as an individual and as a social being. In brief, it will contradict God's design for human nature as can be read from natural law or as it is explicitly spelt out in divine law. Hence, Pope Paul VI made the following plea to legislators, in his encyclical *Humanae Vitae* which, as we have seen, dealt mostly with contraception, but his words have general application wider than that:

> And so, we would like to speak to Rulers of Nations, because to them most of all is committed the responsibility of safeguarding the common good, and they can contribute so much to the preservation of morals. Do not ever allow the morals of your people to be undermined. <u>Do not tolerate any legislation which</u>

<u>would introduce into the family practices which are opposed to the natural and divine law</u> – for the family is the primary unit of the state. *HV, #23.*

One might object that practices such as contraception, abortion and divorce are so entrenched now that they are seen as civil rights so that any attempt to de-legalize them would be impossible. But if it was lobbying by minorities with support from the media in the past that made these things appear as good and as civil rights, even though the majority saw them to be morally wrong and socially harmful prior to that, why could not a similar counter influence, using the same media, bring about a reversal of thinking, and that, perhaps, more easily now when we have had time to see the bad fruits borne by such evil trees? In the case of abortion, for example, should it not be easy now to point to the similarity there exists between that kind of killing, which goes on in nearly every country in the West, with the killing that went on in the concentration camps of World War II? In the case of contraception we now see its bad medical and social and demographic side effects and how it gives increase to the migrant problem. Again, if also today we hear cries to protect the growth cycles of mother earth should it sound strange then if the world were to hear a new cry to protect the fertility cycles of mother woman?

Pope John Paul, following on Pope Paul, knew that legislators are influenced by their constituents so that the duty of giving legal protection to marriage and of promoting the well- being of the family is a responsibility not just of legislators but of *all* citizens, which includes families themselves also. They, especially families, should actively campaign for good, pro-life and pro-family legislation. So, the pope says:

> …families should be the first to take steps to see that the laws and institutions of the State not only do not offend but support and positively defend the rights and duties of the family…families should grow in awareness of being "protagonists" of what is known as "family politics" and assume responsibility for transforming society; <u>otherwise families will be the first victims of the evils that they have done no more than note with indifference</u>. *Familiaris Consortio, #44.*

In giving this witness lay people, families and then legislators, need a lead and encouragement from their pastors. It is a bit rich of some pastors to sit back and stay silent while expecting small bands of pro-family campaigners and the small, few, committed Christian legislators who might be a minority in parliament to "save the day" for the family. The backlash from the secularists, which will come inevitably, will then hit *them*, the pro-family people, while the pastors can keep their heads down behind a wall of silence and continue to be secure in their *imagined* popularity.

I knew of one case when a priest questioned a legislator about the immorality of what he was legalizing – in this case the availability of condoms for young people. The latter, the legislator, turned round and asked the priest, what *he* and his colleagues in the clergy had been doing for the past forty years if they were really concerned about upholding good morals. He was asking if they, the priests, had been asleep all this time? They had ample opportunity in their preaching every Sunday in the days when churches were full to instil good pro-family morals in their people. So why had they not done so? It was a good question because many priests – though not *all* by any means - had done nothing other than, perhaps, direct people to a website of the bishops where a statement on some issue being proposed for legalization could be found. The issues at hand, be they the proposed availability of condoms for young people, or the availability of divorce or abortion or civil unions for people who are not validly married, or whatever, would be "debated" i.e., "promoted", in the media in a most one-sided way; and yet the response from some clergy was so often one of a near total silence. In some cases this was due to a fear of the inevitable backlash, with Church scandals being thrown at them. In other cases it was due to a false, pastoral sensitivity that wished not to "offend" people who are behaving immorally. In other cases still is was a matter of using the pretext of "engaging in dialogue with the world" in so polite and genteel a way that truth and right had to take a back seat.

But some bishops and priests did speak out: the best example being Cardinal Woytyla in Poland when he was archbishop of Krakow and there was also Archbishop McNamara in Dublin in the 1980s and a few others. The former had prepared a generation of young people in Poland to stand up to the anti-family propaganda of the communists of his time with his *Theology of the Body*.

When pro-family people challenge legislators who are intent on passing anti-family legislation the latter will reply and say that, when framing their legislation, they do not base it on any religious tradition but merely on the wishes of those who elected them, the majority of whom – they may admit – are Christian but who want this legislation nonetheless. Or they may say, with unashamed hypocrisy, that they are personally against this legislation but do not want to impose their Christian views on others who *do* want it, even if these others are a minority. How strange that the *anti*-family people have no scruples about imposing *their* views on those who still hold Christian beliefs, even when the latter are the majority! They will say that these practices, which the Church might consider to be immoral, are now prevalent among "the faithful" and cannot be stopped, so they must be regulated with this legislation, immoral though it be in the eyes of the Church. That these legislators are using their authority which comes from God to legalize what God has forbidden does not even cross their minds no more than the "faithful" who ask them to do this are aware of how "unfaithful" they are. But many priests do not point out this contradiction to their flock.

Vatican II did indeed call for dialogue with the modern world, and it should be a respectful dialogue, but not one which stays silent or goes soft when fundamental human rights or moral issues are at stake. (*cf. Gaudium et Spes, #76*). Surely a priest should be able to frame his words in such a way that he can spell out clearly what is right and wrong without making direct reference to individual persons or parties or saying derogatory things about them. Due to these failures on the side of the clergy and the persistence of those on the other side (often a minority but with great assistance from the media) immoral legislation on various issues got passed in many supposedly Christian countries which had the effect of weakening morality generally and then, in time, the dogmas which underpinned it, so that if today a courageous priest does begin to talk up he will find he is addressing only a small congregation of mostly grey heads and will be bashed from many sides, possibly even by some fellow clergy who have already jumped onto the liberal bandwagon.

Civil Law and Morality

The way back to morality and religion is now more difficult but, nonetheless, enough time has elapsed for people to see what harm all this anti-family legislation is doing to the family itself, first, and then to the wider common good, not to mention the less visible harm to souls when people engage in sinful behaviour. We must begin by being clear on the principles that govern the relationship between law and morality.

Civil law has to have a foundation in morality. Conversely stated: laws which are contrary to natural or divine law cannot serve the common good but will be destructive of it sooner later. This is readily accepted in Catholic teaching but not so in societies which have become pluralist, secularist or atheistic. Secularists will try to say that civil law should be totally separate from any particular religious tradition of morality because otherwise, by grounding it on one tradition, one will be discriminating against people of other moral traditions or none. They know that to enter the area of morality is to enter the area of religion because behaviour springs from belief and they reject religious beliefs to begin with on the pretext of not wanting to violate the principle of pluralism which they unwittingly take to be an absolute.

But this claimed separation of law from morality is false. It says that civil law amounts to nothing more than a set of regulations issuing from the parliament of the day to secure orderly behaviour on the street with no basis in any religious tradition but only in the "supposed" consensus of society at a given time. Yet, on examination, one finds that this supposed consensus, if it is not founded on a recognized religious tradition, is in fact founded consciously or unconsciously on some ideology or other in vogue at a given time and which is being promoted by the media – perhaps, humanism or socialism or nihilism or the absolute freedom of the individual or whatever – which ideologies then substitute themselves in people's minds as a new kind of religion, what might be called a "secularist anti-religion". When legislators, however secularist they may claim to be, enact this law rather than that they are drawing, consciously or unconsciously, on some of these ideologies. So, we are back to some fundamental basis for civil law again deeper than the pragmatic requirement of good order at a given time. The very word "good" itself must have a basis in some moral tradition. The secularists may even admit this but still be opposed to anything that has its foundation in the religion that claims to be one true faith, the Catholic religion – a religion which can substantiate this claim by rational argument if called on to do so - and by such blind opposition to the Catholic religion they show *themselves* to be discriminatory and, therefore, as being by no means pluralist.

We must retrace our steps and get back from this abyss. We must see law as founded on morality, the natural law, which is man's participation in the eternal law. It is a law which all reasonable people should be able to read from an open-minded study of human nature. Nonetheless, people, even after baptism, because they are still weakened by the effects of original sin, will at times disagree on their interpretation of the natural law. So, God, in His provident care for us, has spelt out the principal tenets of this law in the Decalogue, the ten commandments; and because people might still disagree on their interpretation of these also, He has given us the Church and the *magisterium* to provide answers on disputed questions.

But given that the Decalogue has come to us from God in the context of a covenant with His people it means that an acceptance of that morality must take us back to an acceptance of religion again as something underpinning the values of society. The Western world was moral in times past and had good laws conducive to right order, upholding the dignity of the individual and serving the common good of society, because its moral code was a product of the Judeo-Christian religious tradition which came to full flower in the Catholic religion in the Middle Ages and later, until the division of faith that was caused by the reformation.

The resulting Protestant traditions still retained much of that moral tradition for a long time, and Protestant family life was often very caring and Christian because based simply and directly on the precepts to be found in scripture. But the internal fragmentation of Protestantism which followed fast on the reformation inevitably weakened that moral tradition over time. A sense of the absoluteness of objective moral norms began to give way to the subjective, to the relative and the situational which then, in many places, led to agnosticism. With the Enlightenment, next, Christian religion, both Catholic and Protestant, was pushed aside for a Deist understanding of God and a purely naturalist understanding of man. And finally with the Communist revolution God was banished formally and man was reduced to being a mere producer of material things. In the West, though still claiming to be Christian, God was banished informally and man reduced to being a *consumer* of material things. That produced societies that were atheistic and secularist, consciously or unconsciously, in large parts of the world.

We must reassert the fundamental importance of the natural law for all men and have the courage to propose – without imposing – the Church's interpretation of that law.

Media and the Family

The media have great influence and hence great responsibility for promoting the things mentioned above: good housing, the return of work to the home, and good legislation based on a morality of natural law. But they have a contribution of their own to make also so as to be of help to marriage and the family. As said already when talking about various influences on youth, the media has to take responsibility for what it presents by way of entertainment. We spoke then about music, good and bad, but there is also the film and the soap and how they portray marriage. The makers of these latter, will, of course, present both the joys and difficulties of married life if their productions are to be accepted as being in some way true to life. So, they will present the phenomena, for example, of marriage breakdown and infidelity in their story plots. They can present these things as the new normal that "everyone is doing", which they do too often; but they could also, if they had the will, present these things as destructive, affecting everyone adversely, so that the viewers will seek ways to avoid these sufferings. Sadly, producers seldom present their stories in this latter way.

The screen does not merely *portray* married life, it also influences it, and those behind the cameras have a responsibility in this regard. It amazes me that film producers and media people generally, when they portray breakdown and infidelity as the new normal, are not aware of the kind of society they are shaping for *their own children and grandchildren* who will be the next victims of these evils. Are the takings at the box office of more account than the wellbeing of these, their own descendants, and the common good of society?

Spirituality of Marriage and the Family

A Goal beyond the Natural

When the Christian family is in a healthy condition it is not the case that the members merely "do things right" according to the commandments and Church teaching or that the spouses "hold together" somehow for fifty years or more. Much more than that happens because a family is a living thing, dynamic, and, like all living things, it is growing and is heading towards some goal and is radiating outwards while doing so. But towards what goal in the case of the Christian family? A purely naturalist answer would say simply that the children will grow up, will marry in their turn and give rise to a third generation, the grandchildren, while the old couple will eventually die off. And so, round and round goes the cycle of life and death. But the Christian sees beyond this to the supernatural, to the life of grace and *its* goal. The priest who prepared the couple for their wedding will not be content merely with ensuring that all the papers were filled in properly and that the marriage was celebrated validly. With the blessing he gives at the end of the ceremony he asks God to keep them together in a union that will be happy and fruitful: that they live in God's grace and fulfil its primary and secondary ends and that their children coming after them will do the same in *their* turn.

But is that all that there is to a living out Christian marriage? No; for Christians there is a still more ultimate, overall aim which is that the couple bring each other, hand in hand, along the road of life and return to the One who created them and, hopefully, with their children and grandchildren following behind them later. While travelling this road they radiate the grace of their sacrament outwards for those around them to see. Pope Pius XI says in *Casti Conubii* that married love must rise above the fulfilling of the natural ends to the overarching end of the spouses growing in holiness in imitation of Christ:

> This outward expression of love in the home demands not only mutual help but must go further; <u>must have as its primary purpose that man and wife help each other day by day in forming and perfecting themselves in the interior life, so that through their partnership in life they may advance ever more and more in virtue, and above all that they may grow in true love toward God and their neighbour,</u> on which indeed "dependeth the whole Law and the Prophets." For all men of every condition, in whatever honourable walk of life they may be, can and ought to imitate that most perfect example of holiness placed

before man by God, namely Christ Our Lord, and by God's grace to arrive at the summit of perfection, as is proved by the example set us of many saints". #23

Put differently, their married life is a path to holiness and to final union with God through Christ as the way, being led along by the Holy Spirit. To say this is to say that marriage, though natural for all men and women who choose it, is also for Christians a vocation; that therefore there must be such a thing as a distinctive spirituality of marriage alongside that of priests and religious. Here Pope Pius XI was anticipating the Vatican II theme of the universal call to holiness.

The Three Stages of Spiritual Growth

It is God who takes the initiative in all of Christian living by sending us His Son and the Holy Spirit who sanctifies us in a life of grace. Spirituality, then from our side, is our response to that grace which has three stages: the purgative in which we turn away from sin; the illuminative in which we grow in knowledge and virtue; and the unitive in which we draw ever closer to God.

For priests and religious the purgative requires that they live celibacy and complete chastity and that they are detached from or renounce material possessions. For married people it requires that they live an *analogous* chastity that renounces unnatural sex and attachments to material things in excess of the requirements of their state in life. This brings us back to the need for them to practice natural family planning. For the priest to believe that he is leading the married couples of his parish on the road to holiness while not putting these challenges before them is simply to deceive them into thinking that one can draw close to God without first renouncing sin. It is like saying that a boat can set out to sea without cutting the ropes that are tying it to the land.

The illuminative stage requires a growth in knowledge and virtue for the priest or religious but which, again, is analogously similar and different for married people. Everyone is called to be virtuous but the virtues needed in a mother looking after a sick child are different to those, for example, of a priest in the confessional looking after the sick soul of a penitent.

And finally, union with God will require the frequenting of the sacraments and time spent in prayer, but again analogously similar and different for people in different states of life: the married man or woman will not be able to spend the same amount of time in prayer as, for example, the monk or nun in an enclosed order. *Their* time may be Sunday Mass together with the family and then family prayer, perhaps the rosary, together at night around the fireside. We made these comparisons already when talking about the spirituality of the priest in an earlier chapter.

Spirituality has to be centred on Christ, truly God and truly man because He is the way to the Father. By receiving His grace in the sacraments Christians are "divinized", given a participation in the divine nature. Then, in addition, Christ has His three offices of king, prophet and priest, and married people participate in these also and live them out analogously.

They share in His kingly role, first of all, by denying themselves daily so that they have mastery over their own desires and emotions but also by the various deeds of service they perform in in the home and in their work places. They also exercise their kingly role by engaging in pro-family politics as we mentioned earlier. Of this Pope John Paul says:

> The social and political role is included in the kingly mission of service in which Christian couples share by virtue of the sacrament of marriage....*FC, #47*.

Parents share in Christ's prophetic role when they teach their children their prayers and their catechism in the home and also when they speak up for Christian values in public life and in their work places, in the school and, more generally, when they engage in various kinds of evangelical enterprises to make the faith better known in today's secularist world. St John Paul again:

> To the extent in which the Christian family accepts the Gospel and matures in faith, it becomes an evangelizing community. Let us listen again to Paul VI: "The family, like the Church, ought to be a place where the Gospel is transmitted and from which the Gospel radiates. In a family which is conscious of this mission, all the members evangelize and are evangelized. The parents not only communicate the Gospel to their children, but from their children they can themselves receive the same Gospel as deeply lived by them. And such a family becomes the evangelizer of many other families, and of the neighbourhood of which it forms part." [*Evangelii. Nuntiandi, 71*]. *FC, #52*.

Then, they share in Christ's priestly role when they frequent the sacraments and when at Mass they bring along their achievements and sufferings, their sacrifices of the week, and place them on the patten and the chalice at the offertory to be taken up by the priest so that at the consecration they will become the body and blood of Christ. Thereby they are joining their sacrifices in the home and the workplace to those of

Christ on the cross for the redemption of mankind. When they receive Communion then they are strengthened to go out again for the tasks of the coming week.

> Just as husbands and wives receive from the sacrament the gift and responsibility of translating into daily living the sanctification bestowed on them, so the same sacrament confers on them the grace and moral obligation of transforming their whole lives into a "spiritual sacrifice." *ibid., #56. (cf. Sacrosanctum Consilium, #59).*

The Way Forward

Christendom was not a paradise. There were evils in those days also and bad rulers at times. But, still, some kings and queens of that era were saints, and there was general agreement on right and wrong in countries of different cultures because all those cultures were different expressions of the fundamental religious beliefs of those people which were mostly Catholic. Those days are gone and we are now in what is called a pluralist, secularist society. But, as explained above, that term "pluralism" is often merely a mask for a new uniformity of another kind of religion or rather an anti-religion which worships man instead of God and makes him, man, to be the sole arbiter of right and wrong, of what is now termed "acceptable and unacceptable".

Our situation now is more like that of Christians of the pagan Roman empire when these people, our ancestors in the faith, were a persecuted minority in that society, a small but committed band of believers, dedicated to Christ, who gave wonderful witness to Him and His law, even to the shedding of their blood. But that blood, to recall a well-known saying, became the seed of many more Christians until, after some centuries, we find the flowering of the great Christian, Catholic civilization of the Middle Ages.

The West, the living civilization of the countries of Europe, the Americas and those countries colonized by them, has a soul and that soul has been the Judeo-Christian soul, the Catholic soul in its fullest form. Either it resuscitates that soul or it will perish and precisely because it was, and still is a Christian soul, a soul whose inner logic is that of dying and rising in imitation of its Founder, we can hope for a new Christendom even if its material base will be different due to the advent of technology and all that came with it. The popes have been calling for this return to our Judeo-Christian roots since the middle of the twentieth century and there are many young people yearning for this already who are beginning to see through the illusion of secularism and materialism. In order that such a return will come to pass it is our task today, to keep the light of faith alive in this new darkness, just as the Irish monks did in the dark ages that followed the fall of the Roman empire, and to sow new seeds of the ever old, ever new gospel, with good pastors to water them with their preaching and sacraments until God will bring them to full flower in another new Catholic civilization.

We can *hope* for this resurrection of the Catholic spirit in the West again but we can *not* sit back passively. Man must co-operate with grace, and if we fail to do so in this trial of the West, then the West will be lost to the faith similar to the way the countries once converted by St Paul were lost to Islam at a later time. What will likely happen then is that the centre of gravity of the faith will move to Africa or Asia and flourish there anew. Or, could we be now in the end times, expecting the return of the Lord when all seems lost, and the setting up of His kingdom? But, then, this is not the first time in history that all seemed lost.

Towards the Kingdom

Whatever the location of the Church in the near future Vatican II tells us that the ultimate goal of the Church is the kingdom of God. (*Lumen Gentium* and *Gaudium et Spes*). She is a pilgrim people on the march to that goal. In her, the kingdom is already present in mystery and is growing till it blossoms forth at the eschaton. People in religious life stand before us to give us a foretaste of what life will be like in the kingdom where we will see God face to face and praise Him unceasingly along with the angels and saints - where we will have glorified, risen, physical bodies but love each other unselfishly in a non-physical way. All people, especially lay people, are called to prepare the world around them so that it will become material for this kingdom, this perfect reign of God in all hearts and in all of creation. They do so by doing their work and by living out their various responsibilities in the home, in the workplace and in the wider society in a Christian way. But they must remember that the kingdom is, nonetheless, not a merely human achievement but a work of God, a grace, which is why scripture describes it as the new Jerusalem *coming down from above* (Rev.21). We contribute to it from our side down here, but it is God who gives it from above. Families too, precisely as families, have their own contribution to make to the kingdom. St John Paul again, quoting *Lumen Gentium*:

> What the Council says of the laity applies also to Christian spouses and parents, especially with regard to the earthly and temporal realities that characterize their lives: "As worshippers leading holy lives in every place, the laity consecrate the world itself to God." (*LG, #3,4); FC, #56*.

The principal joy of the kingdom is the direct vision of God; but it is also a social or horizontal joy because of the perfect communion that will be there between all the blessed in the holy city. Even though the marriage-bond of husband and wife will no longer remain in the kingdom, but, instead, the great marriage that it signified, i.e., that of Christ and His bride the Church, nonetheless, all those bonds of love that existed in the family here on earth, once they have been purified of all selfishness, will endure and shine all the more brightly in the kingdom so that parents will have the added joy of seeing their children and grandchildren beside them there, no longer gathered round the fireside of their earthly home but round the Lamb in in the kingdom in unending adoration.

Conclusions:

1. The harm to society caused by the undermining of the family since reformation and the French revolution should be a spur to Christians to work towards a rebuilding of the family by campaigning for legislation based on sound morals, for good affordable housing, for a reuniting of work and home, for greater financial supports for families and other such things.
2. To engage on this rebuilding is not to try to go back nostalgically to the Middle Ages but to draw again from the ever valid principles of the Judeo-Christian tradition in order to give them new application in the world of the new technological infra structure of today. We look back in order to march forward.
3. Of primary importance is the reinstating of God and His religion and His design for marriage and the family. In addition to the measures just mentioned, this is best achieved by the witness of Christian families themselves living out God's design for the family to the full even if those families are few in number.
4. There is a distinctive spirituality of marriage with its various stages analogously lived. The ultimate goal of family life is not just the keeping of God's laws in this world but union with Him at the banquet feast of the Lamb in the kingdom of heaven.

We have been looking at the sacraments from a pastoral perspective. The grace they channel to us will blossom forth in the kingdom of God. We will be saying more on that in the next section.

Part E

Towards the Kingdom

Introduction

We have been looking at the work of the priest in the parish where, for love of Christ to whom he is configured in a special way, he leads, teaches and sanctifies the faithful so as to bring them home to the Father by the working of the Holy Spirit. We have been looking at the roles his lay helpers also play in this work of building up the Church, the body of Christ. It is time now to ask to what end is all of this building up or does it have any end at all other than that of simply keeping things going, or "keeping the show on the road" as I heard one parish priest put it? Vatican II puts the kingdom of God before all Christians as that towards which the Church is straining and that towards which Christians should be aiming in their family lives and their work lives even though the kingdom, at the end, is a thing given by God from above.

Chapter XXXIV

The Celtic Cross

Whither goes the Parish? – a Dialogue

When I am lifted up from the earth I will draw all things to myself. Jn.12:32.

I am the Alpha and the Omega, the First and the Last, the Beginning and the End. Rev. 22:13.

She becomes on earth the initial budding forth of that kingdom. While she slowly grows, the Church strains forward toward the consummation of the kingdom and, with all her strength, hopes and desires to be united in glory with her king. *Lumen Gentium, #5, cf.* also *#9.*

This chapter will take a different format to previous ones, the format of a dialogue between a parish priest and a tourist who is travelling around the West of Ireland. It explores the meaning of eschatology, particular and general eschatology, and shows how they are both necessary and complementary.

Whither goes the Parish?

The story is told of a tourist travelling round the West of Ireland who realized he was getting lost and did not know where the road was taking him. He happened to see an old man sitting on a stone wall at the side of the road contentedly smoking his pipe. So, the tourist stopped his car, let down the window and said to the old man: "Tell me Sir, where does this road go"? To which the old man replied: "Mister, I am living here for the past seventy years and I never saw this road going anywhere. It has always stayed right there where it is"! "But", said the tourist, "if I travel on further, where will I come out"? To which the old man said "You will come right round in a full circle back to this place again. Such is life anyhow, my friend: a big circle that goes nowhere only round and round, and when you come to realize that, you will stop your travelling around and do what I am doing, you will sit on another wall and smoke your own pipe"!

But to continue the story let us say that our tourist travels on further and eventually comes into a small town, the centre of a rural parish, and he passes by the church and he sees the parish priest cutting the lawn, taking care to cut in and around each of the graves of former priests buried there. Even though there are lay people who would gladly do this cutting for him he prefers to do so himself for the exercise it gives him. So, the tourist stops to talk to him and perhaps get some more definite directions.

Let us say, for the sake of our story, that it is the parish of our Fr Smart whom we met in the *King* section of this work, the man who was very proud of the amount of lay involvement he had in his parish even though, as we saw, it was mostly only a Sunday or weekend involvement and, although large in itself in that respect, still engaged only a small percentage of the total laity in that parish. Fr Smart is a bit older now and does not have any curate at this stage due to the fall in vocations. But he is still "running a good show" and even though there is a drop in Mass attendance and in church weddings and in church funerals also, the "involvement of the laity" in and around the church gives the outward impression that all is well despite the fact that those laity are mostly elderly people. So, he can manage without a curate; and, with the number of Masses reduced, the few still being celebrated, being better attended, the church looks more full, which again looks well and allows Fr Smart to continue to pat himself on the back. So, our tourist stops his car, gets out asks for some directions which leads on to a conversation between them because the priest is getting tired of the mowing and the tourist is getting tired of the driving. The tourist begins with a greeting from the window of his car:

Tourist: "Good evening, Father, I take it you are the parish priest around here because curates are a rare species nowadays everywhere in the Western world with the way things are going in the Church. I am a stranger here so you might give me some directions".

Fr Smart: "My pleasure. Park your car and come and sit down here".

There is a garden seat in the lawn at the side of the church and both sit down on it. It is a nice Summer's evening with the sun declining over Croagh Patrick, that majestic pyramid-shaped mountain in the West of County Mayo, a holy mountain and a place of pilgrimage. Their conversation continues:

Fr Smart: "I have care of another parish also, but with the low Mass attendance and a reduction in the number of Masses now it can be done by one priest, for another while anyhow, because I am pushing on in years".

Chapter 34: The Celtic Cross

Tourist: "You refer to the way things are going in the Church nowadays. Tell me just where do you see this parish going from here?"

Fr Smart: "Not wishing to be cynical, Sir, but I am here ten years now and in that time I have never seen this parish (or any other parish as for that matter) go anywhere. It stays put like the road out there and life in it goes round and round, year in, year out. But perhaps you mean to ask me if I am taking the parish on a pilgrimage from here sometime soon, and indeed I am. I will be taking a busload of parishioners to Knock shrine in September, and some years we go to Fatima as well. Every year a bus load goes to climb Croagh Patrick over there".

Tourist: "This is my second time today being told about things staying put only to go round and round. No, I didn't mean a parish pilgrimage to a particular shrine but, now that you mentioned it, such a pilgrimage, in a way, is a kind of symbol of what I had in mind so I will use that example to explain what I mean".

"A pilgrimage, as you know, any pilgrimage, is a spatial symbol of our journey in time through life as we go from this world to the next. As usually understood, that means for most people that we plod along down here as individuals, grow old, die and then, hopefully, go to heaven. But I want to extend the idea to the entire parish - after all, your bus will possibly have about fifty people on board, representative of all corners of your parish - and then I want to extend the idea to the diocese, even to the entire Church so that all of us Christians, taken together, can be seen as a pilgrim people on the march towards the kingdom of God of the end time. Within that wider context I am asking you where this parish might be, as part of the entire Church, on that pilgrimage?"

Fr Smart: "I must admit I never even gave a thought to that question. If each individual can save his own soul at the end of his or her life's pilgrimage what more could anyone ask for? As for the parish itself being on pilgrimage – apart from a bus-load going to Knock – that is a new idea to me. A pilgrimage has the idea of a line going from a starting point straight to a finishing point but I think that a better symbol for a parish is a circle that goes round and round in regular predictability. First, we have Advent, with the Advent wreath, then Christmas with the crib, then Lent with Ash Wednesday, then Holy week when we "put on a bit of a push", then Easter and then the green season when the hay is saved and the turf is cut and hopefully the parish priest gets some of the good turf rather than the bad stuff, and soon we are round to Advent again: round and round to the same point again".

Tourist: "By any chance Father were you a Hindu at one time before becoming a Christian?"

Fr Smart: "I'm enjoying your sense of humour, Sir. We are all cradle Catholics around here and our ancestors before us and the only thing like a Hindu we would ever come across is those guys with the towels around their heads that set up stalls down the street there on a Saturday morning. But why do you ask?"

Tourist: "Because the idea of things going round and round for ever, with no beginning or end, is very much a Hindu thing. I read one time that the Celts as a people originated somewhere over in the Middle East. Their *sean nós* (old style) singing still reminds me of Indian, Hindu singing as it can be heard even today, a kind of long, lonely lament that life, with its unending sorrows, keeps going round and round with fatalistic inescapability. Death then is like the fate of a salt doll that walks into the sea. The individual is dissolved into an eternal state of tranquillity in the divine, understood in a somewhat pantheist sense, as some kind of god or world-soul which is really only the inner spiritual core of the world we see. Maybe there is still something of that in your subconscious, collective memory".

Fr Smart: "Just what are you getting at Sir?"

Tourist: "When I pulled up here I saw you were cutting the grass carefully around the grave of that priest over there, the one with the high Celtic cross over it. (*See the cover of this book*). They are magnificent pieces of work, those Celtic crosses, and in olden times they also served as catechetical lessons in stone because the story of salvation is carved up along the main pillar on all four sides of the cross. But look at the top. What you see is a the cross and the circle around it. Do you know the symbolism of that?"

Fr Smart: "Yes, I do. The cross, of course, is the crucifix, Calvary, and the circle, then, stands for the rising sun, the resurrection. The sun formerly was a pagan symbol because pagans like the Egyptians and the Celts worshipped the sun; but now, for us Christians, it stands for the rising Sun which is Christ Himself at the resurrection".

Tourist: "You are right. I cannot disagree with you on that. But there is something more subtle in those Celtic crosses that you are missing out on and indeed which I would have missed out on also only that I happen to read a bit of Chesterton now and then. I'm saying that the circle had a further pagan meaning which might still be lingering in the minds of people even to this day".

Chapter 34: The Celtic Cross 521

Fr Smart: "Are you are saying that the circle on these Celtic crosses suggests something pagan because a circle is a thing that goes round and round, and that that points to something pagan still persisting in our psyche today? If so, then you are wrong. A circle, does not have to be a pagan or Hindu symbol anymore because it has been taken over and baptised, as it were, by St Patrick long ago. As I said already, it is now the symbol of the resurrection. But, if you want to keep to the idea of the circle as something going round and round, it still continues to be a Christian symbol because, in the end, is not the circle the symbol of eternity, the eternity of God Himself, who has no beginning or end, a life in which we each hope to have a share some day? So, even on this interpretation, it does not have a pagan symbolism now but a thoroughly Christian one".

Tourist: "I can accept all that but there is more. Let us look at that cross again and the circle. Notice that the cross *breaks through* or *breaks out* of the circle in four directions, up and down, left and right".

Fr Smart: "Meaning what?"

Tourist: "Let's give the circle back its pagan meaning again for a moment. It says that things, life, people, the world, indeed the entire universe goes round and round unendingly. Pagans had that idea because they did not have the idea of *creation*, an idea which *we* have from the first line of the Bible: *In the beginning God created heaven and earth*. We would never have got to that idea, either, were it not for revelation. Even the great Aristotle, who *did* believe in God as the supporting cause and the final cause of everything, could not rise to the idea of *creation* - things having a beginning in time - because it implies the idea of the world being made of out nothing, and for him and all the old Greeks that was impossible, because for them it was a fundamental principle that *out of nothing comes nothing*. So, while the circle of the annual recurrence of things still stands, as willed by God: the round of day and night, the round of the four seasons, the daily coming and going of the tide, this year being like last year with people being born and dying *etc.*, God has burst open or burst through that circle with a straight line, a line that begins with creation, finds its middle in Christ and ends with Christ's second coming, this notwithstanding the fact that the Church's seasons do also come round every year".

"To make this clearer, the line I am talking about has its beginning when the Father Creates all things through the Word. It has its middle when the Word became flesh in Christ, died on the cross and rose again; and it will have its end at the Kingdom when Christ returns and hands everything back to the Father. We could use the example of an arrow in flight, time's arrow, going in a straight line from a starting point to a target, a goal, at the end. For us Christians that goal is the kingdom of God, the eschaton, the New Jerusalem come down from above from God. The horizontal beam of the cross, going from left to right, represents that line or arrow".

Fr Smart: "How interesting? But are you forgetting about the other beam of the cross, the vertical one that points upwards and downwards. Is that bursting open the circle also?"

Tourist: "Indeed. That vertical beam, breaking out of the circle upwards, points to heaven above. It signifies, first, that the Christian God is transcendent, that is, He is infinitely above the world of finite things in His being, though present in every atom because sustaining all things by His power. That makes Him to be utterly different to any kind of immanent or pantheist god such as the Eastern religions have and some Western philosophers too in recent centuries like Spinoza and Hegel. More familiarly, the beam going upwards also symbolizes the individual Christian's soul going up to heaven at the end of life. Then, the same beam, pointing downward into the ground, is a reminder that our bodies return to the dust and also that the souls of the damned go down further into hell, below the ground. In sum, that vertical beam tells us that there is more to life than the circle of this material world, even though that world is good because created by God and redeemed by His Son".

"Traditionally such matters were studied under what was called *The Last Things*. They were the topics of death, judgement, heaven and hell, (purgatory fits in here also, though it is not entirely 'last'). They were studied mostly as pertaining to the individual at the end of his/her life, which is why the study was also called "individual or particular eschatology". And that was and always will be very important, the saving of one's soul, to put it simply. That is why devout people pray for a holy or happy death and why St Alphonsus preached such good sermons on that topic. You are well used to those ideas from your school catechism of old and, because of that, I presume you preach about them also here in your parish".

Fr Smart: "I did preach about hell once a few years ago. But do you see that supermarket over there? There was a posh business woman running it at that time and she came to me after Mass one Sunday claiming that I was 'terrorizing' her little granddaughter with such talk: that in school they never hear of hell. She said that she would write to the bishop to complain. Whether she did so or not I do not know. So that was the beginning and end of my sermons on individual eschatology in this parish and I would say that it is the same in most other parishes around here also, except that at funerals we are supposed to guarantee everyone that Granddad is in heaven smiling down on us all, even if Granddad was well known by all to have been a proper scoundrel. At November we talk about the dead "to remember them" whatever *that* is supposed to do for their souls if they are in purgatory! Nothing is said about indulgences lest we offend some possible Lutheran who might happened to be living within a radius of fifty miles of one's parish".

"I didn't press the matter any further, either with her or the bishop, because the name of the game in religion now anyhow in most places is 'keep the customers happy' – a bit like running a supermarket if you think of it. You don't hold on to your customers by selling things they don't like. She herself is gone now as well. She was found dead in her bed one morning without the sacraments, a thing I have noticed a few times about people who unjustly criticize their priests. She was notorious for over charging, and for selling drink and condoms to youngsters. So, I wonder if the 'terror' caused by the few soft words I said about hell was not after all something that upset her own conscience rather than something that upset the sensibilities of her granddaughter. What a pity we cannot phone her up now and ask her where she has landed herself on the other side!!!"

Tourist: "How sad for all concerned, because that nicey-nice stuff is still not holding the 'customers' in the church".

"But to keep to our topic: individual eschatology, even if it *is* preached, is still only half the study of eschatology. The other half is what is called "general eschatology". It concerns what we profess at the end of the *Creed* every Sunday: *the resurrection of the dead* when Christ *will come again to judge the living and the dead* and set up a *kingdom that will have no end*. You had that in your old catechism also, at least a brief mention telling you that, at the end, Christ will return, the dead will arise to be judged, the world will be renewed, the just will then go, body and soul, to heaven and the bad will go, body and soul, to hell. But not too much was said about it because it was presumed that most of us as individuals will have to face our own individual judgement before the end of the world arrives so that it was better to concentrate of *that*, i.e., on being ready for one's own individual judgement, and let the end of the world come whenever it will. Still, the Church never loses sight of any of her doctrines even if at a given time one doctrine gets more emphasis than another. I can remember as a small boy my grandfather often putting the question to me of how we will all fit in the Valley of Jehosophat for the general judgement after we rise from the dead?! And I was not able to answer him. But it shows that the faithful, some of them at least, kept an eye on that doctrine also". [The risen, glorified body is not limited spatially as ours are at present].

"Vatican II sought to restore balance in this matter as in many other matters. The council has been the subject of endless controversy, some people wanting to scrap it entirely so that we can all go back to Trent and others wanting to take it miles forward by trying to have it advocate things that were never in its documents or anywhere else in Catholic tradition with the aim of fabricating a totally new Church with no continuity with our past. But, as I see it, the aim of the council was simply that of restoring the balance in a number of areas of faith in light of the signs of the new times we are now living in as a result of new developments such as our new consciousness of history, the advent of democracy, advances in technology and communications, globalism, urbanization and many more such things. In the matter of eschatology also it sought a better balance better between individual and general eschatology with Christ at the centre. Or, in terms of our Celtic cross, we could say it sought for a better balance between the vertical beam and the horizontal beam with Christ with His cross and resurrection at the centre".

Fr Smart: "So, will you tell me now what that new balance should give us?"

Tourist: "I will try. Let's begin at the far-over left side of the horizontal beam. As said already, we have God's act of creation breaking open the circle at that point. Then we have the creation of our first parents, their Fall, then the call of Abraham which leads to the forming of a people specially chosen from whom Christ would come. That brings us to the centre point. Christ founds the Church, a new people of God who march onwards on their pilgrim way through history till some day they come to the far-over, right-end of the circle and break through it because we will then go beyond history to the second coming of Christ and the setting up of His kingdom, a gift from above, a kingdom of true freedom, justice and peace in which God's will will be perfectly *done on earth as it is in heaven.* True freedom is not licentiousness; it is doing God's will. True justice is not the bland, same-dose-for all of the communist; it is each receiving his/her due. True peace is not the stillness of the graveyard because all graves will be empty then; it is the harmony of full life and joy that results from true freedom and true justice when *every tear will be wiped away and we shall see you Our God as you are. (Preface of the Mass for the dead).* Earth itself will be taken up into heaven then".

"Notice here that while, of course, Abraham was an individual and so also is Christ, I am stressing the idea of a *people*, a pilgrim people, like an army on the march to a definite destination. I grant that we are all individuals and that we must each take responsibility for our own souls individually and that we will die and face judgement as individuals as soon as we close our eyes. But, despite that, is it not also true that we are born into families? We are brought to the church for baptism by our parents, which sacrament incorporates us into the family of God, the Christian community, the Church as a royal, priestly people. We live and grow in interaction with those around us because we are social beings by very nature, and even at the lonely hour of departing this life we still can have the support of the Church which can give us three of her sacraments at that point and, hopefully, we will have our loved one's praying for us at our bedside. And the prayers which the Church recites at that time speak of the angels and saints coming to meet us from the other side to bring us across the divide of death. Seen thus, I think it is very appropriate to speak of the local, parish community as a pilgrim people on the march to the Kingdom of God and not as a disconnected quantity of individuals going round in circles with a few dropping off each year in death".

"The early Christians were known as the 'People of the Way' and also as the 'Children of the Dawn'. Such titles convey to me the lovely image of the holy women of Jerusalem, coming up along the hill of Calvary early that first Easter Sunday morning. They were surely the most devout and faithful followers of Christ from the beginning because they were the ones who stood their ground at the foot of the cross on Calvary on Good Friday evening when all was dark and the others had fled. They were a small group, the very first Christian people, making their 'way' up along the hill of Calvary to the tomb at dawn, just as the sun was rising over the hills of Moab behind them and casting its golden beams up along the dusty, rugged roadway along which the women were plodding. And soon they would meet the risen Christ, the Christ of that first Easter Sunday who is also the Christ of the eschaton, the Christ of the kingdom. The kingdom had begun in Him already because He had just triumphed over death even though it won't be fully realized in the rest of His followers until the end of time, the exception being Mary who would very soon be assumed in glory. Mary is the prototype of the final destiny of the pilgrim Church and I see those holy women of Easter Sunday as the vanguard of that pilgrim Church marching along to meet the same Christ who will come towards them once again and finally at the eschaton".

"When the glory of the end is realized in the rest of the faithful, in the fully completed mystical body of Christ, with ourselves, hopefully, among them, we can say that then the pilgrim people will have arrived at that point on the Celtic cross where the horizontal beam breaks through the circle over at the far right-hand side, the point where history yields to what is trans-history in the risen life of the citizens of the new Jerusalem".

"But more than that, the whole material world will also *be set free from its bondage to decay* then and be called to join in the resurrection of the end time by being purified, transformed and glorified. *(Rm. 8:22)*. Recall Christ's words when He said that when raised up on the cross He would draw all things, *omnia*, to Himself, not just all people with their souls alone, not even with their souls and bodies as well, but even all of creation from the stars above down to the atoms under our feet. This is because of the old principle that the dwelling should befit the dweller: a glorified world for glorified souls in glorified bodies, bodies like that of Christ Himself on Easter Sunday morning, a world like that which is described in the *Book of Revelations* when it talks of *the new heaven and the new earth". (Rev. 21)*.

"We can see now that the two beams of the cross are complementary, the vertical and the horizontal: Christ saves the individual person which means the saving of his/her soul, but that soul is the form of the body and that body lies in the earth because it has come from the earth to begin with. So, the body and the earth will be raised up and glorified also. That, we might say, is the salvation of the vertical. But that person is one of a people in the mystical body of Christ, as said above, a pilgrim people who have marched through history. So, all of that people, that mystical body, has to be saved or gathered up or recapitulated in Christ at the kingdom because He is the *Alpha* and the *Omega*, the beginning and the end of everything, because He is the centre of everything by His cross and resurrection. That, we might say, is how He is the salvation of both the vertical and the horizontal beams in Himself".

"Accordingly, it is perfectly in order for me to ask where all things are heading, where history is heading, what is the end of the universe as a material thing, what is the goal of history taking all people together as one body in Christ in His Church – that is, those of them who heed His call from the cross and follow Him – and then it must surely be in order for me to ask where this parish of yours is going, given that it is an integral part of the entire Church, given that it is the entire Church herself in miniature, localized in this lovely scenic part of the West of Ireland".

Fr Smart: "I'm afraid Sir that you are only one around here who would ask such questions. Do you see that guy who has just pulled up with his truck down the road there? Jo Green is his name. He is a builder. He is loading up another load of cement for a children's hospital that is being built out the road. It is a community effort by him and many others who are raising funds for it because the next nearest hospital for children is many miles away. What do you think he would say if I called him up here to join us and asked him where this parish is heading in the overall plan of salvation history? My guess is that he would tell us that he was busy with his load before it came to stopping time and that he had no mind for such abstractions? Anyhow, he stopped going to Mass a few years ago when the decline set it".

Tourist: "But I bet he still gets Mass said for his parents on their anniversaries each year and I will bet also that at some time in his past either he or his grandfather might have asked questions about the end of the world like the question my own grandfather asked about people trying to fit in the Valley of Jehosaphat".

Fr Smart: "You are probably right. Something of the faith does linger on in people's minds even for a generation or perhaps two, after the practice of the faith has ceased".

Tourist: "You are right and priests should tap into it whenever possible. It is there underneath only to bring it to the fore again".

"But to get back to the cross again: I was saying above that the two beams of the cross are complimentary, the vertical and the horizontal, individual and general eschatology, which means that effective preaching must deal with both. I said also that in the past priests preached somewhat more about individual eschatology so as to encourage each person to prepare him/herself for a holy death, rather than about general eschatology which was presumed to deal with things still too far off. I am saying now that though that preaching was good as far as it went, there was still an imbalance there which Vatican II has sought to correct, especially with its document on the Church called *Lumen Gentium* and its other document, the Church in the Modern World called *Gaudium et Spes*. If the two beams of the cross are complimentary then the neglect of one will, in time, lead to the neglect of the other also and soon there will be no preaching at all on the after-life in any respect. And that, I maintain, is one of the reasons for present day secularism, a world-view that has no place for God or the supernatural, a world-view that priests lament and rail against but without seeking to explore its deeper causes. If there is no after-life or no end goal to history what have we left is only this material world around us, so we have to make the best of that: "eat, drink and be merry for tomorrow we die"; and is not that another way of describing secularism? More than that, people then go on to make a false god or a substitute god out of this world and the things it can offer, wealth, pleasure, success *etc*. Then you have secularism become a kind of anti-religion".

Fr Smart: "So, what are the deeper causes of this secularism? I guess they are many but you might give me a few".

Tourist: "Going through history the Church has been assailed by heresies of all sorts. One of those has been the virus of radical dualism, a world-view that divides reality into good and evil with spirit as good and matter as evil; the soul is deemed good but the body and, with it, marriage and sex, are seen as evil. The underlying philosophy was Platonism which played off the world of the forms up above against the world of matter down below. If you transpose that kind of thinking into Christianity then the soul of the individual alone is all that matters so that it will be saved and rise up vertically to God at the end of one's life. There is not much room for a theology of the world or the earth or the body or of marriage in this view of things or of history as aiming at some goal horizontally. The best thing is to concentrate on saving one's own soul and let the world, history and even other people, literally, go to hell".

"But it is inevitable that such a line of thinking would beget a backlash from the world, a protest as to its own natural goodness even if it is a goodness devoid of grace due to the Fall. Or, instead, paradoxically, that such a world would accept being described as evil and say 'so what, if evil then why not use it for maximum pleasure and then discard it'. Both reactions lead to an ethos of licentiousness and hedonism. This shows how an exclusive and narrowly vertical Christianity leads to fruits that are contrary to true Christianity which has to have both arms of cross, up and down, over and back".

"Another cause of eschatology, even individual eschatology, being lost sight of in preaching is that the Marxists made the accusation that priests were keeping their people in subjection and misery by preaching another world up above, a pie-in-the-sky Christianity which did nothing to ameliorate the misery of millions on the ground as a result of the industrial revolution and its ethos of *laissez faire* capitalism which, in practice, amounted to unrestrained greed by the owners of production who exploited the workers. Hence the well-known Marxist chant that 'religion is the opium of the people'. These Marxists choose to ignore the great charitable works of the Church and her great encyclicals defending the rights of workers. But the accusation stuck so that many priests then went silent entirely on the next life and substituted instead a Christianity of nicey-nice politeness in this life or a Christianity that became entirely social or political".

"Having thus silenced the priests in their preaching, the Marxists then went on to fill the lacuna and give the workers, whom they called 'the proletariat', a new meaning of their work, a new meaning of history and a new goal for it but one that is thoroughly secularist. This was communism, a philosophy of materialism with no God; a philosophy of hatred because of the dialectic which has things which are complementary by nature fight against each other in relations of opposition and even violence. At first, this opposition had employers pitted against employees with the latter urged to rise up and eliminate the former by bloody revolution. Today that same evil principle of the dialectic is advanced under other forms and applied to other complementary opposites, blacks against whites, citizens against government, women against men, wives against husbands, children against parents, mothers against their own children with abortion; and it is done so subtly that its Marxist roots are well disguised because this leopard is good at changing his spots. Hence today one will find advocates of contraception or abortion honestly thinking they are promoting women's right to choose or their right to equality or their right to some other such contrived values, which values once had Christian roots but which now are hijacked and distorted so as to justify all kinds of evil, and neither their advocates or their gullible recipients having any idea of the Marxist roots of these things".

Marxists gain their adherents with the promise of some kind of classless, free, utopian society in the end: a classic example of the false promises of Satan which we renounce on Holy Saturday night, an inversion of the values of the kingdom I spoke of above. I say 'false' because communism has had more than a century to prove itself in many parts of the world and all it has brought is tyranny, bloodshed, economic misery and homelessness to millions".

Fr Smart: "But perhaps you are linking things together that have no causal relationship. Can you say that all these evils come from the single root of communism?"

Tourist: "Have you not heard of the Fatima messages - that Russia would spread her errors throughout the world? It is happening here in your country also. By disguising the source of these errors, communists can spread them all the more successfully; but it is the same dialectic of opposition, hatred and destruction of what is natural, good and God-given which is at work in all these things. But to answer your question, yes, there are other factors leading to the loss of faith. There is a complex of things which interact on each other. A simple thing like the progress of technology, a thing good in itself, still can have a disruptive effect on family life and on old customs which conveyed wisdom and values from one generation to the next. It has to be channelled towards good ends. So also telecommunication and easy travel to mention but a few. But here I am concentrating on the influence of Marxism because of the attention that Our Lady wanted to give to the errors of Russia".

"Even if priests preach nothing heretical but mere pious platitudes about the need for people to be "nice" to each other, that suits the Marxists just as well because that is very weak, harmless stuff which cuts no ice in the real world. It leaves what we might call a 'media vacuum'. They themselves, then, will have already got control of the media and will easily fill this vacuum, influencing the people when there is little or no opposition from the Church but only this nicey-nice preaching. If you are surprised at this, or think it only applies to other places faraway, look at the situation now in Ireland and presumably here also in the West of Ireland. Is it not a fact also that a high percentage of your people here, have, over the years, being voting in referendums for such things as abortion in various measures, divorce and even same-sex marriage, which has to mean, mathematically, that even many of those still going to Mass have been voting for such things and see nothing wrong with it? There is, quite obviously, a split between what your parishioners do on a Sunday and what they do on a weekday in the polling booth, and not only a split, or disconnect, but a direct opposition between the two: Mass goers, the followers of Christ, voting for the policies of the anti-Christ. And life goes on as usual the next day!"

"So, Russia has already spread her errors throughout the world and into every area of life, even into some seminaries because a favourite tactic of Marxism is infiltration. A new party setting up calling itself Marxist will not gain adherents in most places, except from a few well-known radicals, because Marxism has a bad name by now. But if they can infiltrate well established political parties or the Church or the universities, or teachers' unions and especially the media, and work under those banners they will be far more successful. It is an instance of the old rule that evil is a parasite on good".

"The Church opposed this ideology of Marxism with many encyclicals since that of *Rerum Novarum* by Pope Leo XIII in 1891. But prior to the council she had rather little to say about the horizontal, about the goal of history and where the Church, as a pilgrim people, was heading, about the meaning of new phenomena such as technology, democracy, urbanization, globalism *etc*. This lacuna was swiftly and forcefully filled by the Marxists, and the workers fell for it. We might say that for them the horizontal beam has no cross at its centre and it does not break out of the circle of this world but promises a false heaven, a workers' paradise within this world. They, along with their so-called 'comrades', even died for this ideology at the barricades, and, even though its fruits were nothing only totalitarianism and suffering for millions, many today still cling to it because they have not been given anything better from their priests in Sunday preaching or in catechetics. In brief, having first gone soft on the upper beam of the cross, on individual eschatology, we then began to neglect the lower beam, the horizontal beam and the Marxists were quick to take over both and fill them with their crude materialism and their promise of an earthly utopia as the goal of history".

"Yet the Church did not fail the world. With the papal encyclicals and her charitable works she brought great light and help to millions. Many popes condemned socialism and communism. Then with Vatican II, and especially with *Lumen Gentium* and *Gaudium et Spes,* she went further than condemnations and gave the world very positive teaching on the meaning of history. In them she affirms the goodness of creation, but also on its need for redeeming grace because of the Fall; the dignity of the individual made in the image and likeness of God but also the social nature of man as belonging to a people; the centrality of Christ who lived and died once in the past but who is also the *Alpha* and *Omega* of history. She shows us the goal of history as the kingdom of God which is the destiny of the people of God as a pilgrim people marching forward

Chapter 34: The Celtic Cross

towards that kingdom which will take them beyond this world. So she has now given us a truly Christian meaning to the horizontal beam of the cross. However, so many years after the council, that meaning is still largely untapped, so the lacuna continues to be filled by Marxism, by the errors predicted at Fatima but disguised under ever new forms, cleverly presented by the secular media, so that even some practicing Catholics fall for them and think they are advancing human rights and a better society because claiming to be more liberal".

Fr Smart: "Also I see that you know a lot about the inner life of the Church especially when you were talking about seminaries a while ago. Are you a priest or seminarian yourself?"

Tourist. "No, not a priest. I'd be dressed like one if I were. I am an American of Irish descent, Kelly is my name, a typical West of Ireland name I see. My grandparents came from somewhere around here and they often encouraged me to go on holidays to Ireland for the nourishment it would give my faith. They thought that the Ireland they grew up in would continue to hold the faith forever. I have come here a number of times but it is fortunate for them that they are gone now because the changes I see in the lives of people here would sadden them terribly if they were still alive. I entered a seminary but it was a seminary gone off track and I would be gone off track myself also were it not for my parish priest at home in whom I confided when home on holidays and he kept me right. He was sound. He had studied in Rome and advised me to quit the seminary in my own country and to study theology in the University in Rome where he had studied and then to try finding a bishop who was also orthodox. That is where I am now. I'd like to tell you the full story some other time and you might even be able to help me towards finding such a bishop".

It was getting late. The sun was now sinking behind Croagh Patrick to the West and was shedding the last of its golden rays through those eyelets of the Celtic cross where the vertical and horizontal beams break out of the circle. Croagh Patrick is Ireland's holy mountain, a symbol of the faith which that saint brought to Ireland in the fifth century. How ironic that the sun, the symbol of the resurrection, was sinking as our two friends were talking about the sinking faith of Ireland.

Fr Smart put away his lawnmower and invited his guest to come in for tea. He was anxious to hear more of the story of his guest and to learn from him where he thought the Church and his parish, as the Church in miniature, should go from here. He was coming round to seeing that a parish is not just a territory on a map but a community gathered round the Eucharist and that it should not stand still or go round in circles;

that there is indeed a divine goal for the parish as the pilgrim people of God on the march. As to what it means in practice for a Christian people to march forward towards the kingdom of God we will see in the next chapter. If people could see what that means then it might come to pass that it would be the *rising* sun which would once again be seen to shine through the eyelets of the Celtic cross, this time from the East, the place that symbolizes the resurrection for Christians everywhere and perhaps indicate a resurrection of faith for a new generation in Ireland. In the longer term this would have its impact on the entire Western world because at the time of the Celtic crosses it was Ireland which did so much to give the faith to so much of that world. If that was her mission in history once before why should it not be her mission again?

Conclusions:

1. The individual Christian has the goal of saving his own soul and thus of preparing himself for the particular judgment at the end of his life. But he also has a body and is a member of the community of his parish, and of the universal Church which is made present in his parish. In that respect also, as part of his parish he, along with all the others who make up the parish, also has a goal.
2. The parish is not something static nor is its life something that goes round and round endlessly even though the seasons of the Church come round annually. It is a pilgrim people on the march towards the kingdom of God of the end time.
3. Particular eschatology had to be kept in a balance with general eschatology if secularism is to be overcome. Both need to be preached.

If the Church is a pilgrim people on the march towards the kingdom of God, it is fitting that we say more about this kingdom in what follows.

Chapter XXXV

The Kingdom of God

The Church and the Kingdom, the Kingdom and the Parish, the Vision of *Gaudium et Spes,* Preparing the World for the Kingdom, the Kingdom Existence of our Achievements

Then I saw a new heaven and a new earth; for the first heaven and the first earth had passed away, and the sea was no more. And I saw the holy city, the new Jerusalem coming down out of heaven from God, prepared as a bride adorned for her husband; and I heard a great voice from the throne saying 'Behold the dwelling of God is with men'… Revelations 21:1-3 ff.

…the Church has a single intention: that God's kingdom may come, and that the salvation of the whole human race may come to pass. *Gaudium et Spes, #45.*

The Church and the Kingdom

The theme of the kingdom of God is central in the preaching of Christ. We see this especially in His parables. More than that, He identifies Himself with the kingdom. *Know that the kingdom of God is among you. Lk. 17.21.* He said this after working miracles and especially after casting out demons from the possessed. A kingdom is the territory over which a king rules. If Christ was able to control the elements - *even the wind and the sea obey Him, Mt 8:27* - cure all kinds of illnesses and even raise the dead, and if He is God, then it follows that God, who rules all things from the beginning of time, was now also ruling as king in Christ over every level of creation. Hence, we can say that the kingdom of God begins with Christ, though it was also prefigured in the Old Testament in various ways, and it comes to fulfilment when He returns again.

But to rule over every level of creation requires also that He rule in the hearts of men, men who have free will and can say "yes" or "no" to His reign. He called on all to follow Him. As we know, some did and some refused. *But to all who accepted Him He gave power to become children of God. Jn. 1.* Hence, we can say that from then onwards the kingdom continued to grow in the hearts of the faithful, people who often had to pay the price of martyrdom for their faithfulness because the Church has often met with opposition from the world as is the case also today. He had foretold this in the parable of the wheat and the weeds, which tells of the comingling of good and evil, leading to an uncompromising struggle between the two which would go on until the harvest, the final judgment, when good will finally triumph. *(Mt. 13:24-43)*. Later, St Augustine took up this theme with his great work, the *City of God*. Good people and bad people comingle on this earth in the two cities: that of God and that of the world. One cannot distinguish such people when one passes them by on a busy street. But the two cities are different: in the hearts of the citizens of the city of God it is God's will that rules over one's own will, while in the other city it is the reverse.

The Church is not to be simplistically equated with the kingdom of God even though the kingdom is growing and fermenting like a leaven or mustard seed *in* the Church. There are good people who seek to know and to do God's will who are not formally members of the Church by baptism. They too belong to the city of God and the kingdom; and then, there are also people who are formal members of the Church but reject the will of God by knowingly breaking His commandments. Nonetheless, it is still true to say that the kingdom is growing in the Church. *Lumen Gentium* puts it as follows:

> She becomes on earth the initial budding forth of that kingdom. While she slowly grows, the Church strains forward toward the consummation of the kingdom and, with all her strength, hopes and desires to be united in glory with her king. *Lumen Gentium, #5; cf.* also *#9*

When united in glory with her king the Church will openly share the glory He has in heaven, a glory she already possesses imperceptibly in germ by grace, despite the sinfulness of many of her members.

Then, at the eschaton, Christ's kingdom will be seen *coming down from heaven,* ready for the wedding feast of the lamb in the new Jerusalem. *(Rev. 21:2)*. The citizens of this city will enjoy "eternal life", now blossomed into glory, because life in the kingdom is a participation in God's own Trinitarian life and glory which He enjoys from all eternity, a glory once manifest in the Son at His transfiguration and resurrection. Thus, in the end, there is a return to the beginning for the blessed, even to a higher state than what Adam knew in paradise. *(cf. LG #13)*

It is not the case, therefore, that the Church somehow becomes or develops into the kingdom from below by merely human efforts in the course of history. Rather, the kingdom of the end, because it is creation sharing in God's eternal, Trinitarian glory, in a sense, precedes the Church and draws her forward. Christ is standing at the end drawing His bride towards Himself. She, from her side, calls to Him as her Lord saying *maranatha*. That the new Jerusalem, will be seen to *come down* from above signifies that this is a thing of grace, i.e., a gift from above. *(cf.* St. Augustine, *City of God Bk XX)*. It is because Christ, the bridegroom, comes forward to meet His bride that she will be able to withstand the last great onslaught of persecution led by the Anti-Christ.

The Church's relation to the kingdom, therefore, is that she is that kingdom present mystically but she is none the less anticipating and striving towards its complete fulfilment.

> The Church, or, in other words, the kingdom of Christ now present in mystery, grows visibly in the world through the power of God. *ibid., #3*

She leads all mankind towards it, guiding people by her shepherds, teaching them the truth she has from her Lord and uniting them to Him with her sacraments. She teaches them to believe with faith in Christ and His saving deeds, which, in turn, are grounds for hope in His future coming and an incentive to love, both Him and all others, in the present.

In a special way she puts the kingdom before people with the practice of the evangelical councils by some of her members, the religious. *(cf. LG, #43ff; GS, #38).*

Most of all, she makes the kingdom present by anticipation in her liturgy, the liturgy of the hours and especially the liturgy of the Eucharist, when the risen Lord and His sacrifice of Calvary, the eternal sacrifice of the Lamb before the throne, are made present.

In brief, she is the sacrament, the sign and instrument of the kingdom:

> The church, in Christ, is like a sacrament – a sign and instrument, that is, of communion with God and of unity among all men……the sign and instrument of the full realization of the unity yet to come. *CCC, 775, (cf. LG, #1, #9, #48, GS, #45).*

Mary, in her glorified body, already in heaven, stands as the perfect model of the Church in her pilgrimage to the same glory.

<u>The Kingdom Secularized</u>

What the documents of the council describe to us in the above can very simply be called the Christian vision of the goal of the pilgrim people which will be fully realized when Christ returns to call the dead from their graves and judges all people; when the forces of evil are definitively destroyed and His reign is made perfect in the hearts of all *on earth as it is in heaven*. And the earth itself will then be purified, transformed and taken into heaven. The Church has been putting this vision before the faithful from the beginning of her history, in the scriptures, in the writings of Church Fathers such as St Augustine and today.

But when we come to the Middle Ages we find a distortion of this vision in the Cistercian abbot Joachim of Fiore in the South of Italy (1135–1202). He divided history into three ages, that of the Father, that of the Son and finally that of the Holy Spirit. He had a literal understanding of the millenarism of *Revelations 21* and was carried away by the enthusiasm generated by the new religious orders of that age. Thus, he thought he saw the beginning of the fulfilment of the kingdom of God on earth in his own time in what would be the age of the Holy Spirit. His vision was false because the activity of God is one in all ages and cannot be assigned to the different persons of the Trinity in different ages without destroying the very unity of God as St Thomas Aquinas would later point out. Also, the kingdom of God is not something to be fulfilled *within* history but at the *end* of history.

Nonetheless, though this vision of Joachim was false theologically, it continued to inspire thinkers for ages to come in literature, philosophy and theology. It gave rise to a forward looking, progressive, utopian kind of thinking. The sad thing, however, is that such thinking took the form of a secularizing of the truly Christian vision of the divine mysteries and of the kingdom of the God, due to the secularizing influences of the reformation and the enlightenment. One thinks, for example, of Francis Bacon (1561–1626) with his scientism, the idea that once scientific knowledge was applied to matter all our problems would be solved and possibly death itself might be conquered in time. Then there was Hegel (1770-1831) with his philosophy of the great Idea, or mind, coming to consciousness of itself in history by the law of the dialectic, a law of conflict between things and their opposites, until it would find fulfilment in something like the Prussian state of his own time.

Next came Marx (1818-1883) who can be described as the inversion of Hegel such that matter, not mind, was primary; matter for him being the means of production. As a result of the dialectic of class warfare - the proletariat against the capitalists - which would give rise to a great revolution, a classless society would emerge, a man-made utopia with no need whatever of a Saviour or even of God. The proletariat themselves would be their own saviour, following the law of class hatred instead of the law of love, and the communist state would be the new paradise. The party leader would make himself to be the new god by the cult of his own personality. This, in fact, is how many in communist countries would come to see their leaders even though those men were tyrants like Stalin or Mao. It is not irrelevant that Marx, though baptised, had a Jewish background with its influence of messianism.

Darwin (1809-1882), then, with his evolutionism was adding to this secularist hope with his theory that life was progress from matter to life and to ever higher – and it was presumed – ever better forms of life with no need of God either at the beginning or end of the process. One could say that Marxism was an application of this kind of thinking to economics.

And all the while the Church was presenting the world with individual eschatology, the vision of the individual saving his own soul regardless of the goal that the world and history might be pursuing, if any. But the Church did organize great charitable works and provided workers with truly solid charters of their rights in her encyclicals. All of this was good as far as it went. But more was needed: a Christian vision of the goal of history was needed to counteract the secularist visions which had captured and enslaved the minds of millions. The Christian vision - never lost but dormant - came with Vatican II, especially with the documents of *Lumen Gentium* and *Gaudium et Spes* as said in the previous chapter. But even fifty years after the council that vision was still dormant, and distortions of it were being pursued instead. So how can it be given effect in the universal Church and, for our purposes, in the parish? That is still a question waiting for an answer.

The Kingdom and the Parish

All things that act do so for an end. The planets, inanimate things, go around the sun, unknowingly serving their Creator as their end. The birds build their nests acting for an end not rationally perceived but known by instinct which, again, is in them from the Creator. Man can apprehend an end as being good by his power of reason and pursue it freely by his power of will. It is God who gives him these powers and the ability to know, by using his reason, that God Himself is his ultimate end. Prior to arriving at his ultimate end man can chose many proximate ends as means to his ultimate end. But he can also lose sight of his ultimate end and get lost in a life of endless sampling of proximate ends which lead him nowhere. He can settle for a humdrum, day-to-day existence living only to survive until tomorrow, or he can have a vision of greater things.

But what about the Christian and his/her end if he is to go beyond the natural? As we have seen, he can make the saving of his own individual soul to be his entire goal and to hell with the body, the world and even his neighbour. But that is a distortion of Christianity because it is very incomplete and most uncharitable, as we saw already, even if it *is* important to be concerned for one's soul. The Christian is a member of the Church which is not an abstraction but the mystical body of Christ living in the parish community. So, our question then becomes: what is the goal or vision of the parish seen in relation to the kingdom of God? More specifically: what is the goal of people in the parish when they see themselves not just as individuals but as members of this community of faith? What hope does this faith give them not just for themselves individually but for that community itself also as they go about their daily duties? More specifically still: when Jo Green comes to town to buy a load of cement for the new hospital that is being built out the road does he see any supernatural dimension to what he is doing beyond that of earning a wage for himself and his family? He will not have any such vision unless his parish priest can give him such. But does the priest himself have any such vision to begin with?

We saw already that Fr Smart had the vision of a well-functioning parish because he had a lot of laity (so as to be in keeping with what he thinks the "involvement of the laity" is all about), and mostly women (so as to be in keeping with today's feminist ideology) doing all kinds of things around the church, mostly at weekends, but with little concern for what they will be doing for the rest of the week. It is a vision indeed and he is giving it effect but, again, it is a distortion of what Vatican II is saying because incomplete and even Gnostic or docetist in a new way, i.e., in the way it ignores life in the real world of politics, culture, work, business, education, health *etc.*, and ignores that goal which is the kingdom and to which history is heading.

Then there is the young priest, full of energy, newly arrived in a quiet or remote parish who is determined to "shake up" the whole place and make it "buzz" with activity. So, he throws himself into training football teams, organizing concerts, taking the old people on bus tours, helping young people start up little business enterprises, helping farmers start up a vegetable co-operative and many other such things as long as his energy will last. Great. He does see, rightly, that there is more to the parish than the weekend Masses, that one must develop the material and the bodily as well as the spiritual and the soul. He is praised as the one who did indeed shake up the place and got things going. But what is his vision? If it is only to create a "buzz" and inject a bit of life into the place it will all fizzle out when he himself begins to suffer from burn out. And if it doesn't, there is the danger that he will get carried away by the heresy of activism or become so absorbed in his achievements that he forgets about the spiritual and become a mere social worker or development officer or politician. He needs a truly Christian vision to aim at so that this won't happen, a vision in which all of his earthly activities, good indeed, will have their proper place in relation to the ultimate and not become ends in themselves.

The Vision of the two Priests

I would like to return here again to two of the priests whom we met already in an earlier chapter in the *King* section of this study who were great social organizers, but

Chapter 35: The Kingdom of God

who were very faithful to their duties as shepherds, teachers and sanctifiers also, and see what their respective visions were.

The first was Canon John Hayes. As we saw, he founded a parish-based, self-help movement of community development called *Muintir na Tíre*. Very simply a *Muintir* branch would have the people of a given parish identify their needs and organize to solve them by neighbourly cooperation. That might mean cooperating to drain a river that was flooding good land, or building a parish hall or starting a small industry to give employment or whatever.

His vision was based on the family, which institution was strong in Ireland in those times due to the high practice of faith and the absence of the plagues of contraception and divorce. For Canon Hayes the parish should be a family of families with self-sacrificing family love as the basic social value. One could also call him an apostle of unity getting people to co-operate instead of fighting each other in the aftermath of a civil war. His vision could be described as a forerunner of what later St John Paul would advocate as a "civilization of love".

The second priest we encountered was Fr James McDyer in the North West of Ireland who promoted parish-based co-operatives. I knew him personally and was able to ask him about the vision that motivated him. Very simply he said he was trying to save his parish by having people develop its natural potential with co-operative effort. In spiritual terms he said he was trying to give effect to the corporal works of mercy which requires that we take care of the body as well as the soul. He also described his vision as that of a Christian socialism by which he did *not* mean state ownership of the means of production, something that *kills* local initiative, but the people of a parish having shared ownership of such things as the parish hall, small business enterprises cooperatively run, a play-ground for children and other amenities that would be of benefit to all in the parish. Again, as with Canon Hayes, it was a vision of charity given practical effect in the small-scale, local economy for the good of all and for the glory of God. And as with Canon Hayes, he was also a man of devout faith very committed to the Mass and the sacraments and all the practices of traditional Irish Catholicism.

I am not aware of either priest talking about the kingdom of God as the vision that motivated them but both were aware of the call of such popes as Pius X and Pius XI to "restore all things in Christ" which is much the same idea because it envisages Christ being king in all areas of life. They also referred to the encyclicals of *Rerum Novarum* and *Quadragesimo Anno* and would quote from them as it suited them, for example on the subsidiarity principle of the latter encyclical which is very relevant to the small parish that is trying to do things for itself.

Both priests knew well what it is to carry the cross when trying to lead one's flock forward. They had financial worries when trying to get new enterprises going and met opposition from politicians who felt they were stealing the limelight from them, and opposition at times also from the very people they were trying to help. They remind me of the grumbling of the people against Moses in the desert when he was trying to lead them on to better things but still would not follow, and also of the One who came later who cured the lame and the blind, fed the crowds and even raised the dead and was "rewarded" by being put to death on a cross. That explains also why the Mass was very important to both priests: they were living out that sacrifice in their own daily lives until they died themselves from the stress of their efforts, having given of their all.

The Vision of *Gaudium et Spes*

Both of these priests were able to see that there is more to religion than saving one's own individual soul even though they fully agreed that each of us must give an account to God individually at the particular judgement. The respective visions that motivated them were simple - a social, practical applications of the gospel law of charity in a parish setting with a view to "restoring all things in Christ". I would argue that they were anticipations of what the Church would later put before us in greater richness and fullness in *Lument Gentium, Gaudium et Spes* and in the document on the laity *Apostolicam Actuositatem* when these talk about the laity preparing the world for the kingdom of God.

One would think, then, that what these priests were doing should have received a great boost when these documents of Vatican II emerged so that we would thenceforth have an even greater involvement of the laity in transforming the world so as to prepare it for the kingdom. But, instead, what we got was an "involvement" that was limited to the sanctuary at the weekend, and, worse still, an "involvement" of a directly anti-Christian kind when Catholic laity would be found voting for laws which promote every kind of immorality most damaging to marriage, the family and the parish, the Church and society.

Gaudium et Spes confronts an understanding of spirituality which would say that to be holy one must forsake the world, or, at the least, have a minimal involvement with it so as to be more free to save one's soul. This is what was traditionally called a *fuga mundi* spirituality, an understanding of holiness dominated by the monastic ideal such that the monk became the apex or model which all Christians should try to imitate as far as their circumstances in the world would allow. It must be admitted that this was, indeed, the model of spirituality right up until St Francis de Sales made a breakthrough with his little classic *The Introduction to the Devout Life*. There he shows that the one size-fits-all monastic ideal does not work because it does not "fit" the bishop or the married layman or the single girl or the ordinary man in the street such as the "butcher or baker or candlestick maker." To try to make of all these people wear or take on the monastic model would be chaotic. St Francis says:

> The practice of devotion must differ for the gentleman and the artisan, the servant and the prince, for widow, young girl or wife. Further, it must be adapted to their particular strength, circumstances and duties. Is the solitary life of a Carthusian suited to a bishop? Should those who are married practice the poverty of a Capuchin? If workmen spent as much time in church as religious, if religious were exposed to the same pastoral calls as a bishop, such devotion would be ridiculous and cause intolerable disorder. <u>Yet this foolish mistake is often made</u>. *Introduction to the Devout Life, Part I, Ch. 3.*

<u>Rightful Autonomy of earthly Things</u>

This foolish mistake *was* made for quite a long while, indeed even into the 20th century. Underlying it was the idea that if man were to engage with the world to develop it he would somehow be setting himself up as a rival to God. This would indeed be the case if the agents were atheists deliberately setting out to build a secularist paradise or a new Tower of Babel. And that happens. Consciously or unconsciously such people are relying on a metaphysics that is not able to understand the idea of a finite world existing alongside an infinite God because created and loved by Him. The autonomy of earthly things would seem to them to demand the rejection of God and that is the choice they make. *Gaudium et Spes* resolves this problem by distinguishing a false understanding of the autonomy of earthly things from the true autonomy:

> If by the autonomy of earthly affairs we mean that created things and societies themselves enjoy their own laws and values which must be gradually deciphered, put to use, and regulated by men, then it is entirely right to demand that autonomy. Such is not merely required by modern man, but harmonizes also with the will of the Creator…But if the expression, the independence of temporal affairs, is taken to mean that created things do not depend on God, and that man can use them without any reference to their Creator, anyone who acknowledges God will see how false such a meaning is. For without the Creator the creature would disappear. #36

When Christians understand that the world of finite things exists precisely because God so willed it to exist and *saw that it was good* and loves it, they can also see that He willed it to have a rightful autonomy by which things would have their own natures, with their own laws and a real causality though, of course, in dependence on Him. They will then be able to see that their own activity in the world, provided it is morally good, is a furthering of the divine will for the world in co-operation with God and not a rivalry over against Him. Hence the document says:

> Thus, far from thinking that works produced by man's own talent and energy are in opposition to God's power, and that the rational creature exists as a kind of rival to the Creator, Christians are convinced that the triumphs of the human race are a sign of God's grace and the flowering of His own mysterious design. For the greater man's power becomes, the farther his individual and community responsibility extends. Hence it is clear that men are not deterred by the Christian message from building up the world, or impelled to neglect the welfare of their fellows, but that they are rather more stringently bound to do these very things. *ibid., #34*

However, in thus encouraging Christians to get down to the task of "building up the world" in all those areas of life in which providence has put them, in their homes and work-places and in their various careers, the Church of Vatican II was certainly not tilting over to the other extreme of having them "baptize" any and every kind of human activity as being in harmony with God's plan, because this would amount to a simplistic equation of earthly progress and the growth of the kingdom, which, in turn, would often amount to a baptizing of what is sinful, because much of what is considered to be earthly progress *is* sinful because motivated by sheer greed, pride and the desire for power. It would, in effect amount to an idolizing of the world which would then become a second Tower of Babel. Hence the council warns:

> Earthly progress must be carefully distinguished from the growth of Christ's kingdom. Nevertheless, to the extent that the former can contribute to the better ordering of human society, <u>it is of vital concern</u> to the kingdom of God. *ibid., #39.*

They are called to build up the world by promoting what is just, loving and truly respectful of human nature as found in each individual and of the common good of society. They are to make the law of God as found in nature and in divine revelation to be the underpinning law of society, to penetrate the world with a Christian spirit and to bear witness to Christ and His law of love in everything:

Since they have an active role to play in the whole life of the Church, laymen are not only bound to penetrate the world with a Christian spirit, but are also called to be witnesses to Christ in all things in the midst of human society. *ibid., #43.*

When lay Christians are thus engaged in Christianizing the world they are living out their own distinctive spirituality. They are growing in holiness by doing this, by being thus engaged in the world, not *in spite* of being thus engaged, as a *fuga mundi* spirituality would have them believe. They will be living the mysteries: they will be living Trinitarian lives with their practice of charity. They will be perfecting creation by developing the world in various ways, but doing so by respecting the God-given natures of things. They will be extending the incarnation into the depths of the earth when grace will permeate nature all the more due to man's dominance of nature by people in a state of grace. They will be living the redemption by carrying the cross with all the suffering and opposition which their efforts will entail, and they will be preparing the world for the kingdom to come by making Christ and His law effective everywhere so that God's will is done on earth, more and more, as it is always done in heaven.

In doing so they will also be living the three traditional stages of spiritual growth, the purgative, illuminative and unitive but again in ways that are analogously suited to their life situations. They will be engaged in the world but will be purged more and more of selfish attachment to it. They will be illumined by growing in the knowledge of the faith and by making progress in the virtues that are most proper to lay people, for example marital chastity in the family and justice in the work place. Finally, they will make time for prayer as their own time schedules will allow so as to unite themselves ever more closely with their Lord. But what it means to prepare the world for the kingdom needs some further explanation.

Preparing the World for the Kingdom

We have seen already how the Church relates to the kingdom. She does so as a kind of sacrament of it because the kingdom is growing within her. Here we want to see how our work, specifically, and our earthly endeavours generally, relate to the kingdom. Let us first clear away some mistaken notions on this.

The scientism of Francis Bacon would have man bring about a utopia on earth by applying scientific knowledge to matter. Diseases would be cured; famines would cease; the standard of living would go up and eventually death itself might be conquered. But history since the time of Bacon has shown what evils science has also facilitated by its very efficacy – two world wars, for example, with an efficacy that killed millions of people; nuclear weapons, with two atoms bombs exploded already killing hundreds of thousands; and human malice, always there, now given ever wider extension.

To the extent that science does improve man's lot materially and medically – and it certainly does - the end gain, even if it saw the elimination of many evils, would still be only a kingdom of man, not of God. Marxists, we saw, promised an earthly utopia (never realized anywhere) by means of class hatred and revolution, means which would be explicitly atheistic, while accusing Christians of doing nothing for human wellbeing. In response then, there is the temptation for Christians, stung by this accusation (false though it be) to try to outdo the Marxists and all other utopians by creating a *Christian* utopia here on earth but still one confined to this earth, that is, by setting up the ideal state with the best of scientific advances, the best social welfare system, the most equitable distribution of wealth but still a political regime of this world only. One might indeed wish for a state governed by a king like St Luis IX of France or St Elizabeth of Hungary and be tempted to call that the kingdom of God. But, welcome though such a regime might be, it would not be the kingdom of God. Those rulers were indeed saints but many of their subjects were not and in any case those regimes, though they were just and cared for the needy, were still temporary, fragile and subject to eventual failure, as history showed. They were good but still could not be called the kingdom of God.

But have such regimes as were ruled over by these saints, then, any relevance for the kingdom of God? Did they make for any relation of earthly endeavor to the kingdom of God? Do we simply say that they were feeble preludes or anticipations of the kingdom? Is it the same with our best efforts today? To take a concrete example: in the last chapter we saw Jo Green loading up a truck with cement for a new children's hospital that the entire parish had contributed to building. In what sense can we say that his efforts or the hospital itself when finished, or the efforts of those who gave donations towards it, will be a contribution to the kingdom of God, which kingdom will not appear in its fullness until the Lord returns at the end of time? Do they in any way contribute towards the kingdom? One answer to that question is to say that they do contribute by reason of the good intentions of these people in making these efforts, that such good intentions will stand as merits in their individual souls which will earn them many graces before they each die and corresponding rewards in the next life. True indeed. I cannot deny that. But if that is the full extent of their contributions then we are back solely to an individualist eschatology again with no relation to general eschatology, to the kingdom of the end. Put differently, my question is: can these efforts to build this hospital, and the hospital itself when built, be in any sense a contribution to the kingdom of the end? One other answer, negative again, is to say that such is impossible for the simple reason that such efforts are transient actions and that the hospital itself, even if it endures for a hundred years, may well be demolished long before the kingdom of the end arrives. But *Gaudium et Spes seems to say otherwise above* when it says that anything we do that makes for a better ordering of society is of "*vital* concern to the kingdom of God". It goes even further and says:

> For after we have obeyed the Lord, and in His Spirit nurtured on earth the values of human dignity, brotherhood and freedom, and indeed all the good fruits of our nature and enterprise, we will find them again, but freed of stain, burnished and transfigured. This will be so when Christ hands over to the Father a kingdom eternal and universal: 'a kingdom of truth and life, of holiness and grace, of justice, love and peace'. *ibid., #39.*

So, we can affirm that our efforts to do good in the here and now, though temporary and fragile, will become contributions to the kingdom of the end. This might sound novel but in truth it is saying only what I often heard old people saying long before Vatican II: that we take nothing with us out of this world when we die *except the good we have done*; that that good will go on ahead of us into the kingdom and in some way be a contribution to that kingdom. The good in question may be good works understood as good deeds or the fruits of those works understood as the things achieved by them.

How our Achievements make a Contribution to the Kingdom

To affirm that our earthly efforts, our work and the things produced, do make a contribution to the kingdom calls for some further explanation as to just how this happens. It is not the case that our achievements will somehow *evolve* in the kingdom of God by themselves with time, nor do we make or produce the kingdom by ourselves. That would be a kind of Pelagianism and would give no part to God. A better example can be had from farming. The farmer prepares the ground and sows the seed but it is God who gives the growth as a gift. Yet the farmer's contribution is important. Scripture gives us a building example in the Psalms: *if the Lord does not build the house in vain do the workmen labour. Ps 127.* The Lord is the real builder but the workmen must also do their part. St Thomas uses this example also: Christians by their good works are like the under workers on a building site constructing an arch but it is the master builder who must put in the keystone at the top at the end. Otherwise the arch will collapse. (*cf S. Th. I, q.38, art.3, co*).

This examples points up the *gratuity* of the kingdom as ultimately a gift coming down from God as the primary agent but they also point up the importance of human effort, man's contribution, something willed and welcomed by God. It is not that the work is divided half and half between Christ and His Christians. Christ, as God, is responsible for the entire work, but nonetheless He gives His followers their rightful, full and proper part in the enterprise, albeit with Him sustaining their every effort. Thus we see our achievements as the building blocks in His kingdom, taken up by Him when He gives them the form of His own risen glory, there to shine forth as the jewels of a glorified world for eternity.

Practical consequence

The practical consequence of this for Christians, especially for lay people working in the world, is that it should encourage them, first of all, to pray for the coming of the kingdom because it is foremost a thing of grace *coming down from above*. This we do every time we say the *Our Father*. Then it should encourage them to work hard at whatever is productive of genuine good, of that which promotes the true welfare of mankind both as individuals and as communities locally, beginning with the family, then in the parish or neighborhood, and then in one's country, and even extending out from there onto the international, global scene to further the common good of the entire human family. They should do this by using their talents to develop all natural, God-given resources, by promoting good laws that are in keeping with the moral law and by making the law of charity to be supreme so that witness will be given to Christ everywhere and that He will be king in their hearts in a civilization of love.

Even if many of their efforts are obstructed or destroyed by the powers of evil, or fail, or pass away with time, they will still be encouraged by the belief that they will go before them so that they will find them again "freed of stain, lit up and transfigured" in the kingdom of the end. Compare the hope that such a vision gives to Christians to that which Marx gave his followers with his classless society born of hatred and revolution and which has proved to be a total lie, a false promise and a dismal failure everywhere it was tried.

We saw in the last chapter how Jo Green and his community were working to build a hospital for children. Obviously, they had a vision, what could be called a "humanitarian" vision, that was motivating them. But at the same time, we heard that he and many of his friends had stopped going to Mass, which means that they saw no connection between their humanitarian vision and the Christian vision of the kingdom of God proposed to all of us by *Gaudium et Spes*. The connection is that the Mass is an anticipation of the banquet feast of the kingdom of the end because the Christ, who is made present to us at the consecration, is the glorified Christ who will come at the eschaton to take all that is good in our efforts and the world itself to Himself and give it a share in the same glory. Jo Green and his friends are hopeful that the new hospital will serve the sick for many years to come, perhaps a century or maybe even more, but what if they could have the hope that it, and the good that will be accomplished in it, will be taken up by the Lord for eternity when He comes and that they will find all that good before them when they too pass over into His arms? What a much richer vision that is and what a new appreciation of the Mass it gives!

This takes us to the practical consequences for priests. If Jo Green and his friends are to have that vision it must be given to them by Fr Smart in his preaching and, prior to that, it should be given to them by their teachers in their religion classes at school. If not, the split between faith and the world will continue and the lacuna will be filled by secularist ideologies of various kinds which the secularist media will disseminate.

We saw above the kind of visions which motivated Fr Hayes and Fr McDyer and how they came near to that of *Gaudium et Spes* by anticipation. We saw also how they tried to give practical effect to those visions by leading their people in great efforts to develop their parishes economically and socially. I am not suggesting that every parish priest must, therefore, become expert at draining rivers or starting small businesses or founding cooperatives. Much depends on the kind of parish he has care of. Inner city parishes of high rise flats do not lend themselves to that kind of activity and even some parishes that are rural are already places of full employment with all kinds of social amenities available to them. In some underdeveloped places, where there are few people with professional training, people will turn to the priest for leadership in different areas of life from sport to business to culture, while in other places they have able lay leaders with various qualifications who can, and therefore should, take such a lead instead of the priest doing so. Some parishes are merely dormitory residences to which workers come home in the evening from their places of employment perhaps many miles away.

Then there is the matter of the natural talents of the individual priest. One priest might well have a talent for starting small business while his successor has no such talent but does see the need for it in a parish that is under populated and will help by giving encouragement to those who *will* take the lead. His successor again might be a talented sportsman and uses that to organize the young so that he can get to know them pastorally with a view to evangelizing them and forming them in the virtues that are needed in good sportsmanship first and then as good workers for the kingdom.

But whatever the kind of parish or the talents of a particular priest he must be a preacher of the word, and preach in a way that shows people, wherever they live or work, how what they are engaged in for most of the week in their families and places of work can be a path to holiness for them because making a contribution to the kingdom of the end. He must first instruct them in right and wrong so that they will break with sin, a prerequisite for any progress in holiness. He must show them how their various occupations and engagements can be their distinctive ways of living the mysteries of the faith. He must encourage them in making the gospel underpin all that goes on around them wherever they are so that they will be creating a civilization of love for everyone. He must advise them that such efforts will require a taking up of the cross, but that doing so is a central part of Christian living as they, both as individuals and as communities, march forward towards the dawn of the kingdom.

It will also require that the priest organize classes in Catholic social teaching. He may never have the opportunity to go inside the factories or offices where his parishioners are working, as worker priests or deacons might do, because of constraints of time and distance, but from his base in the parish he will have given them the catechetical tools with which they, as lay people, will be able to do what is most proper to them, which is to transform those places in a Christian way and make Christ present in them. That will also require that he show his people how to be firm and militant when secularist media or anti-religious governments or lobby groups try to undermine what is Christian. He will have to support them when they inevitably get backlash from doing so. But the weapons they use should be those of the gospel: courage and hope combined with patience and charity.

The Kingdom Existence of our Achievements

A question still remains as to what kind of existence our earthly achievement will have in the kingdom of God, a thing which takes us beyond history into the eternity of God? How can we find again these human values and the fruits of our enterprises when their existence in time is so contingent and when the conflagration before the end of the world will be so destructive? Vatican II does not answer such questions specifically but it points us towards an answer when it says:

> Then the human race as well as the entire world, which is intimately related to man and achieves its purpose through him, will be perfectly re-established in Christ. *Lumen Gentium,* #48

Because of the relationship of the world to man, as finding its apex in him, and then of man to Christ, in whom all things will be recapitulated, we can say that our efforts will rise also and live again *as related to the risen Christ*, head and body, in the glorified cosmos.

This still does not enable us to say exactly how the hospital that Jo built will perdure in this new eschatological kind of kingdom existence if perhaps it has been demolished many years prior to the end. There is continuity but also discontinuity between our present earthly existence and our future kingdom existence, something scripture talks of when it says that *eye has not seen nor ear heard and which has not entered the heart of man the things God has prepared for those who love Him. 1 Cor.2:9.* As a result, our speculations about things in the kingdom must needs be limited and inadequate. At any rate, to go any further is to go beyond the limits of what Vatican II enables us to know definitively at present in its documents but, nonetheless, it gives us a vision which is beautiful, inspiring and full of Christian hope.

Conclusions:

1. The kingdom, foreshadowed in the Old Testament, begun in Christ, is growing in the Church and will come to full glory in the eschaton. The Church is a sacrament, sign and instrument of the kingdom leading all men towards unity with God and each other in Christ.
2. Earthly progress relates to the kingdom, not by "producing" it by mere human effort as in an earthly utopia, but as moving towards it, contributing to it, because drawn by Christ, sustained by His grace, and accepted by Him as an offering which He glorifies at the end.
3. The kind of earthly progress which is thus accepted must be the fruit of human effort which is morally good and directed towards the values of true justice and brotherhood, of benefit to the true perfection of the individual, the family and contributing to the common good of all.
4. The kind of existence which these efforts will have in the kingdom can best be understood in the perspective of their relationship to the risen Christ, head and body, and in the perspective of the renewed cosmos, the dwelling befitting the dweller.
5. Christian lay people need this vision of their efforts contributing to the kingdom of God and it is for the priest and the catechists to give them this. Otherwise, their understanding of eschatology will be merely individualist, limited to saving one's own soul, and the lacuna will be filled by other visions of a secularist kind, illusory and harmful.

In our march towards the kingdom, the fullness of which might still be a long way off, we need some lights on the hills in front of us. What they might be we will see in the next chapter and what kind of society we should aim at having in the meantime.

Chapter XXXVI

The Dawn of a New Christendom

Fuga Mundi, New monastic Witness, Islands of Faith

You are the light of the world…. a city built on a hilltop cannot be hidden. Mt. 5:14.

He calls some to give clear witness to the desire for a heavenly home and to keep that desire green among the human family. *Gaudium et Spes, #38.*

The vision being put forward in the preceding chapter stands in contrast to that of a vision or spirituality which concerns itself solely with the individual soul as it tries to disentangle itself as much as possible from engagement with the world, even if one is living in the middle of the city, because the world, being material, is deemed to be very sinful, and by so disentangling itself it will be able to pass the test of the particular judgement. That spirituality is often labelled as *fuga mundi*, "flight from the world," and the monk and monastic life was usually held up as being the model of this. His vows of poverty, chastity and obedience were seen as knives that cut a person off from matter, the body and from freedom so that he could become as "angelic" as possible.

In this chapter I wish to show that this was a distorted understanding of monasticism, that while some are indeed called to withdraw into a secluded kind of spiritual life "far from the madding crowd" that their calling is a very positive one, not just on its own terms but in relation to those of others also whose calling is to be in the midst of the secular world.

Fuga Mundi correctly understood

Is the understanding of monastic spirituality given above - a flight from the evil world - correct? Not at all. If it were, it would follow, then, that we should reject the monastic tradition entirely, a tradition with a history of two millennia behind it, a tradition which produced many saints and which conferred immense benefit on the Church and also on the world, even in material terms, especially at times when the world was in darkness during the centuries that followed the fall of the Roman empire, a tradition which was largely responsible for that blossoming of civilization which then followed in the Middle Ages and which is still an inspiration for people today. To do so would mean cutting off something that is not only *beneficial* to the life of the Church but *essential to it*, hence it would be a contradictory, self-defeating exercise. Also, if we were to hold on to this understanding of the monastic tradition it should follow that we reject the very world around us, the place where the Lord has placed most of us and where he expects us to grow in holiness. [1]

One can indeed find in the writings of some monks and religious things that reflect this very negative understanding of *fuga mundi*. But that is merely a caricature resulting from an undue influence of Platonist or Neo-Platonist philosophy and of the negative Gnostic, Manichean and Docetist theologies of the early centuries.[2] Nonetheless, it is a theology that would surface again and again in later centuries as Albigensianism and Jansenism, the latter drawing on St Augustine for its source but with a narrow interpretation of him. We looked at this already in our *Prophet* section when talking about the true understanding of chastity, and later when talking about marriage.

That kind of thinking, an excessive dualism which pits the spiritual against the material and the soul against the body, is, as we said before, like a virus that recurs and infects Christianity every so often and then, by reason of the swing of the pendulum, begets a reaction of a naturalism such as we had, first with the renaissance, and more fully, later, with the enlightenment. We see the effects of this still today because it is one of the main causes of secularism, a world-view without God in which everything is permitted. Paradoxically, that too leads to a downgrading of the body, as was said in the previous chapter, when it is treated as a mere object of pleasure in an age of hedonism.

What traditionally was called a "*fuga mundi*" spirituality can, if properly understood, be seen in a very positive light. Most of those early Christians who left the city and fled to the desert did so to give themselves more fully to God by lives of prayer and penance and by practicing the evangelical councils more perfectly so as to be unhindered in their love of God. They were indeed fleeing from places where there was much distraction and sin, such as the big cities of the Roman empire of those times, because they were not suitable habitats for what they were embracing. But they did not reject creation or the city *as such* or the body or the neighbor or marriage because they saw all these things as good because created and given to us by God, though tainted by sin as a result of the Fall. In the remoteness of their desert cells, and later in their monasteries, they were praying and doing penance for the world and not just for their own souls so that the world would be saved and, in time, taken into the arms of God at the second coming of Christ. Furthermore, remote as they were from the cities, they still were not remote from each other because they were always conscious of belonging to their respective communities by their common rule, even if scattered here and there geographically in the desert, depending on where they had

Chapter 36: The Dawn of a New Christendom

built their little cells; and, of course, they were conscious of belonging to the universal community of the Church at all times. Moreover, people from the cities would seek them out for their prayers and their advice which was gladly given.

Their practice of the evangelical counsels was not negative, not destructive of anything truly human but only of sin which has infected human nature in everyone. It was positive, then, because a help to charity, which is the essence of the spiritual life. It enabled them to free themselves from inordinate attachments to property (by the vow of poverty), the sinful excesses of bodily desires (by the vow of total chastity) and from the self-will of egotism (by the vow of obedience) which things would pull them away from a pure and disinterested love of God and neighbor.

Religious people love one another with sincere affection that is bodily as well as spiritual because it takes account of man's physical and emotional make up, not stifling these things but controlling them properly, putting them fully under the control of intellect and will, so that their love would be pure but never finding expression in physical relations with others. That kind of love here on earth is a pointer to the kind of love that exists between the persons of the Trinity from eternity inasmuch as it is a love of self-giving of one to another (the Trinity is in no way bodily of course), and to the love the just will have for each other in the kingdom: bodily indeed but with bodies that are glorified and free from any taint of lust.

Recognizing this positive kind of *fuga mundi* spirituality which the monks had taken on, people from the cities would come out to visit them and ask them for their prayers and their counsel on all kinds of matters, not only spiritual but material as well, and they would bring them gifts in thanksgiving for favours received. Later, Kings and emperors would visit monasteries, endow them with lands and money, defend and promote them because they saw the benefits they were conferring on their kingdoms, spiritually with their prayers, culturally with their works of art, academically with their schools, medically with their hospitals and socially with their hostels and with the employment they gave to many round about. It is said that Charlamange even borrowed things from the rule of St Benedict for his own civil rule in his kingdom. Then consider the great material benefits they bestowed on the world by their innovations in agriculture, their draining of rivers, their planting of trees and their development of iron works and herbal medicines. Men and women with a hatred of the world would hardly do such things. On the contrary, they were preparing the world of their time for the kingdom of God of the end and providing their contemporaries with a foretaste of that in their communities. That said, it must be admitted that there were some with distorted views of spirituality who were negative towards the material and extreme in their actions.

The Need for monastic Witness today

If the monastic and religious life generally is essential to the life of the entire Church, as providing all Christians with an example of what it is to follow Christ more fully, then it follows that that life is needed as much today as ever, if not more so. *Gaudium et Spes* recognized this and gave us a positive vision of religious life, and especially of contemplative life, but in a balanced way that recognizes the complementarity of this with other callings also:

> He calls some to give clear witness to the desire for a heavenly home and to keep that desire green among the human family. He summons others to dedicate themselves to the earthly service of men and to make ready the material of the celestial realm by this ministry of theirs. Yet He frees all of them so that by putting aside love of self and bringing all earthly resources into the service of human life they can devote themselves to that future when humanity itself will become an offering accepted by God. *#38.* (*cf.* also St. John Paul II. *Vita Consecrata*).

The kingdom of God, growing in our midst at present, is still ahead of us in its full reality because we do not know when Christ will come again. Christ, at times, spoke of a coming that would be very soon but also, on other occasions, of a coming that would be very late.[3] But His constant warning was to be *awake and alert because you do not know the day or the hour* because when it does come it will be *like a thief in the night.* (*1 Thess. 5*). People live mostly in the short term and if something promised is too far away there is the danger that they will lose hope or fall asleep like the ten maidens of the parable. (*Mt.25.1-13*). To provide against that, God gives us the monks and the religious in their cells and their monasteries to provide us with foretastes in advance of the kingdom. They are like lights on the hill, sending forth the first beams of a new dawn, glimpses in advance of the full light of the kingdom which is still ahead in terms of time but present already, liturgically, in the Eucharist and growing by grace in the hearts of the faithful.

We need these lights. Hence, given the organic nature of the Church where all the members are different in their talents and charisms, but interrelated so as to be of service to each other, it must follow that we do not "play off" the religious life against the life of the pastoral priest and his helpers in the parish, or either of those against the lay life; rather must we see their relatedness and interdependence. That is why monasteries and religious houses in times past have been havens of spiritual refreshment and support for pastoral priests and for lay people as well, and why they would visit such places at weekends and for longer periods to do retreats. It would be mistaken to see such priests and laity as trying to "escape", even if briefly, from their duties in the "big, bad world". Rather, they should be seen as going there for spiritual strength, advice and encouragement, for a "charging of the batteries" as it were, so that they can return to their duties with renewed faith, hope and charity, to take up those duties along the paths on which Providence has placed them which duties sometimes are joys but which at other times are crosses which they must carry in order to be saved and find their Lord.

The priest then is not a monk "let out" in a parish but a man with a distinctive spirituality of his own by which he grows in holiness when he leads, teaches and sanctifies his people so that they, in turn, can grow in holiness in their families and places of work and entertainment. But he has the example of the monks with their prayer when he reads his breviary and the example of their penance when he carries the crosses that are peculiar to a life of caring for people in the parish.

The lay people are not monks or religious either, but the tradition of third order religious tells us that they too can borrow from the monks in their example of prayer and penance but, again, not in ways that will have them flee the world but in ways distinctive to them as people who have the mission of Christianizing the world around them where they are. Accordingly, while working hard to develop this world of the present in a way that makes it more human for everyone, lay people will not become engrossed in it to the point of idolizing it but will be detached from things, living simple lives of frugal comfort because they will be keeping their eyes fixed ahead on the eschaton of the end, *having nothing though having everything,* in St Paul's words *(2 Cor. 6:10).* Doing this is not a contradiction but one of those healthy paradoxes that are characteristic of all Christian life.

<u>Renewing the Monastery</u>

For most of the past two millennia, and even today, the monks have engaged in work that was mostly manual and did so as a means of providing for themselves and those whom came to them for help from round about. They did so also for its spiritual benefit of being a remedy against idleness and of developing what God had given them in creation. It was mostly agricultural in kind, though monks also engaged in other manual activities as varied as carpentry, brewing, baking, printing and tailoring - to mention only a few such activities. Their work was agricultural for the obvious reason that that was the work of most people prior to the industrial revolution and, more so, because it is a very fundamental kind of work, so much so that some economists will argue that most other occupations depend on it one way or another and that, conversely, when the farmer is suffering those in other occupations will be suffering soon after.

Be that as it may, the fact is that the industrial revolution has happened and that now we are in the midst of the information technology (IT) revolution, which is the field of employment of more and more people, along with the many service industries that have developed. I see a challenge here for the monks to adapt to these modes of work also so as to Christianize them in their monasteries and thus give a lead to lay people to do the same in their places of work. There is a monastery of Cistercians in the US in a place where the monks found many trees growing on the surrounding land when they arrived there. The monks, instead of clearing the trees to make room for agriculture – as one would expect Cistercians would do - began instead to use the wood as raw material for a little industry of their own to makes coffins, (how cheerful indeed! but a product that will always be in the demand at this side of the eschaton!). I believe we need more such examples of the monks leading the way in new kinds of work and showing how such enterprises can be run in a truly Christian way.

Widening out further from the monastery, what I have in mind is an area of countryside surrounding the monastery where the people are working together under the inspiration of the monks to create entire districts of a truly Christian kind. Such a district might be made up of a number of parishes, and the priests in them would be helping to give effect to new Christian enterprises, at least by their teaching on Catholic social principles if not by more direct involvement, if time would allow them, so that they would not be taken away from the administration of the sacraments and the management of their parishes.

What I am proposing is not something new but a revamping of what happened when Christendom was coming to be. During the dark ages of the barbarian invasions, after the fall of Rome, it was the monks with their monasteries who kept the light of faith and learning alive in isolated places, which monasteries soon became the centres of civilization in the surrounding areas because towns grew up near to them and many of the lay people actually worked on the lands of the monasteries. As time went on those monastic districts spread in influence and coalesced with other such districts so that soon entire provinces and then whole countries came under their Christianizing influence. Thus did Christendom get going. Along with that, the secular priests served the people in the surrounding parishes, being helped by the monks in various ways.

One might object and say that we still have some monasteries and religious houses today but without them having these effects in the areas around them, that instead, vocations to such houses are in decline in the West. I would argue that that is due to a failure of these communities to embrace the vision of the religious house as a light on the hill pointing forward to the kingdom and that that, in turn, is due to the remains

Chapter 36: The Dawn of a New Christendom

of the Jansenist virus that denigrates everything human, that embraces penance for its own sake and that seeks an individualist perfection of a disembodied, spiritualist kind. I say "the remains" because with the shake-up which followed the second Vatican council, (but again not due to the council) that Jansenism, now a past phenomenon, has begotten the opposite reaction of an irresponsible liberalism and a crude hedonism which has infected religious life in many places, destroying true community life, giving rise to scandals and stifling new vocations. This takes us back again to the question of how religious life generally and monastic life in particular is to be understood by candidates for that life in light of a correct understanding of Vatican II. Let us take some hypothetical examples.

Three candidates enter a religious house. We will call them by the well-hackneyed names of Tom, Dick and Harry. Tom is seeking to grow in holiness but does so by "crucifying" the body with the most extreme of penances. He rejects even the most innocent pleasures of the senses such as the singing of the birds on a Summer's morning and a modicum of simple food at breakfast and does so to the point of endangering his very health. The body, he believes, has to be thus crucified because it is the seat of all evil desires. He is engaging in what we already heard Jacques Maritain call "angelic suicide" - trying to so free himself, not only from what is sinful but from human nature itself so that he comes to be as near to being angelic as possible.

At the other extreme there is Dick who is a lazy fellow hoping for a good time on the bandwagon of religious life and complains that there are so many rules. In any case, rules or no rules, he will compensate for what he sees as the negativity of the evangelical councils by indulging himself in any way he can get away with.

Then there is Harry who takes on severe penance also, not at all because he sees the body as evil but simply to respond to Our Lady's call at Fatima that people would make sacrifices in reparation for the sins being committed in our time and also to curb any evil inclinations that come from his own heart so that he can grow all the more in holiness. Self-denial for him is a pruning away of the bad branches of vice in himself so that the good branches of virtue and can grow all the better. He knows too that he must carry his cross in the meantime but it is a cross understood in a positive way as leading to the resurrection, not a thing of suffering for its own sake. He prunes his vices and carries his crosses under the supervision of a prudent spiritual director so that he will not endanger his health or go to extremes. He is aware that many of the sins of our time are due to the errors that Our Lady had predicted would spread from Russia, which errors can loosely be called "communism" and the many other ideologies that are variants of this. In all of this he has something positive motivating him: the vision of the coming kingdom of God for which he longs and for which he prepares by fostering every authentic human value in himself, in his brothers in his community and in the world around him as far as his influence can extend.

Then there may be others in the community who have no particular vision, true or false, but simply that of carrying the day with as much ease as possible. There has to be rules, many rules for such members. Otherwise, there will be total disorder with everyone "doing his own thing". But the observance of such members achieves little if they have no vision of what they are doing. For those who *have* a vision, rules are no problem and not even necessary. St Paul would say that in their case love fulfils the law, regulations or no; or to paraphrase St Augustine, they can love and do as they will. Their rule is charity internalized and enlivened by grace.

All of these are members of the same community with much the same daily duties to fulfil and the same time-table to follow; but see how different their inner lives are due to the different visions that each has of what religious life is all about. The spirituality of Tom and Harry might seem similar, materially or externally because they both see the value of penance, yet formally they are very different, as different as truth is from falsehood. From a purely secularist point of view Dick might seem to have the best life of all but his spirituality is a fake. I would argue that not all religious had the right vision in the past, that we are still suffering from the blindness of a very negative, dualist vision, but that Vatican II gives us guidance as to how to get it right in the future with the more positive vision it puts before us, the vision of the kingdom ahead.

Islands of Faith

If or when we do get it right we can, I believe, get on to creating what I will call "islands of faith", a term I am using to indicates a support structure which Christians have need of today so that they can come together to be of support to each other in living the faith. The need is becoming greater every day as Christians find themselves living in a world that is becoming more and more hostile to what they believe is due to a large-scale, current apostasy. This has many causes going back to the breakup of Christendom which happened with the Protestant revolt and which then advanced further soon after with the naturalism of the enlightenment. Today this hostility is gaining force from the ideologies of secularism and of a pluralism which would have us believe that one can mix all kinds of people with very different beliefs and none into one society as in a melting pot and that with only the fake ideals of unlimited freedom and unlimited tolerance of everything, even of things objectively evil, we can have a coherent, stable society supportive of what is truly human. We can see before our eyes now that the false freedom and tolerance being propagated today leads soon enough to anarchy because civil law has no longer any foundation in human nature or in God's revealed law, and that this then leads to a new tyranny because people cannot live with anarchy for very long, so that a dictator will soon rise up and take control so as to restore order. But he will do so at gunpoint, by force. Napoleon, Hitler and Stalin are but a few examples from the past. He will be a fore runner of the anti-Christ if not that evil man himself.

The proponents of this kind of evil regime want an of "open" society, where national borders are supposed to give way to an amorphous globalism in which people of traditional Christian beliefs are told to shelve or suppress their beliefs lest they "offend" those who come in across their borders when the latter have totally different beliefs or none. Belief in objective, revealed truth is then supposed to give way to subjective, private opinion, and objective morals are reduced to a relativism that depends only on subjective feeling, which is ever varying and which can lead to any kind of behavior depending on different situations.

I have dealt with this already in the *Prophet* section of this work when talking about pluralism in the classroom so I won't repeat all of that here. I am simply making the point that a religiously or culturally amorphous, undifferentiated globalism does not work and will only lead to a new barbarism in a totalitarian society, and I am offering this idea of islands of faith as the antidote for Christians. I will probably be accused, then, of proposing a kind of *ghetto* Catholicism exclusive of all other peoples, a Church that is looking inwards when it should be looking outwards and missionary. Not so. Experience shows that when the host Catholics practice their faith openly, sincerely and unapologetically, incoming migrants of other beliefs come to embrace Catholicism freely and gladly because they see its truth and beauty in practice. The very word "Catholic" means "universal", that is, a religion designed from above to be welcoming of all who wish to embrace it whatever their race or country. If we go deeper still to the first truth of faith, the Trinity, which is a *communio* of self-giving love of the three persons going "outwards" from one to the other, and then "outwards" again to the world in missionary fashion when the Son and Holy Spirit are sent, we have a further reason for seeing these islands of faith as outward looking and missionary. They are missionary when they seek to extend their circles of influence outwards and when they welcome those who come to them. But to do that successfully they must also be inward looking in the sense of consolidating their own faith amongst themselves, in order to be strong in that faith and not faint hearted or lukewarm in it as so often is the case today when faith is diluted and then tacitly denied so as not to offend any non-believers.

Given all this, even so, if incoming migrants do not embrace the faith, for one reason or another, they should still be allowed freedom to practice their own religions provided that doing such is consistent with the moral law and the common good and does not undermine the ethos and traditional practices of the host country. They should be treated with respect, justice and charity because whatever their religion they too are in the image and likeness of God and are called by His Son to a life of grace.

These islands of faith, I would argue, should have a monastery or religious house at their centre and have a number of parishes surrounding them with both priests and people drawing inspiration from life in the monastery so that they can march forward as parish communities, led by their priests, towards that kingdom of the end, the kingdom which is already anticipated and modelled for them in those religious houses in their midst. These places will be islands of *faith* because the inhabitants will draw strength for themselves and their families from the faith that they share in common, the Catholic faith handed down from the apostles. They will also be islands of *hope*, of Christian hope and not that of worldly ideologies, because they will see the light of the monastery pointing them to the dawn of the kingdom; and they will be islands of *charity* because of a shared love for God and for each other that is fed from the Eucharist and put into practice in daily life.

As to the material infra structure of this society I would hope that it would embody the idea of distributism, the idea that people would find it attractive to come out from the big cities to live in small villages and little hamlets in the countryside with as many people as possible having their own independent, small holdings for growing food and small, family industries for the production of other things and the provision of various services, thereby giving maximum independence to each family and individual but with a high degree of co-operation between all, which is simply charity in practice in economics. The priest would have his own humble dwelling in their midst.

Hopefully these islands will then extend outwards in all directions as more and more people see their value and coalesce with other islands around them as happened in the Middle Ages and that a new Christendom will begin. But should it be the plan of divine providence that history will come to an end before such a new Christendom comes to fulfilment, nonetheless, given the strength that comes from unity, Christians in these islands, will still be better fortified for that final onslaught of the anti-Christ which must happen before the end and, being purified all the more by the suffering it will entail, will be all the more ready to receive the embrace of the Lord when He appears from on high to set up His kingdom of the end.

Conclusions:

1. In an age when people are historically conscious, we must not only look up to the mystery of the Trinity, to live its *koinonia* love amongst ourselves, or backwards towards creation so as to develop and perfect it but we must also

look forward to the eschaton, to the kingdom of God of the end, to prepare the world for it. We need this as our vision.

2. This should give us hope to double our efforts to improve this world for the good of those around us, but in a spirit of detachment and humility, knowing that all is from God, in Christ, and must be given back to Him again so that He can be *all in all*. (*1 Cor. 15:28*).

3. Understood correctly, and in line with Vatican II, religious life is not a rejection of a world as a thing bad in itself but only of what is bad in a world that was created good by God, though sinful in many respects due to the Fall and subsequent sin. The religious house is a light on the hill, a beam of the dawn that betokens the kingdom so that priests and people will engage in this world in a way that fosters every human value but in a spirit of detachment from it also so as to avoid any kind of idolatry.

4. Islands of faith, of course, presuppose faith in those who would try to construct such things but this, in turn, provokes again the question Our Lord posed when on earth: *When the Son of Man comes will He find faith on earth. Lk. 18:8.*

5. The calling of the pastoral priest which has him lead his flock, as individuals and as a community, towards the kingdom of God is a truly great thing. This is true whether he be the bishop of a great city diocese or a country curate in a remote place. He is a Moses of the New Testament leading his people to the promised land of heaven. He is a small instrument in God's great plan of salvation, a small worker in a great vineyard, small but valued by His Master who called Him to give this lead, the One who died and rose again for him. To be such an instrument in such a great drama that is so much bigger than oneself, is a great thing; and if the priest carries out those duties with pastoral charity he can hope to hear the words *well done good and faithful servant… enter the kingdom prepared for you. Mt. 25:21,34.*

6. All together, in our different callings, religious, priests and laity must pray and work for that kingdom in a spirit of faith, hope and charity. But we must remember that this kingdom is a gift from above and that it is God's glory which we must seek in the end.

End Notes

Chapter I The Mysteries of the Faith and Models of the Church.

1. Those who bash the institutional Church will keep on repeating that "the Church has to change" and are seldom challenged by media people as to what they mean by this. Mother Theresa was once asked about this said that yes, indeed, it must change beginning with you and me living holier lives!

Chapter II The Church, Universal and Local

1. In the Irish tradition there is a lovely scene of parish patriotism in a book called *Knocknagow* or the *Homes of Tipperary* by Charles Kicham. The local hero Matt the Thrasher takes on an English captain in throwing a weight at the sports and shouts "All for the little village" and wins. Irish football is also parish based unlike soccer in other countries where the club is a business enterprise with "fans" from very diverse places. In the English literary tradition H. Belloc is an exponent of local patriotism.
2. By having people disconnected from the family and from any local place of belonging Marxists can more easily dominate and manipulate them.

Chapter III The Kingly Office

1. There is a kind of blind assumption today that because there has been a trend of democratization in the West from the reformation, via the French revolution to the present that this must of necessity be taken on board by the Church also so that she too becomes a democracy. This is despite the fact that Plato saw democracy as the last step before anarchy (*cf.* his *Republic*). Instead, it should have people ask the deeper question of just why Christ did *not* structure His Church as a democracy.
2. In the background here is the question of the relation of jurisdiction in the Church to the sacrament of holy orders: authority is from God, through Christ and apostolic succession and then from the bishop to the priest but does it come formally through the sacrament of holy orders? It raises questions about the exercises of the offices, *munera*, of a bishop or pope should he decide to retire. It is a debate I do not intend to go into here except that the documents of Vatican II seem to give an affirmative answer to this question and tie jurisdiction closely to sacramental power.

Chapter IV The Kingship of the Laity and of the Ordained

1. The 1973 *Instruction* from the *Congregation for Divine Worship and the Discipline of the Sacraments* speaks of the vestments which the <u>priest</u> who carries the Blessed Sacrament may wear during a *Corpus Christi Procession*, while *canon 943* again says that the minister of exposition of the Blessed Sacrament is a priest or deacon. There is also the Instruction *Redemptionis Sacramentum* of 2004 warning against "pastoral assistants taking on themselves what is proper to the priest or deacon". These documents do allow for exceptional cases when no priest or deacon is available, but the exception should not become the rule.

Chapter V Shepherding the Flock

1. A person who likes reading detective stores will know that Sherlock Holmes had the method of observation and deduction. But observation is more than simply seeing. Two people going up the same street *see* the same things but one *observes* more than the other.

Chapter IX The Priest in the Vineyard of the World

1. Some popes saw themselves as the successors of Ceasar in Rome. Cardinal Richelieu was happy to support the reformers in Germany if that would weaken the empire even though the emperor was Catholic. That, Richelieu thought, would then strengthen France.
2. It so happened in the same parish that I was given the key of the nearby creamery for safe keeping in case of "some emergency" which, fortunately, never arose.
3. It did happen that once there was what was supposed to be a painting of New York hanging on a wall in a museum in Germany for forty years. It looked like a grid, hence the resemblance to New York was difficult to see. However, it was hanging upside down in the museum all those years until someone found a photo of the same picture in the artist's studio which was hanging right side up there forty years previously – and none of the culture vultures had noticed.

Chapter X Evangelization and Preaching

1. The non-Christian people are potential Christians; they have a natural openness to the grace of Christ and actual graces from Him may already be at work in them moving them towards a full acceptance of Him, but we still cannot call them "Christians" in the proper sense, even if anonymously. I wonder what Rahner would say if an Arab told him (Rahner) that he was an anonymous Muslim!
2. The Congregation for Doctrine and the Faith under Cardinal Ratzinger (later Pope Benedict XVI) issued a document in 2000, *Dominus Iesus*, affirming the centrality of Christ and His Church for the salvation of all peoples.

Chapter XI The Sources of Preaching

1. Another example that comes to mind of this meditative knowledge of scripture is a sermon by Cardinal Newman when he takes what seems to be a very short, banal or "theologically empty" sentence from St Paul in which he tells Timothy not to keep himself to drinking only water but to take some wine also for the sake of his health, *(I Tim. 5:23)*. But Newman weaves a beautiful meditation on abstinence from it. *Parochial and Plain Sermons Vol VI, sermon 3*. Given that all scripture is inspired there can be no such thing as a theologically empty sentence in it.
2. If the story of Jonah is mere legend in the sense of fable then how does one explain the fact that people were venerating his tomb in Israel for centuries until it was destroyed in recent wars? Furthermore if one accepts it as historical and reads Jonah's prayer one sees that he is seeking deliverance from *Sheol* and from the "pit" which strongly suggests that he actually died and was brought back to life again, as against him merely surviving inside the whale which would then make of Christ's resurrection a mere resuscitation, that is, if the former is to be accepted as a sign of the latter.
3. For example in scripture we have St Paul telling us that Christ was the spiritual rock which followed the Jews in the desert. *(1 Cor. 10:4)*. Origen and Clement of Alexandria are great examples of the spiritual sense, of allegory, in the Fathers.
4. By feminists I mean women who make their own desires to be an absolute in disregard of objective morality. By comparison, I have the greatest respect for women who are faithful to the Church's teaching and contribute so much to the life of the Church not just by their work on Church councils but by their

formation in virtue of their own children in the home. The Church is greatly indebted to such women.

5. There is an underlying question here of whether or not a person brought up in no religious tradition whatever would still have a moral sense and perhaps behave morally at times at least? He would indeed have such a sense due to the basics of the moral law being imprinted by God in every human heart (*synderis*) even though he is not consciously aware of this. But this, to begin with, implies the existence of God as the supreme lawgiver and thus implies a relation of the moral person to this God which he may not be able to articulate for himself.

Chapter XII Preparation for Preaching

1. Vianney, St John. *Sermons of the Cure D'Ars* UK: Mediatrix Press, 2016.

Chapter XV Education for Chastity

1. *Educational Guidance in Human Love.* London: Catholic Truth Society, 1983. *The Truth and Meaning of Human Sexuality.* London: Catholic Truth Society, 1996

Chapter XVIII A Love for Truth

1 From the anti-modernist oath of Pope Pius X one can see clearly what is forbidden in modernism:

"I sincerely hold that the doctrine of faith was handed down to us from the apostles through the orthodox Fathers in exactly the same meaning and always in the same purport. Therefore, I entirely reject the heretical misrepresentation that dogmas evolve and change from one meaning to another different from the one which the Church held previously. I also condemn every error according to which, in place of the divine deposit which has been given to the spouse of Christ to be carefully guarded by her, there is put a philosophical figment or product of a human conscience that has gradually been developed by human effort and will continue to develop indefinitely".

2. An example of faith acting as a negative corrective of reason would be its insistence on an individual active intellect in each person, which accords with scripture, as against the theory of a pan intellect for all men as some claim that

Aristotle was teaching. An example of faith acting as a positive help to reason would be that of *Exodus 3* where God speaks of Himself as *I am who am*, an idea philosophy would hardly ever have attained to by the natural light of reason alone and which it expresses as the *Actum purum esse*, the perfect act of infinite being.

Chapter XX Baptism

1. When children from other parishes are coming for first confession, first communion and the later sacraments the parish priest of the host parish must see to it that they will produce evidence of baptism. Also, it can happen that people of non-Christian religions such as Hindus or Muslims may ask for confession or for the anointing of the sick when they hear of its healing effects but are not baptised. This cannot be granted but they should be received with pastoral care and the reason for the refusal should be politely explained to them.
2. Thus to say "John, *we* baptize you in the name of the Father …" is invalid. If John later became a priest his ordination and subsequent Masses would also be invalid. Yet this has happened more than once.

Chapter XXI Confirmation

1. In Ireland, about that time, there were some very far-seeing people who foresaw the rise of the new rock culture (or anti-culture) and foresaw how inimical this would be to what was there already. So, they organized themselves into a body called *Comhaltas* to protect and promote Ireland's traditional music, song and dance. They have had considerable success but still not enough to withstand the emerging rock culture because it was coming in on the young on all channels and was becoming worldwide.

Chapter XXIII Eucharist – Pastoral Considerations

1. Ironically, a converse row blew up in India amongst the adherents of the Syro-Malabar rite in the early 2020s. In that rite the priest had been facing the East, *ad orientem*, for centuries until Vatican II. Then he began facing the people, and everyone seemed to be happy with that, novel though it was, until the archbishop of one diocese in Kerela wanted to return to having the priest face the East again, but this caused a furious revolt by both priests and people in Kerela, some in favour, others against.

2. In 2020 the USCCB, the US bishops' conference, issued a *Guide for Liturgical Hymns* stating what kind of hymns were not suitable: hymns that show 1) Deficiencies in the Presentation of Eucharistic Doctrine 2) Deficiencies in the Presentation of Trinitarian Doctrine 3) Hymns with Deficiencies in the Doctrine of God and His Relation to Humans 4) Hymns with a View of the Church that Sees Her as Essentially a Human Construction 5) Hymns with Doctrinally Incorrect Views of the Jewish People, and 6) Hymns with Incorrect Christian Anthropology.

Chapter XXIV The Loss of the Sense of Sin

1. St Alphonsus says the following: "The devil does not bring sinners to hell with their eyes open: he first blinds them to the malice of their own sins. Before we fall into sin the enemy labours to blinds us that we may not see the evil we do and the ruin we bring upon ourselves by offending God. After we commit sin he seeks to make us dumb that, through shame, we may conceal our guilt in confession". *St Alphonsus Liguiri, The Spiritual Guidance,* https://catholicinsight.com/the-spiritual-guidance-of-saint-alphonsus-maria-de-liguri/ It is also and old trick of Satan to lift the veil of the evil of peoples' sins when they are dying so that they will despair of seeking forgiveness.
2. Rev. Richard Wurmbrand (1909 -2001), a Lutheran pastor of great integrity who suffered under communism, provided evidence in a booklet that Marx was a Satan worshipper.

Chapter XXVIII The Sacrament of Holy Orders

1. In November of 1995 the then Congregation for the Doctrine and Faith released a statement saying that the Church's prohibition of women's ordination "requires definitive assent...(and) has been set forth infallibly by the ordinary and universal Magisterium.".
2. The terms "liberal" and "conservative" come from the realm of politics and belong there. They are out of place in the realm of theology. The two important terms of comparison there are "faithful" and "unfaithful", i.e., adhering or departing from what we find in scripture and the two thousand year tradition of the Church which is not frozen but always developing but always in organic continuity with what has gone before.

Chapter XXIX The Spirituality of the Secular Priest

1. St Thomas would say that character resides in the soul as a spiritual power of an intellectual kind, because to worship is to pray and to pray is an act of intellect, c*f*. his *S. Theologiae, III, q63, a3*. Others like Alexander of Hales and St. Bonaventure would say it resides in the entire soul as a *habitus.*
2. See Gilson, E. *Reason and Revelation in the Middle Ages.* New York: Charles Scribner's Sons, 1938. It gives a good account of this swing back to a narrow Augustinianism after the time of St. Thomas.
3. Trochu, F. *The Curé D'Ars.* Westminster: Newman Press, 1949. In this book Trochu relates how a sincere fellow parish priest came to the saint complaining that despite his best efforts his flock were not responding. The saint asked him if he was taking on certain penances which he, the saint, proposed to this priest. Should he try these penances he would see results.

Chapter XXXI Marriage Undermined

1. Mis Smith has been a great apostle of marriage and of natural family planning. See for example her book *Why Humanae Vitae was Right: A Reader.* San Francisco: Ignatius Press, 1993. It contains articles by herself and many other people.

Chapter XXXII Marriage Supported

1. Simone de Beauvoir, the French feminist, exemplifies much of this ideology. See for example her book *The Second Sex*, 1949 and other books.
2. See J. Dominian. *Marital Breakdown.* Middlesex: Penguin Books, 1968. It is a good book on the psychology of marital breakdown but somewhat vague on the morality of contraception and divorce, though Dominian was a Catholic. He died in 2014.

Chapter XXXIII Marriage in the Wider View

1. Other big names in *distributism* were G.K. Chesterton and Hillaire Belloc in England, Fr. Harry Bohan in Ireland. Then there was the Sydney Institute in Australia. The original inspiration for d*istributism* was Pope Leo XIII's encyclical *Rerum Novarum*, 1891 and that of Pope Pius XI forty years later, *Quadragesimo Anno.* The idea is to give the small man as much ownership as possible of

the things he needs to live – land or machines - so that he will have as much independence as possible instead of the state owning what he needs to work with (socialism) or big corporations (capitalism) owning them. Under capitalism he is at the mercy of the big corporation which can fail or move to another country at short notice. Under socialism he is at the mercy of the state which owns all the means of production, and possibly even his house, and has him come cap in hand for whatever crumbs it choses to give him after the elite of the party have been taken care of. *Distributism* tries to give him as much autonomy as possible by having him be master of the means of production of those things which we all need for basic living in frugal comfort and by having him trade with others nearby for the things he cannot produce himself.

Chapter XXXVI The Dawn of a new Christendom

1. In his letter *Vita Consecrata* Pope John Paul II makes it clear that the religious are and always were essential to the life of the Church. "In effect, the consecrated life is at the very heart of the Church as a decisive element for her mission, since it "manifests the inner nature of the Christian calling" and the striving of the whole Church as Bride towards union with her one Spouse". *#3*.
2. John Cassian is a great source for information on the desert fathers in his *Conferences* and *Institutes*. He travelled round the deserts of Egypt and Syria collecting stories and saying from them which are of great wisdom. One does, indeed, find in his collected stories a few of a negative, radically dualist kind. But they are the exceptions. In more recent times an Irish lady called Helen Waddel wrote a little book called *The Desert Fathers* which makes for a good summary of Cassian's findings and is very readable. It is published by *Penguin Books,* 2009 and by other publishers also.
3. Christ speaks of an early coming of the kingdom for examples in *Mt.10:23; 16:28*; and *24:32*; and then of a delayed coming in *Mt. 21:33-44; Mk. 4:30-33;* and *Lk. 21, 24.*

Reading Church Documents

Documents of Vatican II, 1962 – 1965

Those most quoted were: *Lumen Gentium*: The Church, 1964; *Sacrosanctum Consilium*: Constitution on the Sacred Liturgy, 1963; *Gaudium et Spes*: The Church in the Modern World, 1965*; Inter Mirifica:* Decree on the Instruments of Social Communication, 1963; *Optatam Totius*: Decree on Priestly Formation, 1965; *Apostolicam Actuositatem*: Decree on the Apostolate of the Laity, 1965*; Presbyterorum Ordinis:* Decree on the Life and Ministry of Priests, 1965; Gra*vissimum Educationis:* Declaration on Christian Education, 1965. These documents were published in London by Geoffry Chapman Ltd., in 1965 but are easily available on the internet.

Documents Post Vatican II

Code of Canon Law. 1983; Catechism of the Catholic Church 1994.
Compendium of the Social Doctrine of the Church, Pontifical Council for Justice and Peace Vatican City: Libreria Editrice Vaticana, 2004.

The Popes

Leo XIII, *Diuturnum, 1881;*
- *Immortale Dei, 1885;*
- *Rerum Novarum*, 1891;

Pius X, *Pascendi Dominici Gregis*: On the Errors of Modernism, 1907.

Pius XI, *Casti Conubii*: On Christian Marriage, 1930;
- *Quadragesimo Anno*, 1931.

St Paul VI, *Evangelii Nuntiandi:* Evangelization in the Modern World. 1975.
- *Inter Signores On the Admission of Women to the Priesthood*, 1976.

St John Paul II, *Catechesi Tradendae*: On Catechesis in our Time, *1979*;
- *Familiaris Consortio*: On the Role of the Christian Family in the Modern World, 1981;
- *Laborem Exercens*: On Human Work, 1981;
- *Familiaris Consortio*: On the Role of the Christian Family in the Modern World, 1981.
- *Salvifici Doloris*: On Suffering, 1984;

- *Reconciliatio et Paenitentia*: On Reconciliation and Penance in the Mission of the Church Today,1984;
- *Redemptoris Mater*: Mary Mother of the Redeemer, 1987;
- *Christifideles Laici*: On the Vocation and the Mission of the Lay Faithful in the Church and in the Modern World, 1988;
- *Mulieris Dignitatem*: On the Dignity and Vocation of Women on the Occasion of the Marian Year, 1988;
- *Pastores Dabo Vobis*: On the Formation of Priests, 1992.
- *Ordinatio Sacerdotalis,* On reserving priestly ordination to men alone, *1994*

Pope Benedict XVI, *Spes Salvi*: On Christian Hope: 2007. Pope Benedict XVI trilogy on *Jesus of Nazareth* is good on the central figure on Christ himself and in this study on the redemption. See his volume on *Holy Week*. Vatican City: Libreria Editrice Vaticana, 2011.

Other Church Documents

The Religious Dimension of Education in a Catholic School, Congregation for Catholic Education, London: CTS 1988;

Truth and Meaning of Human Sexuality, Pontifical Council for the Family. London CTS, 1996;

General Directory of Catechesis, 1997.

Instruction on Certain Questions regarding the Collaboration of the Non-Ordained Faithful in the Sacred Ministry of Priests. Interdicastery, Vatican city: Libreria Editrice Vaticana, 1997.

The Priest, Pastor and Leader of the Parish Community, Congregation for the Clergy. 2002.

The Fathers of the Church

The writings and sermons of St John Chrysostom, especially his writings on marriage are still as relevant today as they were in his time. For example his *Sermon on Marriage; Homily 12*, 20, 21 reflecting mostly on *Ephesians 5;* his *How to Chose a Wife*. See St John Chrysostom, *On Marriage and Family Life*, Popular Patristic Series, New York: St. Vladimir's Seminary Press, 1986; *On the Priesthood.*

St Augustine. *On the Goods of Marriage;*
- *The City of God Bk XIV;*
- *On the Shepherds, Sermon 46.* The Sermons of St Augustine are rich in insights for preaching on a wide variety of topics.

Pope St Gregory the Great, *Pastoral Rule*. New York: St Vladamir Seminary Press, 2007. This is of direct relevance to any study of pastoral theology,

Elizabeth A. Clark. Women in the Early Church in *Message of the Fathers of the Church Vol 13*. Minesota: Liturgical Press, 1983.

St. Thomas Aquinas.

His writings are a wonderful source for all of philosophy and theology, *especially his Summa Theologiae* of which there are various editions and which are also on the internet. His *Commentary on St John's Gospel, Ch 10* is directly relevant to pastoral theology.

Sermons

As well as those of St John Chrysostom and St Augustine above there are also those of St John Vianney, see his *Sermons of the Cure D'Ars*. Cork: Mercier Press, 1960. Then there are the *Parochial and Plain Sermons* of St John Henry Newman, available on the internet. The series of Wednesday audience talks on marriage by St John Paul II which became his *Theology of the Body* is now a well known classic, translated and published in many places.

Books

Aumann, J. *Christian Spirituality in the Christian Tradition*. London: Sheed and Ward, 1985. - *Spiritual Theology*. London: Continuum, 1980.

Bohr, D *The Diocesan Priest*. Minesota: Press, Liturgical, 2009.

Dulles, A. *The Priestly Office*. New York: Paulist Press, 1997.

- *Models of the Church*. New York: Random House, 1974.

The writings of Avrey Dulles are good especially on matters relating to the *King* and *Prophet* sections of this study.

Gilson, E. *Reason and Revelation in the Middle Ages*. New York: Charles Scribner's Sons, 1938.

Kempis, T.A. *The Imitation of Christ*. Reproduced many times in many different publications. It is a spiritual classic which, though rather other worldly, contains many gems of spiritual wisdom, especially on the carrying of the cross. Also Book IV contains some beautiful meditations on the Blessed Sacrament.

Leeming, B. *Principles of Sacramental Theology*. London, Longmans,1955/56. This is an old classic on sacramental theology which has stood the test of time before and after the council.

Newman, J.H. *Essay on the Development of Doctrine*, published in various places. It provides a good response to modernism even though some have tried to use it to justify that heresy. Rahner, K. The Theology of the Symbol in *Theological Investigations Vol 4*.

- *The Church and the Sacraments*. Freiburg: Herder, 1963.

Schillebeeckx, E. *Christ the Sacrament of Encounter with God*. London: Sheed and Ward, 1999.

Smith, J.E. *Why Humanae Vitae was Right: A Reader*. San Francisco: Ignatius Press, 1993.

Trochu, F. *The Curé D'Ars*. Westminster: Newman Press, 1949. This is a very fine comprehensive study on the saint.

Vorgrimler, H. *Sacramental Theology*. Minesota, Liturgical Press, 1992. Walsh, L. *Sacraments of Initiation*. Chicago: Hillenbrand Books, 2011.

The Author

Fr Richard O Connor, D.D., is an Irish priest, ordained in 1976, who worked in the diocese of Kerry for many years. He was also head of philosophy in All Hallows seminary in Dublin from 1981–1983 and has been a professor of theology at the Angelicum University in Rome from 2008 to the present.

www.ingramcontent.com/pod-product-compliance
Lightning Source LLC
Chambersburg PA
CBHW060256240426
43661CB00060B/2807